Jeremiah O´Donovan Rossa

O'Donovan Rossa's prison life

Six years in six English prisons

Jeremiah O′Donovan Rossa

O'Donovan Rossa's prison life
Six years in six English prisons

ISBN/EAN: 9783741196263

Manufactured in Europe, USA, Canada, Australia, Japa

Cover: Foto ©Andreas Hilbeck / pixelio.de

Manufactured and distributed by brebook publishing software (www.brebook.com)

Jeremiah O´Donovan Rossa

O'Donovan Rossa's prison life

O'DONOVAN ROSSA'S

Prison Life.

---·•·---

SIX YEARS IN SIX ENGLISH PRISONS.

---·•·---

THE AMERICAN NEWS COMPANY:
NEW YORK.
1874.

DEDICATION.

TO THE IRISH CONVICTED FELONS,

1865-1870.

FRIENDS:

To you and to your memories I dedicate this book. Representing, as you do, the different parts of Ireland—even its exiled children—I hold you as the truest representatives of its people, their aspirations, and their aims. Scattered, as you are, over the world—sharing what seems to be the common heritage of our race—with some still bound in the enemy's bonds, and others in the embrace of the grave, I collect you here to offer you this humble tribute of my esteem and remembrance.

Yours very sincerely,
JER. O'DONOVAN ROSSA.

TO

Name	Sentence.	Birthplace.
MICHAEL O'BRIEN	Death	Co. Cork.
MICHAEL LARKIN	Death	Co. Galway.
WM. PHILIP ALLEN	Death	Co. Cork.
MICHAEL BARRETT	Death	Cork.
JOHN McCLURE	Death—Life	Dobbs Ferry, N.Y., America.
THOMAS FRANCIS BOURKE	Death—"	Fethard, Co. Tipperary.
PATRICK DORAN	Death—"	Dublin.
JOHN McCAFFERTY	Death—"	Sandusky, O., America.
EDWARD KELLY	Death—"	Cork.
EDW. O'MEAGHER CONDON	Death—"	Mitchelstown, Cork.
WM. P. THOMPSON DARRAGH	Death—Life (died in prison)	Ballycastle, Antrim.
PATRICK MELADY	Death—Life	Dublin.
JAMES F. X. O'BRIEN	Death—"	Waterford.
THOMAS CULLINANE	Death—"	Ireland.

DEDICATION.

	Sentence.	Birthplace.
JOHN O'BRIEN	Life (still in prison)	London.
SERGEANT M'CARTHY	Life (still in prison)	Fermoy, Cork.
THOMAS CHAMBERS	Life (still in prison)	Ireland.
JAMES DARRAGH	Life (still in prison)	Ireland.
JAMES WILSON	Life (still in prison)	Ireland.
MARTIN HOGAN	Life (still in prison)	Ireland.
PATRICK KEATING	Life (still in prison)	Ireland.
THOMAS HASSETT	Life (still in prison)	Ireland.
MICHAEL HARRINGTON	Life (still in prison)	Ireland.
ROBERT CRANSTON	Life (still in prison)	Ireland.
JAMES KEILEY	Life (still in prison)	Ireland.
THOMAS CLARK LUBY	20 years	Dublin.
JOHN O'LEARY	20 "	Tipperary.
MICHAEL SHEEHY	20 "	Cashel, Co. Tipperary.
MICHAEL CODY	20 "	Dublin.
JOHN SHINE	20 "	(still in prison) Ireland.
EDMOND POWER	15 "	Tralee, Kerry.
JOHN F. KEARNS	15 "	Cork.
JOHN FLOOD	15 "	Baldoyle, Dublin.
JOHN DEVOY	15 "	Naas, Kildare.
EDWARD DUFFY	15 "	(died in prison) Ballyhadereen, Mayo.
PATRICK F. LENNON	15 "	Dublin.
PATRICK LOMAN	15 "	Ireland.
PATRICK WALSH	15 "	Charleville, Co. Cork.
WILLIAM G. HALPIN	15 "	Co. Meath.
RICKARD O'S. BURKE	15 "	Dunmanway, Cork.
JAMES M'COY	15 "	(still in prison) Ireland.
THOS. DELANEY	15 "	(still in prison) Ireland.
"PAGAN" O'LEARY	7 "	Macroom, Cork.
WM. MACKEY LOMASNEY	12 "	Fermoy, Co. Cork.
DENIS DOWLING MULCAHY	10 "	Redmondstown, Tipperary.
C. UNDERWOOD O'CONNELL	10 "	Frankfort, Kings Co.
BRYAN DILLON	10 "	(dead) Cork City.
THOMAS BAINES	10 "	Co. Sligo.
DANIEL BRADLEY	10 "	Cork City.
MORTIMER MORIARTY	10 "	Kerry.
GEORGE F. CONNOLLY	10 "	Dublin.
JOHN LYNCH	10 "	(died in prison) Cork.
CORNELIUS DWYER KEANE	10 "	Skibbereen, Cork.
WILLIAM F. ROANTREE	10 "	Leixlip, Dublin.
EDW. PILSWORTH ST. CLAIR	10 "	Warwick.
GEORGE BROWN	10 "	Glenowrin, Co. Down.
THOS. M'CARTHY FENNELL	10 "	Kilballyowen, Co. Clare.
JOHN WARREN	15 "	Clonakilty, Cork.
CHARLES J. KICKHAM	14 "	Mullinahone, Tipperary.
JOHN BOYLE O'RIELLY	15 "	Co. Meath.
AUG. ELLICOTT COSTELLO	12 "	Killimore, Co. Galway.
JAMES O'CONNOR	10 "	Glen of Imael, Co. Wicklow.
CHRIS. MANUS O'KEEFE	10 "	Ireland.
WILLIAM MOORE STACK	10 "	Tralee, Kerry.
PATRICK BARRY	10 "	Co. Cork.
JOHN HALTIGAN	7 "	Kilkenny.
MICHAEL O'REGAN	7 "	Rosscarberry, Cork.
TERENCE BYRNE	7 "	Dublin.
JOHN COGHLAN	7 "	Cork.
WILLIAM O'SULLIVAN	5 "	Kilmallock, Limerick.
EDWARD BUTLER	5 "	Dublin.

DEDICATION.

Name	Sentence.		Birthplace.
Andrew Kennedy	5 years		Nenagh, Tipperary.
Hugh Francis Brophy	10	"	Dublin.
Thomas Duggan	10	"	Ballincollig, Cork.
Michael Moore	10	"	Dublin.
John Kenealy	10	"	Gleannlara, Co. Cork.
John Bennett Walsh	7	"	Ireland.
Denis Cashman	7	"	Waterford.
Jeremiah Ahern	7	"	Ireland.
David Commins	7	"	Ireland.
Simon Downey	7	"	Ireland.
Denis Hennessey	7	"	Kilmallock, Co. Limerick.
Eugene Lombard	7	"	Cork.
Morgan McSweeny	7	"	Ireland.
Joseph Noonan	7	"	Ireland.
Patrick Reardon	7	"	Kilmallock, Limerick.
John Sheehan	7	"	Kilmallock, Co. Limerick.
Eugene Geary	7	"	Ireland.
Patrick Mears	10	"	Ireland.
Peter Maughan	10	"	Moate, Westmeath.
Patrick S. Doran	7	"	Kilmacow, Co. Kilkenny.
Bartholomew Moriarty	7	"	Ireland.
Henry Shaw Mulleda	7	"	Naas, Kildare.
Patrick Ryan	5	"	Merthyr Tydvil.
Martin Hanly Carey	5	" (dead)	Eyrecourt, Co. Galway.
William Murphy	5	"	Cork.
John Carroll	5	"	Ireland.
Charles Moorehouse	5	"	Ireland.
Daniel Reddin	5	"	Dunleary, Dublin.
Thomas Scally	5	"	Ireland.
John Brennan	5	"	Ireland.
Timothy Featherstone	5	"	Ireland.
James Walsh	5	"	Ireland.
Stephen Joseph Meany	15	"	Ennis, Clare.
Michael Stanley	10	"	Dublin.
John B. S. Casey	5	"	Mitchelstown, Cork.
Thomas Daly	5	"	Kilmallock, Co. Limerick.
Patrick Dunne	5	"	Dublin.
James Flood	5	"	Dublin.
Maurice Fitzgibbon	5	"	Kilmallock, Co. Limerick.
Thomas Fogarty	5	"	Kilfeacle, Tipperary.
Luke Fullam	5	"	Drogheda, Co. Meath.
Laurence Fullam	5	"	Drogheda, Co. Meath.
John Goulding	5	"	Ireland.
Patrick Leahy	5	"	Ireland.
Patrick May	5	"	Slane, Co. Meath.
Michael Noonan	5	"	Kilmallock, Co. Limerick.
Jeremiah O'Donovan	5	"	Coolflinch, Cork.
Cornelius O'Mahony	5	"	Macroom, Cork.
James Reilly	5	"	Ireland.
Robert Wall	5	"	Ireland.
— Davitt	14	" (still in prison)	Ireland.
— Wilson	7	" (still in prison)	Ireland.
Pat. J. Hayburne	2	"	Dublin.
David O'Connell	2	"	Tipperary.
Edward Fitzgerald	2	"	Tipperary.
John O'Clohissy	2	"	Dublin.
George Hopper	2	"	Dublin.

	Sentence.	Birthplace.
WILLIAM CURRY	2 years	Kildare.
GUNNER FLOOD	2 "	Ireland.
JOSEPH TOMPKINS	1½ "	Dublin.
JAMES TOMPKINS	1½ "	Dublin.
JOSEPH BROWN	1½ "	Dublin.
JOHN WATSON	1½ "	Dublin.
EDWIN FORRESTER	1½ "	Ireland.

CONTENTS.

CHAPTER I.
Introduction—A View of Ireland—A Semi-Political and Semi-Religious Chapter.

CHAPTER II.
Ireland's Suffering—Providence—Famine—Our Fathers' Crimes—'98 and '48—Protestants and Catholics—Egotism—The Phœnix Society—Mr. Stephens' Visit to Skibbereen—Joining the Revolutionary Society, May,'58—American Aid—Drilling—Police Hunts—Too Fast for the Irish Americans—Arrests December, '58—Extra Police—Meeting with William O'Shea, Tim M'Carthy, Jerry Cullinane, and Denis O'Sullivan—Bantry Prisoners—Lodged in Cork Jail.

CHAPTER III.
Oakum and Solitary Confinement—Black Bread and Leek Porridge—Eating in the Dark—Mock Trial in Prison—False Swearing about Drilling, etc.—"Marching in Military Order"—Patrick's Day in the Dock—Sent Back to Prison Again—Plead Guilty—Jury Packing—Lord O'Hagan—Patriotism of the Irish Bar a Sham—First Working of the Revolutionary Movement in '58—Mortimer Moynahan—"Steeped to the Lips in Treason"—Centres and Circles—Opposition of the Clergy—Absolution Refused—The Jubilee—The Bishop and Dr. Doyle—Give to Cæsar What's Due to Cæsar—The Police Spy System—Altar Denunciation—Rev. Mr. O'Sullivan's Information to the Government, and Mr. Sullivan's (of the "Nation") Note of Warning—The Evil Effects of Curiosity.

CHAPTER IV.
A Glance Over Six Years—Eviction—Fidelity of the People—"Shoneen" Snobbery—The Patriotic Bishop O'Hea—Rifles and Pikes—English Hypocrisy—Surrender—Polish Demonstration and Prince of Wales' Illumination—Tearing Down the English Flag where there was not much Danger in the Way—Threats—The "Irish People" Newspaper Denunciations—Calumnies—A Hard Job for any of the "Fratres Feniores" to Get Married—No Absolution—Father Leader and his Gross Insult, which Ended in Marriage.

CHAPTER V.
Seizure of the "Irish People"—Arrest and Search for Papers—The Ballybar Races—Story Telling—Little Jealousies—Ordered off to America—In Court—Nagle and the Detectives—Richmond Prison—Religion and Routine—Stripping—My Cell—My Board and Lodging—My Wife's Visit and Dr. Cullen's Slanders—"Mad Dog" and Barry the Crown Prosecutor—The Lower Castle Yard—Preliminary Examinations—High Treason and Hanging—Stephens' Escape—Seizure of my Defence Papers—The Trial—The Packed Jury—The Packed Bench—Keogh and Fitzgerald—Conviction and Sentence for Life—Search for my Treasonable Documents.

CHAPTER VI.
Convicted—The Black Van and the Cavalry—Mountjoy Convict Prison—Dressing, Registering, Shaving and Photographing—Sympathetic Tears—For-

bidden to Write—A Bed, but no Sleep—My Government Acquaintance—The Convicts' Priest—Religious Books—A Blinker Pew in Chapel—Feeling My Pulse and Fit for a Journey—Meet the Convicts O'Leary, Luby, "Pagan," Moore and Haltigan—Tight Irons—Departure—More Sympathizing Tears, and a Few Opinions on "Peelers" and other British Pensioners—Old Dunleary—The Convict Ship—"Respectable" People—A Word of My Companions—The "Pagan" and His Work—Soldiers and Arms.

CHAPTER VII.

In England—Christmas Eve—London—Pentonville Prison—Stripped of Flannels—Clothes Searched—Naked—Cell and Cell Furniture—Solitary Confinement—Cold and Hunger—Christmas Fair—My Trade and Occupation—Reading the Rules—Forbidden to Write—The Doctor—Airing or Exercise in the Refractory Yard—My Library—The Prison Directions—Dreams of Happiness.

CHAPTER VIII.

Arrival in Pentonville Prison, London—Stripped—Deprived of Flannels—Fixed in my Quarters—Bed and Board, Etc.

CHAPTER IX.

Lodged in Portland—Boots and Books—New Cells—Rain Down—Director Fagan from Cork—His Letter Regarding us—No Catholic or Irish Warders to Have Charge of Us—The Broad Arrow—"Amulets or Charms"—The Wash-House—Stationary Tubs and Soap Suds—Dodging About for a Clean Job of Work—Pumping and Picking Linen—Denis Dowling Mulcahy Our Priest—His Sermons and Psalms—A Sunday in Portland—Parade and Salaams—Oil and Blacking—"Orderlies" and Slop—The Evil Eye—Forbidden to Walk or Stretch in My Cell—Bread and Water—Dietary Table.

CHAPTER X.

Removed from the Wash-house and Sent to the Quarries—Nobbling—I Become a Quarryman—"Reported" and "Degraded"—Tried and Condemned Without Witnesses—Privy Cleaning—Rain Down in Our Cells—Earning Marks—Eighteen Months in Prison After Death—Cannot Speak High or Low—"Do You Defy the Prison Authorities"—Pat Barry's Jugglery and Punishment—Donald Bane, the Scotchman, and His Razor—"Cannot You Fellows Shave Each Other"—Michael O'Regan Joked and Charles Kickham Shoved by Gunning—William Roantree's Illness—Martin Hanly Carey Breaks a Finger, and the Doctor Makes Him Work with One Hand—I Try to be as Good as an English Gentleman Convict and Tear My Clothes—"Mutiny"—I'd "Suck Another Man's Blood"—Michael O'Regan and the Prison Priests.

CHAPTER XI.

Visits—Demands for Visitors' Expenses—Devils—My Wife and Child in Prison—My Memorandum Book—My Wife's Poems—My Letter—Fear of Publicity—Compromise with the Governor—My Love Letters on a Slate—Determination to write Surreptitious Letters—Convict Lynch—His Gift of Pen, Ink, and Paper—"Conspiracy" to Break Prison—Michael Moore's Failure—Hugh Brophy's Failure—Myself a Hypocrite—Lynch Detected in Carrying my Letter—Punishment of Him and Me—Try again—My Amour in Prison—Brings Bread and Water and Endless Punishments on Me—Jerry O'Donovan, of Blarney—Rev. Mr. Zanetti—The Devil—Ireland's Soggarth Aroon—Zanetti Giving Evidence before the Commission—The Evil Eye—A Petition on "Think Well on It," and what came of it—Writing in the Dark—Cat's Eyes—My Memorial to the Secretary of State.

CHAPTER XIII.

My Carriage in Waiting—My Breakfast—Fight for my Dinner—Journey to Millbank Prison, London—Thoughts of Escape—Supper—Reception Ward

CONTENTS.

—Installed in Office—Tailoring and Theft—Letter Writing—Scrubbing Floor—Pump Handle and Crank—Punished for not doing Two Things at the Same Time—Oakum Picking and Picking Coir.

CHAPTER XIV.

Association with English Convicts—Working the Pump—Irish and English Poverty and the Priest—Eating a Warder—Getting Bread at Prayers—Task Work—Wetting Coir—Punished for obeying Orders—Lying Warders and Gambier—Extensive Seizure—All my Writing and Writing Material Captured—Change of Quarters and Bread and Water—Bully Power's attempt to Bully Me—Separation from other Prisoners—The Soldier Prisoners—Telegraphing through the Walls—Honor amongst Thieves—A "Cedar" Lost and my Search for it—Johnny O'Brien and the Irish Republic—My Prison Poet—Turn your Face to the Wall—New Confederates—The Red Blood of Ireland will Rise in England—Reflections—The Road to Freedom Dangerous—Lord Macaulay's New Zealander—Swallowing an Ink-Bottle—Stealing Paper—John Devoy and other New-Comers—Swallowing Power's Pencil—Skeleton Weight.

CHAPTER XV.

Wife's Visit—Lies about Letters—Knox and Pollock—A Castlebar Man Stealing Ink for Me—Stealing Paper—A Narrow Escape—My Love Letter and the Sham Inquiry—Lying Again—Lord Devon's Commission—Writing amongst Fleas—Punished for having my Task Work Done before Time—Refuse to go to Punishment Cell—A Terrible Choking and Dragging—I Barricade my Door—It is Broken in—Four Months' Cells—Meeting John Devoy—Taken Ill—Dr. Pocklington—My Body covered with Boils—Effects of Low Diet and Confinement—Meditated Mutiny and Outbreak—The Devil Visits Me—Reflections on "Burke and Froude"—My Books Taken Away and Returned Again—I Threaten to Destroy Cell and Muffle my Gaslight—Volunteering to Western Australia—Manchester Rescue—Soldiers Guarding Us—Out of "Punishment" and in it Soon Again—Meeting James Xavier O'Brien—Patrick Lennon—Stripped Naked Every Day—Breaking Spy-Hole and Door—Handcuffs, Bloody Wrists, and Dark Cells—Throttling and Threatening—Eating "on All Fours"—Break my Spoon and Wooden Dish—Stuff the Key-Hole and Have a Little Fun, and Get More Bread and Water for it.

CHAPTER XVI.

Christmas Day on "Bread and Water"—Telegraphing to John Devoy—An Archbishop on Stephens' Escape—Sowing Distrust—The Handwriting on the Wall—The Bible in the Blackhole—A Thief Feeds Me; his Letter and his Present—A Stem of a Dhudeen—Refuse to have my Picture Taken, except the Queen sends for it—Manchester Murphy and Michael O'Brien—A Night on the Hills of Connaught—"Fenianism" and "Ribbonism"—Edward Duffy meeting with his Mother—Application to see him Dying Refused—Preaching—A Wail—Meditated Mischief—A Change for the Better only a Preparation for one for the Worse—Journey to Chatham Prison.

CHAPTER XVII.

Reception in Chatham—I Must Learn Drill or go to "Jilligum"—Association with Thieves—Stone Breaking—Wheeling Rubbish—Yoked to a Cart—Light Work, Light Wages and Light Diet—"Cos" and "Jobbler"—Pratt—A Prison Spy—I Smash my Window—Refuse to pay Salaams—Rev. Mr. Duke, Protestant Chaplain—A Cedar—Cosgrove Punished and Degraded on my Account—I Learn the Prison "Slang"—Bearla gar na Saor—Made an Accessory to Theft—"Scotty's" Presbyterianism—"I'll Make Some one pay for this yet"—"Ah, Get Out"—"Insolence and Irreverence" at Chapel—Richard O'Sullivan Burke and Henry S. Mulleda—An Escape from Having my Neck Cracked—I "Strike"—Throw my Hammer over the Wall—Five Warders hold me Salaaming to the Governor—He'd Treat me with Contempt—My Resolution, my Prayer and my "Salute" to the Governor—Satisfaction—Hands

Tied Behind my Back 35 Days—Bloody Wrists—"Blood for Blood"—The Pursuit of Knowledge under Difficulties—Father O'Sullivan—The Destruction of Popery in 1866—A Book out of Date—Director Du Cane—Giving Tit for Tat—I Break up the Special Party—"Jobbler's" Good-bye—The Thieves' Kindness—Flogging Prisoners—Meet Rick Burke and Harry Mulleda—My Sentence Read—Released from Irons.

CHAPTER XVIII.

My New Cell—The Music of the Waters—Handcuffs and Blackhole Again—Break My Model Water-Closet, My Bell-Handle, My Table, etc.—Gambler's Visit and Hypocrisy—Deprived of My Bed and Bible—Verse-Making—My Readings and My Wife's—Deprived of Bed and Body Clothes—A Struggle—Knocked Down, Stripped, Leaped Upon, and Kicked—A Reprieve—Meet Halpin, Warren, and Costello—A Strike Against Clipping and Stripping—A Family Quarrel—"Erin's Hope" and Her Heroes—Grass Picking—Rick Burke and Harry Mulleda—Wood-Chopping—Warren Chops a Finger—Detected Letter—Wrongfully Imprisoned Ten Days—O'Hara's Letter—Kept from Chapel—Extraordinary Precautions—Ludicrous Position at Prayers—Release of Costello and Warren—Arrival of John M'Clure, John Devoy, and Captain O'Connell—Brick-Cleaning in a Refrigerator—The Cup of Halpin's Affliction Flown Over—His Illness and the Doctor's Indifference.

CHAPTER XIX.

New Arrivals—John M'Clure—American-born Irishmen, and Irish-born "Sprallareens"—New Work—Stocking Mending—"Fox and Geese"—Lies of Bruce, the Secretary of State—Superstition and the Bible—Halpin "Joining the Service in a Good Time"—He Strikes Work, and Keeps his Hair on his Head—Mr. O'Connell's Sore Foot and Dr. Burns—"I Don't Like to be Here at All," and Warder Browne—The Tipperary Election and the Terror of the Authorities—John Mitchells Remarks—Visit from McCarthy Downing, M. P.—Colonel Warren and Patrick's Day—The Soldier Prisoners—Mr. Blake, M. P., and Australia—Mr. Pigott's and John F. O'Donnell's Visit—Mr. A. M. Sullivan—His Opinion on the "Coup D'Etat," and My Opinions on Him, and on His "Story of Ireland"—Ireland Over the Water.

CHAPTER XX.

A Chapter of Letters—The Belmont Fund—T. F. Donovan, Wm. R. Roberts—Maurice and Kate Spillane—Courtship After Marriage—Love and War—My Wife's Letter to Mr. Gladstone and His Reply—Her Letters to Me and My Replies—Apprehensions of Both of Us Committing Suicide—A Romance of Real Life.

CHAPTER XXI.

The Commission of Inquiry—Lord Devon Chairman—Examination of Directors, Governors, Warders and Prisoners—Official Falsehoods—Mr. Bruce, the Hon. Secretary of State, a Convicted Liar—The Commissioners Agree in Their Report, but the "Doctors Differ."

CHAPTER XXII.

One of the Commissioners in Irons—Letters—Mr. Gladstone and Mr. Bruce—Mr. M'Carthy Downing—"Amnesty"—Banishment by "Victoria, by the Grace of God"—A Private Letter and My Reply—Leaving Chatham and Leaving Halpin Behind—The Cuba—Forbidden to Touch Irish Soil in the Cove of Cork—Arrival in New York—A General Jubilee of Welcome—I Must be a Tammany Man or Cease to be an Irishman—I Rebel Against This, and Sacrifice my Popularity to my Independence—Irish-American Politicians and American Politics—Collector Murphy—Emigration—Tammany War Cries; "Grant and Murphy," "Murphy and Grant"—I Commit Political Suicide with the Irish People by Running Against Tweed, and Kill Myself Entirely by Becoming a Commune and Joining Tennie Claflin.

PREFACE.

IT is a sorry admission to be obliged to make, but it is the truth—and we believe that the policy, no less than the duty, of those who seek to reconcile the people of England and the people of Ireland is to state the truth, the whole truth, and nothing but the truth, on all questions at issue between them —it is the truth, then, we are sorry to say, that the complaints so angrily and persistently made in Ireland for the last three years, regarding the treatment of Fenian prisoners detained in English jails, have been, if not literally maintained, certainly in their substance justified. Those statements, advanced in the House of Commons by members of Parliament, and in memorials addressed to the Government by Irish municipalities, in the most formal and serious manner, in which such charges could be raised, have been met by the ministers especially responsible and by the prime minister himself, with an indignant and categorical denial. At last, however, on the occasion when Mr. Gladstone promised to "liberate" these prisoners in the event of a cessation of the aggrarian disturbances which prevailed in

---

The above article is copied from the London *Spectator*, and inserted here as a preface. It covers briefly the ground which I will travel over in detail. The writer of it will never be suspected of partiality towards me, and, therefore, in presenting this book to the public with introduction from my enemy, I trust in some measure to silence captious criticism, and leave data from which to judge of the truthfulness of my statements.—O'DONOVAN ROSSA.

three or four Irish counties last March, he also consented to the appointment of a commission to inquire into the charges brought against the prison officials. That commission has reported, and its report justifies some of the worst charges advanced against the administration. It is a simple matter of fact that in one case, the case of O'Donovan Rossa, punishment was carried to the extent of torture—torture of a novel kind, certainly, but quite as brutal as the boot, and protracted with a vindictive pertinacity unprecedented, we hope and believe, in this century on this side of the equator.

Mr. Gladstone saw a great many shocking things in the prisons of Naples, and he recorded them in terms and in a tone which thrilled the hearts of all civilized men. But if it had been his lot to see one Italian prisoner, one of Poerio's rougher and less cultivated comrades, who, for an act of insubordination to his jailor, had, without further warrant than that official's will, had his hands manacled behind his back, except at the hour of meals and the hours of sleep, for thirty-four continuous days, in what words would he not have painted that long agony of artificial paralysis and unmanning ignomony! How he would have described the exquisite torture of depriving a being made in God's image, for the coarse offence of a moment's fury, through more than one whole month, in the full heat of the Neapolitan midsummer, of the use of his hands, of the organs, that is to say, which, after his brain, are the most active, intelligent, and indispensable agents of his life! Consider the incessant series of services which the cunning of a man's hand renders to him in the course of one whole day, and then imagine the state of a man shut up alone in a cell for thirty-four successive days, and those the thirty-four hottest days of the year, with his hands pinioned at the loins! A man in such a state is at the mercy of the meanest insect in creation. The wasp may fasten on his eyelid, or the bug burrow in his ear, and he cannot help himself. If tears flow from his eyes he cannot brush them off. The sense of personal filth, which is the sorest trial of prolonged and relaxing illness, is enforced on a man in the full vigor of an unusually robust constitution, at the time of a year when the air of a cell is like the air of an oven. Suppose such a man to be suddenly attacked with sickness, that he burst a blood vessel, that he has a fit, that he vomits violently, that he is attacked by cholera, how is he to summon help? He may be too weak to cry so that his voice shall pierce walls and bars, or to ring the bell, if indeed a bell be provided, with his teeth. It is here that the spirit of torture which originally suggested such a punishment as handcuffing behind the back most distinctly reveals itself. A man handcuffed in front would be equally secured from doing violence to himself or others—and for such a reason only, it is manifest, ought handcuffing or the strait-waistcoat to be employed on the prisoners of a country pretending to consider itself Christian and civilized—but handcuffing in front does not reduce a man to such a condition that, where his state is not like that of a cripple, it is more or less like that of a corpse. We wonder what may become the favorite attitude of a man whose hands are strapped behind his back for many hours a day, and many days together. The ingenious violence that is done to some of the most delicate and complex nerves, muscles and vessels in the body is such that he can hardly escape incurring the liability to aneurism, or anachylosis, or some form of paralysis. Poerio was chained. But a man who is chained can at least lie down or sit down with tolerable ease. A man who is handcuffed behind the back can only lie down on his breast, and that in a form peculiarly injurious to the lungs and heart. Unless his cell happens to be purposely provided with a low stool, he cannot, we imagine, sit down without very great discomfort. Kneeling is of the few bodily adjustments possible to him, the one that, perhaps, can be longest endured, kneeling with one shoulder leaned against a wall, varied by walking backwards and forwards, and counting the few possible paces, and trying to multiply them into miles; we dare say that is the way O'Donovan Rossa dodged mortal disease, and kept his reason during those thirty-four days. This miserable man was not a minister of State, like Poerio, but he was, so far as the will of one of the greatest of the Irish shires could so make him, a member of the British Parliament. This charge of torture was made. It was denied again and again, but it was a true charge; and the people of Tipperary marked their sense of its truth by sending the name of O'Donovan Rossa to the head of the poll at the next election. This was a turbulent and ungracious manifestation of opinion, no doubt; but there was much more excuse for it than we thought at the time. That the provocation given by O'Donovan Rossa was of a very gross character, and that he was a most difficult subject to manage, need hardly be said. Prison discipline must be maintained over political offenders as well as over pickpockets. Flog, if necessary; if it be still more necessary, introduce martial law into our prisons and shoot. But let whatever punishment is inflicted on any man, however guilty or unworthy, who bears the character of a British subject, be a punishment according to the spirit as well as the letter of English law, and according to the custom of the Courts of the United Kingdom. If a police magistrate at Bow-street were to take it upon himself to order a thief thirty times convicted before him to be handcuffed behind the back for thirty days, how long would the Chancellor allow such a magistrate to hold a seat on the bench? Shall it be tolerated that the governor of a jail is to use the power that is given him for the purposes of restraint until the punishment inflicted becomes by accumulation one of the most truculent forms of torture ever employed? If it be necessary let us return to severe penalties; but let such methods of punishment, even in regard to our Irish political prisoners, be inflicted only after an act of Parliament has been passed for the purpose. We hanged the governor of an island for employing torture in the last century. Have we so degenerated as to allow the governor of a jail to use it under Queen Victoria? Unfortunately this case, though by far the worst, is not the only case in which charges brought against the administration of the prisons were substantiated to the satisfaction of the commissioners. The governor of Portland, Mr. Clifton, charged O'Donovan Rossa, on the ground of an intercepted paper, "with an attempt to carry on a love intrigue by letter" with the wife of another prisoner. The paper in question was addressed to "Mrs. Mary Moore, for Mrs. O'D.," and was evidently intended for O'Donovan Rossa's own wife. The governor, however, chose to regard the insertion of the words "for Mrs. O'D." as "a subterfuge," and took occasion to inform the prisoner Moore of the relations which he believed existed between O'Donovan Rossa and Mrs. Moore. The commissioners having gone into the case carefully, at O'Donovan Rossa's request, hold him "clear from the imputation of any endeavor to carry on a love intrigue" and regret that the governor acted under "misapprehension." They find, moreover, that the governor neglected until he was brought before them after an interval of four years, to compare the letter incriminated by him with Mrs. O'Donovan Rossa's letter to which it was a reply. Had he done so, they add, "such a comparison could not have failed to prevent him from harboring such a suspicion, or communicating it to others." It is well for Mr. Clifton that he does not form such suspicions, and communicate them to others outside the walls of his jail. Were he to do so, he might find that his "misapprehension" might not be so lightly regarded by a jury of British husbands. In estimating O'Donovan Rossa's want of respect for the majesty which clothes the person of a British jail governor, we submit that this wholly unfounded charge against his moral character deserves some slight consideration. Who can wonder that such a charge should work like madness on the brain of such a man as this O'Donovan Rossa? In all that we read of him we discern the elements of an essentially Southern temperament—a nature capable of sudden fits of fury, but not the less capable of generous and noble conduct. Had Mr. Gladstone met a lazarone of such a type in the prison at Naples, so tortured in the body and in the soul, manacled by the back for a month, morally dishonored in the face of evidence for four long years, he might well have said "*Ecce homo!* Such is the manner of man such a system as exists in Naples naturally produces." A soft word had power to do with this dogged Irish rebel what manacles could never have done. The Commissioners drily record that "an opportune appeal to his better feelings by Captain Du Cane in October, 1868, proved more effectual than a long previous course of prison discipline; and, with one exception, in the December of that year, he has not since been subjected to any further punishment."

The Commissioners, we regret to add, find that grave charges brought by other convicts were well founded. They find that, having arrived at Pentonville in mid-winter, they were at once deprived of the flannels which they had been supplied with in the Irish prison from which they came. The report that O'Connell, suffering from disease of the aorta, or heart (medical authorities differ on the point whether it is his heart or his aorta that is affected; but he is, besides, subject to "nervous paralysis of the head," and he has steadily declined in weight to the extent of twenty pounds since his imprisonment) was put on bread-and-water diet in close confinement seven times, being evidently "unfit to undergo such discipline." Five of this prisoner's letters were suppressed. The Commissioners think the letters ought to have been forwarded, erasing such parts as the authorities considered objectionable. The prisoner, Mulcahy, a man of good family and remarkable talents (he was one of the principal writers of the *Irish People*), while suffering from spitting of blood, was kept to hard labor at Portland, and the hard labor was stone-dressing; but it was also proved to involve the practice of carrying large slabs of stone on the back. After about three weeks of this work the spitting of blood ended in hæmorrhage from the lungs. The Commissioners think that this prisoner was, on the whole, "not fit for hard labor." Mulcahy, it is added, "was never reported for misconduct, nor ever punished," unless, indeed, carrying slabs of stone on the back when a man is spitting blood is to be considered punishment. In the cases of the other prisoners who came before the Commissioners, some complaints were substantiated, some held not proven; but taking a general view of the whole report, we must not hesitate to say, that the case of the Fenian prisoners against the authorities has been, on the whole, established; that at least one of those prisoners was treated with a degree of barbarity which it is grievous to contemplate; that they were all subjected to inconsiderate and unnecessary severity; that the conduct of the officials incriminated by the report calls for further action on the part of the government; that by some of these officials the government was misled so as to make untrue statements in Parliament; that the facts of the case, as revealed by the report, deprive the amnesty of the claim to be considered in any degree as "an act of pure clemency;" and that it is impolitic, and indeed, impossible to maintain the principle, for the first time applied in the case of these prisoners, that political offenders should be submitted to the same usage as burglars and footpads.

CHAPTER I.

INTRODUCTION—A VIEW OF IRELAND—A SEMI-POLITICAL AND SEMI-RELIGIOUS CHAPTER.

SOME persons have the gift of writing agreeably upon disagreeable subjects, and it would take one of these gifted people to make an interesting and pleasant book out of a very unpleasant kind of life—that is, prison-life in England.

I don't presume to think it is generally believed that prison-life in England is worse than prison-life anywhere else; indeed, I believe the opinion prevails that it is better. Englishmen labor very zealously to put themselves in a favorable light before the world, and if they cannot do so by showing any superior merit in themselves, they will attempt it by pointing out the demerit in others. They pry into nearly all the prisons of the world; opportunities are afforded them for learning how the inmates are treated, and I admit that they have done good in many cases by throwing light upon deeds of darkness. But all this time their own prisons are closed to every curious inquisitor; no foreigner can enter an English prison and ask a convict how he fares. It is here that the genius of this people displays itself in showing up the barbarity of other civilized people and drawing a sanctimonious veil over its own.

As this book may fall into the hands of readers who know little of Ireland and its wrongs, it may not be amiss to say something of the cause of my imprisonment. To those who know anything of history it is known that for seven hundred years Ireland is cursed with as cruel a government as ever cursed the earth. In the twelfth century the Normans had succeeded in conquering England, and coveting Ireland, they laid their schemes to conquer that too. They were intensely Catholic, but in the pursuit of conquest they never hesitated, in any country, to ravage convents and monasteries; but in several cases they were religious enough to endow these institutions also, when doing so would further their ends, or when an object was to be attained by showing the church that they were turning the plunder of their neighbors to a holy use.

The English interest was always able to persuade Rome that the Irish were bad Catholics, and that they required reformation. At the present day, when England is Protestant, it is able to do this, and to get Bulls and Rescripts denunciatory of my countrymen.

Seven hundred years ago an English king making such a representation to the Pope of Rome, received from him authority to possess Ireland for the purpose of improving the morals of its people, and during these seven hundred years has the Irish people been waging a fierce fight against the efforts England has been making to "improve" them off the face of the land. England always brought in the name of religion to aid her in the conquest. At first professing Catholicity, she had her English priests in Ireland proclaiming that it was no sin to kill an Irishman, and one of them went so far as to declare before a council that he would celebrate Mass on a Sunday morning, after killing one, without making it an act of confession.

Then came the Reformation, and she commenced to persecute the Irish Catholics and root out the whole race, because they would not become Protestant, for she thought that, by becoming Protestant, they may become less Irish or more English. For a time the words Protestant and English were synonymous; also the words Irish and Catholic, and hence arose that curse of religious antagonism which, for three centuries, blighted the prospects of our people for independence. The English interest was represented by Protestantism principally, and the interest of nationality by Catholicism— so much so that Catholic Irishmen came to feel that, in fighting against Protestantism, they were fighting against England, and, in fighting for Catholicity, they were fighting for Ireland. The priest was the person most sought after, most persecuted by the English, and the most loved, most looked to, and most protected by the Irish. He became the guide and the controller of their action, and he was ever faithful in defending and leading the people to defend the interests of the Church. The faith and the spirit of liberty in the people were not crushed, and, in the growing enlightenment of the present century, England—for the purpose of maintaining her dominion— has thought proper to change her policy. She now patronises the Church, hugs to her bosom its dignitaries, and trusts that they— having influence over the people—will keep them from rebellion. Some of those dignitaries have labored hard to do this in the movement for which I was imprisoned. It is in times of peace that the Church flourishes, and, in the interest of the Church, many will not blame the clergy. Few will blame them, too, for opposing a rebellion where the necessary means of success would not be forecalculated; but, where I could be at issue with them would be in the matter of their opposition to us while providing the means, and few will deny that we had that opposition in Ireland during the past thirteen years. There was no diocese in Ireland where the men who were organizing means to fight England, were not denounced from the altars and sent away from the confessionals unshriven. It is right also to add that there was no diocese in which there were not many priests to bless the laborers and wish Godspeed to the work; but the tongues and hands of these clergymen "were tied" as they themselves would say, by the higher ecclesiastics, while the "bad priests," as we called them, were allowed full scope to denounce us and brand us as infidels before we were any way unfaithful.

In making these observations wholly regarding the action of Catholics toward the independence of Ireland, I must not be understood as excluding the efforts of other religious people in that direction. During the last century many Protestants and Presbyterians were sent to the scaffold and the convict-ship for daring to maintain that they, as Irish-born men, should have an independent Ireland; and in the late revolutionary movement we had a blending of all the sects for liberty. This was as disagreeable to the bigots as to the English enemy. A union of creeds does not seem desirable to Church or State, and both united in assailing those who were bringing it about as traitorous and disreputable. The State had some reason to attack them, but the Church had very little ; for those who were banded together to fight for civil and religious liberty would be the first to stand in defence of their faith if any foe threatened their altars. The Catholic members of the organization found themselves, at the outset, denounced by Catholic priests; and this gave birth to a strange feeling in the breasts of young men who grew up looking upon a priest as the embodiment of hostility to England. They considered that in resolving to battle for the rights of their native land, they had taken a noble resolution, and, in swearing to do so they did not feel, between themselves and their God, that they had committed a sin. But finding themselves condemned, nay damned, for this act, afforded them food for reflection, and what wonder if some of them disregarded the denunciations and labored on? I did. I saw that the time was gone when the priest and the people were as one persecuted. I saw that the priest was free and comparatively happy, while the people were still enslaved, and decidedly miserable. The tradition that my boyhood received of fighting for my religion is fighting for my country, and in fighting for my country I was fighting for my religion, was broken; for here I had sworn to fight for Ireland, and I was set upon as an enemy of Catholicity. The calumny is kept up ; but I can afford to live it down. The politico-religious faith of my fathers is taken to pieces, and as the Irish head of the Church believes that in fighting for Ireland now I am not fighting for Catholicity, I must presume, on the other hand, to believe that in fighting for Catholicity I am not at all fighting for Ireland. I don't put my country before my God ; but I put it before religious ascendency of any denomination. The Church has many defenders, and needs my aid as little as she need fear my hostility ; Ireland has few, and I am beginning to fear they will not be able, unless aided more earnestly than they have been, to work out her immediate salvation.

I do not write my book as a champion of religion, or as one who would assail it. I write neither as a Catholic nor as a Protestant. I come before the public merely as an Irishman, wishing to see my country free for all religious denominations; and wishing to see, for the purpose of overcoming them, all the obstacles that stand in the way of its freedom. If I speak of the interference of religious people in its political concerns, it is not from choice, but from necessity. I hold it absolutely impossible for any one to speak truly of the movements of the people towards independence if he ignores the religious elements that are set in motion to sway the people to one side or the other. Religion and politics are as yet in Ireland inseparable. I should like to see the man who could give a history of the one without touching on the other. I could not do so; and as I am going to tell the whole truth, and nothing but the truth, I am not going to attempt such a story; but I will "nothing extenuate or aught set down in malice."

As this professes to be an account of my prison life, I ought, perhaps, to have you, my readers, inside the prison walls long ago, but I do not think it improper to have a little chat with you beforehand, so that you may understand the cause of my imprisonment and judge whether or not I was deserving of it. If I was, I suppose I will have very little of your sympathy in connection with my suffering. But it is not for sympathy I write; and as to my suffering, it may not be much more in prison than the suffering of many who were out of prison. In order to achieve anything men must be prepared for suffering, and if they are not, and do not dare it, they will lag behind. Men must be ready to brave all they will hear from me, within and without the prison, if they mean to free Ireland; and if the words of my experience be of no use to the present generation, they may be to the next or the one after the next. I will end this chapter with a quotation: "Providence, in order to accomplish its desires in all things, requires a lavish expenditure of courage, of virtues, and of sacrifices—in a word, of man himself; and it is only after an unknown number of unrecorded labors, after a host of noble hearts have succumbed in discouragement, believing the cause to be lost, it is only then that the cause triumphs." We, it seems, have not made sacrifices enough yet; but from the amount of discouragement we have had, we would be warranted in believing in our triumph being immediate if we had faith in the writer of the quotation.

CHAPTER II.

IRELAND'S SUFFERING—PROVIDENCE—FAMINE—OUR FATHERS' CRIMES—'98 AND '48—PROTESTANTS AND CATHOLICS—EGOTISM—THE PHŒNIX SOCIETY—MR. STEPHENS' VISIT TO SKIBBEREEN—JOINING THE REVOLUTIONARY SOCIETY, MAY, '58—AMERICAN AID—DRILLING—POLICE HUNTS—TOO FAST FOR THE IRISH AMERICANS—ARRESTS DECEMBER, '58—EXTRA POLICE—MEETING WITH WILLIAM O'SHEA, TIM M'CARTHY, JERRY CULLINANE AND DENIS O'SULLIVAN—BANTRY PRISONERS—LODGED IN CORK JAIL.

IN the face of all that Ireland has suffered and all the sacrifices she has made to attain her liberty, I cannot attach much importance to the concluding sentences of the last chapter. I do not attribute the misfortune of our slavery to Providence; as little do I attribute the "famine" of '47 to that Power. We are bound down by England. She has the strength to rob us of the produce of our soil till we are reduced to famine diet, and I should be thinking very ill of our people, and very ill of our Creator, if I attributed our state to anything else but a temporal tyranny, living and acting in this world in which we live.

What have our fathers done out of the way that they should be scourged with a rod of iron for seven hundred years? What have they done against God or man more than England has done, that we, their children, should be sown broadcast over the wastes of the world—many of us to perish unheard of and unknown—nay, desirous, alas! not to be known? It may be irreligious to doubt this "will of God" in our bondage, but I would rather be considered so than do violence to my own feelings in my opinions of His justice.

Within the last century our country has been full of adventure in resistance to her opppressor; but we have not had the preparation necessary to resist successfully.

In '98 we had some brave fighting; but many of us acted timidly while a few of us were fighting bravely. For instance, the County of Wexford was up in arms, and the other thirty-one counties of Ireland remained looking on—standing on the fence to see how the fight would go. If successful, they would come in with a helping hand, and with their hurrahs, when neither were wanting; but they didn't or wouldn't come in the nick of time, and the Wexford men were overpowered. Had their action been imitated by the men of every other county in Ireland, we would to-day have a different story to chronicle, and we would have no necessity to keep appealing to our people to act in concert and to work unitedly.

In '48 there was another uprising, and another failure, in consequence principally of not having arms to put into the hands of the people, who sprung forward to use them. It is noteworthy, in view of the efforts of the enemy to perpetuate religious dissensions amongst us, and to make the word Protestant synonymous with the word Englishman, that the men who were most prominent, and who suffered most in the advocacy of the cause of Irish independence during the periods I speak of, were Protestants; and it is but equal justice to the Catholic portion of the community to state that they respected these men and reverenced their memories more than they did men of their own creed. The names of Tone, and Fitzgerald, and Emmet, and Davis, and Mitchel, and O'Brien will live as long in the future, and be as dear to Irishmen, as any other names in their history.

After the English government had crushed the movement in '48, Ireland appeared spiritless and politically dead. Charles Gavan Duffy left the country in '54, saying he left the cause of freedom a corpse on the dissecting table. But, like the seed put into the ground, it must only have been rotting to produce new life; for a few years after we find it in vigorous existence again, and the authorities putting forth all their strength to overcome it. My own experiences now commence, and, like all writers who have anything to say of movements in which they took part, I must become a bit of an egotist. I can not tell the rest of this story without saying something of the writer of it. It is no matter to you, kind reader, whether I like to talk of myself or not; the thing has to be done in order to carry out my arrangements, and I am not going to shrink from my duty, even though the doing so might be a relief to me.

In the month of May, 1858, one of my companions called into my residence in Skibbereen and asked me to take a walk with him, as he had something of importance to communicate to me. I went out, and during our ramble up the Steam-mill road he informed me that on the preceding evening he had received a note of introduction from a stranger, given to him by a mutual friend in Bandon. The stranger told him that the Irishmen in America had resolved to aid us at home in achieving the independence of Ireland, and the aid was to consist of arms and of men. If we had a certain number of men sworn to fight, there would be an equal number of arms in Ireland for these men when enrolled, and an invading force of from five to ten thousand before the start. The arms were to be in the country before the men would be asked to stir; they would not be given into their hands, but they were to be kept in hiding-places until the appointed time, when every Centre could take his men to the spot and get the weapons. As soon as we had enrolled the men willing to fight we were to get military instructors to teach us how to do so as soldiers. I jumped the proposition of "joining;" and next day I inoculated a few others whom I told to go and do likewise. The stranger who came to the town that May evening was Mr. Stephens, and I was promised an introduction to him in a short time if I would work well. We had a society in Skibbereen at this time called the Phœnix National and Literary Society. It was a revolutionary one, though not oath-bound, and we were contemplating affiliations in connection with it in the neighboring towns around at the time I speak of. We gave it the name Phœnix to signify that the nation was to rise again from its ashes. We had about one hundred members, and before a month had elapsed from the day of Mr. Stephens' visit we had over ninety of them enrolled in the new movement.

Before the autumn months had passed away we had the whole district of country in a blaze, and in October we had a drill-master sent to us from Dublin. He had served a period in the American army, and well and truly he did his work amongst us, despite all the police watchings and huntings. One night we were on a mountain side, another night in the midst of a wood, another in a fairy fort, and another in a cellar. We had outposts on every occasion, who signaled to us of any approaching danger, and in the darkness of the nights many things were signalled as dangers which were quite harmless; and we had many adventures in scattering which were subjects for our amusement at the next meeting. In Loriga wood one evening the sentry gave us the signal to scatter, and we ran in the direction opposite to that from which we apprehended the danger. I was the second man; he who was before me got up on a ditch and made a leap to cross a large dyke at the other side of it, but he slipped and didn't get across clear. As he lay at the other side I leaped upon him, the next man leaped upon me, and before a minute nine or ten of us were sprawling in the dyke. In these drillings we departed from the programme of organization, for we brought more men together than ought to be known to each other, and this we had to do to keep them in good humor, for when it was known the military instructor was in the district, every company was calling out for his attendance, and as he couldn't be everywhere we had only to bring the men everywhere to where he was. The first man who learned the art from him and became his assistant, and his substitute when he was gone, was Colonel P. J. Downing, now of Washington. It is said that people in America are a fast people, and the Irish there are not exempted from the benefit of the expression; but in Ireland, when it was a question of uniting to fight against England, we were too fast for our brothers across the Atlantic, for we had the men ready to fight before they had given us the arms to do so.

The Government took alarm and they took measures to have a number of us arrested and cast into prison. About four o'clock on the morning of the 5th of December I was roused out of bed, and I found my house surrounded by police. I was taken to the station, and there I met some twenty others of my acquaintance. Many of them had left my house only a few hours before, for we were sitting up doing the honors to one of our company, Dan M'Cartie, who was leaving town next morning to discharge the duties of brewer in Ballinasloe, and, as we met in the police barrack, we commenced joking at the ominous appropriateness of the last song sung by Mortimer Moynahan:—

> "Hurra for the wild wintry weather,
>   While the nights pass so gaily along,
> As we sit by the fire altogether,
>   And drown the loud tempest in song.
> Hurra! let the peals of our laughter
>   Arise and be heard far away,
> Our lives may be gloomy hereafter—
>   Then let us be glad while we may.
>
> "Hurra for the wild wintry weather—
>   The summer has bright leafy bowers;
> But, 'tis thus, round the fire altogether,
>   Young and old spend their happiest hours.
> Hurra! let us all swell the chorus
>   'Till it rise and be heard far away;
> Perhaps some dark cloud gathers o'er us—
>   Then let us be glad while we may."

A number of extra police had been sent from Dublin to Skibbereen two months before our seizure. These were on duty every night in all parts of the suburbs of the town, and, though we were on duty too, they never, by any chance, surprised us at our drillings. The night of the arrests the police of the surrounding villages were drafted into the town. The authorities were terribly alarmed; they apprehended that we had arms and that we would resist, when we had very few weapons and didn't dream of fighting till we got the orders. Each of us was handcuffed between two policemen going from Clonakilty to Bandon, or, to express myself more clearly, two policemen were handcuffed to every one of us. In the Bandon prison we met some men from Bantry, arrested on the same charge as we were, and on their way to Cork Jail. We were huddled into cells flooded with water at nine o'clock in the evening having been travelling all day under rain, and having received neither food nor drink, and now we wouldn't get a bed nor bread. Next morning we found ourselves in Cork Jail, awaiting evidence on a charge of conspiracy.

CHAPTER III.

OAKUM AND SOLITARY CONFINEMENT—BLACK BREAD AND LEEK PORRIDGE—EATING IN THE DARK—MOCK TRIAL IN PRISON—FALSE SWEARING ABOUT DRILLING, ETC.—"MARCHING IN MILITARY ORDER"—PATRICK'S DAY IN THE DOCK—SENT BACK TO PRISON AGAIN—PLEAD GUILTY—JURY PACKING—LORD O'HAGAN—PATRIOTISM OF THE IRISH BAR A SHAM—FIRST WORKING OF THE REVOLUTIONARY MOVEMENT IN '58—MORTIMER MOYNAHAN "STEEPED TO THE LIPS IN TREASON"—CENTRES AND CIRCLES—OPPOSITION OF THE CLERGY—ABSOLUTION REFUSED—THE JUBILEE—THE BISHOP AND DR. DOYLE—GIVE TO CÆSAR WHAT'S DUE TO CÆSAR—THE POLICE SPY SYSTEM—ALTAR DENUNCIATION—REV. MR. O'SULLIVAN'S INFORMATION TO THE GOVERNMENT, AND MR. SULLIVAN'S (OF THE "NATION") NOTE OF WARNING—THE EVIL EFFECTS OF CURIOSITY.

IN Cork Jail we were lodged in separate cells, and got oakum to pick. We asked were we obliged to work before we were convicted, and we were told we should work unless we paid for our maintenance. Half a dozen of the men made arrangements to get their own food, and the rest of us thought we would inure ourselves to hardships; but we could not eat the fare we got, and this, with the solitary confinement imposed, starved us out of our resolution "to suffer and be strong." The bread was made from rye wheat; it had the appearance of brown hand-turf, and you could squeeze the water out of it. The porridge was about the same color, but it was flavored with leeks, which made it disgusting to look at, for, when you drew your spoon out of the bowl, you drew up one of these leeks half a foot long, and unless you had gone through a course of starvation—as I had gone through in the English prisons—your stomach would refuse to receive it as food. One of the prisoners said he could manage to eat it in no way but by keeping his eyes closed while at it.

After being a week in this prison, we were told that the charge would not be ready against us for a week. The second week passed by, and then we learned the cause of our arrest. We were led into a room in the prison, where sat four gentlemen awaiting us. Two of them were stipendiary magistrates, and the others, Sir Matthew Barrington, and his assistant, crown prosecutors. We were told there was a charge of conspiracy against us, and that one of the conspirators, seeing the wickedness of our project, and regretting his part in it, had come forward to give evidence. In a word, they had an informer to swear against us. He was brought into the room, and most of us recognized him as one we had seen before; his name was Dan Sullivan *Goula*. He swore that he saw me drilling three hundred men on a by-road, within a mile of Skibbereen, one night at ten o'clock. He swore he saw me another night drilling some twenty men in a room in the town, but everything he swore was false; he never saw me drilling these men, nor did these drillings ever take place; but he saw me in the room with the twenty men, and he swore against every one of these twenty that they were present the night of the three hundred. This was for the purpose of having every one arrested who could prove the falsehood, and he was instructed to swear this way by one of the stipendiary magistrates, Fitzmaurice. This gentleman had a great character for breaking up what are called Ribbon societies in the North of Ireland, and for getting informers amongst them, and a few weeks before the arrests in Skibbereen he was sent to that town on special duty. One of the prisoners, named Tim Duggan, hearing how *Goula* was telling lies of him in his presence, made a move as if to approach him; the informer cried out that Duggan was going to strike him, and the prisoner was threatened with all kinds of punishment if he attempted to intimidate the witness from giving evidence. We were represented by a very clever solicitor, Mr. McCarthy Downing, who is now member of Parliament for Cork, and it is but justice to him to say that throughout these cases he did us invaluable service in defeating the attempts of the Government to suborn more witnesses against us. He demanded that the gentlemen of the press should be allowed into the prison, to be present at the proceedings, but his demand was refused, while at the same time the slavish writers of the Anglo-Irish journals were obeying the behests of the Crown, and representing that all kinds of horrible things were being brought to light concerning this horrible conspiracy.

According to English law, the evidence of an informer, uncorroborated, is insufficient to detain men in prison, and the meanest shifts were resorted to to get other evidence. The police had been watching after us for months, and could adduce nothing illegal against us; but now they were threatened by this Fitzmaurice that if they did not make informations to corroborate *Goula* they would be deprived of their situations. This was after the first week of our imprisonment, as I since learned from some of the policemen who swore against myself, and before the end of the second week a dozen of them had sworn something against us. One young "peeler" swore that he saw Denis Downing marching through the streets of Skibbereen "in military order;" and when our solicitor, in cross-examination, asked him who was walking with the prisoner, he answered: "No one but himself!" So that walking through the town with an independent tread was considered by this protector of the law as something that would corroborate the informer in what he swore about the drilling.

All the men arrested were released on bail except myself and five others. We were condemned to remain in prison to await trial at the March assizes. The March assizes came, and we were ready for trial; but the Government would not try us. They brought us into the court on Patrick's Day, '59, and ordered us to be sent back to prison again to await trial at the assizes of the following July. Our counsel asked if we would not be admitted to bail, and they were told not. Back we went to prison, and remained there till July, and then they would not try us, but threatened us with another postponement of trial till the succeeding March unless we pleaded guilty to the charges against us, in which case we would get our freedom. We had been refusing to do this since the first assizes, because we knew that we could disprove the evidence of the informer. Our prosecutors knew this, too, and though they were eager for our conviction, they doubted their success before the public court, even with a packed jury. They had tried Daniel O'Sullivan (Agreem) with a packed jury in Tralee, and had him sentenced to ten years' penal servitude; and now, as a last resource of getting their ends of us, they offered to release Agreem if we would plead guilty, and to this we consented.

It is not easy to get the better of your enemy when he has you under lock and key. The English law presumes that every man is innocent until he is proven guilty; but in political cases in Ireland the practice is quite the contrary, for every man is treated as guilty until he proves himself innocent. We were eight months in prison, and it would never tell for the justice of the great nation that she had subjected us to imprisonment so long, with the Habeas Corpus Act unsuspended, unless she could show that we were criminals; therefore, it was necessary to get us to put in the plea in vindication of the justice of our incarceration. Perhaps we were wrong in relieving the Government from this odium; but we relieved ourselves from imprisonment, and also relieved him who was committed for ten years. We were to appear for judgment on this plea of guilty—if we were ever guilty of a repetition of the charge against us; but we were to get fourteen days' notice to appear, and during these fourteen days we were at liberty to leave the country if we liked. I want this to be remembered when I come to speak of my trial before Judge Keogh in 1865. We were released from prison in July, 1859, and the authorities were so mean as to keep Dan O'Sullivan (Agreem) in jail till November, though his immediate release was promised to us.

Talking of jury packing, I am reminded of what late Irish papers bring under prominent notice—that is, Lord O'Hagan's advocacy of the bill for that purpose now passing through the English Parliament. He was our counsel at these Phœnix trials; and in the defence of Dan O'Sullivan he spent eight or ten hours in denunciation of the packing of juries against his client. But Lord O'Hagan, the great Catholic champion, is now on the English side of the House, and the Irish and their claims to anything like justice or fair play may go to Jericho. When I hear these Irish lawyers at their law dinners prate of the patriotism of the Irish bar, I feel that I have heard the most sublime humbug that man ever listened to. Dowse, who made a most patriotic speech in defence of John O'Leary, was next year prosecuting John O'Leary's companions and denouncing his principles.

As information that might temper future action in Ireland may be drawn from my experience of the proceedings that led to my imprisonment in 1858, and from the manner in which this informer Goula turned up, I may be allowed to trespass upon my reader's attention a little while I relate what may be of interest to him should he ever desire to do anything for Irish freedom in the way of fight.

I lived in the most southern town of Ireland, and with the assurances given us of a struggle in the immediate future, and the belief that all Ireland was working towards its success, we resolved not to be backward, and we worked with all our energies in getting recruits for the Irish revolutionary army. He who did most in extending the work through the district was a young man named Mortimer Moynahan, who is now battling with the world in the great city of New York. He was manager in the office of Mr. M'Carthy Downing. This attorney used to attend every sessions in every town in the district; he did the largest business of any lawyer in the circuit, and used to take Moynahan with him as an assistant. Every client had to approach the big man through Mortimer's hands, who marked out all who had any sort of Irish spirit in them, and swore them into the revolutionary movement at night when the business of the law was over; so that he was working legally by day and illegally by night. When Attorney-General Whiteside was prosecuting him, a few months afterwards, he described him to the jury as "one who was steeped to the lips in treason." Before we were six months at work we had the organization started in every corner of the south of Cork and in a part of Kerry. The man who swore me in was first appointed Centre of a circle comprising 820 men, which gave him the direction of those men; then I grew big enough to be appointed another Centre; then Moynahan, and then two others for the remoter country districts around. Fenians in America may talk of the aid they have given the men at home; but I can tell them that the men at home spent out of their own pockets, in working up the organization, more money than the Fenian Brotherhood collected altogether. The first check we met was from the Catholic clergy. Our men came to us telling that they were driven away from the confessionals, and would not get absolution unless they gave up the oath.

We asked them did they think they committed a sin in taking

an oath to fight for their country's freedom, and when they said they did not, we told them to tell the priests that they came to confess their sins and not their virtues, and to ask the priests if they had sworn to fight for England against Ireland, would they not get absolution? The priests were getting vexed with us, and we were getting vexed with the priests. The most amusing stories were afloat of how simple country boys argued with their clergy on the subject of fighting for Ireland. A pastor one day told his penitent that the society was illegal, when the penitent softened his confessor's heart to give him absolution by exclaiming: "Yerra, father, what do I care about their illegal? I care more about my soul."

In July, 1858, there was a Jubilee in our place. The young men were going to their duty, and the priests were discharging their duty in sending them away without the Sacraments. I found myself some twelve miles from home one day, and meeting a priest, who knew me, he asked:

"Jerry, did you do the Jubilee yet?"

"No, Father," said I, "there's no Jubilee for me; I'm outside the pale of the Church."

"How is that?" said he.

I told him, and he replied:

"Ah, that's no sin. I'll be in Skibbereen on Saturday, assisting the other priests; come to me, and we'll have no difficulty about the matter."

I did go to him, and he was as good as his word. The Skibbereen priests and the Skibbereen bishop were still persistent in opposing us, and I determined to have a talk with his lordship, whom newspapers love to style the patriotic Bishop of Ross.

I went to confession to him and told my sins, after which he asked me if I belonged to an oath-bound society, and I said I did.

"Then," said he, "I can't give absolution."

"Oh, my lord," said I, "I don't seek absolution for that; I was at confession since I joined the society and got absolution; the priest told me that such a thing was no sin."

"It was a sin," said he, "and that priest participated in it; and go away from me and don't come any more."

I went away, but that day week I went to him again, and, as I knelt down in the confessional, the first words he said were:

"Didn't I tell you not to come any more to me?"

"My lord," said I, "it is not to you I come but to the confessional. I came here to confess my sins to God, through you; and you cannot refuse to hear me."

"You should have more humility in the confessional," he replied.

To make a long story short we got talking on the political question. I remarked that Dr. Doyle said, that if a rebellion raged from Malin Head to Cape Clear, no priest would fulminate a decree of excommunication against any one engaged in it; when the bishop hastily said—

"Ah, I know more about Dr. Doyle than you do; and go on with your confession."

I did as he directed, and we parted amicably. He told me to come again to him in a week, but I was in Cork jail before the week elapsed. The bishop was true about Dr. Doyle, for I read his life, by Fitzpatrick, in prison, and if I had read it before I would not quote the great doctor in defence of oath-bound societies, or of any societies aiming at the destruction of British rule in Ireland.

Some of the priests took occasion to denounce our work from the altars, too. I was at Mass that Sunday, at the end of October or the beginning of November, when the Gospel of the day contains a recommendation to give to Cæsar what is due to Cæsar, and Father Beausang laid hold of it to show that we should give tribute to England, and denounced the wicked men who were in his parish administering oaths for the purpose of doing work in opposition to the text. I have ever considered, and will ever consider, this preaching a perversion of the text. "Give to Cæsar what is due to Cæsar" was said to confound those who were devising schemes to accuse Christ of some offence. The coin that was shown Christ did not belong to Cæsar, and it was not given to Cæsar, whose image was on it, but to the man from whom it was received. If Dr. Anderson was charged to-morrow as a man of doubtful loyalty, if he was asked if it were lawful to pay tribute to Victoria, and if he asked a coin of the realm and made use of similar words as the Bible contains, he would not give or send the coin to Victoria, but to the person who showed it to him. If the British flag floats in Ireland, and if the impress of British dominion is on the land, nevertheless it is not English nor England's by right; it is Irish and belongs to the Irish, and it will be theirs yet if they act like men and repudiate the political teachings that would educate them as slaves.

England's police system in Ireland is one vast spy system. More than half of these police are Catholics, and some of them have to attend every Mass in every chapel on Sundays. The priest speaks of a secret oath-bound society to his parishioners; the policeman goes to his barrack, and his first duty is to make a report of what the priest said and send it off to Dublin Castle. I may safely say that it was through this channel that the authorities had any certainty of the spread of revolutionary work. Then the newspapers took up the cry; and, in accord with the newspapers giving what information they could glean by exchanging confidences with friends and by all other means, some priests were giving private information to the Castle.

I have in my possession evidence to convince any one that one priest gave information, and I will give that evidence. I am not going to tell how we got possession of it; that can only be told when the secret workings of our machinery can be made known. I know the correspondence is genuine. I know how it came into our possession. I know that this priest who wrote it was not condemned by his bishop for doing so; but that will not be wondered at when it is known that his lordship is the charitable Kerry gentleman who said, "that hell was not hot enough nor eternity long enough for those Irishmen" who were giving so much trouble to England.

Father O'Sullivan, of Kenmare, does not deny this correspondence; indeed, I believe he justifies it. I, a few weeks ago, saw communications between him and the editor of the Dublin *Nation* on the subject of giving first information. The priest was, I think, first in private, but the paper was first in public. Both, no doubt, satisfied themselves that they were doing the best thing they could do, but I blamed the layman more than the priest, for something more was expected from him. He professed himself a fighting man for Ireland if there were fighting means. We were trying to organize the means, and we thought he should not be the man to come forward and expose us. If his house was on fire, and if his friends rushed into danger to save his furniture or his family, he should not be the first to pitch stones at them and knock them off the walls. He considered the movement would destroy or involve Ireland more than it would redeem it, and he must have liberty of opinion. I considered, and still consider, that Ireland will never be free from English rule unless by a secret oath-bound conspiracy in the British Islands, but a more unscrupulous one than the one we had. Here is the priest's correspondence, and a pretty piece of business it is:

"Kenmare, October 5, 1858.

"MY LORD—Having discovered in the latter end of the week that an extensive conspiracy was being organized in this parish, and was imported from Bantry and Skibbereen, I deemed it my duty at both Masses on Sunday to denounce, in the strongest language, the wickedness and immorality of such a system, and its evil consequences to society. Before evening I had the satisfaction of coming at a good deal of the workings of the system, and even got copies of the oaths, which I send at the other side for the information of the Government.

"I was led to believe that 700 or 800 persons had been enrolled here, and some 3,000 in Skibbereen: the former I know to be a gross exaggeration, and I suppose the latter equally so. Before I come out on these deluded young men—the names of some of whom I have—I advised the magistrates of the facts, and they, too, have probably advised with your lordship.—I have the honor to be, &c.,

"JOHN O'SULLIVAN.

"Right Hon. Lord Naas, M.P."

"Kenmare, December 11, 1858.

"MY LORD—Since I forwarded to you copies of the oaths that were being administered by the misguided young men, some ten or a dozen of whom were arrested here yesterday, I beg to assure you that I lost no opportunity of denouncing, both in public and private, the folly and the wickedness of their proceedings.

"Nay, more, I refused to hear the confession or to admit to communion any one person who had joined the society until they should come to me, 'extra tribunal,' as we technically term it; and there, not only promise to disconnect themselves from the society, but also give the names of every person they knew to be a member. It was rather difficult to accomplish the latter, but I did; and having thus come at the names of these deluded young men, I, either with their parents or with themselves, showed them the insanity of the course they had been following. Almost every one of those now under arrest have been last week at their Christmas confession and communion; and, though it may be no legal evidence of their being innocent, to any one acquainted with the practice and discipline of our Church, it is *prima facie* evidence of their having solemnly pledged themselves to disconnect themselves from the society.

"I beg to assure your lordship that since the 3rd of October—the Sunday on which I first denounced this society—not even *one single person has joined it*; and, had the thing taken root or progressed, I would have been as ready to advise you of its progress as I was of its existence. So completely extinct has it been that more than once I proposed writing to you to remove the *extra* police force, seeing them perfectly unnecessary.

"Under such circumstances, I make bold to ask your lordship to interfere with his Excellency for the liberation of these foolish boys—for boys they are. They have got a proper fright, and I make no doubt that an act of well-timed clemency will have more effect in rendering them dutiful subjects hereafter than would the measure of the justice they certainly deserve.

"If they be treated with kindness they will be thankful and grateful, and doubly so if the thing be done at once, and in a friendly and fatherly spirit; but carry out the law, and you will, of course, vindicate it, but you certainly will have confirmed a set of young rebels in their hostility to her Majesty's Government.—I have the honor, &c.,

"JOHN O'SULLIVAN.

" Right Honorable Lord Naas, M.P."

The next letter is to a school-fellow of his, who was partner to Sir Matthew Barrington, the Crown prosecutor. Mind how he talks of the "brats":

"Kenmare, December 16, 1858.

"MY DEAR PAT—It never occurred to me that the prosecution of these young men here would come before you so soon; so I was waiting the approach of the Assizes to put before you the part I took in it. The moment I got hold of the existence of such a foolish conspiracy here I advised the magistrates of it, who could scarcely believe me.

"I denounced it at both Masses on the 3rd of October, and such a surprise was it on the congregation that they most unanimously voted me either mad or seeking to work upon the fears of Trench, who is still going to all and most unworthy lengths in opposing the convent.

"Immediately after denouncing, a party came and gave me copies of the two oaths I enclose you. I dreaded him, and to save myself I mentioned the facts to the magistrates. Trench at once sent to me for a copy, and, feeling he only wanted to make a call at the Castle, I was inclined not to give it; but then, on the other hand, I feared to withhold it, as he would be but too glad to have so much to tell Lord Lansdowne and the Government.

"'The two Simpsons dined with me the same evening, and Richard advised me to send a copy to Lord Naas by next post, but to withhold the copy for Trench until the post after, and then let Trench make a fool of himself by sending up his "Eureka" to the Government. I did that, and see Lord Naas's reply. On the arrest of these young men I wrote to him a letter, a copy of which I send you, and if he has sense he will take my advice. Let him prosecute these lads, and the excitement that will follow will have no bounds. The people are already talking of giving them a public entry—of raising a subscription to defend them, and thus the excitement will be tremendous; whereas, if the brats be sent home at once, all this will be anticipated. I beg of you to do what you can to carry out this view of it. The Government may be quite satisfied that, since the 3rd of October, there has been a complete stop to it here; and if any of the unfortunate boys have moved in it since, I am not to be understood as having the slightest pity or feeling for them. Say, if you please, what we ought to do; and do what you can for these poor, deluded boys. Would you advise me to write to Sir Charles Trevelyan, or to the Lord Lieutenant, or would you advise a public meeting and a memorial here?—My dear Pat, &c.,
"JOHN O'SULLIVAN.

"P. D. Jeffers, Esq."

"Kenmare, December 17, 1858.

"DEAR SIR MATTHEW—I wrote to Pat Jeffers yesterday, and immediately after heard from Mr. Davis; he was on his way to meet you. Had I known so much. I would have reserved my letter to Pat for you. About the 1st of October I had the first intimation of the movement of these blockheads. I denounced it at both Masses on the 3rd, and before the evening of that day I had the satisfaction of getting copies of the oaths, which I at once forwarded to Lord Naas, and for which I have his thanks.

"I would stake my existence that from thenceforward not a single individual joined the society. I send you a copy of the letter I wrote to Lord Naas upon the arrest of these young lads, as conveying what I would impress upon you now ; and I will only add to it that the less you make of the whole matter the more you will contribute to the peace of the country in general. Require heavy bail from them, and that bail they will get ; but then you will elevate a pack of silly boys to be great patriots, and attach a significance and importance to the whole matter it really does not deserve. Great sympathy for the young chaps exists here by reason of their youth; and if you go to any extremities with them, it will not only give great dissatisfaction to the people, but it will confirm the young fellows in their hostility to the Government, whether they be guilty or not. I beg of you, therefore, as you value the peace and welfare of the country, to let them out, either upon their own recognizances or upon very moderate bail, and you will find it to be the most effectual stop to this very silly movement.—I am, dear Sir Matthew, &c.,
"JOHN O'SULLIVAN.

"Sir Matthew Barrington, Bart., Tralee."

"Kenmare, December 26, 1858.

"MY LORD—Now that an investigation has been had as to the nature and extent of the Phœnix Society, I venture to call your attention to a letter I took the liberty of writing to you on this day fortnight. I have just read the evidence of the approver Sullivan in the *Cork Examiner*, and he states 'he had been at confession with me, and that I advised him to break the oaths.' *The man never confessed to me. I never exchanged a word with him. He is not a parishioner of mine at all!* If all his evidence be as true as this much it is of little value.

"Looking, therefore, at the unsupported evidence of this fellow, at the youth of the lads led astray by him, and, above all, at the fact of the society having been completely extinguished since I first denounced it on the 3rd of October, I venture again to ask your lordship to interfere with his Excellency for a free pardon for these foolish parishioners of mine. It will be the most perfect extinguisher he can possibly put on it.

"If you call them up for trial a large subscription will be made up to defend them; for their youth, with the innumerable perjuries of the approver, has created much sympathy for them, and great excitement will be kept up here until the assizes. If they shall be acquitted a regular ovation will be the consequence, while a conviction cannot entail a very heavy sentence on such striplings. If his Excellency will graciously grant them a free pardon he will attach them faithful and beholden to her Majesty, and we shall hear no more of this absurd, wicked, and foolish society. I am quite sure, also, that you must be aware that it was my active interference suppressed the society so immediately here; and, though I incurred much odium in the beginning, all parties now admit I was their best friend. This, I think, entitles me to some consideration on your part; and be assured that, if I had the slightest reason to think that a prosecution would tend more to the preservation of the peace and the dignity of the constitution than what I ask now, I would be the foremost in recommending it. I therefore confidently ask for a free pardon *for the whole* of my poor, deluded parishioners ; because, if the thing be done at all, it ought to be done in a free and generous spirit, making no distinctions or exceptions, because without pronouncing on the guilt or the innocence of any of the parties, I am perfectly satisfied and convinced not one of them had the slightest connection with the society from the day I first denounced it.—I have the honor, &c.,

"JOHN O'SULLIVAN.

"The Right Hon. Lord Naas, M.P."

This information, or this oath, which the priest sent to Dublin Castle, was obtained under the following circumstances : A young man went to confession to the Rev. Mr. O'Sullivan, and the priest ascertaining that his penitent belonged to the society, asked him out into the chapel yard, where he questioned him again, and extracted from him a copy of the oath. This was—to use the words of the priest—getting the information *extra tribunal;* but I doubt that there are many priests or laymen who will approve of the use made of what was so obtained.

When the Castle authorities got the first information in October they set to work to get an informer, and they succeeded in getting one in Kenmare. They sent him to Skibbereen in order that he might be able to make the acquaintance of some men there, and swear against them. We, in Skibbereen, knew he was coming to see us, and the friends in Kerry told us to be cautious of him, that he was a suspected individual, got into the society by one who did not know him well. This informer went once to a fair in Bantry, some 20 miles from home; he was sworn in Bantry, much to the annoyance of his neighbors, who would never have trusted him so far, but now that he was in, they had to make the best of it. When he came to Skibbereen a number of our young men went to see him through curiosity—all to pass an opinion as to his honesty or perfidy—and he swore informations against every one to whom he got introduced. But all he swore was false, and his employers knew it. They will never scruple to carry out their ends by falsehood, and here we are not able to meet them. They did not care how they got us to prison so they had us there. They knew that they could then have the better of us. They worked hard to get criminatory evidence against us and failed, hence our release without trial after eight months.

CHAPTER IV.

A GLANCE OVER SIX YEARS—EVICTION—FIDELITY OF THE PEOPLE—
"SHONEEN" SNOBBERY—THE PATRIOTIC BISHOP O'HEA—RIFLES AND
PIKES—ENGLISH HYPOCRISY—SURRENDER—POLISH DEMONSTRATION
AND PRINCE OF WALES' ILLUMINATION—TEARING DOWN THE ENGLISH
FLAG WHERE THERE WAS NOT MUCH DANGER IN THE WAY—THREATS—
THE "IRISH PEOPLE" NEWSPAPER DENUNCIATIONS—CALUMNIES—A
HARD JOB FOR ANY OF THE "FRATRES FENIORES" TO GET MARRIED—
NO ABSOLUTION—FATHER LEADER AND HIS GROSS INSULT, WHICH
ENDED IN MARRIAGE.

My release from one prison in 1859 until my re-entrance into another in 1865 runs over a period of six years—full of incident and adventure sufficient to make a book in itself.

It will not do to make one book within another. I can make a second one, if, after reading the first, my readers judge that I am any hand at all at book-making, so I will devote no more than one chapter now to my knowledge of the movement during the half-dozen years I speak of.

While I was in prison landlordism played some pranks with my family. The ownership of my residence and place of business was disputed by two parties; the man from whom I had the house rented lost the lawsuit, and the other, getting a court order to take immediate possession, ejected my family; and when I came out of prison I found the old house at home gone, and the inmates in a strange one. My business was suspended, and I set to work to put the wheels in motion again, but it was a difficult job to bring as much water to my mill as it had before. Then, landlords themselves and rich people traded with me; now, the poor people and the peasantry alone stuck to me. It is believed that the lower you descend into the bowels of the earth the hotter you will find it; and it is said, side by side with this, that the lower you go amongst an oppressed people the warmer you will find them, the truer and the more ready to make sacrifices for freedom, friend or fatheland.

I believe this to be true. I know the Irish people now, at least in Ireland, for it is not so easy to know them in America; and I would trust my life in anything for Ireland to the poorest of them sooner than I would to the richest. I travelled England, Ireland and Scotland in connection with the revolutionary movement; I met the poorest of our people in the small villages and in the large cities; I whispered "treason" and "rebellion" to them night after night for years. I was three months awaiting trial in Dublin prisons; any amount of money would have been given to any one who would come forward to swear that I was seen in such and such a place on such an occasion, and though I could count by thousands the humble people I had met, not one of them came forward to take the English bribe. I would not run the same gauntlet amongst the rich. How often have I been told by some of my well-to-do friends, who knew what I was at, that I would find these people selling me; and how often have I contemned their vaticinations. How often have I told them that it would be well for them if they were willing to do as much for Ireland as the men they were despising; and how often to the sneering expression of "what have they to lose?" have I replied, "they have their lives, which are dearer than anything you could lose."

But then "it was not respectable!" but why did not the "respectable people commence it, or come into it, and make it respectable? It is the very same thing to-day in the city of New York. The "respectables" won't do anything with the "ragamuffins" who are willing to do something for Ireland, but they have no objection in the world to shake hands and make high-fellow-well-met with them— nay, to condescend to fling them a few bones when fat meat is wanted for our more respectable cousins, and when the poor man's vote will help to get it. This fat meat idea came into my head while thinking that it may be time for me, as the French say, to return to my mutton.

I recommenced my pursuits, political and commercial, a few months after my release from prison, and I found it much more difficult to be successful in the legal than in the illegal one. To transact the political business I could meet the people anywhere, but to do the commercial matters the people had to come to my house, which many were afraid to do for a time, in the fear that their landlords would be down on them for having any association with such a desperate character; for, of course, the stock-in-trade lies were told of us, that we were going to massacre landlords, and overturn altars. And some of the ministers of the altars did their parts too, if it is proper to think so from the fact of the "patriotic" Bishop O'Hea's challenging a man and his wife in the confessional for frequenting my house. The man told me that he was challenged, and told me that his wife told him that she was challenged. They both live still; I am not going to tell their names. I did not hear that any others were put through a similiar operation, but I suppose there were others. It is well for a man to suffer for his sins in this world; better than in the next. I might have been a greater sinner than the ordinary run of mortals around; I know I am not a lesser one; but certainly I did not show much more scandal than many others who had not the ire of the Church on them. Perhaps it is a very great crime to teach the people to be independent of priests in politics; this I did do, and this I will do as long as the priests oppose any organization of means to rid Ireland of English rule, and I believe no organization will do it that will not be oath-bound and secret in and about Ireland, and that will not avail of all and every means that is deemed necessary to attain the object.

One branch of my business was the spirit trade, or as I am writing in America, the liquor trade. Licenses for this are renewed every year, and at each renewal the police came forward to have mine annulled. They put me to trouble, expense and annoyance. I always appealed to a superior court, and as no charge of keeping an irregular house could be urged against me I came away with my license.

The authorities had frightened the simple portion of the community by our arrest, and I found the people under the impression that if any kind of military weapon was found with them they would be sent to jail. It was hard to disabuse them of this, and I took a practical method of doing it.

I was in possession of an Enfield rifle and bayonet, a sword and an old Croppy pike, with a hook and hatchet on it, formidable enough to frighten any coward, and these I hung up in a conspicuous part of my store; yet this would not even satisfy some that I could keep these articles with impunity, and I had many a wise head giving me advice. But when I have satisfied myself that a thing is right, and that I make up my mind to do it, I can listen very attentively to those who, in kindness, would advise me for the purpose of dissuading me from a course inimical, perhaps, to my own interests, while at the same same time I can be firm in my resolve to go on as soon as my adviser is gone. The arms remained in their place, and on fair-days and market-days it was amusing to see young peasants bringing in their companions to see the sight. "*Fheagh! fheagh!* Look! look!" would be the first exclamation on entering the shop; and never did artist survey a work of art more composedly than would some of those boys, leaning on their elbows over the counter, admire the treasured weapons they longed to use one day in defence of the cause of their fatherland.

At the end of a few years the people were fully persuaded that they could keep arms in defiance of the police. It would answer the ends of government very well, if the authorities by keeping the people scared, could keep them unarmed without the passing of arms acts and other repressive measures, that look so very ugly to the world. If England could keep her face clean—if she could carry the phylacteries—if she could have the Bible on her lips and the devil in her deeds, without any of the devil's work being seen, she would be in her glory.

My pikes were doing great mischief in the community it seems, and rumors were going around that others were getting pikes, too. Tim Duggan, whom I spoke of as being in Cork jail, was employed in my shop. Tim should be always at some mischief, and, taking down the pikes one day to take some of the rust off them, no place would satisfy him to sit burnishing them but outside the door. This he did to annoy a very officious sergeant of police, named Brosnahan, who was on duty outside the store. Next day I was sent for by my friend M'Carthy Downing, who was Chairman of the Town Commissioners, and magistrate of the town. He told me that the magistrates were after having a meeting, and had a long talk about what occurred the day before. Brosnahan represented that not alone was Tim Duggan cleaning the pikes, but showing the people how they could be used with effect—what beautiful things they were to frighten exterminating landlords and all other tools of tyranny. Mr. Downing asked me would I deliver up the arms, and I said certainly not. He said the magistrates were about to make a report to the Castle of the matter. I said I did not care what reports they made; the law allowed me to hold such things, and hold them I would until the district was proclaimed.

"Now," added he, "for peace sake, I ask you as a personal favor to give them up to me, I will keep them for you in my own house, and I pledge you my word that when you want them I will give them to you."

"Well" replied I, "as you make so serious a matter of it you can have them."

I went home, I put my pike on my shoulder, and gave another to William (Croppy) M'Carthy. It was a market day, and both of us walked through the town and showed the people we could carry arms, so that we made the act of surrender as glorious as possible to our cause, and as disagreeable as it could be to the stipendiaries of England.

These are small things to chronicle but it is in small things that the enemy shows a very wary diligence to crush us. Inch by inch she pursues us, and no spark of manhood appears anywhere in the land that she has not recourse to her petty arts to extinguish it.

In the spring of 1863, the Poles were struggling against their tyranny, and we conceived the idea of having a meeting of sympathy for them in Skibbereen, and carried it out. We prepared torchlights and republican banners, and we issued private orders to have some of our best men in from the country. The authorities were getting alarmed, and they issued orders to have a large force of police congregated in the town on the appointed night. During the day the "peelers," as I may inoffensively call them, were pouring in, and as they passed by the several roads the peasantry crowded in after them. The rumor went around that we were to be slaughtered, and men from the country came in to see the fun. The town was full of " peelers" and peasants, and to have another stroke at the big fellows we got handbills struck off, calling upon the people not to say an offensive word to any of the police, that they were Irishmen, like ourselves, and only obliged from circumstances to *appear* our enemies. We posted these bills and employed boys to put them into the hands of the police. There were six magistrates in the town, and the stipendiary one, O'Connell— a member of the "Liberator's" family—was in command of the forces. They thought to intimidate us from carrying out the programme of our procession, and we felt bound to maintain the confidence of our people by proceeding according to our announcement. They recognized in our meeting of sympathy for the Poles a meeting of organized hostility against England; they knew that bringing the masses together and allowing them to see their strength and union would create confidence, and that is what they wanted to kill. And, to be candid, it was necessary for us to humor the peculiarities of our people some way. They are ever ready to fight, ever impatient for the "time," and when the time is long coming they are drooping and restless without stimulants.

The officers of arrangement moved from the committee-rooms. The committee were armed with wands and marched in front, towards the place where the vast assembly of people were formed in line of procession, with the torches in their hands.

The wives of the police and the police themselves had been sent to the mothers of some of the young men on the committee, telling them that the police had orders to fire on us; and the mothers implored us, on their knees, to give up our project. We went on; and, as we proceeded to move, the magistrates came in front of us, with the police behind them, and stopped the route of our march. The Castle agent, O'Connell, addressing himself to Brosnahan, asked—

"Who are the leaders of this tumult?"

And the police sergeant answered—

"Here, they are, sir; Dan M'Cartie, Mortimer Moynahan, Jerry Crowly, Con Callaghan, O'Donovan Rossa, James O'Keeffe, &c."

O'Connell—"I order this assembly to disperse."

Committee—"For what?"

"For it is disturbing the peace of the town."

"It is you who are disturbing the peace of the town. We are peaceful citizens met here to demonstrate our sympathy for a people struggling against tyranny. Do you say we have no right to do so, or that we must not walk the streets?"

"You are meeting in an illegal manner; I will now read the Riot Act, and if you do not disperse before fifteen minutes you have only to take the consequence."

He read the Riot Act; after which we asked—

"What do you see illegal in our procession?"

"That red flag," pointing to an equilateral triangle banner.

The Committee—"Take that flag down. Now, Mr. O'Connell, do you see anything else illegal?"

O'Connell—"Those transparencies with the mottoes."

Committee—"Take those transparencies away. Do you see anything else illegal, Mr. O'Connell?"

"Those torchlights."

Committee—"Put out those torchlights. Do you see anything else illegal?"

"You had better disperse."

Committee—"Do you tell us, now, that you come here with your authority and your armed force to tell us that we must not walk through the streets of Skibbereen?"

"I do not."

The committee ordered the band to play up "Garryowen" and to march on. The boys did so; the magistrates moved aside; the police behind them opened way, and the procession marched twice through the streets, and ended the demonstration with the reading of an address.

The marriage of the Prince of Wales in '63 came on in a few nights after we had the Polish sympathy meeting in Skibbereen, and some of the loyal people of the town illuminated their houses. There was a public news-room in the Prince of Wales' Hotel, and as the loyalists paid the proprietor £7 for lighting the house, those of them who belonged to the news-room held a private meeting and passed a resolution that the windows of that room should be illuminated too. So they were; but some of the Committee of the Polish procession were members of the news-room, and when they heard that it was burning with loyalty, they went to the room, called a meeting, pointed to one of the rules which excluded politics from the house, and denounced those who held a hole-and-corner meeting to introduce them there that day. A crowd was outside the hotel listening to the fight inside, and cheered and groaned according as the several speakers spoke. One of the loyalists said it was a mob meeting. "Then we may as well have mob law," said I; and, making for the windows, I tore down the transparencies, the fil-dols and the English banners, and threw them into the street.

Some one may ask what has this to do with prison life? Well, not much, perhaps; but it has to do with the movement for which we were put in prison. That movement generated a spirit of manhood in the land which the enemy could not crush, and cannot crush if we do not prove ourselves dastards. Acts of hostility, similiar to those I speak of, were occuring everywhere; and, if the people had only arms to back their spirit, they would do something worthy of them. The Gladstones know this, and use all their ingenuity to keep the dangerous weapons from the people, lest—as one of them said lately—the people would hurt themselves. But, "beg, borrow, or steal" them, we must have arms before we can have our own again.

After those occurrences in Skibbereen the stipendiary of the Castle, O'Connell, and Potter the Inspector of Police, came to me one day and told me they had instructions to give me notice that if I did not cease from disturbing the community I would be called up for sentence, pursuant to the conditions of my plea of guilty. I told them they should first show that I violated any of those conditions; that they should prove me guilty of the practices of drilling and the other things sworn against me at the time of my imprisonment; and that while, to their eyes, I was acting within their own law, I did not care about their threats.

Some time after I received an invitation from James Stephens to come to Dublin and act as manager of the *Irish People* newspaper, which was about to be started. I accepted the position, and we were not a month at work when we experienced a most active opposition to the sale of the paper from some of the priests. As manager of the business department I can safely say that there was not a county in Ireland in which we had not some clergyman denouncing our principles. I travelled the whole country from that little lake on the top of Fair Head in the north, to that deep pool that sleeps in the bosom of the mountains round Loughine in the south; from the Hill of Howth in the east, to Croagh Patrick in the west; and north, south, east and west we had some one to assail us as enemies of our race and name. It was just as Michael Doheny said when he was hunted:

"Thy faith was tried, alas! and those
Who periled all for thee
Were cursed and branded as thy foes,
Acushla gal machree."

Our agents were bullied, and when bullying would not do, were threatened with hell and damnation; where both failed the trade of the man was threatened; and I know one district in Waterford where a priest was in league with the magistrates to refuse spirit licenses to publicans who sold the *Irish People* newspaper; and the Centre for Kilkenny told me that the penance enjoined in confession on some of his circle of accqaintance was that they should not read the *Irish People*.

Perhaps some of those priests ought not to be blamed for denouncing our paper if they believed many of the things they said of ourselves. A priest of Ballycastle, a little town on the north coast, near Rathlin Island, in preaching to his congregation one day, in 1864, said, while denouncing our paper and our society, that the opinions some of us held on marriage were that if a man did not like his wife he could put her away and take another, and put the second away and take a third; and that one of us had carried out his opinions so vigorously on that matter that he was at that time taking a trial of the ninth wife. A few weeks after the reverend gentleman said this I was at Mass in his chapel, and, on my way to M'Donald's Hotel, my companion—Mr. Darrragh, who died in Portland Prison—told me this story of the gentleman I saw celebrating Mass.

When I was on this trip in the North of Ireland, I was instructively amused in the town of Ballymena at something which may be learned from the following anecdote:

One of the most active workers in the town had been going about with me to some of his friends in the mountains between Ballymena and Cushendal, and he never showed any symptoms of fear or concern lest any particular individuals should see him walking with such a suspicious-looking stranger as I was, till one morning that we were going to Randalstown to see some fellow-laborers in the cause. We were walking up and down the platform of the railway station awaiting the train; policemen and detectives were on duty there, and magistrates were walking around, too. He was telling me who was this man, and that man; there was a relative of "Finola's," and here was a cousin of William Orr's, when all of a sudden he bounded away from me and ran behind a railway wagon. The train was about starting when, coming toward me, I asked him what was the matter.

"Ah," said he, "didn't you see Father Lynch coming up; he knows me well, for he has been at me about the paper and the organization; knowing that you were a stranger he would immediately suspect what we were about, and I thought it better he should not see us together."

This was a sad reflection to me all the way to Randalstown, to think that this Irishman defied all the myrmidons of English rule while working for Ireland, and only quailed before him who should be Ireland's truest friend. While living in Dublin many stories came to my ear about the efforts some of the priests were making to arrest the progress of our work. Some of them might not be thought worthy of credence, and I myself pitched upon one, which I held in my mind as a little exaggerated, and that was that certain priests refused to marry men who were connected with the revolutionary movement unless they "gave it up."

I do not know whether a desire to test the truth of this had anything to do with getting into my head, about this time, the idea of marrying, but the notion got there; and, as it was associated in my mind with the picture of a pretty poetess, I could not put it or the image of the little woman out of my head. Indeed, to be candid, I did not try to do so, but, on the contrary, cultivated her acquaintance up to securing her consent to marry me. She lived in the South of Ireland and I lived in Dublin. I should take with me a license from the priest of my parish. The Rev. Mr. O'Hanlon lived within a few perches of the office of the *Irish People*. I went to see him, and took George Hopper with me. He introduced my business to the clergyman, and the clergyman, after satisfying himself that I was a marriageable man, proceeded to write my license. After writing a few words he stopped and said:

"I must make this license informal."

"How is that, father?" said I.

"Why," said he, "you haven't been at confession."

"But I am ready to go to confession to you."

"Oh, I could not hear your confession, now that I know you."

"Couldn't you hear a confession of my sins?"

Priest—"I could; but as I know you belong to the *Irish People* I should ask you certain questions, which you should answer, and which would make it impossible for me to give you absolution."

"And does belonging to the *Irish People* put a man outside the sacraments of the Catholic Church?"

Priest—"There is no use arguing the question Mr. O'Donovan. My hands are tied by this paper here, and by my instructions from Archbishop Cullen." And then he proceeded to read the printed paper referred to, in which the *fratres Feniores* were talked of side by side with the Freemason *fratres* and the *fratri Carabonari.*

"Well, Father, said I," "you had better make out a license as best you can, and if it be in order to say so, you can state that I offered to go to the confession to you and that you couldnt't hear me." "Very well," replied he. And taking the scrap of paper from him when he had done, I shook hands with him, and bade him good-bye.

I took the train for the south of Ireland, and I began to reflect that I was going into the diocese of the Bishop of Ross, and into the Parish of Father Leader, both of whom knew me well, and both of whom I knew, from previous experience, would place every possible ecclesiastical and lay obstacle in the way of my "making myself happy." I thought to myself I had better stop in Cork and try to make the matter all right there before I got to Clonakilty. I did stop and I strolled into a chapel near the Northgate-bridge, under the shadow of the Bells of Shandon. There was no priest there; but I learned that by going up to a convent, which was at the back of the chapel, I could see a priest. I went up and was introduced to a Dominican Father. Dressed in his white woollen robe, he sat down and I knelt at his feet. I ended, perhaps badly, perhaps not in the proper spirit; anyway, it was with a desire to conform to the education of my youth and "the custom of the country." And ending, I said: "That is all, Father," when he immediately asked:

"Do you belong to any secret society?"

"No."

"Do you belong to any society in which you took an oath?"

"I do."

"What is the object of it?"

"To free Ireland from English rule."

"You must give it up."

"I must not."

The old fight went on for ten or fifteen minutes. I got up from my knees and asked him if he would give me a certificate stating that I had been to confession to him, but that he could not give me absolution.

"That I could not do," said he, "without your permission."

"I give you permission," said I; "nay, I ask you to state the reason why you would not give it to me? I am no way ashamed of it before man or afraid of it before God, and if all my other sins were forgiven I could face him fearlessly on the last day with nothing to account for but that for which the Church excommunicates me."

After hard pressing I got the certificate from him, and I left the chapel thinking I would leave myself and my sins to the mercy of God in the future, and that it would be a long time again before I would trouble such priests.

I went to Clonakilty. I met the little poetess. Her father very reluctantly consented to our marriage, and, after consenting, I told him the difficulties that may be put in our way by Father Leader. He went to the priest, paid him the marriage money, but in view of my advice to him he was cautious enough at first not to tell him who the intended husband was. He called the second time for the "permit" to the curate to marry us, and learning that I was the happy man, he asked him to go back and bring him my license. The license was brought him, and he immediately pronounced it informal, and said I should be sent to the bishop. The bishop lived some twenty miles away, and I told my father-in-law that I had to leave for England the next day, and that unless I got married without delay I should leave Clonakilty without doing so, and only asked him get back the marriage money from the priest, and to bring himself and his daughter to Cork to get us married. The priest told him to bring both of us up to him; and when this was announced to me, I told both of them that unless they were firm in telling the priest they would adopt the above course, in view of the necessity that obliged me to leave Ireland immediately, that we could not get the better of Father Leader, and both agreed to be firm in the matter.

When we reached the priest, he questioned me as to my license, my residence in Dublin, and my residence in Skibbereen. He said I had lived my life in Skibbereen; that my family was there now; that it was from that parish I should have my license; that the one I had was informal and of no use; that I should go to the Bishop, and that it was entirely out of his power to marry me, as things stood. To this I replied that I had lived in Dublin for the past eighteen months; that it was my recognized residence; that if the license was informal it was no fault of mine, as I had made every effort to harmonize things with the requirements of the church; that I had no time to go to see the Bishop, as I was leaving Ireland the following day, and if he could not marry me I should have to go to Cork to get married.

"What!" Do you think that Miss Irwin would give such scandal in this parish as to leave it with a strange man, without getting married?"

"I am not a strange man in this country. I want no scandal in connection with me. I want to get married, and if you put difficulties in the way, I hope Miss Irwin will assist me to overcome them."

Mr. Irwin—I believe if you don't marry Mary Jane that she will go to Cork to get married. I have given my consent to the marriage, and if you will not marry them, I will permit her to go."

Father Leader—"That matter rests with Miss Irwin herself. And now, Miss Irwin, I ask you—you who have received a convent education—will you cast such a reflection upon those holy nuns who instructed you? Will you give such scandal to the girls of this parish as to leave it with a strange man without being married to him? I now ask you would you leave it without being married if I did not marry you!"

Miss Irwin—"I would!"

Father Leader (addressing himself to me) said:

"Oh! whatever be your hostility to our poor old Mother Church, that has protected us and promises to protect us through all ages —whatever you do to create disrespect of the ministers of our holy religion, and to corrupt society, leave us—do leave us one thing : *leave us the virtue of our women.*"

By Jove, didn't I feel this to be hard? But the man who said it was a priest, and there was no strength in my arm. He is dead, and God be merciful to him; but my wife and her father are alive to bear witness to the truth of what I say. We got an order to the curate of the parish to marry us, and "if *we* don't live happy that *you* may."

The following poem is part of the labors of my prison life. From it, it may truthfully be inferred, that the lady and I "made the match" without the knowledge of her parents; that when they heard of it they decided it was an unwise undertaking; that by their advice she wrote to me, saying that the matter was at an end, and not to write any more; but I threatened her with a breach of promise case, or the visitation of my ghost in case of my dying of a broken heart, frightened her into re-changing her mind:

THE DUTIFUL DAUGHTER.

A dutiful daughter won my heart,
  And after winning it, cruelly said,
I write to tell you that we must part,
  For papa and mamma won't have us wed.

Mamma asked me last night to sing,
   As we sat in the parlor after tea ;
But as I played, she noticed the ring—
   Then I told the truth, when she questioned me.

She said she liked you well as a friend,
   And wished none better than she wished you.
And telling papa—he said it could end
   In nothing but ruin to the two.

He knew you never were inclined to save ;
   He knew you never were a miser, nor poor ;
He knew that all you could hope to have
   Would keep a wife, but would keep no more.

That cares come on in a year or two,
   Which young people marrying never see ;
And 'twould be as much as you could do
   To get us both bread, butter and tea.

That half the miseries of this life
   Were caused by people who rashly wed ;
That he was to blame who took a wife,
   Unprepared for others, who'd cry for bread !

I never saw papa so troubled before ;
   I never before saw mamma cry.
I told them I'd think of our marriage no more,
   For they know more of the world than I.

Then papa said he would write a letter,
   To tell you the matter was at an end ;
But mamma thought I might write the letter,
   And send the ring in it—which I send.

As this is my last—I'll say adieu ;
   I never looked into the future before ·
What papa and mamma say is true.
   Good bye ! good bye. Don't write any more.

This is the letter that causes the smart ;
   This is the letter that nurses the pain ;
This is the letter that pierces the heart ;
   This the letter that burns the brain.

Bright dreams of Paradise, where have you gone ?
Odors of fairy bowers, where have you flown ?
Cupid plucked summer flowers, where are you strewn ?
   Am I lost, am I left in the world alone ?

O'Donovan Rossa's Prison Life.

I can't rest, I can't eat, I can't sleep, I can't pray—
  Can do nothing but drink—oh! I would'nt much grieve
If death would but come in a natural way,
  But God in His mercy ordains that I live.

I'm like a wreck on a sea-washed rock,
  That every wave heaves to and fro;
I'm like a lightning-stricken oak
  With its source of life all charred below.

All mankind should pity and come to my aid;
  For the race would die out if some men hadn't spirit
To marry until they had fortunes made—
  With odds against having an heir to inherit.

Will anything alter the state of my mind?
  I find myself tempted to go on a spree—
Or go making verses—I'm strongly inclined
  To appeal through the Press for sympathy.

CHAPTER V.

SEIZURE OF THE "IRISH PEOPLE"—ARREST AND SEARCH FOR PAPERS—THE BALLYBAR RACES—STORY TELLING—LITTLE JEALOUSIES—ORDERED OFF TO AMERICA—IN COURT—NAGLE AND THE DETECTIVES—RICHMOND PRISON—RELIGION AND ROUTINE—STRIPPING—MY CELL—MY BOARD AND LODGING—MY WIFE'S VISIT AND DR. CULLEN'S SLANDERS—"MAD DOG" AND BARRY THE CROWN PROSECUTOR—THE LOWER CASTLE YARD—PRELIMINARY EXAMINATIONS—HIGH TREASON AND HANGING—STEPHENS' ESCAPE—SEIZURE OF MY DEFENCE PAPERS—THE TRIAL—THE PACKED JURY—THE PACKED BENCH—KEOGH AND FITZGERALD—CONVICTION AND SENTENCE FOR LIFE—SEARCH FOR MY TREASONABLE DOCUMENTS.

ON the evening of the 15th of September, 1865, as I was talking to some friends in No. 82 Dame street, Dublin, Mr. Patrick Kearney rushed in and said the *Irish People* was seized, exclaiming, "What are we to do?" He had fight in his eye, and I saw that the most welcome words to him would be instructions to resist the police. But, with very few arms, I knew we could not fight that night; and I told Paddy Kearney, who had a number of fighting men at his command, that we had nothing for it but to keep quiet, and that I would go up to the office. I was expecting that this swoop would be made, and always taking precautions to keep no papers about me, I searched my pockets, and gave a few business receipts and a small pistol to Mike Moynahan. I lived across the street, and when I left my residence an hour before, I left my wife packing up her trunks. I was under orders from Mr. Stephens to go to America, and I was taking my wife to the south of Ireland next morning. I had always given her instructions to destroy any papers connected with the organization that she may find about the house, but there was one document that I told her to preserve, and this she sewed into the leather lining of her pocket-book. The thought struck me that it was better to destroy that too. I told the boys about me that I would run over to speak a word to my wife, and then go to the *Irish People* office; but as I was going across the street two detectives pounced on me and said I was their prisoner. Each had clutched a shoulder of me, and they were so excited that their nervous tremor kept shaking me.

"All right, gentleman," said I, "but you need not be so much afraid, or grasp me so tight."

One of them stuck his hand into the side pocket of my coat and pulled out nothing; the other followed suit; and then they conducted me through the Lower Castle Yard to Chancery-lane Police Station. I was the first in. They took me to the searcher, turned my pockets inside out, and found no treasure but my money, which they returned to me. By and bye others were brought in, and by twelve o'clock we had a company of about twenty, amongst whom was Captain Murphy, who kept us alive by proclaiming himself "a citizen of Boston," and protesting against his illegal arrest. At twelve o'clock, George Hopper, John O'Clohissy, myself and a fourth party were huddled into a privy and kept there till twelve o'clock next day. The compartment was about seven feet square —a receiving cell for a drunken man or woman; the lid was broken off the closet; we had no bed, no room to stretch or walk about; so that our first night's imprisonment did not open under very encouraging auspices. But I had many a worse night since—many a one to which the first was a paradise.

When my two guardians had secured me they made for my residence, and turned everything upside down in search of papers. They took a lot of old Irish manuscripts belonging to Nicholas O'Kearney, a Gaelic scholar, lately deceased. These they took away, and I never saw them since. I had a revolver, and they took it with them too, though, at the time, it was perfectly legitimate property. James O'Connell O'Callaghan was in the house when the detectives arrived. He came to tell my wife that I was arrested, and, asking her were there any dangerous papers around, she said not, except one she had in a safe place. He told her, however safe the place was, that it was safer to put it in the fire; so she ripped open the pocket-book and burned the treasure. It was a letter of James Stephens', and I may as well tell the story of its preservation here as anywhere else.

I had many letters from him during the course of four or five years; but this was the only one that cost me an unpleasant thought, and made me fear that I was about to lose his friendship. Some one may ask why I should fear to lose the friendship of such a man, and I say for the simple reason that I liked him; that I believed he was going the right way to free Ireland; and I saw him working in the direction through all kinds of difficulties and under circumstances that would paralyze the spirit of an ordinary man. I worked with him, or under him, if people will have it so. I believe I have even since been looked upon by some of my friends as too friendly to him, and particularly since his failure this prejudice follows me. I am told by friends that I believed in him with a religious belief, and did everything that he wished done. It is true I was obedient, but this obedience never degenerated into subserviency. I did everything I was told; but James Stephens never told me to do anything that my heart was not in, and my own judgment did not tell me was promotive of the cause of Irish independence. I did many things without his instructions; but with them or without them, I am not ashamed of anything I did in connection with the revolutionary movement in Ireland, England and Scotland.

The nature of the document my wife had hid, and which James O'Callaghan made her destroy before the detectives came in, will be learned from the following narrative :

In the first week of September, 1865, the races of Ballybar were to come off near Carlow. The men in the organization availed themselves of gatherings of this kind to meet and discuss all questions affecting their interests. At the previous races I had been with Mr. Stephens himself, at Ballybar, and now the Carlow men wrote to Dublin, asking that some one should be sent down, and that Rossa was the person they wished to meet. On this occasion I should ask to be relieved if delegated to go, for I was a short time before at the Navan and Trim races ; I was tired of running about, and my wife was beginning to look even blacker than she does look at my being out nearly every night. I received a letter in the *Irish People* office, and it being my duty to forward it to the Boss, I did so. In the evening I got a note asking " why should those Carlow men attempt to dictate to him the proper party to be sent down? they should be taught that they could not do that, and it was for him to determine who was the fittest party to meet them." I could not go, and he bade me write to them to tell them so, and told myself to be in readness to start for America on the following Friday.

If he had learned that I had written to the Carlow men, asking them to write for me, he might be justified in sending me such a letter. I had been to America in July; I was asked to go again in August; but I, by permission, delegated the commission to another.

I was a new married man, I was not yet tired of my wife, and I wished to show her that I had something in me besides those rambling propensities which the exigencies of the occasions created, and which, from the memories of those times, she still imagines I am largely possessed of.

In deference to my own wishes and to hers I did not go in August, but now I saw there was nothing for me but to go. I took the letter to her and told her she may see it was not a matter of choice now ; that from what she could read, in the tone of it, she could see that my sphere of usefulness was closed in Ireland. My easily-earned, unmerited, and worthless popularity was getting me into a scrape. I fancied Mr. Stephens showed signs of a little jealousy, and I, having something perhaps of the nature of woman in me, felt hurt and pained at seeing this passion aroused in my partner, when I had not an impure or disloyal thought in my head, and when he had little cause from me, and less danger. I told my wife to preserve the letter, and this is the one she burned the night she was packing up to go home preparatory to my going to America.

About twelve o'clock the day after our arrest we were taken out of our privy, locked up into one of the black vans, and conducted to a police office. Vast numbers of people were in the streets, and the detectives found in the crowd that surrounded the van as we were coming out, many whom they suspected of connection with us, and arrested them. About thirty of us were in the dock, and I saw around me the proprietor, the editor and sub-editors, the printers, porters and reporters of the *Irish People*. The authorities had burst open the premises, seized all the papers and materials, and had them carted off to the Castle, had taken possession of the establishment, and left police in charge of it. They tore up the boards, arrested every man that came to inquire after anything about the concern, and refused admittance to our wives. They seized Mr. O'Leary's bank book, laid an embargo upon the money in the bank, and refused to allow Mr. O'Leary to draw it until his counsel made a motion in court for it. They knew that in this they were acting illegally, and refused to act otherwise without obliging us to have recourse to their own law to make them do so.

The prosecuting counsel, Mr. Barry, appeared in court, and, addressing a stipendiary magistrate who sat on the bench for the special occasion, charged the prisioners in the dock with conspiracy, made some observations as to our fell designs against Church and State, priests and landlords, and wound up by saying that the ends of justice demanded that we be sent to prison for a week, without disclosing the evidence against us, as other parties were implicated who were not yet in the hands of justice. The evidence was so voluminous that it would require a little time to arrange it. The magistrate granted what he asked, and we were remanded for a week.

The prosecutor left the court; we were delayed in the dock about an hour, and here something occurred that set me thinking about the informer, Nagle, who was also a prisoner. The detectives were around us. I knew some of them, and I asked if they would not allow my wife in, who was outside the door. I was told it could not be done. I heard Nagle make a similar request, and the detectives went out and brought in Mrs. Nagle, who remained talking to her husband over the rails for some minutes. A bad thought came into my head, not about the woman, but the man; but I banished it in a moment, and set the favor down to the detective's personal friendship for him. To be suspicious is not characteristic of our people. We consider every man honest until he plays the rogue with us at our expense, and I am seriously thinking of going on the opposite tack of thinking every one a rogue until I prove him an honest man, at least I'll try and study myself into the disposition if I get time to study in this busy New York, or if I can change this bad part of my good nature.

Into the black van again, amidst the encouraging huzzas of the crowd; up towards Richmond Prison; the big black gate opens; the cars rumble over the pavement; we are taken out, and we find ourselves locked in. I am taken into a large hall, and in a line with my companions we are registered as inmates, and all goes on smoothly until we come to the religious part of the business. Mr. O'Leary, Mr. Luby and myself are in the room together. I am asked what my religion is, and I say I am an Irish Catholic. They have no such denomination on their books, and I must register myself as a Roman Catholic. I was Irish, not Roman, but this would not do; there was the printed heading of Roman Catholic on the register, and I should sign my name under that. I offered to go to the chapel, but they would not let me go to church or chapel unless I signed the register, and this I refused to do. Mr. O'Leary adopted a similar course, and I think Mr. Luby. We were left in our cells while the others were at prayers, and then it was industriously circulated to our prejudice that we refused to be of any religion, which so far corroborated the slanders that were uttered against us, and will be ever uttered against every people who dare to do anything against an established tyranny.

The next part of the performance was to strip me naked, take my clothes aside, and turn the pockets of them inside out. An inventory of my stock was taken. My pocket-book, my pencil or my knife would not be returned to me. I was shown into a flagged cell, seven feet by six, which contained no furniture but a stool, and a board stuck into one of the corners of the wall to serve me as a table. I was told I would be allowed to pay for my board, but if I did not pay I should work. Mr. O'Leary occupied the cell next to me. The jailor communicated between us, and we agreed to pay for our maintenance. No such luxuries as wine or porter or spirituous liquor of any kind would be allowed us if we desired to indulge in them—not even tobacco or snuff. We got one hour's exercise every day in the open air, and the most rigid precautions were taken lest we should have any conversation during this hour. We were made to walk six paces apart, and ordered always to keep our faces to the front. This was treating us to convict life before we were convicted. I often thought to kick against it, but I did not like to make myself singular in company or to set a bad example.

The time of remand passed by, and we were preparing to go to the court to hear what was to be sworn against us; but the court visited us in prison, in the person of a magistrate, who informed us that we were remanded for another week; and when that week was passed we were taken into the Lower Castle Yard to be confronted with our accusers.

My wife was allowed to see me in the presence of the governor of the prison, and at our interview we were obliged to speak loud enough for him to hear what we said. She told me of all the terrible things that the papers were saying about us. Archbishop Cullen himself came out in a pastoral against us, and aided the Crown work by abusing the prisoners. Our natural enemies were bad enough ; but when the sanctity of the Catholic Church corroborated the slanders of the English enemy, we were pretty badly off.

When the head of the Catholic Church in Ireland said that " *we proposed nothing less than to destroy the faith of our people, to seize the property of those who had any, and to exterminate the gentry and the Catholic clergy,*" I suppose it must be true ; but *I* don't believe one word of it. England's work was done, however innocently or religiously the holy man did it. This is one paragragh of his pastoral, and not the worst one:

"If the charges lately made against the originators of the movement had been made known, every one would have been filled with alarm at their introduction into the country ; for they are said to have proposed nothing less than to destroy the faith of our people by circulating works like those of the impious Voltaire, to preach up Socialism, to seize the property of those who have any, and to exterminate both the gentry of the country and the Catholic clergy. Whatever is to be said of such fearful accusations—which we hope are only founded on vague report—it is too certain that the managers of the Fenian paper, called the *Irish People*, made it a vehicle of scandal, and circulated in its columns most pernicious and poisonous maxims. Fortunately they had not the wit nor the talents of Voltaire ; but, according to appearances, they did not yield to him in anxiety to do mischief, and in malice. And hence, it must be admitted, that for suppressing that paper the public authorities deserve the thanks and gratitude of all those who love Ireland, its peace and its religion."

Here was the cry of "mad dog" raised against us with a vengeance ; and what wonder that after this the pious Catholic and Crown prosecutor Barry would follow up the slander at the preliminary investigation for the benefit of the public indigdation. Here are some of *his* words, as reported :

"The design, as manifested from their writings, both public and private, as will be proved in evidence upon the trial—the design took the form, not as on former occasions of a somewhat similar character, not of a mere revolutionary theory, not some theoretical scheme of regeneration by substituting one government for another ; but it partook of the character of Socialism in its most pernicious and wicked phase. The lower classes were taught to believe that they might expect a redistribution of the property, real and personal, of the country. They were taught to believe that the law by which any man possessed more property than another was unjust and wicked ; and the plan of operation, as will be found to have been suggested, is horrible to conceive. The operations of this revolution, as it is called, were to be commenced by an indiscriminate massacre—by the assassination of all those above the lower classes, including the Roman Catholic clergy (here the prisononers, O'Donovan Rossa and O'Leary, looked at each other and smiled), against whom their animosity appears from their writings to be especially directed, by reason of the opposition which those clergymen thought it right, as Christian ministers, as Irishmen, and as men of peace and honor, to give to the projects in question."

The Lower Castle Yard is one of the strongholds of the English in Dublin. With all their power and pretence of greatness they were afraid to take us into one of their ordinary courthouses, and went through the farce of trying us with closed doors, refusing to admit our wives and sisters who were outside the gates. The reporters of the press were, however, admitted with the express purpose of giving publicity to the calumnies and the terrible things with which Barry, the prosecutor, assailed us; but which he was never able to establish. It was necessary to paint us black, in order to justify the illegality of the arrests, the illegal seizure of the *Irish People*, and the tyranny and despotism that characterized every act of the Executive regarding us. When England was fighting in India, the English papers, in order to justify the attrocities, attributed all kinds of demon tricks to the barbarous Sepoys. Women were sawn across between deal boards, who were afterwards seen in England, without the sign of a saw's tooth in them. When it was thought the Irish were going to fight, Hugh Rose, who operated in India, was sent to Ireland; and to pave the way for his process of pacifying Ireland, it was necessary to tell horrible tales of the blood-thirsty Irish. These same tales will ever be told in the English interest whenever an enemy is battling against England. The things that are "expedient" for England to do are diabolical when done by others. She must have a monopoly of all means necessary to her ends, and she would scare others away from her own practices, lest they should meet her on equal terms.

She will tar and feather, blast and burn, dislocate and disembowel, blow from the cannon's mouth, assasinate and murder, as it suits her purpose; but I suppose this is as little as she ought to be allowed to do for protecting other nations from such practices by her denunciation of them. Barry denounced the men who meditated imbruing their hands in the blood of pious priests and lenient landlords; but the men could not open their lips because they were represented by counsel, and this counsel was bound, under penalty of severe reprimand, to act with due decorum and not interrupt the counsel for the Crown while making a statement, which he should get credit for having evidence to sustain.

I took the precaution to tell the counsel not to consider himself engaged for me, that I would conduct my own defence and now and again I pleased myself by saying something that displeased the bench. I never like to have my tongue tied when I hear people telling lies of me, and when I see them pretending to administer justice to me by endeavouring to cut my throat.

This was the first time we saw Nagle come forward to swear against us. He had been employed folding papers in the *Irish People* office, and he had, he said, engaged with the detectives eighteen months previously to give information. He had very little to swear, but the Government do not want much once they want victims. The machinery of their law can accommodate itself to every necessity that arises, or to any demand made upon it, whether to convict an innocent "rebel" or to acquit a criminal loyalist.

It was one of the beautiful things connected with our treatment that, whereas, we were charged with conspiracy, and that the evidence against any one of us could be legally urged to convict all, though all may be unacquainted with the individual and the acts of the individual in question, not one of us would be allowed to communicate with the other before those preliminary investigations. My deeds were evidence against John O'Leary and Thomas Clarke Luby; but Thomas Clarke Luby or John O'Leary would not be allowed to speak to me about means of defence, which accounts for such passages as these in the report of our trials:

O'Donovan Rossa, addressing the Court, continued—"This is the way the *Irish People* has been seized, and the way we have been treated. Yesterday we wanted to have an hour's conversation in the presence of an officer of the prison, and we sent this message to the Governor:

"RICHMOND PRISON, Sunday, October 1, 1865.

"SIR: In taking measures to prevent us from speaking or communicating with each other, the Government, we consider, are precluding us from the means of defence. We were before the Crown Prosecutors yesterday, and many things came under our notice that demand our consideration for a short time before we are taken before them to-morrow again. We ask that we may be allowed to confer during an hour or so. Did the matter rest with yourself we may expect you would see the justice of granting our request; but if Government has given orders to the contrary, of course we cannot expect it.

JOHN O'LEARY,
O'DONOVAN ROSSA,
T. C. LUBY,
JAMES O'CONNOR,
GEORGE HOPPER."

"Well, the Governor sent a message saying that he could not grant our request himself, but would send a copy of our communication to the authorities; and, that if they gave him liberty he would give us the opportunity we asked. Under these circumstances I think we were treated very harshly. If we were charged with murder, or the assasination with which Mr. Barry opened his statement, we could not be worse treated than we are. We defy you to prove us criminals. We defy you to bring evidence to show that we were in association with this Nagle or Petit."

We would not be allowed to consult with each other. We were taken before the paid magistrate, Mr. Stronge, who had his instructions in his pocket how to dispose of us. He and the counsel on all sides were very anxious that the prisoners would keep their mouths shut, but the prisoners were not inclined to do so, as the following extracts from the papers of the time testify:

Mr. Stronge—"I consider it to be my duty to commit the five prisoners—Jeremiah O'Donovan Rossa, C. Manus O'Keefe, Thomas Clarke Luby, John O'Leary, and James O'Connor for trial on a charge of high treason. It is my duty to ask them if they wish to say anything in reference to the charge. They are not obliged to say anything unless they desire to do so. Whatever they say will be taken down in writing, and may be used as evidence against them on their trial. I may remind them—what, indeed, may almost be looked on as an impertinence in me to say—that they are represented by very able and judicious counsel, and it is for them to consider whether it would be wise for them to say anything."

Mr. O'Leary asked to be permitted to make a statement.

Mr. Sidney, Q.C.—"It is right to say that any statement he makes is not made with my concurrence.

Mr. O'Leary—"Certainly. When first we appeared before this court, Mr. Barry said the Government was not proceeding against us from any fear of the so-called Fenians; but, as well as I could understand him, because certain weak-minded persons, I suppose including my Lords Bandon and Fermoy—were afraid. Now, I do not care to enter into any detail as to the manner in which the Government has treated us since our arrest; but I may say that a Government which has been so very spiteful must be somewhat afraid."

"O'Donovan Rossa said he supposed there was no use applying to be admitted to bail. As regarded the *Irish People* office, which had been seized, he understood that guards had been sent to the office, who received all the letters and transmitted them to the Government."

Mr. Barry, Q.C.—"I believe letters are anticipated."

O'Donovan Rossa—"They are received and sent to the Government. This, I say, is more despotic than the conduct of the Russians in Poland, or the Austrians in Italy."

Mr. Stronge said they were charged with being guilty of the high crime of treason; and the newspaper publication, and everything connected with a conspiracy—every weapon wielded by those persons, was seized by the Government. They were charged with conspiring to upset and overthrow the Government of the country, and it was not likely the Government would allow them to continue to avail themselves of the weapons by which they sought to overthrow it. He was really surprised that O'Donovan complained of being deprived of those weapons; the complaint, he thought, was quite unreasonable.

Mr. Luby—"I must say you said any government in Europe would behave precisely—"

Mr. Stronge—"I did not. I said any government at either side of the Atlantic."

Mr. Luby said that during the present century, not since 1803, had any government adopted so harsh a measure, except where martial law was proclaimed.

Mr. Stronge—"You are now committed on the informations made before me."

O'Donovan Rossa—"We have not seen the informations on which we were arrested."

Mr. Stronge—"You cannot refer to them; they were not resorted to here. They have not been seen. They are not essential."

O'Donovan Rossa—"I understand you circulate reports that you got information from the American government?"

Mr. Stronge—"I cannot discuss that question with you."

O'Donovan Rossa—"I think I can speak upon Mr. Barry's speech, though you may desire to shut me up."

Mr. Stronge—"Do you deny this charge or not?"

O'Donovan Rossa—"I beg your pardon, sir; I want to make an observation with regard to Mr. Barry's opening statement. You can tell me I shall not if you wish."

Mr. Stronge—"I don't want to shut you out from making an observation."

O'Donovan Rossa—"Or explanation. He charged the parties connected with this—the parties charged here—with holding the opinion that no man had a right to hold more property than another. I deny that he could prove it by any article in the paper. And then, talking about massacre and irreligion, and articles connected with it, and priests and their assassination, it is certainly a novel thing in the history of the world to have an English Crown prosecutor coming here to preach such things to the Irish people."

Mr. Luby—"Those statements were mere platitudes, intended for the constituency of Dungarvan."

O'Donovan Rossa—"Mr. Barry brings matters forward that he has got since we were arrested, and he says: 'Under these circumstances, it was impossible for the Government to forbear'—that is, that it was impossible for the Government to forbear making the late seizure after getting evidence which they did not get till after they made that seizure. I do not expect justice here. This is a prison. I would ask you to go back with me, if your imagination can go back so far, to Poland, and imagine a correspondent writing from there to the *Times* newspaper such a letter as this, headed, 'Seizure of a Newspaper.' I will read it for you."

Mr. Stronge—"Is this by way of defence?"

O'Donovan Rossa—"It is."

The prisoner then read the following allegorical letter, which was manifestly intended to put his own case and that of his fellow prisoners in what he imagined to be the most forcible manner.

"WARSAW, September 30.

"On the night of the 15th instant, the Russian authorities marched a company of police and a division of their spies to Parliament street, and halted at the office of the *Polish People* newspaper. The officers in command demanded admission, and, the doors not being opened, they gave orders to have them broken. A search was made through the house, and none of the officials being found, all locks were broken, and books, papers, printing materials, and all matters portable were taken to the Russian garrison. While the police were inside the house, a company of the spies were posted outside, who arrested and conveyed to prison every suspicious person who was attracted to the spot through curiosity or interest. Before next day nearly all connected with the establishment—from the porter to the proprietor—had been arrested; many who never entered the place had also been lodged in prison. It was fortunate for the inhabitants that no individual had resisted arrest, as the commander of the city had all the military under arms, with rifles loaded and capped, in case of any resistance.

"A guard of police was left in charge of the office. They receive all letters and communications coming there, and transmit them to the Russian Governor. It is thought that the authorities expected to seize information which would lead them to the capture of a large amount of military stores, as the Polish exiles in America have been talking of an army of liberation for Poland, and of sending war material into the country. Simultaneous with this proceeding, orders have been issued to the Russian officials throughout Poland to seize every military-looking man wearing American boots; to have him searched and detained until the Governor is communicated with, and his will made known regarding the prisoner. In furtherance of these orders, large bodies of police are stationed at the frontier, on the American side; and every returning emigrant found in possession of a pistol, a military book, or any memento of the American war, is put under arrest. The Russian Government, some time ago, gave the Poles a kind of constitution The present proceeding is in violation of that—in fact, it is a complete revocation of it. The Governor of Poland, who must be a Russian, has, through his press, circulated a report that this despotic seizure of a newspaper, and all men and materials belonging to it, was made on information received from the American Government; but this is doubted by many, as some forty men are now in prison a fortnight, and it is known that two of the Russian magistrates are in daily communication with the spies and professional swearers, who are always at hand for use. Indeed, it is known that one of the latter left St. Petersburg a few weeks ago, telling an acquaintance of his that he was going to Warsaw to do a bit of business. Though it is

a principle of law in many countries that a man charged with a crime
is presumed innocent until proved guilty, it is different in Warsaw.
The moment a man is arrested on a political charge he is presumed
guilty and treated accordingly. Though he might not be brought
before the public tribunals for four, eight, or twelve months, there
is no bail taken for his appearance; he is sent back to his dungeon
and treated as the caprice of the Governor of Poland may suggest.
The men in this case have been in solitary confinement all hours of
the day and night, save two. During one of these they leave their
cells in the morning to wash, and the other, at noon, to walk about
a small yard. This time the guards are doubled on them to prevent
their talking, and they must keep a certain distance from each other.
They are also prevented from having any communication with the
outside world.

"They are to be removed from one prison to another to-day, in
order to appear before the officials who have been preparing the
charge against them. The prisons in Warsaw are generally governed
by the Municipal Council of the city; but it is the privilege of the
Russian Governor to take the government of them into his own
hands, which he generally does on occasions of this kind. The
newspaper writers of Poland would be loud in their denunciations
of such despotism if they saw the English Government acting this
way in Ireland, or the Austrian Government in Hungary; but Russian
influence and patronage blinds them to every act of tyranny in
their own unfortunate country."

You should see how the paid officials were biting their lips as I
was reading this. They attempted to silence me a few times, but I
persisted in my right to defend myself in the manner most pleasing
to me. Before we came to this court it was, of course, decided by
the authorities that we were to be sent back to prison again, and
back we were sent, to await trial on some future occasion.

One day the Sheriff of the County came to the prison, and I,
with some others, were brought before him. He unfolded his parchment,
and gave us notice that the charge of Treason Felony against
us at first was withdrawn, and that we were to be tried on the 29th
of November for High Treason. On this occasion I experienced
that ugly sensation which men fond of the world are supposed to
experience when they, in health, are told they must die. I
hanged myself on that day, and what harm if I say that I did not
like the operation, and that I felt myself a bit of a coward. I went
through the whole ceremony in imagination, and survived it; and
if the reality of the performance had to be gone through afterwards,
I believe I would have gone through it well, even though it would
have killed me. The scare was past; I had died, and I felt able to
go through the rest defiantly. Always make up your mind for the
worst and you will be able to go through anything that comes your
way in a better manner.

Day by day, for two months in Richmond Prison, we were put

through the same routine of solitary confinement and an hour's solitary exercise in the open air, save and except that, instead of being exercised with my companions walking five yards apart around a ring, I was put into a separate yard and exercised by myself.

During the first fortnight an attorney named Ennis had been attending upon us. He had a large business in the police courts and feared this would be injured by continuing to be our solicitor. While with us he did the best he could, but if the magistrates in the courts he pleaded in took it into their heads to be adverse to the success of his suits, they could ruin his reputation and himself in a short time, and we thought it was only reasonable to allow him, at his own request, to withdraw from our defence. He told us the best attorneys we could employ, and we were about writing to some of them when I received a letter from Councellor P. J. Smyth, now member of Parliament for Westmeath, offering us his professional assistance. On this particular subject our jailers gave me permission to consult Mr. O'Leary in their presence, and he decided I may write to Mr. Smyth accepting his kind offer. I wrote, and in a few days after I had a reply from him stating that he called to see us and was refused admission at the prison gate. I thought this was a monstrous thing. I sent for the governor and asked for an explanation, and I was told that the authorities would not allow Mr. Smyth to have any communication with us; he was a suspicious character, not considered very favorable to the maintenance of English rule in Ireland, I suppose. He sent me word again, saying as he was denied permission to assist us himself, he would recommend to us the assistance of Mr. John Lawless, an attorney on whom we could rely. I wrote in accceptance of it, and Mr. Lawless was introduced to us.

The time of James Stephens' release from prison came, and as much has been said of that by many, I may have a word to say about it too. It has been stated in a "Life of James Stephens," published in America, by some one that was intimately acquainted with him, that the basis of his escape from Richmond was an agreement with a jailer to effect it for a sum of £300. Now, I do not believe one word of this; but I believe that the men who effected his escape, and who could as easily effect the escape of the whole of us at the time, were men who would not move one inch in the matter for mercenary motives; and I am able to state that they got no money, or made no money agreement for his release.

The day before that of his escape, one of the prison officers, in passing my cell, whispered to me, "The little man will be out to-morrow night." "Are you sure of it?" asked I. "Certain," replied he, and added, "Have you any message to send him?" to which I answered, "No."

Next day our attorney, Mr. Lawless, visited us, and as the time of trial was approaching, it was deemed necessary that Mr. Stephens and Mr. Duffy should meet Mr. O'Leary, Mr. Luby and me. The solicitor made the application to the Governor of the prison, and the Governor allowed Mr. Duffy to be brought to our consultation room, which was Mr. Luby's cell; but Mr. Stephens would not be allowed to approach us. We remained in conversation for half an hour. Duffy whispered to me that Stephens was going out that night. I whispered it to John O'Leary, and, as we were parting, Mr. Lawless said he would renew his application for an interview between Stephens and us next morning. We said the meeting was absolutely necessary, inasmuch as our trials were to come off on the following Monday.

We shook hands and parted. In my cell I could not help dwelling on the meditated escape. I thought I could keep awake all night, and keep my ears open to hear the least noise; but the powers of sleep stole a march upon me, and kept me entranced in the midst of soldiers and jailers and United Irishmen, till the real jailers came to my cell about three o'clock in the morning, and woke me by the noise they made in opening my door to see if I was safe. The alarm was given, and the question now with me was—" Did he escape, or was he caught in the attempt?"

The noise and bustle, and the continual running of jailers about the wards could not enable me to decide one way or another, and, knocking violently at my iron gate, I told the officer who was passing by that this noise was preventing me from sleeping, and that I should report it to the Governor in the morning. One word borrowed another; my keeper's observations told me something wonderful had happened, and I concluded the bird had flown.

At eight o'clock next morning Mr. Lawless visited and informed us of the terrible news of Mr. Stephens' escape, at which I opened my eyes and mouth in amazement. We talked of the coming Commission, and of the propriety of having no counsel to defend us in case the Crown packed the juries and persisted in pursuing towards us a course against which our counsel were battling. This was agreed on between Mr. O'Leary, Mr. Luby and myself. A part of the programme was that counsel were to throw up their briefs if certain just things were not allowed by the judges; but this they could not agree to do when things came to a crisis, and the project of no defence was given up.

Thomas Clarke Luby was the first man tried, or rather convicted, for political trial in Ireland is a farce. John O'Leary was the next; and the putting of them through the portals of twenty years' penal servitude occupied four days for each. I was called up after them, and as I was placed in the dock, the usual question was put, if I was ready for trial, to which my counsel answered "Yes." "I beg your pardon, gentlemen," said I, at which the counsel started, opened their eyes, and adjusted their spectacles. "My lords," continued I, addressing myself to the judges; and here the gentlemen of the long robes looked at me forbiddingly, as if I should not speak. "My lords, I had papers prepared for my counsel connected with my defence, and these have been seized by Mr. Price, the Governor of Kilmainham prison, and would not be returned to me. It is reasonable for me to suppose that there are some channels of communication between Kilmainham prison and the Castle of Dublin, and I suspect that these papers have been put into the hands of the Crown prosecutors. I now ask for them, and I am not prepared to go on with my trial until I get them." There was a kind of murmur in the court. My counsel looked as if they were relieved from the imprudence of my talking. Judge Keogh asked where was the Governor of Kilmainham, and, as he was not present, it was ordered he be sent for. The work of the law was brought to a stand-still; prosecutors and judges looked at each other a moment, and the question was asked, "What are we to do my lord?" and the lord decided that the prisoner O'Donovan Rossa be put back, and another prisoner be brought forward. The Attorney-General and the Solicitor-General, and the host of assistant generals that were around, held a consultation, and then addressed the court to the effect that as the case of Michael Moore was a short one, they would put him on trial; but he was not brought down to court that day, and the van would have to be sent for him. There would have to be a delay of an hour or so, and during this time the court took a recess.

I was taken back to the waiting apartment, and told my story to Charles Kickham, Charles O'Connell and James O'Connor, who, with me, were selected as the most deserving victims after Thomas Clarke Luby and John O'Leary. I told them I had other plans in my head that would keep them from being convicted at this Commission anyway, and we had a laugh over the matter. Michael Moore was sentenced to ten years' penal servitude next day, and I was again brought forward.

I got my papers in open court from Governor Price. Judge Keogh administered to him a rebuke, and told him it was quite improper for him to make any use of the papers of any prisoner, but this impropriety afterwards appeared to have been legalized, if we may judge so from the number of times during the succeeding trials that Governor Price seized upon manuscripts of prisoners to have their handwriting identified and sworn to, on many occasions, I believe, before Judge Keogh himself.

When I was put forward a second time, and asked if I was now ready for trial, I showed that it was necessary for me to have witnesses who were mentioned in these papers of mine that were seized. Mr. Price had them in his possession a week, and during this week I could do nothing towards preparing for my defence.

The judges and the prosecutors could not get over the reasonableness of my demand. The black van was put into requisition again. I was put back; there was a repetition of the recess; and another short case was got in—John Haltigan, the printer of the *Irish People*. It was now Friday evening, and I thought I had a fair field to keep the court engaged till Thursday, when the judges were advertised to open the Commission in Cork city. Kickham, O'Connell, O'Connor, Moore and myself were brought to the Court on Saturday morning. Mr. Haltigan was sentenced to seven years, before one o'clock, and a third time I was brought into the dock. The High Sheriff came into us a few times during the forenoon, and, in the blandest tones, wished to know from me if I were ready for trial that day. I knew he was sent by the "big wigs" to worm me; but, while I was very civil in answering his questions, I made the answers convey as little as possible, and kept my mind to myself, which all men—and, indeed, all women, too—ought to do in critical times, if they have any mind worth keeping.

The judges asked me now if I were ready for trial, and when I said yes there was a rustling of papers and a pleasant appearance of business upon every face, except the faces of those who were sure that my doom was already sealed.

One official proceeded to call the jury panel, and one by one, as names were called whose owners could not be relied upon to bring in a verdict of guilty, the jurors were told to "stand aside." My counsel were challenging on my behalf, and I was twenty times on the point of telling them to desist—to withdraw, and leave me to my fate; but "propriety," or awful respect for "the majesty of the law" prevented me. I was most anxious to assert and vindicate the right of every man who was called there to act there—in a word, I was mad to have something to say to this jury-packing, when I was to be packed off myself by it; but my tongue was tied by my having counsel to act for me, and this was making me feel uncomfortable with myself.

The jury was duly packed, the first witness was called and put through, the second witness was examined and cross-examined, my discontent was growing, and before the closing of the day's work, when I attempted to say something and was silenced, I resolved to throw up my counsel and to commence my own defence on Monday morning.

Again when I stood before the judges, and when they and the lawyers were proceeding, in the usual legal form, to "try" me, I handed in a paper requesting the counsellors to withdraw from my defence. The newpaper report of the trial says that—

"Pierce Nagle was sworn, and was about to be examined by the Solicitor-General, when the prisoner interrupted the proceedings by saying that he wished to address a few words to the court.

"Judge Keogh said that the interruption could not be permitted. If the prisoner had anything to say he should communicate it through his counsel.

"Mr. Dowse said that counsel had no control over what the prisoner wished to say. He understood that he wished to inform the court that he did not desire to be defended by counsel.

"The Prisoner—I have seen the course the Crown has adopted in proceeding with my trial. I heard the jury being called, and I heard the words "stand by" to thirty or forty gentlemen. What did that mean? It meant that the Crown was determined—

"Judge Keogh—We cannot permit this.

"The Prisoner—I believe this trial is a legal farce, and I won't be a party to it by being represented by counsel.

Mr. Dowse said they were quite ready to conduct the prisoner's defence, but, under the circumstances, they would at once withdraw.

"Judge Keogh—I have to express my regret that the prisoner has not left himself in the hands of the able counsel who has hitherto defended the prisoners.

"The Prisoner—I fully concur with your lordship with regard to the ability of the counsel. I want to know what are the papers and documents on which the Crown will rely for my conviction.

"The examination of Nagle was being again proceeded with when Judge Keogh suggested that Mr. Lawless should take a seat near the prisoner, so as to be able to assist him with the documents.

"The Prisoner—I don't want the assistance of Mr. Lawless at all, I only want the documents."

But if I did not want the assistance of counsel Judge Keogh wanted I should have it; for in having it I was precluded from being anything in the play but a silent, foolish-looking spectator. "His lordship" quickly silenced me as above when I was going to tell him I would do my own defending, and now he ordered Mr. Lawless to sit by my side to instruct me. I said I did not want his instruction, but it was no use. Mr. Lawless took his place convenient to me, and I commenced to cross-examine Nagle.

He was swearing to my handwriting in an account book; Chabot, an expert was also after having been examined as to it, and as I was to have this latter gentleman examined again I was putting Nagle through every line of the writing. There was also in the book the handwriting of James O'Connor, Dan Downing and Con O'Mahony. The expert and the informer swore contradictory things—what one pronounced mine another pronounced another's, and I had great fun with Judge Keogh in the length of time I kept Nagle at the handwriting of the different entries. His lordship repeatedly asked had I not examined enough, and I repeatedly said "no." At length he decided I should go no further, and I decided that I would, because that when any book or paper was put in evidence against a prisoner, it was the prisoner's legal right to go through the whole book or paper if he desired. I asked that Chabot and other witnesses be put out of court while any witness was under examination. They were put out, but I afterwards learned that some of them were placed so that they could hear what was going on.

Going back to the newspaper reports—

"The Prisoner asks—As I intend to examine Mr. Nagle as to the handwriting and the signature, and as there was an expert here,

I wish that he would be put out of court, and also any witness you intend to examine in corroboration of what he says.

Judge Keogh—Certainly. Is Mr. Chabot here?

The Solicitor-General—He is not in court. He is in the office, my lord.

Judge Keogh—See that all the Crown witnesses are kept out of court.

Prisoner—And those detectives that the Crown intend to examine, so far as they have to do with the corroboration.

Judge Keogh—They have nothing to do with the case.

Prisoner—Oh they have, my lord.

Judge Keogh—I don't think they have."

All the papers of the *Irish People* office were seized. The Government selected as many of them as would tell against us; but there were others there that would explain and clear away many things, and these I wanted to get for my defence, but could not get them. I contended that I should have for my use as many of the documents as did not contain matter which the Crown could urge as criminatory against us. The judge quibbled and lied in saying that "all the documents required by the prisoner should be forthcoming at the proper time;" for though the prisoner was four days on trial he never got one of them. Here is the passage:

"The prisoner stated that there were certain letters found at the *Irish People* office which he would wish to see, particularly a business letter which would explain charges against him now.

Judge Keogh—You will have any letters that you require, or that were produced by the Crown.

The prisoner observed that he had heard Smollen state the other evening that there were letters found in the *Irish People* office which might not be of use to the Crown, but which might be of use to the prisoner.

Judge Keogh intimated that all documents required by the prisoner would be forthcoming at the proper time.

Nagle was one time discharged from the *Irish People* office by James O'Connor. He applied to Mr. Luby to be taken back. Mr. Luby had him restored; and as I was cross-examining the informer as to the state of his conscience in swearing away Mr. Luby's liberty, he felt a bit puzzled, and hesitated before giving me a reply. I repeated the question two or three times to no effect, when the court was startled from its solemnity, and myself somewhat refreshed, by what the following describes:

"Prisoner.—Do you believe in your conscience that in swearing against Mr. Luby, who treated you so kindly, you did anything that you must answer for to Almighty God some day?

" (The witness hesitated for some time.)

" A voice in the Gallery—Answer.

" Mr. Justice Keogh—Who spoke in the gallery?

" Crier—This is the gentleman, my lord.

"Mr. Justice Keogh—Let that person be removed from Court instantly, and do not allow him in again."

The fight with the judges as to my right to have Nagle's opinion on every item of my private account book is described pretty accurately in the papers of the time. My object was to examine Chabot after Nagle on the same items and to show the jury, or at least the public, the contradictions of the two witnesses, but I was not allowed to carry out my object.

"Judge Keogh again interposing, told the prisoner he thought the line of cross-examination he was following was not calculated to serve him. He had been reluctant to interrupt him, because he desired to afford him every opportunity or cross-examining the witness."

"The prisoner, however, continued his cross-examination of the witness in relation to the book.

The witness mentioned other articles which he believed to be in the handwriting of the prisoner. The first ten entries are in the prisoner's handwriting; also, the thirteen last entries on same page.

The prisoner was continuing to cross-examine the witness when

Judge Keogh said—I have allowed the greatest possible latitude —an extravagant latitude—to the examination. Only a portion of this book has been put in evidence by the Crown. You have gone through a large number of entries. in it, merely asking the witness questions as to the handwriting of these entries. The Court think that you have gone far enough in this line of cross-examination, and I cannot allow the public time to be wasted with it.

The Prisoner—When a book or any writing has been put in as evidence once, I believe the whole of the book or writing can be examined. I believe this, my lord.

Judge Keogh—If at any time you (the prisoner) during the trial, wish to put any relevant question with regard to this book you can have the witness recalled. But I now, once again, tell you that I will not allow the public time to be wasted by irrelevant questions.

Prisoner—The public time is mine as well as yours, my lord. (To the witness)—Look at that writing.

Judge Keogh—Don't look at that writing.

Prisoner—Do you see that entry about the Midland Railway?

Judge Keogh—State the question to the Court you wish to put, and not to the witness.

Prisoner—I am bound to examine the witness myself.

Judge Fitzgerald—I beg your pardon. My brother and myself are both satisfied that this is a new attempt to waste the public time, and we cannot permit it to be continued.

Prisoner—Well, I am not satisfied. Twenty years is a long

time, and I want to spend a couple of days as best I can. I want to get the rule of the court in writing.

Judge Keogh—You have already heard the rule of the court, and we will not allow it to be carried on a moment longer.

The prisoner again essayed to put to the witness several questions in refereuce to entries in the book, when Judge Keogh interposed by saying that if the prisoner did not put relevant questions the witness should retire."

At another stage of the proceedings it was necessary for me to have those papers which Judge Keogh, a few days previously, said I *should* have; but on my applying for them I found I could not get them. The judge got out of this part of the business by saying he had made the order, and that is all he could do. Possibly the Crown Counsel, in the meantime, examined the documents, and, finding that they would be useful to me, held them back.

"Mr. Charles Chabot was examined by Mr. Barry as to whether or not several documents produced to him were in the handwriting of the prisoner, and also as to whether or not his handwriting was attached to the deed, and to certain checks.

The prisoner said he could not cross-examine this witness without the aid of certain documents which had been seized at the *Irish People* office.

Judge Keogh—Do you decline to proceed with your cross-examination now?

Prisoner—I don't decline to proceed with my cross-examination; but you have seized papers belonging to me which I require.

Judge Keogh told the prisoner he was entitled to ask the witness any questions he thought proper now that were relevant to his defence. Any documents that the Crown had they were ready to produce.

The Solicitor-General—We are, my lord.

The prisoner said that there were documents in the *Irish People* office that were now in the possesion of the Crown, and which were necessary for the purpose of cross-examining the witness.

Mr. Lawless said that the documents the prisoner referred to were those named in the order made by his lordship on Thursday night. Notwithstanding that order these documents had not been given up to him (Mr. Lawless).

Judge Keogh said he could only make the order.

The prisoner said he referred to the documents sworn by the detective as being still in the *Irish People* office.

Judge Keogh—The constable swore that he left a heap of papers and letters in the *Irish People* office; but they could have no connection with the examination of the present witness.

Prisoner—I know that they *can* have connection with the examination of this witness, and I want them.

Judge Keogh—You must go on with the cross-examination of the witness, or he will be allowed to retire."

And here is another passage, showing how I was shut up:
"The prisoner then examined the witness at considerable length as to the interviews he had with Nagle, until Judge Keogh again interposed, and stated that it was trifling with justice to be occupying the time of the court in that manner.

Hour by hour and day by day the battle went on ; and, reading over the proceedings of the trial now in order to get extracts to illustrate some remembrances I have of it, I am tempted to give more than I intended. It may be stale to many who read the papers at the time; but how many youngsters are grown up since to whom it may be intereresting? Besides, if this book is ever read by any one after my day—and where is the book-writer who does not think his book will live?—these lengthy passages about my trial may not be the most uninteresting portion of it to the reader who reads me—dead.

After the examination of many witnesses, the papers say :
"The prisoner then proceeded to address the jury. He said it was hard for him to say anything to them. No overt act had been charged against him, and no criminal act had been proved against him. When he heard the Attorney-General, on last Saturday, tell thirty gentlemen to 'stand aside,' he considered that he (the Attorney-General) looked upon them as persons who would not bring in a verdict of guilty; and he also took it for granted that when the jury was sworn the Attorney-General looked upon those sworn as men who *would* bring in the verdict. That observation was not complimentary to the jury, but he could not help it. As to trial by jury, it might be the jury's duty to give a verdict of guilty, but it was also their duty to protect the prisoner from tyranny. The Executive Government were taking harsh measures against them. As they had outraged all law, and had recourse to dark courses of despotism, the jury should protect the prisoners, and not condemn a man to penal servitude when nothing that was wrong was proved to have been done. If a man should say that Ireland, Hungary, or Poland should be free—but they could not be free unless they fought for freedom—would he be guilty of 'treason-felony?' A judge might feel it his duty to tell them that if a man said so, he should be found guilty; but, in that case, trial by jury was a mere bulwark of tyranny instead of the safeguard of liberty.

"The great crime against him, he said, were the words 'Jer' and 'Rossa,' and having known Stephens, O'Mahony, O'Leary, and Luby, whom he felt it an honor to know. Having then alluded to Mr. Justice Fitzgerald's address to the jury in one of the cases disposed of, in which his lordship said that the documents found with the prisoner at Queenstown disclosed the object of his mission to America, the prisoner continued to observe that no matter who it was had made the address to the jury, there was never such a jumbling statement made, nor one more devoid of foundation or contrary to evidence. The testimony of Nagle and Dawson the previous day showed there was evidence to prove he could not have lost those documents at all.

"He would now read an extract from a speech of Mr. Potter on the subject of the Jamaica massacres and the execution of Mr. Gordon. The prisoner read the passage, which was to the effect that in order to justify the massacre of the black population in Jamaica, calumnies were published of them representing them as contemplating hideous crimes. The same course was adopted during the Indian Mutiny; the soldiers were worked up to the perpetration of acts of cruel barbarity by accounts of insurgent crimes, but it turned out that many of the accounts were false, and he (Mr. Potter) took it the same was now the case in Jamaica. He (the prisoner) told the jury the same was the case with regard to the statements made about Fenianism in Ireland. On this subject he read an article from the *Irish People* newspaper. In this article it was stated that conquest was always accompanied by calumny. The conqueror was never contented with his victory, but represented his slave as a dog in order that he might flog him like a dog. Their English masters loudly proclaimed that the Irish were no better than savages—that what appeared oppression of them was simple justice. The English even affirmed that their Irish slaves were not human beings. They denied the claim of the Irish to humanity, the better to reduce them to the condition of beasts. Forty of the Cromwellian soldiers were actually found to swear that a number of the Irish killed at Cashel were found to have tails. The jury were sitting there for no other purpose than that of the Attorney-General pointing out to them the prisoners who had tails. The *Irish People* newspaper had striven to put an end to religious differences, and unite all religions against England. The beautiful policy of the English Government has been to use religion for the purpose of conquest. It was amusing to see how the Government could get Dr. Cullen and Dr. Trench, and all the doctors to abuse the Fenians.

He (Rossa) wrote a letter to Sir Robert Peel last week about procuring him proper facilities for a trial, and suggested to him that he should resign his situation if he had not the power of correcting these things—and, by-and-bye, he did resign. The prisoner then proceeded to read the following extracts from his letter:

"I am keeping you too long, Sir Robert; but ere I let you go I'll take you to have a look at the Piece that has been prepared for the end of the Play. Judge Keogh is to try us. Well, you know —or, if you don't, you will know—that the *Irish People*, since its commencement, has been writing down agitation, and has been writing up Judge Keogh as the sample of the benefits derived by the Irish people from tenant leagues, parliamentary agitation, and episcopal politics."

"Of the many allusions to his lordship throughout the journal here is a specimen from the number of March 26, 1864:

"'Mr. Justice Keogh (what a curious combination of words!)

speaks of cowardly men who, in their closets, wrote violent and inflammatory stuff which led others into such acts as were subjects of these investigations, but who themselves shrank from joining in the dangerous practices they led others into.

"'It must have been rather refreshing for the learned judge's audience to hear him coming out in the appropriate character of *Censor morum*. But has the high-flying moralist never heard of men who spoke violent and inflammatory stuff, and swore rhetorical oaths which they never kept? Has he never heard of men who now sit in the high places of the land who were once, if not the accomplices, at least the intimate associates, of forgers and swindlers? But it is a waste of time to bandy words with Mr. Justice Keogh. To be sure, he is a judge—but so was Jeffreys, so was Macclesfield, and so was Norbury.

"'Now, you know Judge Keogh is not an angel, much less a saint. Indeed he has as little chance of canonization as you or I have, so long as Dr. Cullen is considered an authority in the Catholic Church, for the archbishop has denounced us all severally in several pastorals. The judge is only a human being like either of ourselves, subject to all the little irritating annoyances which afflict human beings, and subject to be impressed with dislike of those who treat him with contempt. Selecting him as the judge to try the persons connected with the *Irish People* may be quite in accord with the rest of the proceedings, but it cannot tend much to impress people with a feeling of respect for the administration of justice. But as it is law the government seems most desirous to administer, there is no doubt but in selecting Judge Keogh to administer it to us, they have selected the most proper person. The two points which I present for your executive consideration, Sir Robert, are the restrictions here, and the admission to bail, on either or both of which I shall be most happy to hear from you, and remain, your obedient servant,

"'JEREMIAH O'DONOVAN ROSSA.'"

The prisoner then went on to read extracts from articles which appeared in several newspapers pending the trial of the prisoners, and which, he alleged, had been published to prejudice them in the minds of the jurors.

[The reading of the articles occupied more than an hour and three-quarters.]

Having concluded, the prisoner said—If there was any gentleman connected with the Continental press in court he begged that he would take down the words from the London *Times* of the 14th November last:—"Treason is a serious thing; and these men are undoubtedly guilty of it." He thought the publication of those articles in Dublin sufficient to justify any court in removing the trials from Dublin. He would now read the affidavit that had been made for the purpose of the motion. Mr. Lawless had gone for a copy of it.

Mr. Justice Keogh—I cannot allow it to be read. We have given you very considerable latitude indeed. I may say to you at once that everything you have read is irrelevant to the case, and wholly beyond the bounds of all evidence. But, as you are undefended, we have given you every possible latitude. If counsel appeared for you here, and attempted to do what you have done, we would not permit it for one moment. You have now occupied two hours in reading those articles, and we cannot now allow you to read the affidavit, which would be only a repetition of everything that you have gone over. Proceed to address the jury. It is unnecessary to wait for the affidavit.

Prisoner—I will ask no concession from your lordships but what the law allows me. Give me the pamphlet of the Chicago Convention.

Mr. Justice Keogh—Certainly; give him the pamphlet.

[The pamphlet in question was handed to the prisoner.]

Prisoner—Give me whatever other books have been given in evidence.

Mr. Justice Keogh—There is only this account book.

Prisoner—Was there not a drill-book?

Mr. Justice Keogh—I believe so.

Prisoner—Let me have it.

Detective Officer Dawson brought in a copy of the drill-book, and placed it on the ledge of the dock.

Prisoner—Am I not entitled to read all those books produced against me?

Mr. Justice Keogh—Anything material to the issue you are entitled to read; but you may as well understand, once for all, that you will not be allowed to fritter away the time of the court, or occupy the time of the court, jury, and public, to make a defence when you are not making any.

Prisoner—The time of the public has been given to try me.

Mr. Justice Keogh—You will go on until every human being will have seen that you have got every latitude; but when you have gone so far as that no human being in the community can say but that you have got the utmost possible latitude—latitude never given to prisoner before—then I will stop you.

Prisoner—There never was before such a trial as mine, either in the judges trying me or——

Mr. Justice Keogh—Proceed now.

Prisoner—I will read the pamphlet. Garbled extracts have been read against me, and I am entitled to show they do not bear the interpretation put upon them.

The prisoner then proceeded to read the pamphlet. Having gone through about twenty pages, the foreman of the jury (Mr. Vaughan) said—

I am requested by the jury to state that if the prisoner would mark any portions of the pamphlet which he thought bore upon the case for his defence, they would give them the same consideration as if he had read them.

A Juror—What he is doing now is greatly against him.

Prisoner—I am reading the pamplet to show that it has nothing to do with me.

A Juror—We are quite willing to sit here as long as it may be necessary to fully and fairly investigate the case, but we can consider this pamphlet in our room.

Another Juror—Occupying so much time in reading what does not concern the case is enough to stir up an armed insurrection amongst the persons in court (a laugh.)

Prisoner— I am entitled to read it.

A Juror—Only a portion of the book is in evidence.

Prisoner—I don't see how the book can be considered in connection with me at all. You can only blame the Crown for putting in such books against me, but as they are in I will read them.

A Juror—We are only making a suggestion to you.

Prisoner—Do you think the book has anything to do with me?

Mr. Justice Keogh—You cannot question the jury. I may tell you that in point of strict law you are entitled to read it—every line of it—if you choose.

Prisoner—If the Crown withdraw the pamphlet I will give it up.

The prisoner then proceeded to read through the pamphlet, which consisted of about eighty octavo pages of small print, and which contained all the proceedings of the Chicago Convention, the constitution of the organization, and the statutes by which the members were bound. Having concluded, he said:

Now, gentlemen, I will not further occupy your time; but——

Mr. Justice Keogh—Before you go further, it is scarcely necessary to remark to the public press the grave responsibility that would attach to the publication of that document which the prisoner has read, under the pretext that it would form a necessary portion of his defence.

Prisoner—I have used the document to show that there was nothing in it which could concern me. Are there any other pamphlets proved in evidence?

Mr. Justice Keogh—No.

Prisoner—There is a drill-book.

Mr. Justice Keogh—There is; but only the finding of it in the *Irish People* office has been proved. None of it has been read in evidence.

Prisoner—Is it not right to show the jury the nature of the book? The book has been produced by the Crown to influence the jury.

Mr. Justice Keogh—You can make any observation on that book you please.

Prisoner—Have you seen this book, gentlemen?

A Juror—We have not.

Prisoner—Then I submit I have a right to show them what sort of a book it is.

Mr. Justice Keogh—Proceed with your address.

Prisoner—Two volumes of the *Irish People* have been produced in evidence.

Mr. Justice Keogh—That is quite a mistake. The volumes have not been given in evidence; but certain articles in them have been proved, the particulars of which were furnished to your solicitor.

Prisoner—I understand that all the articles were put in. The Crown counsel having quoted in a garbled manner several articles, I think that I am entitled to read them all.

Mr. Justice Keogh said the prisoner was entitled to read all the articles which had been read in evidence, and also all articles which tended to explain or qualify them.

Prisoner—I submit that as I am charged with publishing this paper, I have a right to show all the articles to the jury that they may judge from all the publications what sort of a paper it is. I don't mean, of course, to read the advertisements (a laugh); I only mean to read what is necessary for my defence.

Mr. Justice Keogh—You will proceed with your address to the jury, but you will understand that it shall not degenerate into absolute abuse.

The prisoner said that in opening the case the Attorney-General had referred to a copy of the first publication of the *Irish People*, to show that he was the manager of it. In that paper was an article headed "Isle, Race and Doom." Was he to be precluded from reading that article?

Mr. Justice Keogh—It is quite competent for the Attorney-General to show that you were manager of the paper without permitting you to read all the articles.

Prisoner—The jury cannot tell what the paper is unless they hear it read.

Mr. Justice Keogh—Well, sir, proceed at once. You have been addressing the court for four-and-a-half hours, and you shall have every further opportunity, but there is a limit to all things.

The court then adjourned, and on resuming the prisoner repeated his request with reference to the court allowing him to read the whole of the articles which had appeared in the *Irish People*.

Mr. Justice Keogh said he could not allow any such thing. He might read those articles which had been used against him, and other portions of these publications which might go to explain the articles relied on by the Crown.

The prisoner then asked the Crown to withdraw the charge of assassination made against him by Mr. Barry, and then he would content himself with alluding to the articles put in evidence.

Mr. Justice Keogh—Proceed with your address to the jury, sir.

The prisoner said that he should show that the charge was false, and also that the charges made against them by the Dublin press, which, he said, prejudiced the public against them, were false.

(The prisoner then read several articles from a file of the *Irish People* newspaper.) He was proceeding to read one, headed, "England on Ireland," when

The Attorney-General said—This is not an article in the indictment.

Judge Keogh—I have looked through the article and read some of it as it appears in the same paper and bearing on the article I read; but it does not qualify that article. You can look at it, and if you like you can read it, but you will see whether it prejudices your case.

Prisoner—I am glad you have the paper, at all events.

Judge Keogh—I have the paper.

The prisoner then proceeded to read the article, which was, he said, written in reply to English articles abusing Ireland. In replying to these they were to be excused for getting up a little spirit. They—the jury—would say the same themselves. If their country were run down by Englishmen they may likely themselves become somewhat plucky, and say something that, perhaps, the judge would say was treason-felony. He would now read an article headed "Tall Talk." In the paper of November 28—

Judge Keogh—We have looked carefully over the article and find that it has no reference to the case.

Prisoner—Then you will not allow me to read it?

Judge Keogh—No.

The prisoner said he would read the article headed "Bane and Antidote."

Judge Keogh said it was not mentioned in the indictment.

The prisoner said he wished to read it for the purpose of showing that it was not right to be tried before his lordship.

Judge Keogh—That at once settles the question. You cannot read it.

Prisoner—Well, I will read the article of the 5th of December.

Judge Keogh—We cannot allow you to read it.

The prisoner then referred to an article entitled "National Self-Reliance," which, he said, ridiculed the idea of inviting foreigners to come here and invade the country. That was one of the charges against him. That article stated that if fifty thousand French or Irish-American soldiers landed in Ireland, and that the people were not prepared for them, they would be swept into the sea by the British troops in less than three months. That was true and he believed it.

Judge Fitzgerald said that he had read an article headed "A Retrospect," in which the spirit of the other article was a great deal exaggerated. He should tell him that they would not allow the court to be the means of spreading articles which were treasonable, and certainly seditious.

The Prisoner—The English jurors who are here for my protection—

Judge Fitzgerald said it could not be read.

The prisoner said he could not consider it right to have a packed bench trying him.

The Attorney-General protested against this court being made the medium for the dissemination of treasonable doctrines. It should not be allowed in a court of justice.

Judge Keogh—The prisoner is entitled to make any observation on them he pleases, and he is merely reading them.

The prisoner said he had a right either to read them or make observations on them, according as it pleased him.

Judge Fitzgerald said he wished to mention that he trusted the good sense of the press would indicate to them the propriety of not publishing these articles in any paper.

Prisoner—I will read all the articles in the indictment. I will claim my right to read every article in that indictment.

The prisoner then read the article headed "The Approaching Crisis," observing, *en passant*, that he would read to-morrow the articles which would explain those that he was now reading. After reading some more articles, he proposed to read from the *Irish People* "John O'Mahony's Letter to Bishop Duggan."

Their lordships ruled that this could not be read, as it was not in evidence.

The Prisoner—Am I not charged in connection with John O'Mahony?

Judge Keogh—You have heard the ruling of the Court.

The Prisoner—Oh, very well; we will return to it again. He then commenced to read an article headed the "Chicago Fair," when

Mr. Lawless, solicitor, who sat near him, observed to him that in reading these articles he was making the speech of the Solicitor-General.

The Prisoner—So I am, and my own speech, too. Having read a number of articles, he came to one in which there was a passage that every man had an object to accomplish, namely, to make "every cultivator of the soil the proprietor in fee simple of the lands and houses of his fathers," and this, he contended, did not mean to deprive any man of his land. He proposed to read an article on "Military Books," in answer to a correspondent.

Judge Keogh—We have looked through this article, and we would be only making this court of justice a means of propagating treason if we permitted that article to be read. We cannot allow it.

The prisoner urged that he ought to be allowed to read it.

Judge Keogh—You have heard the order of the court. We cannot allow that article to be read.

The prisoner having read the article "Priests in Politics," he expressed a wish to read the letter signed "A Munster Priest," on which article he said that letter was written.

Judge Keogh asked him for what purpose he proposed to read that letter?

The prisoner said he wished the jury to understand the article.

Judge Keogh said he might read the letter in question.

The prisoner proceeded to read the letter, when he was interrupted by Judge Keogh, who said: You have read enough of this letter, purporting to have been written by a priest, to show the nature of it; but we really think that to allow you to continue to read it would be propagating the worst kind of treason. I will act upon my own responsibility, and will not allow the further reading of that letter.

The Prisoner—What use is it for me, then, to try to explain these articles.

Judge Keogh—There has not been the slightest attempt from the beginning to the end of your address, now of seven hours and a half's duration, to qualify, pare down, or soften a single article; but, on the contrary, everything has been addressed to the jury to exaggerate them.

The Prisoner—If this was treason, why was it not prosecuted before?

Judge Keogh—Proceed now; I won't allow it to be read.

The Prisoner—I say it is my right——

Judge Keogh—The ruling of the court is that it shall not be read.

The Prisoner—You gave me liberty to read the letter.

Judge Keogh—I gave you liberty to read it to explain the article; but I now perceive that it is quite inadmissible.

The Prisoner—You change about; you rule one thing now and another thing afterwards.

Judge Keogh—If you don't proceed I will terminate your right to address the jury, and that peremptorily.

The prisoner, on coming to an article on the Cork trials, said he claimed his right to read it.

Judge Keogh—It has nothing whatever to say to the charge.

The Prisoner—Oh, yes; there is something about Cornelius O'Keane brought up here.

Judge Keogh—That does not make it admissible as evidence.

The prisoner then proceeded to refer to an article headed, "The Regeneration Scheme," and said before he read the article it would be better for him to read the letter by Dr. Moriarty first.

Judge Keogh—We will not allow any such thing to be done.

The Prisoner—But the Attorney-General charges me in his speech with—

Judge Keogh—Proceed with your address. We won't allow it to be read.

The Prisoner—Very well, I will go on now, but I reserve my right to read these things before I am done.

The prisoner then proceed to read the article, and, on coming to the passage about the freedom of Hungary, said it was not to free a country that was a crime, but to attempt to free a country and not to be successful, that was the crime. Now, he said, after reading that he had a perfect right to read the letter about Dr. Moriarty.

Judge Keogh—Proceed, now, sir, with the next document.

The prisoner then read an article headed "Peace in America." At the conclusion he said:

It is now six o'clock, my lord, and I suggest that we close for this evening.

Judge Keogh—Oh, certainly not. The Court will proceed.

The Prisoner—I am now speaking for eight hours, my lord, and the Court closes every other evening at six o'clock.

The jury intimated a desire to proceed.

Judge Keogh—What is the wish of the jury?

The foreman said to proceed.

Judge Keogh—Proceed now, sir.

The Prisoner—Why, it is like a '98 trial—a regular Norbury case?

Judge Keogh—Proceed, sir.

The prisoner then proceeded to read other articles, and on coming to one in which allusion was made to the advancement of "Keoghs, Monahans and Sadliers," said—"And now, gentlemen, I will address you a few words. I say that indictment has been brought against me, and that man (Judge Keogh) has been placed upon that bench to try me; and if there is one amongst you with a spark of honesty in his breast, he will resent such injustice. That article has been brought against me in the indictment; and do you all believe that that man on the bench (Judge Keogh) is a proper man to try me? He has been placed there to convict me. There, let the law now take its dirty course," said I, and saying it, I flung on the table the large volume of the *Irish People* out of which I was reading.

The prosecuting counsel were quite unprepared for my sudden stop, and when I declined to take any more part in the proceedings they and the judges decided that they would adjourn the court until next day.

The last day of my appearance in court was Wednesday, the 13th of December; the judges were advertised to open the Commission in Cork on the 14th, and I felt satisfied in having occupied them the time I intended. As the *Evening Mail* said, in justification of the legality of my course, "the Crown's game was a fast one, but mine was a slow one," and I had a right to take it as it pleased me. This is the closing scene:

"His lordship next called the attention of the jury to a letter which had some reference to Paris. Now, he had a notion of his own that conspiracies of this kind would be dealt with in a very different way in that capital. The Frenchman would clutch at once with a strong hand all those who dare interfere with his authority.

The Prisoner—That is a nice address to a jury.

The learned judge went on to say that he was sure military schools would not be allowed to be established in Paris. The prisoner stated, and it was not an unusual circumstance, that he assumed the name of O'Donnell going out to America, because he had many friends there, and did not want to be bothered with their invitations. He also said he had business transactions with the export of whisky from Messrs. Wyse & Murphy, Cork.

The Prisoner—I have the papers.

Mr. Justice Keogh said there was nothing inconsistent in the prisoner having business transactions of the kind. He came home on the 21st of July; he landed that day at Queenstown. The date was important. On the 22d of July the bills of exchange and the letters were found at the terminus of the Kingstown Railway. The evidence showed conclusively that it was not the prisoner who dropped these documents.

The Prisoner—Mr. Justice Fitzgerald said in his charge it was."

Mr. Justice Keogh said it was impossible the prisoner could have dropped them. The jury, however, had it that the prisoner went out to America by the name of O'Donnell, and in the letter in question O'Mahony speaks of his regret at parting with O'Donnell, and requesting him to be sent back "in view of cordial and prompt action."

The Prisoner—Suppose it was O'Donovan Rossa that was alluded to, but that he did not act upon the letter—did not go back but remained in Dublin, as the police proved—have you nothing to say to the jury upon that?

Mr. Justice Keogh—That is a very proper observation.

Prisoner—Yes, I think it is.

Mr. Justice Keogh—Certainly, gentlemen, you have a right to regard that observation of the prisoner; but, of course, you must also take into account the letters relating to the prisoner's departure for America; that he went by the instructions of Stephens under the circumstances stated.

Mr. Lawless—Your lordship will remember that Nagle said he saw the prisoner's name over a house in New York.

Mr. Justice Keogh—Yes, that is so, in 1863; but I do not think it has much bearing on the case.

Judge Keogh having read and observed upon other letters then referred to page 5 of the account book, in which, among other entries in the prisoner's handwriting, was one that he had given "£25 to J. Power," that was Stephens, to travel.

The Prisoner—On that page there are payments to Cherry and Shields, of Sackville-street, to Alexander, of Mary's-abbey, and other people.

Judge Keogh said that was certainly the fact. The prisoner himself directed Nagle's attention to another item, which had not been used by the crown. An entry of £3 7s. 11d., and 10s. 9d. for postage on Chicago papers kept in the Post-office.

The prisoner said the explanation of that entry was this, that the paper not being registered at first, the papers addressed to Chicago were kept in the Post-office, and after some months they were all got in a bundle, and those were the sums paid upon them.

Judge Keogh said that was a natural and very proper explanation, and he was delighted the prisoner interrupted him to make that explanation.

The Prisoner—As I said before, if I could get the papers the Crown have kept, I could explain a great many other things and——

The Attorney-General interposed, and said he objected to the prisoner being allowed to address the jury in this way.

Judge Keogh said the prisoner could not be allowed to repeat statements over and over. He then proceeded to tell all about Robespierre and the revolution of his day. One word as to these abominable articles. He was glad to see the spirit of the real public journalism of this city which did not report the articles the prisoner read here yesterday in the expectation that they would be published —they did not allow them to go forward to contaminate the moral atmosphere of this country. "Every man a sovereign and the rulers the servants of the people," the great constitution of America was founded by Washington and maintained by Madison and Adams, and its Senate was adorned by the eloquence and unrivalled abilities of Webster and Henry Clay. Gentlemen, I send these papers to your box. If you believe that that wild confederacy existed, and that the prisoner at the bar was a member of that confederacy, you ought unhesitatingly to find him guilty. Let there be no words bandied about assassination in actual or massacre in general. I leave this case to your arbitration; I believe whoever reads these trials in a calm and tranquil spirit, will say that if we have erred at all it has been on the side of indulgence to the accused!

The Prisoner—You have told them to convict me.

Clerk of the Crown—Remove the prisoner.

The jury retired at half-past one o'clock.

THE VERDICT.

At thirty-five minutes past two o'clock the jury returned into court, and the prisoner was again brought into the dock.

Mr. Geale—You say that he is "guilty" on all the counts.

The Attorney-General—I have now to ask your lordships to pronounce judgment on the prisoner, and in doing so I have to refer you to an entry on the calendar, by which it appears that this prisoner was arraigned and pleaded "guilty" in July, 1859, at the Cork Assizes, to an indictment of a character precisely similar to the present—an indictment of treason-felony. He at first pleaded "not guilty," but afterwards withdrew it, and was released on the condition that he would appear when called upon to receive sentence. Having regard to the lapse of time, I thought it more fair and constitutional not to call the particular attention of the court to that entry, and ask the court to pass sentence without a trial, but to allow the present case to take its course. I think it right now to call attention to the record of the former conviction by the Clerk of the Crown for Cork.

Mr. Justice Keogh—Has the prisoner anything to say? You pleaded guilty to a similar indictment at the Summer Assizes of '59.

Prisoner—My lord, that is a small matter. I have to say I was arrested in '59, and charged with an offence, but everything that was sworn against me was false. I believe Mr. Whiteside was Attorney-General under the Derby Government, and through our attorney we were told that if we pleaded guilty, Dan O'Sullivan (Agreem), who had been transported, would be released. We would not do so until July, when there was a change of government, and on the second day of the assizes we were discharged. You can add anything you like to the sentence you are going to pass on me if it is any satisfaction to you.

Mr. Geale—Jeremiah O'Donovan Rossa, you have been indicted and found guilty of compelling her Majesty to change her measures, and stir up and incite foreigners to invade this country. What have you to say why sentence should not be passed upon you?

The Prisoner—With the fact that the government seized papers connected with my defence and examined them—with the fact that they packed the jury—with the fact that the government stated they would convict—with the fact that they sent Judge Keogh, a second Norbury, to try me—with these facts before me, it would be useless to say anything.

The observations of the prisoner created a profound sensation, to which audible expression was given in court.

Mr. Justice Fitzgerald—We will retire now for a few minutes.

After a short absence, their lordships came into court, when Mr. Justice Keogh passed sentence as follows:—Jeremiah O'Donovan Rossa, you have, after a most patient trial, been found guilty by a jury of your countrymen of the offence which is charged against you in this indictment. You have been found now twice guilty of the same offence—once upon your own confession nearly six years ago—and now by a verdict of your countrymen. We have investigated and considered the details of the evidence as affects your case, and we have contrasted them with the degrees of guilt by which your co-conspirators were affected. We have considered whether there could be a distinction drawn between your case and those of the others who have been tried, but the more we have done so, the more we have been bound to arrive at the conclusion on the evidence that has been brought before us that you entertained those criminal designs at a period long antecedent to *them*. On the occasion on which you pleaded guilty the indictment to you must have entertained those designs—and that is so far back as 1859. You may have entertained them immediately after your liberation from custody—there is no evidence of that—but you certainly, on the clearest evidence, have been connected with these transactions so far back as the year 1863.

The Prisoner—Ah! I am an Irishman since I was born.

Mr. Justice Keogh—We have on the clearest evidence that, so far back as 1863, you were the most trusted of the friends in this conspiracy of James Stephens and John O'Mahony. No unprejudiced man who has listened to these proceedings can arrive at any other conclusion than that the jury were imperatively coerced to find the verdict which they have arrived at. I shall not now waste words by trying to bring any sense of the crime of which you have been found guilty to your mind.

The Prisoner—You need not. It would be a useless task for you to try.

Mr. Justice Keogh—But it is our duty—and the public interest require it—that a man who once experienced the clemency of the Crown, and who afterwards violated his good faith, and proceeds again to conspire against the institutions of this country, shall not have again the opportunity presented to him of entertaining such designs and projects. We could have drawn no distinction favorable to you as between your case and that of the prisoners Luby and O'Leary, who have been convicted of a similar offence; and our attention having been called by her Majesty's Attorney-General to this plea of guilt entered on your behalf in the year 1859, for the identical same offence of which you have been found guilty here to-day, we have no discretion left except to pass upon you the sentence of the court—that you be kept in "penal servitude for the term of your natural life."

The Prisoner—All right, my lord.

Mr. Geale (Clerk of the Crown)—Put him back.

The prison officers, who were assisted by a large force of police, pressed the prisoner from the front of the dock. As he turned round he saluted some friends in the gallery, and, with a smile, proceeded by the underground passage from the dock."

There were many comments adverse and otherwise on the course I pursued in court. There is no necessity for me to give the opinions of the flunkeys, of the constitutional agitators, and of the admirers of that *palladium* of British Liberty—trial by jury. They all agreed that I had acted disreputably, shown myself a fool, a madman, or a man of inordinate vanity. I, myself, do not believe that I was either mad, foolish, or disreputable; but I may be a bit vain, for who is there who has not some little mixture of foible or frivolity in that compound of passions that go to make up his human nature? If men that I respect—men that have suffered for the cause for which I suffered—approve of my action, it is all that I desire, and it is to me worth all the praise or censure that the lickspittles of England or the enemies of Ireland could favor me with.

John Mitchel, who can write as well as any other man, wrote as follows:

"Paris, December 22, 1865.

"Your readers must have followed with intense interest the reports of the trials (as they were called) in Ireland. Our poor friends who have been called upon this time to stand before courts and juries have all behaved nobly; but to my mind the conduct of O'Donovan Rossa was the noblest of all.

"It was very imprudent in him to take this course, and, in fact, it brought on him a sentence for life, instead of twenty years. But at any rate, he did the thing that was right, and just, and manly."

The *Evening Mail*, a Protestant journal, that occasionally gleams with a ray of Irish nationality, came out thus:

"THE TRIAL OF O'DONOVAN ROSSA—'CROWN CLEMENCY.'

"We do not think the crown lawyers excercised a wise discretion, either as regards their own convenience and character or the public service, in bringing O'Donovan Rossa to a new trial at the present Commission. These gentlemen, however, thought otherwise, and they must not now object to such criticism as their conduct of the case may seem to require. This, we must say, appears to us ill calculated to secure the ends aimed at by these prosecutions. When the prisoner undertook to defend himself it would, in our opinion, have been at once the shortest and the wisest course to have permitted him to do so with the fullest latitude, as to means and time, within the limits of the law.

"In our opinion, therefore, it was imprudent, as well as somewhat ungenerous, to refuse any of the papers which he represented necessary for his defence. His argument that, when out of all those seized at the *Irish People* office a certain selection only had been put in evidence for the prosecution, there was a presumption that the remaining might be evidence for the prisoner, was at least plausible; yet the Crown lawyers resisted it, and did not, until the last moment, if at all, place the papers actually referred to in the indictment in the hands of the prisoner's solicitor.

"We must say, also, that some portions of the prisoner's cross-examination of witnesses objected to seemed to us to be perfectly relevant, and to display considerable insight and acumen. We may mention, as an example, his cross-examination of the informer Nagle upon an account-book, which was supposed to be a blind 'starting' (as Nagle termed it) of new evidence for the prosecution, but which turned out afterwards to be very skillfully designed to break down the testimony as to the handwriting of the expert, Chabot. A good deal has been said about the time occupied by the prisoner's defence, and the expedients he resorted to for the purposes of delay; but he answered the criticism when he reminded the Court that the time belonged to him for defence as indefeasibly as it belonged to the Crown for prosecution. It must be recollected, too, that if the game of the Crown lawyers was the short one, his was the long one, and that he was as fully justified in playing out his to the best of his ability as they were in playing off theirs."

The *Irishman* said:

"The public interest in the Fenian trials, which had begun to flag, were revived by the unexpected announcement that O'Donovan Rossa would defend himself. The innovation naturally excited as much horror among the gentlemen of the long robe as the intrusion of the shoe-strings into the ante-chamber of Louis XVI. created in the mind of the court usher. That the determination was a comparatively wise one, however, could scarcely be doubted by any impartial spectator of the vapid farces presented by the learned counsel for the previous prisoners under the name of defences. We say comparatively, for probably it would have been the wisest of all for Luby and O'Leary to plead guilty at first, as they virtually did at last. Nevertheless, the acuteness, vigor, and even good humor with which the prisoner conducted his case yesterday contrasted very strongly with the quibbling hair-splittings and irrelevancies of the professional lawyers."

And the *London Times*, in mortified admiration at the spirit displayed by the prisoners in general exclaimed: "*It would seem that self-reliance, self-confidence, patriotism, and even justice, were confronting the judge and the informers at the bar.*"

And so they were.

I was transported for life, and, looking over every thing that was urged against me, I fail to see anything that the law could honestly urge against anyone as an offence. The prosecutors urged that I was intimately acquainted with John O'Leary and Thomas Clarke Luby, and that I was the trusted friend of John O'Mahony and James Stephens, to which I replied that I was proud of their friendship and acquaintance.

It was urged against me that I was the treasurer of a fund subscribed for the defence of Cornelius Dwyer Keane, a man who was awaiting trial on a charge of swearing in men, and I showed that it was perfectly legal to see about the defence of prisoners, and that the law itself provided counsel for a man who had no means to provide it himself.

It was urged against me that I went to America in June and came back from America in July, and I asked where was the treason in that? But then they had documents which were lost and found in Kingstown, from which they attempted to show that my journey was in connection with treasonable designs. One of the judges, in charging the jury in Mr. Luby's trial, went so far as to say that it was I who lost these documents, but I proved by their own detectives, who were watching me these days, that I was on my way from Cork to Dublin at the time those papers were found.

There was an entry in my private account book, which I kept in the *Irish People* office of two pounds to Denis Hayes, for Stephens. This Stephens was a young son of mine, and I gave Denis Hayes two pounds to buy clothes for him. But Judge Keogh, in charging the jury, told them to look upon this money as paid to James Stephens and criminatory of me. The *Irish People* was not registered at first for transmission abroad, and the newspapers were all detained in the post office without our getting notice of it, till a friendly clerk came and told me. We got the paper registered. It cost five pounds to restamp all the numbers that were directed to Chicago. I had this entered on my book as "Postage paid on Chicago papers," and Judge Keogh told the jury to look upon this as postage that I paid for distributing the Fenian pamphlet of the Chicago Convention.

A fellow named Petit came from England to the office of the *Irish People* to entrap me. I was on my guard, though he had a letter of introduction. His telling me that he was sent over by the friends in England to drill men in Ireland was sufficient for me, as I knew we had hundreds of men already who could act as drill-instructors if they were needed. This Petit swore against me, and in his informations he stated that while he was in the room with me I took Charles Kickham into a corner of it and commenced whispering to him something which he (Petit) could not hear. This was one of the informations on which I was prosecuted; but they would not bring Petit forward, because they learned that Charles Kickham was very deaf and could not be spoken to, less whispered to, without using an ear-trumpet. Nagle also made informations against me, which were false. They were read against us at the preliminary investigations. I had made arrangements to show the perjuries of the fellow. The Crown prosecutors must have learned this from the seizure of my defence papers; and when I came to examine the informer on his original informations, Judge Keogh coolly told me that these were not put in evidence against me.

I was baffled every way by their jugglery; but I baffled them a little, too. A counsellor named Coffey, who was engaged for my defence when I was in prison in '59, was now acting barrister. He was on circuit through the country, and everywhere he held his sessions he was trying to frighten the people by telling them that the Government had twenty informers to swear against us, whereas they were at their wits' end to get one at all, outside of Nagle.

They got a person named Gillis to swear against Michael Moore at the preliminary trial, but by the time the Commission came on he refused to swear according as they desired, and they sentenced him to five years' penal servitude.

Few men had travelled as much of the organization as I, few men were so generally known in it; the authorities knew this, and they were mad that I had gone through so much without their being able to catch up any traces of my work that they could bring against me.

They thought I should have papers somewhere to be seized, and they searched everywhere. They invaded the house of my father-in-law, who lived two hundred miles from Dublin, they turned his furniture upside down, turned the drawers inside out, and even went up the chimneys, without getting anything but soot. The only one thing they could bring legally against me was my signature to legal documents as publisher of the *Irish People*. On this they held me responsible for everything published in the paper. I signed this document in their own courts, in presence of their own witnesses, and they brought it forward against me to convict me of conspiracy. I told them that under a Russian despot or a French tyrant justice would be satisfied and vengeance appeased by the punishment of the proprietor or the editor, or any one responsible party; but English vengeance was a horse of another color—it should even ride rough-shod over the printers who dared to set such treasonable type.

They also seized the used up correspondence that was thrown into the waste-basket and prosecuted the writers; they seized the books that contained the names of the subscribers—things that we could not avoid having—and these subscribers they put into prison.

On the 24th of June, '65, I left the Cove of Cork for New York. I took with me dispatches from James Stephens to John O'Mahony. When I arrived on the 5th of July I learned that Mr. P. J. Meehan and Mr. P. W. Dunne were going to Ireland on business connected with the organization. They were to examine into things on the other side, and were to report faithfully. A meeting of the Council of the Fenian Brotherhood was held at the house of Mr. William R. Roberts, at which I attended. and heard read those despatches which I brought. This is not the place to tell what passed there. Mr. Meehan and Mr. Dunne were to sail on the 12th, and as I had my business done I determined to sail with them. John O'Mahony wanted to keep me in New York, as he said many inquiries were made about Ireland which he could not answer, and my being in the office would do much good. I told him I would not stay for any consideration, as I had no instructions on that head. He asked me to remain for a month, during which time he would write to Stephens and have a reply, but this I would not do. I was strongly of opinion that there was to be a fight in Ireland. Now; I do not say that I was mad to be first in that fight; perhaps in cool blood I would think myself safer out of it, but I was anxious to stick up to my own expressions and to what people expected from me, and that was not to be safely out of the way when there was any danger around.

General Wolfe once told his mother that he thought the good opinion others had of him would bring him to an early grave, for he felt himself inferior to what was thought of him by his friends.

Yet to act up to their estimate of him, he thought that in case of danger he would have to be superior to himself, be first in the fight and first to fall, and thus predicted to himself an early death, which he had at Quebec. I have not extraordinary fighting courage, nor would I feel warranted in rushing into dangers because my friends may think I would do so, but when I commit myself to a thing I like to act up to it. I knew I had committed myself to be in the fight in Ireland, and I would not give it to any one to say that I had been safely in America while it was going on.

John O'Mahony told me that as I would not stay he would give me a note that would send me back as soon as I handed it to Stephens. But I told him I would not be the bearer of any note that I considered complimentary to myself, and refused to take it.

"Then," said he "I will send it by the others, and Patrick will take it down."

I was on board the Cuba when Patrick J. Downing came alongside on the tender, handed me the note, which I handed to P. J. Meehan. Something has been said of John O'Mahony having refused to pay my passage back to Ireland, and that it was P. J. Meehan paid it, part of which is true and part false. John O'Mahony did not refuse to pay my passage; but it was stated to me by P. W. Dunne, in O'Mahony's presence, that the party going to Ireland had engaged one passage more than they wanted, and that I would fit in there. And after I gave Colonel Downing's message to P. J. Meehan he took me to the purser of the ship and paid for my passage. This money, of course, I looked upon as Fenian money, for I knew that Mr. Meehan was the bearer of funds to Ireland.

Going into the Cove of Cork I told Mr. Meehan that as I left Ireland in a troublous state, and not knowing but there may be a rigorous search on landing, it would be well for him to give those papers he had to his sister or Mrs. Dunne, who accompanied us. He told me they were all right, that he had sewed them up between the soles of one of his carpet-slippers. Next day he lost these papers in Kingstown, where he went to deliver them to James Stephens. Pursuant to the caution given him, and his own promptings, he thought it better not to have those papers in any pocket of his, and he fastened them with a pin, as he told us, inside the waist of his drawers. The pin slipped out, and the letters slipped away unknown to him. The charge has been made against him that he lost these documents intentionally, and much contention has, I understand, been in America about them. All I say is, that the matter was discussed at a Council meeting in Dublin, that I gave it as my opinion that he lost them honestly, and that I have no evidence since to warrant me in changing that opinion. Parties may say what they please of Mr. Meehan on other matters; it is only right for me to say so much of him on this.

CHAPTER VI.

Convicted — The Black Van and the Cavalry—Mountjoy Convict Prison—Dressing, Registering, Shaving, and Photographing—Sympathetic Tears—Forbidden to Write—A Bed, but no Sleep—My Government Acquaintance—The Convicts' Priest—Religious Books—A Blinker Pew in Chapel—Feeling my Pulse and Fit for a Journey—Meet the Convicts O'Leary, Luby, "Pagan," Moore and Haltigan—Tight Irons—Departure—More Sympathetic Tears, and a few Opinions on "Peelers" and other British Pensioners—Old Dunleary—The Convict Ship—"Respectable" People—A Word of my Companions—The "Pagan" and his Work—Soldiers and Arms.

Now I am a convicted felon, and I am to experience the benefits of those institutions which England has established to civilize those who are so barbarous as not to appreciate the many blessings to be derived from her "glorious British Constitution," and from a peaceful and obedient resignation to her benign laws.

Five minutes after the condemnation I was ushered unto the black van, in fact it had been waiting for me two hours, the horses ready harnessed and the soldiers equipped, to escort me to Mountjoy Prison. Before I went in I shook hands with the police who had been keeping watch over me in court for the previous fifteen days, and I will not deny that they looked as if they were sorry for me. The van rattled through the streets, the soldiers galloped at each side of it with sabres drawn, and in less than half an hour the world closed upon me, and the first light of a very dark life dawned upon me inside the portals of Mountjoy. The soldiers were lounging about the entrance yard; they ran to the steps ascending the doomed palace as the *cortege* approached. I came out, and, with as kind a look as I could give, and as light a step as I could take, I passed through them. I always go in for being civil to those who can help myself or my country; and, if I don't get anything by showing my better nature, why, then, I go in for being otherwise.

I was ushered into a room, my clothes were prepared for me, I was divested of everything I wore belonging to a free man, and, after examining my naked body—to be sure that I had nothing concealed—I got my outfit. It consisted of a shirt, a flannel drawers and waistcoat, a grey vest, jacket and trowsers, a pair of stockings, a pair of shoes and a cap. This was not a complete outfit. I was short a pocket handkerchief and a neck-tie, but orders were issued that I was not to have these.

I am sure that in the certificate of conviction sent with me to prison a "bad character" was sent with it in consequence of the course I pursued at my trial, if I may call it a trial. After being dressed I was taken into the registry office. My height I believe was five feet nine inches and a half, my hair was fair, my eyes were blue, my mouth and nose were—well, I will not say what they were —I always thought I had a handsome mouth and nose, at least I thought others thought I had, but my admirers on this occasion were people of very little taste, and their opinion on these things is not worth much to those interested in such matters; however, they wound up with describing my features as "average," and sent me from their department to the next manipulator. He escorted me to my cell, and giving his commands to two others, they came, one holding a candle and the other a razor. The first gentleman told me "sit down on that stool there," and drawing a scissors out of his pouch he commenced clipping away at my beard. Whenever he had occasion to say "hold up your head," "turn your head this way," or "turn your head that way," he said it in as gruff a voice as he could command, and I obeyed in silent admiration of the power that I was now subject to. While using the scissors on my face he scarred me a little. He asked did he hurt me, and I said, "Oh, governor, never mind." The man with the razor next came on, and as he moved, my eyes fell on the face of the man who was holding the candle, and they began to swim in their sockets. It was the first time I got soft during my imprisonment; but when I saw the tears streaming down the cheeks of this Irish-hearted jailer who was holding the candle, I could not restrain my own from starting.

After being shaven I was led to have my picture taken. The photographer had a large black-painted pasteboard prepared, with my name painted across it in white, and, pinning it across my breast, he sat me in position. I remained sitting and looking according to instructions till he had done, and he never had the manners to tell—what artists never failed to tell me—that I made an exceedingly good picture. The rules are read to me, and I see that one of them says that I can write a letter on reception into prison. I ask for pen, ink and paper, and I am told that I cannot have the benefit of that rule, that there are special instructions in my case, and that I cannot write until there are special orders. The first day of my imprisonment, here are these special instructions to treat us exceptionally. I would not grumble or wonder if, as political prisoners, it were exceptionally better; but no, it was exceptionally worse than the worst criminals of society. I respectfully demanded that I be allowed to write to a member of parliament about the illegal conduct of the judges at my trial. No, no; I could not write, and I may as well put the thought of doing so out of my head.

I went into prison determined to bear all things patiently, determined to obey in everything, as I conceived that the dignity of the cause of liberty required that men should suffer calmly and strongly for it; but the more obedient and humble I was, the more my masters showed a disposition to trample upon me—the more they felt disposed to give us that annoyance which had no other object but to torment us.

I have often asked myself what was the motive of worrying us as they did, and—waiving the question of killing us or driving us mad—I see no other object in view but that of making us so tired of our lives that we would beg for mercy, or beg to be let alone; and that would be a great thing for the English Government to have to show to the world, that here were those Irish revolutionists, who were so stubborn in the dock, now on their knees. The Irish in America, and the Irish all the world over, would feel humbled, and, if our own spirit would allow it, it might be as well that we had given them reason to do so, in view of the little good we appear to have done outside Ireland by doing differently.

My cell was about ten feet by seven. It contained a water-closet, a table, a stool, a hammock-bed made like a coffin and about two feet broad at the top, a salt box, a tin box, a tin pint, and a spoon. I got a pound weight of oakum to pick the first day, and I picked about two ounces of it, which was not bad for a beginner. I went to bed at eight o'clock, and, immediately after, I was roused up and ordered to put out my clothes through the trap door. This also was something that was not required of ordinary prisoners; but in consequence of the flight of James Stephens from them, they were afraid the fairies would fly away with us. Every fifteen minutes of the night the trap-door of my cell was opened by two officers; one of them held a bull's-eye lantern towards my head, and if he did not see my face he kept calling me until I put in an appearance. Then there were two soldiers outside my cell window who kept calling "all right" to each other every half hour.

This continued night after night. For ten nights I was here I never got an hour's sleep. I read of some Eastern tyrants that tortured their prisoners by preventing them from sleeping, and I experienced that torture under the government of these sanctimonious people who denounce it to the world when it is inflicted by any one but themselves.

My breakfast was gruel and milk; my dinner and supper bread and milk; and two days in the week we got meat for dinner. I got an hour's exercise in the open air each day, and in this matter I was treated exceptionally also. The ordinary prisoners were exercised in companies, but I was exercised alone, save that in the ring in which I walked there was a goat tied by a rope to a stake.

Two warders and a soldier kept guard, and the goat seeing I was so lonely seemed to take compassion on me; for as I approached the part of the circle where he was tethered he would run towards me and butt gently with his head as if he desired to make my acquaintance. Sometimes I had to catch him by the horns to put him off my course, for I could not step off a flag which was about eighteen inches wide and ran around inside the iron-railed enclosure. The warders ordered me to go round without having anything to do with the goat; they would order the goat, too, but the genial little soul seemed to despise them and their regulations; he did not care for the rules and would be refractory by running to meet me, so that they put him out of the yard altogether.

The second day of my residence in Mountjoy my cell-door opened, and who came in but an Irish priest. I was only a short time out of the world, and yet I well recollect how delighted I was to see any one belonging to it, and to see a priest, too; for, perhaps, the dormant tradition of my younger days was revived, that it was in periods of darkness and difficulty the Irish priest clung to the Irish people, and I felt as if I could forget the past, if the pastor could do so, and be friends for the future.

He told me his name was Father Cody, and that he was a Kilkenny man.

"Then," said I, "you have the honor of belonging to James Stephen's county."

We had some half an hour's talk, much of which I do not now remember. He looked at the oakum I had to pick, and told me I need not worry myself with it at first, but do a little. He asked me had I any books, and I said no. Then he told me he would get me some, and going out, he brought me in a new Testament, a Prayer-Book, and the Lives of the Saints, and "Think Well of It." I got no secular book, and if I did I could not do much with it, as my mind was not sufficiently calmed down for study. The priest asked what induced me to take the defiant course I did at my trial, and I said I saw myself doomed, and thought I might as well have the value of my money out of them as be standing in apparent awe, silently looking on at the farce of giving me a trial. As he was about to leave he said:

"Well, on my word, I'm so disappointed in you."

"How is that, Father?" said I.

"Why," replied he, "I thought, and we all thought here, that you were crazy, or that you were one who had some kind of ungovernable temper that no reason could control."

I smiled at the words. He bid me adieu for that day, saying he would call next day again. The door closed, and I found myself in the congenial society of my own thoughts.

I knew that Pagan O'Leary, and Mr. Luby, and Mr. O'Leary, and Mr. Haltigan, and Mr. Moore had preceded me to Mountjoy

Prison, but I never could get a sight of them. For the hour during which I was exercised, I strained my eyes in every direction that I could give a squint, but I never got a glance at one of them. I was taken to chapel on Sunday, but I was put into a box which had blinckers at each side of it; I could see only the backs of the other prisoners. I believe my companions were placed in similar boxes alongside of me. These compartments are arranged for very refractory characters, and before we had time to acquire any prison reputation at all we were ushered into them.

It was on Christmas Eve, the eleventh day of my conviction, that at four o'clock in the morning, the bull's-eye patrol ordered me to get out of bed; he threw my clothes in through the trap-door, and told me to dress in a hurry. He handed me a piece of bread and a pint of milk, and told me to waste no time in eating my breakfast.

"What is all this about, Governor?" said I.

"Never mind what it is about," answered he; "do what you're told and ask no questions."

While I was engaged in carrying out that part of the order which related to my breakfast, the door was opened and three or four persons, dressed in men's clothes, came into my cell. One of them—that was not Dr. M'Donnell, who always spoke very civilly to me—felt my pulse and pronounced me fit for a journey. Out they went without any ceremony, and left me thinking that I was going somewhere, but whereto was the puzzle. A few minutes after I was ushered into one of the large halls and placed alongside of five other men. I could not take a good look at them, as I was adhering to the orders always to look to my front and never turn my head sideways. I thought I would become a splendid prisoner, and get a most excellent character for myself by obedience to the rules and adherence to the precepts. When I was a young man a young girl once flattered me by saying I had the happy gift of making myself amiable in every society in which I mixed. This was at a time of life when my mind was susceptible of impression, and she made this impression on it—so much so that I never go into any company without thinking that I can make myself very agreeable, and never know till I am told afterwards by some acquaintance, more candid than she of my early days, how very ridiculous I make myself. This feeling of mine followed me into prison, and did not forsake me for years. Not until I had been worn down to a skeleton, and the old flesh worn off my bones, and the old thoughts worn out of my mind did I come to learn that all the arts of my nature could not make me agreeable company. My jailers could never see in me the gift that the arch little girl flattered into me. All my efforts to be amiable were of no avail. I found that I had been cheating myself, and I had to change my tactics. But I will come to this by and bye.

When ranged alongside the other prisoners I took advantage

of the officer's eyes being off of me to open my ear wide and whisper to the man next to me, "where are we going?" He replied, "I don't know." I knew his whisper. I looked at him, cried out, "Luby;" he replied, "Rossa," and we had a little shake hands. The officer frowned at us, but I got a little courage, and I thought it was not much harm to look at Mr. O'Leary, and the Pagan, and the others, giving them a nod of recognition, though it was with difficulty I recognized them. The handcuffs came; Luby was next to me; they were fitted on him first and then I was tied to him. His hand was very small, and I told the jailer that the irons were too small for my hand, but he was in a hurry and could get no others, so I had to suffer to feel my wrist bound in an iron that was crushing the bones of it.

The order came for us to move, and we were conducted into the "black van." Six jailers were put in with us. We were all locked up; the wheels rumbled over the pavements of Dublin; the cavalry galloped alongside, and on we we went for an hour or more, not knowing to what quarter of the world we were bound. The irons were tormenting me, and as the horses stopped I remarked that it was not at all necessary for my safety to bind me so tight. One officer said he could do nothing in the matter; he turned the bull's eye of his lantern to look at my hand, and as the light fell on the face of another jailer beside me, I saw the tears streaming down his cheeks. I know the man's name, and I know the name of the other man whose sympathy showed itself in his eyes while I was being shorn, but it would not do to mention names here; these men may be jailers still, and I am not going to injure them. What I witnessed in them only tended to confirm an opinion I long entertained—that a red coat, a green jacket, or a jailer's livery may cover as Irish a heart as any in Ireland. If we had any kind of a decent fight many of these would have wavered in that allegiance which the poverty of their pockets alone forced them into, and turn to that allegiance which they sucked in with their mother's milk; and I for one do not blame them for not being the first to start into rebellion, nor will I have a hard word to say even to those who, in the English service, were my captors and my prosecutors. They may live, they may even die in the enemy's service and doing the enemy's work, but I will give them credit for wishing to serve their country, or wishing they had a country to serve. That these will not be the first to commence hostilities to England I am confident, and I am just as certain that the comfortable and well-to-do classes will not be the first either.

In Ireland the United Irishmen were not considered respectable by the "respectables," because it was the poor people worked up the society. It commenced below and worked its way upwards to a position of respect; it did not commence above and work down, for the snobbery above could not condescend to communicate with the masses. Snobbery had something to lose, and said that the "mob' that were risking their lives had nothing to lose and aimed at getting possession of what snobbery possessed.

The movement was not respectable, said our "respectable" folk, and they never tried to make it so by coming into it themselves.

The same thing had been said in America of the Fenian movement, and the "respectable" Irish patriots there never set to work themselves to establish what, according to their views, would be a respectable movement. They can complain and cavil very well at what they dislike, and make their disliking an excuse for their inaction, but they never do anything else It is useless to be wasting words upon such folk; their existence does not commence in our day or in our nation; they have existed in all times and amongst all peoples, and we will have to do our work without them; nay, against them, for they will permit nothing to be done or own nothing is good that is not done by themselves.

When I speak of the poor people having to fight the battles of every country, I am not to be understood as saying that we had none to fight the battle for Irish independence but those "who had nothing to lose." The snobs, the *shoneens* in Ireland who could be so grand as to drive a one-horse gig, though they could hardly afford to pay for the oats the *staggeen* of a horse would eat, would sneer at the independent farmer or mechanic—though he could buy him out of house and home, his *staggeen* and his gig into the bargain, and quadruple his brains, too—working for the cause of Ireland. The misfortune is, here and there, that fallen fortunes are not respectable; and, though we can afford to talk and sing of the martial deeds of Fion MacCumhail and the chivalrous glories of Brian the Brave, we cannot afford to do anything practical in emulation of them: *that* would entail labor, and, perhaps a little sacrifice, and we need not undergo this while we can purchase the name of patriot and make profit by it in a cheaper manner.

This morning of my removal from Ireland, when I was taken out of the "black van," I looked around me to see where I was, and I found myself on the pier of Old Dunleary. The steamer was before me, ready to sail for England, and between me and the steamer were two rows of soldiers, between whom I and my companions wended our way to the ship. It was a dark December morning, and the appearance the redcoats presented through the mist told us it was considered an occasion of the greatest importance. Arrived at the boat, I had the honor to be helped on board by the Dublin detectives who had arrested us. They were there to see us off, and to see whatever else would be interesting to them in the prosecution of their labors for "maintenance of law and order."

The ship sailed. The day was breaking as we were parting from that land whose soil we were to tread no more, unless against the will and power of those whose rule has been a curse to it for centuries. I had my feelings on the occasion, but I kept them in my breast, where I always—well, nearly always—keep them, when I can do no good by keeping them elsewhere.

I was about an hour at sea when I thought it was time for me to make a little noise about those irons that were crushing my hand.

My wrist was quite swollen. I showed it to the jailers and I asked if I could not have some relief now that we were safe out of Ireland. The Deputy-Governor of Millbank Prison came, with six of his jailers, to the Irish shore to take charge of us, and I asked if I could not see the officer in command, in order that now, as we were going to a free country, I might be supplied with freer irons.

Whenever I felt sore or sad about my treatment in the hands of those people I always made it a point never to make my sorrows known; and as well as I could I laughed and joked away many things that were galling to me, and that were meant to be so. This annoyed my masters more than anything else, and my own friends could not understand how it was becoming in me to be gay under such very serious and solemn circumstances; and to this disposition of mine I believe I owe the fact of my wife not being a widow to-day, for had I given way to passion on every indignity being heaped upon me, I would have burned myself up long ago. On the occasion of my asking for "freer irons as we were going to a free country," I was reminded by one of my companions that it was a most unsuitable time for a display of wit. This put a damper upon me. I don't know that it wasn't it made me sea-sick, for I began discharging my stomach immediately; indeed it may have put some grave manhood in me also, for I *demanded* that I should see the superior officer immediately, or I would try and get something to break the irons. Captain Wallack came, examined my hand, said the handcuffs were a little tight, had me untied and chained to Michael Moore, and having released Pagan O'Leary from Mr. Moore, he had him tied to my partner, Mr. Luby.

I cannot land on the shores of England for a few hours, and as I have spoken of my companions here, I may occupy the rest of the voyage in speaking a little more of them.

I have spoken of the name of O'Leary twice, and it is necessary to be understood that I speak of two distinct characters that have sometimes been confounded one with the other. Pagan O'Leary is not John O'Leary, nor is John O'Leary the Pagan. It would not be easy to find two men more different from each other, or any man more ready than either, each in his own way, to risk life in an honest, earnest endeavor for Irish independence. John O'Leary was editor of the *Irish People*. The two other writers of it were Charles J. Kickham and Thomas Clarke Luby. They were three men whose acquaintance, whose friendship, and whose esteem any man may feel proud to have, and I would feel proud to be worthy of. If I would say that at the time I was working with them I loved Kickham, admired Luby and reverenced O'Leary, I would be saying what I thought of them, and thinking this is all the clue that I can give my readers here as to the characters of the men. My pen is too poor to do them justice; they still live, and I hope will live to do something worthy of their ambition to serve their country.

The Pagan is a soldier, and I do not know that he aspires to be anything else. But he has also a capacity for other work, if we may judge from his labors in Ireland. He had gone from America to Ireland three times to fight, and three times he had not got the chance of firing a shot. He was arrested at Athlone in November, '64, and charged with attempting to swear English soldiers into Irish revolutionists. It was urged at his trial that he had been traveling through Ireland and corrupting the army, and he was sentenced to seven years' penal servitude. He had a wonderful influence over these soldiers, and if his work and that of others who worked in the same department had been vigorously utilized in '65 we might have a different story to tell to-day.

The Pagan did not cease his work in prison ; he made friends there too ; and some of them proposed to Edward Duffy and myself to effect his escape before conviction. We communicated the proposal to "The Captain," and he decided that it would bring the strength of our organization too much under the notice of the Government, and that it was better policy to leave one man to suffer than to make an alarm and give the Government grounds for adopting repressive measures which would interfere with the steps we were taking to relieve the national suffering.

The Pagan was in Mountjoy Prison before my arrest, and I attempted to get at seeing him, but was not able to succeed. One day I found myself in possession of a ticket giving permission to visit the place of his confinement, and proceeded there with my plans arranged to try and get a word or a whisper with him by hook or by crook. I found myself and Cornelius Dwyer Kane and a few others inside the prison walls, and a few officers detailed to show us round. We went to look at the chapel, and, as it was there I had meditated to sound my purpose, I asked the guide about the several religious denominations, and told a tale of an institution I knew that gave protection to a man once who would not belong to any religion unless there was a Pagan temple in the place.

"Oh," said he, "we have just such another case here."

"Here in Dublin!" said I, in amazement.

"Here in this very prison," replied he.

And then he proceeded to tell me about the Pagan's refusal to belong to any religious denomination; but when they kept punishing him for the offence he at length consented to attend the Roman Catholic place of worship.

"Is he out of his mind?"

"Well, I don't know, for I have not much communication with him ; but I suppose he is."

"And do you allow him to associate with the other prisoners?"

"Oh, no; he is in a separate cell by himself. I will show it to you by and by when we are passing."

"By Jove, I should like to have a peep at such an odd character."

On we went. I had my mind fixed on that cell where the Pagan was confined, and one of my hands was playing with a few silver crowns I had in my pocket, when a prison bell rang, and the Governor sent word to us that as some of the prisoners were about to go to prayers he was obliged to ask us out; but if we came at a more propitious hour he would be very happy to afford us longer time for observation. We left without having attained our object, and I did not enter Mountjoy Prison again till I entered it a convict.

CHAPTER VII.

In England—Christmas Eve—London—Pentonville Prison—Stripped of Flannels—Clothes Searched—Naked—Cell and Cell Furniture—Solitary Confinement—Cold and Hunger—Christmas Fair—My Trade and Occupation—Reading the Rules—Forbidden to Write—The Doctor—Airing or Exercise in the Refractory Yard—My Library—The Prison Directions—Dreams of Happiness.

The telegraph must have carried the news that we were bound for "the land of the brave and the free." for, as the ship approached Holyhead, the pier was crowded with spectators. The company of soldiers, who accompanied us from Ireland, were drawn up on the quay, and we ran the gauntlet between them to the railroad carriage that was in waiting for us. After a few hours we arrived at Chester. One of our keepers was called out by the officer in command, and coming back, he brought a meat-pie and divided it between us. My two hands were bound to those at each side of me; they would not unbind me while I was eating, and whenever I put my hand to my mouth the hand of some one of my companions had to accompany it. Not alone for eating they would not loose my hands, but they would not loose them for anything else. It is some hundreds of miles from Holyhead to London. Our journey took from four o'clock in the morning to eight o'clock in the evening. One might think that once we were in England our masters would have no scare about our safe-keeping; but no, the scare never left them, and they never left us to the ordinary vigilance to which other convicts were left, though they were continually telling us that there was no difference between us and them. These people preach very much to others about propriety and decency of behaviour, while they outrage every principle of both in their treatment of those whom they hold as their enemies. When we went to the closet on board the steamboat, the sentinel kept opening the closet-door every half-minute lest we should attempt an escape through the pipes or through the port-hole, and they would not for any consideration allow us off the railroad car while we were on the journey from Holyhead to London.

It was Christmas eve, and at every station we could see the filled hampers that were being taken to their homes by the merry people of "merry England," who were going to have a happy Christmas. How could it be helped if we had sad thoughts at the reflection that those near and dear to us were to have a poor time of it. Some very nicely regulated minds can derive pleasure under any circumstances from seeing people happy, but I confess that on this occasion my equanimity was not much improved by witnessing the gaiety of a Christmas time that I could but very poorly enjoy. How often in prison did I feel inclined to bear testimony to that truth the poet sings—

"That sorrows' crown of sorrow is remembering happier things."

I have no doubt that, as another poet sings, the memories of the pleasant past are always pleasant when you are in a position to repeat the enjoyment, but locked up in prison, and debarred from all the world's enjoyment, the recollection of the jolly times I had spent in the past did not come to me with any soothings for the gloomy present.

Our train arrived at Euston-square Station, London, about 8 o'clock in the evening, and there was a little army of jailers and policemen waiting for us on the platform. They had with them two of those vans which are kept for transferring criminals from the courts to the prisons, and into these we were ushered. So close a place of confinement I was never in. The compartments were about two feet square, and I was locked up in one of these after having been unbound from the others and getting a whole pair of handcuffs to myself. The horses galloped through the streets of London, and I got no glimpse of light again till I was taken out of my coop when inside the gates of Pentonville prison. As I was ascending the steps to the front door of my future residence one of the jailers that was in waiting to receive me caught hold of me by the shoulder, and, as he clutched me, said, "Get up, Paddy." Talk as you may of bearing imprisonment properly, and with that submission which becomes a man, you cannot talk my blood into coolness or good behavior under certain provocations; it will get hot and rush to the head, as it did when the fellow addressed me with his "Get up, Paddy." My first impulse was to stop his tongue with a blow, and my being a convict, or my being in prison, or my being in the midst of my enemies, would not have prevented his getting it, if I were not manacled.

The governor of the prison took a look at us as we stood in one of the large halls, and having examined the papers that were brought with us, gave us over to the petty officers to be put through and located. We were ordered to strip as we stood in line, and I threw off my shoes, my jacket, trousers and vest. Thinking this much was enough, I stopped, and one of the surveyors cried out, "Why don't you strip?" I asked him had I not taken off as much as was necessary, and he said, "No, take off those stockindgs an that shirt," and in a short time the six of us stood naked on the flags.

There we were in a row, quite naked before the gaze of these officials, and then commenced that examination of us which cannot well be described, but which left an impression on our minds never to be effaced. These English people speak of their sense of decency—nay, they have laws in the interest of morality that punish wanton exposure of the person, but such gross ruffianism as attended our entrance into a residence in the civilized city of London is something that should be put an end to, even in a convict prison.

I had been blessing my stars on account of the removal from Ireland to England, for now I thought that the fears of our masters were removed, I could have rest and liberty to write to my family. I gave the English credit for their magnanimity and for their desire to treat us decently when their scare was over, but "if I live to be as old as Methuselah" they'll never have such credit from me again. The first practical experience I had in England of their dark designs regarding us was in the dressing of us. They took our Irish clothes away when they had stripped us, and opposite to where we stood were six little parcels, placed each about three feet apart from its neighbors, which turned out to be our six suits of clothes. Number one in the line of prisoners took number one of the parcels, number two two, and so on until we were all supplied. The first thing I looked for were the flannels, but I looked for them in vain. I asked where was the inside clothing, and was told there was none. I remarked that I had got flannels in Ireland, that I had just taken them off, and I asked that if new ones were not given to me I may be supplied with the old ones, but all to no use. Our reception had been prepared for us, and the doctor of the prison had decided that we were to have no flannels at reception. This was the most cruel treatment, for it was mid-winter and the snow was covering the ground. To give any idea by words of the cold I experienced, is what I could not do, and when hunger came with cold it is surprising that so many of us lived the time through.

When the six of us were dressed we were led to our cells, and no two of us were placed in the same ward of the prison. I asked the warder, who had charge of me if I could not have a warm drink of some kind, as I felt fatigued, and cold and thirsty. He said he would get me my supper in a few minutes, and that is all he could do. He lit the gas, and, putting the key in the door before he shut me in, said he would be back in a few minutes. The few minutes passed, and back he came with a piece of bread and piece of cheese. "Officer," I said, "where is the warm drink?" "Warm drink!" exclaimed he, as if in surprise at my presumption, "there is your warm drink," pointing to a water tap that was fixed over the water closet which the cell contained, "there is your pint and you have everything in your cell that is necessary for you. I am going to leave you now for half-an-hour while you are eating your supper, at the end of that time I will be back, and let you have your body-clothes made up in a bundle to put outside the door as well as every moveable article of furniture you have in your cell, for there is nothing to be left with you during the night that can be taken away from you." "All right, governor," said I, "I'll try to do the best I can for you." He turned his big key upon me, and I turned my attention to my supper and my bed. I took the tin vessel and turned the tap and drank a pint of cold water. I filled again and finished a second pint. The bread and cheese remained untouched for want of appetite, and then I proceeded to make my bed. That consisted of a board seven feet by three, with a few other boards about eight inches high nailed on the head by way of a pillow; a mattress about half an inch thick, not quite so hard as the board, two sheets, a blanket and a rug. I made my bed, and it was making a hard bed for myself, but I suppose I had been at that a long time. I took off my body-clothes and folded them up nicely, according to instructions, so as to have them ready to put outside the door when the officer came. The table, the pint, the timber plate, the timber spoon, the timber salt cellar, the towel, the soap, the stool, and the Bible were the only moveable articles in my cell, and these I had arranged in proper order to put outside the door when the orders came. I always liked to get the character of being a good boy. I am terribly weak in desiring that every one that I have anything to do with should have a good opinion of me, and be thoroughly pleased with me, and on this occasion I had worked so diligently to make a good impression upon my keeper that I was a quarter of an hour standing undressed in my bedroom before the door was unlocked. I put out my furniture article after article, and every article I put out was counted and noted by the guardians. The name of one of them was Webber, and some way or other getting a civil word from him I commenced talking to him about an Englishman named Webber whom I knew at Skibbereen. He spoke rather civilly, and I thought if he was to be my keeper I could get along pretty well with him, but he was not left long in charge of me. My light was put out, my door was locked. I lay on my bed, and tried to warm myself by wrapping the clothes tightly around me, but all to no purpose. I could do nothing better than shiver the whole night through. Six o'clock in the morning came, my door was opened, I got a lamp to light my gas, took my clothes and my furniture, and commenced the day's work. But except dressing and eating there was no work to be done this day, for it was Sunday. I got my breakfast, which consisted of a pint of cocoa and eight ounces of bread; the drink I swallowed greedily, but I could not touch the food. Dinner hour came at twelve o'clock. I got eight ounces of bread and four ounces of cheese, but my stomach refused to receive either of mem. Supper followed at five—this came in the shape of six ounces of bread and a pint of porridge, and that was our Sunday course at Pentonville while we remained there. At half-past seven o'clock the bell rang to prepare for bed, the previous night's operation had to be gone through—my little room was gutted of its contents, my body clothes were laid outside, and I was left nothing but that comfortless bed and board. To sleep here was nearly as impossible as in Dublin. It is true I was weary and wanted sleep, but the intense cold I felt kept me shivering and shaking. However, if the cold was bad when first you went to bed and tried to go to sleep, it was far worse when, after a few hours of uneasy slumber, you awoke still shivering and shaking with the terrible prospect of shivering and shaking for several hours before the time to get up and get back your clothes. In the way of metaphysical discomfort I do not know that I ever experienced anything worse than these early morning hours in Pentonville.

Doubtless, what I went through afterwards *was* far worse as regards bodily pain; but then I had become as it were wedded to suffering. But I must let the future speak for itself. What I have here to speak of is the horrible sensation of cold in the morning in those cheerless Pentonville cells. It was not so much the intensity of the cold, for probably the cold was not so intense, as the abominable feeling of always awaking cold, and the hopeless and helpless feeling that there was no prospect of going to sleep again, and no possible way of getting warm till the bell rang and you were allowed to get up and put on your clothes. The remembrance of these physical sufferings is, as a general rule, excessively fugitive and short-lived—you are hungry, thirsty, hot or cold, and you feel sharply and forget quickly; but I do not think I shall ever forget those Pentonville mornings. Few people would find the occupation of blackening a floor a very pleasant one; but I can assure my readers that I felt very positive pleasure in scrubbing my cell until I brought back the warmth to my benumbed body, and the power of active thinking to my half torpid brain.

To brighten this black floor required vigorous exertion with the two brushes that were supplied to each of us, and though I went to the work with a will, for the purpose of bringing the blood into circulation, when the job was done an exhaustion ensued, for which a healthy man would be laughed at if he was working in company; but my readers must always bear in mind that English prison discipline would not allow us more food or clothes than was barely necessary to sustain life, and when I was not able to eat this food during the first days of my residence in London, matters went pretty hard with me.

Some mornings, hard as I worked at the floor—which was made from a composition of some black stuff—and willing as I was to work for my own purpose, I could not please my warder. He kept continually telling me that I should put "more elbow grease on it. When he spurred me I took the spur and brushed the harder.

Seeing, I suppose, that I was a rather tractable individual, and willing to do my best, he one morning put his hand in his pocket, and pulling out a piece of something like shoemaker's heel ball, said, "Here, rub this to the floor, and brush it well off afterwards, and you will have less trouble in bringing on the polish. I am not allowed to give this to the prisoners, and you will take good care not to use too much of it at a time." I thanked him, and showed by the life I put into the scrubbing-brush as he stood looking at me that I appreciated his kindness.

The second day I spent at Pentonville was Christmas Day. My Christmas breakfast was eight ounces of bread and three-quarters of pint of cocoa. My Christmas dinner was four ounces of meat, five ounces of bread, and one pound of potatoes; and my supper seven ounces of bread and a pint of porridge. The dinner was given to me in a tin having two compartments, in one of which was the meat and in the other the potatoes. The porridge and the cocoa were measured into my own pint, which, with everything else I used, was to be brightened up after each meal. I was allowed a knife, a plate, and a spoon. The knife was a bit of tin about four inches long and an inch and a-half wide. The spoon was a timber one, substantial enough by its thickness to fill my mouth, and the plate was timber also. I had a comb and a brush about two inches long and one in width; but as I never saw the like of this brush before, and did not know whether it was intended for a hair brush or a nail brush, I seldom or ever used it. I had two leather knee caps to wear when I was polishing the floor, and these, with my stool and table, constituted my household furniture.

In one corner of the cell was a kind of open cupboard fixed in the walls, on which my bed-clothes were to be placed, nicely folded to a regulated height and breadth. My towel was also to be folded up in a particular manner with my bit of soap in the middle of it, and open to the view of the "principal," who came in every morning to see if everything was in order. It took me an hour to fold these things, and if they were not folded so as to please the officer, he pulled them off the shelf and threw them about the floor, ordering me to go at them again. A man does not like to have any of his handiwork treated with contempt, and when I thought I had my cell made up in the nicest manner possible, it tested my patience to see this gentleman come and toss everything upside down. Indeed, I believe he did it for the very purpose of testing it, and I made up my mind that that was to be proof against every irritation.

My gas burner had a little brass tip, and this was to be kept brightly burnished. The water-pipe, turned one way, flowed into my washing basin, which was also of brass, and turned another way it flowed into a close stool which was fixed in my narrow and badly-ventilated apartment; all the brasses connected with closet, and tap and washing apparatus had to be kept shining bright: the timber cover of the close stool, the table, the stool, the plate and the spoon had to be kept nearly white as snow.

Christmas day passed rather heavily on my hands. It was one of those dark London foggy days, and my window being made of thick semi-transparent glass, which sunlight will not penetrate, and that will let in as little daylight as possible, it may be imagined that I had a gloomy time of it.

At night my ribs and my hips felt the proximity of the hard board, so much so that after a time the skin on those parts of my body on which I was accustomed to lie became quite rough, and I found that in the kind of sleep I got I learned to roll mechanically from side to side every fifteen minutes or so without waking. I have not thoroughly got rid of the habit yet. I have read of a saint who, when he was in the flesh, was obliged to lie upon iron spikes, and so accustomed did he become to lying on such a bed, that when he was relieved from the necessity of doing so he could not sleep upon a softer one, and went back to his iron couch for repose. It is here that I find myself lacking the virtues that go to make a saint. I never sigh after the *clawr bug dale* of my procrustean bed, nor would I ever care to go back to it. Yet it has not such terrors for me as that I would not run the risk of embracing it again with a fair chance of success in the attainment of the object of my ambition—a chance that will come with better auspices when better spirits come, or broader or better views come into the minds of those who profess to be working to bring it about, and then it is not the bed of an English prison I would risk, but that of a prison from which there is no earthly release.

Tuesday morning, the 26th December, '65, dawned upon me; the bell rang to get out of bed at six o'clock, the little trap door was opened, and a little lamp was handed to me to light my gas with, and my breakfast followed. There was an air of business, or a noise of business in the whole concern just now, that I did not notice either of the preceding two days. It was the first working day since we came, and there was a pretty busy time of it in installing us in office. At nine o'clock I was conducted from my apartment to the centre of the large hall of the prison. By-and-by I saw John O'Leary approach me, and one after one my companions appeared from different parts of the prison till the six of us stood in line. The deputy-governor, a gentleman named Farquharson—if etiquette will allow me to call him a gentleman—made his appearance with the rules and regulations in his hand. In the bustle of preparation to do some important business, John O'Leary whispered to me "This is hell." "Yes," said I, "hell open to sinners;" and a hellish-looking place it was, this prison of her Britannic Majesty, with all the spirits that had liberty to pass to and fro, having the gloomy, grizzly air of the unfortunate little devils that we are told keep watch and ward in the dark corridors of the prison of his satanic majesty.

We were marched into line, and being called to attention, Farquharson stood opposite, and commenced to read the rules. Our caps were off, our hands and feet in the military position, and if one may judge by our motionless behavior, we were as attentive as possible. Here, as in Mountjoy, one of the rules declared that every prisoner could write a letter on reception, and here, as in Mountjoy, this rule was set aside for our benefit, for when I asked to write, I was told that I could not do so until special instructions came in my case. I was beginning to get cured of the notion that we were brought to England for the purpose of receiving generous treatment, and I began soono to realize that these great people positively brought us to their country for the purpose of having us more surely under their thumb, and being better able to persecute us without fear of exposure, besides having the pleasure of witnessing their victims undergoing their tortures, and fretting under the wanton annoyances to which they subjected them. We were to be as ordinary prisoners—no difference between us and any other convicts—yet, the ordinary rules were set aside, and special instructions received to treat us worse than the thieves and murderers of England.

When the rules were read for us, we were measured and weighed, and I heard the officer cry out, "Jeremiah O'Donovan Rossa five-nine-and-a-half, eleven-eight." The "eleven-eight" told me I had lost some twenty pounds of my flesh since I left the world. Back to our cells again, every warder taking his own prisoner with him, my door was locked, and no sooner locked than opened again with the order to strip off everything but my trowsers and shoes. I obeyed orders. "Here now," says my guardian, pulling down my bed that was nicely folded, tossing it about the floor and keeping the rug in his hand, "take this and put it about you." I did so. He stood at the door and directed his eyes to a particular part of the prison; the signal came, and pointing to me with his club to go on before him, I advanced. "Forward," "Look to your front," "To the left," "Right," "Look to your front," "To the right," and thus he drove me through the corridors and around the corners until he cried "Halt" opposite a cell, which contained a loom and an individual dressed in civilian's clothes. In I went, and the individual ordered me to take off the rug. He felt my pulse, examined my chest, and went at me like a doctor of the establishment, and as I had made up my mind to have a word with that gentlemen when I met him, I asked if I might ask him a question, and his reply was yes. "Are you the medical officer of the establishment?" "Yes." And getting this affirmative reply, I said, "Doctor, when I arrived at this prison I was stripped of the flannels I had and got none in exchange. I asked for some, and was told that you had ordered none for us; I feel intense cold, and I make an application to you for more clothing."

"I cannot give you any more than you have."

"Very well. I have discharged my duty to myself in making the application."

"That will do."

"Right about face," cried my jailer, at the instant, as if he knew that the "that will do" of the doctor was the signal that I was polished off; and in a few minutes I was locked up in my cell and dressed myself. By-and-by the door was again opened and the order again given to prepare for exercise. I stepped outside the door, and as the order was given to open my jacket, to open my waistcoat, to take of my shoes, to take off my cap to unbutton my braces, to extend my hands, and keep my feet apart, I did each in turn, and the warder, as the prison phraseology has it, "rubbed me down"— that is, he put his two hands at the back of my neck, and felt the collars all around; he slipped his hands inside my unbuttoned braces, till his fingers met behind my back, then he manipulated every inch of my body, front and rear; he seized one arm of mine between his hands, and felt it down to the tips of my fingers; he did the same to the other; then he laid hold of a leg and searched along till he came to the big toe, and after repeating the process on the second leg, he finished by rubbing his palms over my cropped skull. "Button up;" "forward;" look to your front," "to the right," "to the left," "halt." I stood, and while the gate was opening, I took a side squint and saw Pagan standing about thirty yards behind me; his officer had ordered him to halt, lest he should come too near me. I saw by the precautions taken to keep us from getting a look at any other prisoner that the orders regarding us here must be very stringent, and that they were special and exceptionally severe, even in the manner of giving us the hour's exercise. In this prison all the convicts on first reception are exercised, or rather aired, in one large yard. Here there are three circles, one within another, the arc of each being a flagging about eighteen inches wide. The convicts walk on these flags, and in three different places between each circle there are raised pathways, on which the officers walk, and have a view of the whole ring. The prisoners walk about four paces apart, and if one of them is detected attempting to pass a whisper or a sign of recognition to another he is immediately sent into his cell and held under report for punishment. I did not get my hour's airing in this yard; the place I was taken to was one specially built and meant for the taming of refractory characters, and before they gave us any trial, or even a chance to become refractory, they treated us as such. A man's clothes or cell furniture are not taken from him at night unless he has attempted to escape or to break his prison; a man is not sent into the coach-wheel for his airing unless he has been sent back from another prison to be kept in solitary confinement all hours, in doors as well as out of doors, but none of these preliminaries to punishment seemed to be required in our case.

It was taken for granted that we were bad, and we got the benefit of what the worst state of things would allow. To make you thoroughly understand what the coach-wheel yard is, you may imagine a large wheel, 100 feet in diameter, lying on the ground, it has fifty spokes, and on every spoke there is built a wall ten feet high. Between every two of these walls one of us is confined for an hour each day. The rim of the wheel is an iron grating, around which the Governor walked occasionally and obliged us to give him a military salute. Toward the centre of the wheel a door enters or opens from every compartment, and within the stock or the hub of the wheel is a room in which the officer keeps a watch upon the convicts.

If the victim of the law stoops to pick up a pretty pebble, or stops to scratch a word on one of the bricks, he is challenged immediately, and it is surprising the number of people who risk the challenge, if one may judge from the number of scratches on the brick wall, which is alive with observations of all 'cinds. One stone bears the record of the conviction of "Stepeney Joe," and the unmentionable offence for which he was convicted; another tells how the pig was sent back to Portland and the piggish crime he committed; a third brings the news how "the Prince's gal" after the Prince was "lagged" went to live with "Crow;" a fourth informs the solitary public that the governor is a brute, and so on to any number and every variety of running commentary upon things in general. 'Twas a recreation in solitude to read the evidence of live beings being around, even though you did not see them, it was the dead wall speaking to you, and though the language had not the chastity of death about it, still it brought you more cheer than if there were no traces of life to be seen. You came to read "cheer up"— "cheer up," so often, or, at least, I came to read it, that I felt myself growing sympathetic towards the writers. During my time in prison my masters sought to punish me by putting me in close association with them, and I as often kicked against it; but let me here confess the truth, I would choose their society before the society of my own thoughts in dark solitude; and if I often spurned it and went back to the loneliness of my cell and the poverty of bread and water, I did it more in opposition to the authority that would degrade an Irish "rebel" to herd with its criminals than from any choice I had for my own company. If you who shudder at the thought of contact with the vilest of human beings test the strength of your horror and contamination by two or three years' solitary confinement, you may change a little. The sight of a human face, no matter how deformed, and the sound of a human tongue, no matter how vile, is a gladsome thing to me, if I am any considerable length of time out of reach of either.

I like the Frenchman, his remark was good.

> ' How sweet, how passing sweet, is solitude,
> But give me still a friend in my retreat
> Whom I may whisper—' Solitude is sweet.' "

When the first hour's exercise was over in the refractory prisoner's yard, I was ordered to my cell, with every precaution taken that I should not see any one else on my way to it. One of the prison schoolmasters calls, and says it is necessary to classify me, in order to give me suitable reading. He tells me to read a little for him, then he puts me down as No. 3, and he leaves me a book about birds' nests. I thought I should be blessed in getting something to feed my mind on, but what he gave me was of little use. Class 3 was a class of very moderate attainments, and he thought there was no use giving me heavy matter to read. I suppose that, in going through the exercise he gave, the cold made me shiver and stutter, and made him judge I had learned my primer. I was supplied with a set of religious books, consisting of a "Garden of the Soul," a "Think Well on It," a "Poor Man's Catechism," and a "New Testament." The schoolmaster also gave me a grammar and an arithmetic, which, with the religious books, I could keep always with me, and told me the other book would be changed once every fortnight. He left me a slate and pencil, and said I would get one hour's schooling every week, and he would call to see what progress I was making, but this schooling we did not receive until we were about six weeks in the prison. After the schoolmaster was gone a most important individual visited me in the shape of a Prison Director. He was accompanied to the cell by the Governor and three of the warders, and the moment the door turned on its hinges, the three sub-officers cried out, one after another, "Attention, attention, attention!" I stood to my feet, my cap was on my head when the key was turned in the door, and I left it on. I was ordered to take it off, and I did. The Governor told me I should never wear my cap while in my cell; that I should always keep it hanging on the bell-handle, and [that [it was only given to me to be worn out of doors. I said that my head was shaven so close, and my clothing was so light, that I felt intense cold and felt more comfortable with my cap on. The Director said I had as much clothing as the regulations allowed—that, if more was necessary, the doctor would order it for me, but that the discipline of the prison should be maintained before every thing else. The big man's name was Gambier, and he and I became afterwards very much acquainted with each other. 'Twas no social acquaintance, but one in a line of business. It was his duty to order the infliction of punishment, and mine to go before him to hear the indictment against me. He was a tall, smooth-tongued old gentleman of about seventy, with very white hair, a glass eye, and a large red, jolly-looking nose, which I could never look at without thinking of the good old times of Irish whisky punch and jolly company. He could order you fifty lashes on the bare back and twenty-eight days on bread and water, in the most pathetic tones of regret that your bad behavior and the necessity of maintaining discipline called for it; and you'd think his glass eye, as well as his unglazed one, was swimming in tears over your misery.

Captain Gambier gave orders to put me to tailoring, and told me the more obedient I was and the more industrious, the better it would be for myself. I asked him if I could not write that reception letter, which the rule on that card—pointing to the regulations on the wall—says every prisoner is entitled to write on his arrival. He said he had no power to allow me to write, but that, no doubt, a time would come when I would be allowed.

Some fifteen minutes after this party left me, an officer brought me needle and thread, a thimble and scissors, and told me to practice stitching on a piece of jacket stuff he laid on the table. "Sew it all round, and when you have one circle of stitches made make another circle an inch farther in, and so on until you have the whole piece sewed up. When you have practice enough to enable you to stitch pretty well, I will give you a jacket to make; but stop, I must cut this thread shorter." "Why, Governor," said I, "'tis short enough already?" "That's no matter," said he, "I must obey my orders," and he cut my skein of housewife thread to about twelve inches in length. This was lest I should have thought of manufacturing any of it into a rope for escape. 'Twas an annoyance to be threading my needle after every few stitches, but 'twas foolish of me to get annoyed at trifles of this kind. My time belonged to my owners, and if they set me threading needles all day, I could not grumble; 'twas not about my work they cared, but about worrying me.

Tuesday's dinner was four ounces of meat, five ounces of bread, and a pound of potatoes. My appetite had not come to me yet, and I did not feel at all in good humor. I had seven or eight small loaves of bread accumulated in my cupboard; the officer told me that was against the regulations, and I should either eat them or have them removed, as the law did not allow more than one day's bread to remain in the cell of any prisoner. I told him I could not eat it, and on his asking me if I would permit him to take it away, I replied; "of course, yes." As he was counting the loaves, I said, "where, Governor, is Mr. Webber. I have not seen him since the first night?" Did you know Mr. Webber?" he inquired. I answered "No, but I knew an English namesake of his." "Well," added he, you won't see Mr. Webber here for awhile again." From the few words that were heard to pass between Webber and me the first night it was feared we knew each other; he was advising me to keep quiet, to do everything I was told, and that in a short time I would get used to the place. I thought he spoke kindly and I thanked him; but some other officer listening made a story of it, and he was removed.

The history of one day—*Vitam continet una dies*—contains the history of nearly every day of prison life; the same cheerless food; the same solitary confinement; the same dreary monotony; except that if you grew discontented with any of these things you could have a change for the worse in dark cells, bread and water, handcuffs, or anything that way you desired to choose as a variety ; and I grew into such a state of mind that to get a change, even from bad to worse, was a kind of relief to me.

The rising at six was the same every day of the week; the breakfast of eight ounces of bread and three-quarters of a pint of cocoa was the same; the polishing of the floor, the making up of the bed, the searching before getting the hour's airing, with an additional hour every second day; and the same searching when returning to your cell; the eternal stitch, stitch, stitch, with the spy stealing around in soft slippers, spying in occasionally to see if he could catch you idle, and report you; the supper of seven ounces of bread and one pint of porridge at six o'clock; the hour and a-half's work afterwards till you prepared your bed and had your furniture to put outside the door, and your clothes packed up to put out at eight, when the gas was turned off, and you were left to twist and turn to ease your ribs till morning.

'Twas all the same in everything, except the dinner, and in this there were four changes a week. Two days there was a quarter of a pound of beef; two days a quarter of a pound of mutton. One day, Thursday, a flour pudding that would take the stomach of an ostrich to digest. One day, Wednesday, a pint of soup, without any solid meat, and Sunday four ounces of cheese for dinner, without meat or drink, unless you chose to drink water.

You were supposed to be at work from breakfast hour in the morning until half-past seven in the evening, except that you had one hour for dinner; and if you were in a mood for study this left you fifty-five minutes to read, for with the ravenous appetite you were sure to get, if you were not in a dying state, you could devour all the food you had in less than five minutes. After the first three days my appetite returned to me, and my craving for food became intense; it was the greatest imaginable pleasure to me to have enough to eat. Many a day and many a night I regretted having allowed the warder to take away those six little loaves of bread that accumlated in my cell after my arrival; and often did I say to myself what a fool I was. For four years this feeling of hunger never left me, and I could eat rats and mice if they came in my way, but there wasn't a spare crumb in any of these cells to induce a rat or mouse to visit it.

In reading books of battle and adventure when I was a little fellow I never could realize to myself that any condition of existence would make me eat dead horses and dead cats, such as besieged armies were described as eating, but my prison life did away with the boyish notion, and I do not now wonder at any story of cannibalism when the stomach craved food. I used to creep on my hands and knees from corner to corner of my cell to see if I could find the smallest crumb that might have fallen from me when I was eating my breakfast or dinner some hours previously. When I had salt in my cell I ate it for the purpose of assisting me to drink water to fill my stomach. It was often a question of deep consideration for me whether water contained any nutrition, and the fact that the people who tried to break my spirit by starving me left an unlocked water-tap in my cell made me decide in the negative.

I do not think I had one hour of calm, easy sleep during these years—that is, if it be true that sleep to be calm and refreshing must be unaccompanied by dreams. My whole prison life was a life of dreams, and the night portion of them was not the pleasantest. Well, some of them were pleasant enough, till the awaking brought me the bitter disappointment—a disappointment intensified by the knowledge that I had no possible chance of realizing in my sober senses the imaginary pleasures which the vision had given me. Well do I remember in awakening from these dreams the efforts I made to snooze myself back in order that the god of sleep might vouchsafe to me a continuance of the dreamy pleasure that was escaping from me, and often did I, on fully awakening, smile at these endeavors to cheat the devil out of his due, or, in other words, to cheat the British Government out of the measure of punishment they had exacted from me.

The platefuls of bread and butter that I ate some nights would be alarming to any physician, were he to see me eat them, and as for hams of bacon, there would be no keeping account of them. My mind must have received impressions of punch and mulled porter somewhere, for I found myself indulging in one or the other occasionally, till the sound of a bell, or the clanking of keys dashed the pewter or the tumbler out of my hand.

Hunger had one time brought me to view things in such a philosophical manner, that if when eating my eight ounces of bread I found a beetle or a *ciarogue* cracking between my teeth, instead of spitting out in disgust what I was chewing, I would chew away with the instinctive knowledge that nature had provided for the carrying away of anything that was foul and the retaining of what was nutritious from what I swallowed. So much had the feeling of hunger taken possession of me, that, day by day, I found myself regretting that I did not eat more of the good things of the world when I was in society, and my teeth would water at the recollection of a leg of lamb or mutton. This is not to be wondered at when it is understood that starvation was a part of my punishment, and that I had experienced the sobering influences of bread and water for a period of five hundred and sixty days, during the first three or four years of my imprisonment.

I did not pretend to my persecutors that I felt the least inconvenience from all they were putting me through; but I suppose they knew very well that I could not but feel miserable. Their business was to make me so, and make me beg for peace or mercy, and my part of the game was not to give them the satisfaction of letting them see that I cared about their punishment. I had all along a secret feeling of defiance that sustained me when they were illtreating me. It did not show itself on the surface, for I was habitually polite, except on two or three occasions, that their outrages got the better of me; then the spirit broke out and pitched them and their rules and regulations to the devil. I had a feeling that I would have to succumb to the ordeal in the long run, and I took a resolution I would make my death as dear to them as possible; that they were treating me, and should treat me, in a manner that would disgrace them if it were known; and then my efforts were directed to make it known, or to leave such evidence on record as would have a chance of coming to light at a coroner's inquest. As, in making these remarks, I am going before my time, I think I had better pull myself up, and in another chapter go regularly through my course at Pentonville.

CHAPTER VIII.

ARRIVAL IN PENTONVILLE PRISON, LONDON—STRIPPED—DEPRIVED
OF FLANNELS—FIXED IN MY QUARTERS—BED AND BOARD, ETC.

On the Wednesday after my arrival in Pentonville I was in regular working order; the master tailor who examined my stitching thought I did it very well, and brought me a waistcoat to make. The principal officer of the ward brought me a button and told me to sew it on the breast of my jacket just opposite my heart, and when this was done he handed me a round little board on which was painted the number 26. A leather strap was nailed to it, and he told me to attach it to the button and never to take it off. This 26 was the number of my cell, and it was to be my name in prison. I was newly christened, and the name of Rossa was to be heard no more. 'Twas 26 here and 26 there and 26 everywhere. The governor of the jail and the deputy-governor visited 26 every day, and the number was ordered to stand to attention and stood erect. The jailer that accompanied the deputy-governor told 26 several times that besides standing to attention he should salute the superior officers by raising his hand to his uncovered head: 26 listened patiently, but he always seemed to forget the instructions when the superior officers came, for when the orders were given to stand to attention, he stood with his hands rigidly fixed to his sides. For this he was often reprimanded, but they did not inflict any further punishment for the dereliction of duty.

A bell rang at eight o'clock every morning, and I heard the whole prison moving, but did not know for a time what was up. I made bold enough to ask an officer what was the matter, and I was told it was going to prayers. "And cannot you take me to prayers?" said I. "No," he answered; "there is no service in the prison for Catholics; Millbank is the place for that." When the Governor came round I begged leave to ask him a question, and he gave me permission. "I understand, Governor," said I, "that the prison rules accord religious service to all convicts, and how is it that I am kept from chapel?" "We have no Roman Catholic service here," he answered; "but I understand the Directors of the Prison are taking measures to have a priest visit you." Friday came, and I got my dinner of four ounces of mutton with a pint of the water in which it was boiled. I asked what was my religious registration in the prison, and I was told it was Roman Catholic. Then I asked if I could not have a fish dinner or some dinner other than a meat one on Friday, and I was told I could not. "You'll be very glad before long to eat that on a Friday," said the officer, shutting the door in my face, and it was very true for him. But I did not eat it that day, and when he came round for my tins after dinner I put the meat and soup outside the door. "Can't you keep the meat," said he, "and eat it to-morrow?" "No," I said; "I should eat it to-day if I kept it in my cell;" and smiling at me he shut the door more gently than he did before.

Whatever part of the faith of my fathers I had lost, I had up to this retained the practice of abstaining from meat on Friday. I believe if I had not been put to prison I would have through life adhered to this abstinence—not, perhaps, so much from religious scruples on the matter as from feelings of respect for the memory of the father and mother that reared me a Catholic, or for some hallowed recollections of the Catholic associations of early home and its surroundings. This was one link of the chain that I was not going to give up, even though Cardinal Cullen had visited me with the major excommunication of "bell, book and candle light," but though clinging to it, it would, I suppose—if his Eminence had just grounds for excommunicating me—be only clinging to a straw.

I was shaved three times a week by one of the warders. The ordinary prisoners, as I afterward learned, were allowed to shave themselves, but the razor was never entrusted into my hands while I remained in this prison. It was a most unwelcome job to the warder, also; one of them would go through it pretty smoothly, but two or three others of them would give me an awful scraping. Occasionally a convict takes it into his head to release himself from prison by cutting his throat; and so many of them took it into their heads lately to cheat the Government in this matter, that the authorities had decided to abolish the use of razors altogether, and now the prisoner's beard is clipped with a scissors once a month.

I got a bath once a week. The water was warm, but very dirty. The bathing pool was a long trough, over which were erected sheds to prevent the prisoners communicating, but there was nothing to prevent the water in which the prisoners at each side of me were washing themselves from flowing in to me. Our legs could touch each other under the sheet iron that kept us apart, and I hardly ever took a bath that I hadn't some unfortunate fellow thrusting his leg into my compartment for the purpose of picking up, or rather of *kicking* up an acquaintance.

I chanced one day to get next Charles J. Kickham in one of these places; I saw him as I was passing the door of his crib. I entered mine, stripped off with all the haste I could, jumped into the trough, and stuck one of my legs as far as I could into his compartment, poking it about until I touched him. I spoke to him as intelligibly as I could with my big toe, and he seemed to understand me, for he gave it a shake hands; to do this he must have dived down a bit, so I drew back my foot, and, taking another dive, thrust my hand in and caught his; but he gave me such a squeeze as would have made me scream, if my head were not under water, or if the fear of calling the officer's attention were not before my eyes. The next day I came to bathe I thought it was Kickham that I saw again in the same place, and I endeavored to renew the acquaintance. There was somewhat of a repetition of the previous day's work. I dressed in a hurry, and as the officer had his back turned I got out and cried, "Ready;" but before I spoke I had snatched at the hand of the other man who was dressing. He grasped mine affectionately, but as our eyes met I saw it was not Kickham I had, but some poor fellow that was blind of an eye, and in possession of a most pugnacious-looking face. At this period I was getting my hour's airing in the ring with the ordinary prisoners, and the new acquaintance never lost sight of me. It amused me often in passing him, to notice how amiably he would try to look at me, and what an expression of friendship would beam in that solitary eye which his head contained. I reciprocated the look as well as I could. I suppose he was a thief, but that is no matter—he was certainly a prisoner and a human being, and here we stood upon equal terms.

I took advantage of one of the Governor's visits to my cell to renew my application to be allowed to write, but he had not the authority to permit me. I asked him "could I write to the Secretary of State," and he said "that was a matter I could bring before the Directors." I wished to know how, and was informed that they met in the prison once a week, and any prisoner could, on application to the Governor, have his name put down to see them. "Then, Governor," I said, "you'll please take my name," and the Governor told me it was out of order to take it on that occasion—that I should tell my officer, and my officer would take me before him next day, and he would make the order to have me see the Directors, if my business was legitimate. So far so good. I gave my name to my officer, my officer took me to my Governor, my Governor heard my application to write to my Secretary of State, and put my name down to see my Directors, and when my Directors came I was conducted into their august presence. There were about nine of them in the room; they gazed at me as I entered and took my position in front of a large table, in obedience to the order of "Stand to attention."

I swept my eyes around till they rested on Captain Gambier—the old gentleman who sat at the one end of the table in the position of Chairman. The officer who conducted me in cried out: "Treason-felony convict, Number 26, Jeremiah O'Donovan Rossa, penal servitude for life," and as he ended, the Chairman asked bluntly: "What do you want?" "To write a letter to my wife." "We cannot permit you. Do you want anything else?" "To write a letter to Mr. Stansfield, Member of the English Parliament."

"We cannot permit you. Do you want anything else?"
"To write a letter to the Secretary of State."
"Granted. Do you want anything else?"
"Can you give me any information regarding the religious service which the rules say all prisoners must attend, for I can see nothing of the kind in this establishment?"

We have made arrangements to have a priest visit you, and he will give you any information that is necessary on the matter. Do you want anything else?"

"No, thank you."

"Number 26, right-about face," and right-about I faced and marched toward my cell in obedience to orders.

A few days after, the door of my cell was thrown open and in came a priest. I was very glad to see him. "'Twas a cure for sore eyes" to see any one or anything that had not the color of the prison, and as the holy father closed the door behind him, I felt myself growing big with joy that I had some one I could speak a word to.

But I was soon chilled by the cold, icy words of this disciplinarian. My readers may expect that I was not long speaking to him before I asked him something about Ireland, and as soon as I did he promptly told me that I was not to ask him anything that did not appertain to his prison duties. The conversation turned back on religion again, and again I offended by asking some irrelevant or irreverent question. Father Zanetti stamped on the ground and told me that his honor was at stake, and not to be trespassing upon it. A third time I offended by asking him could he tell me anything that he might have seen in print about my wife and children, and a third time he told me that I must not ask him any questions about the world or anything in it. He told me he would bring books from his prison, and do everything else for us he could consistent with his duty. A fourth time I offended by asking him if he would convey a remembrance from me to my fellow-prisoners, and he left me, carrying with him, no doubt, the opinion that I was a very refractory prisoner. The next Thursday he visited me, and while my mind was yet wholly troubled about the world, he would have me turn all my thoughts to religion. I told him candidly that I could not as yet get my mind to travel in his groove, that it was too much impressed with the troubles of this world to turn suddenly toward the next, and that I would rather hear something which it was in his power to tell me about Ireland than anything he could say to me about hell or Heaven. "Father," said I to him, smilingly, "this is my hell, and you refuse to give me a glimpse of Heaven." He smiled and shook his head. I turned the conversation to the state of my library, asking him what he could do for me in the way of books. He would see about that and tell his man in Millbank to make out a list of books from the Catholic library in order that they may be forwarded to Pentonville for us; he would try to have each of us get one of them every fortnight, in addition to the one we were getting, and I became quite elated at this, because the little book I had was worthless.

Before he left me this time he made another attempt to turn my thoughts to religion, and I told him I was put outside of the pale of the Church by some of the priests of the Church. "How is that?" said he. "Simply that I have been refused the sacraments, that I have been turned away from the confessional, for the reason that I have pledged myself to assist in freeing Ireland from English rule."

"Oh, you are mistaken, that is not the reason. The reason is that you belong to a secret society, whose leaders are in league with Mazzini and the heads of the wicked societies of the Continent."

"I think you are mistaken, Father Zanetti; as far as I know, and I think I ought to know something on the matter, the society in Ireland was not in communication with any of those people or any of those societies you speak of, and if your information as to the wickedness of the Continental societies are only as reliable as what you say of our society in Ireland, I do not think much of it."

"Are you a secret society condemned by the Church?"

"It is said we are, but I strongly doubt the justice of the condemnation. The Church knows our object, and we have no bond of secrecy in the oath. It is purely a military organization, and the Church ought not to condemn an Irishman for taking an oath to fight for the freedom of his native land; it does not condemn an Irishman who swears to fight for England, and necessarily for the enslavement of his country."

"But England is an established government, and you would not be justified in opposing it unless there were extreme oppression, and that you had the necessary means of success."

"There is no question of the oppression, and as to the means of success, we were only organizing them with the intention of not fighting till we had them, when some of the clergy set their faces against us."

"Well, we'll have a talk on that some other time, and now let me ask you to be prepared to go to your duty the next day I come round."

He was in good humor now, and I said to him—

"I don't know about that, Father; if I were to think, as some of my friends and relations think, I'd hardly believe you to be a priest at all."

"How is that?"

"Simply because they consider a priest is one to administer comfort and consolation in every situation of life, and if I could tell them I asked you a question about my family, and that you refused to answer me while able to do so, they wouldn't believe it of a Catholic priest, and would be inclined to tell me that you were not one."

He shook his head, as much as to say, "You're cute, but you won't get a thing out of me," shook hands with me. and saying he would bring me a book next week, departed. The next week came, and with it came his reverence, bringing the book. It was a double-columned volume of Lingard's History of England, and I hugged it to my bosom on seeing the large amount of reading that was in it. I parodied for it the old Irish song in praise of whiskey, where the lover of it, embracing the bottle, exclaims :

> Mo bhean agus mo leanbh thu,
> Mo mhathair agus m'athair thu,
> Mo chota more iss mo rappar thu,
> Iss ni scarra may go bragh leath.
>
> My darling wife and child are you,
> My mother and my father, too,
> My big great coat and wrapper new,
> And I will never part you.

Father Zanetti told me that he had made arrangements with Canon Oakley to say Mass for us every Wednesday and Sunday, and, as he himself would come every Thursday to visit us, the week would be pretty well broken. Should any one notice that I speak too often of the priests or of the ministers, let them understand that they were the only Christians I met in my prison life, and the only persons to break its monotony. I could see no other man who had not the prison livery on him, and, as for seeing a woman, the Lord bless you! I was for about two years at one time without laying my eyes upon the face of an angel, and nearly three years without hearing the voice of one.

The day the priest brought me the History of England, I had a long talk with him again on my religious duties. He urged me, now that I was imprisoned for life, that I could do nothing in the outside world, and that I may as well give up the oath and become a good Catholic.

"And Father," said I, "can I not be a good Catholic unless I give up the oath?"

"No."

"Then I fear I'll never become a good Catholic."

"If you were on your dying bed, wouldn't you give it up?"

"I would not."

"And you'd damn your soul for eternity?"

"I don't believe that God would damn my soul for that; if all my other sins were forgiven but that of swearing to fight for the liberty of my country, I would face my Creator with a light heart."

"But how can your other sins be forgiven when you will not avail of the graces God offers you through His Church and His ministers?"

"I have only to trust to God entirely, when I find that the sacraments of the Church have been denied to me for doing that which I believe to be the noblest and the most sacred thing a man can do."

"Well, I am sorry for you; your heart is better than your head; I will pray for you, and I ask you, as a special request, to pray for me."

I saw immediately that this was for the purpose of getting me into a praying mood, and as he pressed me to promise him, I did so. He then told me that in these prisons they did not alter the prison fare on Friday's for Catholics, but that the church had given them permission to eat meat on those days, and that no fasts need be observed. I did not tell him, nor did I tell you yet, I believe, that I had been a "Friday dog" for the past two weeks. Hunger and reflection in solitary confinement had got the better of my scruples, or rather of my pride, in sticking to this practice of the old faith of my fathers. The first Friday I put out my meat, the second Friday I kept it in my cell and ate it on Saturday. I did not think there was much merit in doing this, and the third Friday I "broke the pledge" quite deliberately by eating the four ounces of mutton and drinking the pint of mutton water with which it was surrounded.

It may be proper that I should call this broth or soup, in accordance with discipline, but inasmuch as I am now outside of its controlling influence, I use the expression mutton water. It had barely the taste of the meat, unless, indeed, you were fortunate enough to come in for a chance of getting a pint from "the top of the pot," and I smile now at thinking of the haste with which I would run to my canteen when the door was shut to see what luck I had. The bill of fare says that your dinner for Friday is to be one pint of soup made from four ounces of mutton "boiled in its own liquor," together with this four ounces or what remains of it; every hundred pints of water and every hundred quarters of a pound of meat to be flavored and seasoned with a few ounces of onions and pepper and salt, and this was more savory to me at that time than the most spicy dish that could be set before me now at Jude's or Delmonico's.

The meals were given to the ordinary prisoners through a trapdoor. This was about eight inches square. It was locked outside, and when the turnkey opened it he thrust it in and laid the vessel thereon.

If the prisoner was not ready to take it off the moment it was laid on, and shut the trap at the same time, he subjected himself to a report, and a report is always the forerunner of punishment. In giving the meals to me and my fellow-prisoners our doors were always opened, and two officers were present. This was lest any one officer, approaching us by himself, would give us information, or lay himself open to be corrupted. They nailed up our traps one day, and every stroke of the hammer on my door struck me as being a fastener on me. Those great English people would not even trust their English jailors with us without making them act as spies upon each other. That is the very thing that would corrupt an Irishman; his blood would rise mountain high if it was plainly set before him every day that he would not be trusted in the discharge of his duty; but the Englishman bore it throughout with the most Christian resignation, and took it all as a matter of course. And even among the best Irishmen this sensitiveness of theirs works mischief often. In political organizations say, something is necessary to be done that it is not necessary to tell to more than one or two, but, by-and-by, the thing spreads, it comes to the ears of Mike Fitzgerald, and Mike Fitzgerald immediately demands of some authority why he wasn't told of it as well as Jim O'Brien—was not he as well to be trusted?—didn't he work as long, and didn't he do as much work as any one else?—to say that anything should be done now without telling him of it, when others were told. And so the grumbling goes on, to the infinite injury of all harmory and good order.

One Sunday morning my door was opened, and my officer told me to prepare for chapel. I told him I was prepared for anything, and he ordered me to bring my prayer-book and my stool. "Now, forward; march." And on I marched through halls, around corners, down stairs, and along dark passages, till I found myself halted opposite a little altar. It was in the basement of the building, where the dark cells are located.

Two large dykes were dug along the sides of the dark hall for the purpose of laying pipes in them, and the prisoners were sitting, each on his own stool, about one yard apart between the two mounds of earth that were thrown up. A warder with his club in hand stood in the door of each of the dark cells, and if a side squint was noticed from one of us, the gentleman who noticed it shook his stick at the offender.

The priest came out of one of the dark cells that was near the altar; his eyesight was bad, and he had to be led by the hand by his clerk along the boards that crossed the dyke. It was a meet chapel—or would be—for Irish rebels of the olden time; those who were hunted for adhering to their religion or to their country when the cause of religion and the cause of country were one; the cave in the rock; and the light glittering on the priest's garments and brightening the darkness, were here to awaken the traditions that our youthful memories had stored. My eyes were fixed on the prayer-book, according to discipline, but my mind was fixed elsewhere, and I was rambling through the graveyards that grow around the old abbeys of the old land, when the warder punched me in the side with his club to make me aware that I should not be kneeling when all the others were standing, and the priest reading the Gospel. I was the last man that was taken into the cave, and when Mass was over I was the first man taken out. The officer made a motion with his club toward the rear. I took up my stool and marched away, without having seen the face of one of my companions.

Sunday was to me the gloomiest day of any of the week. On other days I kept myself occupied, or tried to do so, by counting every stitch I put along the back of a waistcoat, every stitch I put along the front, inside and outside; every stitch I put around the collar, and around the waist; the button and button-hole stitches were counted too, and I figured a sum total of the number of stitches I put in every waistcoat made by me. This was the way I provided myself with mental exercise, a sort of exercise that was very much needed—more needed, perhaps, in solitary confinement than physical exercise.

While I was taking my hour's airing one day, some one came into my cell and took away one of my library books. I made a noise about it, as if it was stolen, and that I wished to get out of trouble by reporting it, and was told that it was taken away by orders, because the law did not allow a prisoner to have more than one library book, and as the priest had given me one a few days ago —contrary to regulations—the matter should be corrected by taking it away. Here was bad news again, but it was a change in affairs, and, I think, every change in prison life, whether for bad or good, tends to promote health—that is, if the change for the worse is not a very wicked one. I know that for the variety the change afforded in a monotonous existence, I often sacrificed what imprisoned people would consider a happier state, but as I am yet only in the first months of a course of five or six years, I will keep the particulars that suggest these thoughts till I grow older in my career.

That Sunday, when I came from chapel without being able to see the faces of my companions, I grew very gloomy. The book was gone, my needle and thimble were gone, and I had no stitches to count. The day was a dark, gloomy one, and the cell, which was a darkened one, was darker than usual. On some foggy days gas has to be lit in these cells to give the prisoners light enough to work. God's sunlight is artificially kept out in order to punish the criminals, and among these England classed us, and into the criminal cells she stuck us. Suicide and lunacy form a very large item in the effect of England's treatment of her convicts, and I don't wonder at it. I am writing now of a very dark day in prison; I found myself out of all resources, and I had nothing for it but to go on verse making. "The poet and madman nearly are allied," and if you wish you can believe that I was on the road to distraction when I made such verses as the following. However, don't be too hard on me if you see no brilliancy or bright idea in them—remember what I am telling you about the gloom that enveloped me even on the sunniest day:

I have no life at present, my life is in the past;
I have none in the future, if the present is to last;
The "Dead Past" only, mirrors now the memories of life,
The fatherland, the hope of years, the friend, the child and wife.

Then am I dead at present? Yes, dead while buried here—
Dead to the wife, the child and friend, to all the world holds dear;
Dead to myself, for life is death to one condemned to dwell
His life-long years in exile in a convict prison cell.

Though dead unto the present, I live in the "Dead Past,"
And thoughts of dead and living things crowd on me thick and fast;
E'en when reason is reposing they revel in my brain,
And I meet the wife, the child and friend, in fatherland again.

The goddess on her throne resits—the cherished dreams are fled—
Were they but phantoms of the past to show the past is dead?
Past, Present, Future, what to me!—how little man can see—
Am I dead unto the world?—or the world dead to me?

God only knows. I only know that which to man He gives,
The love of Liberty and Truth—the soul, the spirit lives;
And though its house of clay be bound by England's iron hand,
It freely flies to wife and child, and friend and fatherland.

I wrote this pacing my cell in a diagonal line from one corner to the other. By taking that course I made my line of march about one pace longer. I did not give a right-about nor a left-about face when I wanted to turn round, for I found that would put a *megrim* in my head, but I went straight for one of my diagonal corners, and when I had reached it I paced right straight back again, heels foremost, and when I had a couplet of my beautiful poem composed I halted to pencil it down on my slate.

Twice a week the searching officers came into my cell and turned everything upside down and inside out, looking for something and finding nothing. I had to strip to the buff in their presence, and when they examined me quite naked they left me to dress up again and to arrange my things in the nicest order.

I managed to keep in my cell two little bits of slate, each about an inch square, but it would not be nice to tell where I hid them. I kept them for the purpose of communicating with my friends, and we held communication in this manner. We were all exercised in that yard which I called the coach-wheel, where I could learn, by throwing pebbles over the wall into the compartment that was next to me, and getting a pebble thrown back in return, that there was some one there. I threw a bit of slate with a few words scratched on it. At the first throw it would contain my name, with the words, "Who are *you?*" and, if he was any one I knew, we kept throwing backward and forward while the hour lasted. I watched to see when the officer's eyes were off me to write a few words, and I suppose the same instinct that guided me guided my correspondent. The Pagan was the person I fell in with the oftenest, and he was at a disadvantage, inasmuch as he could not read well without his spectacles. Sometimes he would take my bit of slate to his cell with him, and it might be three or four days or a week before I could strike him again and have a reply. In taking in my tablet and bringing it out I hid it in my neck-tie, just opposite the apple of the throat. This was the only spot that used to escape the fingers of the jailor in searching me. If he found my treasure it would be high treason, and I do not know to how many days' bread and water it would subject me.

All the prisoners got one hour "at school" every week. During this hour the cell door was left open, and the schoolmasters perambulated the wards, calling in to every cell to see how the scholars were progressing, and to loosen any knotty question that might impede their progress. This hour's schooling was not conceded to us until we were a month in prison. My door was unlocked and thrown wide open, and left open without any one coming into my cell. This was an extraordinary occurrence with me. What can it mean, thought I, and not understanding what it did mean I remained sitting on my stool stitching away for the dear life. In about a quarter of an hour a respectable-looking old man came in asking, " Why are you not at school ?"

"At school," said I, starting up and making for the door.

"Stop, stop," said he, laying hold of me, "where are you going ?"

"Going to school," said I. "Where is it ?"

"This is your school," said he, "you are not to leave your cell. Where is your slate ? Are you able to do any figures ?"

I told him I could do a little, and, laying hold of the slate which lay on the little table, he asked, "What figures are these ?"

"They are the number of stitches I put in the little waistcoat I made."

"Are you obliged to keep an account of them ?"

"No, but I keep the account for mental exercise."

Turning the other side of the slate he asked, "What sort of a sum is this ?"

"That is a sum in interest."

"Certainly not, this sum is not worked by any rule in interest. What £42 7s is this at the foot ?"

"That is the amount of interest a hundred pounds will bring in one year by Loan Bank interest in Ireland."

"You must be wrong, no bank interest is so high as that; how do you make it out ?" And saying this he sat down on my stool, and I bent down alongside to show him.

"That first item of one hundred pounds is the banker's, and he lends it to a hundred poor struggling people—a pound each. For lending the pound, each gives him one shilling, which gives him a return of five pounds the first day; he lends this five pounds again and gets five shillings more, which he keeps in his bank till that day week. He has now, as you see, one hundred and five pounds at interest, which is to be paid back to him at a shilling a week from each of his debtors. The next pay day he gets one hundred and five shillings, which, with the five shillings he has in stock, makes £5 10s.; he lends five pounds of this and gets five shillings' interest, which he adds to the ten shillings and keeps in his bank, as he has not a full pound to lend. He gets in a hundred and ten shillings next week, and he lends six pounds, keeping eleven shillings in his bank, and so on till at the end of the year he has, as far as I can make out, £42 7s. interest on his £100."

"But do you tell me that kind of work is in operation in Ireland?"

"Yes, and in very many places, and the poor are glad to have the benefit of it."

"Well, God help the poor people;" and suddenly turning the conversation as if he did not want to dwell on it, he asked, "How are you off for books?"

"Very badly. "I get but very poor books from the librarian; little things that are not worth reading, and which I can read in one day. I am obliged to have recourse to such exercises as you see on that slate for the purpose of keeping my mind engaged."

"What class are you in? Is this your card? Third class?"

"Yes."

"Well, I'll put you in a better class, and the officer will have to give you better books."

I thanked him; we had a few words more, the bell rang, the hour for school was up, he bid me good evening, and when the librarian came round the next day he looked at my card and gave me a better book than he was in the habit of giving me.

Shortly after this improvement in my condition, the door was thrown open another day, and another strange gentleman entered, announcing himself as the chaplain of the prison, and after asking me if I had a wife and children, where they were, how they were situated, and how I felt about them, he opened a book and showed me a letter lying open in it.

"Oh, that's my wife's writing, sir."

"Yes, it is. I have got this letter to give you, and you're to get a leaf of paper to write a letter in reply."

I thanked him as kindly as a happy convict could, and he bade me adieu, hoping I'd get along well.

I have the letter before me now, and, to put a little variety into this dull writing of mine, I think I may as well let you read it. There is never much novelty in reading private letters that are intended for the public; but this that I am going to give was never intended for the press, and will be a kind of break in what I am going through. Besides, I don't care to make this prison life one dark gloomy chapter of all its ills and annoyances. I mean to go through it on paper with the same light heart that I tried to go through it with on the ground. If I painted the devil here as black as he is, which I cannot do, because I lack the ability, and if I kept my readers all the time on bread and water, on chains, dark cells and solitary confinement, I may in America be making converts to that apathy which exists among "repectable," well-to-do Irishmen, who don't want to sacrifice anything or run any risk for the cause of oppressed Ireland.

But I won't do that; I'll make prison life as entertaining and as interesting as possible for them, and I'll break the monotony of it now by giving my wife's letter.

The Government brands come first, and they run: "No. 3411; Jeremiah O'Donovan Rossa; A. 2. 27; H. F., Deputy-Governor, F. F. P."

"17 Middle Mountjoy street, Wednesday Night.

"MY LOVE, MY DARLING HUSBAND: I could not write to you before, my mind was so unsettled by a few disappointments, and it would have been too bad to vex you with a desponding letter. Indeed, Cariss, my conscience accused me of having indulged privately in very unhappy feelings. I wish you could have power to look into my heart and give me absolution. Some day you may listen to my confession, and pity all the weaknesses I wouldn't own to any one else in the world but you. You know I would not give my "confidence" to any friend, and my thoughts are sometimes more than I can calmly bear alone. I get credit for bearing up well, but I feel myself a hypocrite after. These few days a better spirit than usual is uppermost with me; I am hopeful again, or I should not have taken a pen to write to you. I *could not* write to you any way but truly as I feel. I could not tell you I was happy, or even resigned, if I did not believe in being so, and I was not so a week ago, though to-day I am.

"Now, Cariss, about the children. The last, I suppose, I may put first, the wee one, that makes me sigh for you at every time I feel its presence. I don't know whether I'm most happy or most miserable about it. 'Tis all I have of you, and if things turn out badly it will be the only thing I'll care to hold my life for. The rest are well. I sent money to Mrs. Healy, as she sent me a message that she had seen or heard nothing of the money Denis O'Donovan says he sent to a friend for the children's use. Father Lucy or Mulcahy, I don't know which, was saying something about adopting one of them. Murty Downing offered to take two. I do not think well of either offer. I was to see Father Cody to-day, and he advised me to leave them as they were for awhile. I'll have to do so I'm afraid. It seems the office was not in debt to you more than £75. I got £20 of that three weeks ago; could get no more since, but 'tis no matter, as I did not decide on any school for the boys yet. I have not got your clothes from Kilmainham; the Governor has no amiable feelings for you, and puts me to the trouble of applying for an order at the opening of the Commission here. Shall I write to Denis O'D. and ask to *whom* he sent that missing money. I think I will. I spent an unhappy Christmas at Mr. Hopper's, in Kingstown, and dined here at my lodgings in 17 Middle Mountjoy street on Christmas Day. I thought of you all night, and cried myself to sleep and dreamland near morning. Two years ago I sat in a circle of father, mother, brothers, sisters and friends, and I did not dream of you. *One* year ago I sat with you and forgot home and family in your smiles, and *this* year I sat alone and heartweary, with strange faces in the place of those I had loved, and wondered what would the next year bring—more joy or more sorrow? Papa sent me a present of fowl for New Year's Day, so I gathered my friends to eat them. Mrs. Luby and the O'Learys, Maria Shaw and Mrs. Burke, my brother and other gentlemen came. The evening passed very agreeable to all. Poor Mrs. Luby looked absent and sad at times, and I looked round the room and found no place for eye or heart to rest on; but all the rest were in great spirits. The entertainment cost me a little, but it served a good purpose. They will not forget this New Year's Day if we meet to celebrate the next, and God grant we will, my love.

I was dreaming a few nights ago you had come out of prison, and imagination even painted you without that beard I was so fond of. I dropped a few tears specially for that the night you were convicted. Eily is after coming in, and she tells me Mr. Lawless set them right about that money due to you. I have heard other news also that pleases me. Good by, my own. I don't know whether this letter will reach you or I'd write more. All our friends send love to you. Fondly as ever, your wife,

MOLLIE J."

You have read the letter once, but I read it twice, and three times, and four times, and had not done reading it when the cell-door opened and two officers entered. One of them held in his hand a leaf of paper and the other carried a pen and ink. "Here," said the gentleman who had the paper, "is material for you to write a letter in reply to one you have received, but I am instructed to tell you that if you write anything about the way you are situated, about the work you are at, or about the prison officers, your letter will be suppressed." "Then what am I to write about?" said I. "There is the paper for you," said he, laying the leaf upon the table, "and there is the pen and ink for you," taking them from the other officer and putting them alongside of the leaf, "you must know the rules and regulations, and if you do not write according to the instructions you have received, you have only to take the consequences." "*Gu voarih Dhia urruing*," answered I, "what do you say?" "What's that he says," cried one and the other, as if I had said something awful. "Oh," said I, "I'm only saying God help us, as there seems to be nobody else to help us around here." "You'd better mind the rules and regulations," chimed in both, walking away and shutting the door after them.

I wrote my letter and sent it to the Governor for transmission. In four days after, he sent for me and told me there were two passages in it that should be expunged, or the letter suppressed. One of them was that in which I asked my wife to try and get me permission to write to an English Member of Parliament about the manner in which I was tried, and the other was that in which I told her to write me a reply as soon as she could. I told the Governor that he might erase both passages, and he said that would make the matter all right.

We had some conversation on the irrelevancy of asking a reply to the letter. I argued that the rules gave me the right of receiving an answer to every letter I wrote; but he told me that I should take the letter I was after receiving as the answer to the letter I was now writing. In this manner I was cheated out of hearing more fully from my family, and many of my fellow-prisoners were treated similarly, as I learned from them when we met in Portland, the next prison we were sent to.

I noticed on Sunday, at mass, that we had a larger congregation than usual. I was located in my usual position, but I found a man at each side of me, and others behind me. I gave a squint, and I recognized the man at my right to be James O'Connor. I knew that the new recruits were from Ireland, and I was itching to know who they were. When the priest prayed loud, I pretended to be accompanying him, but, instead of uttering prayers to God, I muttered to James—" Where is Stephens? Are they going to have a fight? How many of ye came? Who are those behind me?"—and James kept answering my prayers, till the officer by his side, noticing something, laid hold of him by the shoulder and conducted him back to the end of the congregation.

I learned from O'Connor that Stephens remained in Dublin for months after he was taken out of Richmond Bridewell; that a fight was expected; that fourteen or fifteen of them had come to Pentonville; that the men behind me were Kickham, Brophy, Mulcahy, Kenealy, Roantree, Carey, Brian Dillon, John Linch, Charley O'Connell, John Duggan, Jerry Donovan, of Blarney, "The Galtee Boy," and "some others," as he styled others whom he knew I did not know personally. He made his syllables as short as possible, and he gave me no surnames where he was aware I would recognize the names without them.

Returning to my cell, a prisoner impeded my passage at the foot of the stairs which I was to ascend. His jacket, his waistcoat, his braces were loosened and his arms extended, as the officer was searching him preliminary to his entering the cell, for we used to be put through this search going to chapel and coming from chapel —in fact every time that we were leaving our cell or entering it. Looking at the prisoner I recognized him as Kickham, and had I acted on impulse I would have rushed at him and embraced him before the officers could have arrested me. I did not do so, and when

I entered my cell I got sick; I had checked the natural course of my feelings, they became stagnant somewhere, and I felt most uncomfortable until I found relief by bursting into tears. They flowed, and I let them flow for some ten minutes, but they did not come until some verses of Kickham's came into my head as I was walking madly about my cell, and thinking of the unnatural combinations that sent such men as he into penal servitude. He, an Irish Catholic; yes, as true a one as any priest or bishop that ever denounced the cause for which he suffered; ay, as full of faith, as pious and as moral too. I should like to have Kickham's mind, I should like to have Kickham's faith, for I'd like to have the mind and the faith of such a good and gifted man, but I fear I can never have either. His verses of the *Soggarth Aroon* came into my mind on this occasion I am speaking of; I repeated them in whispers as I paced my cell; they revived memories of olden times; memories rather of youthful days. I felt the hard, unnatural state of things that placed some of the Irish priests in antagonism to those who were ready to risk all for the purpose of freeing Ireland. I felt that we were wronged, bitterly wronged, and, as I was reflecting upon that curse which came to divide priests and people in this cause, rage or some other passion began to burn me. The tears started into my eyes, and I let them flow freely for the first time since I entered prison. This was a relief to me, and I make no apologies for putting in my book those verses that strike so deep into my soul whenever I read or repeat them:

SOGGARTH AROON.

Cold is the cheerless hearth,
    Soggarth aroon,
Sickness, and woe, and death,
    Soggarth aroon,
Sit by it night and day,
Turning our hearts to clay,
Till life is scarce left to pray,
    Soggarth aroon.

Yet still in our cold heart's core,
    Soggarth aroon,
One spot for evermore,
    Soggarth aroon,
Warm we've kept for you—
Warm, and leal, and true—
For you, and old Ireland, too,
    Soggarth aroon.

For sickness or famine grim,
    Soggarth aroon,
This bright spot could never dim,
    Soggarth aroon.
Despair came with deadly chill,
Our last fainting hope to kill,
But the twin love we cherished still,
    Soggarth aroon.

Has poor Ireland nothing left,
 Soggarth aroon,
This last wound her heart has cleft,
 Soggarth aroon;
Ah! well may her salt tears flow,
To think—oh, my grief and woe!—
To think 'twas you struck the blow,
 Soggarth aroon.

We crouch 'neath the tyrant's heel,
 Soggarth aroon,
We're mute while his lash we feel,
 Soggarth aroon;
And, pining in dull despair,
His wrongs we, like cowards, bear,
But traitors we never were,
 Soggarth aroon.

And "stags" you would make us now,
 Soggarth aroon,
You'd stamp on the bondman's brow,
 Soggarth aroon,
Foul treason's red-burning brand,
Oh, doomed and woe-stricken land,
Where honor and truth are banned,
 Soggarth aroon.

To those dark days we now look back,
 Soggarth aroon,
When the bloodhound was on your track,
 Soggarth aroon,
Then we spurned the tyrant's gold,
The pass then we never sold,
We are still what we were of old,
 Soggarth aroon.

Passages in this poem can be better understood when I say that some priests were telling the people from the altars to deliver up to the police any one they found attempting to enroll men in the revolutionary movement.

When I went to chapel next Sunday I was more fortunate than usual in getting a position favorable for observation. I was placed under the stairs, the officers behind me could not see my head, and when I found the eyes of the others off me I managed to get a look at those who were around. I could not for the world make out who Denis Dowling Mulcahy and Hugh Brophy were, though I was intimately acquainted with them in Dublin. The clipping of their hair and beard made such a change in their appearance that I never recognized them until I got a chance of getting a whisper with Hugh, and a chance of getting in the next compartment in the exercise yard with John Kenealy one day, when he told me who Denis was, by throwing our bits of slate to one another over the wall that divided us. By-and-bye I found that Mulcahy had been trying to convey the latest news to us by scratching upon the walls,

A few words were written on one brick, which, taken by themselves, meant little or nothing; but a few bricks further on I found a few words more which made a connection. In this way I learned there was no fight in Ireland, or likely to be; but that there was lots of fighting in America, and likely to continue from the number of leaders and plans they had to free Ireland. I suppose my spirits sank a little, but others had as much reason to be low spirited as I, and I thought I would "never say die." I imagined, for the Irish-Americans, what a splendid thing it would be, and how easily we could free Ireland if we had rifles and cannon of three thousand miles range; then we, or they rather, might take some spot to plant our artillery on, and blow England to atoms—that is, if the American Government would allow them. When I say this I am not sneering at those who would strike at England through Canada, nor am I approving of diverting from Irishmen in Ireland the aid that was contributed to assist them in a revolutionary struggle there, when men risked their lives to strike at England anywhere. I am not going to be hard on them, and particularly when the Canadian prisons chain at this hour the liberties of many such men. I would strike her everywhere I could, but I would rather strike her on her own soil than anywhere else outside of Ireland, for it is on her own soil that she would feel the blows most severely. The Manchester affair and the Clerkenwell affair and the Chester affair struck more terror into English statesmen than any affairs I know; and if she apprehended a repetition on a somewhat larger scale of these things every year till Ireland were free she might be more disposed to loosen her grasp of the old land. If the tables were turned and that we were the domineering power, England, having the element in Ireland that we have in her, would not scruple doing anything to attain her ends, and would have burnt or blown us up long ago. I have conceived these notions since I entered prison; at least they have been cultivated there by the treatment I received and by the spirit displayed toward me and my fellow-prisoners. I find myself in that state of mind that I wouldn't scruple doing anything to destroy the power of such an enemy, and that is no more than meeting England with her own weapons. She will say this is vicious and diabolical, which I admit it is; but if you go to fight the devil you may as well put your hoofs and horns on at once. I remember that in the September of '65 I was entrusted with a document for James Stephens by a delegate from the United Irishmen of a part of England. The substance of it was that in case of a rising in Ireland it was probable England would send all her troops to crush it; and they sought permission to be allowed to give England as much trouble at home as would frighten her and oblige her to keep all her soldiers to protect herself. Permission was also sought to form a Vigilance Committee who would have the special care of any traitors that might turn up, but Mr. Stephens refused both applications; he meant to fight England on honorable terms, and in observance of all the rules of civilized warfare, which England would not do with him, and never did with any country she laid claim to. After reading the paper he handed it to me remarking, "that is a most curious document, and would be interesting for preservation, only for the danger of it." "What am I to do with it," said I. "Do what you like with it," said he, and as my standing instructions were to destroy all dangerous papers that passed to me except such as I was told to preserve, I took a match off the mantelpiece of the room in which we met, and, striking a light, burnt them to oblivion in his presence.

I knew he'd like to have them preserved, and I'd like to preserve them myself, but as he didn't tell me do so I did my duty in destroying them.

The letter which I got from my wife was a kind of load to me to carry, as I could not communicate the news of it to any one else. It is said that sorrows are halved and pleasures doubled by sharing them with another, and I suppose it was the desire to increase my happiness that made me desirous to get a chance of passing the letter to one or more of my companions. I took it with me to exercise every day for a week without noticing that any of my friends were located within a stone's throw of me. At last I found by my sounding that the Pagan was alongside, and tying a bit of a slate to the paper I threw it over the wall. I got the slate back again with the words "all right" written on it, and I felt as happy as a prince that I had been able to let him take a peep at the outside world. I ran a great risk in trying to communicate in this manner, but the relief I felt in doing what I desired to do had always a greater influence over me than the fear of any punishment that might come from detection. If I was sure of being detected I mightn't do the thing, but where there is a way or a chance to succeed in any undertaking my cautionary bumps are not yet strongly enough developed to prevent me from making a trial. More cold-blooded, more prudent, or more wise men would see they had all means necessary to success before they took up any adventure, and where they could not grasp all the means they would not attempt anything. Such men would never free a fallen land, or never free themselves out of prison had they been imprisoned for its sake. In saying this I hold that we ourselves contributed more than any one else to our release by the efforts we made to make our treatment known to the world. England would do us to death if it were possible to do it secretly. She kept punishing us for the efforts we were making to expose her, and increased her precautions to hide us from the world, according as she discovered any attempt on our part to reach the public. We succeeded at length, at least Dennis Dowling Mulcahy and a few others did, in unmasking the hypocrites who were proclaiming that we were feasted on roast beef and mulled porter, at the same time that they had us manacled in the darkest of their black holes and were starving us on bread and water. A cry of indignation arose that burst the prison gates for some of us; for the tyrants felt they were being degraded brfore the eyes of the world; but they were mean enough to hold others on the miserable and false pretext that they were not political offenders. These are the soldiers, and the men arrested in England on charges of transmitting arms to Ireland and rescuing men in Manchester who were charged with promoting revolution in Ireland.

It was eight or ten days before the Pagan could get a chance of throwing me back my letter, and during that time I fell in with John Kenealy, Brian Dillon and John Lynch, and had some correspondence with them over the wall. When I had all the latest news that they had brought from Ireland, the burden of our telegraphs were made up of cold and hunger. We felt both intensely, and when the doctor visited us, as he did once or twice a week, I thought there could be no crueller mockery of my state than his asking me if I used to eat all my food. I applied to him a couple of times, when he visited me, for flannels and for more food. I did not do this in a supplicating tone. I told him that as a political prisoner I had a right to a sufficiency of coarse food and clothing, that I asked him for them as a matter of right, and if the authorities would not give them that I would apply to have my friends be permitted to supply me. He'd say I had as much food and clothing as the prison regulations would permit, and no additional food or clothing from any one outside the prison was ever allowed to a prisoner. This was his invariable reply, and I invariably told him I made the application not expecting to succeed, but in order that I should have nothing to upbraid myself with in case my health failed under this process of cold and starvation.

I awoke from my dreamy sleep one morning about the 1st of March and found myself utterly prostrated. For three days I was laid up with an attack of dysentery. The doctor ordered me medicine, which the medicine man brought me three times a day. Orders were issued that I be kept in my cell altogether; that I get no airing or exercise, but I would not be allowed to stay in bed or abstain from work. An ordinary prisoner would, as far as I have since learned, be sent to hospital under similar circumstances, but there was no hospital for me there or thereafter when seized with any illness. The doctor ordered me a flannel waistcoat when he saw how I was affected. Probably he thought my blood was cooled enough by this time. I asked him if he would not afford me drawers with the waistcoat, and he said he would see, but a sight of them I never saw.

Another change came to me about this time. One morning when I was ordered out for my exercise, I, instead of being first sent to the refractory place, found myself ordered into the large yard where all the thieves were tramping around each other in concentric circles.

Here I found myself in the midst of company, not very select company, indeed, yet behaving themselves pretty decently. It was a change, maybe, for the better, and the variety of features and forms to look upon made it interesting. I had no society before; I couldn't get a look at the face of a prisoner; but now I found myself in a new life, and the question was, whether to take it or kick against it. I was thinking that if I were to be separated from my companions and associated at any time with these very hard characters, I would rebel; but here there was no association as yet. I had to walk five paces distant from my neighbor. I dared not speak to him, nor dared he speak to me, and on this occasion I thought I might as well take the world as it came. I saw Charles Kickham, and John Lynch, and Brian Dillon, and the Pagan, and Michael Moore, and Thomas Duggan, and others in the same crowd, but no two of our men were allowed near each other; four or five thieves were always between them. We often had a wink at each other in turning the circles at certain places. The first circle was about twenty yards in diameter, the second thirty, the third forty, and so on. The man in the inner ring made more circuits than the man in the ring next to him. So that if we did not strike upon each other when we entered the yard at first, we were sure to pass each other repeatedly during the hour. The warders, on mounds raised between the circles and overlooking the men, kept vigilant watch over all, and had their eyes upon us particularly. The Pagan was one time noticed giving me a salute by rubbing his finger down along his nose. I was noticed doing the same, and both of us were told that if we did not keep our hands by our sides, we would be sent in and put under report.

I saw Kickham pulled up one time for having his hands behind his back, with one stuck into the sleeve of the other to protect them from the cold. This was forbidden; one should always walk with his hands by his side, and on cold, frosty mornings, you may see every man on the field with his shoulders and his hands shrugged up in the effort to make the sleeves of his jacket cover the tips of his fingers. Brian Dillon made signs to me one day which put me in bad spirits. Whenever I passed I could notice that he pointed to the ground, and the information I drew from it was that he was sinking into his grave.

John Lynch set me thinking another day; he gave me a regular puzzle, by giving a little jerk to his hand, as if he was throwing a stone; and I at length remembered that day was the 10th of March, that it was the anniversary of the Prince of Wales's marriage, three years before, when the people of Cork broke the windows that were illuminated, and John was tried for being one of the people. As we were passing again I returned the jerk, giving a look of intelligence. He whispered, "Oh, Rossa, the cold is killing me," and it did kill the poor fellow. I missed him from the ground a few days after. He sank under the treatment of the assassins at Pentonville, or rather under the treatment especially ordered for us by the State authorities, he was sent to Woking Hospital, and from there, in a few months after, to the prison graveyard. God rest his soul! is all I can say for him, and I suppose it would be wrong and useless for me to pray to God to blast that assassin regime which crushed it out so soon. I don't pray much, but if I believed in its efficacy in this latter direction, I would pray noon and night and morning. God will not send down fire from heaven to do for us what He ordains man shall do for himself, but which, in the abasement of the noble soul He has given us, we are too cowardly to do. Indeed, some of us are blasphemously base enough to find excuses for not doing our duty by indirectly charging the author of our being with being the author of our degradation. "It is God's will." It is from Him comes all temporal authority; it is He has established British rule in Ireland, and given us Cromwells. I simply say I don't believe one word of it. I can't believe it. Neither can I believe that it is His hand is scattering us over the world. What have our ancestors done that should entail upon us the curse of the Jews? What has the Island of Saints done that its children should be the outcasts of society, the pariahs of the world, the servants of the servants of men? Look at our men when they come to this great America; have not they to begin life, the best of them, the most intelligent of them, and certainly the most virtuous of them, by becoming, what we are sneeringly called, the "hod carriers," the hewers of wood and the drawers of water? Look at our women, the virtuous daughters of our virtuous peasantry; have they not to commence life in this country, have they not to make their first start as "the servants of the servants of men?" And of men and women, how many of them are lost, morally and physically, before they emerge from the probationary state? How few of these become rich and respectable compared to the many who live and die poor and unhappy, much unhappier than they would live and die in the old land?

And there is England that has been cursed by Popes and prelates these hundreds of years fattening upon our ruin, and we, "the chosen people," enslaved and degraded by the accursed. The chosen and the elect of olden times were blessed and promised to be blessed with the fat of the land—that is, the blessing that all people without distinction of creed, class, race or caste seem to prize most, and I could wish to heaven that some curse or blessing would send it to the people of Ireland *in* Ireland, for nowhere else through the wide, wide world could they enjoy it better. I learned some way or another at my mother's knee (I am not going to say that I was taught it), that the poor were the heirs of heaven and the rich the heirs of hell, and that if the state of both were different here so would it be different hereafter. The tables were to be turned entirely. I think some opinion or feeling of this kind prevailed among the peasantry of my neighborhood. I don't say it was that made them poor or kept them poor, at the same time that I think it might have tended to make them contented and peaceable under landlord and all other oppression. To suffer in this world was a passport to a blissful reward in the next. I still hope it is, and indeed partly believe it if we suffer in an effort to upraise our fallen native land, or suffer in any effort to relieve the sufferings of our fellow-man; but when I grew up and saw that the ministers of all religions were more desirous to associate with the heirs of hell than with the heirs of heaven, the prejudices, as I may so say, of my youth passed away, and I tried to become rich, but some stain seemed to remain that prevented me, and prevents me still, and will, I fear, ever prevent me. But, any way, I see no virtue in poverty or slavery, nor do I see that any one else, lay or cleric, sees it either. If possible, I will try to get out of both, and if I cannot succeed, it may be as happy a thing as I can do to return to the old idea, and that reminds me that I ought to return to my story.

Well, the days rolled on—but no, they didn't roll on, they dragged their slow length along in snail-creep fashion, and as for the nights, they wer very little better. The thoughts that troubled me during the day I tried to count out of my head by counting the stitches I put into the clothes I was making, but when the gas was turned off, and when sleep would not come, I could not keep myself from counting over the memories of the past, the friends and the friends' meetings of bygone days. I do not know that it made me anything happier to think of these things. I do not know that I could, under such circumstances, sing—

"Long, long be my heart with such memories filled."

Indeed, as far as I can judge, I think it would be well if my mind became blank, and that it retained no impression of life only what it received since I came into prison. It seems to me that memories of past pleasures do not tend to happiness, unless you are in a position of repeating them should an opportunity offer. If it is impossible for you to repeat them, if you are a pauper, or a prisoner, or a fallen unfortunate character any way, the memory of what you were or what you enjoyed as a virtuous man or a freeman brings more of pain with it than pleasure. So at least, I often thought, and, I believe, felt, those nights that I lay down on my hard bed after my day's communion with my needle and thread. I could make no approach to sleep till about twelve o'clock, then, in my dreamy sleep, felt myself turning to ease my limbs till half past four, which was the usual length of my doze.

Some two months after I wrote the "petition" to the Secretary of State, asking him for permission to write to an English member of Parliament, the governor sent for me and told me my prayer was refused. I wish I had a copy of this petition to put before my readers. I dare say it was not considered humble enough, like another I wrote afterwards in Portland. I managed to retain a copy of this, and I intend giving it in its place when I am some eight months longer in prison.

When coming from Mass one Wednesday morning I chanced to strike upon Mr. Charles Underwood O'Connell. We were ordered out of the chapel one by one and had to keep some twelve paces apart while walking along the passages and corridors; each of us carried his stool between his hands; Charley turned a corner and seeing no one in sight, he, as I rounded the same corner, turned his face toward me, and in a spasmodic whisper said: "I was dreaming about you these two nights past, and you'll shortly hear some important news."

Sitting down in my cell I commenced stitching away without counting my stitches this time. Charley's dreams chimed in so ominously with day dreams of my own that I could not help dwelling on what he told me, and as I played with my thoughts I was startled from my reverie by the turning of the key in the lock. My keeper entered and said "come on." "Where now?" "Never mind," said he, "but obey orders." On I marched till I was halted opposite the door of the Governor's room. "Throw your cap down there," and down I threw my cap. "Why do you throw it down that way?" "Didn't you tell me throw it down." "Silence," and here I obeyed orders. The door was opened from the inside, and the man outside, in a voice that startled me, roared out "Forward."

In a second I stood before the Governor, and he sat before me holding a letter in his hand. Just as I was in position, my accompanying guardian again bawled out, "Number Thirty-four eleven A Two Twenty-seven Convict Jeremiah O'Donovan Rossa, Life," and the Governor in response to that, addressing me, said:

"I have sent for you to tell you that I have received a letter from your wife, but, inasmuch as no letter is due to you, I cannot give it into your hands, yet, as the news it contains is of a family nature, and as the prison rules give us a discretionary power to communicate to prisoners any information similar to what this letter contains, I am able to inform you that on the 30th of April your wife was delivered of a son, that she is not yet strong enough to be out of bed, and that the child is to be christened James Maxwell, after the names of her father and brother," and, addressing my keeper, he added, "that will do." The keeper gave the order of "right about face," and as I raised my hand to him to signify that I wished to speak a few words with the Governor, he raised his club and ordered me to keep my hands by my side.

The Governor asked what did I want, and I asked him if he'd be pleased to allow me read the letter; he said he could not give me possession of it, but on asking him to read it for me, he did, and I thanked him. I then inquired if I would be allowed to write to my wife, and I was told I would not; that the prison rules allowed a prisoner only one letter every six months. I told him I had only written one letter since my conviction, that I was about five months a convict, and that under the circumstances of my wife being ill I might be allowed to write my second letter a month in advance. He informed me that could not be—that I should wait until six months after the date of my last letter before I could write again. "But I was three months in prison before I was allowed to write that first letter which I ought to be permitted to write on my entrance." He couldn't help that; every letter must count from the writing of the previous one, and I could not write for four months longer. I was saying something about this being worse than the treatment of an ordinary thief or pickpocket, but before I had finished he motioned his hand to the keeper, who then roared out his "right about face," and the other warders present making a move toward me, I thought discretion the better part of valor and faced the door. In a moment after, I found myself locked up in my cell, and I am not sure now whether this event of the birth of a sixth son, which makes every father rejoice, was not a subject rather of grief than joy to me. I paced my cell, unmindful of the rules and regulations that forbade me to do so during working hours, but I was soon startled from my meditations by a voice through the keyhole of my door crying out, "What are you doing there? Stop that walking instantly and go to your work."

I sat down upon my little stool, the Bible and the prayer-book and the other religious book lay on the little table before me, and instead of praying as a good man ought to do, I dwelt upon the hypocrisy of these people that supplied me with such books and trampled under foot all the principles of religion they contained. Here was my wife delivered of a child seven months after I had been taken away from her, and they would not allow me to write a line to her! No, I did not pray on the occasion, but I felt it would be a relief to me if I could curse, and if the high authorities who ordered this treatment toward me were within my reach, I do not know that I would not have pitched their Bible in their face and hurled a malediction at them with it.

I have read many stories of the conversion of prisoners confined in solitary cells in the prisons of America and England, through the discipline of allowing them no other book but a Bible while under punishment, but the practice seemed unnatural to me, and I could never realize that equanimity necessary for solid or permanent reformation of the mind through the same agency that tortured the body to bring it about.

I used to read five chapters of my Bible every day, and I made a shift one time to steal a Bible, when, for increased punishment, it was decreed that I should not get a book or Bible for six months, but I well remember that once I could have torn the book in fritters to express my sense of their abuse of it when they starved me on "bread and water" for twenty-eight days in a darkened cell, in which they specially built a privy, leaving it without a cover, and never leaving me in the open air for one hour during that time. I had nothing but the Bible allowed, and I could think of nothing but the hunger that gnawed my vitals and the stench that was thick about me in the warm July days. Yes, I would have torn up that Bible to express my sense of their abuse of it, only that I was sure it would be the first thing they would use in public against me to show what a hopelessly irreligious and desperate character I was. The thoughts that occur to a man in his prison life are a part of the world's history, and if men who have been confined for years would or could give what passes through their minds, philanthropists and those inrteested in the reformation of criminals and their proper treatment would have a better guide to lead them than all the advice that could be given on this head by theorists and philosophers who study human nature outside prison walls.

Father Zanetti came to me a day or two after I heard the news of my getting a young son, and I spoke of the heartlessness of my jailors. Patience, obedience and resignation were his panacea for all the ills of life, and he enjoined me to cultivate them as diligently as I could. He put several questions to me that he never before touched upon, asked if I didn't feel my chest sinking, my breath getting short, and my legs getting weak. I said "Yes" to all. When he was gone, I began to think what it meant, and I concluded there was something in the wind that denoted a change of climate. The following Sunday Canon Oakley, in preaching his sermon to us, touched also upon something new, and when he had ended, I gave a significant look at one of my companions sitting next to me. An officer saw me, raised his stick, and threatened that if he caught me again turning my head aside, it would be worse for me. After the priest withdrew, he commenced badgering me again, telling me if I did not conduct myself properly, he would make me. I was very near breaking out and telling him to keep his tongue to himself, and to conduct himself then any way he thought proper. He annoyed me so much that when I went to my cell I made a resolution that I would not quietly stand such abuse again. Indeed, so disgusted was I with myself for listening quietly to it, that I resolved I would take a look the very next Sunday and give him a bit of my mind if he attacked me. But that next Sunday never came to us in Pentonville, for on Wednesday morning, at six o'clock, we were taken out of our cells and marshalled into line on the same spot as the night we entered. The scales were there before us, and one by one, as we stepped on and off, a record was taken of our weight. I had reduced eight pounds since I came to London, but others had fared worse. Cornelius Keane, Michael O'Reagan and a few more had each reduced as much as thirty pounds. The chains and the handcuffs were brought into requisition. I found myself tied in a chain that held eight of us. It ran through the handcuffs, and a lock attached each of us to a particular part of the chain, so that neither of us could slip away from his position. In this manner we were ushered into a van that was in waiting for us in the courtyard of the prison. Eight more of us were put into a second one, the remainder into a third, the gates opened and we had a drive through the streets of that great city, London.

Having arrived at the station of the railroad that was to lead us to another prison, detectives and policemen were there in readiness to conduct us to our carriages. The three chainfulls of us were escorted into one car, and the jailers who had charge of us took their seats in our midst. One old fellow had charge of the escort; he held the papers and orders connected with us, but he was as grum as a statue, and we could not get a word out of him. The train moved away from the station, and, addressing the commander-in-chief, I said—"Governor, where can we be going to now?" He only shook his head; another officer cried "hush;" a third said there was no speaking allowed; one of the prisoners observed that we certainly ought to be allowed to speak a few words now, a second seconded the motion; Denis Dowling Mulcahy debated the question with the jailers, who were threatening to report us when we arrived at our destination. At length the final arrangement was come to that we may talk a little while the train was in motion, but we were to keep a silent tongue in our head during the time it remained at every station.

Our guardians carried with them two or three canvass bags, and the contents of these turned out to be bread and cheese for dinner.

Orders had been given that we were not to be allowed out of the cars till we reached the end of our journey, which we did about three o'clock in the evening.

The prison vans were in waiting for us at the Portland terminus, accompanied by the necessary amount of guards. I sat in front on the first one, and, as it was moved out, a drunken soldier staggered towards us and said, " God knows, my poor fellows, I pity ye." The jailer roared out, "Get away out of there or I'll have you under arrest immediately," and the poor unfortunate, looking sympathetically, turned his back upon us. Twenty minutes afterwards we were safely lodged inside the walls of Portland Convict Prison.

CHAPTER IX.

LODGED IN PORTLAND—BOOTS AND BOOKS—NEW CELLS—RAIN DOWN—DIRECTOR FAGAN FROM CORK—HIS LETTER REGARDING US—NO CATHOLIC OR IRISH WARDERS TO HAVE CHARGE OF US—THE BROAD ARROW—" AMULETS OR CHARMS "—THE WASH-HOUSE—STATIONARY-TUBS AND SOAP SUDS—DODGING ABOUT FOR A CLEAN JOB OF WORK—PUMPING AND PICKING LINEN—DENIS DOWLING MULCAHY OUR PRIEST—HIS SERMONS AND PSALMS—A SUNDAY IN PORTLAND—PARADE AND SALAAMS—OIL AND BLACKING—" ORDERLIES " AND SLOP—THE EVIL EYE—FORBIDDEN TO WALK OR STRETCH IN MY CELL—BREAD AND WATER—DIETARY TABLE.

Having arrived inside the gates of the establishment, we stood side by side in the waiting-room of the prison. Our chains were unloosed, our names were called, and as we answered we were told to strip. This we did in the presence of the company; and, leaving our clothes behind us, we marched into the bath-room. After going through our ablutions, we found new clothes ready for us, and, being dressed, we were ordered back to the hall from which we came. The old clothes had vanished. If we had anything concealed in them, these were the precautions taken to deprive us of the contraband article. Our names were again called, and, as we answered, each of us got three religious books and a library book. This latter was to be changed once a fortnight, and the religious ones were to be permanent stock. Two school-books were also allowed, which could be changed every three months. Some of us took a grammar and arithmetic, others a dictionary and Mensuration, and more a Euclid and class book. Such books as Euclids and Mensurations would not be allowed to us when we got to the London prison, lest they should teach us anything that would facilitate our escape.

We were in lodged in basement cells which were never before occupied. They were in size 7 feet by 3½, and separated from one another by corrugated iron. The flooring was of flags, the ventilators and windows of cast iron, so that we were surrounded by no very warming influences. Taking with that the fact that when it rained the water poured down into these cells, so much so that I had often to leave my hammock at night and huddle myself into a corner, it can be understood that, however we were boarded, we were not very comfortably lodged.

I have before me now the report of five Commissioners who inquired into our treatment in the Summer of 1870, and I take from it a few questions and answers in corroboration of what I say of this "rain down." Of course the prison officials make the shower as light as they can.

Doctor Lyons, one of the Commissioners, asks—"Is it possible that rain water could have got in and flooded these cells and wetted the bed clothes and beds?"

Mr. Clifton—"It is quite possible that in the extraordinary heavy gales we have here, and the building being built of wood, that there is water sifting through the wood, and it very often happens that a man's blankets may get damp in the night, or slightly wet in a few of the cells that are exposed to the west and south winds. And on these occasions that the treason-felony prisoners have complained to me that these cells were flooded, I visited the cells myself, and there were signs of there being moisture and wet in the places, and the blankets were slightly wet."

Doctor Lyons—"While the cells were in that imperfect condition did you happen to direct that the prisoners should be removed to other cells?"

Mr. Clifton—"I had no other cells to send them to at the time, unless I located them with the other prisoners, which I knew would be so distasteful to them."

To me who knew how very little these jailers accommodated matters to our tastes or our distastes, it was amusing to hear the Governor of Portland say he did not remove us from wet cells because he should put us in the society of thieves, "and that would be distasteful to us." It may be interesting, to give the instructions that followed us to Portland, and to observe that these instructions were written by an Irishman and a Catholic, by the son of a man who was champion of Catholicity and "Emancipation," and an associate of Daniel O'Connell's—William Fagan, Member of Parliament for Cork. And men like him got an "Emancipation" which left us enslaved. It freed themselves from the disabilities which prevented them from filling Government positions—it withdrew their support from the cause of nationality—the cause of the people at large, and opened a way for the Keoghs and the O'Hagans to arrive at a position where they could become the oppressors of their own race instead of remaining with the people and discharging their duty as the assertors or the champions of their country's independence. Not alone is the "lamp that lights them through dignity's way caught from the flame where their country expires," but they are very glad to set the country in flames and their fellow-countrymen in chains in order to find favor with the enemies of Irish liberty.

Mr. Clifton, the Governor of Chatham Prison, is further questioned by Lord Devon as to the instructions he received regarding us. He says he received no instructions until he wrote for them; and till he got an answer he put us in the wash-house:—

"HER MAJESTY'S PRISON, PORTLAND, }
GOVERNOR'S OFFICE, May 15, 1866. }

SIR: I have the honor to acquaint you that I received yesterday twenty-four Irish treason-felony convicts from Pentonville Prison, pursuant to warrant dated 5th inst., but I have not yet been furnished with the instructions as to their treatment referred to in the circular letter of the 9th inst. The Secretary of the Board of Directors intimated to me that they were coming, and merely stated that instructions would be forwarded. Pending further orders respecting them, I have employed them in the wash-house.—I have the honor to be, sir, your most obedient servant,

GEORGE CLIFTON.

To WM. FAGAN, Esq.

A few days afterwards, Mr. Clifton says, I received the letter back with this memorandum in it:

"MR. CLIFTON—I regret that my absence at Chatham prevented me issuing instructions to you on the subject. They are to be located in the last lot of new cells, passed by me as fit for occupation at my last visit.

(Those are the cells, my lord, that you visited in D hall; they were just then completed, and never occupied before.) They are to be worked in a separate party at labor equal to their ability, both as regards their strength and knowledge, and are to be kept and exercised by themselves on all occasions, and full marks to be awarded to them for their labor, except in cases of proved misconduct, and they are to be worked by Protestant officers—English, in whom you have full confidence—and they are not to be employed in the domestic duties of the prison, except as regards their own cells or halls. You must, therefore, locate them on the works in a secure position, where too much attention will not be drawn to their isolation, at the same time in such a position where the safe custody or the officer's honesty will not be tampered with. Due provision will be made for a Roman Catholic priest's attendance, but until one is nominated there will be no objection to one of the prisoners reading prayers to the others.

WILLIAM T. FAGAN."

May 17 1866.

There was a public works prison in Portsmouth where there was a Catholic chaplain, but that would not do for us. Portland was a place where a priest's foot never polluted the soil, and there could be no sympathetic influence there to imperil our safe keeping. These people as you see by the instructions from a Catholic director, would not trust an Irish Protestant near us. No; he must have the English brand upon his Protestantism to make it orthodox when the guardianship of Irishmen was in question. I believe this Mr. Fagan got charge of us at first, for the very reason that the Government intended to treat us shamefully, and if any of their bad work came out on them they would say, "why, we have treated these prisoners like pet lambs: what other proof of our kind intentions towards them can you desire than that we have given the principal charge of them to an Irishman and a Catholic, William T. Fagan?" Mr. Fagan would possibly be a good Irishman and a good Catholic if an Irish Catholic Government were giving him the same salary as he is getting now. He is paid for working for the English, and he is doing their work well, like many other pious, patriotic Irishmen, which is all that I need say of him at present.

The day after our coming to Portland, we were taken to the shoe store to be fitted in shoes and boots. The shoes for Sunday and cell wear, and the boots for public works. But, weren't they boots? Fully fourteen pounds in weight. Those that my youthful imagination figured in reading of the seven leagued ones of "Jack the Giant Killer" were nothing to them. I put them on and the weight of them seemed to fasten me to the ground. It was not that alone, but the sight of the impression they left on the gutter as you looked at the footprints of those who walked before you, struck terror to your heart. There was the felon's brand of the "broad arrow" impressed on the soil by every footstep. It was not enough to have it branded on several parts of your cap, your shirt and vest, your stockings, jacket and trowsers, but the nails in the soles of your boots and shoes were hammered in in an arrow shape, so that whatever ground you trod you left traces that Government property had traveled over it. "I'll put the "broadar upon you," was an expression in use long and many years ago at John Cushan's school. It was the threat of a beating that would leave a mark which could never be effaced, and I never realized the force of this "broadar" till I recognized it in the broad arrow that brands everything animate and inanimate belonging to prison life. The handle of the cat-o'-nine-tails, that opens the poor convict's back is marked with it, as well as the Bible that the minister reads to soothe him when he is groaning in his cell after the scourging. You see it on your comb, on your tin pint, on your tin knife, and if it does not enter into your soul, it at least finds its way into your mouth branded on the bowl of your timber spoon.

It took about two hours to fit the whole of us in boots and shoes, and during this time we were walked about the yard, and allowed to speak to each other two by two. This was the first sunny glimpse we got of prison life; to be allowed to walk about and hear each other's voice, and hear the news that O'Connor, and Carey and Mulcahy and the others, brought, who were in the world three months later than some of us, were things to us the value of which a free man cannot appreciate. I heard O'Leary say it would be grand if this kind of prison life continued. We did not know what disposition was to be made of us, and of course had our speculations on the matter, but the question was soon put outside the pale of the speculative sciences. When we were all foot-fitted, orders were given to halt and draw up in double line. Then the Governor came in front, and to the cry of "hats off," each of us uncovered. He made a short address, hoping we would have good conduct, as he intended to maintain with the utmost strictness the discipline of the prison—that he could be mild or severe according as it was necessary—that he had not as yet received instructions regarding the work we were to be put at, but until he received them he would send us to the wash-house—that the "amulets" or "charms," which were yesterday taken from us, would be held by him until further orders, as he could not permit a prisoner to hold anything that the rules did not allow. I thought some of my companions more religious than I would resent the allusion to the crosses and scapulars they wore; but, as they did not, I did not like to become the champion of the insulted Faith. I asked the Governor if I could write a letter to my family, as the prison rules state every convict can write one on reception, and he informed me that was a privilege not permitted in our case—that we could not write until there was a special permission from the authorities, and here again we were in this matter treated worse than the English thieves and throttlers.

Next day we were taken to the wash-house, and the labor of our convict life in Portland commenced. I did not like the smell of the place; but what is the use in saying I didn't like things? There were the stationary tubs full of dirty suds and dirty clothes, and feeling I would rather have a hand in anything than a hand in them, I "mouched" round to see if anything better would turn up. I laid hold of the handle of a pump, and commenced pumping away as hard as I could. A large water trough had to be filled. I kept at my work for half-an-hour, by which time the tank was full, and as I turned about, wiping the sweat off my face with my check handkerchief, I saw I had gained my point. All the stationary tubs were engaged, and I was detailed to fill the tank whenever it was empty. When this was done my duty was to sort the linens. The broken garments were to be picked out from the unbroken ones and sent to the menders, and the good articles were to be made up into kits, each consisting of a shirt, a handkerchief, a pair of stockings, and a flannel drawers and a waistcoat. Every Saturday night every prisoner got his bundle, and every second week the bundle was *minus* the flannels, the prisoners getting a change of these only once a fortnight. Occasionally, I had half-an-hour or so taking clothes into the drying-room and bringing them out; so that my labor in the wash-house was a little diversified, just what suited me, for of all things I cannot bear in prison life, or in any life, it is to be kept plodding away ding-dong from morning till night at any one occupation. The first week in Portland I made myself a variety of employments, but I had not such a good chance afterwards, while in Portland or anywhere else.

Sunday came, the bells rang for religious service, we heard the parades and the trampings to church, but there was no devotion for us unless we chose to be devout in our cells, where there was no great temptation to be otherwise unless we got into a bad vein of getting discontented with the condition and grumbled at the Fates that offered such hard fare.

We came to Portland bringing with us our registers of "Roman Catholic," and as there was no priest in prison the Governor informed us that one of ourselves would be allowed to officiate on Sundays until a clergymen was appointed. He was informed that in the Catholic Church a layman could not do service for a clergyman, could not say Mass, could not hear confessions, could not give communion, could not do anything that a priest could do for a congregation. He then suggested that one of us might read prayers or a chapter of the Bible in the hall outside of our cells, and as we preferred that to remaining locked up we consented, and made Denis Mulcahy our chaplain. He knelt at the end of the hall on a stool, with his books on a table before him, and repeated aloud for us the morning and evening prayers, a litany, and a chapter of the Bible. It is but justice to say that in the latter devotion he selected those parts of the Scripture which harmonized best with our positions. It was pleasing to me to hear him read from the Holy Book denunciations of tyrants and oppressors, perjurers and liars, and sympathy for their victims, with curses and punishments for liars and perjurers, and blessings for all who suffered pesecution for justice sake.

It was the most treasonable preaching ever I heard, and we had it Sunday after Sunday for eight weeks till the priest came, a Rev. Mr. Poole, Englishman, but priested in Ireland, at All Hollow's College, Dublin, and I wish the college joy of him for anything of Irish life they infused into him.

As I am speaking of Sunday, I may as well give an account of how we spent that day in Portland. The evening previous we had to make preparations for the proper observance of the Sabbath. We stopped work and came into our cells an hour and a-half earlier than usual. Our first preparation was in the bath house, where we got rid of as much as we could of the soil and moil of our week's work. Back in our cells two of us were detailed as "orderlies," and the duties belonging to an orderly's office were to take the sack full of kits and lay one kit down at every cell door, to take the empty sack and go round again to take the soiled linen, the prisoner when giving back every article opening it out, turning it back and front to show there was no unnecessary tear in it; to take the oil and the oil-brush, the blacking and the blacking-brushes to every cell-door, to sweep the hall, and last, though not least, to go about collecting the slops.

With the oil and the oil-brush the convict smeared his large seven-leagued boots, and there is a special watch kept on him while doing this, for many hungry men have been known to drink this oil. With the blacking and the blacking-brush the shoes are polished, and polished brightly too, for if the "shine" is not on at parade in the morning it is a black mark for the convict and for the officer who has charge of the squad. Often have I been obliged to go a second time over my shoes in order to have them pronounced fit for inspection. It is true I often tried to get off with giving them a "Scotch lick," for cleaning shoes in a narrow cell with the door locked and very bad ventilation became odious to me. Taking the dried gutter off them, putting on the blacking, and then working up the "shine," made the air redolent with blacking and Portland stone, and so much did it become impregnated with particles of these, that I could feel them cracking between my teeth. While oiling the boots the door was left open, and you had to do the work standing in the doorway, facing outwards. If you got the oil inside your door you might drink it, but there was no fear of your drinking the blacking. When you got your boots done you shut the door; and, by-and-bye, the orderlies came and put the shoe brushes and blacking under the door. When you had used them you returned them in the same manner.

The usual time for rising is five o'clock, but on Sunday the bell rang at six and when another rang at a quarter past six you were to be up and dressed. Two being detailed as orderlies, the slops are collected by these commissioned gentlemen going round from cell to cell with the bucket. "Doors closed," and at that word of command orderlies and all others are shut in. In a half-an-hour breakfast comes, and the orderlies are out again. Each prisoner put out his pint and plate the last time his door was open; and now the vessels are there waiting for ten ounces of bread and three quarters of a pint of cocoa—the bread often sour and the cocoa often sickening. One orderly holds the cocoa-can, the other holds the pint and plate, and the officer measures out the stuff. Then the orderlies lay hold of the bread-basket, and the officer lays hold of the loaves, placing one at every door. If a prisoner had the distribution of these loaves it would be his fortune while in office. He would be the prince of the ward. Tweed, in the Seventh Ward of New York, when he was in his glory, would be nothing to him. He might put a man on the "pipes" or put a man on the "Boulevard," who would be his henchman on election day. But what was he to the man who had it in his power to make choice of one or two hungry men, to whom he would give crusty loaves or loaves carrying half an ounce more than other loaves, where all the men of the ward were starving?

Such abuses crept into English prison life in the imperfect stage of its discipline; but now that is all changed. No prisoner can give out bread or measure drink; everything must be distributed impartially by an impartial officer, and there are no more quarrels amongst convicts on the grounds of such a one giving the other the worst loaf in the basket. Our breakfasts taken on Sunday morning, we are ordered to the parade. Before we got the priest we all stood at our door with our caps off. The Governor passed by, looking at each of us in turn. It was a stare from head to foot to see if our scalps were bare enough and our boots bright enough. After the chaplain came, we were marshalled at a respectful distance from another gang of English convicts. As the Governor appeared, to the order of "Rear rank, two paces backward," a pathway was made between our lines, through which pathway he sometimes passed, and other times he passed in front. In sleet or in sun our caps had to be kept off during this inspection. One day the Deputy-Governor, Major Hickey, was the parade master. He had passed one party, and as he was on the way to the next gang, I, at the right of the line, seeing he had passed me, put on my cap. He turned and asked why I did that without orders, telling me to uncover again, and I obediently did so; but I was watching after that to give the fellow a hit. I did so in a letter, "a petition," I wrote to the Secretary of State, and he was very gentlemanly to me afterwards. I never got any peace from these people till I treated them with contempt, and I never did this till I saw that nothing reasonable would satisfy them, and that the more I showed an obedient disposition the more disposed they showed themselves to annoy me.

The inspection being over, we were led to chapel—led and driven—for one officer went before us and another came behind. We were in our cells again about half-past eleven, and at twelve dinner was distributed. This was 12 oz. of bread, 4 oz. of cheese, and a pint of water; and the orderlies, having done their duty, were locked in like the rest of us. One officer remained on watch. He walked about in slippers, and sometimes, if your eye was fixed on the spy-hole, you could see the outside blinker of it slowly moving aside, and then an eye glaring in at you. 'Twas an ugly sight, as ugly a one as remains to me of my prison remembrance. Talk what you will of beautiful eyes, but the eyes of an angel would look repulsive to me in such a position. I don't know was it an innate detestation of spying that affected me so uncomfortably at this spectacle; but the eye of a serpent or of a lion fixed on me within my cell would not, I think, make me feel worse than that eye fixed on me from without. To me it was the all-seeing eye; but I was certain that for me also it had in it more of the devil than the Divine.

When the officers came back from dinner we were taken to the chapel for evening prayers, and after chapel we were taken to exercise, as we had two hours in the open air every Sunday. Cells after exercise, and supper at five o'clock, consisting of six ounces of bread and a pint of gruel, supposed to have in it two ounces of oatmeal. You remain in your cell till half-past seven o'clock, the hour for preparing to retire, and in this space of seven feet by three and a-half you are at perfect liberty to amuse yourself any way you like, save and except that you are not to make any noise, that you are not to walk about, and that you are not to take your hammock off your shelf, nor to sling it to stretch upon. Walking about my cell during dinner hour a rap came to my door. I saw the eye at the spy-hole and heard a voice cry, "What are you dancing there for?" "I'm not dancing, I'm only walking to keep my blood in circulation." "You are making a noise in your cell, and you can't do that; you'll have to keep quiet." I sat down on my hard stool, fully persuaded it was a hard place to live in.

Another of my Sunday experiences is that I was located on the side of the hall where all the cells are dark. Here there is no chance of reading, and after some meditation on my situation, I took down my hammock and stretched on it. The eye immediately detected me, and ordered me to replace the hammock. I said that in a dark cell where I could not read or walk I might reasonably be allowed to stretch, and next day I was sentenced to twenty-four hours' bread and water for my insolence and insubordination.

At half-past seven on Sunday evenings the orderlies are out, the doors are opened one by one, and the slops are collected. Shut in again, another bell rings at a quarter to eight, up to which time you are not to touch your bed. Then you set to work to fix your hammock, undress yourself, and be in bed when the eight o'clock bell rings, and all lights are extinguished except those in the body of the hall.

So much for a Sunday. And now as I have spoken of the dietary of one day here, I may as well give the scale for all the days of the week in Portland. I have it before me in the report of the Commissioners of Inquiry, and I may say it looks very nice and spicy in print; but were you to see it in reality and feed upon it for any time, you would think it "flavored and thickened" with something more than "as above."

PORTLAND, PORTSMOUTH, DARTMOOR, PARKHURST, AND WORKING DIETARIES FOR CONVICTS AT PUBLIC WORKS—HARD LABOR.

BREAKFAST.

Three-quarters pint cocoa, containing half oz. cocoa, two oz. milk, half oz. molasses; (bread see below.)

DINNER.

Sunday—Four oz. cheese, bread.

Monday and Saturday—Five oz. of beef without bone, and after being cooked with its own liquor, flavored with half oz. onions, and thickened with ⅛th oz. flour and any bread and potatoes left on the previous day, and three-quarters oz. pepper per cent, one lb. potatoes; bread.

Tuesday and Friday—One pint soup, containing eight oz. shins of beef, one oz. pearl barley, two oz. fresh vegetables, one oz. onions, one lb. potatoes; bread.

Wednesday—Five oz. mutton without bone, and after being cooked with its own liquor, flavored and thickened as above, one lb. potatoes; bread.

Thursday—One lb suet pudding, containing one and a half oz. suet, eight oz. flour, six and a half oz. water; one lb. potatoes; bread.

SUPPER.

One pint of gruel, containing two oz. oatmeal, half oz. molasses or salt.

Bread per week, 168 oz. each—week day, 23 oz. each; Sunday, 30 oz.

CHAPTER X.

REMOVED FROM THE WASH-HOUSE AND SENT TO THE QUARRIES—NOBBLING—I BECOME A QUARRYMAN—"REPORTED" AND "DEGRADED"—TRIED AND CONDEMNED WITHOUT WITNESSES—PRIVY CLEANING—RAIN DOWN IN OUR CELLS—EARNING MARKS—EIGHTEEN MONTHS IN PRISON AFTER DEATH—CANNOT SPEAK HIGH OR LOW—"DO YOU DEFY THE PRISON AUTHORITIES"—PAT BARRY'S JUGGLERY AND PUNISHMENT—DONALD BANE, THE SCOTCHMAN, AND HIS RAZOR—" CANNOT YOU FELLOWS SHAVE EACH OTHER "—MICHAEL O'REGAN JOKED AND CHARLES KICKHAM SHOVED BY GUNNING—WILLIAM ROANTREE'S ILLNESS—MARTIN HANLY CAREY BREAKS A FINGER, AND THE DOCTOR MAKES HIM WORK WITH ONE HAND—I TRY TO BE AS GOOD AS AN ENGLISH GENTLEMAN CONVICT AND TEAR MY CLOTHES—"MUTINY"—I'D "SUCK ANOTHER MAN'S BLOOD"—MICHAEL O'REGAN AND THE PRISON PRIESTS.

After a week an order came to take us away from the wash-house. We were to be sent to work in the quarries; and in obedience to the mandates of Mr. Fagan—"You must therefore locate them on the works in a secure position, where too much attention will not be drawn by their isolation," we were placed in a little valley in view of the Governor's office. He had his spy-glass on us whenever it pleased him, and all diligence was shown in the carrying out of the instruction to place the cherished convicts "in such a position where their safe custody or the officers' honesty will not be tampered with." Mr. Clifton, in his evidence before the Commissioners, says (page 67):—"And as soon as these instructions came down, they were removed to a spot on the public works which you can see from the windows." Oh! weren't these people careful of us! and frightened lest some invisible power would run away with us! "They are to be worked by Protestant officers, English, in whom you have the fullest confidence," and yet the "officers' honesty" was to be watched.

The little valley was within about 300 yards of the main prison; it opened towards the building, which was the only view we had, as on all other sides it was surrounded by high grounds, on which were constructed railroads and tramways. We dare not ascend any of these and take a view of the sea, or the island, or the other prisoners working beyond. We had, however, an opportunity of occasionally seeing some of those as they were taken to hospital or to the dead-house on stretchers, after being maimed or killed or having committed suicide on the works. The first day in the quarries we occupied ourselves in erecting blocks on which we were to dress stones. The blocks were to be three yards part, and I found Luby, O'Leary, and myself on the angles of a triangle. As I turned myself round I found myself at the apex of another triangle, having Denis Dowling Mulcahy and James O'Connor for its base, and so on with each of the others. It was at this time about the middle of May, and we were obliged to work with our jackets off. Some cold days came, and the sea wind blowing in, seemed to cut through me; yet the prison regulations and discipline made it summer season, and we had to work as all others worked. Mr. Clifton says, "I can produce the Secretary of State's reply, in which they were to be treated as other convicts." Our first work was making "nobblers," a nobbler being a stone with five sides dressed and one rough side. When the workman had his rough stone filed down into a nobbler he laid it by his block, called his companion, and both taking the handbarrow, went to the quarry for another rough stone. On one of these trips I laid hold of a sledge, and to warm myself commenced sledging away at a large rock, while my mate was "keebling," that is, knocking the large rough corners off an embryo nobbler. "I think, Rossa," said Gunning, the officer, "you'd make a good quarryman, and you'd better stay here with Brophy." "All right, governor," said I, "anything you like;" for I like variety, and as every one of the laborers had to call a few times a day to the quarry, I had an opportunity of having a word with each in turn. Hugh Brophy and myself were getting on splendidly till the first of my misfortunes came on me in the shape of a "Report," and come it did like a thunderclap, without the preliminary of a flash of lightning. We got up at five o'clock in the morning, had our breakfast at half-past five, and were in the quarries at six. 'Twas a long, weary day, and I always had a splendid appetite for my meals. When you come into dinner you enter your cell, shut the door, and the orderlies of the day are called out, and they lay at the door a canteen containing the dinner. The orderlies are then sent in, and the warder opens door after door, each prisoner taking in his dinner, and the officer taking care not to open one door till the other is shut. Opening my door this day in question, and stooping down to lay hold of the tin, he roared out, "Leave that there; stand outside here, and turn your face to the wall." I obeyed. Michael Moore's cell was next to mine, and opening his door, Mike, as hungry as myself, bowed towards the canteen, and Gunning ordered him to leave it there, and turn his face to the wall. If we hadn't food for the stomach we had at least food for speculation. As all the dinners were taken in, and all the doors locked, the officer coming towards me, cried, "About face, two paces forward, march," and we obeying, he followed behind, giving all the orders that were necessary to send us around corners and through halls till he had each of us locked in a darkened cell. The officer in charge of this dark abode came to me and demanded my boots, my braces, my necktie, my handkerchief, and my cap, taking them away, locking my door, and leaving me asking myself what the deuce can all this mean? But I wasn't left long in doubt; it was a "Report;" my door was opened, and I heard the order "Forward." "My boots, governor," I said; "Never mind your boots," said he, "forward march," and on I went through the flagged hall in my stocking vamps, and my two hands having hold of my trousers to keep it from tripping me. "Halt, right face, forward." I entered by a door that another officer opened, and found myself before the judgment seat of the Governor, with a strong iron railing between him and me, and two officers at each side of it. The judge reads from a large book before him—"Treason-felony convict, Jeremiah O'Donovan Rossa, No. 34, you are charged with speaking to the prisoner in the cell convenient to you." "When, Governor?" "Yesterday evening, at seven o'clock." "Who is to prove the charge, Governor?" "Do you deny the charge?" "I only ask who is to prove it. You certainly are not going to convict a man in England without some one giving evidence." Governor, addressing one of the officers, "Where is the patrol?" Officer, putting his hand to his head, "He is off duty to-day, sir." Governor, addressing me, "The patrol who was on duty outside your window yesterday evening heard you. Do you deny the charge?" "I admit or deny nothing."

Governor—"As this is your first offence, I will not punish you severely, but as the discipline of the prison must not be despised, I order you to be degraded, and I fine you 84 marks; you must not speak or make any noise in your cell while in this prison." "But can I speak at all?" "Yes; you can speak to your companions while at labor, but you must speak so loud that the officer in charge of you can hear you, lest you should be planning anything." I bowed my acknowledgements, and to the orders of "about face," "forward," "left face," "forward," "halt;" "left face," "forward," I kept moving and entered my dark cell again. The door was locked,—by-and-by it was opened and I was handed my dinner, but I had to eat it without knife, or plate, or table, as this was one of the punishment cells in the punishment ward of the prison.

The bell rang at one o'clock, the door was opened, I was told to dress and get ready for labor. I took my boots and in them found my handkerchief, stock, cap and braces. Moore and myself were being marched off when we heard the cry of "stop," "stop;" the officer in charge of us cried "halt," and the other on coming up handed each of us a jacket, saying, "here, give me the jackets you have on and wear these till evening," and, having made the change, we went out and fell in with the rest of the party as they were going to work after dinner.

I had one pleasant piece of news to communicate when we arrived in the "pleasant valley," and that was what the Governor told me, that we could speak while at work, but loud enough for the officers to hear us, lest we should be planning anything. We indulged in the privilege much to the mortification of the officers in charge of us, for a great part of their recreation consisted in checking any of us who seemed inclined to carry on a conversation with his neighbor, but now they were checked themselves, and they appeared to regard it as a curtailment of their authority. Men like to have power over other men. We are all tyrants and need to be held in check by some power outside of our own wills. It was a great thing for those ignorant jailers to bring men like us to account every hour of the day, to shut our mouths or allow our tongues to wag at their will. As we were in the height of our glee at this change in our affairs, Gunning cried out, "See, see, two of yous men will have to come and clean out the privy here," and in obedience to his command the two who were first on his list went at the work. Once every three weeks this unpleasant duty was performed by two of us. Gunning, speaking to me one day, told me I was one of the two who should empty the closet next Monday, and I said I would see something about it first. When I went to the cell that evening I called the officer and told him to take down my name to see the Governor next day, and next day at dinner hour I was taken before him. "Governor," I said, "the officer in charge of us told me yesterday that I should clean a privy next Monday and I desire to know from you if that is work expected from me?" His reply was "Certainly, yes," to which I answered, "All right, Governor," and turned away. When I went out Gunning said, "You went to the Governor to know if you would be made to clean the closet, but now instead of having two of you to clean it once every three weeks, I will make yous clean it every Monday morning," to which I answered, "All right, Governor." But at the same time I was nursing a determination to refuse point plank to do such work when Monday morning came. I told my companions I would refuse, and some of them remonstrated with me. Mr. Luby observed that obedience and subordination were more than anything else in accord with the dignity of the cause of our imprisonment, and in this I agreed with him. John Mitchell submitted to the prison discipline, he said, and did his work like any other convict, but I could never realize to my mind John Mitchell's shoveling the dung out of a privy, and I know I never did it myself without wishing that the Prime Minister of England and the Secretary of State were within the reach of my shovel. There was no satisfaction to me in hurling my indignation at an humble underling of a warder. John O'Leary's argument at length persuaded me to go back of my determination, and it harmonized most with my own feelings. It was, that some four or six of our party had cleaned the closet before me, and my refusing to do it would look as a reflection on their spirit or a presumption of my own superiority.

I wished I had been away from the party, and in a position where I could pursue the bent of my own inclinations without the risk of hurting the feelings of any one I cared about, but I had to take the world as it came, and when Monday came had to clean the privy. I did it, cursing under my teeth, and two years afterwards the memory of this indignity came on strongly, with that of others, to urge me to commit the very undignified act of throwing the water from my slop-pail through the bars of my prison chamber right into the face of the Governor of Chatham Prison when he stood outside the door calling on me to give him a salute, at the very same time that he was starving me on bread and water.

If corroboration be needed of our being obliged to do this dirty work, it is to be found in page 58 of the report of the Commissioners of Inquiry. Mr. Clifton, the Governor of Portland Prison, is under examination, and here are a few questions and answers as given in the book:

" You tell off a certain number of prisoners as orderlies?"
" Yes."
" What have they to do?"
" Clean the privies; carry water inside and put it at the prisoners' doors; clean and wash the steps leading from the landings."
" Are they expected to clean the privies?"
" They take it by turns and wash them out."
" How are the privies in the works outside cleaned?"
" Once a week two prisoners belonging to the party empty them at a spot where the manure is subsequently carted by a contractor."

So much for this part of the degradation. Now let me return to that degradation which was ordered for Michael Moore and me for speaking in our cells.

When we returned from labor that evening our jackets were returned to us, and we found that the regular badges had been torn off the sleeves and others put on, which branded us as refractory. I forget now what was the degrading color of the badge, but I know that Mike's and mine were different from all the others. We were mangy sheep, and we should lead three months of the most regular life before we could get rid of our scabs. The partitions between our cells were made of corrugated iron, and in the one between Michael Moore and me there was a slit alongside the wall through which you might pass a silver shilling. We occasionally had a whisper through this, and the spy outside our window must have heard us through the ventilator on the occasion for which we were degraded and fined eighty four marks each, which is equivalent to fourteen days' imprisonment, and I will explain how. When a convict is sentenced to a term of imprisonment, every day of the term is put down against him as six marks. He is then told that if he is obedient and works hard he can earn eight marks a day. Thus, if his term of imprisonment be twenty days, he can work out his 120 marks in fifteen days. But he may be working fourteen days, and earning eight marks a day, and his officer may report him for looking at another prisoner, or for some imaginary offence, when he is fined as many marks as will put him back to his original sentence. I had a few words with the Governor of Portland one day about these same marks. I was then about ten months under his guardianship, and being before him for punishment, he wound up somewhat as follows:

"I have been looking over your many punishments and your very bad character on the books, and with the number of days on bread and water, I see you have been fined three thousand two hundred and eighty-five marks, which is adding eighteen months to your imprisonment."

"What, Governor," cried I, "do you really mean to tell me that you are going to keep me a year and a half in prison without burying me after I'm dead?"

"What does he mean?" (addressing the officers.) Putting their hands to their heads, they all answered, "Don't know, sir."

"I mean that I am transported for life, and how can eighteen months be added to that?"

"Well, if you don't care about earning your remission, if you don't care about your wife and your children, I can't help you. Take him away." And away I was taken to the abode of "bread and water." A fortnight after we got permission to speak, and to speak loud, the Governor stood over us on the railroad track, and, in our presence, brought the officers to account for permitting us to talk so high, and then the annoyance commenced in earnest. If we talked low we subjected ourselves to reproof and threatened report, and so worried was I at length that on Gunning checking me one day I said to him: "See, officer, I have had warning, and threats, and admonitions enough from you. I know the rules and regulations, you know them too, and when you see me infringe them just report me to the Governor, let him punish me, but let you keep your tongue off me." Next day I was reported, and got my first dose of twenty-four hours' "bread and water," that is eight ounces of bread at half-past five in the morning, with a pint of water; and eight ounces at half-past five in the evening, with the pint of water. No dinner, no bed at night, no open-air exercise by day, no stool or other seat in your cell; all solitary confinement, and this is what, in prison parlance, is called "bread and water."

The first step on the road to misfortune, like the first in sin, is seldom retraced, and my first dose on "bread and water" soon brought others after it. "We'll tame you as we tame lions in England," is a common expression of jailers to their sulky captives. When I saw this starvation process resorted to in my case, my whole nature arose in arms, and I felt that even against *prison* government I could be a rebel too. It was measuring me by the same rule as that by which they measured their thieves and pickpockets; and though we were wearing the same jackets, I had inside of mine some kind of Irish pride which made me wish to have the authorities learn they were mistaken in supposing that the application of this rule to Irish revolutionists was to have the same effect upon them as upon the garrotters and Sodomites of England.

Again and again was I reported for speaking too loud while at work, and bread and water followed each report, till at length orders came that we were not to speak high or low. Warder Gunning having read these orders to us one morning in the quarry, I asked him how long they were to last? and he told me I must not be impertinent. In an hour's time a courier from the prison came out to him and, after going back, we were informed that the order issued in the morning was relaxed to the extent that we were allowed to speak regarding our work. Every two men had hammers, and keebles, and sledges between them; one could ask the other for a tool, or ask help in lifting a stone, or anything necessary about the work. "Governor," I said, "can I say to my comrade, this work is rather hard?" and his reply was, "I have told you to-day before that you must not be insolent." By-and-by an officer called a "principal," who wears a gold band on his cap, came the rounds, and we saw Gunning summon O'Leary before him, then Luby was summoned; I came next. Gunning's charge was—"Mr. Warren, this convict, O'Donovan Rossa, has used gross insolence two times to-day before me; he is defying the rules and regulations and giving a bad example to all the party."

Rossa—"Mr. Gunning, will you please tell the Principal what I said and did to warrant your making such a charge?"

Gunning—"He asked me, sir, in a very insulting tone, how long would the order last that enforced silence, and he asked me if he could not say to another prisoner, that the work was hard."

Principal Warren—"Why, this is regular mutiny. You will have to give up your impudence and insolence to the officers of this prison or suffer for it."

Rossa—"Governor, I have no desire to be insolent or impudent to any officer; the prison rules do not allow me to be so, nor do they allow any officer to be insolent or impudent to me."

Principal—"Send him into the punishment cells."

Gunning—"Here, Mr. Blaney, take Rossa into the cells."

On I marched with Warder Blaney, but as at this time I was stripped to my shirt I was called back to put on my jacket and waistcoat, which were lying by my block. I was dressed and on the march again, when Warren told me to come back and stay at my work till dinner-time, when I could be reported after going in. Warren went away, and after he was gone I proceeded to tell what he had said to me to William Roantree, who was working near by. Gunning approached and said:

"Rossa, do you persist in defying the rules and regulations of this prison?"

Rossa—"That's an improper question, Governor."

Gunning—"Answer me, do you persist in defying the prison rules?"

Rossa—"The question is illegal, and I won't answer it."

Gunning—"Do you defy the prison authorities?"

Rossa—"You know your duty. If I am violating any rule report me to the Governor, but don't be trying to frighten the life out of me by screeching that way at me."

I worked till dinner-hour, but I got no dinner. I was reported for "showing a mutinous disposition," and got my blood a little cooled by getting hard bed and board for a few days. When I came to the quarries again I found some of my friends had been making provision for me. Patrick Barry had brought out a loaf of bread, and the difficulty was, how to have it passed to me, and how I could eat it? He ran danger in bringing it out, and I would run danger in taking it in; for, going out and coming in, every one of us was closely searched. At length Barry and I found ourselves together in the quarry. We seized an opportunity when Gunning's eyes were on some others of the party, and, presto! quick as a lightning flash the loaf changed hands. The next moment my hand was up as a signal to go to the closet, and the loaf wasn't seen since. But Pat Barry got into trouble that day himself. Blaney, the sub-officer, got talking to me. He was a smart little fellow, and was trying to worry me into an admission of saying something I didn't say. I was explaining, and Barry observing "that's just what Rossa said," Blaney immediately pounced upon him for interfering, reported him for insolence, and got him put on bread and water.

The petty tricks resorted to at this time to annoy us are beyond description. Gunning would come into my cell one day and instruct me to keep my spoon resting against my timber salt-cellar at about an angle of 45 degrees, and Donald Bane would come the next day and scold me for not having the spoon laid on the top of the salt-cellar. There was no use in my saying, "Governor, the other officer told me yesterday to keep it the other way." "Never mind what the other officer says; you're always to obey the last order;" and if I said another word there was a peremptory order of "Silence." This Donald Bane was a burly Scotchman, about six feet two, and proportionately stout. He spoke as roughly as he could, for the purpose of enforcing discipline, and, as I didn't like his growl, I thought I'd have a bit of fun with him occasionally. We were shaved every Wednesday and Saturday evening, Donald being the superintendent. In Pentonville the razor was never allowed into my own hand, as the barbering was always done by a warder; but here they were not so particular. Donald came about with half-a-dozen razors, gave one to the prisoner, who gave it back again when he had done, at which time the officer would inspect the face and neck to see if they were perfectly smooth. It was always a kind of torture to me to shave under my chin, and with the spirit

of human nature, I thought as I was scraping away one evening that there was no legitimate reason why I should be my own torturer. I didn't make a clean shave of it, and giving out my razor, Donald said, "Here, let me look at you, hold up your head," and as I obeyed orders he roared out, "What! do you call that shaving?"
"No; I call that holding up my head."
"Take that razor again, and go into your cell." I took the razor, went into my cell, shut the door, laid the razor upon the little table till Donald came round in a quarter of an hour's time. "Are you done with that razor?" "Yes, long ago." "Let me look at you now." "Here."
"What do you mean? Do you mean to tell me that you shaved yourself again since I gave you that razor last?"
"I don't mean to tell you any such thing."
"What did I give you the razor for?"
"I am sure I can't say; you told me take it and I obeyed orders."
"Here, now, take that razor again and shave your neck, or if you don't I'll make you do it."
"Oh, Governor! I shaved my neck as well as I could. It is always a torture to me to do that part of my shaving, and I can't do it any better."
"But you must do it."
"Oh! there is no use in my trying; if you don't consider I am shaven according to discipline, you are at perfect liberty to shave me in order."
"What! *me* shave you!"
"Yes; the officers in Pentonville shaved us regularly."
"Then I tell you that you'll get no officer to shave you here, and now take that razor again and have yourself properly cleaned when I call in ten minutes."
"I'll take the razor, Governor, but inasmuch as I have shaved as well as I could this evening, you may as well take it with you, unless you are prepared to carry out the prison discipline yourself."
He looked at me steadily for a moment or so and I looked at him; then ordering me to shut my door we parted for that evening, but next day he had me taken before the Governor on a charge of refusing to shave and giving gross insolence.
Governor—"What have you to say to the charge?"
"Nothing."
"Did you refuse to shave?"
"No; I did shave."
"Why didn't you shave your neck better?"
"I shaved it as well as I could. This shaving is one of the prison punishments. To me it is a kind of torture, and I don't like to see myself the agent of my own punishment. I believe if the regulations were properly carried out that a razor would never be allowed into the hands of a convict. I have shaved myself as well

as I could, and if you don't like how I enforce the discipline on myself I am willing to submit myself to a closer application of it at the hands of the officer."

Governor—"Cannot you fellows shave each other?"

"I cannot shave myself according to your liking, and I have never attempted to shave anyone else, nor can I do it." Bane got instructions to ask if there was any one in our party who could shave the others. Michael Moore and Pat Dunne consented to try, and after that I submitted myself to their manipulations.

"You, fellows," was not a very unusual expression with this Governor Clifton in addressing us, or, at least, in addressing me, and this studied insult, instead of making me feel my degradation, made me only feel more disposed to despise the meanness of the man.

When the orders came that we were not to speak on the works, Gunning had us to remove our blocks two yards further apart than they were previously, and, thinking I was too comfortably situated with Hugh Brophy, he took me away from the quarrying and placed me in an isolated position, with Cornelius Manus O'Keeffe and Thomas Clarke Luby, at the other two corners of our triangle. O'Keeffe was just after being sent to Portland; he had as great a desire for talking as any one else, and would often try to reach me by a whisper. I could not hear, and I occasionally alarmed him by asking, in an ordinary tone of voice, what he was saying, or trying to say. This brought Gunning's attention upon me, and it was then he used to demand if I persisted in defying the rules and regulations. O'Keeffe was a good Irish scholar, and I tried to draw him out by giving him a word of Gaelic, which was high treason to the jailers. They prohibited us from speaking in our mother tongue even on the days when we were allowed to talk. They called it "slang." I believe it was Thomas Duggan, of Ballancollig, that was severely reprimanded once for speaking Irish, and threatened with severe punishment if he repeated the offence.

But if their ire was raised at our speaking what they could not understand, their wit was aroused occasionally at our Irish names. "Regan," cried Gunning one day, as he wanted to challenge Michael O'Regan about something. Mike never raised his head, but kept picking away with his hammer till the officer, approaching, stood before his block demanding if he did not hear his name called? To which the prisoner answered "No." "Is not your name Regan?" "No; my name is O'Regan." "Oh! then I suppose I must make arrends for that?" said Gunning, walking away about ten paces, and, turning round, he called "O'-O'Regan," and told Mike whenever he forgot the "O" in future to remind him, and he'd put it on on the double the next time. About the time I speak of Charles Kickham was in a very infirm state of health. Five days after he came to the prison he was sent to the hospital. Two weeks afterwards he was sent to the quarries in a very weak condition with running sores on his neck; he was so weak he could hardly stand. I believe I have stated previously that as he leaned against a ledge of rock, while I was dressing a large stone for him, Gunning seized him by the shoulder and made him stand up straight, telling him he should not rest that way during hours of labor. But I am going to speak of something now regarding him that stirred my own blood a little. We were coming from dinner and had to march to the quarry with military step. One officer was walking by the side of the front men and another by the side of the rear. I was behind Kickham, and I did not know where I was till I saw Gunning rush at him, and giving him a shove, staggered him four or five paces out of the ranks. He then laid hold of him and dragged him to the rear. The reason of all this was, I suppose, that Kickham was not keeping the step, and Gunning wanted to arrange matters without calling a "halt." Charles Kickham was taken to the hospital again after a few weeks, and that was the last I saw of him.

There was a shed convenient to the place where we worked, and when it rained hard we were taken there for shelter till the shower was over. All the gangs have similar sheds, and the large bell of the prison rang us a notice to make for shelter whenever the rain was considered too heavy. Hearing the bell one day, and all of us being anxiously waiting for it, as we were wet through, we made for the shed, and the officer ordered us back to our blocks again. He kept us there for over ten minutes; then he gave the order "Break off," and when we were in the shed he said no matter for what reason the bell rang we were never to leave our work until we got orders from him. He himself had oil-clothes on, and we wore our thin suit of convict grey.

William F. Roantree was one of the second next men to me in the quarry, and he was in a very precarious state of health for some time. He put his hand into his boot one day, and when he drew it out it was full of blood; not spotted with it, but as he slanted the palm of his hand the blood streamed off. Afflicted with hemorrhoids, he was in this state for three months before he was allowed to rest in the hospital. He was then declared invalided, and removed to the invalid station at Woking.

Martin Hanly Carey was sledging another day, and as he was drawing the stroke the iron flew off the handle of the sledge. Carey knocked his hand against the rock and broke one of his fingers. He was taken to the hospital. The doctor wanted to amputate his finger, but Carey would not allow him, in consequence of which the doctor would not allow him to remain in the hospital. Martin Hanly was sent out to work the next day with his hand in a sling. He was seated on a heap of stones in a corner of the field, a hammer was given to him, and he was kept there breaking stones day after day for six weeks before he could use the injured hand.

When Carey wanted a barrow of large stones I waited on him for the first two or three days, but the officers seeing that I took advantage of this for the purpose of having a whisper, I was forbidden to approach him in future, and some one else was commissioned to keep the invalid supplied with work. Carey, one of these days, overheard the Governor telling the warder to report some of us for idleness, and next day we were taken before this impartial judge to be sentenced to our several terms of bread and water.

Occasionally there seemed to be a necessity for punishing us to show that the rules were administered with rigor, and the discipline vigorously carried out. Every adverse wind that blew from Ireland brought us a kick or a bark, or deprived us of a bit of our daily bread. Possibly, too, that some English philanthropists were saying we were treated with milk-and-honey kindness, and that, consequently, it was no wonder sedition was rife in Ireland as there were no terrors for the rebels.

All my punishments hitherto had been for talking, but when I was brought up for idleness the Governor read me a lecture, and said "there were educated gentlemen working in the next quarries to me who dressed seven stones a day, whereas we dressed but one or two each. These men he spoke of were brought up gentlemen, and never did a day's work till they came to prison; I should learn to work as well as they did, or, if I didn't, should take the consequences. The discipline of the prison should be maintained."

"Governor," said I, "as you cannot put me in the category of your English educated gentlemen, you must excuse me for not entering into competition with them in the amount of convict labor to be done." I got my dose of bread and water, and when it was taken I came to the quarry with a resolution which no one could understand but myself, and which I did not care to explain to any one.

I went to my block, took my pick in hand, and hammered away for the dear life at my stone. In less than an hour I had it finished. I took another and dressed it in about the same time, and as I was at the third I saw some of the boys look at me now and again to see what was the matter. One of the prisoners helped another in taking the dressed stone to the pile, and in going from that to the quarry for a rough one. The passage way was a path through the party of workers, and going for my fourth stone one would whisper as I was passing him by, "Rossa, are you mad?" another, "are you crazy?" another, "what the devil ails you?" To all of which I never spoke a word, but smiled, till I was passing John O'Leary, who never minced matters, but always came out with what he thought suitable, and when he said "Mr. O'Donovan, that is a very poor way of showing your vanity," I replied, "I agree with you, Mr. O'Leary; but you must agree with me that we are in a very poor place." Gunning roared out, "Stop that talking there." I hurried with my fourth stone to my block, and hurried to have it dressed as soon as possible. Our average work every day was about a stone and a half, or two, and when Gunning saw that I was likely to break this average, he seemed to be getting into good humor. Approaching me, he said, smilingly, "Rossa, you're getting on well to-day."

"Yes, Mr. Gunning; I want to show myself a gentleman convict."

"Oh, I see you remember what the Governor said to you."

"Yes, Mr. Gunning; I want to show the Governor that I can do as much work any day as one of his English gentlemen."

"Hallo! what's that I see there?" (pointing to a large hole in the hip of my trousers, for I had placed the handle of the pick against my side while working, in order to lessen the weight of it while in my hands, and the friction or action of the tool tore a large hole in my pants.)

"Oh! that's from hard work, Mr. Gunning."

"But you must work without tearing your clothes; you must not allow the handle of the pick to rest that way on your hip."

"If I tore the flesh off my bones, Mr. Gunning, I mean to show the Governor that I can do as much work as any of his English gentlemen he has here."

"Now, you'd better stop that or I'll have to report you."

"You may report me or do anything you please, but I'm determined to work away as hard as I can till I have the seven stones dressed." And dressed they were before the day ended.

Coming out from dinner the next time, we were halted in front of the Governor's office and ordered to dress up in lines. He came out and read for us a letter from the Board of Directors giving him permission to allow us to write oftener than the other prisoners if we kept ourselves free of reports; but inasmuch as the reporting was in his hands and the hands of his officers, the privilege availed us but little. If I wanted to write I should, to entitle me to consideration, be two months without a report, and I was never allowed to have such a clear record as that. Two weeks afterwards we were halted in the same place and another letter was read revoking the last one, and stating that we were to be treated as ordinary convicts. After the letter was read the first day Gunning drew the Governor's attention to the hole in my trousers. "Hard work, Governor," I said. "But you must not work with your pick this way," said he, placing his cane on his hip, and moving it with both hands as if he was striking at a stone. Then he gave the officer instructions to report me if he saw me doing it again, and we got our marching orders to the quarry.

I quieted down to my average labor of a stone and a half, and Gunning noticing this, brought me to account. I asked him, "Did he want me to tear my trousers again." He said "he did not, but now that I had shown I could work I should work." "I have shown," I said, "that an Irishman in any position in life can do as much as an Englishman, and that is all I care to show, or care to do here." "Come on with me, then," and on I went till we stood opposite the heap of nobblers. "Where are the seven stones you dressed yesterday?" "Here is one, and here is one, and here is another," and so on till I pointed out the seven to him. "Now, take every one of them and pile them up in front of your block, place three in a line first, put two on them, and put the other two on top." I obeyed orders, and by-and-by I had my pile before me. The boys christened it "Rossa's folly," but I met their jokes by appealing to Gunning to use his authority to make them look upon it as a monument to my industry. I could hardly restrain my laughter at the serious way he would take applications of this kind from me. I pretended to be in earnest, and it was amusing to see the look he'd give when I'd ask him to prevent Pat Dunne and Tom Duggan from laughing at my monument whenever they passed it. "It was hard enough to be threatened with bread and water for doing so much work one day, but to be laughed at by my comrades was a thing I could not stand, and I would take the first opportunity I could get of running away from the prison." "What! —what!—what's that you said, Rossa? running away from the prison, is it? Don't you know that's mutiny?" "Mutiny or no mutiny, Governor, I wish I could see a chance of getting off; I don't like to be here at all."

Some of my friends would gravely bring me to account for joking on such a serious state of affairs as ours; it did not comport with the dignity of our position to trifle with it or look upon it lightly. One would occasionally remark that convict life seemed quite agreeable to my nature, and I suppose my nature must be kind to me, as it moulds my head to rest lightly upon whatever pillow the vicissitudes of fortune place under it. I felt the pains and penalties of convict life as much as many of my companions, but I would not give my enemies the satisfaction to see that I did feel them; and it gave me pleasure to see how disappointed and enraged they were at my smiling and joking at punishments which they know bring a man to the verge of the grave, and in the grave I would be to-day, perhaps, had I carried myself through the torturing annoyances of prison with that gravity which is consonant with dignity and a life of death. There is no better way of frightening away a fairy than to laugh at it. The man or the woman who can do that in presence of a *Leanawn Shee* or a ghoul will never be possessed by either.

> "Let me play the fool with mirth and laughter,
> So let wrinkles come—
> And let my visage rather heat with wine,
> Than my heart cool with mortifying groans."

We had not much wine in our time to heat us, but it was better to try and get the blood do what it could in that line than to be groaning or croaking where there was no one to pity us.

A day or two after the monument of my industry was raised I was in the quarry looking for a stone.

"Here," said Gunning, "take that"—pointing to a large round one about two hundred pounds weight. Hugh Brophy lifted the barrow with me, and as he ascended a step of the quarry the block rolled back upon me and threw me down. I escaped with getting a cut hand, and as I was dressing the wound, the jailer cried:

"Come, Rossa, you're loitering too long about that pin scratch. Catch hold of that barrow again, and take your stone to the block."

"Rossa won't do any such thing, governor; he is not bound to work beyond his strength, and that stone is too heavy for him. Your starvation diet doesn't leave a man much strength."

James Flood came to remove the stone with Brophy, and as they moved off, I walking alongside of them, Gunning again cried:

"Rossa, you're a man that would suck another man's blood."

"I don't believe a word of it; but you yourself look like one who'd do it. I don't think you're warranted in using such language to me in the discharge of your duty, and I'll go to the Governor to-morrow to ask if you are."

To-morrow came, and instead of my having a charge against Gunning, he had a charge against me for idleness, and I had some days on bread and water before I came out again. When I was before the Governor I told him I had a charge against the officer, and he told me I could make no charge while I was under report. It was a week before I could get clear enough to tell Mr. Clifton what Gunning said to me, and then the satisfaction I got was to have the Governor tell me, "I was not to be too sensitive." "Nothing could make me more degraded than I was," and "Did we think the officers were to take off their caps to us." "I think it is quite improper to have such language used towards prisoners," I replied. "You have no right to think here," added he, "you are a convict and must have no will of your own." "Bah!" said I, with as much contempt as I could put into a look, and the signal was given to have me off to "chokey," the convict's name for his place of purgatory.

When Director Fagan came to the prison I went before him, and told him what the Governor said and what Gunning said to me, and both officer and master denied that they had ever said what I have stated. Next day Gunning was removed from the charge of our party and a new officer put in his place.

The first day I met this Mr. Fagan in Portland I had not the least idea he was an Irishman. I didn't even know his name, and whatever I had to see him about I said in the course of conversation, "Governor, if in bringing us from Ireland to England the Government contemplate effecting a change in us, they ought to know that it is not by starvation an Irishman can be changed into an Englishman." I don't know what he said at the time, but when I learned he was an Irishman I thought he should think my words were meant to insult him unprovokedly, and nine months afterwards I told him I understood he was an Irishman, that I did not know it when I met him at first, and if I did I would not make use of some observations he heard from me regarding Englishmen and Irishmen. He told me he did not remember I said anything offensive, and I replied it might look so if I knew he was an Irishman. I was this time under punishment for refusing to pick oakum. He asked why I was not doing my work, and I asked him why I was not getting my food. "But you're under punishment." "That's the very reason that I consider it wrong to ask me to work," I replied; and then asking if he could hear a charge against the Governor for defaming my character, he said he could not, as I was under report, and, turning away from my cell, the door was closed.

It was not much relief to anyone to lose Gunning but to me. Russell came in his place, and though he was not so insolent, he was every bit as well able to worry us. It was he, who, when the rain-bell rang to have us go into the shed for shelter ordered us back again until the orders came from his tongue, and kept us under the shower until we were wet through. However, my nose was not so much kept to the grinding-stone as under Gunning, and I removed "Rossa's folly" to the general pile without Russell's asking me to leave the monument stand. Then I could help this man or that man to bring a stone from the quarry which I could not do with Gunning, as he had detailed one to travel with me, and I had no chance of a word with anyone else. In one of these recreative hours when I used to be holding a chisel while another was hammering at it to split a rock, I fell in with Michael O'Regan, and he commenced telling me his woes. The burden of them was that Father Zanetti would not give him absolution, that Father Poole would not give it either unless he gave up the organization, and as he meant to stick to Ireland it was too bad that he could not go to his duty for seven years. This fidelity to Ireland and the old faith at the same time must have touched some sentimental chord of mind. An Irish peasant, speaking of something he feels bitterly, can put more pathos into a simple story than some of the greatest orators can, and Mike's account of what he was suffering from the English priests putting his duty to his country in opposition to his faith, affected me so much that I threw the chisel out my hand and walked away from him towards my block. It was the second time that I got soft in prison, and from the same train of thought.

Michael O'Regan came to Ireland in '64, on a message from John O'Mahony, and remained in expectation of the fight. He went to the southern coast of Ireland, where he was born, and commenced bringing the men together. He was arrested and sentenced to seven years' penal servitude on a charge of swearing in some navy men, in Castletownsend, who belonged to Queen Victoria's revenue cruiser. His brother, Patrick, came to Ireland a few years before, but finding that things were not ready for a fight, went back to

America and died. Mike and Pat told the mother one day in New York that they would go to Ireland to help the boys there and leave their youngest brother, John, at home to take care of her. "No," said she, "I was able to take care of myself long before ye were any help to me. I am strong enough still to do so, and John must go too, for he will do more good helping ye than helping me."

CHAPTER XI.

VISITS—DEMANDS FOR VISITORS' EXPENSES—DEVILS—MY WIFE AND CHILD IN PRISON—MY MEMORANDUM BOOK—MY WIFE'S POEMS—MY LETTER—FEAR OF PUBLICITY—COMPROMISE WITH THE GOVERNOR—MY LOVE LETTERS ON A SLATE—DETERMINATION TO WRITE SURREPTITIOUS LETTERS—CONVICT LYNCH—HIS GIFT OF PEN, INK, AND PAPER—"CONSPIRACY" TO BREAK PRISON—MICHAEL MOORE'S FAILURE—HUGH BROPHY'S FAILURE—MYSELF A HYPOCRITE—LYNCH DETECTED IN CARRYING MY LETTER—PUNISHMENT OF HIM AND ME—TRY AGAIN—MY AMOUR IN PRISON—BRINGS BREAD AND WATER, AND ENDLESS PUNISHMENTS ON ME—JERRY O'DONOVAN, OF BLARNEY—REV. MR. ZANETTI—THE DEVIL—IRELAND'S SOGGARTH AROON—ZANETTI GIVING EVIDENCE BEFORE THE COMMISSION—THE EVIL EYE—A PETITION ON "THINK WELL OF IT," AND WHAT CAME OF IT—WRITING IN THE DARK—CAT'S EYES—MY MEMORIAL TO THE SECRETARY OF STATE.

Visits from our friends to us were something which the authorities availed themselves of for the purpose of giving us much annoyance. Every convict is allowed one every six months, but if the officers choose to have him on their books as ill-conducted he may never be allowed to see the face of a friend from the outside world. My wife had been writing from Ireland to know if she would be permitted to see me, and the Governor told me one day that as a favor to her, not to me, he was going to grant her permission to come. I told this to my friends, and we thought it would be well if some others availed of her coming for the purpose of having their visit from her, in order that we might glean as much news as we could. Martin Hanley Carey saw the Governor on the subject, and told him the only friend he cared to see was his mother, but as she was old, and could not come to Portland without much inconvenience and expense, he would be obliged if the "visit" which the rules allowed him was granted by allowing him to see Mrs. O'Donovan. She could convey to his mother, who lived in Eyrecourt, County Galway, anything he had to say. The Governor said he would consult the Directors, and in a few days after Carey was sent for, and told that the authorities would not allow him to see my wife. I had given some trouble about these visits some time before, for I had applied to the Governor to know if the expenses of our friends would be paid when they came to see us. "Certainly not," said the Governor, "why should you expect such?" "I don't expect it at all," I said. "Then why do you ask?" "Because I desire to learn how justly the Government mean to act by us. If they left us in Ireland where we were convicted our friends could see us without much expense or inconvenience: they adopt an extraordinary course in bringing us to England; and it is only fair and just that they should pay the expenses of our visitors from Ireland and back again."

"The Government can do what they please with you."

"I know they can! But when ordinary prisoners are convicted in Ireland they are not brought to England; we should have the benefit of the convict law as it stands in Ireland, and if the Government cannot afford to keep us there, where our friends could easily see us when the regular visits were due, they ought to pay their expenses to England as they paid ours."

"The Government are treating you too kindly and considerately. Twenty years ago you'd have been hanged."

"It might be better we were hanged, and certainly it was through no merciful consideration for us that we were not. No political prisoners have ever been treated in any country as we are treated by the English."

"You are treated too well; you have put back the prosperity of Ireland twenty years; thousands of moneyed people have fled from it, and you don't know what ruin you have brought on the country."

Here I laughed outright, and asked him if he would not, as a matter of justice, place my application before the authorities. He said he would, and sent for me in a few days to tell me the Directors had refused to pay the expenses of our visitors from Ireland.

These kind of things varied the monotony of my prison life, and afforded me amusement, too. Any of my friends did not know but that I was serious in this matter of applying for the expenses, and when I would say I was in high hopes of having them granted, and what a grand thing it would be to be putting the Government to the cost of four or five hundred pounds a-year for bringing over all our friends, some of the party would say that they, for their part, would not take a penny of the money, and that they would go to the Governor right off and tell him so. To this I'd reply there was no necessity to be in a hurry in the matter; they could have patience until they'd see how my application would succeed, and they should understand I did not make it for any one but myself, and for my part the more expense I could put the Government to the more I liked it. Many fell in with this view, but the "dignity," "honor," or "humor" involved in the question was very soon decided by the announcement of the refusal.

I was sent for to the Deputy's office one evening to put the name and address of my wife on the visiting ticket. As I was writing an officer came in and reported that a certain prisoner had been very idle all day, and asked what would be done with him. The Principal looked towards me and said, "If a man will not work, neither let him eat;" but, added he, looking at the officer, "as he has a good character give him another chance, and don't put him under report this time." There was no punishment, no torture inflicted on a prisoner that these officers could not back with a quotation from the Bible. "The Devil can quote Scripture for his purpose," and if devils do really "go about like roaring lions seeking whom they may devour," I had the honor of seeing some of them in English prisons, not in the lowest grade of office either, but like the old fellow himself, high in authority.

For days and weeks after sending the ticket I was expecting the visit, and at the end of a month I had nearly given it up, when one day while I was at dinner my door was opened, and I was told, "Come on." "Where now?" I asked. "Ask no questions," said the officer, "but come on." I was taken to the door of the room where I was examined the first day, and as I entered I saw my wife, and in her arms the baby I never saw before.

I hesitated before approaching her, because I heard that in the visiting places there were panels or partitions between the parties. Discipline was so much in my mind that I stood there till she or I would go behind a separating barrier; or perhaps I had pride enough to keep me from making an advance that they had in their power to repel. The officer who was standing by her side said, "You can come up here and speak to your wife for twenty minutes, but if you tell her anything relating to matters inside the prison, or if she tells you anything relating to outside matters, I must end the visit. I sat down and took the baby in my lap, but the little fellow did not seem to know me, though he was then three months old. Indeed, I think his mother hardly knew me. It was the first time she saw me since I was shorn, shaved, and dressed in convict fashion. She felt my hands, which were as rough as oyster-shells, and my face had been baked to the color of an earthenware crock. For the first few minutes I kept talking to the son all the time, thinking what in the world could I say to the mother, and I think we parted without saying much. There was the jailer right beside us, and my tongue was paralyzed. At the end of twenty minutes Mr. Bulwer, the Deputy Governor, entered, and said in consideration of my never seeing the child before he would extend the time ten minutes longer. I had messages from William Roantree, James O'Connor, Denis Mulcahy, and several others, but when I attempted to say anything of any other prisoner I was told I should confine myself to my own case. As we were parting I recollected I had a few notes scratched on a bit of slate in my pocket, and as I took it out the officer seized it. The wife vanished, and I went to work with a heavier heart than ever. I had a load on it I could not unburthen, and I felt it weighing me down.

Not many days elapsed before I got into a scrape with the Governor. He told me he was away from home the day my wife came, and if he was in the prison he would not allow her to see me in consequence of my bad conduct, and the Deputy-Governor trespassed too much upon his discretionary power in allowing me to see her in the reception-room instead of in the ordinary-place. I told him he need not feel very much discomforted on account of any happiness or consolation my wife's visit brought me, and I was very sorry if Captain Bulwer's kindness subjected him to any reproof. The Deputy was one of the most gentlemanly of the officers that I met in prison. I never spoke two words to him, he always did his duty, but in doing it he never gave that haughty, contemptuous look that others would give, and never wantonly wounded our feelings by any impudent remarks. I suppose if he is still in authority it will not serve him to have me say this, but I must speak the truth of all I came across in my prison life. The schoolmasters of Portland Prison were also gentlemanly in the discharge of their duty. The mistake made by those who charge themselves with the reformation of convicts is to give them in charge to brutes, instead of to men with human or humane feelings.

A kind word or a wanton insult to the biggest criminal will have much the same effect on him as on us in penal servitude. The opinion seems to prevail with English jailers that kind words are thrown away upon their prisoners, and the only way to keep them up to the discipline is to lash and abuse them into it. I found these tactics resorted to in our case, and if for nothing else but to show they would fail, and that we had something in us better than the thieves and murderers they classed us with, I determined that there was one man who would go to his grave before he gave them the satisfaction of seeing they could lash him into submission by insult, chains, and bread and water.

As I have not said much about the visit of my wife, and as there is very little poetry in this narrative of mine, let me be pardoned for giving a little of her description of meeting me in Portland. I should wish she had written more flatteringly of me, but I suppose she does not consider me so ugly now.

A Visit to my Husband in Prison.
May, 1866.

Within the precincts of the prison bounds,
  Treading the sunlit courtyard to a hall,
Roomy and unadorned, where the light
  Thro' screenless windows glaringly did fall.

Within the precincts of the prison walls,
  With rushing memories and bated breath;
With heart elate and light swift step that smote
  Faint echoes in this house of living death.

Midway I stood in bright expectancy,
  Tightly I clasped my babe, my eager sight
Restlessly glancing down the long, low room
  To where a door bedimmed the walls' pure white.

They turned—the noiseless locks; the portal fell
  With clank of chain wide open, and the room
Held him—my wedded love. My heart stood still
  With sudden shock, with sudden sense of doom.

My heart stood still that had with gladsome bound
  Counted the moments ere he should appear—
Drew back at sight so changed, and shivering waited,
  Pulselessly waited while his steps drew near!

Oh! for a moment's twilight that might hide
  The harsh tanned features once so soft and fair!
The shrunken eyes that with a feeble flash
  Smiled on my presence and his infant's there!

Oh! for a shadow on the cruel sun
  That mocked thy father, Baby, with his glare;
Oh! for the night of nothingness or death
  Ere thou, my love, this felon garb should wear!

It needed not these passionate, pain-wrung words,
  Falling with sad distinctness from thy lips,
To tell a tale of insult, abject toil,
  And day-long labor hewing Portland steeps!

It needed not, my love, this anguished glance,
  This fading fire within thy gentle eyes,
To rouse the torpid voices of my heart,
  Till all the sleeping heavens shall hear their cries.

God of the wronged, and can Thy vengeance sleep?
  And shall our night of anguish know no day?
And can Thy justice leave our souls to weep
  Yet, and yet longer o'er our land's decay!

Must we still cry—"How long, O Lord, how long?"
  For seven red centuries a country's woe
Has wept the prayer in tears of blood, and still
  Our tears to-night for fresher victims flow!

And flow it seems they must for still fresher victims again, befo e the soil is watered enough to produce a race of men able to strike the tyrant down.

When my wife reached home she sent me a photograph of herself and baby, and a few days after its arrival in the prison the governor sent for me and said he should return it again. I observed it was a very harmless thing to allow me to keep; but, no, it would not be allowed, the prison rules did not permit it, the discipline should be maintained, and my photograph returned. "However," added he, "as you seem to be improving in your conduct lately I'll allow you to look at the picture before I return it." I took it out of his hand, and taking the look, gave it back to him. I afterwards learned that the thieves were allowed photographs, but, then, these were thieves of good character, and unfortunately for me I was in bad repute.

I find in my wife's book of poems, one on the return of the photograph to her, and I will give that, too, a place in my Prison Life.

"THE RETURNED PICTURE.

"[In 1863, while my husband was confined in Portland Convict Establishment, I sent to him a likeness of mine and baby's, taken specially for him, as he had never seen the child, its birth occurring after his conviction and sentence. The following week I was returned the carte, with a polite note from the Prison Governor, to inform me that "Prison rules did not allow convicts the possession of likenesses."]

> Refused admission! Baby, Baby,
> Don't you feel a little pain?
> See, your picture with your mother's,
> From the prison back again?
> They are cruel, cruel jailers—
> They are heartless, heartless men!
>
> Ah! you laugh my little Flax Hair!
> But my eyes are full of tears;
> And my heart is sorely troubled
> With old voices in my ears;
> With the lingering disappointment
> That is shadowing my years!
>
> Was it much to ask them, Baby—
> These rough menials of the Queen?
> Was it much to ask them, give him
> This poor picture, form and mien
> Of the wife he loved, the little son
> He never yet had seen?
>
> Ah! they're cruel, cruel jailers,
> They are heartless, heartless men!
> To bar the last poor comfort from
> Your father's prison pen;
> To shut our picture from the gates
> And send it home again!

Cruel, cruel jailers, and heartless, heartless men are they truly without question, and especially so when their captives are Irishmen who would rid their country of English rule.

Time passed on, and the day came around again when I was allowed to write a letter. This, of course, was written to my wife. I had a mother in America, and I was anxious to send her a line, but these humane English would not, for any consideration at this time, extend to me the privilege of an extra letter. They would not even give me a scrap of paper on which I would write a few lines to enclose in my wife's to the old woman on the brink of the grave. I made a special application for it to the Governor, and he refused me.

My letter was written; it had been given in a few days; the Governor sent for me, and when I was regularly placed in the "stand-to-attention" attitude before him, he said—

"You will not cease complaining; what is the use of your writing these letters? You know I cannot send them out."

"Governor, have you read my letter? I think you must be mistaken. I have certainly uttered no word of complaint, and I don't think I have infringed on any of the rules in anything I have said in that letter."

"I haven't read it; I couldn't read it, the writing is so small. Your letters take up more of my time than all the other prisoners', and you have written between the lines, which is a thing specially forbidden by the instructions."

"Well, that is a thing you might excuse me for, seeing that I have only one leaf of paper, and having such a large family, and so much to say; I can read that letter in five minutes for you, and if you notice anything objectionable in it, as I go on, I will scratch it out."

"Here, then, read it."

I commenced reading, and I ended reading without his objecting to anything, and, as I finished, I said—

"Now, Governor, you see that there is nothing objectionable in it."

"There is no use, I can't allow that letter to be published."

"Published!" cried I in amazement. "Why, Governor, sure the letter is for my wife."

"Oh, but your wife publishes your letters."

"Publish my private letters! you don't mean to tell me she does that?"

"I do, and more than that; when these people come visiting here they publish all they can learn about the prison, and bring a lot of trouble upon me."

"I am very sure that I would not write such a letter as that to my wife if I thought she would publish it, and I am sure she would not."

"Well, if you write on the head of that letter that it is private, and not to be published, I will pass it."

"Oh, certainly, Governor, that's what I will willingly do."

I got a pen and wrote the following words, which I copy from the original letter now before me :—

"Do not, love, make such letters as this public. I do not write for such a purpose. 'Tis rather delicate, this letter, too, as all my letters to you must needs be."

Then comes the printed instructions on the face of the paper in these words—

"Convict Establishment, Portland,
near Weymouth.

"Convicts are permitted to write and to receive letters and visits periodically according to the class which they may attain by good conduct, as follows, viz.: third class every six months; second class every four months, and first class every three months. All letters must be prepaid. Matters of private importance to a convict may be communicated at any time by letter (prepaid) to the Governor, who will inform the convict thereof if expedient.

"In case of any misconduct the above privileges may be forfeited for the time.

"All letters of an improper or idle tendency, either to or from convicts, or containing slang or other objectionable expressions, will be suppressed. The permission to write or receive letters is given to the convicts for the purpose of enabling them to keep up a connection with their respectable friends, and not that they may hear the news of the day. Inquiries will be made as to the character of persons with whom convicts correspond, and if the result is not satisfactory the correspondence will be stopped.

"All letters are read by the Governor or chaplain, and must be legally written, and not crossed.

"Neither clothes, money, nor any other articles are allowed to be received at the prison for the use of convicts, except though the Governor. Persons attempting otherwise to introduce any article to or for a convict are liable to fine or imprisonment, and the convict is liable to be severely punished.

"Neither money nor stamps must be inclosed, as they will not be received.

"No visits allowed on Sundays.

"The convict's writing to be confined to the ruled lines of these two pages. In writing to the convict direct to No. 5364."

The 5364 is in writing. Then there is, with several other brands, the autograph of "George Clifton," without which the letter could not pass out of prison; and, finally, here is the letter itself, which you may have the curiosity to read in order to see what kind of a thing a convict's letter is :—

"August 26, 1866.

"MY LOVE— I am in doubt whether it is better to scold you, or to coax you into sending me what I desire from you at present, and what I have been disappointed in getting. Scolding might be the best if you were as much afraid of my voice now as before, but as possibly you would place the proper value on my growling at you from my cage, I had better give it up and see what I can do the other way. Then, as it was partly by scolding I came into the happy possession of you (unhappily for you now), I would like to continue it, but, perhaps, you are a much wiser and sadder woman than you were two years ago, and not so easily frightened. I will *not* scold you, Mollis. I fear I am not a good hand at coaxing, so I will only ask you coldly, though lovingly ask you, to send me a very, very long, long, letter —six, ten, twenty sheets of paper, what to you! You often gave me so much when I was not in so much want. What matter if they must necessarily be sorrow-laden. I have accompanied you in sunny hours, and cannot I have your company when the rain is falling fast. No political news, all about yourself—how you met the world since, and particularly when you went to Carbery. Who were kind to you and who were cold to you, &c. Did the children realize their position? did they say anything of me? what happened you every day, hour, and minute? for in so much of your life am I interested. If you say you have nothing to write a long letter about, I say write about nothing and that will be something to me. What can I lose, or what can you if your letter be read by others? The governor of the prison must read it, but if it gives no political information or bright expectation, it might be deemed of little interest to any other authority. How many, many things I had to say which I forgot, and many more, as you heard the chief warder say, I would not be allowed to speak of, all too many in the short space of half-an-hour. When you left I felt I had relieved myself very little of my burthen, and then it grew heavier. A little punishment awaited me that day, and I thought I was being taken to receive it when you took me by surprise. I was—to give you a very vicious simile—stricken somehow as a bird is by the gaze of a serpent. *That's certainly more like scolding than coaxing.* Well, anyway, Mollis, I was only *fascinated* by you, exclusive of the baby. All you said and all I forgot to say came before me when you were gone. I did not ask about our fifth son. I must needs speak of him in the fifth person, lest the mention of his name might interfere with the tranmission of this. You know the record of it in my account book was used to my prejudice by the judge. Regarding the four eldest, it is not pleasant that your father has the keeping of them when he has plenty company of his own; but if my brothers or mother sent money for them I would rather they would remain with him for a while than be separated. I often applied for leave to write to my mother—she might die any day, and then I'd feel so sorry that she did die; perhaps thinking she was forgotten by me. I will go to the Governor to-morrow again, and if successful will enclose a note for her, also one for the children. You said some one was going to take one of them, and Miss O'Dowd, the lady of the curls, another. Ned strove to make you jealous one time by telling you I looked at those curls, because he is a jealous dog himself. I forgot to ask you about him, and if John had been ejected out of Coolavin, or if his brother Andy abandoned, as I advised him, the prosecution against Finn the agent. I am allowed to write now as a letter would be due to me if I remained the usual time in Pentonville. I might have had two visits there for my good conduct, which good conduct I was not good enough to have here. I had the misfortune to incur prison discipline punishment for the first time, twice the week of your visit. Such is tolerably supportable and preferable to punishment by harsh words. I often expressed a preference for it if I violated a rule, but never got it till then. It is the duty of an officer to speak to, and bring a prisoner to order, and the prisoner's duty to be silent or respectful; but if anything is said to which an officer cannot reply, he may end by saying—'You are insolent,' 'impertinent,' or worse. I offended and I got punished, which entails forfeiture of all privileges; but the Governor is pleased to restore them to me again, as he has changed the officers and considers I have got into a better disposition and do more work, He tells me he answers letters of inquiry from you as to my health; this, he need not have done—any kindness to you from any one, I think more of than anything regarding myself. You ought to keep a record of such things for me, that they may appear before me if I ever live again. You see that though my life is forfeited to the laws, I cannot banish 'hope, that parasite of woe.' As regards my general health, I believe it has been good save what I told you about my eyes. I had two fits. I conquered the first. I got it by my being deprived of flannels the 22d December. I shivered it off, together with any expectations I had of fair treatment. This day fortnight was foggy; I arose next morning with sore throat. I went to the doctor, he could not see what I felt, and I have been trying to get the better of a severe cold since; I think I'll succeed. Write yourself, and put one from each of the children with your own—their own handwriting and dictation that I may see them naturally. If money be contributed by Irishmen for the maintenance of the families of the men imprisoned I am not so proud as to feel any pain of mind that mine are to be so cared for, but I would fling a contribution in the face of anyone who would tender it as charity. You are one of the trustees of money now, and I refer to this as I am anxious that when you are withdrawing from such trusteeship, you will be able to have your accounts satisfactorily shown. Our enemies always make money a handle to hurl slander.

"The Governor says, as you had a visiting ticket from the State Secretary, you might try again. I would rather you would get liberty to write oftener. If you could get liberty for me to state all regarding my trial, 'twould be well. Our Catholics here are banned too; perhaps 'tis only reasonable that Irishmen should renounce the crimes for which they are made English convicts before they are allowed sacraments by Anglo-Roman priests. I asked to be allowed to absent myself from priest's services. Refused. You wrote a defensive letter after my trial; you used the word 'charity' for the fund; some were hurt. Do you write to Mrs. Keane and Mrs. Duggan, Ballincollig? You ought. Have you anyone to rock the cradle while you write?—Yours, love, ever fondly and faithfully,

"JER. O'DONOVAN ROSSA."

Some readers of this letter may wonder at my publishing that I applied for permission to absent myself from the priest's service. Indeed a few of my friends suggest that it may not be "prudent" to publish it; but I never care to act the hypocrite. I felt so indignant at finding those English priests persecuting our Catholics inside the prison walls, that I thought I would show them what I thought of their work.

I knew if I were allowed to absent myself from service the priest would call upon me for an explanation, and I would have an opportunity of giving him a bit of my mind. My application was refused. It stands on record on the books of the prison, and may be exhumed at some future day to show what a refractory character I was. It certainly would have been brought forward had I succumbed to the prison discipline, and had any question been raised about my ill-treatment at a coroner's inquest.

After three or four weeks I got a reply from my wife. She asked me some questions about monetary matters, and she wrote a special letter to the Governor asking him to allow me to answer them. He sent for me, and said he could not allow me write, but if I wrote the answers to the questions on a slate, and sent it to him, he would have them copied and sent off. I did so, and, on asking him a month afterwards if they were transmitted, "No," said he, "I could not be sending your love letters to your wife; besides, it would lessen your punishment." I went back to my cell, and determined that, right or wrong, by fair play or by foul, I would never stop until I found some means of reaching the world, and getting out an account of our treatment. I became very civil to the warders who had charge of our party, in the hope that I could get so far into their favor as to give me the appointment of going to the well for water, and going to the gravel pit for gravel, which those who were making the altar wanted to smoothen the table. I tried to make myself humorous, and to make myself everything that was necessary to my purpose, and I succeeded in the long run.

One of the warders accompanied me always to the well and to the gravel pit. These places were not within view of the Governor's window. Other warders would come there with other prisoners. The officials seemed as anxious to have a word with one another as the prisoners. They chatted away on their own subjects, and give me an opportunity of whispering what I wanted to *my* chums. I was promised writing material and conveyance for what I wrote, and I became the funniest fellow in the world to my warders.

Just at the same time we fell in at chapel with a good fellow named Lynch; he was a Francis street Dublin man, but sentenced in Bolton for seven years. He gave us writing material, and I went to work to break the law for the first time by writing a "surreptitious letter."

Lynch told us he could get this conveyed to the outer world for three pounds, and that out of the sum we could get ten shilings' worth of tobacco imported. It was such a novel thing to get tobacco here, and as some of my friends desired to have a taste of it, I gave the order for it, with an order on my wife for three pounds. But as I feared that letters addressed to "Mrs. O'Donovan Rossa" would be opened in the post office, I directed this one to the mother of Michael Moore, and on the cover of the envelope I wrote in very small writing the words "For Mrs. O'D." Michael Moore kept watch for me during the dinner hours while I wrote. He lay down on the floor of his cell, and under his door there was as much space as would enable him to see through the hall. Sometimes the slippered officer who kept watch outside would go upstairs to have his peep at those who were in the cells above us. That was my time for scribbling, but as Moore would see the jailer coming down he'd give me a signal and I'd stop.

I kept watch for Moore for many hours in a similar position, and while he was engaged in work far more dangerous than writing "surreptitious" letters. He was trying to break a hole in the wall of his cell large enough to admit him into the yard, through which hole he and I meditated an escape. Hugh Brophy and Martin Hanley Carey were in the two next cells, and if Mike found he was able to do his work, they were to operate about the place where the iron partition divided their cells, and the four of us were to fight our way. We did not intend any harm to man or mortal, but after we made our way into the yard we had agreed if any man came upon us before we had scaled the wall by the aid of sheets, &c., there was nothing for it but to throttle him into quietness in case we could not avoid his notice otherwise. Michael Moore stole —yes—the thief actually stole a small steel chisel out of our tool box on the works, and the thief was the more criminal inasmuch as he was the prisoner most trusted with the distribution and collection of the implements. I don't know where he hid the chisel when he was bringing it into his cell; but I know when he had it there he gave me the signal to lie down on the flags and keep my eye on the hall. I heard him scraping away for an hour, at the end of which time he gave another signal to get up, and then through the little slit that was in the partition he whispered to me that he thought the work would be all right; he had made a hole large enough already to hide the chisel; then he shut it up and plastered the surface with the whiting he had for brightening his tins. The color was very much like the whitewash on the walls, and no distinction could be discerned when standing at the door, as he had shaded the spot by the arrangement of some of his cell furniture. Brophy, Carey, I, and a few others supplied him with all the whiting we got, and day after day for a fortnight he worked at the hole in the wall, and I kept my ear on the floor and my eye to the stairs. He did not, like Baron Trenck, blow away the rubbish through a quill, but he tied it up in the tail of his shirt and made away with it in the quarry. At the end of a fortnight he was half-way through the wall and we were half way to freedom, for of course it never entered our heads to fail once we got out; we were to die game rather than come back to our cells again. But, woe of woes! as my ear was to the flag I heard Mike give a groan. I gave a cough, and he answered it by the signal to come to the slit in the partition. His agonized whisper was—" O God! Rossa, 'tis all up with us; the stones in the middle of the wall are all fastened to one another by stout links of iron, and it is impossible to remove these; we must give it up; lie down again until I shut the hole," and with a *bronach* heart I took my recumbent position.

Hugh Brophy and I had another scheme of escape a short time before this. As we quarried a large piece of rock one day we discovered a large hole under it, which appeared to be a cave. It escaped the officers' detection, and as the stone was removed we covered the hole. We took five or six into our confidence, who were to keep the jailers engaged one day while we examined the discovery. We found it was a fissure between the rocks, and did not extend far, and would do no more than answer for a hiding place. For three or four days after, our friends were sparing their bread and bringing it to hide in the hole till there was sufficient there to support Hugh and me for two or three days. We were to enter, the others were to cover us up and make the floor of the quarry just the same as all around, leaving a few air-holes, which could not be detected except by the closest search. We were to have a few ropes stolen from the tool-box, and if we escaped detection for a few days, the friends were to whisper through the air-holes that it was supposed we had got into the country; then we were to emerge at night and make a raft; launch it on the sea below, paddle our canoe across the bay to the land, which appeared about three miles distant. When the day came that we were to enter the cave we found that two of us could not get room in it by any kind of stuffing, and we had to pronounce the project hopeless. The hole was open, and we had not time to shut it before we saw the Governor approaching from the prison and coming on the path towards us. Quick as thought I pulled up a leg of my trousers, took a rough stone and rubbed it hard along the calf from the knee to the ankle; went into the hole, and gave a roar that shook the quarry. The little bird that sat hatching her eggs in a hole a few yards from us ran out of her nest. The boys and the officers ran towards me, and as the Governor came up he asked, " Why is Rossa sitting there ? " " It seems, sir," said Gunning, " his leg got into that hole and got scratched a little." I was taking off my boot, and I gave a black look at both of them, as much as to say is that all the pity you have for me after escaping with my life ?

The letter which I spoke of as having written to my wife came to be delivered, and I had my plans laid to pass it to Lynch at chapel one Sunday morning, but the first attempt of mine to reach the world "surreptitiously" turned out to be a failure, and brought upon me an endless amount of punishment. When I took my position in the chapel I found Lynch was two seats behind me and not at my side of the stool.

I passed the paper to Patrick Dunne, who was transported on a charge of attempting to swear in soldiers on the Pigeon-house-road, Dublin. He used to do his bit of prison life in as jolly a spirit as possible, and in doing anything else that was not in perfect harmony with the rules and regulations, he did it in as sly a way as it could be done. But on this occasion a principal officer, who was on watch at the back of the congregation, saw some movement on the part of Lynch, and on leaving the chapel, as I afterwards heard, he was arrested and stripped. I was in my cell that Sunday evening, the door was opened about five o'clock, and the warder said " Come on." On I went towards the dark cells, and looking behind me as I was entering, I saw Lynch following in charge of another officer. I had to strip to the buff; my clothes were searched inch by inch, and seam by seam, myself was then searched, nothing was found on me, and I remained in suspense till twelve o'clock next day, when I was taken in *deshabille* before the Governor.

" You are charged with endeavoring to get a letter out of prison surreptitiously to the wife of another prisoner. What have you to say ? "

" The charge is not properly recorded."

" Do you mean to dictate to me how I am to discharge my duties."

" I do not, but I mean to say that the charge, as you have it recorded on the books, is a false one."

" Do you deny the writing ? " (holding up the letter.)

" I admit or deny nothing, but I ask you to take down what I have said."

Governor (motioning to the officers)—" Take him away, and I'll postpone his case till I hear from the Board of Directors."

And the Board of Directors being heard from, I was sentenced to three days on bread and water, and fined as many marks as would add a few months to my imprisonment.

At work on the quarries again I learned from Michael Moore, one afternoon, that the Governor had been serious when he charged me with "writing to the wife of another prisoner," and whether he believed or not I was holding a love intrigue with the wife of Moore, he endeavored to make others believe it. I first looked upon the matter as a joke, but when I came to have it corrected on the prison books, lest it might remain on record and be brought forward at some time to defame my character—for this is a trick that England plays on dead enemies—I found the thing turned out to be no joke at all to me, unless a hard bed at night, and starvation in solitary confinement by day, be considered an agreeable kind of pastime.

Michael Moore made application to the Governor to be allowed to write to his wife, and the Governor asked him if he knew that there was another man in the prison in communication with her.

"What?" said Moore, in astonishment.

"Oh," said the Governor, "I would not have mentioned the matter to you only I thought you knew something about it."

The prisoner insisted on his right to know all, and the Governor told him I had been detected in sending a letter surreptitiously to his wife. Moore affected the greatest indignation, and kept it up till he came out to work, and demanded an explanation from me. As we were at this time forbidden to speak, and as the necessity for explaining away the charge seemed paramount to the necessity of maintaining silence, I, regardless of the jailer's admonition, kept talking to Moore, and the more I talked the more Moore grew dissatisfied. In this manner we cheated the English Government out of an evening's conversation. When the officers went to headquarters that evening they reported that Moore and Rossa had like to have a fight on the works, and I demanded to be allowed to see the Governor next day, to know why he had been telling falsehoods of me to my fellow-prisoners. Next day came, and I was taken to the door of the judgment chamber. I found Mr. Luby, Con Keane, Thomas Duggan, and three or four others waiting for a hearing. I was called in first, and asked the Governor by what authority he told Mr. Moore that I was detected in correspondence with his wife, and he told me by the authority of a letter he had in his possession.

"Cannot you look at that letter, and see on the corner of the envelope the words—'For Mrs. O'D?' Cannot you also see that it is addressed to Mrs. Mary Moore? Now, if you look at your books, and find the record of the letters Mr. Moore has received from and written to his wife and mother, you will learn that his wife's name is Kate, and that it is his mother who is called Mary. If you read the body of the letter you will find allusion to my children, and Mrs. Moore has no children. I ask that you correct this charge on the books, and also correct any erroneous reports you have made regarding it."

Governor—"I'll do no such thing." I believe all these things were subterfuges. I am fully persuaded the letter was for Moore's wife, and I told the Secretary of State so, and I told the Board of Directors so."

"Then you told them what was false."

Here he ordered me to be taken to the cells; the door was opened, and as the jailers were approaching me I stood, looking firmly at him, and said—" You're a mean creature, and you've shown nothing but meanness in our treatment since we came into your hands." Then I was laid hold of, and turned towards the door, where I saw my companions awaiting their call, and with very little ceremony I was shoved through the hall and tossed into a darkened cell.

Next day at twelve o'clock, I was charged with gross insolence to the Governor, calling him "a mean man," and ever so many etceteras. What had I to say? "Governor, you have been slandering me, and placing on record charges against me in Government offices, false charges which may be exhumed for the defamation of my character when I am dead. I suppose you can do what you please with me while I am living, but your torture should end there."

Governor—" I did not, until I got back your letter yesterday, see the words 'for Mrs. O'D' on the corner of the letter; but they were written so small that no one could see them unless his attention was particularly directed to them. If you had acted respectfully when coming before me, and given your answers in a proper manner, you would have fared differently. I will not punish you now further than fining you forty-two marks. That will do" (addressing the officers to remove me).

"Governor, won't you correct the charge on the books and your report to the Secretary of State?"

"You are getting off very easily."

"Will you give me permission to write to the Secretary of State on the matter?"

"I cannot do so. You can see the Director."

"Then I will thank you to put my name down to see the Director when he comes."

"Granted."

This was all very well. I went to work, and felt sure when the Director came I could satisfy him the letter was written to my wife, and that he would correct the erroneous reports made regarding it, but there are many tricks in trade, and the Governor of a convict prison is not without a few in his line of business. The day before the Director came I was reported for talking while at work, and the day he was in the prison I was on bread and water, and, being under punishment, I had forfeited my privilege of making my complaint to the gentleman. It is a part of his duty to visit every prisoner in the cells; my door was opened, I stood to attention, and seeing Mr. Fagan standing outside I proceeded to tell my story. I was told I was forbidden from making any complaint while under punishment, and that the next time the Director would come he would, if I was in good standing, go into my case. But the next time he came I was in punishment too, and the time after and every time till I left the prison of Portland. I knew Mr. Fagan had already examined into the charge of intrigue, and that he had seen it was a piece of bungling on the part of the Governor, and he certainly allowed the Governor to have recourse to the trick of having me on bread and water every time he visited the prison, so as to prevent him from making an official report. When this light dawned on me I made all possible efforts to communicate "surreptitiously" with the outer world, and after various attempts, failures, subterfuges, and punishments, succeeded.

Lynch, in whose possession my letter was found, got three days on bread and water, twenty-five days on penal class diet, and lost three months of the remission he had previously earned. He was to leave the prison a few months after he had the misfortune of falling in with me; but I met him twelve months afterwards in Millbank, and he told me they kept reporting him time after time until they took away every day he had earned, and he had to work out his whole term of seven years. When he came to chapel after the twenty-eight days on bread and water he passed me another lead pencil, and told me, in a note the package contained, that he'd have paper, envelopes, a writing pen, and an ink bottle for me on next Sunday.

Some one employed on the works had heard of his being in communication with me, and of his suffering punishment without "squealing" upon the person who furnished the writing material, and some one else made an offer to him to supply the needful and act as postman for a consideration, which consideration I of course readily consented to have provided. Sunday came; I was on the look-out, and the writing material came safely into my possession. I had two sheets of paper, two envelopes, and a darling little glass ink bottle, three inches long and one inch in diameter.

When I entered my cell and opened my parcel I was delighted; but the joy was not of long duration,, for the fear of detection soon chased it away, as the question arose, " Where in the world am I to hide them?" English convicts are allowed to wear an article of clothing called a shirt; it has, as I may say, two tails, and in the front one of these I tied my treasure. The hour for exercise came, and I chose for my comrade on this occasion Jerry O'Donovan, of Blarney, as I intended to make him my storekeeper and general agent in the nefarious business I had on hand. Jerry had one of the best characters; he was pretty free from "reports," and the warders considered him very quiet and guileless. Not alone was he *from* Blarney, but he had blarney, with all its rich raciness, on his tongue; in his manner that openness and pride of being Irish, and working for Ireland, characteristic of the true Irish peasant; and in his heart that love of faith and freedom, with hatred of those who would trample on either, which is "the salt of our soil," and, indeed, the salt of any soil.

Faith and Freedom, did I say? yes; but in Jerry's case, or in those who had to deal with Jerry's case, the two were made to clash, and the pursuit of freedom, as Jerry pursued it, was antagonistic to his profession of faith as the Rev. Mr. Zanetti professed or propounded it. The priest was for a long time urging the prisoner to give up the oath he had sworn to free Ireland, and to return to the fold; Jerry could not see that this renunciation of his duty to poor old Ireland was at all necessary to his salvation, and refusing to yield to the arguments and solicitations of the holy father, the rev. gentleman with his knuckles tapped him on the forehead three times, saying—" It is in, in, in there you have the devil in you." Some people may consider this very profane—not of me but of the priest—but let them not mind it; he was an Englishman, the son of an Italian, and had not a drop of Irish blood in his veins. I can only laugh at the ridiculous nonsense of such people when they preach loyalty to England, and threaten damnation because we are not loyal. I can listen to an Irish priest, for he is supposed to have as much interest in the country as I have; but when an English priest comes forward to denounce me for undertaking any danger or sacrifice that may be between me and Ireland's independence, I care very little for what he says. I have learned long ago what some of my countrymen seem to want to learn yet, that every priest is not an Irishman. No man can find his way to my heart more easily than the good priest, the *soggarth aroon*, who silently prays, for he cannot publicly speak for the overthrow of English rule in Ireland, and who, if we had a fight on our native soil, would obey the voice of God, as many an Irish priest would, calling upon him through his feelings to rush to the battle's front rather than the voice of Cullens or Cardinals calling upon him to denounce the " rebels " in the name of " the Church." To show how accommodating our Father Zanetti was to the Government, and how he could reconcile the requirements of the State with the obligations of the Church, I will quote a little from his evidence before the Commission of Inquiry. The Commissioners, thinking it would, perhaps, work a greater reformation on prisoners to allow them to go to church than to keep them from it while under punishment, questioned the priest thus:—

" Question No. 13,194—Do you recollect a prisoner of the name of Patrick Ryan, a treason-felony convict, being here? I have not a distinct recollection, my lord, of Patrick Ryan.

" 13,194—He makes a statement to us, and I should like to know whether what he represents has been brought under your notice or not. He says that he was employed to work the pump. He is asked the question—' Did you ever object to work any one day in the week?' And his answer is—' I objected to it once, sir, and that was on a Sunday that I was to receive the Blessed Sacrament, and the officer told me I could not, that it would be better for me to work at the pump, that it would do me more service.' Do you recollect hearing that there was any difficulty thrown in the way of the prisoners receiving the Sacraments in cases of being employed at work? I no not, my lord; but now that mention is made of it, I have some recollection of some prisoner, but who the prisoner was I cannot recollect—making a difficulty of working the pump on Sunday, and stating an objection he had—but whether he was going to Communion or not I cannot remember. I stated to the prisoner —I cannot remember who it was—that it was a work of necessity; that the water had to be supplied to the prison, and that, consequently, the prisoners had to work on Sunday, that it was not an unnecessary but a necessary work, and that, therefore, he should do what he was told and should work at the pump like the rest. I cannot say whether it was Ryan or not, but I remember the question distinctly.

"13,209—If the authorities of the prison, without a positive necessity, prevent prisoners under punishment and infirmary patients from hearing Mass on Sundays, are they not only depriving them of a privilege, but compelling them to forego a duty? I should not classify the two together. I should think it most desirable that prisoners in the infirmary, who are sufficiently well to attend the service of the church, should attend service; but with respect to the prisoners that are in punishment, I should consider that the object that the authorities had of rendering that prisoner's punishment more heavy would satisfy me in regard of the obligation under which he was placed.

"13,210—Do I understand you to say that you can justify the depriving prisoners of Mass as a means of making their punishment more heavy? The authorities believe it is necessary, and I accept their declaration that it is necessary for the efficacy of the punishment, and, in that point of view, I think that it is a justifiable resource.

"13,212 (Dr. Lyons)—Do you think it desirable or necessary that a change should be made in the disciplinary arrangement, so as to allow prisoners under punishment and infirmary patients to attend Mass on Sundays? I should think it desirable if it could be effected without disparagement to the essential discipline of the prison, to allow prisoners in the infirmary to attend Mass, and if the authorities consider that to allow prisoners to go to Mass would not be a diminution of punishment, I should likewise desire that they should go to Mass; but I am willing to accept their declaration that it would be a considerable diminution of the punishment of the prisoners to allow them to go to Mass."

The Sunday I took my hour's exercise with Jerry O'Donovan, of Blarney, I passed my writing material to him, and made arrangements for its safe keeping. He was to cut up the pencils in pieces about an inch and a-half long, to keep one bit on his person, together with a sheet of the paper, and hide the rest on the works. I made up my mind for detection a second time, and made provision for a supply of pen and paper to carry on the game again after I had gone through my punishment.

Indeed, I made provision to carry it on while under punishment, for I took the lead out of one of the pieces of pencil and breaking it up into small bits, I hid these in the seams of my jacket and trousers. So strict was the watch kept upon me now, that I had no chance of writing in my ordinary cell any hour between rising and retiring. The "eye" seemed to be ever at the spy-hole during the breakfast hour, the dinner hour, and the hours between six and eight in the evening. As I stretched on my hammock at night, I racked my brain for some means of writing, and I found two. One was to talk on the works deliberately, with the intention of being sent into the punishment cells. On entering these there is a strict search. You can take no contraband article in with you, and you can find nothing within. You are quite safe here, and, consequently, the eye is not so often on you as elsewhere. I thought that I could carry my bits of pencils in with me, that I could sit with my back to the door, and using the sole of my slipper for a table, write my story upon my closet paper. Sitting in this position, I was too low for the eye at the spy-hole to see me, and if the door was to be un locked by a surprise, I was too lazy, too sulky, or too fast asleep, to get up before I had my pencil and paper stowed away in the seams of my clothes. The other plan was to sit up in my hammock all night, and write away as well as I could. I had as much light from the gas in the hall as would enable me to see the paper; but then I hadn't much stationery, and if I attempted to write close, I might write one line over the other. Communicating my projects to my friends, Martin Hanley Carey told me he had a book in his cell which did not belong to his registry. It was a religious little treatise called, "Think Well On't," and it was not even stamped with the prison brand. Some one of the officers left it with him by mistake; it had large margins to every leaf, and he said I could write as much as I desired on it. I took it and gave Jerry orders to have the pen and ink ready. But he had been making further preparations to assist me. He showed me a little tin article he found in the quarry, which he intended to fashion into an ink-bottle. I told him it looked like a leprechaun's teapot, and that there might be luck in it. It would hold about a thimble full, and before evening he had some of the ink conveyed into it from the glass bottle. Taking it into my cell that evening, and getting safely as far as bed hour, I, when the door was locked for the night, gave Jerry the signal to pass me the writing-pen through a small hole that we made in the corrugated iron partition that divided us. I commenced to write, and the officer on guard commenced his parade through the hall. He wore slippers, and everything was so still I could hear his footfall as he approached my cell. I then used to lie back. If he peeped in he could see me, and if I remained writing he could hear the scratching of the pen on the book. If by any mischance I made such a noise as might attract attention, I commenced to snore for a minute or two, and if no one came I arose to my work again. Night after night I continued my labors, sleeping during my dinner and supper hours. When I commenced my work I could see little more than the leaf I was writing on, but before I had all finished my sight was sharp enough to see that I was writing in straight lines. I don't know was it that, like the cat, I was learning to see in the dark. Nature, perhaps, had sympathy with me, and came to my assistance. I used up all the paper I had, made up my parcels with the proper directions on them, and consulted with Jerry O'Donovan and some others, how we were to hide them until we got an opportunity of passing them out. We decided upon keeping them hid in the wall of the shed in which those worked who were making the stone altar, and into which we went for shelter when it rained. I had two letters written, and on the "Think Well On't" I had copied from memory a petition I was after writing to the Secretary of State. When some of my friends heard I was writing a petition, they began to wonder, and were on thorns to know what I was petitioning for; but I could not tell them, or tell myself. I am bound to do my best to clear myself with you, and as I am giving everything that came across me, I will give a sample of an Irish felon's petition to his English captors.

It was one of the ways that came into my head to get an account of our treatment before the public. A convict, if he is a well-conducted one, has the privilege of writing a petition every year to the Secretary of State, but after my Portland one, the authorities were not very willing to indulge me with the privilege; in fact, they refused it to me repeatedly on the grounds of my being a bad character. My idea was that I would write to the Secretary of State, and that I would manage also to write a copy surreptitiously in the hope of getting it out. In case of failure I had it in my mind to have it communicated to some of the visitors that I had written an account of our ill-treatment to the Ministry, and then some Irish member of the English House of Commons might be able to come at it through the interpellation of Parliament. At the Commission of Inquiry into our ill-treatment in 1870 I called for this memorial to refresh my memory and got it. I managed to transfer it to Captain John McClure, and, as we were allowed pen and ink during the Commission, he took a copy of it on waste paper the day I was under examination. This copy I succeeded in hiding till my release. I brought it with me to America, and will hold it with the certainty of being able sell it for a very high price a few centuries hence.

To the Hon. SPENCER HORATIO WALPOLE, *Sec'y of State.—The petiton of* JER. O'DONOVAN ROSSA.

HUMBLY SHOWETH—That your attention is solicited to the following:—In the early part of this year I wrote to Sir George Grey requesting permission to state particulars connected with my trial to an English M. P. I showed that instructions which I had from my counsel on paper were seized in prison, that papers explanatory of several things urged against me were in the hands of the Crown and would not be given to me; that in charging the jury summoned for my conviction, the judge over-charged them and distorted many innocent matters to my prejudice, as he had to admit when I ventured to interrupt him on more than one occasion. Many other things I referred to, that you may see on reference to my letter to your predecessor, which I suppose he has left after him. About the time of my conviction Englishmen were making some noise about a Mr. Gordon, of Jamaica, who was hanged, without having, as it was thought, " a fair trial" I said to myself (I had no one else to speak to) that if Mr. Gordon, instead of being hanged, had been transported or imported to England for life, he would be allowed to state his case to a lawyer or a member of Parliament. I fancied that a white Irishman might be as dear to a justice-loving England as a colored West Indian. I did not know then that there was in the same prison with me, No. 5,369, who was arrested amongst yourselves in London, on Christmas week, taken to the proclaimed part of the United Kingdom (Ireland), far away from the locality where he was said to have offended and away from his witnesses; brought the following week before a General Commission in Cork and sent back to London, where he had lived for the previous twenty years, after having received a sentence of twelve years' penal servitude.

Sir George Grey refused my request. I do not insinuate to you that this refusal had anything to do with his loss of office! I will only repeat the request now. If you grant it with any other reasonable one the letter may contain, may you hold the distinguished position of Secretary of State as long as you like it; if you do not grant it, you have only to hold the office *as long as you can!*

Macaulay says of Englishmen, that it is not one of their besetting sins to persecute their enemies when they get them into their power. The historian may be right, though I do not recollect that he brought forward any enemy qualified to speak in proof of his assertion. I say he *may* be right, having in view that there is an exception to every rule, and coupling it with the fact, that in the same book he says of my countrymen, "that they were the most hated and despised enemies of his—*hated*, because they were enemies for five centuries, and *despised* because they were conquered, enslaved, and despoiled enemies." Of my experience, while in the power of Englishmen, I will give you a brief sketch. Should it contain anything unpleasant to you, don't take it up personally, or consider me personally disrespectful; but do not wonder if you should find me falling into the sin of contemning British magnanimity when I am told by the Governor of my prison that my treatment is in accordance with the special orders of the Secretary of State. It is no harm to let you know what this treatment is, and give you time to approve or disapprove of it before I make up my mind that so much miserable meanness springs from such a source. As a man thinks of many things in solitary confinement, I, transported from Ireland to England for life, think it possible I may yet become an English citizen, particularly as you think it advisable at present that every independent, honest-minded man should be sent and kept out of Ireland. I can imagine myself having an interest already in seeing that the honor of England is maintained—upon English ground at least. No matter how we use the Bible and the bullet in aid of our mission to civilize the world—no matter how we plant penal colonies—no matter how we run men into prison, or blow them from the cannon's mouth in other countries, let us not stain the liberty hallowed heather of our own land—let us not blight the grass which grows ever green over the graves of the English martyrs, whose blood enriches the soil, by bringing amongst us, for the purpose of visiting with a vile persecution and worrying to death, men who at least are not matricides, or parricides, and who, at most, are guilty of the desire to manage their own affairs—a very heinous crime, no doubt, when we consider how many wise and philanthropic English noblemen and gentlemen are anxious to do the thing for them. Let us not—but hold! it is possible my imagination has trespassed too far upon my citizenship, and carried me too far on the liberal side to be pleasing to you; too far entirely—before I am out of the probation class of that process which is deemed necessary for the civilization of Irish political prisoners—to render me agreeable to any stern advocate of the "right divine." I will beg pardon, break the illusion, and commence my small sketch. With a view to making it as entertaining as possible I asked the Governor if I would be allowed pen, ink and paper in my cell for a day or a Sunday to write "according to the regulations." I thought I might get facilities suited to the dignity of my correspondent; but no, I can have only thirty or forty minutes, or an occasional evening after my day's labor, three or four days apart—in fact, no more than if I were writing to my wife or mother. What wonder then if I am in bad humor, or if I cannot write so as to engage you pleasantly. However, I will strive to conquer all disadvantages, and will do my best to interest you. I dare say you have in your library some volume relating to the prisons of Europe and pictures of European despotism. I can only promise you as full and as truthful a chapter of torturing annoyances as you can find in any of these. If the dark cruelties be absent take into account the extremely high degree of your civilization; and if in any of your almshouses, as your own writers say, "you kill so slowly that none could call it murder," think what it can be in a gaol. Take in your hand, for instance, "Silvio Pelico," and compare as I carry you along. He, I believe, was connected with a journal in Italy; I was connected with a newspaper in Ireland. In order to have it legally registered I had to appear in a court of law, and sign a document in presence of witnesses. Charged with belonging to a secret society, a conspiracy, this document was the only evidence against me relied upon by my prosecutors, and the only legal evidence they had at all to make me guilty. I was sentenced to penal servitude for the remainder of my days. Thus transported to a new life, the first night of it darkened upon me in Mountjoy Prison, Dublin, on the 13th December, 1865. My hair and beard were shorn, my clothes taken from me. I got the felon's dress, and, with my name pinned across my breast, my photograph was taken. Here I noticed the absence of the customary compliments from the artist of my making a good picture, &c. The rules for my guidance were read. I pitched upon one which allows every convict to write a letter upon reception. I asked for pen, ink, and paper, to write to my wife. I could not have them. I referred to the rule, and was told that was for the ordinary criminals. I was put in my cell, got oakum to pick, and one hour's solitary exercise every day. During the ten nights I lay here, I got a little experience of the torture inflicted in other countries upon prisoners by forbidding sleep to them. Guards were calling to each other every half hour outside my cell. The door of this contained a trap, through which I got my food. It was fastened with a chain and bolt, and opened every fifteen minutes by two officers, who held a bull's-eye lantern and shot the light from it full in my face. If I covered my head to avoid the annoyance, they called upon me until I showed my face before they would shut the trap.

On the morning of the 21st, I saw some of my fellow prisoners for the first time. We were put in a van, and when we got out of it I found myself in Kingstown, going on board a steamer for England. The irons were fastened so tightly upon me that my hands were already colored and swollen, and the pain was reminding me too forcibly that I was a prisoner. The poem of the convict came prosaically to my mind, and I began to realize that—

>"Wave after wave was dividing
>Bosoms that sorrow and guilt could not sever."

Altogether, I was getting so disgusted with the voyage, that I began to discharge my stomach. I asked for the officer in charge of us. I showed him the state of my hands from the tightness of the bands, and as we approached nearer to free England he gave me freer irons. I found myself getting into a London prison about eight o'clock in the evening. I thought that in the capitol of a great nation I would be allowed many things forbidden elsewhere, and it was some consolation to me to think I could write to my wife next day. I felt fatigued, cold, and thirsty, and I asked if I could have a drink of some kind, but there was to be no drink for a while. We were stripped of the clothing we got in Ireland, and supplied with the Pentonville dress. We got flannels in Ireland, and we got none here; we asked for them, and were told we could not get them, as the doctor had so ordered. A warder directed me to my cell and brought me a piece of bread and cheese. I told him I did not want anything to eat, but wanted a drink. He showed me a pint and a water pipe, and told me the cell contained every other necessary that was deemed requisite for me—that he would leave the gas lighting for half an hour, during which time I should eat my snpper, make my bed, and have every article of my clothing, except my shirt, made up in a bundle, to be put outside my cell door during the night. I drank a few pints of water. I made my bed upon a board 7 feet by 3, raised at the head by another board for a pillow. I had for a bed, a mattress about half an inch thick, and not altogether as hard as the board. The warder came in due time, and I put out my clothes and every moveable article in my cell, except that comfortless bed. The sufferings of these days was intense. In the cold month of December, and on such an occasion, it was cruel to deprive us of flannels which we were accustomed to wear. Will you find anything like it in the prison life of Silvio Pelico? Some of the men who were treated in a similar manner died.

No. 5,365 tells me that he was present when Mr. Lynch was deprived of his flannels, and heard him tell the warder that unless he got them he would be dead in three months. He, alas! spoke but too truly, but of course he died in the manner Coleridge says— "Killed so slowly that none could call it murder."

For three days after my arrival in London I could eat nothing, and the officer removed the bread that accumulated. The first time I saw the doctor, I asked him would he be pleased to allow me flannels, and he would not. The Director visited me, and left an order that I be made a tailor of. I asked him could I write to my family; He said—No. To Mr. Stansfield? No; but I could petition the Secretary of State if I liked. A few weeks after I did petition him, with the aforementioned result. I did not petition to be allowed to write to my wife, as I felt ashamed to let the Secretary of State see that I thought he could be so small and mean as to deny me a right and privilege accorded to the meanest pickpocket. At length I was handed a letter from my wife, but it was a fortnight in the prison before I got it, and I received one leaf of paper to write a reply. I was told that if I stated anything regarding the prison, or the officers, or the work, or the treatment, that my letter would be suppressed.

Three days afterwards the Governor sent for me, and told me he had to erase what related to my asking my solicitor to get permission for me to write to an English member of Parliament. No reply to that letter was allowed, as the authorities decided that the note of inquiry I received should answer for the reply to a prisoner's letter, and thus several of us were cheated out of hearing about family affairs. This was distressingly painful to me, as I had five children, whose estate was confiscated in my arrest. I represented matters to the Governor, but it was of no avail; he should govern according to his instructions. For the first two months in Pentonville Prison, so far as our exercise and putting out our cell furniture at night were concerned, we were treated like prisoners who had attempted to break prison, but at the commencement of the third month we were sent to exercise with the other prisoners. Some of them were placed between every two of us, and all walked four paces apart in circles, and in silence. The doctor one day ordered me a flannel waistcoat. I suppose he thought my blood was getting cool enough. He often asked me if I was able to eat my food, which looked like mockery to one who as often had reason to tell him he felt half starved, and he always took my answer as indicative of good health. I often thought what a capital chairman he'd make for your board of health in Ireland. An orderly always preceded the Governor and Deputy Governor in their visits to me, and I had to stand to attention with my cap off, but for the Deputy I was ordered to add the additional salute of raising my hand to my head. Why the Governor did not requide this koo-tooing I do not know: perhaps he was enough of the gentleman.

For not raising the hand to the bare head in this prison, Mr. O'Connor was put into a dark cell for three days on sixteen ounces of bread and plenty of water each day. Deprivation of food is a prominent feature in all punishment. On the 9th of May I was taken to the Governor's office and told that my wife had given birth to a son on the 30th April, but I could not write to her until six months after the date of my last letter, and I rejoiced in the event as well as circumstances would permit.

On the 14th May we were mustered for Portland, and we noticed the absence of five of our number. They were broken down in health, and had been sent to the invalid station of Woking. We were weighed, and we learned that some of us had lost as many as 20 lbs. That some of these are not yet sent to the half-way house of death I attribute to their strong-natured powers of endurance, but a little time here is able to work the desired examples. We arrive in Portland in the evening. After several applications for sufficient paper to write to you I am allowed three sheets to do so. I have not spare time to let you know many particulars of our treatment, and must content myself with giving you as much as will enable any clear-headed individual to see the animus towards us. Could I, by my escape from prison, afford you that satisfaction which Dr. Johnson says all people experience at the escape of rebels, and were I never to live in England again, I should form but a very indifferent opinion of the manhood of the country were I to judge of it from what I have seen in this part. Armed authority earns for itself the reputation of coward, when it ill-treats a party bound hand and foot and delivered into its charge. The majority of our masters may not consider the prison rules severe enough for us, and may volunteer a little extra duty. I admit that there are exceptions—men who do their part without making every word and look convey an insult and a sneer. But, perhaps, they are not thus discharging the duty expected from them when in contact with us. Let it, however, be hoped that these exceptions represent a rule.

To be told that we are no better than Sodomites and thieves—that nothing could make us more degraded than we are—that not alone in this world should we be punished but in the next—that it is not easy to kill us, &c., may be nothing—but to be told that we are liars, that we are bloodthirsty, that we are like a lot of old women, that we are better fed than when we fed ourselves, &c., is enough to quicken the blood, even though it be poverty-stricken by bad and insufficient nourishment. A word from us in reply is called insolence and punished as such. This is what you will not find in Silvio Pelico. His enemy never took a cowardly advantage of his helplessness to insult him in his suffering. On the contrary, he says he got kind words and looks of sympathy everywhere in his enemy's country. Yet have we borne all without an ill-word to any one. The sacredness of the cause of liberty and fatherland requires that men should suffer calmly and strongly for it—that cause which I will do you the justice to think you admire when represented by a Hugo, a Kosciusko, a Kossuth, a Garibaldi, or any noble spirit outside the British dominion. Excuse this inconsistency of my expressing myself somewhat like a freeman. You know I am in a land where even the air of the prison is liable to be affected with the taint of liberty. I am not allowed to speak; I am told that even I have no right to think. What wonder, then, if my thoughts overflow a little when allowed to write. On our arrival in Portland the rules were read for us, and these rules declared that prisoners could write a letter upon reception. I asked could we write, and I was told we could not. The Governor told us he could be kind or severe according as it suited the due discharge of his duty. Some of the men had religious emblems, crosses, sacred hearts, &c., momentoes from fond sisters, dear or departed mothers. These amulets or charms, he said, he should retain until further orders. Next day we were taken to the laundry, and until the 19th were kept washing the clothing of other prisoners. We were then sent to the quarries, where we are at present. Mr. Kickham was affected with scrofulous ulcers, and was sent to hospital the second day. After four or five weeks he was brought among us, lodged in one of our dark flagged cells, and sent with us to the quarry at stone dressing. He unhappily is nearsighted and very deaf, and carries an ear-trumpet to enable a person to converse with him; but a warder (I'm afraid I'll slip into saying jailor sometime) has a way of his own of making himself understood. "Keebling" a stone, this sick gentleman sat or leaned upon a ledge of rock while I was preparing it for him; the officer laid hold of him and shook him up, saying loudly, "He was not allowed to rest during working hours." He was another day in the ranks, and not marching with military precision, the warder, while we were in motion, gave him a violent push out of the ranks, and staggered him some paces aside. We are transported on a charge of striving to learn in our own country what you oblige us to practice in this, under pain of punishment—that is, military drill. It is the only thing in which you are kind and just to us—instructing us here in what you forbade us at home, and what may be of use to us some day. Mr. Kickham sank under the system; the ulcers opened; he sent for the doctor, who sent him to the hospital. He grew fit for the invalid station, and we have not heard of him since. Mr. Roantree had hermorrhoids and the blood used to stream into his shoes while at work. Making frequent representations of his condition to the doctor and Governor without effect, he so labored during three months until a representation to the Director got him sent to the hospital. Here he became seriously ill from the loss of blood, &c., and he now fears he is doomed to the half-way house. Mr. Duggan went to the doctor, he got a pill and was told it would eure him, and not to come any more. He was kept at work; two days after he was not able to work, and is now in hospital. Mr. Carey was kebling a stone one day, the iron flew off the handle, and he got the middle finger of his right hand broken; the doctor talked of amputation, and the patient would not have it so. He was sent to the quarry with the sore hand in a sling and spent six weeks breaking stones with the one hand till the other got well. Many of the men were ill from time to time, and wore off their illness without medicine rather than go before a doctor, who thought fit to insult everyone of us who visited him. Several of us were under medical treatment, and receiving extra nourishment leaving Pentonville, one of them, Mr. Keane, reduced two stones there, and being a very tall man, looks very much emaciated. He is bilious, and like others, cannot use gruel for supper. This I know, as I am occasionally in the hall serving out meals, cleaning boots, and collecting slops. He told the doctor of his state, and was informed there could be no special rules for him; that he was getting as much food as any other man in the probation class, and remarked that we were all sick in Pentonville. Mr. O'Leary occupied the next cell to Mr. Keane, and handed him a loaf of bread one day, for which both got punished, and the bread was confiscated to the State. I had occasion to visit the doctor myself—him who appears to belong to the "Jemimar" family. I am not strong-sighted, the glare of the sun on the white stone I am hammering on nine or ten hours every day, and the particles that fly off affect my eyes painfully; but the medical gentleman could see nothing the matter with them. I deemed it well to tell so much, and no more, to the Prison Director, without making any complaint against the doctor or anyone else. I was taken to the infirmary on the Director's order, but the janitor there would not admit me. Both doctors shortly appeared, examined my eyes and held a consultation. Then one of them, addressing me angrily, said—"You made a complaint against us to the Director, but I cannot see anything the matter with your eyes; and turning to the warder, he said, "take him away, and I'll give a certificate to the Governor that will settle the matter."

We have been told by the Director that we were sent here before the usual time for the good of our health. I thank whoever conceived the charitable design, but to us it seems to have miscarried, as cuts and scratches incidental to us at work healed up quickly when we came to Portland, but now they fester and grow angry.

Though you abolished your star chamber in the reign of your First Charles, what I am going to state now would make it appear that the root of it is in the land still, and shoots out occasionally in your convict prisons.

Mr. Moore and I were taken to the punishment cells one day, shortly after our arrival here. I was stripped of my shoes, and led through a long flagged hall, to a room where sat the Governor. He read from a report book a charge against me of speaking in my cell at a certain hour on a certain day. There was no accuser before me except the book. The Governor asked, "had I anything to say in reply." I said "nothing," but that it was possible I did speak, as I had not lost the use of my tongue. He fined me 24 marks, and ordered my clothes to be branded with a mark of degradation, and my companion fared likewise.

My cell is seven feet long and four feet broad, and not at all formed like the dungeon of the Sicilian tyrant, Dionysius. 'Tis true that the rain comes down on me sometimes, and to escape it I am obliged to lay on the flags; but the sound of the voice does not go out by the road the rain comes in. No, there is a small iron grating at the end of a hole opening into the yard, and it is at this hole the caves-dropper outside listens.

On a Sunday, when I am cooped up in this small cell all day, I am not allowed to walk in it. My officer tells me that it is making a noise, and noise is not allowed. I am not permitted to sling the canvas of my hammock and stretch upon it. I did this once in a darkened cell when I had not light enough to read, and I got twenty-four hours punishment diet for it.

The Governor told us we could speak while at work, but that we should speak loud enough for the officer to hear us, lest we should be planning anything; and this same Governor, in a few weeks afterward, and in my presence, called the warders to account for allowing us to speak too loud; and these instructions afforded the warders agreeable exercise for a time in checking us for speaking either too high or too low. Then an order came one morning we were not to speak a word at all, upon any pretence whatsoever. The day this order was issued, an inspecting officer came round; I was called before him, and was called to account for asking the warder, "How long did he think these instructions would last?" I said it looked to me quite a harmless question. He said the order given was wrong, in so far as it was not forbidden to ask for an implement or anything relating to the work. I told him I wished to know to what extent I could go in speaking to another prisoner? if I could say, "Prisoner, this is hard work." He immediately said I was impertinent, and I replied that the prison rules did not permit me to be impertinent to him, nor him to be impertinent to me. He ordered me to be taken to the punishment cells, and on my way in he ordered me to be brought back again.

There is a temporary water-closet near the quarry, and I was told one day I should empty it out the next day. I asked the Governor if this was work expected from me, and he told me it certainly was. The officer in charge learning I had this conversation with the Governor, and knowing that the job was a disagreeable one, said he would make two of us clean it out every Monday morning in future, though it was cleaned only once every three weeks before, and he kept his word with us.

I was carrying a stone on a barrow once. I fell and cut my hand and the doctor plastered it up. A few days afterwards the warder ordered me to remove a very large stone, and when the front man was ascending a step of the quarry the stone rolled back and knocked me down. The warder commenced scolding me, and, seeing another prisoner come to take away the stone, he said, "I was such a man as would suck another man's blood." I asked permission to see the Governor that evening to know if there was any redress for this course of daily insult. If you think there is I refer you to another fruitless effort to find it made by Mr. Mulcahy a few days ago. I was not allowed to make my report to the Governor for a week, and in the meantime I was punished by being put on bread and water on a charge of idleness, insolence and disobedience of orders. As regards the idleness they said I was generally idle; the disobedience of orders consisted in talking while there was a general order not to talk, and the insolence was that when the warder, believing he heard me talk, asked me did I defy the rules? I told him I could not answer what I considered a very improper question, but when I violated any of the rules he could get me legally punished, which I preferred to being abused. When I saw the Governor I reported the warder for using towards me language wantonly provoking, and the Governor told me "I could have no will of my own here; that it was my duty to answer every question put to me; that I was not sent here to be too sensitive; that nothing could make me more degraded than I was; that if I knew the serious consequences of bringing a false charge against an officer—78 days' punishment—I would be slow to do it; that Mr. Gunning's character was too well established in the prison for any charge of mine to affect it, and that he had written for permission to be allowed to divide us among the English convicts." This contrasted rather strangely with the rule that the Governor must at all times be willing to receive the report of a prisoner against an officer.

We are paraded every Sunday, and stand to "attention," cap in hand, while the inspector is passing. Five Sundays ago an officer called Major Hickey inspected us, and I, as usual, put on my cap after he had passed me by some paces. Then he turned sharply around, and ordered me to take off my cap again whilst he was passing the line of English prisoners that stood some distance away. I have noticed that there is no order given to put on caps, but the prisoners put them on after the inspector passes by. When this gallant officer shows such a zeal in humiliating the enemies of his country, I wonder that he seeks them or allows his sword to rust in such a place as a convict prison.

Another time we are at work while it is raining, and the bell rings, as a notice to all prisoners to go under the sheds. We happen to move towards our shed before the officer commands us to do so, and he orders us back again, keeping us till we are well wet, while he himself is protected with waterproof over-clothing.

There are nine articles of tin furniture in each cell, which are to be kept bright and dry at all times. When very wet weather comes we are kept in our cells. The furniture is put outside the cell-door, and, with whiting and brick-dust, gets the benefit of the otherwise idle time. The order for absolute silence being in force, I was reported for talking at my work a few weeks ago, and by a new regulation I am, in consequence of this report, shut up in my cell, and obliged to dust and clean these. I experienced this four times only yet, and the air becomes so impure that I can feel it cracking between my teeth. And speaking to each other is also to be used as a pretext to deprive us of seeing our friends from the outer world, of receiving and writing letters in future. It looks as if the authorities wished to try how much we will bear. I don't know but that it is entirely illegal to prevent us from speaking, if speaking is allowed on the public works in Ireland.

It was allowed here and there at the time of my conviction, and I should have the benefit of the law as it stood then.

Would you please to consult the very able and zealous Judge Keogh, who convicted me, on this point. I rather think his humanity would incline him to giving me the humaner sentence of making my life a short one if he thought my mouth was to be locked up for ever, and that I would not be allowed to speak to a fellow-prisoner, even in praise of the beauties of the system under which we labor, of the benefits of trial by jury in Ireland, or of any other blessing of the glorious British Constitution.

When I applied to the Governor for this paper to write to you I told him, in reply to a question, that I was going to state something to you regarding our treatment, he said, "I do what I can for you fellows, and I consider you are very well treated; too well, considering the enormity of your crime, for you did more to injure your country than can be repaired for a long time, as your own people admit. You caused thousands of moneyed people to leave Ireland, and twenty years ago you'd have been hanged."

I said to hang us might have been the better for us, and that it was rather difficult to hear the natural voice of our own people in Ireland lately.

Only think of a Russian or Austrian jailer telling his Polish or Italian prisoner that he was the ruin of his country when the Governors proclaimed martial law and frightened away a few timid settlers. This kind of observation may be annoying to some temperaments, but as it excites my risibility somewhat, and helps to make the digestive organs do the very difficult work they have to do, I mind it but little.

Now I will present to you another feature of your Christian humanity. My mother is living in America, and I asked the Prison Director for permission to write to her, and could not get it. When writing to Ireland some time ago, I told the Governor that, as my mother was very old and not likely to live long, it was painful to me to think that she might die thinking that she was forgotten by her son. To ease my mind on the matter I asked for the smallest scrap of paper on which to write a few lines to enclose to her in the letter to my wife, and it would not be given to me.

My wife took my children to the home of her father, and she, in writing to me, enclosed a letter from him, which would not be given to me, because, as the Governor said, it contained political paragraphs. I asked to have these paragraphs obliterated.

Several of the prisoners' letters were suppressed because they contained accounts of our treatment.

I had a visit from my wife of twenty minutes' duration, and we were told that the interview would be terminated if my wife attempted to tell me anything of the political world outside, or if I told her anything of my treatment inside the prison walls.

As a general rule, all punishment is inflicted for the purpose of acting as a deterrent of crime, and when any authority inflicts punishment which it is either afraid or ashamed to have known, it is supposed to mean persecution. But I must bear in mind that in governing Irishmen you are not supposed to act in accordance with any known rule. Mr. Gladstone wrote a pamphlet on prisons in Naples, in which he showed that the policy of Neapolitan tyranny required that the political prisoners be subjected to the same treatment as vagabond ones. This, surely, is seeing the mote in a neighbor's eye and blind to the beam in our own. Should you give Mr. Gladstone my card, with a view of his paying me a visit in Portland, I will show him as bad a state of things as he saw in Naples, and if he make a fair inquiry on oath, I will venture to convince him that political prisoners are treated somewhat worse than thieves and murderers in England. Or perhaps you would send the editor of *Public Opinion*, or a Philo-Hibernian such as Lord Cranbourne, or, better still, a philanthropist such as Lord Carnarvon, and I'll engage he'll go back with tears streaming down his cheeks. Do send some one of them, and for the temporal and eternal welfare of mankind in general, and the liberation of all oppressed peoples in particular, petitioner will, as in duty bound, ever pray.

JER. O'DONOVAN ROSSA.

Petitioner will add a postscript as he has been favored with an additional sheet of paper. It is some three weeks since he commenced this petition, and now that the routine of writing is ended he wishes you to understand that he is not so unreasonable as to expect or desire any other treatment than that he is receiving, so long as the happiness of the English people and the interest of the Empire demand that he be "civilized" after the fashion of his friends at Woking, or after the fashion of Mr. Roebuck's New Zealanders. To attend to these interests is your duty; to suffer and be strong while life is left is the duty of petitioner. Petitioner was allowed to receive a letter from his wife six weeks ago; she asked some questions relating to debts and matters connected with the maintenance of herself and children, and she hoped the humanity of the authorities would allow a reply. The Governor told petitioner to write on a slate what he had to say, and he now tells petitioner he could not send the reply, as it would be lessening the prisoner's punishment.

"And this is in a Christian land where men oft kneel and pray. the vaunted home of liberty,"—where every man deprived of it is furnished with a Bible.

My petition was in the hands of the authorities two months before they vouchsafed me an answer. One Christmas Eve I was called out of my punishment cell and ushered into the presence of the Governor. Two English convicts were placed in position by my side, and the three of us having been called, according to our numbers, were told that our petitions had been duly considered, and that there were seen no grounds for granting what we required. I was half ways into a sentence telling the Governor that I did not recollect requiring anything particularly, when he shut me up by waving his hand to the officer, saying "that will do." The officer took hold of my shoulder, and gave me a turn towards the door, sympathetic with his order of "right about face." I had some fun with one of the schoolmasters when I commenced writing this petition. I think I spent three or four weeks at it, as I was allowed to write only two evenings in the week, and about an hour each evening. The schoolmaster took the paper away after I had done with it, and as he brought it after I had done the first hour's writing he said I should have to change the whole thing, as it was written quite out of order. I affected ignorance, and asked him to explain. He said that those petitions had to be written in the third person singular, that I had departed from that regulation and written in the first person: I should put a "he" or a "petitioner" in any place where I had an "L." The schoolmaster was a very nice little man, a perfect gentleman, as civil and as kindly spoken in anything he had to do with us as it was possible for man to be. I did not like to be trifling with him, and I told him plainly that I had used the "he" in that part of the petition which asked anything—viz., in the first line, "The petition of Jeremiah O'Donovan Rossa, Humbly sheweth, That your attention is requested to the following." All I wanted from the Secretary of State was attention to my story, and that story I had to tell in a narrative style. I spoke to the school-master as respectfully as I could, and he very politely said, "Oh, very well, very well, you possibly know best what to do. I don't pretend to instruct you, but to discharge my duty. Go on as you please." I thanked him, and finished my writing without his having anything more to say to me. I did not relax my efforts to get this petition into the world, and lest the copy of it which I had written in the "Think well on It" should be seized, I set to work at writing another copy of it on closet-paper. I used to write four or five sheets every evening, and pass them to Jerry O'Donovan next morning to have them placed in the hiding-hole.

One evening that I was asked to shave I commenced to pare my pencil with the razor. I took a furtive glance towards the door, and there I saw the eye at the spy-hole. I kept looking at it, holding the razor in one hand and the pencil in another, and it kept staring at me. Immediately the key turned in the lock, and Warder Russell stood before me, asking—"What are you doing there?" "Only putting a point on this bit of pencil with a razor." "And is that the use you make of the razor?" "I have nothing else to point my pencil with." "And who allows you a pencil? Where did you get that pencil." "Oh, that's a thing I am not allowed to tell you." "Give me that razor and pencil out of your hands." He took them, went out, locked the door, opened it a minute after with two or three other warders, and ordered me to come on. I went with them. They took me into an unoccupied cell at the other side of the hall and gave me orders to strip, which orders I obeyed. They searched my clothes inch by inch, and found nothing till they came to the pocket of the jacket, out of which they drew three or four sheets of the paper I had been writing on. "What's this?" asked the discoverer. "Don't you see," said I, "that is my closet paper." "But what is this written on it?" "Oh, you can make that out by your 'larnin'."

Orders were issued to march me off to the punishment cells, and there I was lodged till I was taken before the Governor next day. I was charged with misusing the razor and paper given me, with having forbidden articles in my possession, and with many other things connected with these offenses, such as insolence, impudence, disobedience, and insubordination. Asked what I had to say, I said I would give my reply in writing; as I would not get writing materials, I said nothing, and the Governor told me this was such a serious case he would not adjudicate upon it himself, but send it before the Directors, and send me into the punishment cell on light diet until they were heard from. After three or four days, I was sentenced to seventy-two days on bread and water, and an order from the Directors read to me to the effect that I was not to be supplied weekly with the regular supply of waste paper, but was to receive some from the office every time it was necessary "for purposes of nature." Such was the delicate way they put it. The reader may not consider my feelings in detailing matters of this kind, and may not entirely believe me when I say I could never approach one of those officers to ask him for the paper which he every day got for me without feeling a kind of humiliation that I was the occasion of having the discharge of such a duty put upon any fellow-being. I took the scraps of paper to my cell, and wrote upon them as much as I could of my petition with the little three-eight bits of lead that escaped detection in the seams of my clothes. I had no seat or table in those punishment cells, and if I stood or sat anywhere only in one position the officer looking through the spy-hole would see me. That position was sitting on the floor with my back to the door, and how to write here, without a book or a table to lay the paper on, was the question. "Necessity is the mother of invention." My shoes were taken from me, but instead of them I got a pair of old slippers. I planted one of those on my knees; the sole of it turned upwards answered me for a table, and thuswise I wrote what got out into the world, and brought on the sham inquiry by the sham commissioners, Knox and Pollock. I was at work again with my companions, but our masters determined that we should have no peace. The Governor called to the quarry, and saying he heard some talking amongst us as he was approaching, brought the officers to account for allowing us the privilege of speech. We went to dinner, and after returning to work, Jones, one of the officers, said he should report seven or eight of us next day. Some of us asked him if he had orders to do so, and he was honest enough to say he had. Luby, O'Leary, O'Connor, Kenealy, and a few others, told him to take down their names, and he did so. I had no occasion to tell him, for when there was a report wanted and ordered I knew that I would get the honor of being in the crowd. This Jones was a very honest fellow, honest towards us and towards his employers. He was a Welshman, and a military pensioner. He got into a difficulty, on account of which he lost his situation. A prisoner and an officer had some altercation on the works; they came to blows; the prisoner got the better of the officer. Jones, who was in charge of a gang of men near by, ran to the officer's rescue, and made the prisoner prisoner, but as he did not use his sword on the captive and cut him down instead of tying him up, he was given to understand that he was not fit for his situation, and had better resign, which he did. Before he left the prison he told us the circumstances one Sunday that he had us out at exercise, observing,

"I thought it enough to do my duty by saving the officer without killing the prisoner." Thinking that he was in a disaffected or disgusted state of mind at his being thus treated, I suggested the advisability of testing him to see if he would take out a letter from me if I wrote one. Mike Moore approached him on the question, and he proved faithful to his employers. He would take out a verbal word of remembrance from any one of us to any of our friends, he would tell them of the state of our health, or anything that way, but he did not think it would be honorable for him to do the other thing. We respected his scruples and did not press him. Just then we were in communication with some invisible agent who offered to act as a medium between us and the outer world. Our shoes were left in our cells every working day, and Cornelius Dwyer Keane found a note in one of his on a Saturday evening. This note stated that the writer had some sympathy with us, and would convey any message to our friends, and deliver us anything received from them. Con's shoes would be the post-office, and he would call there next day for a reply. A requisition was made on him for a pencil, and the order was left in the shoe; next day it was gone, and the day after the pencil was placed in the post-office. I suggested that the papers I had written should be given to him, but I was overruled by the few others who were in the secret. Any publicity would cause renewed vigilance, and, perhaps, bring about a change of all the officers about our ward, and it was feared our unknown agent may be taken out of our reach. It was decided to get in some tobacco and money first, before we did anything in the way of getting an account of our treatment published, and I had to acquiesce. But trouble came hot and heavy on me a few days after, and continued for a few years. I was taken out of the society of my friends, and never heard how they fared with their postmaster.

The report that Jones said was against seven or eight of us did not come on the day he stated; it was delayed a few days, and then John O'Leary, Thomas Clarke Luby, John Kenealy, Cornelius Keane, James O'Connor, and a few others with myself were taken barefooted before the Governor and charged with speaking while at work. Some of them got off with a reprimand and the loss of a few "marks." John O'Leary, Thomas Clarke Luby, and John Kenneally got each twenty-fours on bread and water, and James O'Connor and myself were sentenced to seventeen days on bread and water, with the additional punishment that when this time had expired we were not to be allowed to work with our own party, but sent into another gang. The seventeen days passed; we were taken from our cells and conducted into a yard where we never stood before. A gang of about forty prisoners were drawn up in line. James was placed at one end of it and I at the other. We were marched off to the quarries, and when the order was given to "break off" for work, James and I sloped towards each other with the intention of having our blocks near each other. Immediately that we did, the officer in command called me to a block in one corner of the field, and told me to work there. I then saw him go to James and take him to the other corner which was farthest away from mine and fix him there. That was defeating our desire to have a word with each other, and I growled in spirit. My first thought was to throw down my hammer and pitch their work to the devil, but second thoughts came on, and brought with them the probability of there being some means to be found amongst these English prisoners whereby I might be able to carry out my design of communicating with the world. They were hard characters most of them, thieves, garotters, and every class of criminal that grows in English society. When the warder had given instructions to James, he returned to give me mine. He told me I was to speak to no other prisoner on the works; when I wanted instructions I was to ask him for them. When I wanted help to lift a stone on the block, the prisoner next to me would help me, and when he wanted help to remove his stone I was to help him. The first evening passed off pretty well, and in spite of all the warder's vigilance I got a chance to make a few inquiries as to whether I could get anything taken out to the world or brought in from it. I was told yes, and I made up my mind to work quietly amongst these till I could accomplish my purpose. One of them asked me if I'd like a chew of tobacco, and on my whispering yes, he said to stick close by him as we were leaving work that evening, and he would pass it to me. I did so, and he kept his word. What he gave me would sell for two loaves of bread in the prison, but the poor fellow never asked me for fee or reward for it, and, moreover, promised me a bigger plug to-morrow. It was about the size of a shirt button, and I kept it between my fingers as I was going into the prison. I intended to get some means of passing it to John O'Leary, but instead of being taken to my cell, I was taken right straight to the bath-house, in order to bathe. I stripped with an officer looking at me, and as he had his head one side, I let the bit of tobacco fall on the floor. When I was in the bath he took hold of my clothes and searched them; his eye fell on the black thing on the floor, and he picked up my bit of tobacco. After examining it he ordered me to dress immediately, and conducted me to a punishment cell. I was left there till dinner hour next day, and then sentenced to seventy-two hours on bread and water, on a charge of having tobacco in my possession. I came out after my three days and three nights, and was surprised to learn that my new associates were aware of what had happened to me. They had opportunities of learning things that political prisoners had not, and many of them knowing that I must be hungry, had been making provision to feed me. One of them spared a loaf, another of them spared a loaf and a piece of meat, and another brought a piece of a pudding for me. The whisper was passed to me to ask leave to go to the closet, and to go there quickly after another man came out. I went and found the loaf of bread and piece of meat which, I am not ashamed to say, I ate, and if I had a slack belly coming out to work that morning, I had a full one going in that evening. There was one Irishman in the party, he was from Blackpool, and was undergoing a sentence of seven years for striking an officer of his in the English army. He was a fine hearty fellow about six feet, with an innocent, honest looking face. He took occasion to come to the water tub for a drink as I went there for the same purpose. I did not see him till I heard the whisper, "God help you, I'll bring you out a loaf to-morrow." As I turned away I looked into his face to see who spoke, and the tears were streaming down his cheeks as they stream down mine now at the recollection of these little acts of kindness from men who were branded as the vilest characters in creation. Yet I refused to work amongst them, but that refusal was dictated by a desire to resent the acts of a Government that would make no distinction between political and other prisoners. They classed us as they classed their criminals, and, as many of these often said to me, they treated us worse. They would make us feel degradation, putting us in association with them, and however humility may become a man in any position of life, I had the rashness to trample it under foot when these mean English legislators required it from me under the circumstances I speak of.

The man who was detailed to help me in the party was not a very agreeable-looking companion; he had a very ill-looking countenance, and, to add to the unfortunate fellow's misfortune, he was blind of an eye. He wanted me to assist him to put a stone on his block, and when he addressed me with "Here, mate, give us a hand with this," I laid my hammer on the block, and, addressing the warder, said, "Here, governor, I don't think I'll do any more work to-day." "What's that you say?" roared he. "I think you heard me," said I. "Do you mean to say you're not going to work?" "I do." "Then, I tell you that you will have to work; take that hammer in your hand." "No," said I, putting as much of the growl into the monosyllable as I could. He turned away from me and sent for a superior officer. Donald Bane came, and much the same kind of words passed between him and me. Seeing it was no use to be at me, he ordered me into punishment cells, where I was duly stripped and searched. At dinner hour I was brought before the Deputy-Governor, Major Hickey. He told me the Governor was absent, and he hoped that I would get on quietly in his absence; he asked me to go to work, and I refused unless he sent me to my own party; he said he had no alternative but to give me twenty-four hours on bread and water. Next day I was sent out again and learned the agreeable intelligence that one of the prisoners was in communication with parties who would send out any communications we had to give. I had very little written but what was in the hands of my friends in the other quarry, which I could not get then, and I determined to set to work immediately to write more. I was put in possession of paper and pencil, which I tried as well as possible to conceal. I struck work again for the purpose of getting into the punishment cell, where, alone, I had an opportunity of writing. The little bits of pencil and the few scraps of paper I had escaped scot-free, and on the sole of my slipper, while on bread and water, I wrote something which I passed to James O'Connor when I came out. James passed it to the prisoner, and I heard nothing about it till Knox and Pollock came to me in Millbank Prison eight months afterwards on a Commission of Inquiry, and gave me to understand that this last thing I speak of as having written had got into the press.

[COPYRIGHT SECURED.]

Here is the letter as I find it printed in the Dublin IRISHMAN, but I supply a few sentences that my wife could not make out when she was copying it for the paper. It was addressed to the London *Star*, but that journal would not, it seems, publish it:

A VOICE FROM THE DUNGEON—REVELATIONS OF PRISON LIFE.

["Every philanthropic work that issues from the English press repeats the name of Howard as one of England's glories, because Howard did much to expose the wretched state of prisoners of his day. Following his example, Mr. Gladstone indignantly denounced the Neapolitan system of prison discipline. Englishmen pride themselves on their sympathy with the sufferings of political prisoners. Unhappily theirs is a telescopic vision which sees the motes in Borisboola Gha, but not the beams in England. We commend the subjoined revelations of prison life to English philanthropists, to Mr. Gladstone, and Mr. Dickens—have they ever read anything more exquisitely sad of its kind? We commend it to Mr. Blake and Mr. Bagwell, the only two of the Irish members in whose hearts one spark of humanity seems to abide, one thought courageously delivered in words, for these homeless imprisoned fellow men. Above all things, we appeal to every man who has a heart to mark this: Mr. O'Donovan Rossa has written the revelation to a London Liberal paper (whose liberalty has suppressed it) for one express and sacred purpose—to clear his name, as a husband and a father, from an imputation as cruel as it was unutterably stupid and improbable. Under cover to another prisoner's mother he attempts to send a tetter to his own wife; it is intercepted, and he, a man with a life sentence over him, is accused of writing to intrigue with that other prisoner's wife. Moreover, this slander is whispered about and told to that prisoner. Therefore, outraged in his most sacred feelings as a husband and a father, and finding it impossible to obtain redress from the officials, O'Donovan Rossa appeals to the hearts and public opinion of Englishmen and Irishmen. In doing so, in making this appeal, to protect his honor—the honor of a father before his family —he may have become liable to punishment. We ask Mr. Gladstone and Earl Derby if they are willing to bear the responsibility of this

—we ask, is there no member in Parliament to speak a word for humanity's sake?"—*Dublin Irishman.*]

TO THE EDITOR OF THE STAR.

SIR—I commenced this scroll on the 19th of January, but whether I am ever to finish it, or whether it will ever reach your hand, I cannot say at present. The first days I came here I could have written a very interesting account of prison life—if my cares and occupation permitted—at least there was plenty material to make an interesting sketch of in the hands of those English philanthropists who do so much good by holding open some of the continental prisons, and allowing the English people to take a peep at the political victims within.

Every week, since my removal here, has only increased the material and lessened my ability to discharge in a creditable manner my duty of correspondent. I call it a duty, because it is incumbent on some one to enlighten the English people as to the treatment of political prisoners at Portland, and I have a life interest in the matter. Time, and paper, and the vigilance of my goalers oblige me to be brief and almost to confine myself to the detail of one particular occurrence which, falsely charged in the prison director's book to the Secretary of State, affects my moral character, and urges me to hazard every risk to set myself right.

On the 26th October I finished a letter to the Secretary of State, in which I gave him an idea of the wanton insult we were daily subject to. At a future time the rulers might say—"Oh, we knew nothing of all this; it was all done by the governor of the prison, and we have dismissed him."

Mr. Gladstone wrote a pamphlet showing that Neapolitan political prisoners were treated in the same manner as thieves and murderers. I offered to show Mr. Gladstone, or any one else sent, that Irish political prisoners are treated *worse* than thieves and murderers in England.

About the end of October I was told that for a trifling compensation, as, under present circumstances, a letter would be forwarded to my family, and seeing that I was prohibited from writing to or hearing from my wife, I availed of the offer. Being supplied with writing materials on the 4th of November, I prepared a copy of the letter to the Secretary of State, and a letter to my wife, both addressed as follows :

"Mrs. Mary Moore, Denzille street, Dublin, for Mrs. O'D." I did not address directly to Mrs. O'Donovan, as I had some fear of post-office interference.

My correspondence was arrested; I was ushered into a punishment cell, and next day, stripped of cap, jacket, handkerchief, boots and belt, was ushered into the Governor's presence, I was determined to take the punishment due to the offense as graciously as possible; but I was rather surprised to find myself called on to answer to a charge of "being detected in an endeavor to carry on an intrigue with the wife of another prisoner." In answer to "Have you anything to say?" I replied that the accusation was wrong, and if he produced the letters he would see it was necessary to change the charge when it was not properly taken down. He told me "I was not to dictate to him." "nor to instruct him in the discharge of his duties," and "did I deny or admit the charge." I said, "as it stands I deny it." He finally said, "Can you deny your letter to the Secretary of State?" and on my saying, "I admit or deny nothing so far," he satisfactorily said, "That will just do me," and wrote that as my reply while I protested. He told me the case was postponed to the next day. I thought it was to afford him time to look over the letters. The governor told me afterwards that "the board of directors had seen my letter to Mrs. Moore, and knew from it what kind of character I was." If the board of directors *did* see the letter in question, and if they did not see in every sentence that it was written to my wife, I would give very little for their brains.

When I asked Mr. Clifton to look at the superscription and he would see "for Mrs. O'Donovan," he said "that was, he believed, merely a subterfuge." He told me he himself had written the report to the Secretary of State and Board of Directors, charging me with endeavoring to carry on an intrigue with the wife of a fellow-prisoner, Mr. Moore.

I would take it for granted, that Mr. Clifton having on record in his book the letters to Mr. Michael Moore from his wife and mother, would know that my letter to "Mrs. MARY MOORE" was addressed to Mr. Moore's mother, who, I learned, occasionally saw Mrs. O'Donovan. The name of Michael Moore's wife is Catherine, and she does not live with her mother-in-law.

The day's postponement of my case was merely time for the Governor to consider my sentence, which happened to be seventy-two hours in solitary confinement on bread and water. This means eight ounces of bread and a pint of water at five o'clock, morning and evening. There is no light or even seat allowed. This I did not deem too hard for the offence, but for one thing or another arising out of it. Thirty-four days and nights in the cells on bread and water and low diet, with the cold of the season, have been productive of the natural, may I say the intended result, on the body at least, and the flesh on my hands is visibly turning into corruption.

I asked the doctor if he would consider it unreasonable that I'd be put to work indoors, in a shed, anywhere out of the frosty air, at the same time showing my hands. He said they were not bad enough yet.

When a prisoner is in punishment the Governor and doctor come to him once a day, to ask if he has any complaint. The person is ordered " to stand to attention," and give the salute of raising the hand to the uncovered head. I "stood to attention" for both gentlemen the first day, and the second, but the herald preceded the Governor the next day, and reminded me that I had not given the salute on the former occasions, and that Mr. O'Connor got three days' bread and water in a dark cell for neglecting this, one time.

When the Governor came I went through all the manœuvres. He asked me had I any complaint, and I replied that I complained the Governor falsified a charge against me; that he refused to correct it, and that he refused to receive my reply on examination. He would not take it down. I reminded him that one of the rules was that he should be at all times willing to receive any charge from a prisoner, but he turned away contemptuously, saying, "You can see our Director if you like." I thought this a poor return for my abject "koo-too-ing," and I began to consider what was the object of obliging me to go through this operation in a place where civility and patience are as much as might be expected from me It was not necessary for any purpose of discipline, for I was alone; when not alone, discipline is necessary, and I have not refused in presence of others to obey such orders. While undergoing punishment in solitary confinement, I began to think these salaams meant nothing more than my humiliation, and with that came into my mind all the vile words of wanton insult heaped on me from time to time by Director and Governor, such as—"Do you think I can believe you convicts?" "I do what I can for you fellows." "You're better fed than when you fed yourselves." "Not alone in this world should you be punished, but in the next." "Thirty years ago you'd have been hanged." "You were not sent here to be too sensitive." "Nothing can make you more degraded than you are." The latter observation was used by the Governor when I went before him on the following occasion: I fell under a barrow of stones one day and lacerated one of my fingers, when the officer abused me, and ended by saying, "I was such a man as would suck another man's blood." I went before the Governor to know if this language towards me was in the order of the officer's duty. When I spoke to the Director about it, he said it was "frivolous." The doctor's visit found me in the humor of these rebellious thoughts. I was stretched upon my *clar bog dael* (soft deal board), with the Bible in my hand, which every cell contains, when the door opened and the officer cried, "Stand to attention and salute the doctor." I sat up and said, "I beg your pardon, officer, but if the doctor is anxious to see me on my legs, he will come in and help me on them, as he seems willing enough to help me off them. I suppose, doctor, you are aware that this treatment is somewhat akin to that which Coleridge says, 'Kills so slowly that none call it murder.'" He said if I studied common sense instead of Coleridge it might be better for me. When I was taken before the Governor next day, I was charged with gross insolence to the doctor; expressions were put into my mouth that I did not make use of, and when I told the exact words that passed, the Governor replied, "I know very well what you said; but I will not be putting down your phillipics here."

"Then," said I, "you know what I said, and you put in the charge what you know I did not say."

"I'll have you punished for insolence if you do not confine yourself to the charge. Have you anything to say as to why you did not salute the doctor?"

"I have, if you take it," I rejoined.

"What is it?"

"Whenever I have been taken before the doctor of this prison I have been treated with insult. On the present occasion I cannot understand paying salaams to a doctor who daily called to see if I were progressing favorably under treatment which he knew, if investigated, was calculated to break down my health."

"This has nothing to do with the charge."

When, to make a long story short, I told him his book was nothing more than a lie, and I was sent back to bread and water.

Next day, when he came round, I told him such treatment merited nothing but contempt. For this I got three additional days' bread and water, in a cell darker than night, and the succeeding day I was sent out to work.

I learned that the Governor had been talking to others about my writing to Mrs. Moore; and having a wife and six children, the possibility of such a report getting into print was not pleasant to me. I sent for the priest, and he, by his manner, made me suspect that he even believed it. The Governor, on being asked by Mr. Moore for permission to write to his mother, remarked: "Moore, do you know there is another man in the prision carrying on a correspondence with your wife?" I sent for the priest again, and it was twelve days before he came. I begged him to do something that would bring on an investigation of the charge, as I was anxious to shield my moral character from defamation. I laid hold of my Bible to give him my last letter from my wife, in order that he might compare it with the arrested letter, but it had been taken out of my cell. I got it afterwards from the warder. I suppose my not having the letter confirmed the priest's suspicions, as, though I asked him to call next day, he did not come until I sent for him again.

When the Director came I was, with others, brought from my work, and when waiting outside his office I was led away again, the Director refusing to see me, as the Governor subsequently told me.

One day, when I was out of punishment, I renewed my application to the Governor to correct this intrigue affair on the books. He would do nothing. Then I asked him to put on record a charge against himself of defaming my character.

He would not let me write to the Board of Directors or to the

Secretary of State, and I ended my charge by saying he had belied me, and treated me in a mean manner. This was in the hearing of some of my fellow-prisoners, who were waiting to see the Governor. He ordered me into a punishment cell, and I had nothing to do but to take my punishment, and pray for patience and forbearance.

On the 24th of December I got three days' bread and water and fourteen days on low diet, for talking to Mr. Keane while at work. He was let off with a reprimand. This, with other things, reminds me of what one of the officers said to Mr. Moore one time of me—"The course Rossa pursued at his trial will not serve him here." Yet I could not say that my fellow-prisoners are not treated as badly as I. Recently I created a necessity for being ordered seventeen days in the cells, by saying to an officer who worried me, that "while God leaves me the use of my tongue, all the rulers of the kingdom would not prevent me from speaking when I thought proper." A prison rule prevents us speaking under various circumstances, but not while at work; and we were told once that we should speak loud enough for the officer to hear, lest we should be planning something.

Mais nous avons changé tout cela! for we are now not allowed to speak high or low.

It seems that our tormentors were not at all pleased by our affecting to take our punishment lightly. It also seemed to have become necessary for some object that we should be represented on the books of the prison as "refractory." Reports had to be got up against us by the officers, and the Governor can specially order us to be *reported*, as he admits he does, in order to make up his books.

The three first of the seventeen days' punishment I had for talking while I was at work, the Governor visited to know if I had a complaint. I had a complaint each day. The last was against the Director, for neglect in the discharge of his duties. All to no purpose. The succeeding day I made up my mind not to notice him, and on the 3d and 5th of January I was arraigned for treating him with contempt, and in answer to "what have you got to say?" I said, "In coming to ask me have you any complaint, and in refusing to take a complaint from me, you make a mockery of your duties. Under these circumstances I am ordered to pay you salaams. I will only say that I am your prisoner, and with my body it seems you have power to do what you please, but my mind and soul is not yours, and I refuse to pay you the required salaam." He'd not take down a single word I said, but ordered me forty-eight hours' bread and water. I was already "doing" the fourteen days' punishment, this time getting twenty ounces of bread and some gruel; but he stopped this, and put me on the new sentence, which, in constitutional England, looks odd, before the expiration of the original seventeen days.

Some Englishmen have written very humorously on a Turkish system of punishment, which, after a man is bastinadoed, obliges him to salute and return thanks to the punishing officer.

"I don't know but that thirty days of this punishment is as destructive to man's health as fifty bastinado strokes. Obliging the man to salute his punisher is, in the civilized world, deemed barbarism, but in England 'tis only "discipline." Besides, there is in England a doctor to superintend the ruin of a man's health. I could understand being obliged to take off our caps to the statue of the Lord Lieutenant every day, if it were placed in our path to the quarries, or to kneel to an effigy of his if placed in our way. This Herman Gessler did at Alfort, and imprisoned Tell for not saluting it. I can't bring myself to relish these salaams to my jailers while they are starving me.

Having another visit from the Director, I asked him to bring in the Governor and receive my explanation, as I was anxious to clear my character of the charge of carrying on an intrigue here. He said "it should be done in the regular manner, and as I was under punishment, he could not do anything that day." "Then," said I, "according as it suits the Governor I can be in these cells every time you visit the prisoners. And are these false reports against me to the Board of Directors and Secretary of State to remain on record in the public offices of the kingdom?" He could not help that," he told me, " he only thought there could be no desire to punish me if I had not violated the rules." I thought differently, and to show him by one small instance the animosity I experienced, told him that I had occasionally on my slate some notes from a book allowed to me, and the officer used to come and blot them out. He asked why I did not report the matter to the Governor. I said the Governor must be a party to it. I told him the officer kept a cell on the lighted side of the hall vacant for five weeks sooner than let me into it, and the Governor said it was serving me right. There were no windows in one side of this hall we occupied, and when a man in a window cell was sent to hospital or to "the cells," the practice was to send from the dark side the man who had the lowest number on the list. I was that man, and when Mr. Mulcahy was removed to Ireland a lighted cell was made vacant, it was kept vacant rather than allow me into it. We are now in a hall containing punishment cells. Up against the window is a sheet of peforated metal, which helps to secure the felon and exclude the sunlight. When I am allowed a book on Sunday, I might, at least, be allowed as much daylight as would enable me to read it, but I am not. The Irish political prisoner in England must content himself with seeing the excellence of the English convict system in print, but feeling none of it.

To add to my punishment, I am sent to work amongst a gang of English felons, away from my own party. James O'Connor is sent with me, but we are put at opposite ends of the gang, lest we should have a chance of exchanging a sympathetic word or look with each other.

The day I was sent amongst these English convicts I refused to work with them, and I intended to take the starving process in preference, but coming up for judgment, and finding the Governor was absent and the Deputy Governor was acting in his place, and being told by him that he was "sorry to punish me, but that no alternative was left him, he should follow the orders left regarding me by the Governor," I changed my mind. I got two days' bread and water and no bed. I went to work next day among them, and determined to get this fugitive letter out and write to my wife, and by so turning the tables on them a little, treat the Government and the Governor as they deserve. My mother lives in America. She is old; and I would not even be allowed to write one letter to her. I have six children. My father-in-law, at the time he wrote to me, in last September, had five of them, and the part of the letter relating to the children would not even be read for me. My wife asked me questions as to debts due to me, and I hoped I would be allowed to answer them. The Governor told me to write on my slate what I had to say. I did, and a month afterwards he said "I could not be sending your love letters." But these are small things, and as I could fill a volume with such trifling annoyances, I will stop. I remember, at a hotel one night, meeting three English tourists, Messrs. Fitzgerald, and Lord, and Ledward of Manchester, and talking politics with them. Mr. Ledward said the Irish were despised because they did not fight for their freedom, and I partly agreed with him. If I could have told him how England treated her political prisoners' he would have been insulted. I suppose nature comes to the assistance of man when he suffers for what he belives a true and holy principle—liberty—and that the mind sustains the body in its sufferings.

> "Eternal Spirit of the chainless mind
> Brightest in dungeons—Liberty thou art;
> For there thy habitation is the heart—
> The heart which love of thee alone can bind !
> And when thy sons to fetters are consigned,
> To fetters and the damp vault's dayless gloom,
> Their country conquers with their martyrdom,
> And freedom's fame finds wings on every wind !"

If you find this an unconnected letter, you will not wonder. It is harder to write here than on a battle-field, for my ears must be open to every lightest tread, and my attention forced from my subject and fixed upon those who are watching me.—I remain, sir, yours, O'DONOVAN ROSSA.

P.S.—Four additional days' bread and water. Some of my fellow-prisoners have reduced two stone weight; I have not weighed myself lately, but even forty days of our "lightening process" in the cell, since the 4th November, makes me feel light-bodied, and light-hearted too, thank God. I wish you would call for a copy of the "letter to Mrs. Moore;" I do not recollect what it contains, but I know my feelings towards my wife, and I venture to say, the man in authority who, after reading it, could write an official report to the effect that it was intended for any other man's wife, is a fool or a rogue. One word more to show how sharply the wind blows here. There is a temporary water closet on the quarry where the Irish felons work; at first it was cleared every three weeks. One day they told me I should do it next. Seeing the Govenor, I asked was this work expected from me, he said "yes;" the officer learning this, and knowing it was a disagreeable task, said he'd make two of us clear it every Monday morning in future, and he has been as good as his word."

When I had this written and delivered it to the prisoner for transmission, I determined to go on the "strike" again by refusing to work amongst the thieves. I was now very much emaciated and reduced in strength. The weather was intensely cold, and I felt as if every blast of wind was cutting through me. Whatever little flesh was on my hands seemed to be rotting off them. I remember that one morning I saw the doctor, and showing him the sores on my hands, asked him if he could not get me work indoors. Looking at them his reply was—"No, they are not bad enough yet. I will order you a pair of gloves." And being taken to the officer who had charge of such articles, I got two jane mittens that covered the hands. They had thumb "fingers" only, all the other fingers were free to play together as they protruded from the large holes at the end of my fashionable gloves. As I got them from the officer and fitted them I smiled, and asked, "What's the price?" and he good-humoredly said, "Oh, never mind, we'll charge them to your account." One morning, in making up my bed, I abstracted the single blanket and wrapped it round my body inside my shirt. I felt very comfortable for a couple of days, but the third day it was discovered, and I had my twenty-four hours on bread and water for "converting the property of the prison to improper uses." Next morning when I went to work I thought it was easier to stand anything than what I was suffering from cold. I laid my hammer on the block and made up my mind that this would be the last time I would work in the party. I don't know how many days I had been in punishment before something occurred that called for a new change of tactics on the part of my masters. The papers which my companions had concealed in the shed in which they worked were by some agency discovered; they found the wall torn down one day when they went out from dinner, and the next morning James O'Connor and I were marched out to work in company with them. All this time the whole of them were working inside the shed, but James and I would not be allowed in; we were ordered to place two blocks some twenty yards outside, and there we were kept in the cold blast, looking at the others under shelter. My first impulse was to kick against this, but the friends told me the papers were discovered, and I worked on till dinner time, knowing that something was to turn up. And so it did.

James O'Connor and I had been away from this place for about a month, and the object of bringing us back there now was to legally identify me with placing the papers there.

When dinner-hour came I was brought before the bar of justice, and charged with destroying prison property, with converting prison property to improper use, with having an ink-bottle and pens and pencil concealed in the prison, and with many other things that made an indictment as long as was made against me before conviction. I was asked what I had to say, and I said "Nothing." This was so serious a case that the Governor said he would not decide the punishment himself, but would send the matter before the Board of Directors, and until they were heard from I should remain in prison—in the punishment cells. In three days an answer came that the Governor was to mete out to me the extreme measure of the law, which was three days on bread and water and twenty-five days on punishment diet. Then there were special orders which were read to me from the Directors. One was that I be deprived of the use of all books, including the Bible, for six months. I had defaced prison property. I had written on a "Think Well On It," and on a prayer-book, but had I a fair trial I would have beaten them on this head, for whereas all books in the prison are branded with the prison mark, the ones I had used were not branded at all; there was no evidence of their being prison property, and all the books supplied to me had been found correct, as marked on my card. But fair play for an Irishman in prison, or out of prison, is out of the question. Twenty-eight consecutive days was the biggest dose of bread and water I had yet, and the time hung pretty heavily on my hands, with nothing to read and very little to eat. I wrote another surreptitious letter, ready to avail of any opportunity that offered for sending it out. These very considerate people gave me work to do while on bread and water: they put a pound of oakum into my cell in the morning, and I left it there all day without picking a thread of it, and in the evening they took it out again. I refused to pick unless they gave me the regular labor diet to eat, and every second day they deprived me of the pint of stirabout and the pound of potatoes which a man gets while on what is called "punishment diet." This I told the Governor was quite unconstitutional. He should not bring in a second sentence to encroach on the first one until the twenty-eight days were up, but he told me he could do what he liked when I would not work. One day he came to my cell with the doctor and Deputy-Governor, the door was opened, and he asked me the usual question—"Had I anything to say to him?" "Yes," said I, "I want you to place on your books a report against the Governor for not allowing me to see the Director the last time he was here, though I was not under punishment." "I'll do no such thing," said he. "Well," added I, "you're a mean, contemptible creature, and

I suppose I'll have to suffer being the sport of such a silly fool."
"What's that he says? What's that he says?" turning to the doctor. "Sport of a fool," said the doctor, turning on his heel, and away the three of them walked. Next day came the usual charge of "gross insubordination," and the usual sentence of punishment. I did not leave out of my head the book record of "writing to another man's wife," nor did I cease making efforts to have it altered. I saw the priest and minister—that is, the Catholic and Protestant chaplains. I explained to them all I thought necessary, and they, as far as I know, took no steps to see me justified. Indeed, from something that happened, I would not wonder if the Rev. Mr. Poole had made up his mind that the charge was true. I kept my wife's letters in a large Bible that I had in my ordinary cell before the sentence was passed of depriving me of the Bible, and it happened that while I was in the punishment cells the officer in charge of the other cells took my letters out of the book. I told the Catholic chaplain one day that I would show him these letters, and that he could compare them with the surreptitious one alleged to be written to Moore's wife. I was to be off of punishment next day, and he was to call to my ordinary cell at dinner-hour. He did call. I took the Bible to give him the letters, and they were not in it. I looked confused, and he looked as if he considered me guilty. He went away, saying he would call again, and did not call. I did not see the priest for some time, and I thought I would have recourse to the plan of preparing a charge against him, in the hope of bringing about an investigation that would clear me of the charge of carrying on a love intrigue. I asked the Governor to take it; he asked me what it was, and I said—"I am registered here as a Catholic. A charge is made against me affecting the morality of my character; the charge is false. It is the priest's duty to protect me in this matter. I have brought the case before him, and he has done nothing. I charge him with neglect of duty." "I won't take the charge," said he, and the door was locked. Next day the priest came into my cell, and appeared rather angry that I should offer such a charge against him. I tried to show him that I meant no harm—not.ing more than to do something which would bring about an inquiry that would give me an opportunity of clearing myself. He took it quite serious, and would not have any explanation I could make as satisfactory, and I told him in the end that if he took it so seriously he may, and that I *did* consider it was his duty to protect his congregation when their moral character was assailed, and to take some steps to help a prisoner to repel calumnies such as were hurled at me. We parted and I did not see our priest since.

Twenty-eight days on bread and water in solitary confinement is a long time. No book to read, no "kitchen" with your food but water, and very little food at that; no one to speak to, no face to look at but the face of a jailer, yet I had to manage as best I could to pass the time. Books that I had read when I was a little boy came to my assistance, and I smile at thinking of the silly things a person will do, or at least I did, to kill time. I think it was in "Schinderhannes, the Robber of the Rhine," that I read of one Karl Benzel dancing with the chains around his feet, and when I used to be lying on the bare boards pinched with hunger and shivering with cold, Karl Benzel would come into my mind, and I'd jump up and go through that ten shillings' worth of dance which I learned from Thady O', till I could barely give a shuffle from sheer exhaustion. Then I'd stretch again and go about making verses. It was in this mood and with such poetic surroundings that I strung together some rhymes about Jillen Andy. I made one verse one day, and kept it in my memory till the next day, when I made another, and when I had the story of "Jillen" I kept tacking on some other verses to it till I had a string of twenty-two or three, and then I entertained myself by reciting them in my cell. The warder would cry out, "Drop that noise," and I'd keep going on. He'd put his eye to the spy-hole and I'd keep declaiming, taking no notice of his attentions. I claimed that that cell was my house, that every man's house was his castle, and so long as I did not make as much noise as would wake the children next door I had a reasonable right to enjoy myself as best I could. I made up my mind for the worst. I saw there was no use in trying to reason them into fair treatment, and I felt considerably relieved and strengthened when I made up my mind to cease to try. But now about "Jillen Andy." I often asked Charles Kickham, when we were on the *Irish People*, to poetise this story of "Jillen." I knew there was no one living man could clothe it in Irish feeling as he could, but he put the task back on myself. My genius did not lie that way. But as idleness is the mother of mischief, I fell into the sin of spoiling a very fine subject for a poem by making verses on it when I had nothing else to do in prison. Jillen Andy lived at the other side of the street in Rosscarberry when I was a child. Her husband, Andy Hayes, was a linen weaver and worked for my father ere I was born. He died, too, before I came into the world, but when I *did* come I think I formed the acquaintance of Jillen as soon as I did that of my mother. Jillen was left a widow with four helpless children, and all the neighbors were kind to her. The eldest of the sons 'listed, and the first sight I got of a red coat was when he came home on furlough. The three other sons were Charley, Thade, and Andy. When I was about the age of twelve Charley was looking at Lord Carberry's hounds hunting one day. Going through some lonesome "airy" place he got a "puck" from one of the fairies. He came home lame, his leg swelled as "big as a pot." It had to be amputated by Doctor Donovan and Doctor Fitzgibbon, and he went about on crutches till he died in the year '65. Andy 'listed, and died in Bombay, and Thade and his mother fell victims to the famine legislation of '47. Thade met me one day, and spoke to me as I state in the following lines. I went to the graveyard with him. I dug, and he shovelled up the earth till the grave was about two feet deep. Then he talked about its being deep enough, that there would be too great a load on her, and that he could stay up and "watch" her for some time. By-and-by we saw four or five men coming in the church-gate with a door on their shoulders bearing the coffinless Jillen. She was laid in the grave. Her head did not rest firmly on the stone on which it was pillowed, and as it would turn aside and rest on the cheek when I took my hands away from it, one of the men asked me to hand him the stone. I did so, and covering it with a red spotted handkerchief, he took out of his pocket, he gave it to me again, and I settled Jillen's head steadily on it. Then I was told to loose the strings, to take out a pin that appeared, to lay her apron over her face, and come up. To this day I can see how softly the man handled the shovel, how quietly he laid the earth down at her feet, how the heap kept rolling and creeping up until it covered her head, and how the big men pulled their hats over their eyes.

JILLEN ANDY.

"Come to the graveyard if you're not afraid,
    I'm goin' to dig my mother's grave, she's dead,
And I want some one that will bring the spade,
    For Andy's out of home, and Charlie's sick in bed."

Thade Andy was a simple spoken fool,
    With whom in early days I loved to stroll,
He'd often take me on his back to school,
    And make the master laugh himself, he was so droll.

In songs and ballads he took great delight,
    And prophecies of Ireland yet being freed,
And singing them by our fireside at night,
    I learned songs from Thade before I learned to read.

And I have still "by heart" his "Colleen Fhune,"
    His "Croppy Boy," his "Phœnix of the Hall,"
And I could "rise" his "Rising of the Moon,"
    If I could sing in prison cell—or sing at all.

He'd walk the "eeriest" place a moonlight night,
    He'd whistle in the dark—even in bed.
In fairy fort or graveyard, Thade was quite
    As fearless of a ghost as any ghost of Thade.

Now in the dark churchyard we work away,
    The shovel in his hand, in mine the spade,
And seeing Thade cry I cried myself that day,
    For Thade was fond of me and I was fond of Thade.

But after twenty years why now will such
  A bubbling spring up to my eyelids start ?
Ah ! there be things that ask not leave to touch
  The fountain of the eyes or feelings of the heart.

"This load of clay will break her bones I fear,
  For when alive she wasn't over strong.
We'll dig no deeper, I can watch her here,
  A month or so, sure nobody will do me wrong."

Four men bear Jillen on a door—'tis light,
  They have not much of Jillen but her frame
No mourners come, for 'tis believed the sight
  Of any death or sickness now begets the same.

And those brave hearts that volunteer to touch
  Plague-stricken death are tender as they're brave,
They raise poor Jillen from her tainted couch,
  And shade their swimming eyes while laying her in the grave.

I stand within that grave, nor wide nor deep,
  The slender, wasted body at my feet,
What wonder is it if strong men will weep
  O'er famine-stricken Jillen in her winding-sheet.

Her head I try to pillow on a stone,
  But it will hang one side, as if the breath
Of famine gaunt into the corpse had blown,
  And blighted in the nerves the rigid strength of death.

"Hand me that stone, child." In his hands 'tis placed,
  Down-channelling his cheeks are tears like rain,
The stone within his handkerchief is cased,
  And then I pillow on it Jillen's head again.

"Untie the nightcap string," "Unloose that lace,"
  "Take out that pin," "There, now, she's nicely—rise,
But lay the apron first across her face,
  So that the earth won't touch her lips or blind her eyes."

Don't grasp the shovel too tightly—there make a heap,
  Steal down each shovelfull quietly—there, let it creep
Over her poor body lightly ; friend, do not weep,
  Tears would disturb old Jillen in her last long sleep.

And Thade was faithful to his watch and ward,
  Where'er he'd spend the day, at night he'd haste
With his few sods of turf, to that churchyard,
  Where he was laid himself before the month was past.

Then Andy died a soldiering in Bombay,
  And Charlie died in Ross the other day,
Now, no one lives to blush because I say,
  That Jillen Andy went uncoffined to the clay.

E'en all are gone that buried Jillen, save
  One banished man who dead alive remains,
The little boy that stood within the grave,
  Stands for his country's cause in England's prison chains.

How oft in dreams that burial scene appears,
  Through death, eviction, prison, exile, home,
Through all the suns and moons of twenty years—
  And oh! how short these years compared with years to come.

Some things are strongly on the mind impressed,
  And others faintly imagined there, it seems;
And this is why, when reason sinks to rest,
  Phases of life do show and shadow forth in dreams.

And this is why in dreams I see the face
  Of Jillen Andy looking in my own,
The poet-hearted man—the pillow-case,
  The spotted handkerchief that softened the hard stone.

Welcome those memories of scenes of youth,
  That nursed my hate of tyranny and wrong,
That helmed my manhood in the path of truth,
  And help me now to suffer calmly and be strong.

And suffering calmly is a trial test,
  When at the tyrant's foot that felon-drest,
When State and master jailer do their best,
  To make you feel degraded, spiritless, opprest.

When barefoot before Dogberry, and when
  He mocks your cause of 'prisonment, and speaks
Of "Thieves," "State orders," "No distinctions"—then
  Because you speak at work—hard bread and board for weeks.

Or when he says, "Too well you're treated, for
  Times were you'd hang;" "You were worse fed at home;"
"You can't be more degraded than you are;"
"You should be punished also in the world to come."

When sneer, and jeer, and insult follow fast,
  And heavenward you look, or look him down,
He rages and commands you to be classed
  And slaved amongst the slaves of infamied renown.

When England—worthy of the mean and base,
  Smites you when bound, flings outrage in your face,
When hand to hand with thieves she gives you place,
  To scoff at freedom for your land and scattered race.

To suffer calmly when the cowardly wound,
  From wanton insult, makes the veins to swell
With burning blood, is hard though doubly bound
  In prison within prison—a blacker hell in hell.

The body starved to break the spirit down,
  That will not bend beneath the scourging rod;
The dungeon dark that pearls the prisoner's crown,
  And stars the suffering that awakens Freedom's God.

Thus all who ever won had to endure,
  Thus human suffering proves good at last,
The painful operation works the cure,
  The health-restoring draught is bitter to the taste.

'Tis suffering for a trampled land, that suffering
  Bears heavenly fruit, and all who ever trod
In Freedom's path, found heavenly help when offering
  Their sacrifice of suffering to Freedom's God.

It was to Michael O'Regan the Governor said "he was better fed than when he fed himself;" to John Haltigan he said, "not alone in this world should we be punished but in the next;" and to myself, "that I could not be more degraded than I was." I must have given an awfully black look at him when he told me this, if my face any way indicated the contempt that was in my mind. I think now that this effort to degrade us, or to make us feel degraded, kept up my spirits wonderfully; there was a kind of a revolt of the mind, it became insurgent, rose up in arms and resolved to support the body.

While I was composing the foregoing verses I made an attempt to steal a Bible. I was changed once a week from one punishment cell to another, either for a change of air or as a precaution against escape. The warder opened my door one morning, ordered me to strip, searched myself and searched my clothes; and when I had put on my shirt he said, "Take the rest in your hands and go into No. 14." I went in; my eyes fell on a Bible that lay on the window, and, quick as lightning, I laid hold of it, and put it under the gutta-percha chamber vessel, which, with a gutta-percha pint, is the only article of furniture in a punishment cell, save and except that Bible, which at the time was forbidden to me. By-and-by the officer came to see if I was duly installed in my new stall, and to lock the door more firmly than I shut it by slamming it out, and allowing the spring to catch me in. He left my cell without noticing anything amiss, and I cannot well give an idea of the delight I felt in thinking that I had something to help me to kill time. I sat down on the floor with my back to the door, read for about an hour, when I was startled by hearing the key turn in the lock. The officer came in, looked around and asked, "Isn't there a Bible in this cell?" to which I grumblingly replied, "There ought to be one there, if the prison rules were carried out." "Have you a Bible on your person?" "I have not." "Now if you have you had better not put yourself to the trouble of stripping again," and saying this he drew his hands all over my person, and was leaving the cell with a look of despair, when giving the gutta-percha a kick my hidden treasure appeared and disappeared with him.

I think my reader and myself have had enough of Portland Prison by this time, and I may as well shift my quarters; indeed, it becomes a matter of necessity with me, as this closing scene will show.

I was under punishment; I refused to work, and refusing I got bread and water every second day, and penal class diet every other day. I refused to go before the Governor to hear this sentence of "bread and water" pronounced against me, as he refused to take down my words in reply to this question of "What have you got to say in regard to this charge of idleness?" I told him it was a mockery to be bringing me before him and asking me this question, when he would not record my reply, and I said, "This will be the last time I'll make my appearance in your presence. You can order your starvation process to go on as much as it will suit the interests of the Government, but leave me at peace in my cell." "I will not, but I'll make you come before me every time it suits me. The second next day, at the dinner hour, my cell door opened and I was ordered before the Governor, in order that I may hear him order I was to get no dinner. I refused to go. Two, three, four, and five officers came; they dragged me outside the door, I laid hold of the iron railings, they could not unloose me; the commander of the forces cried out for the chain handcuffs; one of the officers ran down stairs, and there was a cessation of hostilities till he came up again. The handcuffs were put on, they pulled the long chain, but, unless they pulled off my arms, they could not pull me away from the rails. In as imperative a tone as I could command I cried out, "Here, you man with that key, I order you to open these irons instantly." He obeyed, when I showed him that I had one of the iron bars in my embrace. I was tied again; the five or six of them laid hold of the long chain and pulled. I saw resistance was useless; I walked down the stairs after them, and they led me in monkey fashion into the presence of his Majesty the Governor. He had been listening to the noise, and with the dignity of ignorance he asked, "Why is this man in chains?" Then there was a long charge of my insubordination and insolence, and mockery of the prison authority. I was asked what I had to say, and I said nothing. I was sent back to my cell and got no dinner that day.

At this time I was every second day on bread and water. I got my eight ounces of bread at half-past five in the morning, and I kept this without eating until dinner hour, as I felt it lonesome to hear the dinner bell ring and have nothing to eat. You may talk poetically or metaphorically, or any way you like, of having your teeth water for a thing, but I often experienced the reality when I heard these bells ring, and I knew that the whole prison was eating while I had nothing to eat.

Two days had passed since I was led in chains before the Governor. At dinner hour my door was opened, and I was asked to come on. I refused to go, but on being told that it was not to go before the Governor I consented. I was taken before the clerk of the establishment; a list of the clothes in which I was convicted was read out for me; and on being asked was that correct, I answered "yes." I was told to sign the book and I did. Let not my readers think, as I thought, that I was going to get these clothes. No, it meant only a change of quarters for me. An order had come to convey me to Millbank Penitentiary to undergo a second term of solitary confinement, as my first term of solitary confinement did not seem to have answered the desired end. I was a "refractory" prisoner, and I had to be properly broken in before I could associate with Public Works convicts.

As soon as I had signed the book I was taken back to my cell and ordered to strip. I obeyed, and was led naked into another cell, where another suit of clothes was prepared for me. They brought me a dish of water in which to wash my feet before I dressed myself in the new shoes and stockings of my new suit, for I was to go as clean as possible to my new prison, so that my condition may cast no reflection on the discipline of the prison I had left. When I had dressed I was told to hurry on, and I asked if I was to get no dinner before I left? None. Then I said, "I certainly am not going on a journey without my breakfast." "Come on, come on, and drop that kind of talk, the carriage is waiting at the gate for you." "My carriage must wait until I get my breakfast," said I, "and you may as well take it easy." "Didn't you get your breakfast at half-past five o'clock this morning?" "Yes, but like the Irishman who sometimes took dinner for tea, I take breakfast for dinner, and my loaf of bread is still untouched in my cell." One of them went in and brought me out the eight-ounce roll. I was asked in a softer tone than usual to put it in my pocket and I could eat it in the carriage, as they were in a hurry to catch the train. I obliged them in this, but they would not tell me where I was going to. "Let me take this drink of water," I said, making a move towards my cell, for I had left one treasure there which I was exerting my wits to get at. There was tied up in the corner of my shirt one of those "surreptitious" letters that I had treasured as a reserve in case a chance offered to get it into the world, but I had to leave it in its hiding place, as the officers followed me into the cell, and I never heard of the treasure since. Two or three times I meditated throwing it over the wall, and take chance to have some sympathetic or mercenary friend find it; but the surprise came, and I was spirited away, leaving my week's labor behind me.

As I was passing from the punishment ward, I came in view of the place where the Irish party worked. I stood, and very seriously asked "Pontius Pilate," who was conducting me, if he would not let me down to bid good-bye to my friends. He put his hand on my shoulder, saying—"Come on, now; I thought you had no friends anywhere," and I turned my back on that party of twenty-four, who are scattered now in every part of the world, and many of them in their graves.

CHAPTER XIII.

MY CARRIAGE IN WAITING—MY BREAKFAST—FIGHT FOR MY DINNER—
JOURNEY TO MILLBANK PRISON, LONDON—THOUGHTS OF ESCAPE—
—SUPPER—RECEPTION WARD—INSTALLED IN OFFICE—TAILOR-
ING AND THEFT—LETTER WRITING—SCRUBBING FLOOR—PUMP
HANDLE AND CRANK—PUNISHED FOR NOT DOING TWO THINGS AT
THE SAME TIME—OAKUM PICKING AND PICKING COIR.

When I went outside the prison gate, I found my carriage waiting for me, and I stepped into it without bidding good-bye to the Governor and Deputy Governor, who were waiting to see me off. My two keepers came in after me; the horses started, and I pulled my loaf of bread out of my pocket, and commenced to eat my breakfast. It did not take long to finish it, as my appetite was particularly good at this time. We were at the railway station some twenty minutes before the train arrived that was to convey us. My keepers marched me down the platform, and kept me standing at a distance from all the other travelers. A restaurant was near by, and hearing them talk of dinner I asked for mine. "What," said White, the head officer, "didn't you have your dinner coming down in the coach?" "No, that was my breakfast, and I'll have to get my dinner now as I am travelling." "I don't think you will, for I have orders to give you nothing to eat." "Well, that isn't fair. I left the prison after the bell ringing for dinner. I got none, and now I am taken on a journey without any food." "We can not help that, we must go by our orders." "Orders or no orders, if I have far to go, and that I get no food, I am not going to stand it quietly, now that I am outside the prison walls." Then there was a movement, so that I could see the pistols. The whistle of the train was heard. White went into the restaurant, and returned with a parcel; he and Green conducted me into a compartment of the railroad car; as others were coming in, they wanted to stop them, requiring a compartment for ourselves three alone; but as room was wanted we had to make some for others, the conductor saying "another car would be put on at the next station, and we could have a compartment of our own." When we left the island of Portland and arrived at Weymouth station, this arrangement was made, and as the train moved White unloosed his parcel, the contents of which turned out to be what are called soda cakes. He spilled them out on the seat, and, after eating some of them, said, "Rossa, you can have a few of these if you like." "Thank you, governor," said I, and handing me six of them I took them. Each was about the size of a penny, and it wasn't like making two bites of a cherry, I could make one bite of the six, so ravenously hungry was I, but decency prevailed on me to eat moderately, and I demolished them one after one. Four more of them remained on the seat, staring at me for half an hour, and perhaps I staring at them, till White said, "Perhaps, Rossa, you could make room for these two," and I did make room for them.

By no act of mine could I get out of them where they were taking me, but after traveling for about four hours we stopped at a station where there was a delay of twenty minutes for refreshment, and I could guess from the buzzing around that we were bound for London.

Wanting to stand on my legs and look around, I induced them to let me go to the water-closet. When we came back to the platform the carriage had moved away in order to come back on another track. The passers-by stared at me, no doubt thinking I was some notorious burglar or thief. They might have admired my gray dress, my knee breeches, and blue stockings, that showed off my lank, lean legs to genteel advantage. I noticed a few giving sympathetic looks as they passed by. I thought they may be Irish, and I looked inquiringly at them, but as I did so I was ordered by my keepers to turn my face the other way, and obeying orders had to turn my back on my beholders.

White, the superior officer, went into the refreshment-room, and after a little delay there, came out with a glass of water in his hand. Holding it out to me, he said, "Here, you may be thirsty, and I am sorry I cannot give you anything better." I thanked h m, and after drinking the water, gave him back the glass, which he carried into the refreshment-room. As I was alone with one officer, I thought what a chance there was of "going on the run," if I had any way of getting my hands out of the irons. Even with my hands tied I am sure I would have made the start, only a thought came into my head that I would have a better opportunity of darting off when I landed on the station in London, and I made up my mind that I'd make the attempt at escape when I arrived there, come what would of it. There is no use in your saying "What a foolish idea it was," "How silly of him to think of such a thing." I did think of it and would take action on the thought only precautions were taken that made it impossible. You wise, sensible reader, if you were in my position, might find your wisdom degenerating into the "folly" I allude to. I know that I never found myself unpossessed of it, if any chance presented itself of getting out of my cage. The great hardships within made the outside danger appear very little.

The train that moved away from the station put back, and I was ordered into it.

"What!" said I, "do you really mean to say that you'll take me away from this place without giving me my dinner?" "We can't give you any dinner." "Then I can't go." "Oh, you must." "No, not willingly." One of them put his hand gently on my shoulder, saying, "Come on, there is no use giving us any trouble; we would give you your dinner if we could." With his hand on my shoulder we walked toward the carriage. I sat down inside, the two officers with me, a crowd collected about the window, and as I had an audience, amongst whom might be some one to send the story to Ireland, I kept inveighing against the inhumanity of starving me in prison, and taking me from Portland to London without giving me a bit to eat. White seemed to be giving way and said, "Well, I think I might venture to get you some bread and meat;" but as he laid his hand on the door to go out the bell rang for the train to go off. Just then a little girl with a basket on her arm, who was amongst the listeners, cried out, "Cakes, cakes." "Here, here," said White. He put his hand in the basket and took out two; put the other hand in his pocket and took out a penny. He gave the money to the little girl and gave me the cakes. As I took them into my manacled hands, whatever blood was in my body seemed to rush into my face. I felt it; I felt the thrill through my whole frame. I know there was some impulse toward throwing them into his face, or throwing them out the window, but another impulse counteracted that, in the thought that the man was acting against his orders; that there was some kindness in the act, and the last thing I could do would be to hurt the feelings of a man who did not mean to hurt mine. I suppose if my blood was ever hot, it was somewhat cooled down at this time. I ate the cakes, and never spoke a word till I reached London, meditating on that escape of mine.

Various were the thoughts that passed through my mind, and many were the plans. Assistance should be had somewhere, and I knew it would come if I could get a chance of making myself known. There is no railway station in London that there are not Irishmen about it, who at that time would risk their own liberty to obtain mine. What do we care about getting others into difficulties so long as we can manage to get out of our own. We men are terribly ourselves first, and all the world afterwards. I had in my mind that night, that as soon as I landed on the platform I would make a "bolt;" I would run some way; the best way would be along the railway track if I could get on to it; for there I would be most sure of meeting with the most hard-working Irishmen, the poorest, the truest, and those who had least to lose. I thought I might get some one to recognize my character by crying out "*Cowihr, cowihr!*" "Ireland," "Rossa;" one or either, or all together; but all these thoughts were put out of my head by a new move on the part of my keepers. The train was slackening speed, coming into London; White said, "There is the prison," as we were passing Millbank, and saying so, he put his hand in his pocket and pulled out a pair of handcuffs. As they shone in the gaslight I read in them my death warrant, and as White tied one part of the manacle on my wrist above the other iron that was on it, and tied the other part of it on one of Green's wrist, my spirits fell to Zero.

Here was I, bound to one of my jailers, so that if any attempt was made at a rescue two of us should be taken away, or the hand of one of us should be torn off, if the irons could not be broken.

The train stopped; we came out; went into a carriage; and when we came out again I found myself inside the walls of Millbank prison, London. It was after eight o'clock, and the prisoners were in bed. The officers had retired, but a few were in special waiting for me. I was given up to the man who had charge of the reception ward, and as White was delivering me over, he said to my new guardian, "Rossa had no dinner, and if you have any, give it to him." Millbank: "I have no dinner; the only thing left for him is a nine ounce loaf for his supper.

White—"You may have something extra, for he had nothing to eat all day, and if you have, give it to him." Millbank: "I have no dinner for him. Well, I will try, but I fear there is nothing left. unless some porridge may have remained in some of the tins." White and Green bade me "Good night."

Millbank shut me up in my cell, which contained a table and stool, and six or seven tin cans. By-and-by the door was opened, and my new guardian appeared with a large tin can, out of which the porridge was measured to the prisoners. "Here," said he, "put a few of those tins on the table." I took hold of the whole six or seven, and he cried out, "Stop, stop, I don't think there is much in it." He filled one pint, he filled two, and his tin kettle was drained before he had the third full. "Here," said he, "take that, and you'll be a long time here before you get so much again." I ate my nine ounces of bread and drank my three pints of porridge, all the while thinking of the kind Christian government that went to the expense of telegraphing from Portland to Millbank to give me nothing but bread and water when I arrived, in order to carry out the day's discipline under which I labored when I left Portland. I got my bed and spread it out on the flags. I asked if I could not have a board to put between the stone and the half-inch thick mattress. No; that was a reception cell, and I could have no other accommodation. The old song, "My lodging is on the cold ground," came into my head, but worse than that was to come after.

I did not close my eyes that night—well, literally I did close them in order to force myself into a sleep, but all to no purpose. The chances that presented itself of making an attempt at escape at the refreshment station would not leave my mind; it was one of those chances that never return, and I kept upbraiding myself with folly for not embracing it. Time was when to escape from the myrmidoms of the land was held unworthy of brave men, but that was before the myrmidons laid hands on you. In the revolutionary school in Ireland it was taught by the principal master that no man should run away before he was caught, for in a crisis there

may be a general skedaddle which would bring on general demoralization by the Government circulating that such and such men were to be arrested. These tactics were adopted, too, by the Government, but, to the credit of the men, most of them stood their ground. I believe the history of the world has not on record a country for size and population that produced more devoted men than Ireland produced for the last dozen years—men ready to risk life and liberty for their country's freedom. Nor is there any man in history that I have read of, in a population of five or six millions, who had so many men as Mr. James Stephens had ready to do his bidding in the cause of freedom—willing to venture their lives in the execution of any project he deemed necessary for the independence of his country. How all these men are scattered! How all the hopes that grew with the labors of their early years are blighted, it is painful to see this fourth day of December, 1873. To blame this principal master I have referred to, I will not; one thing alone will I put on record regarding him, and it is, that as tne representative of such men as I speak of, I would like he had shown more "pluck;" I would like when he had publicly promised to be in Ireland at a certain time to fight—that he had appeared there, albeit a man did not accompany him, and even though it cost him his liberty or life. It may be unreasonable to expect this, but only a nobleman in mind will see that something like it was due to the characters of the men who were committed with him in the revolutionary movement in Ireland.

The morning after my arrival in Millbank I was put through the initiatory process of prison citizenship. My height, weight, and color were taken. I was examined by the doctor, registered on the books, and orders were given to put me tailoring. The cell I was placed in was a particularly gloomy one; it was situated in an angle of the pentagon, just behind the chapel, and convenient to the officers' room, within the ward. When I occupied it I looked at my furniture, my tin pint and plate came up for inspection, as I occasionally used one of these articles, when burnished up, for a looking glass. On the bottom of the pint I found engraved the words, "The Artful Dollier," and my heart leaped as if I was shaking hands with Denis Dowling Mulcahy himself. This was the name we called him in Portland, and this was his own writing also. Then, this was the cell Denis occupied when he was in Millbank, and this was the pint he took his porridge from. Hadn't I company? Yes, I had—in that pint that recalled the memory of a friend whenever I used it.

At a quarter to eight o'clock the bell ordered us to make down our beds, and I made mine. At eight a warder went round to see if every prisoner was in his cell, and to turn off the gas. He passed my cell without putting out the light, and, thinking he had made a mistake, I gave a halloo after him. He came back with his, "What's the matter with you?" "Don't you see, governor, you havn't put out the gas." "Never you mind that; that gas is to be left lighting all night, and make no more noise." The burner was only about two feet from the head of my bed, and, as the light was glaring on my eyes, I could not sleep. I thought I would devise something to shade my face. I had a water bucket in my cell, which had to serve the treble purpose of scrubbing tub, of washing basin, and of stool. I took this and planted it by the head of my bed. I then took a large card, about three feet long, by two feet broad, on which were printed the rules and regulations. I made it to stand on the bucket, against the wall, between the burner and the bed-head, so as to screen my face from the light. By-and-bye, the night watch looked in, and roared out, "What have you done there?" "Oh! governor, I could not sleep with that gas-light staring me in the face, and I put the card up as a screen." "Take that card away at once." "Oh! now, governer, what harm is it doing?" "I cannot see your head; take it down at once, I tell you." "If I took it down I wouldn't be able to sleep a wink, and then I wouldn't be able to work to-morrow." "Take down that card instantly, I tell you." "I will not." "Then, I'll soon let you see that you will," and I heard his slippered feet falling heavily in the hall as he moved away. In about five minutes I heard the tramp of several men approaching; they halted opposite my cell, and big Power, the head warder, speaking to me through the slit in the wall, ordered me to take down that card. "Put out the light, and I'll take it away." "That cannot be done, but the card must be taken down." "What harm is it doing, governor?" "That's none of your business; put that card in its place instantly, I tell you." "Oh! for goodness sake, give me some rest, and let me go to sleep." "Go off for the keys." Off the officer went. "Here, come back awhile," and back he came. "See, Rossa, the keys of the prison are given up for the night, and if you don't take down that card we will have to open the door and take it away from you. Once the keys are given over for the night, we cannot get them without a great deal of trouble, and you may as well save us that, for we must take away the card, if you don't." "Well, anything to save trouble," and, taking away the card, I said, "but couldn't you lower that gas a little?" "See, turn off a little of that gas; a little lower; a little higher; there, there, that will do," and away they walked.

As I was doing my share of the "orderly" work next morning I noticed hanging on the wall a card, on which was my name. Opposite was written: "This prisoner to be well watched, and the gas to be left lighting in his cell all night." When I went to my cell I began thinking, and thought I must be a desperate character. Friends ask me, now that I am in the world, "Had I any thought at all of release when I was in prison?" It is said, "Hope springs eternal in the human breast," but the springs of my hope were nearly always dried up by continually witnessing these signs of special anxiety regarding me. I don't know what my masters must have taken me for. If they were not fond of me, they were particularly careful of me. Hoping anything from these people, and acting so as not to have that hope frustrated, would make me their slave—would wear me off my feet. No. I kept myself a free man in prison; while they had my body bound in chains, I felt that I owed them no allegiance, that I held my mind unfettered—that I was *not* their slave.

In this prison of Millbank the prisoners have to do the sweeping and cleaning in turn, and every morning, in every ward, five or six are taken out of their cells for an hour or so to put the corridor in order. I was detailed for service once, but this, it seems, afforded me too much liberty, and an order was passed that I was to be passed over for this service in future.

"I was to be treated like any other prisoner"—that was the stereotyped phrase towards me on every occasion of an interview with the Director, the Governor, the Deputy-Governor, and with every other Governor down to the smallest of these small officials. Yet they managed by their petty acts to deprive me of every little privilege that the convict system accords to its children. My school hour twice a week was confiscated before I was a month in Millbank, and every other privilege that they could confiscate. They pressed so closely on me this time—they screwed me down so tightly that I guessed something was up. I told them they had better screw me into a little needlecase for the Governor to carry in his pocket. Something had scared them. You could see alarm in the countenance of every man in authority. I write now in the light of the world, and I see that on the 7th of March, 1867, there was a "rising" in Ireland. England did not know where it would stop, or whether it would confine itself to Ireland or branch into England. She was terrified. The movement was a secret one, and with all her spies she knew little about it. If she could grasp the whole of it, if she could realize its extent, if it was a large, grand, and powerful constitutional agitation, she could take "constitutional" means to meet the emergency; but she did not know when, where, or how she was to be struck, and hence the alarm. A similar terror seized the English Government in December of the same year, 1867, when an attempt was made to blow up Clerkenwell Prison in London. Horse, foot, and artillery were brought inside the prison walls, and kept there day and night for months. Cannon were placed on the prison square, and every preparation was made in the heart of London to meet an attack from those Irish revolutionists.

I did not escape scot free, for shading my face from the light with the "rules and regulations." Next day I was charged with the offence in presence of the Governor. This man's name was Morish, a big, stand-off, important kind of person, with the air of a disciplinarian. He read me a lecture, and, when he came to speak of my coming to his prison with such an exceedingly bad character,

I gave a kind of smile that made him pause, and pronounce a sentence of "42 marks." I had added a year and a half in Portland to my sentence of life, by the forfeiture of marks, and here was another week put on me. If things go on in this way, thought I, there is poor chance of getting out of prison, either in this world or the next.

Shortly after this first interview of mine with the Governor, two officers came into my cell and ordered me to strip. I was stripped the day before, which I took, as a matter of course, as part of my initiation into the secret masonry of Millbank; but, coming the day after to make me repeat the humiliation, was quite out of order, and I asked, "What's up now?" "No matter what's up, but obey orders—strip." I took off my jacket and trousers, and shoes and stockings, and shirt and wrapper, every one of which they examined and felt inch by inch. I stood before them with the flannel drawers still on me. "Strip off that drawers." "Will you please allow me to put on the shirt before I take off the drawers?" "No, take off that drawers; we will have to see you stripped naked." I obeyed orders again. I turned round; I opened my mouth; I extended my arms and legs. They discharged their duty to the letter of the law, threw me back my clothes, and locked the door.

For three months, day after day, two of these officers came and put me through the same process. I felt it more than anything connected with my prison life; and when the supervision came so close upon me, that, when taking a bath, a jailor had to stand over me, I have no words to describe my feelings of shame. I am not very sensitive, nor very thin-skinned, nor very refinedly fashioned, but I owe to some early association the possession of some very strong prejudices against my fellow-man looking at me in a state of nature. When I was at school, and heard the boys telling stories of how men were stripped naked when they enlisted for soldiers, I imagined it the most awful thing that could be done and there was little fear of my ever becoming a soldier. I once and again reminded some of the authorities that this daily stripping of me conflicted a little with the prison rule, which says, "The Governor and officers must be at all times disposed to cultivate sentiments of morality and propriety of behavior in the prisoners;" but the demands of "discipline," or the Government demands regarding m᛫, required that all rules and regulations be set aside, in order to reduce me to some required standard.

After three months or four, a crisis came, in which I refused to submit to the daily stripping. The clothes were then torn off me by five or six officers; but I will postpone telling the particulars of the adventure, until I come to it in the due course of my narrative. I believe I broke off when I was saying something about my schooling. I was always fond of wandering from that, but now I'll return to it.

When I was in Millbank a few days, one morning the door of

my cell was thrown open, and an old man walked in, handed me a leaf of ruled paper and a writing pen, and walked out again. Then a prisoner who was out as acting orderly came to the door with about twenty little brown stone ink-bottles on a board. "Here, here, hurry on, take one." "What is it for?" asked I. "School, school, school; you're at school now," and after taking my ink-bottle he hurried on to the scholar next door.

I don't know, is it that evil associations corrupt men, or is it that every man has something of the thief in him, and only requires to be placed in certain straightened circumstances to have the faculty developed?—but true as I write, the first thought that came into my head was to steal one of those little brown stone bottles, ink, and cork, and all, and pen, to boot. I had a kind of foreboding that my guardians would not leave me long at school, and I made up my mind not to leave another opportunity pass without making an attempt to avail myself of writing material to help me to educate myself. "Self-help" was one of the books the prison library circulated, and I determined to profit by its teachings, even though learning, treated as I was, might be termed "The pursuit of knowledge under difficulties."

The first day of my schooling, rather the first hour, for it was one hour in each of two days of the week, was occupied in writing my "Jillen Andy" verses on the leaf of paper I got. The schoolmaster came in a second time and told me I could write whatever I liked on the paper, and he would return to take it from me when the hour was up, but he told me afterwards that I should not write verses on my paper; I should write like other prisoners, copy lines or passages from my school books or Bible.

Chance gave me a second day at school, and also gave me an opportunity of retaining my ink bottle when the school was breaking up. I also became possessed of a steel pen by such a *ruse* as this. I noticed that when the schoolmaster came round to give me a pen he had a number of them in his hand, some of which were without nibs. When he left my cell I drew out the nib and put it on the floor, where the shadow from the leg of the table hid it. When he came round by-and-by he saw me idle, and asked "why I was not writing?" I took up the pen handle that lay on the table, and holding it towards him remarked quite innocently that it was not easy to write with that. Had he made any fuss about giving me one with a nib in it, I could have made a little fuss, too, in looking for it and found it on the floor. But he said nothing, only "thought he gave me a good pen," and handed me another.

Being tailoring this time, I had some black thread, which I tied to the neck of the bottle, and the other end to one of the bars of my window. The roofing of the chapel rose to within about a foot of the window, and a gutter ran along it to carry off the rain. In the gutter the bottle lay hid for about three months before it was discovered. Whenever I wanted to use it I hauled in my line, and having used it, put it back to the resting place. I found a bit of a *kippen*, and fashioned it into a pen-handle, tying my nib to it with my black thread, and this I kept concealed between the gas-pipe and the wall.

I applied for permission to write my reception letter, but the governor would not grant it. I reminded him of the rule that said, that every person on being received into the prison, could write a letter, and he reminded me that that applied only to men of good character—not to men who had been sent back from public work for bad character. He said I could repeat the application to the Director if I wished, and doing so, he allowed me to write the letter, but hoped I would confine myself to legitimate matter. The time for writing was during the school hour, and I had not my letter finished the first day. I knew well that it would never pass the consorship, as I was telling all about the treatment I received, and I managed to write two copies on my waste paper before I gave it out of my hands the second school day. I intended sending these copies surreptitiously if an opportunity offered. The next day the Director came, he sent for me and told me he could not let that letter pass, but he would give me a chance to write another. I thanked him and wrote just the same as I had written before. Again he sent for me and remonstrated with me for repeating my offence, ending, however, with the offer of another chance, which I accepted. I was by this time wide awake to some of their trickery. If I refused to write they would put my refusal on record, and thus gain a strong point against me in that battle with public opinion to which I was determined to bring them, if at all possible. If I wrote out a letter, stating nothing of my treatment, while they were treating me in a manner calculated to bring me to an early grave, they, in case I died, and that any question was raised about my ill-treatment, would cry out, "It is all false. Look at his last letter to his wife; see if there is a word in it about ill-treatment" Acting, with the doom of death starting me in the face, I, every time I was allowed to write a letter to my wife, wrote of my prison life. For three years they kept suppressing these letters, during which time she never heard from me. The reflection that she might imagine I did not care about writing to her was painful enough to me, but I had put everything into the fight, and I made up my mind to sacrifice everything before I would play into the hands of such a hypocritical, heartless, merciless enemy as I had to deal with. I tied up the two copies of my letter, each separately, in as small parcels as I could. One of them I had in my straw mattress, and the other in a hole I scooped out in a corner of the cell. This I filled up again so as that it would never be noticed unless a person went looking for unnoticeable holes.

The time came when I was to lose my schooling, and I lost it in this manner. An English convict, born in Kilkenny, occupied a cell next to mine. He was then there under the name of Scott, but he told me that was not his right name. This he wished to be kept a secret, as he did not want Kilkenny folks to know anything about him or his whereabouts. He was only lately convicted, and as we stood inside our open doors in the morning, waiting to have our numbers called to take our buckets of fresh water, he whispered me many stories of the war in Ireland, all of which I greedily swallowed. Not being able to use his food at first, nearly every morning he'd manage to throw a piece of bread into my cell as he passed by it. When I learned that he could tell me everything about Ireland and the "boys" there, I neglected my schooling, to stand near my door and have a whisper with him.

Brown, the officer, used to be up in the centre of the ward occasionally, where he had a view of two corridors, but he put on slippers one day, and creeping softly down, stole a march on Scott and me as we were whispering to each other from inside our doors. We were startled from our *tete-a-tete* by his roaring out, "Put out your brooms and shut those doors," and having taken away my writing material, I shut my door. He opened it again and asked, "Why haven't you put your broom out?" "Where am I to put it?" "Put it outside your door," and putting it out he locked me in. The putting out of your broom or sweeping-brush was to signify to all persons passing by that you were under report and awaiting sentence, and many a time my broom was out. When the Governor sat to pass judgment, I was taken to the corridor, where the offenders are drawn up in line, four paces apart, with their faces turned to the wall. My turn came. I was conducted into the court and charged with talking to Scott during school hour. Asked what I had to say, I said, I'd give my reply in writing, and as I wouldn't get paper, I'd say nothing. The sentence passed on me was, that I get no more schooling while in prison; but Scott was not deprived of his schooling, though it was he did all the talking. His sentence was a fine of 42 marks and a reprimand. Didn't I feel lonesome every day afterwards when I heard the school bell ring, and the doors opening, and my door kept locked! Yes, I did, and concluded that my schooling was forfeited, not so much for punishment, but as a precaution against my getting writing materials into my hands. When the school bell rang, I put away my work and took my slate and pencil to figure away the hour in solitary confinement. I was one day so occupied, when I heard some one at my door asking, "Why is this man idle?" The warder opened the door, and Captain Wallack, the Deputy-Governor, asked, "Why aren't you at work?" "Oh, Governor, this is school hour." "You have been deprived of school, and you must keep to work." "Well, I don't know, I have been often told I am to be treated like any other prisoner; the other man, who was reported with me, has not been deprived of his schooling. I think I may fairly be allowed such privilege as you allow your thieves and pickpockets, and I think it quite illegal to deprive me of what the law says every prisoner must have." "You must not be impertinent here." "The prison rules do not allow me to be impertinent to any one, nor do they allow any one to be impertinent to me." "Put out your broom," and out the broom went for another report. This Captain Wallack was very civil to me from that out; he acted quite gentlemanly, and I treated him quite respectfully. It came within the sphere of his duty to pass sentence of bread and water on me a few times, while the Governor was absent, but he did it without any extra judicial observations. It was illegal to deprive me of schooling, but what did they do to correct this illegality, do you think? The Board of Prison Directors held a meeting, and decided that superiorly educated prisoners—those who were in the fourth class—should get no more schooling, and I was immediately put down as a fourth class man; rather, I should say, I was promoted to it to finish my education, for when I was admitted to Pentonville, some fifteen months before, I could graduate no higher than second class. If this does not prove that I took care of my schooling, it shows that I had some interest to shove me on.

Our cells had to be scrubbed twice a week. You had to go on your knees, but you had strong leather knee-caps to protect your trousers from the flags. Part of the process of scrubbing was to give the cell a finishing touch by rubbing the flags with a kind of soft, white stone, so that when the cell dried it had a nice chalky appearance. This, to my mind, was dirtying the cell instead of cleaning it, for the air was always impregnated with the dust arising from the floor. As I had no instructions at first, I used the stone as a kind of soap, and I gave my finishing stroke by washing it all off. The Deputy Governor, passing by one day, said my cell was very dirty, and I was ordered to scrub it again. I got my bucket of water, my scrubbing-brush, and my soap-stone, and went to work, though I had scrubbed it that morning before. By-and-by, Brown, the ward officer, came in, and said it was dirty still, and asked me to go over it again, and at it I went. In another hour's time he came in, said it was not white enough yet, and told me to give it the finishing touch with the stone, and not to wash off the powder, so a third time I tied on my knee-caps and went to work. Just as I had finished the bell rang for exercise, and I got my hour in the open air. Then the dinner bell rang, and I had my hour for dinner. After that the master tailor came in, and asked me to show him the work I had done all day. "Well," I said, "I have been hard at work, but I have not done much tailoring." Early in the morning he gave me some canvas bags to make, and I had only about a foot of stitching done when I was ordered to re-scrub the cell. Having gone over the work three times, with the exercise hour and dinner hour coming after, I had no time to do the tailor's work. He laid hold of the bag I had been sewing, took out his tape line and measured my stitching. It was only fourteen inches. "And this is all the work you have done since morning, fourteen inches of stiching?"

"I have done other work, for Mr. Brown made me scrub the cell three times, and then the exercise hour came and then the dinner hour, so that I had no time to do any of the work you gave me."

"You should have scrubbed your cell like other prisoners, in the morning before breakfast, and you must get on like other prisoners. I must have my work done, and I tell you, you'll soon find yourself on bread and water if you don't conduct yourself properly here."

"I am conducting myself properly; if you think I am not, you can report me. I prefer it to your abuse."

"Put out your broom," and out my broom went again, to show I was under report and awaiting punishment.

I was taken before the Governor. The tailor was present to charge me with idleness; he had the canvas bag with him to show that I had done only fourteen inches of stitching from eight o'clock in the morning till half-past one in the evening. I was asked what I had to say in reply, and I said nothing, as I would not get pen and ink and paper to put my words on record.

I forget now whether the sentence was marks or bread and water, but there was an addition made to it that the tailoring work be taken from me and that I be put at the punishment work of the prison, which was picking coir, and every day that I did not do the task-work of twenty ounces, I got twenty-four or twice twenty-four hours' bread and water.

At this time all my fingers were bandaged by the doctor. I had been so reduced from hunger and cold in Portland that I came to Millbank with the flesh rotting off my hands. I could use the needle pretty well, for it did not require much bending of the fingers; but when I came to pick the coir I found it required the exercise of all my fingers, and, failing to do my task-work, at first, I succeeded in getting bread and water and no bed at night.

If ever man felt cold, I felt it one of these nights. It was about the 27th of March, 1867, and I had no bed or bed-clothes but a light rug. I would not be allowed to walk about the cell; I had to remain stretched with this rug around me. It was a shivering and chattering of teeth all night through. When I looked out through the hole in the wall in the morning, the house-tops were covered with snow. During the winter season—that is, between the 29th of September and the 25th of March—the prisoner under punishment gets a rug and a blanket, but from the 25th of March to the 29th of September he gets a rug only. The cell has no window, but there is a hole about two feet long and three inches wide to admit a little light, and as my bed-board was under the hole, I found the snow had been drifting in on me all night.

I heard the prison clock strike two. To sleep was impossible, and I got up to walk about the cell. I wore my punishment slippers, and in a minute I heard a voice at the door—"Stop that walking, and go to bed." "I have no bed." "Well, lie down, and don't be making noise." I sat on the board, and communed with myself how to kill time. I took off my slippers, and commenced walking as lightly as I could in my stocking vamps. The watch heard my footfalls, and tapped at the door again, with his, "Didn't I tell you to stop that walking? If you don't go to bed, I'll report you in the morning"—and rather than be reported, I went "to bed," and shivered away the hours until daybreak.

The "rising" in Ireland was on the 7th of March, 1867, and immediately after, there was such a hubbub about me that I guessed there must be something up in the outer world. I was in Millbank a fortnight, and night and day I, the same as every other prisoner, occupied the same cell. But now it was different. When the hour came for going to bed I was taken out of my cell, led through a corridor, then through a few corridors more, and into a cell where I slept all night, with the gas lighting. In the morning I was conducted back to my working cell, and this continued night and day for months till the scare wore away, when they had crushed the rebellion in Ireland. They were not sure that they were not to have a rising in London, and they took these precautions regarding me, lest I should be taken away by force. If I was left during night in the cell which I occupied all day, some officer might tell the boys outside the particular cell I slept in, on the ground floor, or it was more secure to have me in the top of the prison, with as many gates, and bars, and bolts as possible between me and my sympathizers outside. They must have been awfully scared that time, and they must have considered me an awfully important personage.

What I regretted much in this change was, that I lost my bed in which was concealed one of my letters. The mattress and bed-clothes were taken out of my day cell, and I never saw them more. This having happened, I said it was better to make an attempt to send out the other, which was hid in the hole, than to be waiting for a better opportunity, which may never come. I did not know but I might be changed altogether from that cell, and thus loose both my letters. The next day that I was scrubbing my cell I broke my scrubbing stone and ground down a piece of it to about an inch square. I took out my letter and enclosed the stone in it to make it heavy, so that I could throw it over the prison from the exercise yard. I knew there was a road running outside, but I had not much hope of succeeding in getting it out there. There was a garden between the prison and the road, and I calculated if it fell there, some prison officer or prisoner may find it, who, for the consideration that I had stated on the envelope, would send it to its destination. I then had recourse to my ink-bottle that was hanging from the window, and I addressed a note to the finder, telling him to send this to a certain place, and he would get a certain sum of money. I folded it up tidily, hid it away on my person, and went out to exercise when the bell rang. This exercise consists in walking around the yard for a half hour, and in working at the pump for another half hour.

While I was walking about with the party, the principal officer opened the door, and called me, saying, "I want to search you; open your jacket and waistcoat." I did so. "What is this?" "That's one of the six bags I got to make." "And why did you bring it out of your cell?" "I felt cold, and I put it around my waist to keep me warm." "Take it off instantly." I took it off; he took it in, and I was allowed to continue my exercise. I had my letter in my pocket all the time, and, for a wonder, he did not put his hand in it. I knew there was not much time to spare, if I wanted to try my luck in throwing it over the prison, and I made up my mind to try it immediately. Brown, the officer, generally stood at the gate leading into the pumping yard, and, as the prisoners walk around the shed that covers it, the pump comes between the officer and every prisoner, while the latter is going a distance of two or three paces. At this spot I made up my mind to fling away my parcel. Getting it ready in my hand, I, when I came to the place, threw it with all my might. High into the air I saw it go, but my eyes did not follow it, for the officer's eyes were immediately on me; but in a second or two I heard the noise of something falling on the roof. I turned my eyes upwards, and saw my letter fall back into the yard. The prisoner behind me gave a groan, and the one before me gave a curse. The wonder is that the keeper did not hear the noise or notice anything wrong. The letter fell into a corner where cinders were kept. I saw it as I passed by. The snow was on the ground, and there was my treasure on the top of it. I should get out of the ranks to take it, and this looked impossible to do without the officer seeing me. The order came to have us go into our cells. I had only one turn more around the yard. Was I to leave my treasure there and go in? No; I would take it. The officer would, of course, see me, and make a run for me, but I would have it thrown over the house before he could catch me; and, as I was passing the spot, I stepped aside and took up the letter. Stepping into the ranks again, I looked to see if Brown was after me, but he didn't see the move at all, and, as soon as I entered my cell, I placed my treasure in its hiding place. Immediately after, I was ordered to put out my broom, and, when the judge sat, I was ordered twenty-four hours on bread and water, for destroying the property of the prison and converting it to improper use. The destruction consisted in my having put a few stitches in the bag, to keep it tight around my waist.

The next day that I went to exercise I succeeded in throwing my letter over the building without being noticed. The prisoner behind me observed, "It can't have gone beyond the garden; they'll find it and play the devil with you." But it seems it was never found, for I never heard anything of it from that day to this.

I did not forget their punishing me for not doing the tailoring, and scrubbing the floor at the same time, and I asked the Governor to put down my name to see the Director when next he would visit. He came the following Thursday, and I was brought into his presence. His name was Captain Gambier, and I became very familiar with him afterwards. That is, I often came before him in his judicial capacity, and he would speak to me so sweetly that I began to look upon him as a father. But all his fatherly attentions were bestowed upon me in the way or corrections. While pronouncing sentences on me that he knew should bring me on my knees—while he would be writing "bread and water," he would be saying, "God knows I pity you. I am sorry for you." "Four months' solitary confinement on punishment diet, and the first twelve days on bread and water; that will do, take him off." He had a glass eye, and this used to look at me as if it was shedding tears in sympathy with his pitying words, while the other gloated with satisfaction that he had me in his toils, and that it was only a matter of time, in the working of his machinery, to make me anything he desired. It would not do to break a man down, or break him up suddenly. It should be done on English humanitarian or disciplinarian principles—"done so slowly that none could call it murder."

I never could give this Captain Gambier an ill word, for the reason that he always spoke civilly to me. He'd polish up the ugliest dose he could give with his crocodile words, and I believe that I vexed him as much as any prisoner he ever met, for I never lost my temper with him, and I always caught him quietly wherever I found him tripping.

A week or so after the tailor's complaint against me I went before him and represented that one officer set me to work in the morning—that another officer came and put me at other work, and that the first man came and reported me for not doing his business while I was attending to the second man's orders. I told him the whole story as printed in the preceding pages, and asked him to send for the officers. The Governor, who was present, said he at the time asked me what I had to say, and I said nothing. "Do you hear that?" said Gambier. "I do," said I. "And why didn't you make known to the Governor what you make known to me now?" "The Governor had his officers to make the truth known to him. You know that the word of a prisoner cannot be taken against the word of a warder. Rice, the tailor, reported me for idleness. Brown, my warder, knew I was doing other work, I was not idle, and that I was reported for idleness. It struck me that there was some State necessity to have me punished, and made a bad character on your books, and I made up my mind to let the law take its course and offer no obstacle to the fulfilment of its requirements." "Then you are yourself to blame, and you evidently wanted a cause of complaint." I smiled, and said, "Oh, Governor, I don't want to complain at all, but in the blindness of your anxiety to punish me I may have a desire to see how far you will go." This expression of his about my "wanting a cause of complaint" belongs peculiarly to English statesmanship in the Government of Ireland. How often have I seen it stated in the English press that the Irish were more in want of a cause of complaint than anything else. About a fortnight after this adventure with Gambier I was before him about something else, and on his remarking that he had no desire whatever to punish me; that I was treated with every consideration, leniency, and justice; I reminded him of the tailor-scrubbing report, asking him did he call that justice. "Oh, that was your own fault, you refused to give an explanation. You said you wanted to have a grievance." "*I* said I wanted to have a grievance?" "Yes, I have it here entered in the book." "I said no such thing. God knows you did." "God knows, and you know, I did not. I said I wanted to see how far you would go in the blindness of your rage to punish me."

This, I think, was the time I came before him to ask for an increase of diet, and he refused it. I then asked that my friends may be permitted to send me as much coarse food as was sufficient to sustain nature, and this was entirely out of the question. "Well, now, Governor," said I, "I am surprised at that; England would not have a sufficiency of coarse food refused to the political prisoners of any other nation;" to which he replied, "England has no political prisoners now-a-days; you are here no more than any other prisoner, and you are treated like every other prisoner." I again smiled, saying, "Ah! Governor, I think you're a little mistaken; you don't keep the gas burning in the cell of every other prisoner all night, nor do you strip every prisoner naked, regularly, once a day; you don't take every other prisoner through wards, and towers, and corridors, from his day-cell, to sleep in another cell at night; nor do you punish every other prisoner for not doing two jobs of work at the same time; you don't "——" Now, now, that will do; there is no use in your going on with these frivolous complaints. I can't grant your application for more bread—'Refused,'" and as he was writing the word refused opposite my application, I was marched out of the room.

"England has no political prisoners now-a-days." "We were no more than any other convicts.". This was constantly dinned into our ears, until it became "expedient" for the English Government to offer us banishment instead of imprisonment; then she suddenly discovered that those of us whom she decided upon releasing were political prisoners. But she holds to her lying still in the case of the convicted Irishmen who were in the English army, and in the case of Irishmen who were charged with buying arms in England. It is perfectly legal for any man to buy arms in England, but when an Irishman buys them, and when any one swears that they were bought with the intention of having them sent to Ireland to be used there by rebels, the purchasers are sent into penal servitude. Such political prisoners are confined in England to-day, and the English Government is holding them behind the lie that they are not political prisoners. As I write these lines in New York an English historian named Froude is lecturing in the city on the question of Ireland and England. He admits he came over with the view of inducing Americans to take the side of England. There is another celebrated lecturer in the city, a Dominican Friar, the Rev. Thomas Burke, who is talking against Froude, and what I notice in both is that while talking of the 700 years' fight between England and Ireland, and while appealing to the American people, both of them ignore the fact that England holds in her prisons to-day forty or fifty Irishmen whose offence is that they are charged with entertaining a desire to fight for Irish independence if they could get the chance, and that England holds these men behind that lie—that they are not political prisoners. It is no wonder that Froude should forget this in appealing to the American people to be favorable to England, and to see little but justice in her treatment of Ireland, but I do not like that the priest should forget it. I think the strongest point he could make against this Froude before the American people would be to show how these men were detained and tortured in English prisons while the historian was appealing for American sympathy for England against Ireland. But what I like or dislike in the matter is nothing; the priest says he is not a revolutionist, and it is in the interest of revolution I speak. I am sure Froude is not a revolutionist either, and men who rot in prison on the charge I speak of eight years after their conviction, may rot there for all the two eloquent gentlemen care, while they are calling on America to decide between England and Ireland. Froude says he would clasp the hand of Ireland if she had gained her independence, and I believe there is no priest in Ireland who would rather see that independence than Father Burke. I don't know any priest in Ireland that would object to it if gained, but I don't know many laboring to gain it. Notwithstanding that I say this, I believe there are *very many* of them would fight for it if we had the fighting material in the field, but it is not their business to bring it there. The moral I would have Irishmen draw from these observation is this: English historians cannot be Irish revolutionists. Neither can Irish priests be Irish revolutionists openly or actively. Whatever they are in their hearts, they must on their tongues be peaceable. They cannot counsel, originate, or organize a fight.

It is strange what feelings possess a man sometimes. I am vain enough to think this 27th October, 1872, that I am writing words that may be read after I am dead, and may be a lesson to boys whose blood burned about Ireland as mine did when I was younger than I am to-day, though it is dispiriting to think the lesson may be needed after my time. And if I am before my God when these words are read, and if I will have been judged for writing them, I will not be suffering anything for writing with malice or ill-will against the priests or against the people of Ireland, for God is just, and does not punish for an offence what the mind does not contemplate as such. I believe that in the late struggle in the old land we have had much opposition and little aid from the priesthood of Ireland. The majority of them are rebels at heart; the minority pro-English. But in consequence of the discipline or of the government of the Church, this minority could speak, and did speak; the majority could not speak, and had to remain silent. One pro-English priest in a district could denounce us of a Sunday at Mass; six priests, rebels at heart, in the same district, had to keep silent; hence prevailed the opinion that the Church was against the liberty of Ireland. We were denounced as atheists and infidels, which we were not, and if any of us were "unfaithful" there was nothing helped to make us so more than the action of the priests who forbade us the sacraments, sent us away from the confessional, and threatened us with hell and damnation, because we had taken the oath to fight for the liberty of our native land. These gentlemen teach, "Your God first and your country second," which preaching I accept, but the action they took against our movement looked to me as telling us that being true to our country was being false to God, and this I will not accept. To such I may lawfully say, "Yes, my God first, my country second, and you third."

If Ireland was peopled by no one but holy nuns and priests, if it was an island of saints, I do not believe that England would give it its freedom on the score of its sanctity alone.

I know how imprudent it is of me to speak at all of a priest, unless I speak in praise of him; but prudence or imprudence is out of the question with me when the truth has to be told, and when we are face to face with one of the many difficulties that have to be considered and overcome in the struggle against England. I know how easy the names of "Infidel" and "Atheist" can be hurled and whispered around, and I have experience myself of how easily the youthful mind is impressed with a terrible opinion of the man to whom such names are attached. When I approached manhood, I became possessed of nine or ten volumes of the *Nation* newspaper, and it was my political library for a year or two. I became familiar with Davis, Meagher, Mitchell, and the other Irishmen, who left their footprints on the sands of that time, and I well remember how sorry I felt that these men were "Infidels." I used to say, what a pity it is, little dreaming that I, in my own day, was to be the victim of denunciations similar to those which were hurled at the '48 men. And, perhaps, there are growing up in Ireland to-day youths burning with that hereditary love of land, and hatred of its foe, who, reading the clerical condemnation of the '65 men, feel about myself as I felt for Meagher and Mitchell twenty years ago. When they see a Catholic Bishop saying that "Hell was neither hot enough nor deep enough for us," what wonder is it if, with their sympathy with us in the cause we would serve, they may then pity us that we'd serve it to our own damnation. These reflections may be as unpleasant to others as they are to me, and to get rid of them I will end this chapter and begin a new one

CHAPTER XIV.

ASSOCIATION WITH ENGLISH CONVICTS—WORKING THE PUMP—IRISH AND ENGLISH POVERTY AND THE PRIEST—EATING A WARDER—GETTING BREAD AT PRAYERS—TASK WORK—WETTING COIR—PUNISHED FOR OBEYING ORDERS—LYING WARDERS AND GAMBIER—EXTENSIVE SEIZURE—ALL MY WRITING AND WRITING MATERIAL CAPTURED—CHANGE OF QUARTERS AND BREAD AND WATER—BULLY POWER'S ATTEMPT TO BULLY ME—SEPARATION FROM OTHER PRISONERS—THE SOLDIER PRISONERS—TELEGRAPHING THROUGH THE WALLS—HONOR AMONGST THIEVES—A "CEDAR" LOST AND MY SEARCH FOR IT—JOHNNY O'BRIEN AND THE IRISH REPUBLIC—MY PRISON POET—TURN YOUR FACE TO THE WALL—NEW CONFEDERATES—THE RED BLOOD OF IRELAND WILL RISE IN ENGLAND—REFLECTIONS—THE ROAD TO FREEDOM DANGEROUS—LORD MACAULAY'S NEW ZEALANDER—SWALLOWING AN INK-BOTTLE—STEALING PAPER—JOHN DEVOY AND OTHER NEW-COMERS — SWALLOWING POWER'S PENCIL — S K E L E T O N WEIGHT.

On my arrival in Millbank I made an effort to get dissociated from the English convicts, but it was a fruitless one. After a time, however, the authorities had to change their tactics and dissociate me from them of their own accord; then their efforts were to keep me away from them altogether. I went to Captain Gambier one day with this application: "Governor, during my hour's exercise I am put working the pump in company with your murderers and thieves, and I ask to be relieved of their companionship." "Certainly not, you are no more than any other prisoner here, and you must take your exercise the same as others." "Well, what do you say if I refuse to take exercise at all, and remain in my cell during the hour? I don't want such exercise." "You cannot do that; we have to attend to your health, and you will have to obey the orders laid down by the doctor, or be punished." "Then, you will not allow me to remain in my cell, or remain separate in the yard during exercise." "No." "Very well, that is all I want to see you about." "Right about face, forward," and out I marched.

Working the pump was not unpleasant in its way; it tended to develop the muscles, and it gave me a lot of thievish information. Thirty of us were in the gang, and fifteen of us stood at each side of the crank, facing each other. We laid hold of the iron bars hand after hand; the officer cried "On," we worked; our bodies bent, our heads came together at every revolution of the iron, and a whisper of some kind passed. Those professionals could whisper without moving a lip or a muscle of the face, and I took much interest in listening to their stories. They all trusted me; they knew I wouldn't "stag;" and while I was with them I learned how several celebrated burglaries were committed, who committed them and what was done with the "swag." This was a reception prison, and new hands coming in were in great demand for news. I wanted news from them, too, and when I could not get near a new importation, those who could would learn as much as possible from him about Ireland, and come alongside of me next day and tell me how they were going on there. Will I say it? Yes. Nearly half these men were of Irish parents, and their crimes were traceable to poverty and whisky—two things which the Irish people could well afford to get rid of, and which are a curse to any people they afflict.

I was working on the pump one day, and the man facing me was whispering a story about Chatham Prison. He said "It was the hungriest place he was ever in; they felt half-starved and the work was very hard. Many of us," said he, "struck work for more food, but that only brought us more hunger, for the whole of them didn't stick out. I told them there was no chance of getting an increase until we killed a 'screw' and ate him. I offered to kill him if the others would help me to eat him, but the whole of them would not agree to that, and I got so disgusted with them that I was glad to be sent away. You see, there would be no use in us killing him unless we ate him, and until one of those 'Blokes' is eaten they'll keep starving us." I looked at the fellow as much as to say, are you serious, and I believe he was. He became a great friend of mine, would do anything at all for me. When I'd be after spending a few days on bread and water he'd slope his way till he'd got alongside of me on the pump, and then he'd keep giving me sympathy by cursing my tormentors as wickedly as he could.

"They want to kill you. Can't they let you alone as they let us." Another curse, and so on, till he'd wind up by saying, "you must be very hungry. I'll bring you my breakfast loaf to chapel to-morrow." "No, no." "Yes I will, and by heavens if you get me into any trouble by not taking it quickly when I pass it to you I'll have your life." To-morrow morning would come, he'd be seated on the same stool with me and five or six others between us. The officer in charge of us would turn his head, and the loaf would be turned from one to another till it reached me. There was no alternative but to be as quick as another in taking and hiding it, otherwise the whole party might get into trouble.

Some people ask me to-day how I was able to stand all the "bread and water" I got, but I tell you that I was supported by those unfortunate convicts. And I suppose the authorities themselves wondered that their starvation process was not having the desired effect. Barrett, the son of a Bandon man, knew two masons named Murray that I knew in Dunmanway, and he not alone should have me take bréad from him, but, as he was ward cleaner, he would steal pens and pencils, and scrape up bits of white paper for me. Murphy, a Ballincollig man, who was sentenced to five years on a charge of manslaughter, told me he saw me at a certain time at the house of Tim Donoghue, from Ross, in London, and I was there. It was Barrett's uncle who was killed in the fight for which Murphy was sentenced, and when Barrett came to know this, Murphy had to be sent into another party, as they could not live in peace. When he left he had one of my surreptitious letters, as he was expecting to be sent to another prison, and he said he would try and pass it into the outside world as he was passing through it, but I did not hear of either since.

We got a bath once a fortnight, and were taken to it during the time we were at exercise. There were four troughs, with holes in the side boards to let the water pass through all. Four men were called, and when they had bathed and dressed, four more, and so on till all were done. Whether by accident or design, it scarcely ever happened that I was one of the first called, and I never had clean water more than once or twice. The dirty soap suds would scum the surface. Some of the officers in charge would make me strip and go in, but others of them would not press me, contenting themselves with having me wash my feet. This was the only matter remedied by Knox and Pollock. After their visit, and my representation to them on this head, I got clean water every time I bathed.

I could not forget Gambier, and I had to come before him again to bring the conduct and the contrary orders of his officers under his notice. When I was punished repeatedly for not doing my task-work every day, the two officers that came to strip me began talking to me while they were searching my clothes, asking me why I was not picking my quantity of coir. I told them I was doing my best, but the little cords were so small and hard that it was a difficult task. The principal officer said—

"We have a man, Murphy, in another ward, and he can do his work in three hours. When he gets his bundle of coir, he puts it into his bucket of water, lets it soak there awhile, then takes it out and tramples it till he has it softened and torn asunder." Saying this, he took hold of my bundle of coir and put it into my water-bucket. He told me to squeeze the water out of it, and when I laid it on the floor, he trampled on it in the Murphy fashion for a few minutes. I went at it after him, and I found that his preparatory process made the performance of my task easier. But there is a sequel to this story, and here it is. Next week I was placed under report on a charge of wetting my coir, and, as well as I remember now, I think I let the charge go on without making any reply to it; but the following week I went before my friend Capt. Gambier, and charged the Governor with punishing me for acting in obedience to orders. I then told how Cooper, a principal, and another principal, whose name I forget, gave me the instructions about wetting the coir. The two were sent for, and denied every word of it. I asked Cooper if he did not tell the story about Murphy, and I asked the other if he did not trample on the coir, and they put on an indignant face to think they should say or do such things. I think I was getting mad myself to think I was foiled this way, and, as a last resource, I said to the Director— "Why, Mr. Brown, the ward officer, was present, and I ask you, Captain Gambier, to send for this man, and not let him know what he is wanted for till he is in your presence."

Brown was sent for, and his evidence corroborated mine. Then the Governor brought him to account, why he allowed coir to be wet in his ward, and his reply was, that he had no one coir-picking but me, and the coir I got was next to impossible to pick without wetting. Then Power, the head warder, came in with his say, and said he was twenty-five years in that prison, and never saw a bit of coir wet there, which, to my mind, was a big lie, because I learned from the prisoners that the practice was general; however, as charges had to be trumped up against me, practice or precedent was nothing. I told Captain Gambier to bear in mind that not alone was I put on punishment work when no other prisoner in my ward was on it, but I got work that was next to impossible to do, and that I was punished, in doing it, for acting according to the directions of the officers. "It is all your own fault," said he; "why didn't you tell the Governor when the charge was preferred against you?" "No," said I, "I have a desire to have a thorough experience of how you conduct those model prisons of your, and I have no wish to interfere with the requirements of the law in my case." "I see you are getting into a very bad spirit, and instead of improving it is getting worse you are. God knows I am sorry for you." "You may, but be very sure the present style of treatment will never improve me." And so ended this interview with my polished Director.

In May, '67, a change came over the spirit of my dream, but my reader may be sure it was no change for the better. I was at my Sunday's exercise and working at the pump, at a crank, in an isolated corner between two walls, for by this time they had put me away into this punishment corner, thinking I was deriving some information or consolation from the whisperings of the other convicts when mixed up with them while pumping. It was Sunday, and while the crank was going round I heard an order "Halt," and when the halt was made the call of "Rossa," I looked behind and saw two officers motioning to me to "come on." They conducted me to my cell and ordered me to strip. "What's up now, Governor?" "You know well what's up," said one of them, "and we want you to strip." I went through the process and nothing was found on my person or in my clothes. "Put out your broom." I obeyed orders, and when they locked the door I began to ask myself what the deuce can it mean? I made for the window and, woe of woes, there was no black thread tied to the bar—my ink-bottle was gone. I went to the slit under my bed board and my two steel nibs were gone. I searched between the gas pipe and the wall and my writing pen was gone; I went to another hole in the corner of my cell and the letter I had concealed there was gone. There was a general seizure—a clear sweep had been made of all my treasured articles. While meditating on the misfortunes that await humanity, and the "bread and water" that was in store for me, my cell was opened and in marched big Power with four or five jailers. "Tell me where you got that ink-bottle?" The way he stood before me, and the authoritative tone in which he put the question, stirred my bad blood, and, moving close to him, looking up into his face, I said, with as much opposition as I could put into *my* tone, "I will *not* tell you where I got that ink-bottle." He came in with his guards to bully me, but he quailed down immediately and sneaked out, telling the officers to take me on. I was taken to another cell in another part of the prison, and kept there till further troubles removed me again.

When I was summoned to the bar of justice on the charge of having ink-bottles, pens, and letters concealed, I was much amused at listening to Power's complaint as to the insult I offered to himself. "When I asked him, sir, where he got the ink-bottle, you should see the way he swelled up to me as if he would bully me from doing my duty. If I was the commonest man in England he could not speak to me worse than he did. I am twenty-five years in this prison and I never got such an insult. I never came across a more refractory prisoner." I smiled at the compliment. I was ordered seventy-two hours on bread and water, and it was further ordered that I be not allowed to approach any other prisoner, that I be exercised in a separate yard, and that I be taken to chapel in a separate manner. So that this was forcing them to do what I asked them to do at first—to separate me from the other prisoners. My whole fight was, to force them to recognize a difference between us political prisoners and the ordinary convicts, and they were obliged to do so in the end.

I don't know how it came to pass that all my property was seized in my cells. I had two of these cells—a day one and a night one. The night one happened to be situated in the ward where were confined ten or twelve of the Irishmen who were convicted when they were on English soldier service in Ireland.

After going to bed one night I heard some tapping on the wall at the foot of my bed. Hallo, said I, this is a signal from some one, and I set about thinking how to answer it. I turned my bed upside down—that is, I changed my head to my feet, and I signaled in reply. The gas was burning in my cell, and the watch, on coming round, seeing how I had transposed myself, cried out, "What are you doing that way; can't you sleep as every one else sleeps?" "Now, Governor, what's the use in kicking up a noise; don't you know that every one else has no light in his cell. If you put out the gas I will change myself, but I could not sleep well the other way, as the light was full in my face." He seemed to be satisfied, and walked away. I got a chance of signaling a few sentences through the wall, and I learned that the man in the next cell to me was one of the Irish soldiers. We formed a signal to recognize each other at the chapel next morning, and made arrangements to have a long talk next evening, before we went to bed, as I got into this cell half an hour before bed-time, and during that half hour the officers were so busy locking up we could have any amount of conversation unknown to them. But mind, the conversation was to be through the wall, and it was not such a wall as Pyramus and Thisbe had, with a slit in it, through which the lovers could kiss each other, but a strong stone and brick one, built to keep prisoners secure, and keep them apart. But stone walls will not prevent souls from communicating, and prisoners invented a scheme by which they could cheat their jailers out of this forbidden consolation. I learnt this, and through it I became acquainted with Augustine Elligot Costello and Rickard O'Sullivan Burke before I ever saw their faces. I met John Devoy through stone walls, when the authorities were resorting to all tricks to keep me from meeting any one. But these adventures are a year and a-half in advance of Keating's acquaintance. I will not give the details until I come to them in the due order of time.

Next morning, at chapel, I recognized my acquaintance by the signal given to me the night before. He, with ten or twelve companions, were sitting three stools behind me. That night I had a long talk with him. I learned that his name was Keating, and he belonged to Clare; that he was in the Carbineers a long time; that he escorted Thomas Clarke Luby to prison, and also had the undesired honor of escorting John Mitchel on his way to penal servitude in '48; that Foley, who belonged to his party, used to make up my cell every morning after I left it, and that any message I left in it would be found by him and attended to. I told him to tell Foley to look behind the card that was hanging on the wall and he would find a letter from me, which they were to get into the world if they could. It was one of the reserves I had in case a chance offered of passing it out, and I placed it behind the rules and regulations that hung on the wall. That was to be the post-office between me and the soldiers; but the authorities made a seizure of all my post-offices, and I do not know was it here or in the other cell they made the first discovery. Possibly it was in this one, as a principal officer goes around every day on a tour of inspection; if he only touched my card the letter would fall down, and then a general search would be ordered to discover my writing materials. This is the only way I can account for the detection—either that or another prisoner in one of the cells under us might have been listening while we were rapping, and have given information.

I lost the society of the soldiers, and I did not see any of them after that. My cell was changed, my place in the chapel was changed, my place of exercise was changed, and—most wonderful change of all—my closet-paper was changed to old rags.

I think I may claim the honor of driving Gambier, Stopford, Du Cane, Fagan, and seven or eight other prison directors, to their wits-ends. They never had such a case before; they never had to contend with such a persistent effort on the part of a prisoner to make his treatment known. Here they were, twelve men, versed in every appliance requisite to break the most unruly into discipline, having power to starve him into quiet, eternal repose if he could not be brought under any other way. Only think of these cool calculators —representatives of the power that would open all the other prisons of the world to the gaze of humanity—sitting down in council, discussing the measures that were to be adopted to prevent me from making known how they were treating me, and gravely deciding that I was to have no more waste paper for "purposes of nature," but that the warder in charge of me was to supply me with old rags as a substitute.

In my new cell the most vigilant watch was kept over me, yet all the watches in the world could not keep the sympathy of the other prisoners from me, and their sympathy brought me relief. When a man is in such difficulties as make it patent to all around him that there is no possible return to be made for any assistance given to him, you cannot imagine his feelings when he finds his fellow-man so noble as to give him a helping hand. And when this helping hand is extended by those whom society regards as the vilest of its component parts, how noble must the noblest of them be if man had a fair field for the exercise of his humanity. But, after all, there may be as noble elements of human nature in the thieves I met in Millbank as in the Lords and Commons of England. Had the lords been born and reared as the thieves were, and had the thieves been born lords, I would bet "my bottom dollar" that we'd have as good thieves and as good lords as we have at present.

My "character" seemed to follow me to my new quarters, and my new neighbors seemed to know all about me. They knew that paper and pencil, pen and ink were things much desired by me, and as they were sweeping and scrubbing the hall in the morning they would linger outside my door to whisper consolation to me through the slit in the wall. "Cheer up, Rossa, we'll stand to you." He'd pass by, and another would approach whispering, "Do you want a cedar?" I did not know at the time what a cedar was, but as I was in the want of everything that creation contained, I whispered back the reply, "yes," and immediately a splendid lead pencil three or four inches long was hurled in through the slit. Where in the world was I to hide it! The stripping naked and the searching of the cell was to come on by-and-bye.

I should find a hiding place or be detected. There was a slit between my bed-board and the wall; when I probed it with my tin knife I could find no bottom, but, as I could find no other place, I decided on trying this. Where was I to get a bit of thread? Yes, there was the towel; I drew a couple of threads out of it, and, twisting them into one, tied it to my pencil and let it down into the hole. I found bottom, and then I hitched the end of my line to a splinter I fashioned on the edge of the board. This was the first morning I came into my new cell; the report against me came on that day, and I had my three days' bread and water in a punishment cell. When I came back the first thing I did was to run to my hiding-place and see if the "cedar" was all right; but, alas, it was gone. I could not find the end of the string, and the pencil lay in the black hole below. How was I to recover it? Yes, there was one chance, and I would try it. Next morning I brought in a bucket-full of water to scrub my cell; I threw some of it into the hole to see if my cedar would float up. It did not come at the first attempt, and when the waters had subsided I filled the hole a second time. 'Twas no use. I kept working at that hole till I had used up all my bucket of water; no pencil made its appearance. I gave up the search in despair and prepared myself for consequences, as I knew the water was to turn up somewhere. I dried my cell and went to work at picking my coir. In about an hour or so the water had moistened matters, and it began to ooze out from under my bedstead. My cell was soon flooded, and the warder came and asked what was the matter. "By Jove, Governor, I spilled my pail of water to-day, and some of it must have gone down that slit there between the bedstead and the wall." That was truth; I did spill the water, and I took very good care that some of it went down the slit. I never told these gentlemen a lie, but I never told them the whole truth either. I was ordered to dry up my cell, and, as the water kept running out all day, I had to keep drying it up all day. Next morning I was ordered temporarily into another cell, and when I came back to my own I found the slit had been plastered up with cement, and not a hole had been left anywhere that as much as a pin's point could enter.

I whispered my misfortune to my neighbors, and I was not long without another pencil. The greatest difficulty I had was in making them understand that I was in want of as much paper as would enable me to let them know in writing what I wanted. At last they threw me in some brown paper, and next morning I had a note written, telling what I needed. In course of time, we established a post-office in the water-closet, and every morning regularly, for weeks, I found letters there. It was here I got anything like an account of what had occurred in the world since I left it. It was here I first learned how everything had failed; how all the hopes of early years had been disappointed. Johnny O'Brien was in another part of the ward; he had a chance of calling at my post-office, and he gave me a detailed account of how things went on. He was a druggist's clerk in London; he left his situation; went to Ireland and enlisted in a regiment there, in order to teach love of country to the Irishmen who were in it. When the trouble came, he was put in prison, got some kind of a trial, and was sentenced to penal servitude for life. His sentence was read to him in presence of the regiment, and when all the ceremonies of "degradation" were gone through, he gave a hurrah for "the Irish Republic." He was a well-educated, handsome young fellow, about 21 years of age. At the time I met him in Millbank, he told me he would be allowed to rejoin his regiment if he recanted and volunteered for India; but he would not do it. He is still in prison in England. I met him two years afterwards in Chatham, and learned that he was all along subjected to unusually severe treatment. Murtagh and Kavanagh, two other soldiers of the same regiment, were sentenced with him, one to five, and the other to seven years. These are out of prison now, but O'Brien is still in, the Prime Minister of England meanly refusing to look upon him as a political prisoner.

There was a poet in this crowd of neighbors I got into, and one day I found in the post-office verses from him. They were written in the heroic style. I mean in the style that made a hero of me. The poet begged of me to preserve them as a memento of him, but the first thing I did after reading them was to burn them with the gas that was burning in my cell at early morning—for to preserve these verses would be certain destruction to me.

They were written by an Englishman, and taking all things into consideration, they were not very badly written. I was lauded as a man who was suffering for his country, and who even in prison was trying to carry on the fight against the enemy.

When my gang was taken out to get their hour's exercise I was allowed to walk a respectable distance behind them, but on no consideration was I allowed so near the last man as to be able to hear a whisper from him. I cheated the warder sometimes as we were passing through a winding tower down into the lower yard. The last man would loiter behind about the middle of the stairs; I'd step fast to catch what he had to whisper or give to me, while the jailer was locking the tower gate.

We had to pass through a small yard, in which I was left in charge of an officer, while the others were taken to the general exercise ground. When the hour was up my party had to pass through again, and I had to go in after them, but lest any signal should pass between us, I had to turn my face to the wall while they were entering, the officer standing between me and them, so that I would not be able to have even a squint at them. At a particular time a very imperious officer was my supervisor, and he issued his orders in such an impudent tone that I one day refused to turn my face to the wall. He caught hold of me and turned me around, and as soon as his hands were off I returned to the front. He caught me again, and I said, "Take your hands off me." "Turn your face to the wall." "I will not." "You must." "I tell you I will not; you can report me, but you are not allowed to assault me; I am to be treated here like any other prisoner, and I see no one else turning his face to the wall during exercise." He let go his hold of me, but, of course, reported my disobedience to his superiors.

In this little yard was a shed, in which men finished the mats that were made in the cells, and outside the shed three or four men occasionally worked, packing the oakum that was picked. These men saw my row with the officer, and it must have brought some of their sympathy, because, in a few days after, as I was pacing around, I thought I heard the whisper, "Do you want anything?" The man who gave the whisper had his back turned to me, and soon as I was again passing near to where he stood, I trod the ground lightly, and kept my ears open. Sure enough, there it was again—"Do you want anything?"—and the next time I was passing I whispered, "A cedar." Then, for five or six times that I went around, we gave question and answer, and it was arranged that I go to the closet after him next day, and I would get a message from him in a certain corner of it. I went, and found a letter, a pencil and paper. He could get me anything I wanted for a little money, and next day I wrote back, giving him an order for three pounds, payable when presented to a friend in London. I wrote this order so that the three pounds could not be changed to a higher figure, and it was returned to me with a request that I would sign my name on a blank leaf of paper that was given. I gave an excuse for not doing this, and before our negotiations were ended I got into trouble, out of which I was not released for six or eight months.

As I was shaving, I cut my neck, and the blood flowed freely on the flags. There was a little pool of it, and the circumstance bringing to my mind some story of a Duke of Burgundy wounded on a battle-field, exclaiming in French—"See how flows the red blood of Burgundy"—I took hold of my slate pencil, and dipping it in the blood, I wrote on the door of my cell these words—" Le sang rouge d'Irlande coule en Angleterre "—" the red blood of Ireland flows in England."

As I had done shaving, and before I had wiped the blood off the door, the officer came to take me to exercise, and while I was out, the writing was discovered. I was ordered in from exercise before my hour was up, and when I came in I was ordered to put out my broom.

Next day I was taken before the Governor, and while all the officers around looked daggers at me, and trembled with horror at the terrible import of my prophecy, I was charged with writing on my door, in letters of blood—

"The red blood of Ireland *will rise* in England."

"What have you to say to this charge?"
"I say it is false."
"What?" "I say it is false."
"Do you mean to say those words were not written on your door?" "I do."

Then the evidence was taken how one officer went to search my cell, and how he saw the writing; how he went for another officer; how these two went for head warder Power; and how he decided that, as the writing was in Latin, it was better send for a schoolmaster; how the schoolmaster came and went for another schoolmaster; how, in the end, three or four of the schoolmasters together translated the Latin, and how the translation was finally entered on the report book. I told them the translators or some one else gave the words a most malicious turn, and I asked that the sentence be taken down as it was written on the door, but the Governor would make no change. He said I acted wrong in writing anything, and would give me forty-eight hours on bread and water.

When the forty-eight hours were up, I put my name down to see the Director, and when he came, I applied to him to change the record of that report against me. My words were quite innocent—"the red blood of Ireland flows in England"—but when they changed that into "the red blood of Ireland *will rise* in England," they must have a very great desire to misrepresent me. I asked why the original words were not copied, but all the satisfaction I got was to be told that I had no right to write them at all.

I have no doubt but that this terrible prophecy of the red blood of Ireland *rising* in England was sent before a Cabinet Council, and that it did its business in supporting some argument in favor of coercive measures to crush the "rebels" in Ireland and England.

I was coming from chapel one morning, and, being left in a corner of the passage till all the other men would pass to their several wards, I saw a man pass me whom I was sure I knew. I was taken to my exercise ground, where I kept thinking and thinking who that man could be. It was a puzzle to me for a few days, when, looking at him in chapel again, I recognized him as Edmond Power. I set my wits to work to communicate with him, and, having succeeded, I learned that a number were lately convicted and were now fellow-boarders of mine—John Devoy, St. Clair, John Warren, John M'Cafferty, Tom Bourke, Augustine Costello, Edward Duffy, Stephen Joseph Meany, Patrick Walsh, Denis Cashman, etc. I kept my eyes open, and bye-and-bye I got into communication with Costello, who told me his adventure of how he and others came in a small craft from America to Ireland. This craft was three weeks on the coast of Ireland. She first made Sligo Bay, and, not being met there to her satisfaction, she came around to Dungarvan, landed her men, and made her way back to America in safety. It was new news for me to hear, and I made the most out of Costello till the fates put us out of each other's reach.

Power prayed at chapel three or four stools away from me, but there was soon a cordon of communication established between us and bulletins passed regularly. I got a parcel one morning about the size of a marble. As prayers were ended, and I was leaving my seat, Power's eyes and mine met, and I saw him put his finger into his mouth; this I took to mean that I was to keep the message in my mouth, so that if I was suddenly seized upon I could swallow it. I knew there was danger somewhere around, and, as I got into the exercise yard, I made a signal to go to the water-closet. When there I opened my parcel, which contained a bit of lead-pencil and a note, in which I was informed that in consequence of some discovery there was the closest search going on, that he (Power) was stripped three times the preceding day, and that I was to keep the bit of pencil safe for him. I destroyed the note after reading it, and I secured the pencil in the collar of my shirt, near to where it buttoned, so that, if taken by surprise, I would, when unbuttoning, have the best chance of being able, unnoticed, to pass the little parcel into my mouth.

I was not allowed much time for reflections, for immediately two officers appeared on the ground. "Rossa, come on this way." The way led into the tower, and there they ordered me to strip. "Well, well, this is the newest thing yet—stripping in such a place as this; what in the world is up now, that you could not take me to my cell and strip me there?" And as I was talking I commenced stripping with a hearty good will, so as to keep them engaged and make them less watchful. I had the jacket, trowsers, and waistcoat given to them in less than a minute, and as I was unbuttoning my shirt-collar the bit-of pencil passed, as the jugglers say, "by a slight turn of the wrist," from its hiding-place into my mouth. It would not do to keep it there, for the mouth was to be examined too. I had to swallow it. The first effort failed, and I found I had to give it time to moisten before it would go down. The searchers found nothing, or noticed nothing, and I this time escaped my merited share of bread and water.

The chief medical officer of the establishment was a Dr. Gover, and I thought I would have a trial of him on the question of the starvation of an Irish political prisoner in an English prison. One day that he came around on his examination tour I represented to him that I was not supplied with a sufficiency of coarse food, a thing which I thought no civilized nation refused to its political prisoner. After some conversation on my punishments, and on the weight I lost on account of them, he decided he would have me weighed, and if I was reducing in weight he would consider my application. Now, you must know it was next to impossible I could reduce in weight since I came to Millbank, for I was so reduced coming there, from the cold and hunger I experienced in Portland, that I could not go down much further.

I was a mere skeleton of skin and bone. The first day Dr. Gover weighed me I turned the scale at 145 pounds and three-quarters; the next time it was 145, and the third time 146. Dr. Gover said he would be very happy to give me more food, but, as this was about my weight coming to Millbank, I had reduced nothing under his charge, and, as there was so much particularity about my treatment, he should allow the discipline to take its course; but some months after, I think, he put a veto on my getting further punishment, which was in a short time again re-vetoed by Captain Gambier, my genial director.

CHAPTER XV.

WIFE'S VISIT—LIES ABOUT LETTERS—KNOX AND POLLOCK—A CASTLEBAR MAN STEALING INK FOR ME—STEALING PAPER—A NARROW ESCAPE—MY LOVE LETTER AND THE SHAM INQUIRY—LYING AGAIN—LORD DEVON'S COMMISSION—WRITING AMONGST FLEAS—PUNISHED FOR HAVING MY TASK WORK DONE BEFORE TIME—REFUSE TO GO TO PUNISHMENT CELL—A TERRIBLE CHOKING AND DRAGGING—I BARRICADE MY DOOR—IT IS BROKEN IN—FOUR MONTHS' CELLS—MEETING JOHN DEVOY—TAKEN ILL—DR. POCKLINGTON—MY BODY COVERED WITH BOILS—EFFECTS OF LOW DIET AND CONFINEMENT—MEDITATED MUTINY AND OUTBREAK—THE DEVIL VISITS ME—REFLECTIONS ON "BURKE AND FROUDE"—MY BOOKS TAKEN AWAY AND RETURNED AGAIN—I THREATEN TO DESTROY CELL AND MUFFLE MY GASLIGHT—VOLUNTEERING TO WESTERN AUSTRALIA—MANCHESTER RESCUE—SOLDIERS GUARDING US—OUT OF "PUNISHMENT" AND IN IT SOON AGAIN—MEETING JAMES XAVIER O'BRIEN—PATRICK LENNORD—STRIPPED NAKED EVERY DAY—BREAKING SPY-HOLE AND DOOR—HANDCUFFS, BLOODY WRISTS, AND DARK CELLS—THROTTLING AND THREATENING—EATING "ON ALL FOURS"—BREAK MY SPOON AND WOODEN DISH—STUFF THE KEY-HOLE AND HAVE A LITTLE FUN, AND GET MORE BREAD AND WATER FOR IT.

I was taken out of my cell one day, and led through corridors I never traveled before. Something new must be up now, thought I, and true for me, because as I was ushered into a place that resembled a menagerie for wild beasts, a door opened, and my wife stood before me. But we had to keep a respectful distance from each other, as two strong wire screens separated us. She was in one compartment with big Power accompanying her; I was in the other with *my* guardian, and we had twenty minutes to talk across the dividing space with these two listening, and the head warder interrupting the conversation whenever I touched upon the treatment I was receiving.

My wife was going to America to earn a livelihood there; she wrote to the Governor of the prison, asking him to tell me she was coming to see me before she sailed, but he never told me a word of it; she took me completely by surprise, and this was what the authorities desired, so that I could have no story prepared for her. She told me she wrote a letter to Portland six months before, informing me of her intention to emigrate. I never heard of such a letter, and Power said it never came to the prison, but six months afterwards I learned they were telling me lies about it. I was asking the Deputy-Governor some questions about the suppression of my letters; he referred to this one that came with me from Portland, and after several applications to the Director he allowed me to have a part of it to read and be given back again. The bare twenty minutes was allowed for my wife's visit. There was no chance of having a shake hands at parting. Her last words were—to have hope, and not to let my spirits sink. It puzzled me to know why she would speak this way, particularly as she spoke the words with a firmness that indicated there was some reason to have a hope. She now tells me she was at the time fully confident of being able to succeed in having me stolen out of prison. She had borrowed a hundred pounds to effect my release; she had the money with her. She had impressions on wax of the keys that opened several of the doors which stood between me and the world, but in consequence of the many removals of me from one cell to another, the men who were assisting could not get command of all that was necessary. She had to give up the endeavor; paid back the money, and went to America.

She told me there was to be a Commission of Inquiry concerning our treatment, but she was immediately ordered to give me no information on that subject. The public might want to have a little light thrown on the matter, but it was absolutely necessary to keep me in the dark, so that I would not be prepared for what was coming. Everything was to come on me by surprise, so as to disconcert me, and render me unable to defeat "the ends of justice."

And didn't this Commission of Knox and Pollock take me by surprise?—and wasn't I disconcerted? Yes, truly; and often have I laughed at the position it caught me in, and the escape I had from detection while committing the most heinous crime of writing on forbidden paper with forbidden paper and ink.

One morning at chapel, while the priest was repeating the litany, and the prisoners responding aloud, I heard a voice behind addressing a few words to me at every response, and I cocked my ears to allow as much as possible of the whisper to enter. "Have mercy on us," cried the congregation. "I'll get you paper," cried the voice behind me. "Have mercy on us,"—"and pen and ink." "Have mercy on us,"—" our baker can send the letter," and so on, the prisoners in our neighborhood responding louder and louder, when they noticed we were communicating. When I was leaving the chapel, I took a glance at the man that was whispering to me, and next morning I noticed he was two or three seats back of me. By-and-by, when the responses were being given, word was passed to me to "get ready," and in the bustle of rising from our knees, something was passed to me which I covered with my check pockethandkerchief. After getting to my cell, I opened my parcel; it consisted of a letter, a writing pen, a sheet of paper and envelope, and a piece of thick flannel rag scturated with ink. My first move was to put out the red end of my signal board through the slit in the wall, to signify that I wanted to go to the water closet, and in my hiding-place there I secured all I got except the letter, which I brought back to my cell to read. The writer was a Castlebar Irishman; he had heard of the straits I was in for writing material, and he had made arrangements with a fellow-prisoner who worked in the bakehouse to get a letter conveyed out for me. He would keep me supplied with ink, because he got schooling, and when the ink-bottle was left with him to write, he could steal the ink into the flannel rag.

At this time I had in my hiding-place an abundant supply of fine white paper—five or six sheets of it, but this I stole myself. In going to chapel I was taken out of my cell and made to stand in a corner till all the other prisoners had passed. The warder stood in view of me, but I stood in view of the warder also, and when he turned his head aside I turned my eyes to take observations. I noticed on the shelf a large book in which he kept an account of the work. I opened it, one-half of my body and one hand in view of the officer, while the other hand was preparing to commit a theft. I saw the book was not paged, and that I could take sheets out of it without the loss being noticed. I was the last to go into the chapel from my ward, and the first to come back. My cell was near the corner where the book lay; the officer kept his eyes on me till I turned the angle; I was then to enter my cell and shut the door before the other prisoners would pass; but one morning, as I passed this angle, I paid my respects to the account-book, and, quick as lightning, tore out five or six sheets.

Having shut my cell-door, I took a fit of coughing in order to make a noise while I was tearing the paper into a convenient size, and when all was right, I put out my signal-board to get to my hiding-place.

About a week after my wife's visit, I was in full blast writing away in my cell, about ten o'clock in the morning, which was the hour I found myself subject to the least observation. My tin pint contained a squeeze of ink out of the flannel rag; I had my pen in hand, scrawling for the dear life on a leaf of paper laid on my slate, when tramp, tramp, I hear the approach of officers. I stuck my paper and writing-pen inside the waist of my breeches; the keys turned in the locks, the doors were thrown open, and big Power cried, "Come on, come on." "Wait now, governor," said I, " till I go to the water-closet." "No, no, you can't; we are in a great hurry." "Well, then, if you are in a hurry, the quickest manner you can get on with me is to let me have my way a little; so you may as well let me go to the closet." They did let me, but they stood at the door of it, and I had no chance of further concealing the pen and paper I had on my person. I was led into the Governor's room; the warders withdrew, and I stood at the bar before two gentlemen who sat inside. They introduced themselves to me as Messrs. Knox and Pollock, and informed me they were commissioned to ask me some questions regarding my prison life.

I questioned them as to how they were appointed, and what were the circumstances that called for their inquiry. They would not tell me; but I was not long under examination before I saw that something I had written got into the world, and caused a little trouble. They questioned me principally on Governor Clifton of Portland, and my letter "to another man's wife," and I found out that Mr. Clifton had gone back of his words, and had been telling them lies. I asked, if this was to be a fair and honest search after truth, that I be brought face to face with Mr. Clifton; that the Portland prison books be produced, together with the correspondence, and I would convince them my words were true and his false.

They had examined Mr. Clifton, they said, but he was now out of town; they would, however, see him again, and may call to see me in a week's time, but I never saw them since. I was for about four hours under their examination, and as I saw the proceedings coming to a close, I made a move to adjust the pen and paper that were still inside the waist of my breeches. I saw they were getting alarmed when they noticed me fumbling with my hands.

I really believe, from their frightened looks, that they apprehended I had some concealed weapon with which I was about to assault them, and to allay their fears I told the truth; that I was caught writing, and got no time to properly conceal my pen, which was distracting my attention all the time I was talking to them. They said I may regard anything that may pass between them and me, as if it passed between the priest and myself at confession; they would not tell on me; but I did not much mind at the time whether they would or not, for I was certain that the ink I left in the pint would be discovered in the cell by some warder, and that I was in for the punishment anyway. But for a wonder, it escaped observation, and I escaped that day with all my munitions of war.

These gentlemen, Knox and Pollock, were extremely polite to me; you'd think butter would not melt in their mouth, so sweet were they. I thought I gave them every satisfaction We parted apparently on the best of terms, and yet in their report they, in a peculiarly English fashion, cut my throat as if they had never given me a kind word.

Here are some extracts from it:

"We now come to the main grievance—namely, that the Governor had charged treason-felony convict J. O'D. Rossa with writing a love-letter to the wife of another convict, Michael Moore. As a fact quite unconnected with this occurrence, the convict, Michael Moore, asked for permission to write a letter to his wife. The Governor, wishing to know whether Moore had any participation with Rossa's letter, replied, '*This is very strange, only a day or two ago Rossa* tried to pass out a letter to your wife.' He said nothing to him about love-letters or any such thing; Moore flew into a passion, and Mr. Clifton was convinced from his manner that he had nothing to do with Rossa's letter, and so the thing passed off. The book and letter were forwarded to the Directors in London. A few days afterwards, when the Governor saw Rossa in his office, Rossa charged him in the most insolent terms with having accused him of writing a love-letter to Mrs. Moore. Mr. Clifton replied that he had told Moore he had written a letter to Mrs. Moore, but said nothing about a love-letter, adding words to the effect that he did not mind telling him (Rossa) his own opinion, that when a man writes a letter to another man's wife, begins with the words 'my love,' fills it with expressions of strong devotion, signs it with his name, and forwards it in a surreptitious way, the facts had an awkward look.

"Mr. Clifton expressly added, in speaking to Rossa, 'A reason the more which makes me think this was never intended for your wife is, that I have far too high an opinion of Mrs. O'Donovan Rossa to think for a moment she would aid you in infringing the prison rules.'"

That passage from Knox and Pollock's report, referred to the funny charge made against me of writing a love-letter to another man's wife. They, on examination of the papers, could not but have seen that it was the silliest charge ever made. Yet, these sham inquirers having only the one object of whitewashing the Government, will not say a word in favor of the truth. They say, "*Mrs. O'D. will scarcely stand for Mrs. O'Donovan Rossa, and the further explanation that Mrs. Moore was Moore's mother, not his wife, sounds unsatisfactory,*" while they had the book record before them, showing that Moore's wife's name was Kate, and his mother's Mary.

"On June the 3d we visited Millbank Prison, and as our sole object there was to converse with treason-felony convict J. O'D. Rossa, we need not dwell at any length upon the arrangements of the prison.

"Rossa himself admitted that he had nothing particular to complain of, except that he had on various occasions been reported for punishment unjustly, as he conceived. He complained that everyone was unjust to him; it is but fair to add that everyone complained of him in turn. He had the most ingenious contrivance for concealing fragments of paper, for hanging ink-bottles out of his cell window by wires, and obviously managed by hook or by crook to maintain tolerably active relations with the external world. He has driven matters at last to this point that he has been remitted as a thoroughly unmanageable subject from Portland to Millbank, and at Millbank the authorities are obliged to keep him, even at hours of exercise, apart from his fellows. A short time since, he concocted a letter, stuffed full of the most absurd accusations against everybody, and contrived, no one knows how, to convey it to another convict who was about to be removed. The letter was to be dropped on the railway, and was addressed to the editors of any one of three or four papers. It contained the story of his wrongs, and was to set the country in a blaze. We could not but regret, as we saw this fine active young man before us in the prime of manhood, and in strong, vigorous health, that such energies of mind and body had been misapplied, and that the end of all was a convict's cell, and a duel between himself and the authorities, whether they could retain him in prison, or he could set them at defiance and effect his escape. His letter contained the usual farrago of falsehood and exaggeration. He said in it that he had been denied the privilege of writing to his poor mother in America; it turned out that he had never asked permission to do so at all. He complained to us that he had been reported for abstracting at the tailor's work a portion of cloth and concealing it beneath his jacket; it turned out that he had done so, but he said he had not intended to hide it; he had just put it out of the way for temporary purposes. The convict Rossa is a dangerous man and must remain the object of increasing anxiety and vigilance to the authorities. The senior warder at Millbank, a man of no mean experience in convict life, said that in the whole course of his career he had never met with the equal of this most unfortunate man, Jeremiah O'Donovan Rossa. He has no ill-usage to complain of; no severity but of his own making. He must mend his ways or abide his fate."

We have the honor to be your obedient servants,
"ALEXANDER A. KNOX,
"GEORGE D. POLLOCK."

The falsehood and misrepresentation in the foregoing are wonderful. I told them I had no complaints—that I scorned to make complaints about anything I was made to endure, but would make every endeavor to let the public know the truth, and they turn this into—
"Rossa himself admitted that he had nothing particular to complain of."

"A short time back he concocted a letter stuffed full of the most absurd and unfounded accusations against everybody, and contrived, no one knows how, to convey it to another convict who was about to be removed. The letter was to be dropped on a railway."

Everything in that letter was as true as that Knox and Pollock were false; and look at the justice of these two English "gentlemen" making such a report to the public, while they never asked me a question as to whether the accusation in the letter was true or false. They took the words of my jailers, or took their own words, to suit their own purposes.

"He said in it that he had been denied the privilege of writing to his poor mother in America; it turned out that he never had asked to do so at all." Good Heavens! how these people can lie. I had asked this permission as often as there are fingers and toes on me. I had even begged a small scrap of paper from Governor Clifton, in which I would write a few words to my mother, and enclose it in a letter I was writing to my wife, and he would not give it to me.

They say I told them I had put the tailor's cloth away "for temporary purposes," when what I told them was, that I put it around my waist when shivering with the cold. But they would not admit in their report that I said anything about feeling cold, for some of our men died from the effects of it, and that was one of the things Knox and Pollock had to whitewash.

There is no use in wasting any more of my time. with these worthies; I believe them to be willful liars, even though they are English Commissioners and big English " gentlemen."

After this Commission was over the authorities commenced " to put the screws on me" in earnest. Every day and night I was worried in one way or another. The cell in which they lodged me at night was full of fleas, though it is but justice to say that my prison life in England was otherwise pretty free from attacks of this kind of minor vermin. In this particular cell I got out of bed one June morning about three o'clock. I could not sleep, and having my writing materials with me, I planted myself with my back to the door, in a position that the watchman could not see me. It was not long till he appeared, and cried out through the slit:

"Where are you?"

"Here," said I, standing up, holding a prayer-book in my hand, as if I was reading it.

"Go to bed."

"I prefer sitting up."

"But you can't sit up; this is Sunday morning and you can't be out of bed before six o'clock."

"Well, I know that, but I cannot sleep with the fleas."

"I do not care about the fleas; you must go to bed or be reported."

"Very well, then, I'll go to bed."

And to bed I went, taking my writing material with me, and making every exertion I could to finish my letter. I wrote under the blanket, and had the clothes so arranged that if he stole a march on me and looked in through the slit he could but see, before I saw him, that I was only hunting the fleas.

But now came the turning point of my life, the winter of my discontent, the gross injustice that made my whole soul rise in arms against them, and pitch their discipline and themselves to the devil. They punished me for working too fast; they gave me forty-eight hours on bread and water, because I had my task-work finished before the appointed time. I got twenty ounces of coir to pick each day. The officer gave it to me to pick at four o'clock in the evening, and took it away from me at the same hour next day. In giving it to me a cord was tied abut it, and in giving it out I bound it in the same cord, so that he could place it tidily on the scales to

be weighed. I had my bundle made up at fifty minutes past three, and, feeling quite at ease with myself and every one else, I stretched on my bare bed-board with a book in my hand, but I was immediately startled by the voice of big Power, roaring out:
"What are you doing there?"
"Reading."
"Reading! Why arn't you at work?"
"Oh, Governor," said I good-humoredly, and thinking I had him on the hip this time, "my work is done."
He opened the door and called Percival, the ward officer, and brought him to account for allowing me to be idle. "No man should be idle in that prison. I should keep my work on hands till the regular hour, or, if I had it done before that hour I should ask for more," and he wound up his declamation in favor of law and order by ordering me to "put out my broom."

Next day I was taken before the Governor and charged with idleness. Power told his story and I told mine. The judge was a man with whom I had very little influence; he said it was a serious breach of discipline, and sentenced me to the darkened cell for two days. I asked him to appeal the case to the Director, but he would not do any such thing.

"Then said I, "I'll not go to the dark cell, nor will I do anything else in obedience to your rules and regulations while you treat me so outrageously."

"Take him off," and off I was taken. As I was passing the tower that led to the punishment ward the officer cried "To your left."

"No," said I, emphatically, for I was in a rage, "I'll go right straight to my own cell."

They let me walk into my ordinary cell, shut the door, and came back by-and-bye with big Power and four or five others. I required them to use no more force than to lay hands on me; that done I would walk quietly with them, but I would not yield obedience to a simple order. The six or seven of them came into the cell. Power ordered me out. I said "No," and the instant the words escaped my lips, Cooper and Brown sprung at me and seized me by the throat. They clutched me so tight that I could not even relieve myself by a screech. I was thrown down and dragged into the lobby. The hands were released from my throat, and Beresford, seeing that this gave him an open for a blow at my head, raised his club to strike, but Power caught him by the arm saying, "Don't strike him yet." They turned me, face foremost to the ground, then caught my hands and legs and dragged me on. Did't my arm joints catch it? By Jove, I felt as if they were twisted out of me. When I was laid opposite the door of the dark cell, I was ordered to strip, and I refused. The whole of them went at me, and as I resisted they had a little trouble. A civilian, who was working as a plumber in the ward, came to their assistance; at last the clothes were torn off, and I lay on the flags naked. Their work was done and I crawled into my quarters, they throwing the tattered garments in after me. The forty-eight hours passed and when I returned to my cell I was ordered to "put out my broom again." "Put it out yourself if you want it," said I, and out they put it. Next day I was asked to go before the Governor, and I refused to go. Power came, but he could not come into my cell, as I had placed my bucket in a corner between the door and the wall. "I'll soon make you come," said he walking away, and in a minute I heard a tramp as if a regiment was coming. I had a massive earthenware chamber vessel, and as I heard them coming, I smashed it on the flags, and put my towel around a few large pieces of it. The bucket would allow the door to open just as wide as would admit a man's head, and, as sure as I write, if I could get a chance at the head of that Brown or Cooper, who lacerated my throat a few days before, I would give either or both of them the benefit of my loaded towel. But neither Brown nor Cooper was brought this time, and I would not strike anyone else. Chief Warden Handy would parley with me, but all to no purpose. I would not take away the bucket. He would put his head in, but I would warn him not to press further. At last he got enraged, and cried out—

"Knock him down if he attempts to strike anyone."

"Now," said I, "You keep away, too, and if you want to get a chance of knocking me down, bring Brown or Cooper up here."

Some warders that were brought from other wards would take a peep at the wild animal inside through the spy-hole, and catching hold of my pint of water I said—

"Now, if any one else stares at me through that slit, I'll dash this water in his face. An Englishman's house is his castle, and I am not going to have mine invaded with impunity."

Captain Wallack, the Deputy-Governor, came, but all to no purpose. As a last resource, they sent for the priest, and, as I would not let him in except on condition of exacting a promise from all the others that none of them would enter until he had gone out again, and I had perfected my barricades, he went away, and they sent for the blacksmith of the establishment, who came with a sledge and crowbar. He battered away at the door and broke it into smithereens, and, as he had torn it off its hinges, I cried out:

"Hold on now, Governor! that will do; I think I may as well make an honorable surrender," and, taking the bucket away, I let them come in. A few of them caught me by the collar and gave a little chucking, but it was not much, as the Deputy-Governor was present. In a few minutes I stood before my judge, and was charged with resisting and assaulting six officers in the discharge of their duty, three days before. The Governor said he would refer it to the Director, as it was so serious a charge. I was brought back and lodged in the cell next to the broken one; but they took away the bucket that was in it, lest I should raise another barricade. My broom was out for three or four days, till the Director came, and as

I was led into the place where we stand till we are called to go before him I saw one man there with his face turned to the wall. I had to pass him and stand three yards below, with my face turned to the wall too; but, instead of passing him by, I grasped him by the hand and cried, "Hallo, Devoy, is that you—how are you?" "Oh, pretty well; how are you?" The officer interfered, and as I was taking my position I said, "This is the place to civilize a fellow, isn't it?" "Never mind, we'll have a day for this yet." "Why, I think you did not know me at first." "Know you," said he, laughing; "why, I don't know who you are yet." "Not know Rossa?" "Great God! are you Rossa?" and by this time the officer was dragging me down to another ward to separate us.

Here was John Devoy, who knew me for years, who parted from me two years before, not recognizing me now. I thought he would know me boiled in porridge, but I suppose I was this time considerably "boiled down."

My turn came to go before the Director, and when at the bar of justice the indictment was read against me—"I had resisted the officers in the discharge of their duty." "I assaulted them." "I refused to be stripped." "I refused to do anything." "What had I to say to the charge?"

"Governor," said I, "will you please ask those officers if either of them can show you any of the signs of my assault?" Neither of them could, but all said I was extremely violent, and would assault violently were I not restrained.

"Now, Governor," added I, pointing to my neck, which was covered with scabs, as they had torn the flesh off of it in the choking they gave me four days before, "look at this and you can see marks of assault."

"Oh," replied he, "that is what you have to expect here when you resist the officers in the discharge of their duty."

Being asked again what I had to say to the charge, I said I'd give my reply in writing, and writing materials for such a purpose were out of the question.

Gambier spoke of my increasing bad conduct, and I spoke of his increasing persecution, in punishing me for idleness when I had performed all the task work assigned to me. Then they harped again upon the string that was tying my bundle of coir; big Power growling out, "No, sir, he didn't pick that string."

"Ah, trash," said I, "don't be going on with such nonsense. You all seem to be in a great fix to get excuses for starving me, but I'll relieve you of that difficulty in future, for it will be a long time again before I pick a string, or do a stroke of work for you."

"I'll see that you will," said Gambier, as he ordered to have me taken away. I was conducted to a punishment cell, and the Deputy-Governor followed and informed me of my punishment. It was four months solitary confinement in a darkened cell, on penal class diet, with the first twelve days on bread and water, together with which

I was obliged to pick oakum, but for these four months I never picked a thread of it. The bundle was put in every morning, and it remained untouched till evening, when it was put outside my cell door, where it remained till the next day dawned, to get another day's lodging inside, and so on till the end of my four long months.

No "kitchen" with your food, no milk, no meat, no tea, no coffee; you were very fortunate if you got enough of salt to make "dip" for your "pratees" and porridge.

The first twelve days on bread and water brought me two very severe attacks of something like cholera. The first of them seized me in the middle of the night; the watchman hearing me groaning and vomiting asked if he would call the doctor. "You need not mind," said I, "your doctors know very well that this treatment is meant to break down my health, and I am not going to give them any trouble." He, however, reported the case, as by-and-by the doors were opened, and in walked Doctor Pocklington, having only his pants and shirt on him. He said he would send me something to stop the retching, and change my diet for a few days. I got hot milk for breakfast and supper, and rice pudding for dinner, or rather as dinner, for the pudding was the only dinner I got. It was very nice and sweet, and great was my regret that I could not keep this on my stomach; it was so seldom I got anything nice, that I sorely lamented the loss of it.

I think it was three days this diet continued; I was somewhat recovered then, and the bread and water commenced again, and again came a relapse of my illness, which clung to me for four or five days. Doctor Pocklington was as kind as man could be. I don't know what his feelings towards me were, but I feel kindly towards him for the promptness with which he came to see me those nights, and from the fact that I never heard an unpleasant word, nor saw an unpleasant look from him those twelve months that I was in Millbank prison.

After the twelve days the four months' punishment diet commenced, and coming to the end of the time I found my body covered with small pustules, like little boils. Not an inch of me was free from them, and they looked very ugly with their white heads.

At their first appearance I showed them to the doctor, and he said it was the natural result of the food I was getting, of confinement in a darkened cell, and of want of exercise. A fortnight afterwards, as the officers were stripping me, one of them named Cooper opened his eyes in wonder at the appearance of my skin.

"What," said he, "did you not show them to the doctor?"

I told him I did, but as the doctor said it was only the natural result of my punishment, I thought I might as well let nature take its course.

"When the doctor comes round next show them to him again."

"Indeed I will not," said I.

"Then," added he, "I will have to make a report of the case."

He did report it, and I was taken to Dr. Gover's office, and ordered to strip, and after this chief doctor looking at my condition, he ordered me to dress and be taken to my cell.

I afterwards learned that the Medical Department had a fight with the Directory Department about my treatment. Gambier wanted to continue my punishment up to the requirements of discipline, no matter what became of my health, and after the four months had expired I believe I would have got more bread and water for not working during the time only the doctors interfered.

I know Doctor Gover told me he was trying to keep me off of punishment, and hoped I would assist him by good behavior, to which I replied "that I needed to be treated only like any other prisoner, to act like any other." I have nothing harsh to say of the doctors of Millbank; they gave me a glass of magnesia three times a day to help me to digest my punishment diet; they acted like gentlemen; but I have something different to say of the doctors elsewhere.

For the first three or four days I had company in the punishment ward, as John Devoy and St. Clair had been undergoing a sentence of four months in penal class when I came to be classed with them. This they had got on a charge of attempting to break through their cells; and they did make such an attempt; but, as in unsuccessful revolutions, got punished because they did not succeed. When the Director asked John Devoy was he sorry for his offence, John told him he was sorry that he failed. He was undergoing this four months, and seemed not to be yet satisfied that he had had a fair trial of himself in the way of escaping, for one day he attacked two warders who were superintending him while he was sweeping his cell; he knocked one down with a blow of the brush handle; the second blow was warded off by the other's club; the brush handle broke; the officer ran to give the alarm, and John seeing the cause was lost again, commenced to dress the wound of the officer he had knocked down, and allowed the wounded man to have the credit of locking him up before the others came. It was when he was brought before the Director for this offence that I met him in the passage way and shook hands with him.

We had daring spirits in Millbank prison about this time, and with the means of communication we had, we were forming a plan to seize upon the officers' armory and make a fight. It was a desperate idea; but with all that had been ever said about the Irish never making a decent fight, but always making *fiascos*, we had pledged ourselves that in this affair we were to fight to the death. In case of any sudden alarm that would interfere against our escape, we were to leave a mark after us, by burning up everything that we could burn, London itself if possible, so that these English governors would have a lesson given them regarding the propriety of bringing Irish political prisoners to London in order to herd them with their thieves.

I know that I counselled the most extreme measures; my spirit was galled, and I was ready to make any sacrifice, even that of life, for the sake of revenge. If I could lay the city in ashes I would do so, even though my bones were reduced to ashes with it.

General Halpin was in a part of the prison that we could not easily reach when we were speculating on this mutiny, and before we could communicate with him thoroughly, Clerkenwell was blown up; soldiers were brought to guard us, and other changes were made that obliged us to give up the project.

In consequence of John Devoy having used his broom in the scuffle with the officers, the handles were cut off of all the brooms in the prison, and in sweeping your cell you had nothing to lay hold of but the stump that held the tuft of hair.

In the month of July the weather was very warm, and the air of those cells was almost unbearable. To give us a little ventilation, the trap doors were left open during the day. This was customary every Summer, but John Devoy, and St. Clair and I destroyed the custom by availing of it for the purpose of whispering news to each other when we thought the warders were absent.

I discovered one day that an officer was playing eaves-dropper as John and I were talking. I heard him slingeing down closer to my door, and as it was necessary to make his presence known I cried aloud, "John, there is some fellow here alongside of my door listening." By-and-bye all our trap doors were closed, and we lost the little current of air and little conversation we were enjoying.

It was about this time that the devil took it into his wicked head to notice I was in prison, and pay me a visit. He did it in the shape of womankind. You need not imagine that the woman came into my cell, or that I saw the devil there, and hurled my ink-bottle at him as Martin Luther is said to have done when he was in prison; but if what theologians say about the old gentleman be true, he was with me to a certainty—albeit, I have not much faith in the possibility of his getting out of hell.

Father Burke says—"The devil understands every age better than anybody else, after the Almighty God. He tries to entrap the young men into secret societies, to make them swear away their manhood and liberty by secret oaths, and make them pledge themselves—puts an obligation on them—the fulfillment of which would involve crime or imorality, perhaps even bloodshed and murder." With the latter part of this sentence I have nothing to do further than to say I look upon it as mere Cullen clap-trap in so far as it relates to secret societies amongst Irishmen against England, but with the former part of it I must have a little connection.

"The devil understands every age better than anybody else after Almighty God." Well, I suppose it is my duty to believe it on such authority, even though I am very chary about putting the devil on anything at all like an equality with God. I believe in God, but I defy the devil, and I cannot at all bring myself to give his satanic majesty the omnipotent power and omnipresence I give my Creator. I find it hard to believe the devil can be everywhere, or that he has power to circumvent the Lord in the purposes for which He made man. Passing all that by, and getting into the phraseology of the times, let me say that the devil came into my prison cell in the shape of a woman, and never ceased worrying me for three or four years. Why he did not lay siege to me the first few years I do not know. Perhaps it was that my mind was occupied with the hopes and fears attending upon a fight in Ireland, and when that was pronounced a dead failure the ground lay fallow and the weeds sprung up.

But certain it is that "the Old Boy" did attack me, and never more vigorously than when I was in the most miserable condition. On starvation diet, and in a black-hole cell, where not a ray of light could enter, the old fellow would scroodge his way in to remind me how pleasant it would be, *even there*, to have female company.

Unlike some of the saintly men of old, who were similarly assailed in their solitude, I had no virgin snow nor spiked girdle to embrace. My comforter for a time was an algebraic question or a proposition of Euclid, which I took to bed with me and worked away at till I fell asleep; but, as if my jailers knew that I helped myself in this manner, they took my Euclid and my Algebra from me on the plea that I could have no books because I would not work while on punishment.

The devil, seeing, I suppose, how I was fighting him, must have gone to Gambier and instigated him to deprive me of the books. But I did not give up the fight so easily. I told the jailers if I did not get my school-books I'd give them no peace—I'd break everything I could—in other words, I'd keep away the devil by playing the devil with everything. I gave them a few days to consider. During this time Father Zanetti told me that Gambier was talking to him about school-books, and asking him whether I would be more incorrigible with them than without them, to which the priest replied that he supposed it would not make me worse to get them. Next morning I took the cover of my bucket and I made one big stroke at the thick bull's-eye that was built into the wall to let in the gaslight. The officer immediately made his appearance, demanding what I was about. "What about my Euclid and Algebra?" said I; "if I don't get them I'll knock this spyglass of yours into triangles." He told me to stop awhile, and in a few minutes he came back with the books.

I had played them another trick the night before. They were treating me as bad as they could treat me, and in my case there could hardly be any change for the worse, and, if there could, it should be a change that would bring me some variety, and, consequently, some improvement; then, I had no reason to fear anything from them. Even in this punishment cell, from which they shut out the light by a strong perforated iron blind, they should keep my gaslight burning all night. When the prison was locked up, and the extra officers had retired, I got out of my bed, and with my clothes I stuffed the bull's-eye so that a ray of light could not enter. The officers, on noticing the darkness, made an alarm, and four or five of them came parleying with me immediately after. I wanted no night-light; they would not allow me the daylight, and I did not want their gas when I wanted to sleep. I should be treated like any other prisoner, and when they took away my books I would take away their lights, to assimilate my treatment to that of other prisoners. The end of it was I unmuffled the bull's-eye on the promise that they would ask next day if my books were to be restored to me, and restored they were.

It was while I was undergoing these four months' punishment on bread and water that a proposition was made to me of volunteering to Western Australia. Yes, " volunteering:" that is the word. The Government were so kind now as to condescend to pretend to give me a will of my own.

The door of my cell was thrown open one day, and Governor Morish stood outside the gate with paper and pencil in hand—

" I have come to know if you will volunteer to go to the penal settlements of Western Australia ?"

" Volunteer, did you say, Governor ?"

" Yes."

" To go there as a prisoner, and be a prisoner when I get there ?"

" Yes."

" I will do no such thing."

" Why, all the other prisoners are going."

" That's no matter to me. You, I suppose, can send me too if you like, or do anything you please with me, but I'll do no volunteering for you."

" But the Government will not send you otherwise."

" Then I'll remain here with the Government. I prefer to receive their tortures and starvation in the heart of England than in the wilds of Western Australia. If you are taking down names you can put me down as not volunteering. I am a prisoner, and in the hands of the authorities. They can do what they please with me; but whatever they do must be at their own responsibility."

" Then I am to put you down as not desiring to go ?"

" It is not a question at all of my desiring to go or not to go. I know well the authorities care very little about my desires. They will study their own convenience, not mine. I do not know what their motives are in sending me to Australia; but when you tell me I am to be a prisoner there, I prefer to be near you here, where I can make my wants known, than thousands of miles away from you —away amongst the savages, where there may be orders to ' civilize' me in the fashion that you are doing it here in London. No, Governor, I will give the authorities no excuse. Put me down as saying, 'I am in the hands of the authorities; they can do with me what they please, but I will do no volunteering anywhere.'"

He penciled something on his paper, walked away, and the warder shut the door.

Any change of life at this time to me would be a God-send, and I was hoping I would be sent to Australia; but I would not give them the satisfaction of volunteering to go there. If anything happened to us, they would say we volunteered, and, for my part, I did not want to put it in their power to say this. I felt a kind of pleasure in seeing them treat us brutally in England, and I could not enjoy this feeling, under similar treatment, in the Antipodes.

But, as I guessed, my desires in the matter were nothing. In a few days the Government doctor came and inspected me, and in a few days more it was officially announced to me that I was to be sent to the penal colony of Western Australia. I got a sheet of paper to write the farewell letter to my wife. I wrote, but it was pronounced unfit to be let out. I wrote a second, against which the same sentence was pronounced, and then I learned some way that the Australians were sent off and I was left behind.

The secret of this is, that between the time the Governor first spoke to me about going and the time of the ship's sailing, Colonel Kelly and Captain Deasy were rescued from the police in Manchester. This changed the mind of the Government, and it was considered as well to keep some of us in England as send us out of it.

I cannot put out of my mind the vexation that entered it on account of the manner in which Father Zanetti met me one day, when I asked him a question as to whether John O'Leary and Thomas Clarke Luby were sent off or not. They were in Portland, a distance of some two hundred miles, and more unsurpassable barriers of locks and keys and stone walls divided us. I would feel more lonesome if I heard they had gone further away from me. I asked the priest to grant me one request, one day he came into my cell. "What was it?" "To tell me if O'Leary and Luby were sent to Australia." He stamped his foot upon the floor in a rage, saying: "Don't be asking me such questions; don't you know my honor is pledged, and that I cannot answer you?" That was the last question I ever asked this scrupulously honorable man, who was a perfect type of the union of Church and State—a priest of God and a priest of the English Convict Government, too.

My four months' penal class in penal servitude had expired, and I was taken down to my ordinary cell. If I got coir to pick again I would refuse to pick it, but they brought skeins of coir cord and asked me to keep winding them into balls. There was no talk of task work, and I went on pretty comfortably for some weeks. I went to chapel every morning, and there I got acquainted with James Xavier O'Brien. There was no formal introduction, such as "Mr. O'Brien, Mr. O'Donovan; Mr. O'Donovan, Mr. O'Brien," but the prisoners who sat between us communicated to me who he was and to him who I was, and then we looked at each other and slyly nodded. In course of time we came to pass letters to each other, and he was instructing me in many things about the "movement" in Ireland.

One time that himself or his cell was searched, a letter of mine was found, and it brought me to misfortune again. My name was not signed to it, yet that was no matter, as it contained evidence to show that none but myself could be the writer. I had stated that I applied for a visit and got permision; that I sent a ticket to Richard Pigott and a lady friend, and that Gambier, the Director, was "as hypocritically civil as possible in granting it." I was brought before Gambier; he held the letter before him. "And so," said he, "you say I was hypocritically civil!" "Now, governor," said I, "you want to make me admit it was I wrote that letter. I avail of my legal privilege, and will admit or deny nothing. You prove your case; but this you may be sure of—that if what you hold in your hand was written by me it contains nothing but the truth." "Then I will stop your visit, the ticket of which has been sent to Mr. Pigott!" "Oh! you may do anything you please." And orders were immediately given to write to Dublin that I had forfeited the privilege granted to me of a visit. I was taken away, but, instead of being taken to a punishment cell, I was taken into the yard to take my hour's exercise. I concluded that I had escaped this time without getting bread and water; for once a prisoner offends against discipline, there is nothing for him but the restraint of "durance vile" until he passes through the purgatory that washes that stain.

It is wonderful how these people, with all their hatred of Catholicity, have introduced into their prison punishment the very dogmas of the creed. They sneer at purgatory, absolution, and indulgences, and at wiping away the stain that remains after sin, after the sin itself is atoned for; but they retain the very essentials of the creed in the management of their convict system. Here is an instance. A bit of lead pencil is found secreted in my cell; I am sentenced to three days' bread and water, and am fined 84 marks. I pass over my three days' bread and water, and the 84 marks add 14 days to my imprisonment. A visit is due to me every six months, and a month after the report I ask for my visiting ticket as it is due. The books are looked over, the stain of sin is found against me. I am reported and punished for having a bit of pencil, and must remain three months purging myself of that stain before I can obtain any privilege. I must remain two months after it without writing a letter, even though my writing time was due that day I was reported. I can, if I wish, apply to the Director to grant the indulgence, but he can, if he wish, refuse it.

From the day I entered this prison until the day I was punished for having my work done ten minutes before the time, I was stripped naked every noon time. I then "struck" against stripping daily, and the practice was given up. I gained a point here, but it was not gained without suffering and sacrifice, and I believe England will never surrender anything to anyone who is not ready to put these into practice against her.

The day my letter was found with O'Brien I was stripped three times. I went through the process without resistance, because I knew I had nothing contraband about me, and I was anxious to learn what was up. Nothing was found in my place to warrant a charge against me. I was taken before the Governor and charged with some of my writing being found in the cell of another person. Being asked what I had to say, I said, "Nothing." I was put into a darkened cell to await the Director's decision, and after three days I was taken out and told he had ordered that I be kept from Mass and morning prayers during the rest of my time. I was four days in my ordinary cell winding my balls of twine, and as the officers came around I kept twitting them about introducing the old Irish penal laws into prison, and protested against the illegality of keeping me from chapel when I was not supposed to be under punishment. If I was to be persecuted, I demanded it in a disciplinary form. At six o'clock the morning of the fifth day my doors were opened and I was ordered to come out. Out I came, and was conducted to a punishment cell. "What is this for?" said L. "What is my offence, and what is my punishment?" But I would not be told. Breakfast came, and I got my eight ounces of bread and my pint of water. Again I asked for an explanation, and was told I would know soon enough. I was getting a little wrathy. The regulations declare that before a prisoner is put under punishment, he must be told the duration of it, and the offence. Sir John Davies says there is no people in the world who more love to be treated legally than the Irish. I suppose I have some of this national feeling, and though it was English law I was under, I felt this time I had not the benefit of it, and that I was being treated illegally.

When the officer said you will know soon enough, I determined I would, and said "*that* I will." I laid my bread and water on my bed board. I took off one of my slippers, and with the heel of it I smashed the spy-hole of the door. The alarm being given, a half a dozen warders were on the spot immediately. I was placed in handcuffs and conducted to another cell. No sooner were they gone, than I gave the trap-door a kick, and it gave way, with all the surrounding irons that were fastening it. I then put out my handcuffed hands, drew back the bolt, and opened in the door. The man in charge, hearing the noise, made towards me, and ordered me to shut the door. "I prefer it open," said I. He put in his hand to pull out the door, but I was further in than he, and had more power to keep it open. He shook his club at me, and I told him he may as well keep quiet, that I wanted a little air, and would keep the door open as long as I could. Stamping his foot, and bobbing his head at me at every word, he emphatically shouted, "Shut

—that door—I say." "I will not—shut—that door—*I* say." He went off, and soon returned with a principal officer, who unlocked the gate. The first fellow dashed in, caught me by the throat, pinned me to the wall, and raised his club to strike me. My hands were tied. I could do nothing but cry out, "Coward," and he did not let the blow fall. I was mad. I lost my temper for the first time, and when he had loosened his grasp of my throat, I foolishly swore, "By heavens, I'll make you pay for this yet." Yes; for a fortnight afterwards, if I caught that man where I could fling him down the stone stairs, I could deliberately murder him. I say deliberately; for I had made up mind to do it in order to be tried for the offence in open court, where I would have an opportunity of exposing the treatment I was receiving. I forget the officer's name; it was something like Agden; but if I could catch him or Brown or Cooper on a stairs, any time during a few months that I was in the humor, I would fling them over the bannisters.

I am not boasting or "blowing" now. I am only writing my prison life, and showing my reader the state of mind I was in. One time more, while I was in prison, did I lose my temper, so far as to wish I had a weapon I could fight with. I did not care what odds were against me, I would strike. It was when the warders kicked and leaped upon me in Chatham.

After breaking the trap door, I was put into the blackhole cell or twenty-four hours.

It was an underground cellar, the time of the year was about the 20th of December, and it was piercingly cold.

I got a rug and blanket, but no mattress. When I turned from one side to another the clothes turned with me, and I could not arrange them, as my hands were tied. To add to my comfort, I was longer than the width of the cell, and I could not get a full stretch of my legs. When the morning dawned—or rather when my breakfast of bread and water came, for there was no dawn of day in this hole—I felt one of my wrists very sore, and I told the warders to tell the doctor I wanted to see him, as the irons were unnecessarily tight.

The doctor came, and when I raised my wrists up to the lantern I found them covered with blood. "Oh, sir," said one of the jailers, "he has been only using violence to himself, and the doctor pronounced the irons not unnecessarily tight. I must have slept something during the night, and in my twisting and turning, cut my hands.

The funniest thing in the world is walking in those cells. When I was a "greenhorn" in them I'd find my nose or my forehead bobbing against the wall. My eyes were no use to me, and I soon learned to use my elbows instead of them. When I stood up to take my walk I placed my back to the door and my elbow to the wall, paced forward with my head thrown backward, and backward with my head thrown forward, always taking soundings with my elbow.

I was told my punishment this time was six days on bread and water, and twenty-one days on penal class diet, for writing a letter to James O'Brien. The blackhole cell is truly a black one, where no ray of sunlight ever enters; the punishment cell, a darkened one, where a perforated metal sheet keeps out the full light. When I knew my sentence, my passion was over, and I got into good humor. I made a most solemn address to the officers one day in these words: "Now, governors, I am here a political prisoner in England; by all the laws of civilization, and by all the rights of man, I am entitled to as much coarse food as will sustain life, and to an ordinary prison cell that will admit God's daylight. I know it is not in my power to command the food, but I can do something to get myself light; and to take all preliminary steps towards the maintenance of peace, I ask you to take away that iron blind before I proceed to do it myself." The officers smiled at each other. "Then, you won't do it?" "Now, you had better keep quiet." "Then, if you won't, it's my duty to go to work at it," and laying hold of my wooden spoon, proceeded to delve out little bits of cement till the spoon broke. It was left with me to eat a pint of stirabout that is given every fourth day to a prisoner on bread and water. The pint of stirabout coming, I asked for a spoon, and was told the Governor had issued an order that I should get no more spoons while I was in prison, because I broke the spoon I got. The doors were locked, and I was left in the darkness with my hands tied and my pint of stirabout. I put the dish to my mouth, but it was not running stirabout, it was thick, and would not come near my hungry lips. Oh, no, it should not escape me that way. I was determined it should find its way to the blackhole, and I found there was no way to get it down but to lay the dish on the floor, and lay myself resting on my knees and elbows. You may call this eating "on all fours" if you like, but it is the way I had to take my dinner that day, and when I had it taken, I, to mark the circumstance in my memory, turned the bowl upside down and leaped upon it, and broke it into pieces. Having done this, I found myself laughing at an idea that entered my head, and, as I enjoy a joke at all times, I proceeded to perpetrate a practical one now.

The officers visited me every two hours during the day and night. They opened the three doors and entered the cell to see if I was dead or alive. I thought it would be a good thing if, when they came again, I could make them stay with me till my time was up. It was this made me laugh, and it is better to laugh at misfortune any day than to cry at it; so, taking a piece of the broken dish, I broke it into smaller pieces with my teeth, and commenced stuffing the keyhole of the inner iron gate. It was fully loaded when my friends came to look after me. "What is the matter?—this key won't work; show here the lantern," said Beresford, and as he looked, he cried, "Well, well, to be sure."

Awls, and wires, and corkscrews, and gimlets were got before they could get out all my little wooden sparables. They spent eight hours at the work, while I kept begging of them to go away and let me live in peace. When the door was opened, my time was up, and I was taken back to my blind cell.

When the twenty-seven days were passed, I got twenty-eight days more for breaking my dish and spoon, and breaking the wall, and writing on it; then I got fourteen days for something else, so that from the 20th of December till the 24th day of February—the day I was taken from Millbank to Chatham—I was on bread and water.

CHAPTER XVI.

CHRISTMAS DAY ON "BREAD AND WATER"—TELEGRAPHING TO JOHN DEVOY—AN ARCHBISHOP ON STEPHENS' ESCAPE—SOWING DISTRUST—THE HANDWRITING ON THE WALL—THE BIBLE IN THE BLACKHOLE—A THIEF FEEDS ME; HIS LETTER AND HIS PRESENT—A STEM OF A DHUDEEN—REFUSE TO HAVE MY PICTURE TAKEN, EXCEPT THE QUEEN SENDS FOR IT—MANCHESTER MURPHY AND MICHAEL O'BRIEN—A NIGHT ON THE HILLS OF CONNAUGHT—"FENIANISM" AND "RIBBONISM"—EDWARD DUFFY MEETING WITH HIS MOTHER—APPLICATION TO SEE HIM DYING REFUSED—PREACHING—A WAIL—MEDITATED MISCHIEF—A CHANGE FOR THE BETTER ONLY A PREPARATION FOR ONE FOR THE WORSE—JOURNEY TO CHATHAM PRISON.

The several incidents and reminiscences of the past few months of my prison purgatory will comprise this chapter. The punishment referred to in the last one commenced on Christmas week, and on Christmas day I found myself on bread and water. The bell rang for dinner. I heard the doors opening, and I began asking myself was it possible that these Christian people, who were so strong on the Bible, would leave me on Christmas day without my dinner? That was the very thing which was possible. Discipline proved stronger than the Christian spirit. My door was passed, and I was left to dine upon my hungry thoughts. I did not fare very sumptuously or very pleasantly, and, as I had nothing to feed upon, I set my wits to work to get something to do. I wanted occupation—something to take my mind away from the dinnerless reflections. I had an iron screw in my pocket that I picked up when I kicked open the trap-door some days before, and with this I set to work to take down my metal blind, and, though I kept at it till I sweated, I did not make much progress. I lay down on my bed board exhausted; I rapped on the wall to know if there was any prisoner within hearing with whom I could hold a conversation and kill time. I got a response from a cell underneath me, and I asked the signal question: "Who are you?" to which I got the response of a J and an O, and a H, and an N, and a D-E-V-O-Y— "John Devoy." I signalled back "Rossa," and both of us rapped a *Te Deum* on the wall before we commenced conversation. Hungry as I was at the time, I would rather have made this acquaintance than the acquaintance of the best Christmas dinner I ever saw.

We talked till the time John had to go to evening prayers, but there were no evening prayers for me, as I was undergoing punishment. When he returned we talked again till bed-time, when he was changed to another cell. Next morning he was brought back, and we renewed our acquaintance. Our conversation was all about Ireland and the "movement." He was one of the men that took James Stephens out of prison; it was into his arms he was received when he slipped off the prison wall, and I got the full history of the affair from him. It is strange to find it industriously circulated in America that James Stephens was taken out of prison with the connivance of the English Government. I have heard it time after time, and so have many others. A friend was telling me he was one evening in the society of some gentlemen, lay and clerical, where the question came up. An archbishop asserted that Mr. Stephens was let out by the Government. The friend made some observation, which would imply that he held a contrary opinion, when the right rev. gentleman silenced him by some such observation as this: "Don't contradict me, sir; I have reason to know what I say is true." The good bishop was imposed upon by some one in the interest of England. It is our enemy's business to circulate the canting falsehood that, "if you put one Irishman on the spit, you'll get another to turn him," or that you cannot get an Irishman at all whom English gold will not purchase to betray his country. James Stephens was taken out of prison by men who were true to Ireland; and, whatever can be said of him in other respects, this, at least, may be said of him, that he is as free from the taint of English gold, and as unlikely to be corrupted by it, as any man who has ever spoken of his name.

For three or four weeks I was, to my infinite delight, allowed to remain in this particular cell over John Devoy's. I had the four walls of it covered with writing, and as they apprehended I would disfigure in a similar manner every cell I went into, they thought it better to allow me remain in the one I was. It was amusing to see the inspectors come in and take notes of the handwriting on the wall.

"This is the land of Bible hypocrites, where they starve and worry men to death under medical superintendence, so that none may call it murder."

"We will not kill those Irish rebels publicly, but starve them privately."

Then in another corner they would read: "With one hand they reach to me the Bible, and with the other the bit of bread that starves me slowly."

And this was literally true. When a prisoner was put on bread and water, the Bible followed him to his punishment cell, and if he was changed from one cell to another, the Bible followed him. One time that I was taken to the blackhole, Cooper brought my Bible in his hand, and as he was about to lock me in, I said, "Aren't you going to give me my Bible?" "Why, sure you have no light to read it." "But can't you leave me one of those lanterns?" "I wish I could. *Your Bible will be left here outside the door* till your time is up, and then it will be taken to your other cell," and saying so, I saw him lay down the book at a corner of the gate.

I could feel more satisfaction had they carried the farce so far as to allow me keep the book in the blackhole. But the worst of it was, they never told how long or how short I was to be kept in this place, and I was too much on my dignity to ask them, for by evincing any solicitude on the subject I would be giving them the satisfaction of seeing I felt their treatment.

I was as quiet as a lamb during the time I was holding communication with Devoy, but they occasionally tried my temper by taking my pint of stirabout from me and putting me on bread and water, because I would not work unless I got the ordinary prison diet and ordinary cell.

"Stop that knocking, there; what are you doing that for?" they'd often cry out, as they would catch me telegraphing to John Devoy, and I'd tell them I was trying to strike up "Garryowen" on the wall, as I had no other way of killing time. Whenever I noticed myself watched I tried to turn the knocking into the playing of a tune.

At last I was removed from this cell, and finding myself located where I had no communication with any one, I amused myself by repeating all the pieces of poetry my memory could supply me with.

"Stop that noise, there!"

"What's that you say?" said I, as I was thus interrupted going through one of Davis' poems.

"Stop that noise there, I say."

"Oh, by Jove, I won't. I'm making no noise that disturbs any one else."

Next morning I was taken before the Governor and charged with making noise and swearing in my cell. There it was, down in the Governor's book, that when I was told to stop that noise I vehemently swore out, "By Jesus, I won't." I told the Governor it was an expression I never used in my life. But explanations were out of the question; I should not say, "By Jove," or anything else, in my cell, and had to take my punishment. I asked him to remove the expression "By Jesus" from the record, as not belonging to me, but all to no use; there it had to remain, to show visitors, directors and others, what a desperate character I was.

I soon got a comrade in the cell next to me. He was after escaping from Portsmouth prison, and was after being recaptured; he was sent alongside of me to indulge in six months' penal class. He could "knock" on the wall, and we became great friends. One day I was sentenced to bread and water; when I came back from the governor, he knocked, and asked me "what luck?" I told him; then I heard his bell ring; he was allowed to the closet, and when he came back he ordered me to go to the closet immediately, and take a loaf that he left there; if I didn't the officer would find it, and he would get "dosed," as he said. I obeyed orders, and as I was returning from the closet I had the loaf in my pocket. Before I entered my cell, two officers met me, who were coming to take me to another cell to spend my term of bread and water. I had to go with them and strip outside the door. I was questioned why I had this bread in my pocket, and I told them "for safety." They broke it in two halves and threw it in after me. When I had dressed myself, I took my bread, and to my surprise I found a piece of brown paper sticking out of one of the pieces. How it escaped detection I do not know. I read the note; the writer told me I should not starve while he had a bit of bread to spare, and every day they would put me on bread and water, he'd leave a loaf for me in the same place where he left this. His father was from near Limerick, he said, and was evicted by the landlord; himself was born in England, and he offered his family wrongs as an excuse for his own conduct towards the people that legislated him and them into ruin.

He told me he wrote this letter with a pen that he made out of the sprig of a broom, and he got his ink out of a bit of coal that he powdered and mixed with water. This was different to the receipt John Devoy gave me for getting ink. It was to be produced at the expense of my blood; but the question was, from what part of the body could the most copious supply be drawn with the least degree of pain, and after many experiments he learned it was in wounding a particular spot inside the nostrils.

Nugent's term of punishment had expired before mine, and again I was without a companion. He was a very active person, and could do more work in cleaning and keeping things in order than many others. For this reason he was detailed with another prisoner to keep all the wards and corridors in order, an officer superintending both of them. I got an hour's exercise every penal class day in a small yard set apart for refractory prisoners. A door shuts you in, and in this there is a round hole through which an officer can look to see are you "all right." I was pacing round this coop when a whisper of "Rossa" came through the hole. I approached and saw my late penal class companion and another prisoner standing to attention; the two of them looking as innocent as angels.

They were opposite the door, they did not move a muscle of the face, or give a wink to me, and I knew the officer's eyes were on them. I took another turn around and gave another peep, when Nugent pouted out his lips to signify that he had something in his mouth for me. What could it be! Oh, of course, a bit of lead pencil. I watched the hole and shortly saw something drop in from the tips of two fingers. I made for it, and what was it do you think? A bit of the stem of an old pipe. He had been sucking consolation out of it, and now he parted with his treasure and gave it to me to suck. The market value of this bit of a *dhudeen* was two loaves of bread, but I could pay nothing for it, yet here was its possessor giving me a clear surrender of it without any expectation of fee or reward, besides his running the risk of being detected in transferring the property and suffering more therefor. There *is* "honor among thieves," and noble traits of character too, and this is one of the instances of it.

The English people have lately cried out against the ill-treatment of political prisoners in France, and the London *Times* sent a commissioner to Oberon, who found out that the prisoners had one cause of complaint against the Government in the fact that the tobacco supplied to them was not as good as it ought to be. England would never think of asking herself how she treated her political prisoners as regards tobacco. Oh, no!

"'Tis you're the sinner always—she's the saint."

Tobacco for *her* prisoners is a thing out of the question—"'tis a nuisance," "'tis an injury to them," and three days is the lightest punishment that is given to a prisoner, as was given to myself, for being found in possession of as much of it as would weigh a barleycorn.

"Come on, come on," said Warder Power to me one day as he opened my door. On I went, and was brought through the square in which the soldiers were on parade. I was soon landed in a room which turned out to be the photographic department of the establishment. The artist had his glasses ready, and sat me down on a chair opposite the picturing instrument. As soon as he had fixed me in position, and taken his hands off, he made for the machine and and I stood up.

"What do you stand up for?" said he.

"What would I sit down for?" said I.

"To take your picture."

"My picture?"

"Yes; sit down there again," and he made toward me to place me in my position.

"Now, wait awhile; who wants my picture?"

"We want it; sit down."

"You? Do you know I have a wife?"

"What do you mean?"

"I mean I have a wife, and you have made her awfully jealous of me by circulating a report that I was holding an intrigue with another man's wife. I don't want to make matters worse than they are now by sending my picture into the world; if my wife saw me with any other woman, it may cause a separation for life."

"Why, what a foolish man you are; don't you know that these photographs are for the prison authorities, and that they do not leave the prison?"

"Oh, I could not rely upon that, and my mind would be uneasy. The prison authorities have the original, and I will give them permission to come and look at me whenever they please."

"Come now, come now, anb don't be so foolish; you will only be bringing additional trouble on yourself," and here he gently laid hands on me to coax me into the chair.

"Oh, no, governor, no; there is no trouble to me like trouble of mind, and if I allowed you to take my picture I could not help thinking it would get into the hands of other women, and that my wife would hear it."

"Then you absolutely refuse to allow your picture to be taken?"

"Unless I see that it is absolutely wanted, and that I have guartees it will not be improperly used."

Here three or four of them pressed me to sit down. I sat down, and as soon as they had their hands off me I stood up and replied to their persuasion thus—"See now, governors, there is no use pressing me further; there is only one condition on which I will allow my picture to be taken, and that is this—that the Queen write to me for it, and promise she will not let it out of her own possession."

I was taken back to my cell, and the next day I was again taken to the photographer, with the same result as before. Clerkenwell Prison was after being blown down this time; alarm reigned everywhere around. Soldiers were brought into the prisons, our rescue was apprehended, and our photographs were wanted for the detectives in case we were taken away; but as I was this time undergoing all the tortures they could inflict upon me, I knew they could not treat me worse, and I would not give them the satisfaction of letting them make a picture of me.

A change now came; I was sent from one side of the pentagon to another, and my new cell was somewhat of an improvement upon those I had before. It had no iron blind, but had a small window containing two panes of glass, and away out of my reach, near the ceiling, nine feet high. The warder opened it in the morning to give me fresh air, and many an anxious wish I had to indulge myself with a look at the world outside. I'd leap and catch the sill and strain myself, but light as my body was it was too heavy a weight for my hands to sustain, and I'd drop down after a few seconds. Bringing all my wits to work on the situation, I was at last able to attain the height of my ambition, and have not only a look into the world, but a whisper with an old acquaintance. I piled up on one another all the things I could lay hold of. My gutta-percha pot was the foundation stone, at meal time my stir-about dish was next, then my gutta-percha pint, and my jacket and vest on top of these, each folded up so as to afford me as much height as possible, and on top of all I placed on the edge a timber plate which was a resident of the cell and was not removed when I entered, though I had no use of it. It was as nice a feat as you could well imagine, to see me plant my toes on the rim of this plate and keep hanging to the sill for a quarter of an hour at a time while holding a conversation with a prisoner in another cell. My hands would get tired and then I'd lean on the structure underneath more heavily than I ought; the pile would totter to its base. My first attempt to open up communications proved a success, but a melancholy success, from the information it brought me. When I had raised myself to the position that I could see the windows of the other cells, I strongly whispered—" Is there any one there ?" After three or four repetitions of this, a whisper came back, " Who are you ?" " Rossa." " Rossa ? Surely ?" " Oh, yes, who are you ?" " Murphy of Manchester. I met you there, don't you recollect, in '64 ?" Then we had some words as to how and where we met, which I cannot tell here. I remembered him very well, and asked what brought him here ?

" Why," said he, " don't you know ?"

" No," said I, " how could I know ?"

" Did not you hear of the three men that were hung at Manchester ?"

" No; who were they, or what about ?"

" Didn't you hear of Kelly and Deasy being rescued ?"

" No, no; what Kelly and Deasy ?"

" Colonel Tom Kelly and Captain Tim Deasy."

" Is it Tom Kelly that was in Dublin ?"

" Yes. He and Deasy were arrested in Manchester, and we rescued them. One of the police was shot, and three men were hanged for it, and seven transported. You must have known one of them that was hanged, Michael O'Brien, of Cork."

These last words staggered me; the pile that was under my feet fell; I clung to the window-sill, and asked—" Is it Mik O'Brien ?"

" Yes, yes; you knew him; he belonged to the National Reading-room there, and went to America, and came back to fight."

I heard no more, but dropped to the ground. Here was Mike O'Brien dead—hanged! Mike O'Brien! one of my oldest friends in the organization, one of the truest and one of the noblest; as artless as a child, as devoted as a lover, and as courageous as a lion. Dead—hanged! 'Twas too bad. I first made his acquaintance in Cork in '59; I met him at the Crown Hotel, and was introduced to him by a relative of mine, Denis Downing, both of whom were then doing business in the establishment of Sir John Arnott. Denis was arrested in Skibbereen in '58 on a charge of being connected with the Phœnix Society. The movement was then in its infancy, and Denis was in his infancy, too—16 years of age. A year or two after his release from prison, he came to America; went into the war there; raised himself to the rank of captain; lost a leg at the battle of Gettysburg; was marshalled into the regular army after the war, and stationed in Washington; got into ill health; got leave of absence to Ireland, and died there. Mike O'Brien came to America, too, and hearing that Denis Downing was in the war, made towards him. Denis's brother Patrick, now Colonel Downing, of Washington, also imprisoned in '58, was commanding in the 42d Tammany regiment. Mike O'Brien met the brother; they were going into a fight; he should go with them; and providing himself with arms, went into the engagement as a volunteer, and came out of the battle without a wound.

I met him in New York in '63. One day he said to me, "Rossa, I must get more knowledge of the use of arms. I'll never be able to do much if I do not know how to fight. I'm determined to learn more than I know at present, and I have made up my mind to join the 13th New Jersey."

"Now, don't be foolish. What good are you to Ireland if you're killed?"

"There is no use of talking. I have made up my mind to this thing, and I will go. Will you come and see me off?"

There was no use parleying. I went and saw him off. I saw him take the oath, the recruiting sergeant tempting myself by saying I would make a splendid soldier. I saw him on the train that took the recruits to the regiment's headquarters, and that is the last I saw of Mike O'Brien. Oh, God! to have that man hanged as a criminal. Yes, he was one, but as noble a one as Emmett, as Tone, or Fitzgerald, or any one who died for the cause of country.

Murphy whispered to me that Captain M'Cafferty and St. Clair, and a few others I knew, were in the pentagon, and within my hearing. I did not know any of them but St. Clair, and I felt timid about calling their names, lest they might be doing the *role* maintaining a good prison character, and averse to doing anything against the regulations. I whispered their names a few times, and as I got no response I did not trouble them further. I knew St. Clair. I met him in London in '64. He had then the character of being imprudent, in so far as he used to march his men in military order through the streets. He was in penal class with John Devoy and myself on a charge of attempting to break the prison, and when Murphy told me he was somewhere in the vicinity I called his name.

He heard me; he was at the other side of the pentagon, and instead of whispering across when he recognized me he bawled out a congratulation on our meeting. It drew the attention of the officers upon us, and got our quarters changed.

In my next cell Mike O'Brien's death preyed upon my mind for a few days, and as I lay on my bed board one morning, when the prisoners were coming from chapel, one of them put his lips to the ventilator and whispered, "Duffy is dead." "Duffy is dead!" Ned Duffy dead! Another of the confessors of the faith. The man who gave me the whisper was Lynch, who was detected in Portland prison in trying to pass out the letter to my wife, which I had directed in the care of Mrs. Moore. He was then within a few months of being released, but in consequence of being detected in trying to assist me the authorities laid it on to him; the warders kept reporting him for imaginary offences; he lost all the remission he had previously earned, and had to work out the whole term of his sentence. He was now in Millbank preparatory to being released; and learning that I was in the same ward, put himself in communication with me.

I had traveled the West of Ireland with Ned Duffy, and we had many a strange adventure. We found ourselves one night traveling through bogs and brakes somewhere in that triangle of ground within the three towns of Ballaghadereen, Boyle, and Ballymote.

The meeting place was on a hill within view of some rocky eminences that are full of caves. I think they are called the Keish Mountains. Our guide on the occasion was Shemus Andy.

We were to meet four or five hundred men, but there was some mistake made in the naming of the place, for we only met about half of them, the other half having assembled on a hill some three miles distant. This we discovered after we had ended our business about midnight.

Our men knew that the boys from the other district must be somewhere, and a few of them shouted a peculiar call; then there was dead silence, and in the stillness of the night a reply was heard from a place three miles distant. Our men then gave a general shout of parting, which was immediately returned, and we broke up, scattering in different directions.

A very serious question was to be determined this night. Another certain society was in the district, and the members of it were averse to the Society of United Irishmen being introduced. Our men were beaten at fairs and markets, and on the highway, whenever they were met by the others. This had been going on for a few years; but now that the United Irishmen had got strong enough to command respect, and to overpower the others, some of them wanted permission to *force* the other party to join them—to actually beat them into the ranks of the Irish revolutionary army. Ned Duffy and I would not allow it; we counselled peace, and told them their forbearance in their strength would have a better effect, that it was better to use persuasion than force, that there were many good men at the other side, and instanced the case of themselves, who were bitterly hostile to joining at first, but who were now ardent workers in the good cause. There was nothing preventing any one of them from being a member of both societies. There was, however, one difference—that the other was got up to defend the people from aggression, while ours had the object of making war on the aggressors and destroying their rule in the country. We admitted to our brotherhood all Irishmen, of every class and creed, who would swear to fight for the independence of their native land; they admitted to theirs only members of a particular creed. They were sectarian and defensive against the enemy; we were national and agressive—organizing our means to fight.

All seemed pleased with our interview, and it was satisfactory to learn shortly afterwards that the two societies were working harmoniously together.

Edward Duffy was this time—March, '65—in delicate health; yet he traveled night and day, and was up late and early. His heart was in his work, and to see it prospering sustained him. One night we were passing by his mother's house. "Hold," said he to the driver, "there is light in the window; they are up yet, and we'll go in." The mother kissed him, saying, "Eddy, won't you stay with me to night?"

"No, mother, I have to be in Balla at a certain hour."

"Oh, you'll kill yourself."

"Not yet awhile, mother. Good-bye."

They kissed each other again, we mounted our jaunting-car and went to meet the boys, who had word of our coming.

I had a look at Edward Duffy once while I was in Millbank. It was the time I was allowed to go to chapel, and I saw him one Sunday morning going to Communion. I would give anything to have his eye catch mine, but he never raised his head going to the altar or coming from it. He had somewhat of a stoop in his carriage, and looked as if the treatment was bending him to the ground. When his last days were approaching, an officer of the prison told me that Duffy would like very much to have a talk with me; there was no way of having it by signals, as he was in hospital, and I in punishment; but I said to myself I would do all in my power to gratify a dying wish of his, and I had my name taken down by the officer to see the Director the next day he would visit the prison, and when he came I was brought before him.

"Well, what do you want now?"

"There is a prisoner here named Edward Duffy; he knows my family, and as he is only lately arrived"——

"How do you know that?"

"Oh, Governor, I knew it, and"——

"Is it permission to see him you want?"

"Yes, he"——

"Certainly not, you can't see any other prisoner here; it is against the rules; that will do."

The "that will do" was addressed to the officers, and they immediately gave me the order of right-about-face. But I stood and pressed my appeal, thus—"I beg pardon, one moment. It is six months ago since I had a visit. There is one due to me now, and you sent a ticket to Mr. Pigott the other day, but stopped it again. Now, if you let me see Edward Duffy in the presence of the officers, I will not ask another visit for six months."

"You cannot see Edward Duffy—it is out of the question, and there is no visit due to you, for you have forfeited it by your bad conduct."

I again got the order to march out, and if my morals would allow me to curse, I could say, mentally at least, "Oh, sweet bad luck to you."

Within my own memory, the English newspapers made a great sensation of a story about two comrades, Poles, who were confined in a prison in St. Petersburg; one of them was dying, and expressed a wish to see the other and would not be allowed; he died without this little consolation being vouchsafed to him, and the English press was horrified at "the Russian barbarity." But here was an identically similar case—occurring in the heart of London, under the nose of the Queen, and under the nose of her Ministers, Lords, and Commons, and under the nose of all the pious Tract and Bible Societies that send missioners to humanize barbarous Russians and inhuman savages. In the eyes of England it was not, perhaps, a similar case, inasmuch as she conceded to the Poles the right to rebel, while she considers the Irishman who rebels against such a pious, paternal government as hers, unworthy of the name or treatment of a human being.

Wasn't I raging with passion at the hypocrisy of those Pharisees the Sunday Edward Duffy lay in the prison dead-house, to hear one of those missioners from the tract societies preaching outside my cell door. I candidly admit that I was more inclined to curse than to pray. The punishment prisoners get no religious service. They are not allowed to chapel, and on Sunday one of these itinerant Scripture-readers is allowed into prison to preach to them. The cell doors are opened, and the gates left closed. My door and gate both were left shut in consequence of my being registered as a Catholic, but I heard the preaching.

Ned Duffy's death, following close upon the news of Mike O'Brien's, threw me into a melancholy mood, and for days I lay stretched on the flat of my back traveling, with my eyes closed, through the ups and downs of life, and the queer ways of the world. I got my bed at night, and when I could not sleep I turned my thoughts to rhyming. Let not the critics be hypercritical at my coming in here with the few verses I made—

NED DUFFY.

The world is growing darker to me—darker day by day,
The stars that shone upon life's path are vanishing away,
Some setting and some shifting, only one that changes never,
'Tis the guiding star of liberty that blazes bright as ever.

Liberty sits mountain high, and slavery has birth
In the hovels, in the marshes, in the lowest dens of earth;
The tyrants of the world pitfall-pave the path between,
And o'ershadow it with scaffold, prison, block and guillotine.

The gloomy way is brightened when we walk with those we love,
The heavy load is lightened when we bear and they approve;
The path of life grows darker to me as I journey on,
For the truest hearts that travelled it are falling one by one.

The news of death is saddening even in festive hall,
But when 'tis heard through prison bars, 'tis saddest then of all,
Where there's none to share the sorrow in the solitary cell,
In the prison, within prison—a blacker hell in hell.

That whisper through the grating has thrilled through all my veins,
"Duffy is dead!" a noble soul has slipped the tyrant's chains,
And whatever wounds they gave him, their lying books will show,
How they very kindly treated him, more like a friend than foe.

For these are Christain Pharisees, the hypocrites of creeds,
With the Bible on their lips, and the devil in their deeds,
Too merciful in public gaze to take our lives away,
Too anxious here to plant in us the seed of life's decay.

Those Christians stand between us and the God above our head,
The sun and moon they prison, and withhold the daily bread,
Entomb, enchain, and starve us, that the mind they may control,
And quench the fire that burns in the ever living soul.

To lay your head upon the block for faith in Freedom's God,
To fall in fight for Freedom in the land your fathers trod;
For Freedom on the scaffold high to breath your latest breath,
Or *anywhere* 'gainst tyranny is dying a noble death.

Still sad and lone was yours, Ned, 'mid the jailers of your race,
With none to press the cold white hand, with none to smooth the face;
With none to take the dying wish to homeland friend, or brother,
To kindred mind, to promised bride, or to the sorrowing mother.

I tried to get to speak to you before you passed away,
As you were dying so near me, and so far from Castlerea,
But the Bible-mongers spurned me off, when at their office door
I asked last month to see you—now I'll never see you more.

If spirits once released from earth could visit earth again,
You'd come and see me here, Ned, but for these we look in vain;
In the dead-house you are lying, and I'd "wake" you if I could,
But they'll wake you in Loughlin, Ned, in that cottage by the wood.

> For the mother's instinct tells her that the dearest one is dead—
> That the gifted mind, the noble soul, from earth to heaven had fled,
> As the girls rush towards the door and look towards the trees,
> To catch the sorrow-laden wail, that's borne on the breeze.
>
> Thus the path of life grows darker to me—darker day by day,
> The stars that flashed their light on it are vanishing away,
> Some setting and some shifting, but that one which changes never,
> The beacon light of liberty that blazes bright as ever.

I had completed my poetry and my fourteen days' punishment at the same time, and I was in the expectation of being allowed the light and diet of an ordinary cell; but no, that was not for me yet. I was hauled up before the Director and got fourteen days more for not doing any work the previous fourteen.

Brooding over this subject of perpetual punishment, I thought it was better to bring it on hot and heavy, and as they were worrying me, I made up my mind to have the satisfaction of worrying them. When Gambier was giving me this last sentence an army officer was standing by him with his sword drawn. He was in command of the soldiers who were guarding the prison, and these were all round the pentagon in which I and the other Irish prisoners were confined. When I got my hour's exercise that day, I resolved to break all the windows of the officers' residences that I could. These were common glass and within easy distance of me. As I walked around my little yard I picked up every piece of mortar and pebble that was large enough to do execution, and threw them into one corner.

As I was to go about it at all, I resolved to do the thing well; it would be mean and petty to break only one or two panes, and I was making preparations to make a clean job of it. I would make a noise, anyway, and I thought by this act I would be helping an exposure of our treatment, for many of the soldiers knew me and would speak of the matter outside, the officers would tell their wives, and so forth. All these things passing through my mind led me to the act, but I never committed it, as I was arrested in my preparations. It was necessary to resort to some means to prevent the officers from rushing in immediately after I had broken the first pane, and I proceeded to stuff the keyhole with little pebbles. As I was doing this I was noticed and my game was spoiled. I was taken to my cell, and the next time I got exercise there was not a pebble in the yard, and the officer stood at the door.

About seven days of these fourteen had passed when I found myself taken to a first-class punishment cell, and I got four ounces of meat for dinner. I got porridge for supper with my bread, and in the morning three-quarters of a pint of cocoa. I asked the officer what it meant, and he could not tell me. I was getting the regular working diet, and yet they would not put me in a regular working cell or let me go to chapel. But here is what it meant, as I learned a few weeks afterwards.

This very day that the change was made in my condition in Millbank, another change was made in the condition of nine prisoners in Chatham, but while my change was for the better, theirs was for the worse. They were nine men of "good character;" they were within a year or so of their liberation; they had earned all their remission and conformed quietly to the requirements of discipline.

Yet were they, this day I speak of, taken from their ordinary cells, where they had plenty of light and a hammock-bed to lie on, and placed in the punishment cells, where they had little light and were compelled to lie on the hard boards. The change was a mystery to them, but they dared not complain, as they, each of them, would risk the loss of the few years' remission they had earned by "good conduct."

There were ten punishment cells in the ward in which they were located, and the puzzle to them was, till I came, why it was that the tenth was left vacant. This was left for me to occupy a week after, and these men were thus ill-treated to pave the way for my further ill-treatment, and to render it impossible for me to say I had been treated exceptionally. Such mean dodging, such petty subterfuges were resorted to for the purpose of tormenting me, I can give no idea of; and when you bear in mind that the dodgers were English Prime Ministers, Secretaries of State, and Prison Directors, you may well say England is capable of anything.

The last week I had was a pleasant one, as I could look out of my window and see the prisoners exercising. John Devoy was in a corner cell two stories below me, and we could speak to each other without raising our voices very high. We were whispering one morning during breakfast hour, and we noticed there was some unusual stir. We saw a few prisoners taken from this yard, a few from that, and we decided there was a transfer of convicts to the Public Works. As we were making speculations as to when a change would come for us my door was opened; I was ordered out; and irons were ready for me. In a minute's time I was bound and on my way to a coach which was in waiting. Big Power and two other big warders entered the carriage with me, each of them wearing a belt in which were stuck a short sword and revolver. The prison gate opened before us; we drove through London for half an hour, and I found myself transferred to a railroad carriage. The four of us had a compartment to ourselves; big Power feeling he had me well secured began to get jolly, and talked about my skill in providing myself with writing material.

"Rossa, you can write with anything; but now we are going to a place where they make the closest search possible, and if you have anything about you, just fling it out through the window, and don't give it to them to say that we didn't do our duty."

"Ah, Governor, there's no fear but you did your duty by me, but if you did it by your own conscience I don't envy you; I have nothing about me that will bring you into trouble, but where are we going to, may I ask?"

"You'll soon know," and as he spoke the train slackened speed. I heard "Chatham" cried out; I was conducted to the platform, where other armed men shook hands with my traveling companions; two coaches were obtained, and in another half hour I found myself inside the gates of Chatham Prison, and never saw the outside of them till three years after.

CHAPTER XVII.

RECEPTION IN CHATHAM—I MUST LEARN DRILL OR GO TO "JILLI-GUM"—ASSOCIATION WITH THIEVES—STONE BREAKING—WHEEL-ING RUBBISH—YOKED TO A CART—LIGHT WORK, LIGHT WAGES, AND LIGHT DIET—"COS" AND "JOBLER"—PRATT—A PRISON SPY—I SMASH MY WINDOW—REFUSE TO PAY SALAAMS—REV. MR. DUKE, PROTESTANT CHAPLAIN—A CEDAR—COSGROVE PUNISHED AND DEGRADED ON MY ACCOUNT—I LEARN THE PRISON "SLANG"—BEARLA GAR NA SAOR—MADE AN ACCESSORY TO THEFT—"SCOTTY'S" PRESBYTERIANISM—"I'LL MAKE SOME ONE PAY FOR THIS YET"—"AH, GET OUT"—"INSOLENCE AND IRREVERENCE" AT CHAPEL—RICHARD O'SULLIVAN BURKE AND AND HENRY S. MULLEDA—AN ESCAPE FROM HAVING MY NECK CRACKED—I "STRIKE"—THROW MY HAMMER OVER THE WALL—FIVE WARD-ERS HOLD ME SALAAMING THE GOVERNOR—HE'D TREAT ME WITH CONTEMPT—MY RESOLUTION, MY PRAYER, AND MY "SA-LUTE" TO THE GOVERNOR—SATISFACTION—HANDS TIED BEHIND MY BACK 35 DAYS—BLOODY WRISTS—"BLOOD FOR BLOOD"—THE PURSUIT OF KNOWLEDGE UNDER DIFFICULTIES—FATHER O'SULLIVAN—THE DESTRUCTION OF POPERY IN 1866—A BOOK OUT OF DATE—DIRECTOR DU CANE—GIVING TIT FOR TAT—I I BREAK UP THE SPECIAL PARTY—"JOBLER'S" GOOD-BYE—THE THIEVES' KINDNESS—FLOGGING PRISONERS—MEET RICK BURKE AND HARRY MULLEDA—MY SENTENCE READ—RELEASED FROM IRONS.

My new guardians conducted me to the wing of the building I was to have my apartments in, and as soon as I entered one of them cried out, "Turn your face to the wall." My blood stirred, but I pulled the rein and kept it down to its accustomed motion. Bye-and-bye I was measured, weighed, stripped, searched, bathed, re-dressed, shaven, shorn, and entered on the books. Principal Warder Alison got special charge of me, and, as a matter of course, he should read me a lecture. He told me I came here with a pretty bad character, but he hoped I would become an altered man, and I told him I considered myself pretty well altered already.

"You should see," said I, "what a handsome man I was when I was in the world." And you, reader, should see the confused look he gave. The words entirely disconcerted him in the lecture he was giving me, and he changed the subject to that of "Drill."

"Do you know your drill?"

' Drill," cried I, with an alarmed look, as I darted a pace back. "What do you mean by drill?"

"Did they drill you in Millbank?"

"Oh, Governor, you may say they did; I hope you are not going to drill me so here."

"See, Rossa, what I mean is this—this is a military prison, and you have to pay particular attention to the military orders given, and be very particular in obeying them. We are more exact about that than anything else, and any negligence of duty on your part will be punished severely."

"Do you mean to tell me that I'll be punished here if I don't know my drill?"

"Certainly, yes."

"Why, Governor, that's the very thing I'm transported for—for trying to learn my drill."

"What do you mean?"

"I mean that when I and my friends were on trial, the English Government brought up people to swear against us that we were guilty of the crime of trying to learn drill, and are you going to tell me now that I am to be punished further here in England if I don't know it?"

"Now, I tell you that you'll have to obey orders here, or, if you do not, there's a place convenient called Jilligum, and you'll very soon find your way to it," and saying this he marched me off to my cell.

It was ten feet by seven. I saw my bedstead nailed to the ground, and the pillow of it raised four inches high; the bedclothes were folded, and lay on a thin straw mattress which was also folded. My table was a small board imbedded in an angle of the wall, and my stool was two feet high, the trunk of a tree, fastened to the floor alongside of the table.

There was again that detestable metal screen to darken my abode, with the little holes in it to admit as much light as would enable me to see my misery.

My dinner was brought to me and I ate it with avidity, and after dinner I was taken out to have an hour's exercise. Warder Thompson had charge of me, and gave me a broom to sweep up the exercise yard. Prisoners when at exercise here get nothing to do, and I knew this task was given to me to try my temper. I swept away, and as the officer asked me some question I asked him in return, pointing towards them, "Are not those punishment cells?" He shook his head, as much as to say, "I cannot answer such a question."

I got a sheet of paper the second day to write the reception letter. I wrote it to my wife, and next day I was told the letter would not be allowed to pass as I spoke about my treatment. The third day I was sent to work with the nine thieves I have already spoken of; the youngest of them was twenty-six, and the oldest seventy. They worked previously with all the other prisoners in a place called Mary's Island, outside the prison walls.

In the morning we were sent wheeling rubbish from one yard to another; each had his wheelbarrow, and if I did not fill up mine as full as the rest, Thompson would make me take the shovel again and lay more on. We were allowed to talk moderately. They were all anxious to know who or what I was. "Scotty" was my chief interlocutor, and after a few hours questioning me, he in his broad Scotch exclaimed to the others as we were shovelling the earth into our barrows—"Noo I haw it, heece a bawd characthoor, and we're sent here to keep ham coompany." I smiled, and they all promised to do what they could for me, advising me to keep quiet.

After dinner we were sent breaking stones, the ten of us in a row; each could speak to the man next to him, but it was against orders to extend the conversation farther.

I thought I was going to get on very well here, but such a thought was soon driven out of my head. My first impulse when put amongst the thieves, was to kick against association with them—and when I act on first impulses I generally act right. But on this occasion I had a little curiosity to learn what could be learned from these men, and when I found them telling me to "cheer up," and giving me words of sympathy, I determined to give them a trial and see if I could turn my position to any advantage.

I was not long stone-breaking when I noticed the officer's special attention attracted toward me. I am *kiotach*, that is left-handed, and working with my hammer in that hand the officer ordered me to use the other. I told him I could not, and he told me I should; that I would have to work there the same as any other prisoner. This looked strange to me, and I was hoping it was not an indication that the screws were to be put on here, too; but it was hoping against hope. I saw two left-handed men come into the party two months afterward, and this warder never interfered with their using the hammers with their left hands.

It was awkward to me at first to use my right hand; sometimes

I'd strike the block instead of the stone; and more times I'd strike the round loop of hoop iron with which I held the stone in a fixed place.

"Jobler," who worked near me, told me to strike easier until I became more dexterous. "Your stroke is too light," cried Thompson. I looked up to see to whom he was speaking; it was to me, and I said nothing, but hammered away. Ten minutes afterward "your stroke is too light" sounded on my ears again. I raised my eyes and said nothing but resumed work.

Jobler whispered, "Say nothing, but work away, he's on you," and away I worked, knowing that Jobler's was the best advice I could get under the circumstances.

But what is the use of following good advice if you are in the hands of a master who will not be pleased with the best of good work or good conduct from you.

"Your stroke is too light," came on again, and Jobler whispered, "God help you, Rossa."

"Your stroke is too light," "your stroke is too light," "your stroke is too light," came on four, five, six and seven times without my opening my lips; at last, in as quiet and mild a tone as I could command, I replied, "Oh, officer, the wages are rather light, too."

"You're done for," "you're done for," whispered Jobler, as he struck his hammer successively on the stone.

The principal officer coming round soon after, Thompson had a conversation with him, and "Rossa" was called. I looked, and the irate-looking magnate motioned to me with his sword to advance. I went forward and received a lecture. I, in giving an explanation, raised my hand to illustrate the action of the hammer; the principal immediately raised his sword as if he would strike, and ordered me to keep my hands by my side. This raised the devil in me, and to the next observation he made about my "insolence and impertinence," I replied in as scornful a tone as possible—"The prison rules do not permit me to be insolent to any officer, nor do they permit any officer to be insolent to me." Saying this I gave him as black a look as I could; he turned on his heel, telling Thompson to report me when we went into supper, and I returned to my "light stroke."

That evening when I entered my cell the first thing I did was to unbosom a few scraps of old newspaper which Pratt passed to me during the day.

I was reading about two brothers named Desmond who were on trial in connection with that new gunpowder plot of Clerkenwell. The key turned in my door, I stuck the paper inside the waist of my trousers; Alison and another officer entered, and ordered me to strip. Here was I caught the first day of my noviciate in Chatham, and there is no doubt but that preparations were made to catch me, as Pratt who gave me the scraps of newspaper was afterwards hunted out of the party as being a spy on them. When I went out to work after being ten days on bread and water in dark cells, on telling about what Pratt gave me, Cosgrove, who was "orderly" the evening of the stripping, remembered that Alison went into Pratt's cell before he came into mine to strip me.

I was put under "report," stripped of shoes, handkerchief, cap, stock, and braces, and next day at twelve o'clock I was led into the presence of a slimy-eyed, sneaky-voiced gentleman, and charged with "idleness" and "insolence," and having prohibited articles in my possession. I asked him if it was insolence to tell the officer when he was worrying me with my stroke being too light, that "the wages were light too," and he said, "Certainly, yes." I was sentenced to forty-eight hours on bread and water, fined a number of marks, and forfeited my right to write another letter instead of the one which was suppressed two days before. Taken back to my cell I looked about, and, seeing my punishment gutta-percha pint, I laid hold of it, and dashing it against the thick gaslight pane, knocked the glass and the pint into smithereens. This was acting on first impulse, which, as I said before, was acting right. You might not have acted so, but every man's mind is his kingdom, and I believe I, in troublesome times, retained control of mine by allowing to my subjects—first impulses—self-government, or a little of the management of their own affairs.

The noise of the breaking glass brought on the warders immediately, and in a few minutes I found myself lodged in one of the blackholes. Here I spent my forty-eight hours with scanty food by day and scanty clothes by night. I was again put under report for breaking my cell and my pint, and was sentenced to 72 hours on bread and water. I was satisfied that I deserved this punishment and I went through it quietly, save that I refused to pay any salaams to the Governor and other officers when they came to visit. "Doctor," said I to Doctor Burns, as he visited me in one of his rounds, "do not think that by refusing to pay salaams I mean any personal disrespect. I do not, but I cannot be paying my respects to an authority that is starving me." "Oh," said he, "I don't mind, but the discipline of the prison has to be maintained."

I was lying on the flat of my back another time when Deputy-Governor Hardy visited me. I was undergoing a hard Lenten fast, with very little prospect of an Easter day coming on, and, as the lantern was held into the blackhole, in my grim humor, I said, "Governor, is there any chance at all of getting eggs for breakfast here," and I am reported for being insolent to the Deputy, and asking him for an "*extra* breakfast." That is the way my jailors took jokes.

The Protestant chaplain, the Rev. Mr. Duke, visited me daily, and endeavored to reason me into "propriety." He spoke very kindly, and asked me if I would not grant him a favor. I said I would, if it was in my power, and then he asked me to conform to the custom of the prison in the matter of standing to attention when the Governor called. I told him I would, and I stood in the middle of my cell, with my hands by my side, the next time Captain Powell appeared. I thought this settled matters, and that I would be sent out to work when the three days were up; but no, the outraged authority had to be vindicated, and I got three days more for " gross insolence and insubordination."

Then I was sorry that I had made the promise to the chaplain, but as I made it I kept it, and at the end of ten days I found myself stone-breaking at the side of " Jobler."

While I was in confinement. Cosgrove became possessor of a lead pencil, which he hid in his cell for me. He tied a bit of thread to it, hitched the thread in a corner of his ventilator, and then let the " cedar " fall in through one of the small holes.

One day, as we were coming from dinner, we were halted in the hall; nine or ten officers were detailed into the ward, then we were stripped to the buff, but nothing was found.

I told my story about the piece of newspaper Pratt gave me, and then Cosgrove swore out—that that scoundrel Pratt was a spy in the party.

He knew that Cosgrove had the pencil, he gave information to Alison, and that is the reason we were searched. Cosgrove did not escape; he was called away from us an hour after dinner, his cell having been searched closely, and the pencil found.

He got forty-eight hours on bread and water; was degraded for two months, and lost some of his remission. " Degradation " and loss of remission to him was something. He was in the first class, and had roast meat for dinner and tea for supper, now he had to be satisfied with such fare as I had—boiled meat, and gruel instead of tea for supper.

It was funny to me to see all the other prisoners getting tea in the evening, while I was brought a pint of cold gruel. I was a solitary bad character till Cosgrove was reduced to my level, and then there were two pints of gruel brought into the ward. Cosgrove asserted that his pencil could not be found only that some one gave information. He charged Pratt with being the informer, and also charged him with the worse offence of betraying a stranger and a persecuted man by giving me a newspaper and then telling Alison I had it. He cursed him to hell and damnation, and threatened he would have his life.

None of the party would speak to Pratt after that; he complained to the Governor he was afraid of his life, and he was taken away from us. Though any of these prisoners were not allowed to associate with the others, they were even kept in a separate corner by themselves when they went to the Protestant Chapel, yet they managed by signs to communicate to the others that Pratt was a blackleg, and such a cry was raised against him that he had to be sent to another prison.

There was sent to us in Pratt's place a little dark-featured man, who was a pattern-maker from Bradford, and was undergoing a long sentence for burglary. He had learned three or four languages in prison, and was otherwise very intelligent. One day he asked Jobler to change seats with him, in order that he might speak to me. Jobler did so, and immediately Thompson brought the two of them to account. They told him it was commonly done, and they never saw it prevented before, but he peremptorily ordered them to take their own places and stay there.

Jobler's name was William Crane. He belonged to Hampstead, London; told me he saw John Sadlier dead on the Heath, but did not believe he was John Sadlier at all. He entertained me with stories about the Derby and other great races, where thieves would attend in organized gangs; told me how watches were "prigged," and how other robberies were committed, but hoped I would never divulge any of those secrets of the profession if I ever chanced to get into the world.

He and the others would often talk in professional slang, and the secret of that he would not tell me, but, from my constantly listening and observing the result of the conversation, I at last hit upon the key, and he was very much surprised when one day I told him something in slang.

Cosgrove was the recognized head of the party; he was as well built and as handsome a man as one would wish to see; he served in the English militia, and was now serving her Majesty on account of committing a burglary in Nottingham. He was the only man of the party I made freedom with. I used to call him "Cos," but used to "mister" the others whenever I had any occasion to speak to them. Our work inside the walls was varied. We piled brick, piled timber, emptied lime carts, and all the other carts that brought material into the yard.

If "Cos" ever caught me behind a pile, out of the officer's view, he'd go on with tricks of jugglery, and he often made me laugh heartily at pretending to swallow stones and bricks. He one day made me accessory to an attempt at theft. We were tearing down an old shed, in which one of the officers had an office. "Cos" and I were on the top of the shed, tearing the boards, and Jobler and Andrews were taking them away; he saw a coat belonging to one of the warders hanging below in the office.

"By Gollies," said he, "there may be a pencil or a piece of tobacco in that." He signaled to Jobler, and, telling him to be on the watch on one side, told me to keep an eye on the other, and cough if Thompson was coming around. He then jumped down, and was up in a minute again, cursing the old coat because there was nothing in the pockets.

These three months of my prison life were not at all uninteresting, and I had plenty of variety, because there was not a week passed that I had not a day or two on bread and water.

Besides the punishment that came to me from the desire of the authorities to keep me in hot water, I gave myself three days in the cells every month. This was as a kind of protest against working in association with thieves—a kind of compromise to keep myself all right between my convict duty and my conviction.

As I was by myself I did not fear I was showing a bad example; but if any more of my fellow treason-felony prisoners came after me it would be stated by the authorities that I was in association with English prisoners, and never refused to work with them.

The authorities did a very wrong thing in the way they acted when I was kept in the cells.

While the prisoners were never allowed outside the wall that surrounded the building when I worked with them, every day that I was kept in punishment they were taken out. They were thus given to understand that their rigorous treatment was owing to my presence, and if relieved of me they were relieved of the extra vigilance and confinement that made the time more than usually miserable. Several of them applied to the Governor to be sent back to the ordinary part of the prison, and only one succeeded.

This was "Scotty," and he went a cunning way about it. When all other resources failed, he suddenly discovered that he was a Presbyterian, and that he should by right attend the Presbyterian service instead of the Episcopalian. He sent for the Presbyterian clergyman, and told him he wished to attend his own place of worship in future.

These nine men were taken to the Protestant Church every morning, and closely watched, lest they should have any communication with any of the other prisoners. To take "Scotty" by himself to another congregation would require another guard, and it was easier to remove him from the party than have so much trouble. He was, therefore, sent away and a Protestant taken in his place.

I was breaking stones one day, along with the youngest man of the party, and Thompson challenged both of us for being rather idle.

He kept talking to the Englishman a long time, and evidently worried him much. The latter never said a word, but when Thompson moved off he turned his head to me and said: "By Christ, I'll make some one pay for this yet." That is, when his time was up, and when he'd go out into the world, he would have satisfaction off of society for the humiliation he was subjected to in prison.

And I found this was not an uncommon thing in the minds of convicts.

'Tis a sad kind of reformation, but it is not to be wondered at, because the first element of discipline to be learned by these prisoners is that manhood is to be trampled under foot, and that you are not to have any mind or will of your own no more than the brute with the bit in his mouth, whose movements are guided by the driver pulling the reins.

I did not take the officer's reproofs as silently as the Englishman. I told him if he did not consider I was doing enough of work he could report me to the Governor, but I did not want his abuse.

Next day I got two days on bread and water for my "insolence." I asked the Governor if he really considered what I said "insolence," and he said he had not the least doubt of it.

Following close on this, I was "insolent" again under the following circumstances:—

When we leave our beds in the morning, the officer lights the gas, and leaves it lighting until the breakfast is served. When the gas is turned off, there may be light enough in an ordinary cell, but in our punishment cells there is very little light. I made a special application to the Governor on this head, and he gave me to understand the gas would be left burning in our cells after it was turned off in the rest of the prison. Next morning, when the gas was turned off, and darkness came across the page of the book I was reading, I rung the bell, and the officer coming, asked what I wanted.

"I want a light," said I.

"You have the same light as any other prisoner." "I have not, for I am in a dark cell."

"You have the same light as any other prisoner in the ward."

"That is nothing. This is a punishment ward, and as we are not supposed to be under punishment, we ought to be allowed as much light as would enable us to read, as all the prisoners are allowed."

"Now, you had better shut up, and not be making noise, or if you do not, you'll soon find yourself in a darker cell." Then he moved away, and as he was going down stairs, he kept talking at me, "as if I was better than any other prisoner, and as if he didn't know who I was," &c, to all of which I said—"Ah, get out."

Next day I was up before the Governor, charged with this "insolence," and Snell, the officer, denied he ever said a word to me, and that my hurling the "get out" at him was quite unprovoked. I asked the Governor if he would examine the prisoners next to me, for they all heard the fellow scolding, but the Governor said he could not take the word of a prisoner against that of an officer, and I got my forty-eight hours for my "insolence."

"Irreverence at chapel" was another of the heinous crimes put on record against me on those prison books. Two strange men were taken before me to chapel one Sunday. They came out of my ward, and they turned out to be Harry S. Mulleda and Ricard O'Sullivan Burke, who were convicted on a charge of purchasing arms in England. The chapel door was not open as we arrived at it. Rick Burke attempted to give a look at me some four paces behind him, and he was immediately ordered to look to his front.

Our chapel this time was a hall of the prison, with cells at each side. Every prisoner brought his own stool with him, but we had no stools, and we had to take them out of the adjacent cells. When I was placed in position I found myself in a line of one, removed at a respectful distance from the line of five or six. Sitting behind me were the two strangers. How to get a look at their faces was the question, and getting it was the "irreverence." I was sitting on my stool while the priest was preaching. When I had to kneel down, I had to move backwards, keeping my face towards the altar; but, instead of doing this, I gracefully turned around the stool, so that my sight would sweep over the faces of the two men behind me. I did not recognize either of them. When I went back to my cell I was ordered to put out my broom, and the next day I was ordered the two days' punishment for looking at my friends.

"Jobler" tried to know for me who were the two new prisoners. He used to scrub the passage-way outside of the cells, and, getting a chance for whispering, he questioned them as to who and what they were. He had the news for me the next time I went to work, and then I said it was time for me to make up my mind to stop working altogether in my party. They were sent on to Chatham for the purpose of drafting them into my gang after they had done a little probation, and I thought I would not set them the example of working in it. An accident had like to happen me one day. I was very near getting my neck broken, and I availed myself of the event to go before the Governor and ask him to give me work in my cell, or anywhere that I would not be in association with the special class selected for my company. This was my application: "Governor, I was yesterday yoked to a cartload of stones. A noose of the rope was drawn over my neck, while two prisoners were detailed to the back of this cart to prevent it from heeling over. But it did heel over; the shaft of it flew high in the air, and the rope which was around my breast was suddenly jerked away from me. It was a wonder it did not hitch on my neck; had it done so, it would have ended my troubles with the Government in a manner that would be quite satisfactory to you all. I deem it quite out of order to place me at labor in any position where my life is endangered, and I now ask to be removed from this party. I will pick oakum, or do anything that you require of me, in my cell."

GOVERNOR—"I cannot place you at any other work. I am acting under particular instructions regarding you, and nothing is left optional with me to do in your case; if you wish, I will lay your application before the Directors, but more I cannot do."

"Very well, Governor, I will wait till their decision can be known."

Captain Du Cane, Chairman of the Board of Directors, visited the prison a few days after, and I was brought into his presence. I told my story, and asked to be changed. He could not do it as he was acting under the instructions of the Secretary of State, but he would do what he could to give me protection, and this is what he did: He ordered the prisoners to be seated four yards apart when they were breaking stones, and ordered that they should not speak to each other; and, also, when it was necessary to draw stones, that I be left to my work, the others going to draw the cart.

The prisoners were mad at being kept so far apart, and prevented from killing time by conversation, and some of them began to look black at me as being the cause of their discomfort. One magnanimous fellow said if he were in my place he'd fling himself down the stairs or commit suicide some other way rather than be keeping nine innocent men in perpetual torment.

On the morning of June the 1st we were placed at work, surrounding a large heap of small round stones that must at one period of their lives have been washed by sea or river water; we were not allowed to sit down, but were permitted to place one knee on a stone and strike at the small stones with our hammers. It was not a very agreeable position to be working in, and I had previously made up my mind to make a final "strike" that morning, and bid farewell to my companions. Warder Thompson and a principal officer were standing on a pile of wood that overlooked the pile of stone, when I stood up, and asking "Jobler" if he thought I could throw that hammer over the prison wall from where I stood; while he was looking at me in amazement I gave the hammer a fling with all my might.

The warders approached, and, asking what I did that for, I told them I wanted the hammer no more as I had finished my work in that place.

Next day the war commenced in earnest, and I got three days on bread and water. I told the Governor I would work no more in the party, and he told me I should. I told him I would pay him no more salaams, and he told me I should. I told him, another time, it was not to him I meant to be so disrespectful, but to the Government that was sending him his orders to treat me in such a manner, and he told me he would treat me with contempt. The three days passed by, and then I got three days more for not saluting the Governor and for not having my tins bright enough. When these had passed, I got a repetition of the dose, and they kept repeating it day after day until the 17th of June, I refusing to work among the thieves and refusing to salaam the Governor.

On the 15th I told him I would not come into his presence any more, that it looked too much like a farce to be bringing me before him day after day to ask me what I had to say, when at the same time he would not record anything I said, and he told me I should come. Next day I refused to go, and five or six warders came into my cell and dragged me into his "jndication room," as they called it. When I entered, they let go their hold of me, and I rested against the wall with my hands crossed, and one leg across the other.

I was ordered to stand to attention for the Governor, and I made no movement other than to keep standing against the wall.

I was laid hold of, and brought forward to the rails. One officer caught my left hand and held it down by my side, another caught my right; another came behind and settled my heels and toes in position, and then caught me by the shoulders and straightened me up. I smiled, and said to the Governor it would be worth his while to have a picture of this taken for the edification of those English people who are so fond of picturing foreign customs and manners. The three or four men who had hold of me kept me in position till the Governor had passed his sentence of 48 hours' bread and water, and I then told him I would take the first opportunity I could get of practically protesting against this use of physical force to make me pay salaams to him.

I went to my cell, and was raging at the thought of these people laying hands on me for such a purpose, and of there being no ways or means to get myself avenged of them. The Rev. Mr. O'Sullivan, the Catholic chaplain, came in, and the tears rolled down his cheeks as he counselled me to bear all patiently, and offer my sufferings to God as satisfaction for my sins. "Father," said I, "do not talk to me that way; there is no use in my thinking this offering would be worth anything in the sight of God, because it is very unwillingly I undergo what I suffer, and I would not undergo it if I could. If I offer anything to God, it must be something that I voluntarily suffer—something that I feel the loss of, or that will really be a sacrifice. I will not be a hypocrite to God by making Him an offering of what is worth nothing—what I would not wish to have to offer, and what I would gladly avoid having." The priest left my cell, and, as he did, a thought flashed across my mind and brought with it an opportunity of making an offering to God, and also of paying to the Governor such a compliment as would afford me human satisfaction. I fell on my knees in the middle of my cell and repeated these words: "Oh, Almighty and Eternal God, I offer Thee, in satisfaction for my sins, the punishment and suffering that will come to me on account of this act which I contemplate committing to-morrow." I got up off my knees and felt relieved. The load was off my heart already. I had my satisfaction; for I had determined when the Governor came for his salute to-morrow to have my slop-pail full of water, and to pitch it right into his face, and, once I had made up my mind to do it, it was done. Next morning, when I took my pail to the water-tank, I brought it back to my cell half-full.

Twelve o'clock came. I heard the Governor going his rounds, and, as he was approaching my cell, I crouched in a corner to bring him as near my gate as possible. The inside door was unlocked and thrown in, then an iron gate stood locked between me and the parties outside, and I was supposed to "stand to attention" in the middle of my cell. The officer outside cried, "Attention; salute the Governor." The Governor looked through the bars to see where I was and as he did, he got my salute right full into his face. It was the fairest shot I ever saw, and while the water was streaming down his clothes—" That," said I, " is the salute I owe you;" and then laying hold of the timber door, I slammed it with a force that shook the building. " Oh, sir, 'tis clean water," said Brown, condoling with him, and he was truly at the time a fit subject for condolence.

I do not pride myself at having done this act; I once thought I could not be guilty of it, but prison life changes a man, and the treatment I received changed me into doing many things I thought myself incapable of when in the world. But I should have some satisfaction at the time for the indignities heaped on me, and if I could make the Secretary of State or the Prime Minister of England the recipient of the salute I gave the Governor, it would have increased my peace of mind. Their treatment of the Irish political prisoners was wanton and uncalled for. It was not a political necessity to associate us with thieves and murderers; it was to show their affected contempt of us and of our cause, and to try and force us into feeling degraded. While I would humbly apologize to the individual whose lot it was to become the recipient of such an indignity, I would tell the authorities that treated us as I have been describing that the salute was richly deserved, and that "it was only the reflex of the treatment I was receiving." This I told them when I was in their toils—when Capt. Du Cane, in passing sentence upon me, said it was a brutal act. I had made up my mind to fight it out with them, because I had pledged the punishment that was to come of it as an offering, and I would say or do nothing to mitigate the amount.

The day of the assault I remained in my cell, as cool as a cucumber, and I was allowed to rest there quietly too; but next morning, about ten o'clock, Principal Warder Alison, with two other warders, came and told me they had orders to put me in handcuffs. " Here, then," said I to Alison, who had the irons, holding out my hands. He took hold of one, another took hold of another; they brought them behind my back and bound them there. I said nothing or did nothing on the occasion that would warrant any violence, yet they were disposed to be very rude if they got any excuse.

At twelve o'clock Brown and Douglas brought me my dinner. They took off the irons, and I thought they were going to leave them off until I had dined, but that would be too generous a thing; they tied my hands in front and left me to eat as best I could.

As soon as I had eaten they came into my cell and unbound me, but only for the purpose of carrying my hands back and putting the manacles on behind. At two o'clock I was taken out of my cell, and my irons were taken off. My shoes, my cap, my stock, my handkerchief, and my braces were laid before me, and I was ordered to dress myself.

I did so; my hands were again tied behind my back, and I was led into the yard to take an hour's exercise, a special officer having charge of me. The hour being up, my hands were untied, and, giving up my shoes, braces, stock, cap, and handkerchief, I gave my hands to the warders to have them again tied behind my back. At six o'clock I got my supper; my hands were again brought to the front, and, after having supped, were taken to the rear.

At forty-five minutes past seven the handcuffs were taken away altogether, and I was left in peace till morning. At fifteen minutes past five, next morning, my hands were tied behind my back; half an hour afterwards they were untied and tied in front, in order to allow me to take my breakfast, and, having taken it, they were bound behind and kept there till dinner time or the hour's exercise, according as either came first.

This is a history of one day's tying and untying. It continued day after day for thirty-five days, and before a week of the time had passed I could count eight bloody marks on my wrists. I got these from the bitter, vindictive spirit of two of the warders—Brown and Thompson. Whenever these came to change the irons they always made the "dogs" bite by allowing the spring part of them to rest on my hands when handcuffing me. I showed my hands to Doctor Burns; he asked Principal Warder Allison, who was present, "How could that happen?" "Oh, sir," said he, "that will happen to the most careful officer. I have often 'nipped' a man myself, and could not help it." "I see, I see," said Dr. Burns, and there was no more about it, only that Thompson and Brown nipped away every chance they got. These two were consummate scoundrels. "Ah," said I to Thompson one day, "you're a mean wretch," as he was unbuttoning my trousers from my vest, after having bound my hands behind my back. I had no braces, and I had no hands to keep my trousers from slipping off, as I walked about my cell. I gnawed two holes with my teeth in the front of my vest, and to these I buttoned my trousers. Brown reported me for tearing my clothes; the vest was taken away, and I got it back immediately after with two little patches sewn in where I had made the button-holes. I gnawed away at it again, and made two holes more, and the next time that my hands were changed to the front I buttoned myself. Thompson came to change the irons behind, and noticing my trousers buttoned, he went to the trouble of unbuttoning it. I was afraid that to torment me they would resort to the trick of cutting the buttons out altogether. My body clothes were taken from me every night and placed outside my cell door, and every morning I took them in. Thompson opened the door one morning, and as I was stooping to take them up, he kicked them into my face. Now, there is no use in my friends or my enemies saying I had not patience; I had. Thompson had his club, but at the time I did not much care for *that*. I could throttle him before he could use it, but it could never be proved that I did not make an unprovoked assault upon him, and the other warders would be up immediately and beat me to death or next door to it; for, in consequence of the assault I committed on the Governor, the whole of them at this time were anxious to get any excuse to have at me.

When they were putting on the irons, after dinner once, they gave me a very wicked bite, and the blood flowed so freely that it dropped on the floor. I could lay the forefinger of one hand on the wound that was made in the wrist of the other, and, with my back turned to the door, I wrote these words—"Might I not cry out 'blood for blood.'"

Father O'Sullivan came in soon afterwards, and seeing the blood writing, he exclaimed: "Oh! that is terrible, you'll only make matters worse for yourself. Wipe it out, I ask you."

"No, Father O'Sullivan, I'll let it stand and take the consequences."

"No, no, you must wipe it out before it is seen."

"I will not."

"Well, then, I'll do it," and so saying he drew from his pocket a white handkerchief. I thought it too bad to let him soil it, and I promised to clear the thing away as soon as he left the cell.

The Established Church was yet established in these prisons, and was the source of much annoyance to me in the way of books. I was very often under punishment and on probation for punishment—that is, I was a day under half-and-half treatment until my sentence was passed, and during this day I was not allowed to have my ordinary library book, but received one from the penal class library. In Chatham all these penal class books were what I would term "Souper" books; all tending to show Catholics the errors of their ways, and many of them showing to a certainty when Catholicity or Popery was to come to an end. During the thirty-five days I was in irons I was in this probation class, and I was annoyed that I could get no book to read but these bigoted things. I got hold of one of them one day. It was authored by a Rev. Mr. Jones, and written in the year 1848. He had a chapter in elucidation of the prophecies of Daniel, and he showed there as clear as mud that Popery was to come to an end—was to be finally wiped off the face of the earth in the year 1866. I was reading this in my prison cell in the year 1868, and I was after seeing the new appointment of a priest to Chatham Prison since I came there, in the face of the fact that there never was a Catholic chaplain appointed to the prison before my arrival.

No matter though we suffer and scatter, we are truly "spreading the faith" and strengthening it, and, whatever little consolation Irish revolutionists may draw therefrom, let the religious Irish rejoice that "out of evil cometh good," and let them also feel less bitterly towards us, bad people, who are at least considered worthy of being made the instruments of that good.

I sent for the Protestant chaplain—the Rev. Mr. Duke—and he came immediately.

"Mr. Duke," said I, "you had never a regular Roman Catholic chaplain in this prison till this year?"

"No," said he; "what of it?"

"Does it not look as if Catholicity was growing instead of decaying?"

"Well, I don't know; what are you coming at?"

"Well, Mr. Duke, here it is. I am registered as a Catholic, and, in consequence of the established regulations of the prison, I can get no book to read when I am awaiting punishment but one abusing Catholicity and predicting its downfall. I don't wish you to think me bigoted, but I think I hold now in my hands a book that will warrant you in giving me something secular to read, as I am in a bad frame of mind for religious training. This is a book written in '48 by the Rev. Mr. Jones, and explaining the prophecies of Daniel. He explains that Popery must come to an end in 1866; this is 1868, and, with what is before your eyes and mine, you will readily admit that the book is two years out of date, and should not be in any library. Here is the passage."

He read it and said, "I'll try and send you a few books out of the regular library, from which you can choose one." As he was going away I said, "Mr. Duke, will you please leave me that until I get the other?" "Oh, no," said he; "I'll take this with me, and send you the schoolmaster as soon as I can see him." He kept his word, and I chose from the books the schoolmaster brought D'Aubigne's "History of the Reformation."

"The history of the world is the annals of the Government of the Sovereign King."

That, I remember well, is one passage in the preface of the book, and it set me thinking—thinking of all the things that could be charged to God, if everything that the tyrants and scoundrels of this earth committed was His work. I won't believe it even though I be damned a thousand times over for disbelieving—damned by people in this world I mean—not by God. I can reconcile to my views of the Godhead, "the falling of the sparrow," and the falling or numbering of "the hairs of the head," for I believe God omniscient as well as omnipotent, and I believe He has established laws for the regulation of the universe, and not alone do sparrows and hairs fall, but men and women fall when they clash with those laws, and then I believe God will bring them to account how they have spent their time, hoping he will have mercy on all—none being in more need of it than myself.

I kept D'Aubigne in my cell until the irons were taken off me. The book was a large one, and though I had not plenty of reading for the time, still the schoolmaster brought me no other book that I could read. Not that he did not bring me some books that I would rather have than re-read the History of the Reformation, but they were more newly bound, and would not lie quietly on my block without shutting up, or the leaves turning over before I wanted them to turn.

D'Aubigne was an old volume, and a little hacked, and when I laid it open on the block and turned over a leaf with the aid of my tongue and lips, it remained open until I had it read and chose to turn over another. There was no position in which I could read only by laying the book on my stump-of-a-tree-stool, then turning my gutta-percha pot upside down, and sitting on it with the stump of a tree between my legs. Not having the use of my hands, I used my tongue and lips instead of them, in managing the book.

It was a hot Summer and it was hard to pass the day without a stretch. I should lie on one of my hands whatever way I lay down, and I felt my arms pretty unmanageable at first.

But, by-and-by, they got used to the pressure on them. I fell asleep a few times and woke with the arm that was under me entirely benumbed, no feeling in it, and could not stir a finger. The weight of the body on the hand had stopped the circulation of the blood, but by rubbing it to the wall, and to the body for some time, sensation and motion were soon restored.

The days were so warm, and the heat so oppressive in my cell, that I thought it would be a relief to me to leave my jacket off, and allow myself to be handcuffed in my shirt sleeves, and thus I presented my hands to Brown one morning when he came with the irons.

"Where is your jacket?"

"There it is on the block."

"Put it on."

"I think my hands would be more free without it, and the days are so very warm that I think I will leave it off to-day."

"You must wear your full dress. Put on your jacket, I say."

"I will not, I say."

He put on the irons, and at dinner time when the Deputy-Governor, Mr. Hardy, came around, he reported me to him for the offence, and the insolence I gave him.

Captain Hardy said jeeringly, "You had better take off your pants, too, and go naked," to which I replied—

"You would like, perhaps, to have such a thing to report against me, and it seems you want it, when you leave me nothing to keep up my pants with, and when you loose them when I manage to tie them to my vest." This seemed to be quite a proper answer for him, as he and his accompanying officers left the cell without making another observation. I believe the authorities thought about this time it was useless to be trying to civilize me to the level of their convict worthies.

This salute I gave the Governor was *caucused* and counciled over, and the "Ring" must have said to themselves "there is no use in our being at this man; we are only getting ourselves into disgrace and difficulties day after day; we must try some other course." A week after the "salute," Jobler, who was in the next cell to me, knocked on the wall; I knocked in return and listened.

"Good-bye, Rossa; remember me and Cos."

I was rapping back something when I heard the doors unlocked, and the whole party marching out with bag and baggage.

"Good-bye, Rossa; remember me and Cos."

The tears started into my eyes—they even went further than my eyes, and I let them flow. You that have never been in my position can never know the feelings that started them—perhaps I could not well analyze them myself; but there they were, let moralizers, and philosophisers, and kleptologisers say what they will of it.

These men treated me with kindness. When I met them, after spending days on bread and water, "Cos" and "Jobler" would have arrangements made with a few others of the party whom they trusted to give me their dinner bread as we were going up the stairs. I would not take it, and then "Cos," being orderly, would slip his meat out of his tin and throw it in through the bars of my gate as he was filling water into my can, and this would be done at the risk of the officer seeing him, and, if seen, he would lose three months of his remission, and be reduced from roast beef and tea to boiled beef and porridge for a few months more.

Fourteen days of the thirty-five had passed, and, as I had eaten my dinner, the irons were not put on as usual. I was thinking if the torture could be at an end when the door opened and I was conducted to the "judication" room, where sat in the seat of judgment Captain Du Cane, the Chairman of the Directors.

He read the charge for me, and asked me what I had to say. I said that when I was brought before Captain Harvey, the day after I committed the offence, he told me I would get a sheet of paper to make out my defence for the Director. I got no sheet of paper since.

"You can't have it. Have you any reply to make?"

"I'll make no reply except on paper."

"Do you admit the offence?"

"Oh, certainly—yes."

"I am sorry to see that instead of improving, you are only getting worse."

"And worse I'll be getting while you're getting worse."

"This act of yours is a most brutal one."

"It is only just the reflex of the treatment I am receiving."

"That will do," he said, addressing my conductors, who conducted me back to my cell.

I was left for an hour with my hands free, and I thought a new sentence had been passed and the irons laid away. But that was not so; they came as soon as Du Cane had settled his business, and the doubt as to what my punishment was to be was perplexing. Next morning I heard the triangle being placed outside my cell window where the prisoners were always flogged, and as I heard the whistle of the lash strings in the air, and heard the victim's cries as his back was cut, I was nerving myself to go through the same operation.

I was prepared for anything, and though I never much liked flogging, I felt some sort of satisfaction at thinking these people would flog me. I knew the act would both degrade them, and stimulate Irishmen to greater exertion to be avenged.

Du Cane had decreed my sentence that day, but it was twenty-one days afterwards before it was announced to me, during which time I was kept in irons, though I was as quiet as a lamb.

I say this because there is a prison ordinance which says that irons are only to be continued on a prisoner while he continues to be violent, and that in no case are they to be kept on longer than seventy-two hours without a special order from a Director. When Captain Du Cane was questioned by the Devon Commission, as to why these irons were kept on me for thirty-five days without any extra order, he got out of the dilemma by saying that the seventy-two hours meant consecutive hours, and that the order had not been violated, inasmuch as I never had them on at a time for more than fourteen consecutive hours. In a word, he admitted squarely that a coach-and-four could be run through the ordinance, and that the irons could have been kept on me for a life-time, so long as they were taken off at night, without violating a letter of the law, though he admitted the spirit of it might be violated.

When I come to speak of this Commission at length, I will give some of Du Cane's quibbling evidence.

Here is a copy of his judgment sent to Colonel Henderson, whom Du Cane succeeded as Chairman of the Board of Prison Directors, when the other was appointed to the command of the London police force:

"*Defence of prisoner Rossa.*"
"*Declines to make any defence except in writing.*"
Sentence on prisoner.

"Colonel Henderson—The prisoner is without doubt guilty of the very foul and insubordinate conduct alleged in the charge. The Governor of the Chatham Prison is, as is well known, as temperate and judicious a person as it is possible to find; the officers in the immediate charge of the department in which the prisoner is, are selected for their judgment and fidelity; nevertheless, he is, as stated in the evidence, and as his misconduct sheet shows, constantly committing acts of insubordination and resistance towards his officers, and every available punishment has been tried in his case, without effect, nor does kindness have any better effect upon him [oh, Holy Moses, what kindness I got from them]. He would in the ordinary course be punished for the offence he has committed by flogging, but it is thought that this punishment should not be inflicted without special authority. If it should not be thought advisable to inflict it, I can only suggest that he be sentenced to twenty-eight days' punishment diet in close confinement, and be placed in the penal class for six months; also, that to prevent the chance of his repeating outrages of this description on the officers of the prison who are obliged to visit him, all moveable articles and utensils are removed from his cell, and whatever is necessary being made a fixture, and that he be kept in handcuffs in the day time. It is for consideration whether the prisoner should be allowed to remain in this prison after having committed such an outrage on the Governor, especially if it was decided that the severe punishment for such offences shall not be inflicted.—Signed, "E. F. Du Cane, 1.7, '68."

And then Colonel Henderson, taking a week to consider and to consult the Ministry whether the prisoner should be flogged or not, writes:

"I am unwilling to resort to corporal punishment in the case of this man, whose conduct savors of imbecility, except in the last resource. Carry out the Director's punishment, twenty-eight days' punishment diet in close confinement and six months' penal class, and remove all moveable articles from his cell.—Signed,

"E. G. W. Henderson, 7.7, '68."

These people would be only too glad to flog me if they could carry out the "discipline" unknown to the world, but they knew the story would get abroad and do them more mischief than they could do me good. Not a fortnight passed by me in this prison that the shrieks of flogging the unfortunates did not make my flesh creep.

The first three or four strokes generally brought piercing wails, but, after that, till the two or three dozen were given, I heard no more, though I heard the whips slashing against the naked back. An odd case may arise where a prisoner would utter no cry, and this person would be a hardened wretch in the estimation of the jailers, while his fellow-prisoners would look upon him as a hero.

I managed a few times, by putting my fingers in the holes of my iron blind, and drawing myself up, to have a look at the ceremony of flogging. There was the triangle—three bars of iron coming together at the top and extended and stuck into the ground at the bottom.

The prisoner's hands were lashed above, and, I suppose, his feet —which I could not see—were tied below. The two doctors, the Governor, the Protestant chaplain, and several warders stood around. The prisoner was naked to the waist. A burly jailer swayed the cat-o'-nine tails—nine pieces of hard cord tied to a stick about a foot and a half long. Every stroke he gave he drew the cords through his hand to clean away the flesh or blood that may be on them, and also to make them even for the next stroke. A principal warder cried out aloud "one, two, three," and so on, till a dozen were counted; then, to relieve the first man, an assistant flogger took the lash, and began at "thirteen," going on till he came to "twenty-four," when the other took his turn, and became relieved again at "thirty-six," if the victim was to get more than three dozen. 'Twas an ugly sight, suitable only for ugly people. Wasn't my whole flesh creeping and cursing one day as I saw an unfortunate fellow tied up with his head hanging on his shoulder as they were slashing away at him, while the high officials were looking on with umbrellas over their heads and mats under their feet to protect them from catching cold or catching any other discomfort from the drizzling rain!

Du Cane tells Henderson that the Governor of my prison "was as temperate and judicious a person as it was possible to find." Of course he was! Where could you get a Governor of an English convict prison who was not so?

And the officers around me were "selected for their judgment and fidelity." Undoubtedly. And what did that mean? Simply that they were such officers as would be faithful to their masters' behests, and would give no quarter to the prisoner. Du Cane's sentence also decrees that the prisoner is to be kept in irons during the daytime, and here was left an open to keep me in irons for seven months, but that was not done, for the day the bread and water commenced the placing me in irons ended.

About a week after Du Cane's visit I was changed from cell No. 6 to No. 13, and next day, when I got my hour's exercise, I saw two large holes broken in the wall of No. 6. It occurred to me they were making some preparations for my permanent location there and I was right, for as I was passing my guardian officer he was talking to Principal Warder Alison. Both of them were looking at the holes, and Alison said, in a self-satisfied tone, loud enough for me to hear, "I think he will be brought to his senses now." They were building an iron closet in the cell, and otherwise making it iron proof; but you must wait for its thorough description until I come to occupy it.

While the changes were making, I, as I said before, was lodged in No. 13, where I spent a most agreeable time. The two cells over me were occupied by Rick Burke and Harry Mulleda, and I was not long in making their acquaintance.

As we could converse with each other by knocking on the wall, I kept myself occupied all day by sitting upon my gutta-percha pot and telegraphing on the brick with my knuckles, and, when they got sore, with the knob of my handcuffs. The two above me had to work; they were laboring for their daily bread, and I had to engage each of them in turn, so as to give one time to pick his oakum while the other was giving me news.

I had about a fortnight of this life, when No. 6 was duly finished, and my Lenten season commenced. Deputy-Governor Hardy and Alison, and two other officers, entered No. 13 one evening, the Deputy holding in his hand a large sheet of foolscap, which he began to read, and as he began, he stopped, saying—"Had we better not read it in the other cell?" "Yes, sir, yes." And turning to me, Alison gave the order to "Come on," and as we stood in my old—but now new—quarters, Hardy proceeded to read my sentence. I have not the exact words, but this is the substance. I was to be kept in that cell, and never let out of it, for twenty-eight days. I was to get eight ounces of bread and a pint of water at half-past five in the morning, and the same at six in the evening, and every fourth day I was to have a dinner consisting of a pint of stirabout, a pound of potatoes, and a quarter of an ounce of salt. I was to be allowed no books, except the Bible, and my clothes were to be taken from me every night, and given to me every morning. "You may take off the handcuffs now," said Hardy to Alison, as he finished reading. I was unbound; they made a free man of me, and when they left, I proceeded to examine the new improvements in my old habitation.

CHAPTER XVIII

MY NEW CELL—THE MUSIC OF THE WATERS—HANDCUFFS AND BLACK-HOLE AGAIN—BREAK MY MODEL WATER-CLOSET, MY BELL-HANDLE, MY TABLE, ETC.—GAMBIER'S VISIT AND HYPOCRISY—DEPRIVED OF MY BED AND BIBLE—VERSE-MAKING—MY READINGS AND MY WIFE'S—DEPRIVED OF BED AND BODY CLOTHES—A STRUGGLE—KNOCKED DOWN, STRIPPED, LEAPED UPON, AND KICKED—A REPRIEVE—MEET HALPIN, WARREN, AND COSTELLO—A STRIKE AGAINST CLIPPING AND STRIPPING—A FAMILY QUARREL—"ERIN'S HOPE" AND HER HEROES—GRASS PICKING—RICK BURKE AND HARRY MULLEDA—WOOD-CHOPPING—WARREN CHOPS A FINGER—DETECTED LETTER—WRONGFULLY IMPRISONED TEN DAYS—O'HARA'S LETTER—KEPT FROM CHAPEL—EXTRAORDINARY PRECAUTIONS—LUDICROUS POSITION AT PRAYERS—RELEASE OF COSTELLO AND WARREN—ARRIVAL OF JOHN M'CLURE, JOHN DEVOY, AND CAPTAIN O'CONNELL—BRICK-CLEANING IN A REFRIGERATOR—THE CUP OF HALPIN'S AFFLICTION FLOWN OVER—HIS ILLNESS AND THE DOCTOR'S INDIFFERENCE.

My cell was a model one, and, as the jailers left, I lay down on my guard-bed and took a survey. The thick pane of glass that was stuck in the wall to allow me a little gaslight was protected on the inside by a plate of perforated iron worked into the wall, and also another plate protected the spy-hole. My guard-bed was changed from lying across the cell to lying on a line with the door, and, as the ventilator was on a level with my shoulders when I lay down, I found it very unpleasant at night. The bed was changed in order to make room for the erection of a water-closet, which was the beauty of my habitation. It had no cover, and the seat was a thick stone flag, while all the other surroundings were iron. It was made, and the whole cell was made, to resist any attempts of mine to break it; but, after a few weeks, I made a breach in the fortress.

The ordinary mortar with which the prison was built had been chiselled out from the bricks to the depth of an inch, and burglar-proof cement inserted instead. New pipes had been laid, and a water-tap placed inside my cell, which I could turn when I wanted to let the water run. This tap was one thing which I was allowed control of, and after a little reflection I proceeded to make the best possible use of it. It was a patent one, and, turning it as far back as I could, I took a stretch, and as the water spouted away I imagined myself on the banks of a purling stream. In half an hour or so the warders discovered there was something wrong; they had no water in the ward, and the waste was traced to my cell. They came in, and Alison, making for the tap, asked why I let the water run. I told him to keep the closet all right; he kept turning and turning, but could not turn it to the proper grade. He then pronounced the tap out of order, and sent for the engineer. This gentleman came, and pronounced the machinery all right. As soon as they were outside the door I let the water run again, and they returned again. Alison threatened all kinds of punishment, and I told him they were doing their big best already, but in spite of all, I intended to enjoy myself, and as there was a fine old Irish song called the music of the waters I would enjoy as much as I could of it by allowing that water to run till the river ran dry. Half an hour passed and Alison made his appearance with a pair of handcuffs. "Now," said he, "we'll quieten you," and, tying my hands behind my back, I was led into the blackhole. I was kept there for two days and two nights, and when brought back to number six I found the tap had been changed from the inside to the outside, and when I wanted water I had to ring the bell, when a warder would come and let it run for a few seconds.

English prison law declares that a prisoner is not to be put in irons unless he is violent; and some people are so good-natured as to believe this law is obeyed to the letter. There was not much violence in turning a water-tap and talking of the music of the waters, but Lord Devon's Commission will not have it so. Here is what they have to say of an offence of such a "grave character": "The actual statement was that he was manacled for 35 days. It is to be observed that having been released from handcuffs at 2 p. m., July 20, he was, for a further offence of a grave character committed in the interval, replaced in manacles on the same day at 4:15 p. m., and they were not finally removed until noon on the 22d."

When the handcuffs were removed this time I told Alison I'd break the closet if he did not put a cover on it, and he defied me to do so. I had no weapon, but, looking around, my eyes rested on the bell-handle, and I made an effort to break it; 'twas no use trying to do so with my naked hands, but I thought there may be a better chance by taking off my jacket and twisting it about the knob.

When this was done, I gave a long pull, a strong pull, and a pull together, when the bell handle and myself sprawled upon the floor. I knew the jailers would be in on me soon, and as the doors were opening I hurled the piece of iron against the closet basin, and knocked a piece of it off.

This was one breach made in the fortification. I got the black-hole again for a few days, and when I came back I had a bell-handle that could not be broken; but I repeated my resolution to break the closet. I found a bit of the smashed crockery, and with this I scraped away some cement and pulled out a piece of brick, with which I made another breach in the citadel before I was detected. My next adventure was to pull my table out of the wall, and I showed them pretty clearly that I could knock their cell into a cocked-hat in less than no time. After a fortnight's warfare of this kind Gambier, the Director, visited the prison, and he came into me, accompanied by half-a-dozen warders. They made motions as if they would protect him from an assault, but he very blandly said, "Oh, never mind—Rossa won't hurt me."

He then told me, in his silveriest tones, that he was very glad to have some very good news for me—that my wife was doing very well in America, that he saw newspapers with accounts of her readings, and that he met my attorney, Mr. Lawless, a short time ago, who told him to tell me my children were all right, too. As he was talking this way he laid hold of my arm, and my whole frame trembled at feeling him touch me with a butcher's hand. His fingers could not find much between them but skin and bone, and, with all his kind words, he left the prison that day, having given orders that I was to get no bed that night.

Up to this I got my bed at half-past seven o'clock every evening, but as I was in general insurrection, I refused to take it away every morning to the bath-room, on the plea that my bed was taken out of my cell during the day for the purpose of punishing me, and that it was not right for me to be the agent of my own punishment. Sometimes I'd remain lying down until the warders would come and pull the bed from under me. The Deputy-Governor was continually threatening, that unless I removed my bed in the morning I would not get it at night, but the threat was never carried out until Gambier came, and that night and the night after I lay in the black-hole without anything to cover me. But worse than that has to come on yet, when I come to the time that they not alone deprived me of my bed, but deprived me of my body clothing also.

They acted illegally in depriving me of the bed, and when I had two nights' experience of this deprivation, I took it on the third night when Alison offered it to me, on condition of my promising to carry it out in the morning.

I maintained that they were lowering themselves and their dignity in exacting any promises from me, that discipline required my punishment whenever I offended, and no parleying was in order. We also compromised about the cell. I was to abstain from assaulting the closet, on conditions that disinfectants were thrown into it a few times a day, and Douglas got a large bottle of the stuff, which he used whenever I required it.

During these twenty-eight days on bread and water I got no books, but they were so liberal as to allow me to retain my Bible, and so little thankful was I to them for this, that it often came into my mind to tear the book in pieces, in order to show my contempt for their hypocritical regard for it, when they were treating me in all other ways in a wholly unchristian spirit.

But if I tore the book they would use that act against me—they would tell the people in the world that I did such an outrageous thing, and did it in the spirit of irreligion; and the religious folk, Catholic as well as Protestant, English as well as Irish, who had been always opposed to revolution or "Fenianism," would hail this as something to harp upon in sustainment of the calumnies they had always hurled against those connected with the movement. Thoughts of this kind restrained me, or I would have destroyed the book in order to save it from the desecration that came upon it by living in a place where it was used as if in mockery and derision of all its teachings.

About a month after this time, the authorities, thinking I was deriving some consolation from "the Word," decided that that was to be taken away from me, too. Captain Hardy and Alison came into my cell. The former asked the latter if I was yet refusing to work. He said, "Yes;" then the Deputy, pointing to the book, said: "Why is he allowed books, then?" "Oh, sir," says Alison, "that was a mistake of mine; it is my fault. I should not have allowed him any books while he refused to work"—and taking hold of the Bible, he walked away with it.

The following verses, strung together during those cold nights and hungry days in the blackhole, will show how much my mind was filled with their Bible hypocrisy:

> My prison chamber now is iron lined,
> An iron closet and an iron blind.
> But bars, and bolts, and chains can never bind
> To tyrant's will the freedom-loving mind.
>
> Beneath the tyrant's heel we may be trod,
> We may be scourged beneath the tyrant's rod,
> But tyranny can never ride rough-shod
> O'er the immortal spirit-work of God.
>
> And England's Bible tyrants are, O Lord!
> Of any tyrants out the cruelest horde,
> Who'll chain their Scripture to a fixture board
> Before a victim starved, and lashed, and gored.

They tell such tales of countries far away,
How in Japan, and Turkey, and Cathay,
A man when scourged is forced salaams to pay,
While they themselves do these same things to-day.

The bands, the lash, the scream, the swoon, the calm,
The minister, the Bible, and the psalm,
The doctor then the bloody seams to balm,
"Attention, 'tention," now for the salaam.

I don't salaam them and their passions roll,
Again they stretch me in the damp blackhole,
Again they deal to me the famine dole,
To bend to earth the heaven-created soul.

Without a bed or board on which to lie,
Without a drink of water if I'm dry,
Without a ray of light to strike the eye,
But all one vacant, dreary, dismal sky.

The bolts are drawn, the drowsy hinges creak,
The doors are groaning, and the side walls shake,
The light darts in, the day begins to break,
Ho, prisoner! from your dungeon dreams awake.

Attention, "'tention," "'tention," now is cried,
The English master jailer stands outside,
And he's supposed to wear the lion's hide,
But I will not salaam his royal pride.

"Rossa, salute the Governor," cries one,
The Governor cries out—"Come on, come on,"
My tomb is closed, I'm happy they are gone,
Well—as happy as I ever feel alone.

Be calm, my soul, let state assassins frown,
'Tis chains and dungeons pearl a prisoner's crown,
'Tis suffering draws God's choicest blessings down,
And gives to freedom's cause its fair renown.

Secret instruction from the authorities to the prison governor.)

That we are base assassins, he says so,
And liars and hypocrites, 'tis well to know
That he's at least an unrepenting foe,
To cast him out as far as we can throw,
Is now our bounden duty. This we owe
To England's Majesty. Then keep him low,
Yet treat him doctorly—be sure and slow,
Leaving no record anywhere to show
That aught but nature gave the conquering blow,
And once cast out from this our heaven below,
What care we if to heaven above he go!

English writers are fond of turning into ridicule Eastern magistrates, who require a prisoner, after being bastinadoed, to return thanks to the man who beats him. When an English prisoner is released from the triangle, he is hurried to his cell, the doctor follows him to balm his wounded body, and the clergyman to psalm his wounded soul. As each of them enters the warders call out, "Attention!" and if the victim is able at all to stand he is obliged to come on his legs and pay a salute to the gentlemen. The practice is to be laughed at in heathen Turkey, but is nothing more than "discipline" in Christian England.

When my twenty-eight days' bread and water had expired, the six months' penal class diet commenced, and they gave me oakum to pick in my cell, and an hour in the open air every day. I took the hour, but I did not pick the oakum, on the grounds that it was against my principle while undergoing punishment, and for not working they took away my hour's exercise from me, and put me back every alternate day, and sometimes two days at a time, on bread and water. They capped the climax of their punishment now, when, besides putting me on bread and water in the black hole for forty-eight hours, they decreed that I was to get no bed at night, and that I was to be stripped of my body clothes.

Alison came to my cell at locking-up hour, and asked me to put out my clothes. "I will not," said I, "unless I get a bed."

"You can get no bed; that is the order, and we must get out your clothes."

"That is assassination work, and I will be no party to it. I will not give my clothes."

"But you must give your clothes, and we will soon see that you must."

Saying which he walked off, and returned accompanied by warders Hibbert and Giddings.

The foregoing conversation was repeated, and when I definitely said, "No, I will not give them," the three of them rushed at me. I tried to keep them away by holding them at arm's length, but made no attempt whatever at striking them, and they struck my hands with their clubs to make me let go my hold whenever I caught one of them. I was soon overpowered and lying on the ground, with Hibbert's knee upon my neck. You might have seen a butcher trying a pig for the measles; it was in exactly the same manner that Hibbert took charge of my head and neck while Alison and Giddings were pulling the breeches off me. It was necessary to turn me from one side to the other, and necessary for Hibbert to take his knee off my neck while this was doing; but, as I was on the flat of my back, he gave a leap, and, with his knee foremost, came down on my chest. It was a treacherous, murderous act. The air shot up my throat as it would through the neck of a full-blown bladder if you leaped on it. The sudden compression of the chest caused this, and the blade-bones must have been very strong and elastic to bear such a strain.

When they had stripped me they were leaving the cell, and I proceeded to raise myself from the floor, but Hibbert, who was the last going out, turned back and gave me a kick which threw me in against the wall and cut me in several places. I was so excited, and I think I should have shown myself a fighting man that night if I could lay hold of any weapon to strike with.

My door was locked, and in a minute or two they came and opened the trap to see how I fared. ." Ah, you assassin dogs!" cried I, as I laid hold of my gutta-percha pot and flung it at the lamp; but the hole of the trap-door being too small to allow it to go out, I seized three little loaves of bread which I had as a reserve against hunger and hurled them one by one at my enemies.

You will, perhaps, say I could not be very hungry when I had bread to use as bullets, but I was this time experiencing the natural effects of protracted starvation—a loss of appetite. When I got my little loaf of bread in the morning I had no extraordinary mind to eat it, and, having a lively recollection of the hunger I experienced at previous times, I left the bread uneaten as long as I could, in case one of the ravenous attacks came on.

All that night of the assault I felt my chest sore—felt sore in different parts of my body, and heart-sore, too. Rick Burke and Harry Mulleda were in the cells over me; they heard the noise and kept rapping to know what was the matter, and when I was composed enough I answered them. We kept knocking for half the night, and their sympathy was a balm for the wounds of the flesh as well as of the spirit.

In the morning I sent for the doctor, and when he brought me from the blackhole into the light of the hall-way I saw my chest black and blue and swollen. I got some liniment to rub to it, and by degrees the soreness and swelling went away.

As soon as Alison, and Giddings, and Hibbert saw I was under medical treatment on account of their assault, they entered on the books a charge against me to the effect that I had assaulted them in the discharge of their duty, and this charge remained for two months on record before I was called upon to answer it; then Captain Du Cane, the Chairman of the Board of Directors, came to the prison, and I was brought before him to make my defence.

He asked me what I had to say, and I said nothing, but smiled. " Now," said he, " could not you get on in prison like any other of your fellow-prisoners? They are all doing well—every one of them —and when I was telling some of them in Portland, the other day, how foolish you were for yourself, they were sorry for you."

This was all soft sawder in my eyes, and I said at once that things were going to take a new turn, but I would not say anything to interfere with the course they thought proper to pursue towards me. My reply was, " When have I been treated like any other of my fellow-prisoners? Have I not been separated from them in Portland and sent to work amongst thieves? Have I not been separated from them in Millbank and sent to work amongst thieves? Have I not been sent here, and a special party of thieves prepared for me, who were treated exceptionally severe, so that I, working amongst them, could not be able to say I was not treated like others?"

"But if I give you a chance now, will you promise to do better?"

"I cannot promise anything; but if I am treated like a human being I have no disposition to give trouble to any one."

"Well, let us forget the past, and to turn over a new leaf I will remit the rest of your punishment, and send you out to work tomorrow with Halpin, and Warren, and Costello."

"Do you tell me that Halpin, and Costello, and Warren are here, Captain Du Cane," said I in surprise.

"Yes; and I am now going to give you an opportunity of changing your conduct."

"Well, Governor, it will be a change anyway to be sent to work with them."

I knew well that Halpin, Warren and Costello were in the prison, because I had seen them through the holes in my blinds the first Sunday they came, as they were exercising in the yard outside my window, and I was mad at the sight, too, for they were walking around one after the other some four yards apart, instead of being exercised in couples, and allowed to talk as all the other prisoners were. I thought they should have pluck enough to kick against such treatment, and I was vexed at seeing them submit so tamely with all their "Yankee notions." But they did strike afterwards, and Warren and Halpin often made me laugh at the way they kicked against the discipline, so that I was repaid for the chagrin I experienced on first seeing them. And at the time Du Cane was speaking to me, they were on the strike, having refused to work under the petty irritating annoyance of the warders.

I had been holding telegraph communication with Costello during the previous fortnight. He got laid up with a sore leg, and the doctor, instead of sending him to hospital, sent him into the cell next to mine, so that I had an opportunity of learning through the wall all that was going on. I had an opportunity before that also, because when I found these friends in the same ward with me, I managed to get myself into the blackhole, so as to be in the neighborhood of their cells. Costello was the first that my telegraph communication reached; he was over my blackhole; he had a lot of news for me about my wife giving readings in America, and as she and I had had no communication for a few years, I made the blackhole my favorite abode. I managed to do this by giving readings myself. As soon as my forty-eight hours in the underground cellar had passed, I was taken up to my No. 6, and as soon as I was there I commenced giving a recitation from Davis, or some other poet, when I was immediately pounced upon for making a noise, and taken down again. This was what I wanted, and before I got tired of hearing what Costello had to say of my wife, they got tired or got ashamed of keeping me so long in the blackhole. It looked as if they gave me up as a bad job, for in the end I could not get myself sent to the dungeon any more. I might dance, sing, or recite, and they would not notice me, and then I in my turn got tired of declaiming and singing. I felt that I had the victory over their "discipline," and I was so magnanimous as to ask for oakum to pick, and when I commenced to pick it they gave me a library book to read.

The morning after Du Cane was speaking to me, I was sent out to work in company with Augustine Elliott Costello, and we were given in charge to Warder Pepper. He took us to the tool-box, and gave us two shovels, two pick-axes, and two wheelbarrows, and then sent us to wheel a heap of broken stones up along a deal board on top of another heap. When Costello and I broke ranks after being marched out, we shook hands and spoke, "You're Costello, I suppose?" "Yes, and you're Rossa?"—to which I nodded assent. Then we had—"How are you?" "Glad to meet you," and all that kind of thing all round. "Where are Colonel Warren and General Halpin? The Director told me I was to be sent to work with them and you." "Oh, they struck work some days ago. The three of us were breaking stones here till I got sick. Then they struck, and are now in the cells." "By Jove, that looks like a breach of contract. The Director told me I was to be working in company with them, and now they are not working at all."

Here Costello laughed, and Pepper chimed in a word, saying he thought Halpin and Warren would come out when they found I was out. This Pepper, it seems, had been worrying Halpin and Warren in the fashion in which Thompson had been worrying me.

"Their stroke was too light," and he kept telling them they should strike harder, till at length they threw down their hammers, and refused to strike any more. It was intensely cold at the time, coming on November, and sitting on a pile of stones all day long was not the very pleasantest occupation. Warren, Halpin, and Costello were separated when they came to the prison. One was sent to work with one gang of thieves, another with another, and the third with a third; but the three kicked against this, and the concession was made of allowing them to work by themselves.

I worked so hard the first day I came out that Costello asked me if I was going to be a driver on him.

I was reduced to a skeleton and as pale as a ghost, and that is no wonder, for I was in close dark confinement since the 1st of June. To counteract the effects of the cold on me, I ran the wheelbarrow up the hill as fast as I could, but I soon exhausted my little strength, and after an hour or so Costello's reproofs were not necessary to make me go easy.

Halpin and Warren came out to work the second or third morning after Costello and I commenced our labors.

People talk of prison life as if there was no brightness in it, but that is all moonshine. There is no condition in life in which man meeting his fellow-man—of kindred spirit—will not feel rejoiced. I will not grow so fervid as to say that the moment of my meeting Warren and Halpin in prison was "the happiest moment of my life," but this I will say, that meeting them was a great pleasure to me.

Colonel Warren and Captain Costello were amongst the volunteers that came to Ireland in the "Jackmel" or "Erin's Hope." They landed in Waterford, and were arrested the first day they set foot on Irish soil.

The fact that this small ship was three or four weeks on the coast of Ireland fully demonstrates that a number of men and arms could be landed in that country in spite of the vigilance of the English navy. Her commander, in making his official report when he took her back to America, says: "During eighteen of the twenty-four days I was in British waters, I was sought for by the English fleet stationed there, and in proof of their vigilance (!) and efforts I give the loss of the three following vessels—lost in hunting for us—taken from the English Naval Register: The Lapwing, first-class gunboat, lost in Killala Bay; the Revenge, also a first-class gunboat, lost on Daunt's Rock; and the third, a second-class gunboat, foundered in a gale of wind off Cape Clear. And yet there is no point of the coast at which I stopped during this time but where I could land any amount of men and arms were there preparations made to take them from me, and the military officers that were on board will affirm this statement.—JOHN F. KAVANAGH"

The following is the muster-roll of this little ship, and as they all, with one exception, are worthy of honorable mention, I will hand them down to everlasting posterity in this little book:

Brigadier-General James E. Kerrigan, Infantry, commanding military detachment.
Brigadier-General W. J. Nagle, Infantry, second in command.
Brigadier-General John Warren, Infantry, third commanding.
Brigadier-General George Phelan, Cavalry.
Colonel S. R. Tresilian, Engineers, first colonel.
Colonel Philip Dougherty, Infantry.
Colonel Patrick Devine, Cavalry.
Lieutenant-Colonel James Prendergast, Infantry.
Captain D. J. Buckley, Cavalry.
Captain M. J. Green, Infantry.
Captain J. J. Hasley, Zouaves.
Captain P. J. Kain, Artillery.
Captain J. E. Fitzsimons, Infantry.
Captain J. M. Buckley, Infantry.
Captain Andrew Leonard, Infantry.
Captain A. E. Costello, Infantry.
Captain W. Millen, Infantry.
Captain Timothy Horan, Infantry.
Lieutenant W. J. Downing, Zouaves.

Lieutenant Robert Kelly, Zouaves.
Lieutenant M. J. Fitzgibbons, Artillery.
Lieutenant W. E. Nugent, Infantry.
Lieutenant M. W. Walsh, Artillery.
Lieutenant A. Downing, Cavalry
Lieutenant J. P. Murray, Infantry.
Lieutenant P. Roach, Artillery.
Lieutenant P. O'Connor, Cavalry.
Lieutenant P. Nugent, Zouaves.
Lieutenant P. Crogan, Zouaves.
Lieutenant J. O'Connor, Zouaves.
Second Lieutenant Daniel Lee, Zouaves.
Second Lieutenant Lawrence Doyle, Zouaves.
Second Lieutenant Michael Fitzgerald, Zouaves.
Second Lieutenant John Rooney, Zouaves.
Second Lieutenant William Sheehan, Zouaves.
Second Lieutenant James Coffee, Zouaves.
Second Lieutenant John Mangin, Zouaves.
Second Lieutenant John O'Brien, Zouaves.
Second Lieutenant J. O'Shea, Zouaves.

List of officers and crew of the brig "Erin's Hope:"

Captain John F. Cavanaugh, commanding.
Lieutenant William Sweetman, Irish coast pilot.
Ensign Henry O'Neill, second officer.
Thomas Hardy, seaman.
John O'Connor, seaman.
Andrew White, seaman.
James Lawless, seaman.
John Mullen, ship's cook and steward.
John O'Connor, ordinary seaman, cabin boy.

The whole strength of the military and naval force on the vessel mustered fifty.

Warren and Costello were released from prison some three months after I fell in with them. They were convicted for words they had spoken and acts they had done in America, and it was their case brought the attention of the United States to the monstrous injustice of having American citizens punished in England for what is said or done by them in America. This law has since been changed, and now no citizen of the United States can be imprisoned in England on account of his political conduct in America.

General Halpin came over to Ireland in 1865. I met him in New York in the July of that year, and I met him often afterwards in Dublin.

The informer swore at his trial that he heard me giving him instructions in the office of the *Irish People,* but this swearing was false, as Halpin never visited the office, and I never gave him any instructions. He kept away from it intentionally and by advice, to keep away the suspicion that would attach to him by association with the very dangerous characters who frequented that place.

Costello, Warren, Halpin and I, having never met together before, met now for the first time, and it was not a very unpleasant meeting either. We chatted and laughed the weary hours away, save on odd occasions, when we'd go over the past, and speak of our failures and its causes. But as the fight was a heritage of our race, and as we were still in the land of the living, we determined to carry it on, "now and for evermore." Even in prison we held it to be our duty to "never say die."

The four of us were sent weeding the yards. We got bits of hoop iron to root up the blades of grass and other blades that grew around, and as we began to grumble at the pains that came in our back from being kept continually stooping, we were furnished with little boards on which to rest one knee while we scraped all around us. Warren and Halpin thought they might as well sit on the boards as kneel on them, and they did so. Pepper remonstrated, but they thought they could do as much work sitting as kneeling, and they remained sitting. When I saw they were allowed to do so without getting punished, I sat down myself, and the four of us worked this way for some weeks, each taking a ridge of about four feet and picking it from one end of the yard to the other. We had a very fine time of it so far as sitting down was concerned, but those Yankee spirits could not rest contented; they began to grumble at the cold, with their fingers and toes getting frost bitten and benumbed. I felt the cold too, and that pretty sharply, for I had not much flesh on my bones, and I did not care how much I could nurse the discontent of the others, but I was a good boy myself. I had done my share of the striking, and while my masters let me alone I would let them alone.

Warren was the first to strike, then Halpin, but the jailers did not strike at them; they let them have their way.

The use of razors having been abolished for some time, in consequence of the many suicides committed, our beards were allowed to grow for a month or two, and when some of us would be giving the moustache a twirl the barber would come on with his scissors to take the saucy curl out of it. Warren protested against this, and refused to put himself into the hands of the scissors man. He alleged that he expected his release shortly, and did not want to go into the world naked. Halpin also protested, and after both of them getting some bread and water they were allowed to go to work, carrying their hair and beards with them. Costello then refused to allow his black curly locks, and the few hairs of a moustache he had, to be interfered with. I delivered my head into their hands and they kept shearing me for some time, while the others were permitted to carry their hair as they liked. Another part of the discipline was to strip us naked once a week, and Warren kicked against this. The officers came to his cell one day, and threatened to use force to undress him, but he said he would use all the force he could to keep himself from indecent exposure. He suggested that if they wanted to search his clothes they could do so on the day when he was taking his weekly bath, and while they could see him naked then, it was quite unnecessary to subject him to the humiliation in his cell. The authorities availed themselves of this suggestion, and as all the others, except myself, refused to be stripped, an order was issued that the weekly naked search was to take place while each of us was bathing. I saw there was a great change in our jailers' demeanor towards us.

The least resistance to an order before this was to be punished with the utmost severity, but now it was against their will—or, rather, against their policy—to put us on bread and water. "The field was fought and won," and, as I saw there were no more battles in view, I became the most obedient man of the party, and the authorities, for their own purposes, gave me the character of being the quietest man in the prison.

Rick Burke and Harry Mulleda, who were undergoing their nine months' term of probation, were sent out to us, and our work was changed from grass-picking to wood-splitting. We were taken into an old shed where lime was stored, and, after each of us fixing a block for himself, we were supplied with small hatchets.

A pile of wood lay convenient, and, after having sawn this into pieces about nine inches long, our duty was to cut it up into splinters about an inch square and tie it into bundles. This occupation was pleasant enough unless you gave your fingers a touch of the hatchet, which occasionally happened to us all round.

Colonel Warren chopped a piece off one of his fingers once, and, instead of our crying at his misfortune, some of us, not thinking he had given himself so wicked a stroke, were cruel enough to laugh at him, which did not at all please him. On the whole, we made ourselves as jolly as possible, and, as we were allowed to joke and tell stories, we passed the time pretty pleasantly. 'Twas a paradise to me compared with the life I had previously led, and I look back now with a kind of affectionate longing for the stories and the prison society of Rick Burke and Halpin.

Warder Pepper had sole charge of us, but soon something occurred that brought him an assistant. It seems he was not considered watchful enough, inasmuch as a written communication intended for the outside world had been found in the prison, and it bore evidence of belonging to us. Rick Burke was the writer of it, but I was immediately pounced upon and charged with the authorship. I was asked what I had to say in reply to the charge of writing that letter, and I said I would give my reply in writing. I was kept during ten days in solitary confinement awaiting the decision of the Board of Directors, and then I was released and admitted to the companionship of the wood-choppers, after being informed the Directors did not consider there was evidence enough to convict me.

The six of us were taken to chapel every morning, and we were accommodated with two stools near the altar rails. Two warders guarded us, one sitting on each stool, having his legs spraddled across the end of it, and looking at his three men. Another stool was left vacant behind us, and back of that were the rest of the prisoners. A partition about six feet high ran up through the chapel dividing it into two parts, and at the other side of it seats were arranged similar to those we sat upon. The man next to the partition in one front seat could, when he knelt down, whisper to the man next to the partition on the other side, and by availing ourselves of this possibility we opened up communications. I sometimes held conversations here with Johnny O'Brien when the priest was reciting the litanies, and we were supposed to be responding aloud. A man named O'Hara, and a few other Irishmen, belonged to the party, occupied the front seat, and they made arrangements to supply us with pen, ink and paper as well as to forward whatever we wrote to our friends. The material was given to us; Rick Burke wrote the letter, and it was safely passed into the hands of our correspondents at chapel. One of them whose time was up, and who was about to be released, hid it in a photograph which he was allowed to keep in prison. He told his secret to some one else, who informed on him; his picture was broken, the concealed letter was found, and the unfortunate man, losing his remission, was obliged to spend the whole term of his sentence in prison.

O'Hara wrote to me some months ago, and as his letter tells pretty clearly the story of this incident of prison life, I give a copy of it here:

BARKISLAND, NEAR HALIFAX, YORKSHIRE,
ENGLAND, DEC. 15, 1872.

MR. O'DONOVAN ROSSA.—*My Dear Sir:* The writer takes the opportunity of communicating these few lines, hoping to find you in good health, as it leaves me at present, thank Providence for His clemency to me.

My dear sir, I am after getting my discharge from the bleak and barren shore of "Terra Del Fuego," after serving five long years there. I read the *Irish People* previous to my incarceration, which was on the 9th of December, 1867. I was sent to Millbank, and there I got acquainted with A. Costello and poor Captain Warren. The writer happened to be in the singing class every morning, and was in the habit of carrying messages from A. Costello to Warren through a friend of mine. Once I wrote to Costello a letter, worked with black thread, in lieu of black lead. I was sent to Chatham in 1868, and there I saw you, Costello, and some others. My heart bled when I heard of the treatment you were undergoing. I spoke to a fellow prisoner about you, and he told me the authorities would not let you write home to your dear friends. But he told me that he was going to be discharged in a fortnight, and that he could take a note out for you, providing he could get one from you.

I asked him how he could manage to do it, and he told me that he could put it in the inside of his mother's portrait, which portrait he would get a few hours before being searched. So my heart leaped with joy at the thought of getting a letter out of the prison. At that time I used to go up to the front seat to sing every morning, and of course you and your other brother sufferers were at the front seat also at the other side of the partition. But when we knelt down we could see each other. So next morning I took jolly good care to get next to the partition when we knelt down to pray. The partition divided me from poor Burke, and I told him as brief as possible how things were, and he told me that you would be in his place next morning, as he would tell you all about it. So I saw you next morning, and gave you a little bit of black lead pencil and some paper I tore out of my geography. You returned me that paper about the 22d of November, 1868, with some closet paper. It was to R. Pigott, Esq. I gave this paper to this Roger Rogers. But unfortunately he told a villain of the name of Witicam, who communicated with the prison authorities, and the result was that I was dragged out of my cell on a Sunday night, and taken to the Governor's office, and stripped to the skin, and got another suit of clothes, and was taken to the separate cells. All the time they were taking me I wanted to know what it was for. They told me I knew all about it. So they locked me up.

The next day I was brought before the Governor and charged with clandestinely corresponding with Fenians. Of course I denied all about it, so I was sent back to my cell to wait for the Director; but next day I was brought before him again for dirty tins and got three days' bread and water.

Captain Harvey, the Deputy-Governor, came to see me every day, with four or five officers, and made me stand to attention, of course. I used to ask him what I was here for, and he told me I knew all about it. He would say every morning, "Come, O'Hara, I want you to make it simple and clear and get out of it." But I had the one tale—I had nothing to make clear or simple. I knew very well they could do nothing to me; they found nothing on me.

But Rogers paid dearly for not keeping his own counsel. They found the note on him, and, of course, they would punish him for it.

So I had the old parson at me, likewise Captain Fagan, to tell all about it; but I told them I knew nothing about it, and, if I did, I would swing like Barrett did in May, at Newgate, before I would sell my poor unfortunate countrymen. So they left me in my cell to undergo punishment.

I remember seeing some of the State prisoners exercising on Monday, the 14th of December, 1868, in the yard, when their attention was drawn to a place in the corner of the yard where three unfortunates were after getting the whip. I was doing three days for not finishing my oakum. I happened to look through the ventilator. When I saw some State prisoners walking around the yard I could not help giving vent to my feelings by shouting through the holes in the sheet-iron to "cheer up." I had no sooner shouted than in comes the principal officer and caught me. He said, "All right, O'Hara." I got another dose of three days; so I went on like that for twenty-nine days before I was sent to Portsmouth. I was not long there till Harvey was made Governor; then I was in for it. To wind up, sir, I had to do every day of my sentence, which expired on the 5th of this month.

I was convicted of "manslaughter" on the 6th of December, 1867, so I thought to let you know all about that case.

Father O'Sullivan used to visit me often. I hope, dear sir, that you will excuse this writing, and send me a reply as soon as you can make it convenient.

Give my respects to Costello. I hear that poor Warren is dead; the Lord have mercy on him. No more at present from your affectionate friend,
JOHN O'HARA.

This discovery that we had writing materials alarmed the authorities, and they set their wits to work to counteract our efforts to get our case before the public. How I can smile at the hypocrisy of those English legislators when I find them talking of those dark dungeons and the hideous deeds of the prisons of other nations, while theirs is open to the public, and everything done is above board. What did they do now, do you think? Simply this: they kept us from religious service nine or ten days, during which time they were making a doorway in the gable end of the chapel. When it was finished we were admitted through it in charge of the warders, and placed in the next corner. Then while the service continued our keepers sat on the stools in front of us, their backs turned towards the altar, and their faces turned towards us. A properly regulated mind, or a very religious person might pray under such circumstances, but I candidly confess that I could not show much signs of devotion with these gentlemen looking straight into my face.

And, then, when any of our party went to Communion there was such a parade as turned the whole eyes of the chapel towards them. The communicants amongst the other prisoners, who were up half the length of the chapel from us, were allowed to approach the altar without any of the warders stirring from their seats; but when one of our party went up one of the warders followed him through the chapel, and stood over him with his club or his sword drawn while he was receiving the Sacrament, then gave him the "right about face," and followed him down again in the same fashion.

It was the most ridiculous exhibition of English official fear ever witnessed, and would be ludicrous were it not in connection with religion.

And more than that, when on Good Friday there is a ceremony of kissing the cross, every other prisoner left his seat and went up to the altar; but, regarding us, orders were issued that we should not go up, but that the priest should come down, and down through the chapel he would come to us.

Then when we were leaving or going to chapel, or going or coming from work, one of the three officers would go as a herald before us, and, when he turned a corner, if he saw any one in sight he would turn back and order us to halt, and go forward again and order the others to retreat or get out of view. It often afforded us amusement to see the fix they were in occasionally. Our *vidette* would come in view of a brigade of cooks, a brigade of dish-washers, a brigade of tray-carriers, and several other brigades that had to deploy in the yard through which we had to pass before and after meal times. Doors had to be reopened, and steps had to be retraced, but sometimes this strategic genius failed, and the whole party could not disperse in consequence of some avenue having been shut up and the key-holder gone. Then, after a council of war, it would be decided that those remaining on the field should turn their faces to the wall and do us the honor of turning their backs upon us as we passed their lines.

If England had treated us rightly she would not be so scared at having our treatment known.

Her first policy was to mix us up with her criminals; to rub us up close to them, so as it were that we should feel degradation.

Now we had changed all that to such an extent that she would not allow one of them to look at us, so much afraid was she that some sign or signal would be given to convey to the world an account of her assassin treatment of us. We had all along been fighting against being associated with thieves and murderers, at least I had been, and had forced her, in spite of her teeth, to keep us separated.

During the time the door was being broken in the gable end of the chapel we had some slight skirmishing against the discipline. The priest would visit us every morning after he gave the regular service; our doors were opened and we were ordered to come into the hall to pray. Halpin, Warren, and Burke and Costello refused to leave their cells. They said it was a mockery of religion to pray where three open water-closets were conveniently in view, and while there was the ordinary chapel for all the prisoners.

I came out and knelt down, and Henry Mulleda came out. I think Costello and Rick Burke left their doors open and knelt down in their cells while the priest prayed outside, but Warren and Halpin would not give any countenance to this exceptional treatment, and slammed out their doors as soon as the warders opened them. This continued for ten or eleven days, when the chapel was ready to receive us, and then we were led there and kept there in the fashion I have already described.

In January, 1869, Augustine Costello was taken away from us, and on the 4th of March John Warren got his marching orders. We had not as much as a good-bye with them. The six of us went into dinner one day, and we came out without Costello. During dinner hour he was removed from his own cell to one under mine. I heard the clank of chains, and by-and-by, hearing some knocking on the wall, I learned that he was in irons and going to be taken somewhere. There happened to be a writ of error in his case. He was taken to Dublin, and two months after he was released from prison.

We were working at brick-cleaning one morning when a warder called out, "Warren, come on this way." Warren went on, and that was the last we saw of him.

Cleaning bricks was far more unpleasant work than splitting wood, and much colder, for we had to handle them in frost and snow.

Besides this, we were located in a shed of corrugated iron that was specially built for us, and so constructed that we could not get a sight of any one passing through the yard. It faced the high wall of the prison, so that not a ray of sunshine could enter to soften the rigor of the cold, and here we were kept clipping the old mortar off of bricks from day-dawn until nightfall. Halpin called it the refrigerator, and, if you were hard-hearted enough to laugh at a free American citizen bound down to his best behavior in an English prison because of his conduct in America, you could laugh at Halpin hopping from one foot to another to warm his toes, while his hands beat time with his brick-chopper; but he did not stand it long. Laying down his chopper one morning, he turned to the warder and said:

"Mr. Mabbot, the cup of my affliction has flown over."

"What do you mean, Halpin?"

"I mean to do no more of this work. This refrigerator is enough to kill a saint. You can send me into the cells."

"What's the use in being in those cells? Might you not as well stay as you are and try and spend your time as well as you can?"

"No, I can't spend any more time this way. You will please send me in."

"I don't like to be reporting you. If you feel cold take an occasional run up and down on those boards in front of the shed, and that will warm you, but don't be going into those cells."

This was a great concession. A short time ago Halpin's words would have been a gross breach of discipline, severely punishable, but he "joined the service in a good time," as Mabbot afterwards said, and his bad conduct was winked at on this occasion. We prevailed on him to take a little bit of a run to warm himself; then each of us took a similar exercise, and Halpin remained in our company.

He had caught a severe cold in another prison, and was this time affected with a very bad cough. At night and all through the night, we could hear it echoing through the wards. The doctor sent him to hospital, but his doing this seemed to interfere with the existing orders to keep us at all times to ourselves, and not let us in view of any other prisoners. An iron screen was put outside on his hospital cell window; but this did not seem to meet the requirements of the authorities, and Halpin was sent back to us after a few days. During the three winters he was in Chatham this cough attacked him, and this Dr. Burns, who was charged with torturing and paralyzing Daniel Reddin, would not give him any hospital treatment other than allowing him an hospital spittoon in his cell, in order that he might judge how the cough progressed, from the increase or decrease of the quantity of blood thrown up.

CHAPTER XIX.

NEW ARRIVALS — JOHN M'CLURE — AMERICAN-BORN IRISHMEN, AND IRISH-BORN "SPRALLAREENS"—NEW WORK—STOCKING-MENDING —"FOX AND GEESE"—LIES OF BRUCE, THE SECRETARY OF STATE—SUPERSTITION AND THE BIBLE—HALPIN "JOINING THE SERVICE IN A GOOD TIME"—HE STRIKES WORK, AND KEEPS HIS HAIR ON HIS HEAD—MR. O'CONNELL'S SORE FOOT AND DR. BURNS—"I DON'T LIKE TO BE HERE AT ALL," AND WARDER BROWNE—THE TIPPERARY ELECTION AND THE TERROR OF THE AUTHORITIES—JOHN MITCHEL'S REMARKS—VISIT FROM M'CARTHY DOWNING, M. P.—COLONEL WARREN AND PATRICK'S DAY—THE SOLDIER PRISONERS—MR. BLAKE, M. P., AND AUSTRALIA—MR. PIGOTT'S AND JOHN F. O'DONNELL'S VISIT—MR. A. M. SULLIVAN— HIS OPINIONS ON THE "COUP D'ETAT," AND MY OPINIONS ON HIM, AND ON HIS "STORY OF IRELAND"—IRELAND OVER THE WATER.

When we came in from the refrigerator, one evening, we found that three additional cells of our ward were occupied, and, by knocking on the walls, discovered there were new arrivals from Millbank. Next morning I was orderly, and, as I was on my rounds, I had a shake hands with John Devoy and Captain Charles Underwood O'Connell. I did not know the other arrival, as I had never met him, but he turned out to be John M'Clure, who was arrested fighting by the side of O'Neill Crowley, at Kilclooney Wood, and sentenced to be hanged.

This John M'Clure was born in America, of Irish parents, and, having served in the American army, he came to Ireland to fight. He was the most unpretentious of any one of the men that came over; he was unassuming, quiet, and inoffensive, but that did not prevent him from doing as much fighting as any of them. Whether he was put, or put himself, in the way of it, I cannot say. Many Irishmen, passing judgment upon the American-born sons of our countrymen, will say they are no good for anything connected with the Irish cause; but if they could be judged by John M'Clure, I only wish that all Irishmen in and out of Ireland were born and reared as he was, so that the cowards and *spallareens* of our race may grow up brave and decent men. And nowhere do this cowardice and meanness spring into more luxurious growth than in America. The man who was a slave at heart in the old land, when he comes here finds himself rid of those necessities that educated him into subserviency at home.

But what use does he make of his adventitious freedom? Does he avail of it to further the cause that he was afraid to touch in the old land? No: he becomes a blatant, parading patriot; a kind of *buailumskeh*, beating the bushes and wearing green scarfs and ribbons to show there is no man braver than he; but to make his action here consistent with his conduct there, he is the first to sneer at any practical work in the line of what is known as Fenianism; he will have much sympathy with the "poor servant-girls who have been cheated out of their hard-earned dollars," and he will denounce the "swindlers and vagabonds who have cheated the people," as a knavish excuse for his doing nothing for the people's cause.

M'Clure, Halpin, Devoy, Burke, O'Connell, Mulleda and myself worked for a few days in the refrigerators; but then one of the directors visited the prison, and arrangements were made that we be kept at work inside in our punishment ward. The Governor had his adjudication room here, and over this court-house was a small room, about twelve by eight, into which we seven were put, with two warders in charge of us. Our occupation was mending the stockings of all the other prisoners; these were given to us after being washed, but after we turned them inside out such a quantity of sand and dust escaped from them as nearly suffocated us. Nine of us were cooped up in this small space; the Summer came on in a few months, and, after repeated protests to the doctor and Governor, we got them to take down a partition that divided us from another small room, which change made the quarters more airy and less disagreeable.

Halpin struck work, and refused to darn any more stockings in consequence of being refused the privilege of some letters and visits which the rules accorded to ordinary prisoners. He got three days on bread and water for the first refusal, but that did not prevent him from laying down his darning-needle again when the warder handed it to him on the fourth morning. We thought his punishment was to continue for such a gross offense, but it did not; the authorities were by this time pretty tired and sick of their attempts to civilize us by ill-treatment, and they let Halpin alone. Every morning his needle and thread were handed to him; he graciously received them from the hands of the warder, and as graciously laid them down on the stool as soon as he got them. Then he occupied his time and amused us by telling stories all day long. His bad and idle example had an evil influence on myself, and I suggested that we would invent something else to kill time. It would be pleasant if we had a draught-board, but, as we had not, we fashioned one by making a " fox and-geese " on the stool, and we made men out of bits of coal and scraps of paper.

An attack was made upon me on account of playing with Halpin, but I never heeded it. I worked a little and played a little; I did not like to appear to be too daring, or to be playing drafts in defiance of the rules, and as we heard the Governor or other superior authority coming up-stairs, I would say, "Now, Hal, let us draw a veil over our infirmities," and one of us would spread his handkerchief over the fox and geese. Of course, all this was reported to the authorities, but as they winked at our delinquency, we winked at the warder's orders to "stop that game." When going to dinner we hid our "men" in a stocking, and coming back we would sometimes find them stolen away, but as we had always bits of coal, or thread or paper about us, we would make new men, Halpin jocosely grumbling about the trouble the "thieves" were profitlessly putting him to.

This game was a great recreation to me. The pain that troubled me in the back became very intense at times. It became more and more lively according as I allowed my mind to dwell on any of the serious matters that affected me in the world, and I had no escape from suffering but to fly away with my thoughts to something trifling. Either that or something hostile to the powers that governed us: but while they let us alone I was content to let them alone, and live a life of peace.

State Secretary Bruce, when questioned about this time as to my ill-treatment in prison, said in his place in Parliament, that I was now the quietest man in the prison, and hoped that that would satisfy Sir John Gray and the other inquirers. Here is the passage as I find it reported in the *Irishman* of June 12th, 1869:

"Another statement is that his appearance is quite changed, and that he has suffered very much from his confinement. Since he became an inmate of Chatham Prison his weight has increased from 103½ to 171 lbs. (Laughter.) His general health is now stated to be good, and he is reported to have the appearance of a man who is in excellent health. After what I have given of this unfortunate man's career [looking over his speech, I find he was after telling twenty-four direct lies of me], it is a real pleasure to say that since September, 1868, the date of his last offence, his conduct has greatly improved, and he has not incurred any punishment. Captain Du Cane, in visiting the prison, told Rossa that his conduct had been outrageous and disgraceful [yes, and Rossa returned him the compliment], and that he was astonished that a man of his position should have been guilty of it. Since then not only had Donovan behaved well and received no punishment, but Captain Powell said, 'Of all the Fenian prisoners now under confinement he is the best behaved.' I trust that this statement of itself will be considered satisfactory by my honorable friend.

"Sir John Gray was understood to express his satisfaction with the statement which had been made."

This was an easy way to get rid of a vexatious question; but, while I was the quietest man in the prison when playing a game of "Bohea" with Halpin, I had my eyes open to the necessity of letting the outside world know there was a time when Mr. Bruce gave me very little chance of keeping quiet, and when he and all his agents were disposed to be very cross to me.

I joked occasionally with the officers on the change of treatment, and it is notorious that we always had the strictest—the most "reliable" ones, as the Governor said—placed over us. Andrews, who was never known to smile in the presence of a convict, would laugh at our stories and tell us laughable superstitious ones when he found the rules relaxed in our regard. He was an old Englishman, but he was as full of old superstition as any old woman I ever knew. He himself cured warts and evils, and warded off many impending misfortunes by manipulating brambles and bushes, and burying bits of meat and cloth.

When I was working with the thieves I listened long one day as three of them were talking of the Bible, and I was surprised to learn that their faith in it was of a nature that some would call superstitious. Old Mr. West, who was one of the three, said he read a part of the Bible every day, and did not think he would have any luck if he didn't. The young fellow, who swore "by Christ, he would make some one pay outside for the way he was treated in prison," said he did not read, but as he kept it in his cell he had the benefit of it, and in that belief he always kept a Bible among his clothes in a trunk when he was in the world. The third, who was a sailor, told a similar story, and then several cases were adduced where the Bible in a man's trunk saved him from danger, and where many mothers put the Holy Book in their children's trunks when preparing for a voyage or a long journey. One story was told of the escape of a man that must have been miraculous. He was no sailor and could not swim, yet he was washed ashore, while numbers of hardy seamen and expert swimmers were drowned. When he communicated with home he learned that his mother had, unknown to him, put a small Bible in a corner of his trunk, and it was that saved him. When this belief is so strong in the minds of the English Protestant peasantry, I wonder that they cast so much ridicule on the belief that Catholics have in the protecting agency of scapulars, Agnus Deis, and other religious emblems of *their* faith. I reasoned this with those thieves, with a view to make them more tolerant, for they had very strange ideas about Irish principles—so strange that they thought our movement was nothing more than a conspiracy among the Catholics to kill Protestants. I thought it well to make so free with them as to correct this notion of theirs, and when they found I was so tolerant in my religious opinions as to allow peole who differed from me a chance of going to Heaven, they pronounced me a fair man, and "Fenianism" a different thing from what they thought it. I should not mind to spend another year of my life in prison, if the authorities gave me the run of the twelve or fourteen thousand convicts they hold in England. Even though they are thieves and Thugs, they, in their way, represent a certain opinion, and it would be worth while to disabuse them of the prejudices against Irish independence that are instilled into them by our enemies—and by theirs in a certain sense.

It was well understood in our prison that any warder placed in charge of us was on the way to promotion if he traveled that way to the satisfaction of his masters. Since my arrival in Chatham, the fellow that had drawn the blood from my hands, and the fellow that had torn the clothes off my limbs, and kicked and trampled me in the blackhole, had received the reward of their faithful services. Pepper and Mabbott, who were with us before Andrews—the *pishogue* man—had received those yellow bands on their caps which indicated their promotion to the rank of principals. In Mabbott's and Andrew's time the test of faithful service was not so much to worry us about work as to keep us so much to ourselves, and so far from getting a look at anyone else as would render it impossible for anyone outside the prison to know anything about us. These were the times the Government were lying in Parliament about our treatment, and sending down their Commissioners to the prison to manufacture lying reports to be read in Parliament concerning us. After Mabbott was promoted from our charge he got the privilege of calling to inspect us every day. At one of those visits he asked Halpin didn't he resume work yet, and, on getting a reply in the negative, I smilingly said :

"Halpin must have some friend here, Mr. Mabbott, that is saving him from punishment. If it was I was to strike work that way, how soon you'd order me off to the dark cells."

"Ah," Rossa, Halpin joined the service in a good time."

On Sundays, before we went to chapel, we were paraded for inspection by the doctor, and some of our company were already getting so rebellious as to refuse to take off their caps when this gentleman appeared. Halpin and Captain O'Connell commenced the fun and kept it going for a few Sundays; some one or two joined in, but I always obeyed the order of "Hats off" till the whole of us came to an understanding that it should not be obeyed, and that if they commenced giving us bread and water for our disobedience we should stand it to the point of starvation rather than uncover ourselves for this gentleman. Next Sunday, when the doctor appeared, he stood before us, and Alison cried, "Hats off," but the hats remained on. "Hats off!" again roared he, in a voice that made my body tremble, but not a hat of the seven stirred. I was glad in my heart at this spirited stand of the *caubeens*. The doctor and his attendants wheeled off, we were wheeled into chapel, and I had much difficulty in muffling my laughter during prayers when thinking of the ridiculous figure the officials cut in presence of our rebellious bonnets. And you should see how proudly and defiantly those "hats" stood. If you had only one laugh in the world you should give it on looking at the one that Captain O'Connell commanded. He had it so firmly pressed on his head that it nearly covered his ears, and you would think the hat and head were inseparable—one could not be taken off without the other. There had been several previous skirmishes with the doctor, in some of which he would appeal to me, as being "a reasonable man." This was amusing, considering the time I had previously given them.

Warren and Halpin refusing to have their hair cut, Alison directed the doctor's special attention to their heads at one of these special parades, and the doctor said to me, pointing to Halpin's crop, "Now, Rossa, you're a reasonable man (he saw my head cropped to the scalp), don't you think he has too much hair on?"

I smiled the reply. "Ah, doctor, you must excuse me for not giving an opinion on the question."

Captain O'Connell elicited from him the strangest admission I ever heard a medical man make.

He was lamed from the heavy boots he wore, and he asked Dr. Burns if he would allow him to wear his Sunday shoes, instead of the working-day boots?

"No," said the doctor, "unless your leg is sore."

"My leg is so sore that I cannot well walk with these heavy boots."

"Can you show me a sore—is there a hole in it?"

"No; but I am sure it will get sore if I am obliged to wear the boots."

"Well, when you can show me a sore in it I'll try and cure it."

"But is not prevention better than cure, doctor?"

"Yes; but in some cases we are not allowed to prevent."

He actually made use of these very words; and, it appears, he spoke in the spirit of those who order the government of these English prisons—the be-praised model prisons of the world. The "discipline" is sure to work a refractory prisoner into a premature death, and the disciplined doctor will not interfere with the course of punishment until he sees there is no recalling the victim from the grave. Then he will take him to the hospital and do what he can to smooth the last few paces of his journey. An inquest is held, and evidence is given to prove that the man had beef-tea, and mutton-chop, and chicken, and chicken-broth, and every delicacy that could be given beneficially to the man's health, but there is nothing to show how his health was destroyed.'

Darragh, of Ballycastle, a friend of mine, who died in Portland Prison, was "sat upon" by twelve of these prison pensioners, and Roupel, the forger, who was an hospital nurse, was brought forward to prove that before he died he had everything he wished to have. The public little knew the foul work behind this bright picture.

"The public like to be deceived," says some old writer, and so it seems, when the world regards these English prisons as models of perfection, and those who manage them the most humane and kind creatures in creation.

There was one officer named Brown who never missed an opportunity of annoying me. He was one of those who made the handcuffs bite me when putting them on, and now that there must have been special orders to let us alone, he could not refrain from issuing orders to me which he knew I would not obey. After supper every evening you have in winter times two or three hours in your cell before you are allowed to go to bed. During this time I read, and, to make myself a little comfortable, I laid my mattress on the floor, and pillowed it up against the block. It was a most luxurious seat, and, with my back thus cushioned and turned to the gaslight, I was quite at home.

But Brown would not let me enjoy myself in peace. He was on night duty, and he'd open my door and order me to settle up my bed in its proper place. My only reply to him would be, "Ah, Governor, I don't like to be here at all."

"Do you hear me telling you to put up your bed?"

"Ah, Governor, I don't like to be here at all."

"Don't you know that the rules forbid you to lay down your bed till the bell rings?"

"Ah, Governor, I don't like to be here at all."

After giving him this answer a couple of times, if he continued worrying me, I remained silent till he got tired, and shut the door. Next night he'd come again repeating the same thing, and receiving the same return.

If I spoke insolently to this fellow he'd be only too glad, for then he could make a big report against me, and insolently he deserved to be spoken to; but as I was otherwise allowed to live in peace I did not want to rouse myself up on account of the officiousness of this small creature, and I therefore treated him with my sovereign convict contempt. I had great fun with him one morning when I was on the black books. My sleeping place the night before was the blackhole, and when he came in the morning to ask me to put out the mattress and blankets I told him the night was not passed yet, and that I would stay in bed till daybreak.

"Get up out of that, I say, and put out your bed at once."

"Now, the best thing you can do is to let me sleep the night in peace."

"Don't you see it is day—did n't you hear the bell ring?"

"If it is day, why have you that lantern in your hand? Don't you see there is no light here?"

"Get up, or I'll report you at once."

"You may report me as much as you like, but I will not get up until it is day."

When a prisoner refuses to obey orders in this part of the prison, three or four officers have to be brought to force him into his duty, and the required number could not be got together until about ten o'clock, so that I cheated them out of three or four hours of punishment. Then they came into my cell, and when I would not get out of bed "till daybreak," they pulled the mattress clean from under me.

In November, '69, it was made manifest to us that something extraordinary had occurred in the world which called for the most extreme vigilance regarding us. The exercise we got in the open air every day was not given to us in the usual place, nor was it given in the same place to us any two consecutive days. One time we were taken into a small yard behind the hospital, to get one hour's airing. Another time into a passage-way, between two buildings, and occasionally into a small enclosure between two gates and two high walls, where the walking around produced a *megrim* in the head. Halpin suggested that we would unwind ourselves every five minutes, and we acted on the suggestion, trying to counteract the dizzying effect of the circular motion, by making a right about face, and walking the contrary way around, until another change became necessary. The secret of our being treated this way was that the Tipperary election had taken place; the rebel spirit there had chosen me as its representative, and a rumor had gone abroad that I and my companions were to be rescued.

Hence the prison authorities were in the greatest alarm. They could not even bring themselves to trust their own employees, and, lest any warder could be able to tell the attacking party where the prisoners could be found exercising any particular day, our exercise ground was changed *every* day.

The Government were really alarmed, and they took all possible precautions to secure us. They put extra locks upon our doors at night, and extra guards around our cells. If the citadel were besieged we could not have been more vigilantly surrounded.

This was ridiculous; but those who mean to fight England may take one or two lessons from it—first, as regards acting on her fears, and the measures that are necessary to strike terror into her, and, secondly, as to the precautions and provisions that are requisite for protection against surprise and defeat.

In spite of all the arts resorted to to keep us in the dark, we had a line of wires laid down that kept us pretty well acquainted with what was going on in the world, and we knew of the Tipperary election before it was officially made known to us in the following manner:

The Governor of the prison sent for me, and, holding a sheet of paper in his hand, said, "I am instructed to inform you by the Secretary of State that the county of Tipperary has elected you a member of Parliament; but I am also desired by him to tell you that that is in no way to change your prison treatment."

I affected a little surprise, and, after some humorous observations, I told him he may as well take down my name to see the Director in order that I may ask that gentleman to have me transferred to Millbank Prison, so that I would be convenient to the House of Commons, and be able to attend to my Parliamentary duties at night after picking my bit of oakum during the day.

The Director came, and I joked with him also on the matter. "Now," said he, "take my advice and don't have anything to say to the authorities. . You are getting on well lately, and you should do nothing to injure yourself if they were disposed to consider your case favorably. If you take my advice, you will keep silent." As he seemed to speak kindly, I spoke seriously, and, thanking him, said I would take the matter quietly. The Government were annoyed enough at what had occurred without my trying to annoy them more. With the officers I assumed the influence of a live member of Parliament. I was to have some of the good ones promoted, and the bad ones reduced to a probation of convict life.

John Devoy was to have a tide-waitership from me if my constituents permitted me to take any such favors.

One or two of my companions took the matter seriously, and thought I would be really taken before the House. They kept discussing what I was to do—whether I would take the oaths, or refuse to take them; become a member, or continue a rebel.

If this were worth a serious thought—if I were taken before the House, I think I would be found talking Irish to them, and it they would not understand me—why ! let them get an interpreter.

I was an Irishman, represented an Irish county, and had a right to be heard in the language of my country. This may be a new idea for the members who are now discussing what is the best thing for them to do in the House; whether to vote or not to vote, whether to go there or remain away altogether. Let them speak Irish, and insist on speaking it in the House. That may be thought ridiculous, but it is not a bit more ridiculous than to think the votes of a hundred Irish members can get an independent Irish Government against the votes, and the prejudices, and the interests of five or six hundred English and Scotch members. If a London Parliament ever grants the "Home Rule" to Irishmen, it will be just such another sham as the "Tenant Right" she grants to Irish tenants. This Tipperary election was, to my mind, the grandest thing of the kind that ever occurred in Ireland. The Clare election was nothing to it as a protest against foreign rule. Here, the great and popular freeman, O'Connell, was chosen by the people; he was amongst the people and addressed them, but Tipperary chose a man who was condemned to imprisonment for life, who was dead in law, and who was subjected to every indignity England could heap upon him in his living grave. There was no compliment intended to me in this matter. I felt myself no better, nor did the people consider me better, than any one else. The whole movement was a protest against England, and a defiance to her Ministry and ministration. Either of the prisoners was as worthy of being chosen as I; yet, there is no reason why I should not feel proud of being the elect—of being considered the most ill-treated and most defiant of the convicted felons. John Mitchel says: "A great event has befallen in Irish history. Tipperary has just done a wiser and a bolder deed than her sister county of Clare achieved forty years ago. That Clare election won, to be sure, what was called Catholic Emancipation, for the Claremen elected the disqualified Catholic, O'Connell, to represent them in Parliament. Now the Tipperarymen have elected the disqualified felon, O'Donovan Rossa, in his convict cell—have elected, amongst all those imprisoned comrades, the very one whom England most specially abhors—because he defied and denounced the most loudly her government, her traitor judges, and her packed juries—elected him as the most fit and proper person to represent them."

Just so. I may well feel proud before my countrymen of having such a commendation from so veteran a hater of English rule in Ireland as John Mitchel, and so may Tipperary.

In December, '69, our company came to be reduced by the removal from amongst us of Rick Burke. He had been taking medicine for the previous week, and was visibly falling away. In the end he seemed to imagine that poison had been administered to him in the drugs, and he was spirited away from us one morning without one knowing where he was taken. A few days before his removal, Dr. Burns, in my presence, told him that possibly what the matter with him was that he was mentally troubled on account of his crime. Rick told him he was not, and the doctor told him he should be. This was the kind of medicine we occasionally got from these doctors. It was hard for a man to keep his patience with them, and only for the large stock of it we had on our hands, we were sure to run short oftener than we did.

Having learned that M'Carthy Downing of Skibbereen was returned to the English Parliament from Cork, I thought it would be well to have a visit from him, and I applied to the Director for a ticket, which I got, and sent him. My idea was to get him to speak in Parliament about having my letters to my wife suppressed. The Government would then state that this was done because I had told falsehoods in them, and if I could have the letters produced and read, I would have attained my object of having the treatment made known. Mr. Downing visited me about the 24th of March, 1869, and I told for what purpose I sent for him. He seemed to be full of the idea of getting us amnestied, and appeared to be very much displeased at a speech that Colonel Warren had made at a banquet in Cork, on Patrick's Day, as it irritated the Government, and interfered with our release. He wished I would express my disapproval of Warren's action, but this I would not do. I said Warren was accountable for his own acts, and if he said or did anything wrong, the law would take hold of him. We had an idea before Warren left us that this would be the state of things if he were released. People would fetter him outside, because we were fettered inside, and we distinctly told him in the refrigerator one day, to tell our friends not to be deterred from any work they thought proper to do in the cause, by a fear that it would tend to keep us in prison. England would keep us in for ever if she thought that by doing so she could keep Ireland from saying or doing anything hostile against her. In the same way would she hold the soldiers she still holds in chains were she confident that keeping them would keep Ireland and Irishmen quiet.

At M'Carthy Downing's visit he asked me if I would promise to leave the country, if released from prison. This was a ticklish question to me. I told him I was sensitive as to anything being said about my seeking my release on any conditions, or about his seeking it from me.

I told him if a choice was given me of going to Siberia, and being my own master, I would prefer to go there to remaining where I was, but that I would promise nothing. After a lengthened conversation on the matter, I said if he gave me a leaf of paper I would give him a reply to his question in writing, and the Deputy-Governor consenting to give the paper, I wrote as follows:

"Mr. Downing, in answer to your question as to whether I would leave the country or not if released from prison, I reply that I would, and also with the understanding that if found in Ireland or England again, without the permission of the British Government, I render myself liable to be recommitted to prison."

I would not promise not to return, and the saving clause I had in this was, that if I did return it could not be said I broke my word.

Mr. Downing said I might make up my mind that whoever would be released unconditionally, I would not. He put the writing in his pocket-book, promising he would make no dishonorable use of it, and I believe he never did; but when I learned, a year afterward, that he showed it to my father-in-law, I was afraid it would bear such a construction as that I sent for Mr. Downing for the purpose of getting him to intercede for my release, and I wrote to him to return me the paper. He did so, and I kept it in my cell. When the Government officials asked me if I would leave the country if pardoned, the reply I gave was to send them this very leaf of paper.

Mr. Downing paid me a second visit a few months after his first, and brought with him another member of Parliament, Mr. Blake, of Waterford. This interview was solicited on their part, as questions had been raised in the House of Commons about my hands being tied behind my back for thirty-five days.

Mr. Downing said I never told him this, which was true, but it was not to tell it I sent for him. I sent for him that he might ask for my suppressed letters in Parliament, which would tell that story and other stories besides.

The question again came up of my leaving the country, and Mr. Blake talked of my going to Australia. He said he had some very influential friends there, and that he would give me letters of introduction to them. I thanked him; but I was so suspicious at the time as to think he was speaking with a knowledge of where the Government wished me to go, and that the friends to whom he would give letters would be also Government friends. But when a man with the patriotic Irish name of Gavan Duffy is dubbed a Sir Charles by Queen Victoria, and held by patriotic Irishmen to be an Irish patriot still, I suppose I will be looked upon as over-squeamish in imagining the possibility of my falling into any hands that would mould the future of my life to anything different or antagonistic to what the past of it has been. I did not say I would go to Australia then. I said my wife and some of my children were in America, and it was probable, if I had a choice of going anywhere, I would go towards them.

Mr. Blake and Mr. Downing questioned me on the subject of having my hands tied for thirty-five days, and I told them it was true.

The Deputy-Governor was present, and he did not deny it. Mr. Bruce, the Secretary of State, said I "was only tied for a part of a day."

Mr. Downing asked the Deputy if he could see the record books, and the Deputy said "Yes."

But, on reflection, he considered he would be acting improperly in showing them in the absence of the Governor, and begged to be excused.

These records subsequently showed that I was bound day after day for the time mentioned. But at one time they were taken out of the prison and kept in London in order to prevent a detection of the falsehoods of the Secretary of State and his agents. When I am writing on the Commission of Inquiry I will go fully into the matter.

I had a visit from Mr. Richard Pigott and Mr. John O'Donnell, and it was that let the cat out of the bag. Through many interruptions of the Deputy-Governor who presided at our interview, I was enabled to tell them as much as would enable them to make a noise when they got home. Mr. Pigott's object in visiting me was to ascertain if I was willing to give evidence in a case of libel which was brought against him by Mr. A. M. Sullivan, editor of the *Nation*. This was the second time the *Irishman* was prosecuted on account of the publication of a letter of mine concerning Mr. Sullivan. I consented to give any evidence I could in the case, and in a few months afterwards a commissioner, accompanied by Mr. A. M. Sullivan, with attorney and counsel for both sides, came to the prison to examine and cross-examine me.

Mr. Luby tells me Mr. Pigott's attorney, Mr. Lawless, thought I went back of my charges on this occasion, but I do not know how that could be thought. I think I was pretty positive in adhering to them.

I was asked if I ever had any personal ill-will against Mr. Sullivan, and I should conscientiously say I never had, and to other questions replied that I knew himself and his family ; that his father was a respected man, and it was with pain I felt it my duty to write harshly of his son. I was asked if I considered Mr. Sullivan to be an honest man, and I answered that I believed him to be a better man in his heart than in his paper, for I had in my mind the necessities that make a newspaper man say and do many things when he is in with men and parties that are in with the English government and support his paper, which he would not say or do were he independent of them and had no paper.

I knew Mr. Sullivan, and took notice of him when he was a young man and I a growing boy. He had a good reputation in his native town, Bantry, and I heard him talk one day in a manner that made me like him. But when he became a newspaper man, he talked quite the opposite way on the same subject. I don't believe his mind changed a bit, but his necessities did.

It was just after the *coup d'etat* in Paris when that tyrant liberticide, the late Napoleon, perjured himself, shot the people down, and killed the Republic he was sworn to uphold. I was a clerk in the hardware store of William Clarke, of Bantry, he sent me up to the Poor Law Union to look after some contracts, and I stood in the waiting-room awaiting orders. Five or six men were talking of Napoleon, and one of them denounced the scoundrel in the most scathing language, asserting that he himself would not have the least scruples in blowing out his brains, and would do it at the moment if he had the chance. I was too young at the time to say anything, but I tell you it added a little to my pride to find Sandy Sullivan holding the same opinion as myself. I never could read his articles in the *Nation* in praise of this same Napoleon, without thinking of that Bantry Boardroom, and without having a holy horror of becoming a newspaper man. I had a presentiment some way that my becoming so would be my ruin, and sure enough it was.

But withal it did not change one opinion of mine. I hold them now the same as I did those "twenty golden years ago," and if I live those twenty more that I am banished from the old land, may God grant that the old spirit will live too.

Another word about the editor of the *Nation*. It is surprising to see with what persistency he has stuck to maligning "Fenianism" and those connected with it, except a few friends of his, such as P. J. Meehan and Colonel Roberts, who would begin the fight in Canada instead of Ireland. He has written a story of Ireland for school-boys, but I trust few of the rising generation will pay much attention to the two last chapters of it. "The politics of despair" is what he calls fighting for Irish independence, and he says "it may be deplored that a considerable portion of the Irish people have lent a ready ear to them."

"We were in a mood to hearken to any proposal, no matter how wild, and to follow any man, no matter who he might be, promising to lead us to vengeance."

"Our policy was strenuously reprehended by every one of the '48 leaders"—which is scarcely true, for Michael Doheny, and Thomas Francis Meagher, and John Mitchel gave some countenance to it—"and reprehended by the Catholic clergy universally."

This is somewhat false. I know Catholic clergymen who did not reprehend it, and Mr. Sullivan knows them too. One of those, known to both of us, wrote to me when I was elected for Tipperary, but I was never told of the arrival of his letter till I was leaving prison; it was handed to me then, and as the following passage is underscored by the authorities to show it was under their consideration, I give it in full:

"DECEMBER 21, '69.

"You remember Father Leader, how he read from the altar, in 1850, a long list of the evictions perpetrated by Tom Marmion. A history of these evictions appears on the papers of to-day in the form of letters from Father Davis and Father Troy. We are making great strides towards tenant right. Farmers will not be contented now with anything short of fixity of tenure at fair rents, but this is more than they will get until our rulers are better educated. Dr. O'Hea is in Rome attending the E. Council. The opening scene in St. Peter's, the splendor of the ceremonies, was magnificent beyond description. There are 800 bishops and mitred abbots. Put out of your mind the idea that they are to deliberate on the condemnation of Fenianism. *You ought to know that the opinions of Dr. Moriarty are neither general nor well received among the Irish clergy. Every day renders it less likely that they ever will be. The current seems drifting rather in a direction quite the reverse!!*"

Every one knows the priests who denounced the movement, but Mr. Sullivan had no necessity to know the *good* priests, nor am I going to "inform" on them, nor even tell him the writer of the letter I have quoted from.

This anti-revolution historian further says—"The first leaders of the conspiracy were not men well recommended to Irish confidence."

I hope the schoolboys who read this will not believe a word of it. To my mind it is false history. They were as well known and as well trusted in their several localities as ever the historian was was an anti-revolutionist, and he was known andt rusted before he then.

"And in the venemous manner in which they assailed all who endeavored to dissuade the people from their plot, they showed they had not alone copied the forms, but imbibed the spirit of the continental secret societies."

This should read—" And in the venomous manner in which they assailed me—A. M. Sullivan—because *I* exposed their ' plot,' &c."

The use of the words "plot" and "continental secret societies" show he is familiar with the phraseology of our prosecutors.

" Up to 1864 the Fenian enterprise made comparatively little headway in Ireland. In America, almost from the outset, it secured large support."

This is entirely false. It was quite the other way, and if the men in Ireland had trusted to themselves instead of relying on the "large American support," things might also be another way to-day.

"There was up to the last a fatuous amount of delusion maintained by the 'Head Centre' at this side of the Atlantic, James Stephens, a man of marvellous subtlety and wonderful powers of plausible imposition; crafty, cunning, and quite unscrupulous as to the employment of means to an end."

This is a splendid fling at a fallen enemy of his, whom the enemy of Ireland has banished beyond reaching him. To be "quite unscrupulous as to the employment of means to an end," is what any man must be who expects to fight England successfully. That will be no more than fighting her with her own weapons, and those who learn a true story of Ireland must learn this. Saying which, I take my leave of Mr. Sullivan and his petty, spiteful story.

Looking back at my prison life, and reading over some verses I made while we were mending stockings, I am struck with the freedom of thought we managed to indulge in while the body was closely confined.

I would be afraid here now to speak the opinions that are found in the following lines. I entertained them when I was in prison, and might entertain them still if I was in Ireland. But here in America, where our Irish are less religious than at home, they are, as if to compensate for their falling off, more bigoted ; and where I am less known than in the old land, a fanatic paper here could on the strength of the stray words in these rhymes get up a cry of "Communist" or "Infidel" against me that would get holy people to execrate me.

Nevertheless, as they were my opinions when I was free to hold them, at a time that I had no fear of the world's prejudices depriving me of my daily bread, I give them here:

> Here's a health to the victims of tyranny's wrong,
> Here's a health to the weak who're oppressed by the strong,
> Here's a health to the men, be their creed what it may,
> Who can say "God Save Ireland" wherever they pray.
> > And let them kneel to God above,
> > In church or chapel, kirk or grove,
> > Here's heart and heart, and hope and love,
> > > For Ireland, over the water.
>
> Our long suffering mother is ravished by knaves,
> And, dishonored, she weepingly nurses us slaves,
> The tyrants have made us a hell upon earth,
> And we labor in chains, while they revel in mirth.
> > We'd hardly be more sorely tried,
> > More scattered through the world wide,
> > Had Christ by us been crucified
> > > In Ireland, over the water.
>
> But we're told our misfortunes are owing to our guilt,
> That we're paying for the blood which our forefather's spilt,
> That England to us is the heaven-sent stroke,
> And we strike against God when we strike at her yoke.
> > This teaching finds us blood-red graves,
> > In lands beyond the salt sea waves,
> > And leaves us crouching, cringing slaves
> > > In Ireland, over the water.
>
> It is said, and I think 'tis by Machiavel,
> That tyrants in teaching the Bible excel,
> In order the better to plunder the poor,
> And make them submit to the wrongs they endure.
> > And thus they offer us the Word,
> > They tell us pray and trust the Lord,
> > And then they rob with fire and sword
> > > In Ireland, over the water.
>
> To our ruthless invaders the creed mattered nought,
> They made heaven subserve every conquest they sought,
> And the Catholics sent by the Popes for our pence,
> Just hit us as hard as the Puritan saints.
> > Since Adrian's grant, 'tis fraud, 'tis force,
> > 'Tis Bulls, 'tis bayonets, foot and horse,
> > 'Tis Cullen's or 'tis Cromwell's curse
> > > In Ireland, over the water.
>
> Can the creeds that love freedom and manhood elsewhere,
> Be fruitful of nothing but slavery there?
> Will the "Protestant Boys" never give us a hope,
> But hugging their fetters, afraid of a Pope?
> > Our Pagan sires our strifes would shun,
> > They saw their heaven through the sun,
> > Their God smiled down on every one
> > > In Ireland, over the water.

Our children of Roman and Protestant birth
Proclaim our disgrace through the brothels of earth,
Yet the preachers preach on, we have nothing to do
But to "carry the Cross" and "give Cæsar his due."
    Christ never said 'twas Cæsar's coin,
    The land is ours, then let us join
    Our hearts and hands across the Boyne,
        For Ireland, over the water.

But the bigots start up to prevent the embrace,
And the phantoms of faction are flung in our face,
"To hell with the Pope"—"Hell with William the Third,"
Then like devils we fight "for the love of the Lord."
    The world's contempt rewards our pains,
    We're slaves, and with our very chains
    We batter out each other's brains
        In Ireland, over the water.

This creed of dissension is nursed in the land,
While the creed of our martyrs is prisoned and banned—
Sheares, Crowley, Fitzgerald, Lynch, Duffy, and Tone,
Emmett, Larkin, and Orr died for Ireland alone.
    For Freedom's cause at Freedom's shrine,
    This was the creed of Mike O'Brien,
    Let it be yours as well as mine,
        For Ireland, over the water.

And then for a struggle to end in success—
When the Keoghs will protect us and Cullens will bless,
For 'tis but for failure that "rebels" are damned,
That scaffolds are mounted and prisons are crammed.
    Come North and South our land to save,
    Can't we be Irish, true and brave,
    And neither Rome's nor Englands's slave
        In Ireland, over the water.

CHAPTER XX.

A CHAPTER OF LETTERS—THE BELMONT FUND—T. F. DONOVAN, WM. R. ROBERTS—MAURICE AND KATE SPILLANE—COURTSHIP AFTER MARRIAGE—LOVE AND WAR—MY WIFE'S LETTER TO MR. GLADSTONE AND HIS REPLY—HER LETTERS TO ME AND MY REPLIES—APPREHENSIONS OF BOTH OF US COMMITTING SUICIDE—A ROMANCE OF REAL LIFE.

If a prisoner is interestingly married, the outside world knows very little how much the thoughts of his prison life are occupied by his wife. The chapter of letters before me now reveals a troubled existence in all the moods and tenses of intense suffering. It was a question with us in Ireland whether men who had committed themselves to the cause of revolution should marry at all. I know many who had put off "the happy day" until the war would be over, but I was not one of them. I married when the work was hottest, and the day after I married I started for England and Scotland to meet the men in several towns who were calling for some one from headquarters to visit them. A few months after returning I was sent to Connaught with Edward Duffy, and spent a month there. After returning from Connaught I was sent to America, and when I came back, my wife, who left her father's house again and came to Dublin, must have had very serious doubts as to whether I intended spending a "honeymoon" at all or not. She had very little of my company during the few months preceding my arrest. I was out of house all day, and, in the excitement of the times, let me confess that I was oftener out at night than I need be, so that, looking at my married life, it is not to be wondered at that the memories of a wife, now widowed, troubled and friendless, should speak bitterly to me of her condition.

The letters I will give in this chapter were never written for publication, and, perhaps, never ought to be published. They are essentially private letters, but as some things in them are calculated to give a lesson to "patriots," I don't mind letting the "patriots" see them.

There are a number of Irishmen in America who parade and pic-nic, and pipe and play in honor, or in the name of the Irish cause, and the men who suffer death and imprisonment for it are immortalized in song and speech in every one of their festive gatherings,

Yet the wives and the children of those martyred or suffering men may be starving for bare want of the common necessaries of life for all the paraders or the pic-nickers may care.

I, in prison, should have been spared the pain of thinking my wife or children were neglected, and so should the men in prison still, be spared that pain, and if Irishmen here were what they ought to be—if their professions of love for the cause of the old land were to have corresponding action—they would have some society to provide for the widows and orphans of those who fall fighting for it. Irish-American patriots cannot fight for Irish independence in America, and if they don't assist and encourage those who mean to fight for it in Ireland and England, they do nothing.

Here is my wife's first letter from America. Let the men of the Irish societies read it—the Fenians and the *Clan-na-gael* included—and ask themselves are they doing anything even *yet*, only "*enacting the 'huge humbugs' that have been in course of enaction from time to time?*"

6 DOMINICK STREET, NEW YORK CITY, U. S. A., July 19, '67.

To JEREMIAH O'DONOVAN ROSSA, *from his wife*, M. J. O'D. ROSSA:

MY DEAR HUSBAND: I sit down to write to you in a graver mood than usual. 'Twas only to-day I read the full report of the Commissioners who investigated the prisoners' treatment, and I must confess to a feeling of vexation and annoyance that you should make yourself so conspicuous amongst men who are supposed to be as sensitive of their condition as you, by the number of complaints you make and by the number made against you. What is the use of bringing so many successive punishments on yourself by impotent defiance of a rule that holds you in its grasp? Who can assist you? or what end is to be gained? It seems so boyish a temper you have become possessed of that I should fail to recognize it in the report, if I did not mark the irritation of your feelings in our interview at Millbank, and the manner in which you "took up" every word uttered by the warders.

Before you come to the end of this letter you will come to conclusions regarding the advisability of submitting to any and every discipline of your prison, and of passing in silence the wrongs you or your friends are powerless to avenge. I believe the Government is using a short-sighted policy in preventing State prisoners from hearing how affairs go on in the world outside. I am sick in my soul of the "huge humbugs" that have been in course of enaction from time to time; of the duplicity, the treachery, the heartlessness, the folly that have characterized the past two years in the history of Ireland; the only redeeming feature being the self-sacrifice of a number of honest men who are called zealots and enthusiasts, and well-intentioned fools, for their pains, by half the world.

I speak and will speak as I have never spoken before to you. It is necessary perhaps that you should have some incentive to act in a more rational manner. O'Leary is a proud, sensitive, high-spirited man; so also is Luby. Yet, with admirable dignity, they hold up their heads and take no insult from creatures who are beneath their contempt. This is wise in every sense. They have less reason to be far-seeing and politic than you, for think what reasons have you? Need I set before you the fact that you have six sons—four of them in my father's house—and likely to remain there if the poor man can keep a house over them, for I have failed in getting any provision for them here. Need I remind you that you have a wife—a sorely wronged girl whom you took in her inexperience and world-ignorance, whom you afterwards with open eyes left unprovided for, and who is at present drudging away her life at writing for a pittance, and wearing away her heart at yearning for the infant who finds a mother at the other side of the great ocean? Ah, Rossa, Rossa, look out and think of these things—think which has most trouble, you who took it on yourself and drew it on me, or I, who, depending on your love to do all that was just to me, find myself a married woman without a husband, a child without a parent, and a mother without a child. Steeped to the lips in poverty and misery and labor of heart and head; far from home and in the midst of friends who are hollow, and strangers who are suspicious and critical of my youth—who suffers most? who has most reason of complaint? I against you, or you against the authorities?

Is there any hope before me? I see none except whatever arises from the writ of error or the politic clemency of the Crown. Towards the expenses of that writ of error, let me tell you, the American people, after four weeks of the publishing of Miss Mulcahy's petition, have given not a single cent. That speaks volumes. The families have joined in an appeal and nothing goes home in answer to it, and the West of Ireland is famine-stricken again and America sends no relief there.

The policy of the Government will, I have no doubt, even if the writ of error fail, order your release on conditions after a little time—always considering you have set up no obstacle to its mercy in your own bearing and deportment. Your whole conduct is defiantly in opposition to your captors, it is said. I ask you again, what is the use? You are the conquered, not the conqueror, and true valor is best displayed in gracefully accepting your defeat. If you escaped to-morrow I solemnly tell you *I would not live with you* unless you atoned to me for the past by minding your own family and your own affairs for the future. You told me before our marriage that I could "simulate and dissimulate." Well, you were right. Every day after that 25th of October opened my eyes wider to the madness of our union, but I loved you and I would not pain you by showing my unhappiness. I looked to the future, disbelieving all your talk of prisons and battle-fields, and I hoped for the life I had coveted after your Fenian business was past and gone. Philosophy came to my aid, and I patiently bore what few wives would bear unreproachfully, and I simulated happiness while my heart was sore, to make you happy. After this continue to act against your own interest, if you love it and me so little as to feel inclined to act so. You would never know this much I have written if I did not think it necessary to tell you, lest, mistaking my mind still, you plunge yourself and me into more misery yet. What is the use of my life if it is to be no more than a distant accompaniment to your protracted sufferings, and where do you think will the strength come from that is to help me to bear it? Strength comes of suffering, men say, but times

"My spirit swoons away in hopeless gloom!"

Up to this time I have in public taken firm hold of the chalice of bitterness you filled for me, and I have drank it down with brave eyes and unflinching breath: but if the draught be deeper and deeper still, my breath may fail, my courage strangle me, or my strength desert me. Save me if you can. I have one good angel far across the water that looks through the eyes of my child, my bright little boy. This angel smiles on me through my sleep, and stretches two tiny hands across the sea, lisping my name, and with tiny feet tries to tread the waves that divide me from him and the sunlight, and the fresh spray gleams on his shining child-hair and over the little ruddy face. While this angel lives on earth a firm anchor holds me to life, but if he goes—my heart sickens, and I pray God spare me so deep a grief and leave me my one object to live for. So far my letter can be of little comfort to you, but I cannot in honesty make it pleasanter. You will be angry, I daresay wounded, but I must be satisfied with that too. If you understand me you will believe me that one pain I give is at the cost of ten, twenty, to myself, for I find it easier to *take* than to *give* pain or trouble.

Here I must break off, but—by-and-by I shall recommence and tell you of my voyage out, my reception here, and what I do since.

Ever affectionately, your wife,   M. J.

FRIDAY EVENING.

Some day I may be sorry for having written this letter. I am sorry for writing it now, but I don't see how it could be avoided. When you write do not reproach me for the words I have said. I do not deserve reproach, and I feel so wronged that anything harsh you would say to me would have a contrary effect to what you would intend. A constant falling drop will wear away a stone, and such a drop has been secretly falling on my heart—which is not stone—for the last few years. It is worn very thin, so thin that another hard stroke would break it.

It would be as well if it did break at once and end the struggle; but yet a spirit of wild defiance sustains it in its despair—a violent outcry against the injustice that would make you, who have enjoyed everything enjoyable in the world, be the means of sending me, to whom the earth's greenness has borne no fruit of pleasure yet, heartbroken to the grave. I won't and I can't die while I can live for choosing life.

What a strange perversity of fancy keeps ringing in my head your lines in answer to my "Forget me, Rossa." Can you remember them? Can you remember that poem they were an answer to, or a sequel to? When I left you, after that interview at Millbank, I went to Dublin and straight from there to Clonakilty. I told you Mr. Pigott offered me money for my passage to America, and I took it, trusting to be able to pay it back as soon as I should arrive here. I have not been able to do so; but as that incapacity and its reason enter in the details of my business here I will let it pass till you know of the journey that preceded it.

I reached Clonakilty unexpectedly to Papa; was received with open arms by the family, and expected to remain some time. I had my passage engaged, and only two days at my disposal. That dear child of mine clung to my neck the whole time, and would not take his dear little arms away, and he waked me in the mornings kissing and patting my cheeks with his rosy fists. Oh, the pain of parting with him. I had been away a month from him, and had only these two days to be with him before leaving him—perhaps for years or forever. Mamma was distracted at my coming to a country where there is neither kith nor kin of mine. My father came with me to Queenstown. The morning I left, your letter to my father came. I can't say that either he or I appreciated the arguments you drew to satisfy his mind that what is is best as far as I am concerned. I know of no qualities my misfortunes have developed except my strength of endurance, and every woman is endowed with a share of that. I wrote verses before I married; it would have been better for me had I never written. Whatever the qualities are you think creditable that have been developed in suffering, I would, with all my heart, have preferred they should forever lie dormant, if so I could lead a pleasant and happy life, and escape my present and past misery. On the 30th of May I was put on board the City of Paris, and the last sight of my father is stamped as with mordaunt on my memory, with a grey, careworn look over his face, a wan shadow on his lips, and lights of suppressed anguish in his eyes. I know as well as if I followed him that he went back to the boarding-house on the beach, and locked the sitting-room door I had left, and sat down to the table with his head between his arms to cry out the agony of his fatherly heart!

It chokes me, this memory. My poor, poor father! I was known on board, and very kindly treated. There were American families, returning from a tour on the Continent, and they made the voyage pleasant to me. A Frenchman, who had been an artist, was my good angel. The first day of the voyage, when I was so sea-sick that after crawling on deck I had to lay down beside a lady, a ward of his, who was sick too, and covered up in rugs and furs, he brought me lemons and ice-water, and folded all the spare rugs he could find round me, and so I spent the first day after the evening we started from Queenstown.

The following day I was able to sit up, and the next I was looking about for something to employ my hands or my mind on. The Frenchman gave me pencil and paper, and I sketched roughly a few of the faces on board. The artist was much pleased, and every other day I sat at one side of him, his ward on the other, and much to the amusement of our fellow-voyageurs we caricatured all who staid quiet anywhere in our vicinity. Then chance brought out my fortune-telling propensities, and I had all the ladies and their escorts on board, including three Church of England clergymen, come begging me tell their fortune. To the end of the voyage I had not a moment to spare. The doctor wanted his likeness taken, with an autograph, and I gave him both; and the artist wanted my likeness, and I sat for it; and the stewardess even wanted her fortune told. There was a good library on the ship—a small one—but some good books—and I read, at intervals, "Hard Times," and some other pleasant stories. Other times the Frenchman translated German legends from a beautiful little book he had. In the nights, after supper, we all gathered aft the vessel, and watched the balls of phosphoric fire that rolled in myriads from the white wake of foam. Then, nearing land, there were pleasant promenades, in the starry evenings, up and down the deck. I will for a long time remember the kind words, the gentle advice, a fine old gentleman from Louisville gave me. I say "old," but he wasn't old; he was light-hearted as a boy, generous and cheery and gentlemanly. His sister and his niece were with him, and the great interest they all took in me arose from the fact of my being at Roscrea School with a cousin of theirs, Gertrude Hackett. They were extremely kind to me, and left me addresses and invitations to their places, whenever, if ever, I should be in their vicinity. I could have gone with that family as governess to Mr. C.'s daughters, but that is something I have many chances of doing. I won't go into any family till I know a little more of America. The last day of our voyage was a stormy one; we were in sight of land, and had to put to sea again with the land swell. Then, in the evening, we got into Sandy Hook. 'Twas Sunday, and we all had to stay on board till next day. I felt very lonely as the tender reached the Custom-House. At sea I had been free from trouble—I had breathed; but with the first step on dry land my cares and perplexities returned. I had been said many affectionate adieus by the new friends of my voyage. They seemed to be all friends, and I looked sadly after them as, group by group, they passed away, and I was left alone. The Frenchman saw my luggage safe and ordered me a carriage, then said good-by and took off his charge in another direction. I was just seeing my things safe in the carriage when Tim Donovan came up, and asked me if a Mrs. O'Donovan had come over in the City of Paris? He stepped into the carriage with me, and we drove to Mrs. Healy's, where I remained one week, and was very kindly treated. It was not pleasant to me to live in any house on sufferance, not even in my father's house; and finding I was putting the family to inconvenience, I left Brooklyn and went to board with an American family in Thirteenth street and Second avenue. To do this I should, of course, have money, so I engaged myself to the *Irish People* newspaper, to supply them weekly with poems or stories, under my name (yours), at a salary of $10 a week, equal to £1 10s. of our money at present. This is very trifling to live on here, and as for sparing anything out of it!! Och, hone! as Joan said.

I couldn't get the money even to pay back to Mr. Pigott, and that frets me. My hopes are thrown to pieces concerning the whiskey money. I couldn't get a cent of it. Denis Donovan says the duty, and leakage, and storage, ate it up. I would mention to you the names of many men who called on me all with big professions, none with material aid, but 'twould make a big list, and the authorities might see it objectionable. Of course I told them of the reason of my journey, all about the children, &c., but civility and a welcome to the hospitality of their house was all I could get from the warmest of your friends here.

" 'Twas very hard the children should be in such a bad way." " 'Twas wonderful they weren't seen to,"—" awful charge for a young woman," &c., &c., without end, but everybody's business is nobody's business, and I got lots of advice and pity, but no assistance. The boarding-house in Thirteenth street I found too expensive for my light purse, so I moved over here to Dominick street, an humble neighborhood, and a house more home-like to me, as they are Clonakilty people who rent it, and they knew my father before I was born. James is here, but his neck troubles him very much. Prison food brought on an ulcer in it. Poor boy, he, too, is the victim of " hard times." All I could do or all he could do, couldn't get him a situation, such a world of hypocrisy and hollowness is it! Just as to me, he was made ever so many promises of employment, but his patrons forgot their words. I met a brother of yours here. He said your mother and all belonging to you in this country enjoyed good health. If you choose to write to your family next, I shall be satisfied to waive my claim to a letter.

I was at Patrick Downing's place in Newark, and if his circumstances would admit I believe I might expect he would help your children. He is a spirited, generous fellow, but his family is increasing and he has not made his fortune yet. I like him well. Denis Sullivan of the *Irish People* has treated me kindly. Him, too, I believe to be sincere, but his circumstances are not too flourishing.

Col. Denis F. Burke and his family have shown me much friendship, but they are only recovering from the reverses suffered through connection with Fenianism. Their kindness is limited to hospitality and the best of good wishes.

I write as much as I can, and presently I shall see if I can't get in on other papers or periodicals besides the *Irish People*.

Mr. Meehan promised to get me into a fancy store as saleswoman, if I chose to go into business. I will write and look round me awhile. I may presently be able to send for your children, and they will be taken to trades or business here without fee.

I may go down to St. Louis to be near these cousins of mine. All the places in the world are the same to me. I have no tie to any part, but I think it would be pleasant to live near relatives. I don't think I have any more to say, only I got a letter from my father and one from Tim since I came here, and I wrote home once. You will wonder why I did not write long before this. I just wished to know what I'd have to say to you from here. I'm six weeks in the country now. The first week I thought 'twas a splendid place, and the second I grew suspicious of big promises; the third I felt cynical and bitter, and so on every day adding to my heart-sickness, and winding in on myself as if I were a spool of silk that had witlessly unrolled and was being shrunk up again by the motion of the world and its frost. I expect you'll write me, when you do write, in a cold strain, to punish me for having different opinions from yours on several points in this letter. I'd say " forgive," but I don't feel I have done anything to be forgiven. I have not room to argue, you see, and must only sign myself fondly and truly

Your wife,   M. J.

One passage of this letter vexed me somewhat. I did not like that my wife should think of me in such a manner as it suited the English Government to represent me to the world. Knox and Pollock would not bring me face to face with my accusers; they would do nothing to do me justice; their duty was to whitewash the Government and blackwash me; and to be asked "if I could not act in a rational manner," or "act like Mr. Luby, or Mr. O'Leary," was something that annoyed me, when I had no chance of explaining or replying.

I was allowed pen and paper to write to my wife, and when I had written the letter it would not be let out, because it contained the explanation I thought proper to give. To nurse my wrath would be only to burn myself up, and as there was no use at all in my committing such a suicide, I began to grow callous regarding what the world, or the wife, or the warders should think of me. Some one tells us, when misfortune hits us hard, the best way to bear it is to hit hard at something else in return, and I will allow my experience to indorse the wisdom of the counsel.

A year and a half elapsed before I heard from my wife again. During this time I wrote two or three letters to her; but, as I harped on the same strings, they were again suppressed. Her prospects, during this time, were growing brighter, and her letter is not so gloomy as the last. She had been turning her talents to some account in earning an independent livelihood, and was beginning to entertain the foolish notion of getting me out of prison by going to law with the devil, when she would have earned a sufficient amount of money to employ counsel.

She puts me into a corner when she says, "Tell me have you really grown so indifferent regarding what I may think or feel at your silence, that you make no effort to win the good-will of your jailers, or the favors extended to your companions in misery?"

At the time I received this letter my jailers were hitting me pretty hard. It was just after they had been chaining and trampling me under foot, and I was not in the humor to write very kindly of them, or very forgetfully of their treatment. I wrote, but this letter shared the fate of the others. Another was suppressed when I tried, six months after; but the next half-yearly letter was allowed to pass.

UTICA, N. Y., December 13, 1868.

MY DEAR LOVE: I do not know why I write to you to-night unless it is that I feel more than unusually "lonely and alone," and memory has been preaching to me little sermons from your life and mine. I have not been fit to write to you for a long, long time. My heart is in the state of a dormant volcano—by avoiding thoughts of you or my child I avoid an eruption; by reflecting a moment on my more than three years' widowhood and my far-away baby, my soul is shaken to its deepest depths—my heart convulsed to the core with discontent. Well, I will not talk of that now. I am taking the only measures my judgment can approve to mend the faults of fortune, and have now at least a partial certainty of success. It would be a long story to tell you, how I came to adopt the profession of elocution. If you ever get free, or if I ever again unrestrainedly meet you without warders by to listen to and comment on my confessions, I'll give you the history of these three long years, years as long as ordinary lifetimes, years that I never expected human endurance could outlive. The little raft of resolution that floated in from the wreck of my fortune three or four years ago, has run steadily on the waves of life. It will soon, I hope, be strong enough to bear you up too. To depart from parallels, I have been giving public readings for some months, and intend continuing to do so till I have acquired a sufficient sum of money to justify me in engaging counsel to re-open your case and appeal it to the House of Lords. You need not think I am "begging" in your name; even if I could descend to that, people's hearts are closed, and I'd be losing time in trying to open them. am earning honestly my income and have gone through a careful training, have studied my role scrupulously, so that at least no one could call me an amateur reader or a very inferior one.

I am excessively impatient to have a line from you. How do I know but you have mentally buried me and caused a resurrection of your dead loves? If what the Governor said was true about your breaking the rules so often, you certainly did not, or do not, care to write to me. I don't mean to write a long letter until I know. Tell me any ideas you may have yourself as to how I could serve you, and *tell me have you really grown so indifferent regarding what I may think or feel at your silence that you make no effort to win the good will of your jailers, or the favors extended to your companions in misery?*

I cannot tell you any home news, as I had not a letter for some time, nor any answer to my two last, and they told me in their last that baby had the whooping cough. Denny wants me to bring him out here. I am writing to him by this mall to get ready for the journey. John is bound to Mr. Lawless, and the two next are at school, I believe, and boarding with Mrs. Duff; I'm not sure. I have no direct way of knowing, as my success in the New World seems to have made me some bitter female enemies at home, and not having ever had many Dublin friends dear enough to correspond with, I'm not always posted on matters occuring there. I enclose my likeness, taken a month ago. I wonder, if you were out and free now, would you love me as well as you did four years ago. I am changed, Caries—harder, imperious, selfwilled and irritable at times. I should love you better now if you have not been spoiled in prison. There is no man living, if I were free to choose, I could love better. Comparison with all the best men in Ireland or America would not injure you; on the contrary, you appear brighter in the scale. But there were some points in your character the little woman of '65 bore most patiently. I would not promise the same forbearance from the matured, self-willed and exigent woman of '68. But I suppose there's time enough to settle the question when you are out of prison.

Faithfully and affectionately, your wife,
MARY J. O'DONOVAN ROSSA.

CHATHAM PRISON, November 2d, 1869.

Well, Mollis, what's the matter with you? It looks as if "absence makes the heart grow fonder" was to be knocked into *smithereens* by us; that is, if we are to judge by our correspondence, or rather by the absence of yours, for I have made some efforts to convey to you at least an assurance of your engaging a fair share of "my thoughts by day and my dreams by night," as the old love-letters say: But my efforts have failed, my letters have not reached you; you begin to fear that I have forgotten you, and you cease to write. Your father tells me these are your fears.

Your own letter of the 13th Dec., '68, tells me so too. I cannot tell you how much I would admire the stand-off dignity of such a passage in your letter as this, were I not so intimately concerned in it: "If what the Governor said was true about your breaking the rules so often, you certainly did not, or do not, care to write to me. I don't mean to write you a long letter until I know;" and as I haven't been able to let you know, you haven't written me either a long or a short letter since. Neither can I now let you know if what the Governor said was true or not. It is for trying to do such things as this that six or seven letters which I wrote for you have been suppressed, and I mean to let the authorities have it all their own way now, and say nothing particular of the past, which would prevent this from reaching you. Your memory is not so bad as not to recollect I told you at that Millbank visit to write to me every two months whether you heard from me or not, and you have written once in two years. Our short married life perhaps did not afford you time enough to know me thoroughly, and probably you may incline to think that my true character is that given by my enemies; yet I do not believe this is so. But why do I say it? Just to give you a bit of a scolding. Should fate place us together again, I should like my happiness to be such as it has been, but you would have to do some great penance to atone for your distrust of my affection.

"How do I know but you have mentally buried me and caused a resurrection of your dead loves?" I recollect your giving me a touch of this once before in the world. I suppose the thought disturbs all men and women who marry "relicts." I have been thinking how to meet this poser of yours, and I could not find a better way than that of asking you, Would your affection for your first-born be divided if he had a little brother? But enough of this now. Your father has, I dare say, sent you my letter, and I am expecting an answer from you every day, consequent upon the receipt of that by you. From the way things were going when I saw you at Millbank I thought I would have to give myself a little ease [by paying little attention to regulations, which seemed to me to have no aim but my annoyance, and a month or so after I saw you I let a little of this gas escape which was burning within me. One day I had my task of work done some ten minutes before the appointed time, and, waiting to have the officer arrive with a fresh lot, I took a book in my hand. I was seen in this position by that jolly gentleman who superintended our interview, and I was punished for idleness. This was the last straw on the camel's back, and I pitched their rules and regulations to Jericho for a time. Of course, the laws had to be enforced and I had to take the consequence. But I felt relieved, and "the fever burning at the core" burned less fiercely. Only for I relieved myself this way I would undoubtedly have consumed myself away—eaten myself. It was a sanitary measure on my part, one necessary to preserve, or at least to prolong, my life. I had not that devotion either for my country or for my wife that Judy Flanagan's lover had for her, when he professed himself willing to "die for her sake." I would rather live for my loves—you and your rival. You understand I have in my mind your poem of "He told me he loved another beside." Mr. Fagan, the Director, told me "they would probably allow me to get those poems of yours if the book was sent, but your father has, it seems, lost the two copies of them which came to Ireland. If you would come to Ireland as your father expects about Christmas, you may desire to see me. I have spoken to the Director about the matter; he says there would be no difficulty placed in your way. Only that you would take it as an encouragement on my part, I would ask to have a ticket sent to you, but really I do not wish you should incur any expense in doing so. A look at me for twenty minutes would do you no good. Don't think by my saying this I have lost any of my beauty or affection. No, Mollis. Hal and John Devoy say I am as handsome as I was the day you fell in love with me, and I don't feel any loss or diminution of the other quality if you would only be reasonable. And I am sure I was very fond of you, but I admit, as I said in the suppressed letters, that I had a very queer way of showing it. I also admit there would be room to make you feel happier, in my conduct towards you from the altar to the prison, but you would fail in any effort of a similar nature towards me. I have often reflected when feeling the dreariness of solitary confinement, how much of it I gave you in Dublin, and how uncomplainingly you endured it. I recollect you were sick one Sunday; I got some medicine for you; I then went out and left you alone till dinner hour. This was almost cruel, and you took it as a matter of course that I had to be out and never grumbled. I understood that I was trespassing rather too much on a wife's privileges at the time. Your "feigning to be happy to make me so" had the desired effect, and made me fonder of you too. Whether I am ever to return you the compliment, God alone knows. I got the letter you wrote to me after your arrival in America, and the poem wherein you allude to your "fossil heart." I got a photograph that accompanied your last letter. I have it fixed on the back of the door—a queer place you will say—but my habits here are such that I keep my door ever shut when at home, and then you are looking over the whole house and its sole occupant. I think I addressed you a couple of times with the salutation, "Ah, you are dead—Mollis." The four boys sent me a photograph of them, too. I have it not in my cell, but I can occasionally get a look at it upon application. Croum is not himself in it, but the others I recognize. Mr. Lawless asked me if I would signify to him my approval of your sending those boys to school to Belgium, and I told him I had already signified to you, repeatedly, that they were at your disposal if you could do anything for them. But I cannot understand the matter. There is something in it to be explained. Can you enlighten me? You cannot have as much money as would insure the continuance of such a course of education. Public funds cannot be so plentiful as to obtain for all the children of my fellow-sufferers such attention, and I do not like for mine more than others can have. Of course, I would like them to have a good education, but with the loss of my ability to do a father's part I surrender the right to speak in affairs that depend on finances. From your father I learn that the squabbles of party have brought you into the ugly circle of contention, too. This I regret as much as I regret anything. I should wish you had kept outside all those disputes. Perhaps you deemed it necessary to secure audiences to adopt a party; if so, it is deplorable. But when you are on your own resources I must give you liberty of opinion, and cannot be thinskinned on the subject of my wife becoming a manly character. As to disputes regarding your father's treatment of the children, I suppose those are what you allude to in your letter of last December. When you become a public speaker or reader you enter that life which excites animadversion, and you must make up your mind to take all the disagreeableness of the position with a strong mind. Let me know all you can. Send me a copy of the worst things that have been said of you. In your letter of July, '67, you said a few things which were hard, such as asking why I could not conduct myself in prison like Mr. Luby, Mr. O'Leary, and others, who were high-spirited men. They (the hard things) might not be so hard if I could tell you why, but when my mouth was sealed the most painful thing to me was to find myself spoken to in this manner. I have no objection that you would open the sorrows of your heart to me, and if you wish to reproach me with neglect of the worldly welfare of my family that is all fair enough, *but have nothing to say about my prison conduct; you can have only one side of the story.* You have not yet had replies to things you asked me three years ago when I was in Portland. Well, some of them remained in my mind, and I will strike them off here.

The unpleasantness between you and Denis O'Donovan—I was to blame for that. I, in Richmond, led you to think that he owed me money, as I wished to have, through him, what was due to me in the office; and the Governor of the prison being watching every word that dropped from me, after the arrests that time, I was not able to convey to you what was the exact thing I meant. Den. acted kindly towards me—I cannot forget that. I did not get the letter he sent you, and I must scold him for writing to you so harshly as he did. If anything remained to be settled between us it could not be more than a few dollars. The amount due to me at the office, when that was pounced upon, was £75 or so; and if that was not paid to you, privately or personally, it has been paid fourfold by the public in the maintenance of my children since, and that is the way I would wish you to look at it. From your father's letters to Halpin and Warren I learned much about you, when I could learn nothing directly myself.

I suppose you have met Col. Warren since his release. We would be more lively if we had him amongst us, but I dare say he prefers to be out. I believe the last words I said to another companion, named Costello, were to write my remembrance to you, if he got himself outside the prison walls at any time. Do not waste money, if you have any to spare, by attempting to get me out of prison by an appeal to the House of Lords. You may as well, as I said to your father, throw your purse into the deep, and say, "See, Cariss, what I do for love of you."

By-the-by, Mollis, I have, these months past, been looking over Italian, and I think of you, of course, when I meet your words. I cannot study hard. About this time twelve months I felt some disagreeableness, up to that unknown to me—a pain in the spine, which became more active whenever I became more studious or contemplative. I bothered the doctor for the first three or four months about it, but he seemed to think nothing of it. I suppose he, in the enlightenment of his profession, only sees in it the natural consequence of this discipline, and I have ceased to be uneasy at its recurrence. Only for it I could enjoy this place now, as I have got some books lately which were not available before.

The Protestant Chaplain has kindly lent me his own Irish Bible, with the permission of the priest. Both are Irishmen, and if permitted to speak of them it would be kindly. They grace the names of O'Sullivan and Duke, and hail from Cork and Kerry. The priest is from Castletown Berehaven. I have read a German grammar this year also, but the other three years of my time go for nothing. Your father says you were in Boston, preparing for a tour to Canada. That is Warren's locality, and if you did not call to see him, he, I am sure, called to see you. He must have made a great "spread" in Cork last Patrick's Day. I had a visit a few days after from Mr. Dowling, and he seemed to think that Colonel Warren played the deuce with our prospect of freedom. Other visitors after followed up in the same strain. But to us this is all moonshine. I think I said to one of my visitors, who asked my opinion on the matter, that if Mr. Warren acted illegally the law was at hand to call him to account, and as to what he would say out of prison injuring us in prison, we were in the hands of magnanimous England, etcetera, and so forth. If our masters cannot manufacture better excuses than such as that they are losing their genius. I believe it is Gibbon says that an enemy respects you in proportion as you arouse his fears. Setting out from this, we try to flatter ourselves a little, "and suck up as much honey as we can out of this vinegar life." It would appear that we are not altogether the despicable, worthless characters which our enemies would represent us. The censors of my letter ought not object to that word "enemy" being used by me. The world has ever used it to express the relations that exist between the conqueror and his victim. I should dearly wish to see all Irishmen and Englishmen in the position of friends. Tell me everything, big and little, about yourself—your pecuniary resources, income and expenditure, etc. I suppose you are aware that I am now located with strangers, I may say—that is, I have none of the old companions of '65.

* * * * * *

The three first came here from America. I wish we had O'Leary and Luby amongst us, now that we are allowed to talk somewhat, but then my wishes could not be realized without depriving others of the pleasure of their company. We are at in-door work all Summer, and only for the cloud of dust around us, it would be more agreeable in Winter than out-door labor. We are mending stockings which, supposed to be clean, are anything but that—at least they do kick up a dust amongst us. We bear with each others' infirmities pretty tolerably.

The only question we cannot agree upon is—how far God interferes or interferes not in the government of the petty things of earth? One points to the passage in Scripture which says that God delivers one people over to another in punishment of their sins, and another, to put a crusher on Him, says: "Now, can you tell me if any of our Milesian ancestors were present and assisted the Jews at the Crucifixion of Christ?" Then the subject can go no further, and we take an hour's exercise. Someway, I cannot write here without feeling sick. The restraint, the effort to avoid some things and seek other things, agrees not with my present constitution. People like to be quoted, and as want of space obliges me to conclude now, I will do so with one of your expressions, and say, "I will not write you a long letter until I know," &c. You will have seen my letter to your father ere you receive this, and I have said in that something for you which needs not repetition here. Give my remembrance to all my friends. Good by, Mollis. God bless you. Be strong.

Yours affectionately, as ever,
JER. O'DONOVAN ROSSA.

In the month of February, 1870, a few months after writing this letter, I had a visit from my wife. There was much talk in the newspapers about an amnesty, and friends had been telling her that we were very stubborn in prison, and would listen to no terms of release; that the Ministry could not be the first to knock under, and that it only needed an approach from the prisoners' friends, with a request for release, to get a favorable answer from Mr. Gladstone.

When I heard my wife was coming on such a mission as this I felt a little trouble-minded. The authorities had been trying during four or five years to reduce me to the level of a thief or pickpocket, and I had been trying to show them they could never succeed. I could write a "petition" myself, and did write some, but to have any one else write or say anything for me is what I would not allow; and when one so near to me as my wife was to write or speak in the matter it would, of course, be taken for granted that she spoke with authority, and, though I had some opinion of her ability to state her case honorably, I could not divest myself of a very uncomfortable anxiety lest anything should be said that would give my enemies satisfaction.

When we met in Chatham I grumbled some doubts as to the propriety of her interfering with "the cause of justice," and she gave me every promise and assurance she would do or say nothing that wasn't Irish and manly. How far she has kept that promise may be judged by the following, which I copy from a scrap-book of hers:

SKETCH OF MY LIFE SINCE 1867—MRS. O'DONOVAN ROSSA—PART III.

There is no reason why I should not tell the terms I was prepared to make for my husband's release. They were honorable enough to meet the approval of the most unbending patriot, and I supposed them complaisant enough also to meet the views of the reputedly merciful Premier. They are contained in the letter copied here which when Mr. Gladstone refused to see me, I laid in Mr. Motley's hands to be by his kindness personally delivered to Mr. Gladstone.

COPY OF MY PROPOSITION TO THE PREMIER REGARDING THE RELEASE OF MY HUSBAND.

LONDON, 15th Feb'y, 1870.

To the Rt. Hon. W. E. GLADSTONE, M. P.:

SIR: You have denied me the favor of a personal interview, and I feel deeply disappointed at that denial. I have traveled more than 3,000 miles in mid-winter for the sole purpose of pleading a cause which you will not hear—the cause of a husband, to whom, were he a sinner against any other government than that of England, or native of any other sod than that of Ireland, I have no doubt your ready sympathy would flow, in recognition of his sacrifices and sufferings for principle and liberty.

This is not the tone in which I should be advised by a practiced advocate to address you, but I am not a practiced advocate, only a young Irishwoman and Rossa's wife, who, even in the depth of her humility and disappointment, cannot find it in her heart to say anything unworthy of her husband or of the cause that he endeavored to advance.

On the other hand, I have no wish to write a single word in vindication of my husband's conduct in anything which the law under which he suffers has condemned. It would be unbecoming in me to advance anything, even in my husband's favor, which it would be contrary to your duty to entertain; nor dare I hope that any words of mine could convince you of the justice, the wisdom, and the policy of releasing my husband from confinement, if your sense of State necessity has suggested an opposite course. But, as far as I can gather from the expressions that have proceeded from your Government on various occasions, it would appear that your resolution in the matter is founded not upon the necessity of inflicting further punishment upon the political prisoners still remaining in confinement, but upon the danger that would result to the public peace by setting them at large. I cannot deny, even to my own mind, that there may be some reason in this view of the case; but I anxiously hope that I have found a solution of the difficulty, which I venture to submit to your sense of generosity and justice.

In my recent visit to my husband at Chatham I solicited and obtained from him the assurance, that to regain his personal liberty he would be willing to submit to any terms, not inconsistent with his personal honor and character, that the Government might propose. He would consent to leave these islands forever under penalty of arrest and forfeiture of his pardon in case of his return without permission. He would prefer to go to America because I have made that country my home; but if the Crown should insist that exile to any other part of the globe should be the price of his freedom, he is still willing to accept the condition, and I am willing to share it.

These terms were extended to Mr. Hamilton Rowan and several others implicated in the insurrection of 1798 by the government of that day, and they were not found to have endangered the peace of the country. It is to be hoped that justice has not grown more unrelenting, or the quality of England's mercy more strained, since that period. Whatever danger might be apprehended in the release of my husband and his fellow prisoners in this country, their influence could not contribute a feather's weight to the balance of good and evil throughout the world, and to whatever part of the world you may assign us a resting place we are ready to take our way.

In submitting this proposal to your consideration. I entreat you to bear in mind that I anxiously, though patiently, await the result; and while feeling miserably unequal to the task of influencing your judgment on such a subject, I yet humbly address my prayers to God that He may show you some way by which you can reconcile your desire to be merciful with your sterner sense of state policy and state justice.

I have the honor to be, sir, your most obedient servant,

MARY J. O'DONOVAN ROSSA.

P. S.—I am about to visit my relatives in Ireland, and trusting a communication may reach me there from you, I append my Irish address,

MRS. O'DONOVAN ROSSA,
Strand House, Clonakilty Co., Cork, Ireland.

MR. GLADSTONE'S REPLY.

11 CARLTON HOUSE TERRACE, S. W., 18 March, 1870.

MADAM: Circumstances not under my own control compelled me to announce in the House of Commons last night, at very short notice, what I should have preferred to communicate to you in the first instance individually and privately—this, namely, that we are forbidden by considerations of public duty to allow any further release of political prisoners until we can procure such a change in the condition of Ireland as shall afford a greater degree of peace and security to the people of that country, now in several parts of it exposed to violence, distracted by alarm, and apprehensive of a dissolution of many of the ties by which society is bound together.

During the interval since I wrote to you I have made inquiry to learn whether there were any particulars which would enable the Government to draw a line in favor of your husband without injustice to others, but I grieve to say I have been unable to discover any particulars of such a character.

You will be well able to appreciate the gravity of the considerations which have weighed upon my mind and the minds of my colleagues and I hope you may join with us at least in earnestly desiring the arrival of better days.

I remain, Madam, your very faithful servant,
W. E. GLADSTONE.

MRS. O'DONOVAN ROSSA.

I have nothing to say to this reply of Mr Gladstone's, but I was so uneasy at my wife having anything to say that I wrote her this a few days after she had visited me:

FRIDAY, February 18th, 1870,
CHATHAM PRISON.

MY DEAR WIFE: Now that your visits and yourself are gone, the afterthoughts come to remind me of how often I interrupted you, and how a few times I made remarks which you did not appear to take as I meant. With a view that you may fully understand me, I have asked and received permission to write to you. In the solitude of this cell I can arrange myself in better order to convey my thoughts than under the bewildering influence of your presence during those angel visits. I did not let you tell me thro' what channel you got a letter from Mr. Fish to Mr. Motley, requesting him to use his good offices in my favor, or who or what put this idea into your head—not the idea of releasing me, but that of having a friendly interference thro' this means which would promote your object. When you told me at your first interview that Mr. Motley promised you an interview with Mr. Gladstone, and when I said that I did not see how you could honorably interfere, I fancied your brow darkened a little, and I thought I may as well let you have your experience, as you were confining yourself to what I stated in my letter to your father regarding what passed between me and McCarthy Downing. When I questioned the propriety of your interference, it resulted from supposing that Mr. Gladstone was not disposed to countenance my release on conditions of leaving the country, with an understanding that I was liable to be recommitted to prison if found afterwards in England or Ireland without the permission of the British Government; and I have a serious objection to see you in the position of offering what there was no intention of accepting. This I believe is the substance of my reply to Mr. Downing last March, when he asked me if I would leave the country, and told me the Government would never release me unless I did. I sent for him to see if he would—as he could in a legitimate manner—clear the way for my suppressed letters to reach you; but he turned upon this subject, and thinking he had some intimation from some authority to interfere, I felt no hesitation in replying to him, and was particular to put my words in writing. He visited me again in July, and told me he made no use yet of the paper I gave him; that he held it as private, tho' I told him I did not begrudge the world to know it. I felt myself in a false position, for I unwittingly laid myself open to have it said that I had given Mr. Downing a private authorization to intercede for my release, and I then wrote to your father directing him to withdraw the paper from Mr. Downing. You have got that letter of mine to your father, and as you tell me that your letter to Mr. Gladstone contains nothing more than what I have stated to Mr. Downing, I have no fear that the honor of old Ireland is compromised by what you have done. Yet you say that having signified to some of my friends in America your intention of paying me a visit and making an endeavor to know if my release could be obtained by my going there, they seemed to think that I should not leave prison on such conditions. By Jove, they are spunkey. I would like, too, to act spiritedly if I could see any object to be obtained by it; but when my blood is not up to the mark I cannot act. I have met hundreds of men who would die for Ireland, but I have often lamented my own deficiency in this respect. I could never work myself up to more than a resolution to risk life, and then even permeated with a strong hope and desire of living. Nature does much for many. I am weak, and whatever I may think of leaving Ireland before conviction, once I find myself in England with 9549 on my arm I find myself also holding the opinion that I do nothing dishonorable or demoralizing by getting rid of the badge, if my masters allow me the choice of doing so by leaving the country. Doing such a thing as this would not, I think, be deemed improper in the Frenchman, the Italian, the Pole, or any other nationality in chains. "But," as the poet asks, "Where is the nation can rival old Erin," &c., &c. You told me you were going home and coming to London again in a fortnight's time, I did not ask you what engagements were bringing you back, and I can only guess that it is in furtherance of my release. If so, I do not approve of it. You say that tho' the Government may be disposed to let me go by leaving the country—as is the opinion of some of your friends—that it would be *beneath* the dignity of a government to propose such a thing to a prisoner; and if I were willing to avail of the conditional liberty, it may be *above* the dignity of my position to make it known; and here between the two you make a place for yourself, and, as a wife, claim a right to interest yourself. While you do nothing more unreasonable than this, I can not place a veto upon your interference. You have written to Mr. Gladstone, and he it is to be presumed, will give you a reply, and if that does not meet your proposal I am decidedly averse to your proceeding further. Perhaps, now that my friends would compliment me with parliamentary honors, the most polite way for me to put it is, that I do not wish you should seek any influence to embarrass the Minister by pressing him to do what he does not intend doing. When you told me my election was annulled by Parliament, but that some of the Irish members were of opinion that the proceeding was illegal and were to have lawyers' advice on the matter, you seemed not to catch the spirit in which I said that the issue was of little concern to me. I meant that any honor conferred on me was that conferred by the people of Tipperary, and any compliment or meaning their vote conveyed was not changed to me by a vote of the House of Commons. Of course if the verdict of my peers in Tipperary were to set aside the verdict of a Dublin jury, the decision that my election was legal, and that as the choice of the constituency I should be allowed freedom of action, would not be a matter of little concern to me, tho' circumstances might not contribute to my enjoyment of that very select society to which Tipperary would introduce me. You let me know once that you had your share of what you called "wife pride." Is it strong still—strong enough to aid you in your hard struggle thro' life? Summon it to your assistance in this emergency. In one of your poems you ask, "But who can love and be wise?" Some of the ancient poets say it is a faculty not often given to the Gods, and with your knowledge of this weakness which accompanies affection, I have rather a firm trust that you will "suffer calmly and be strong."

Our countrymen seem not to be uninterested in our fate, and I am satisfied to let that be decided by the issue of those events over which I have no control. I recommended you not to spend any time at home beyond what you intended. I did this apprehensive of that sickness of heart to you which is caused by deferred hope. The Minister may not answer you decisively, and some of his admirers may suggest to you an unendurable waiting. The wisdom of a Solon advised Governors to keep the people always expecting something, and the people, afraid of losing that something, would be sure to do nothing. Do not, Mollis, waste your energies in this manner, by feeding at the feet of the British Lion on hopes which may be vain. Do not, on the other hand, imagine that I hurry you to America, thoroughly approving of the career awaiting you there. It is some satisfaction to me to know that, thrown on your own resources, you can obtain an honorable livelihood, but, however much your ability and success in public reading may have pleased me, you must grant me the possession of a little husband pride, and that it is not without its alloy of humiliation when I see you "on the stage." But we cannot have the roses without the thorns. I do not know if all husbands feel as I do, but I will confess that my soul is sometimes shaken at seeing a wife that I am rather fond of in a position of life where the most exemplary conduct also requires a shield of the most guarded behavior to protect her from the idle tongue of society. In my parting letters I told you not to tread the ground heavily, to meet the world with as light a heart as you could afford to carry, and I repeat it now, for I have never doubted but that you would fight the hard battle with all safety to your honor and mine. Mr. Fagan visited the prison on Wednesday, and I asked him permission to write two letters to you—one now, and one in reply to one you promised to write to me, and he granted my application. I then spoke of your intention to visit London ere you departed for America, and your expressed intention to try to see me again, and he was good enough to tell the Governor to admit you if you came. I have said before that I am averse to your coming to London if you have no business but to try to get possession of me. I do not presume to have a right or authority to issue *peremptory* commands to you, and in anything I say do not understand that I am speaking peremptorily. I resign the title to speak so with my inability to provide for you, and with the necessity that obliges you to have recourse to your own resources for maintenance. You have entitled yourself to a certain liberty of action, to a right to use your own mind instead of mine in anything you think proper to do, bearing in mind that any liberty which would restore you to me without a name unsullied, such as when you were torn from me, would be a liberty which I could not well enjoy. Our short married life furnishes the most precious gem to my "Sorrow's crown of sorrow," and any visions of the future that steal upon me through these prison bars are woven in with you. If the visions are not to be realized, why then—life is short, the shuttle flies fast, and the silken thread will come to an end nearly as soon as the rougher one that has had experience of the hackle. A few moments only between the Minister and me, the Queen and you, all to receive whatever—let us hope—the mercy of God is pleased to visit us within a world different from this. Do not imagine I want to put a sad thought into your mind. Some friend of mine was friendly enough to give you to understand I cared very little for my domestic associations, and this perhaps tended to nourish that cold, hard feeling towards me, which the absence of my letters had, as you said in yours, planted in your heart. What can I get to express my feelings on this head? Well, only this: That if the spiritual heads of our three creeds, the Popes of England, Rome and Scotland were to visit me in my cell and say, "Rossa, in the blessedness of union, the mysteries of the future have been revealed to us, and in the fullness of spiritual authority we come to offer you a choice of two things: one is, an immediate translation to the paradise of the next life with an eternity of bliss, and the other, a restoration to your wife and children with a darkness thro' which no human eye can penetrate, which will you choose?" I would say, "By your Majesties' leave, the poor little woman might go distracted at hearing that, with my own free will, I left her a lone widow; I'll go to see her, and trust to the mercy of Heaven to lead us thro' the darkness into light."

It surprised me to learn you had no communication with Mr. Lawless about sending the children to school to Belgium. Last July he told me you wanted my permission to have it done. I told him you ought to know, you were at full liberty to act in matters of that kind, but could not see how you were to ensure a permanency, and he did not enlighten me. This I now see was part of the movement that got you to interfere in that lawsuit, and I hope you will profit by the knowledge of it. Young Tim's opinion of me, as seen by his letter, is not a very flattering one; for his mother's sake I will not think any thing harder of him. I suppose legal zeal is hold to excuse everything. I read James Cody's letter and yours; both contain some mistakes. He says that I got ten per cent. interest for money I lent the Irish people. I thought that any Callan man would not think so of me. I do not approve of your thinking to provide for the children who are in Dublin; you could not assure anything permanent. National sympathy is more enduring, and as it has taken the children of imprisoned Irishmen under its charge, I would be expressing a false pride if I said I felt much humiliation at mine being so provided for.

I miss three poems from your book, the Landscape, the Marriage, and an unfinished one which contained, to my mind, a beautiful decription of Glengariff scenery. The editor considered the Marriage good, and intended to publish it, but as you say you almost forget the reality, I must not wonder at your loss of the poetry of it. I do not know that you would now write "What care I?" Whatever I am prepared to concede to you in the way of superiority, Mollis, there is one thing which I cannot concode, and that is the faculty of your loving me as much as I do you. Rid myself of this presumption and do not again fall into the heresy of thinking of me as you have done, of believing what every one is pleased to say of me. Write and tell me as much as you can what you intend doing, &c., &c. The poem "In the Prison," contains a hard line: "Shall base desertion of my country-friend." John Devoy is one of my companions here, and one of those who was led to adopt the course that brings him under this line, and if you asked me to point out a few men who would lose their heads before betraying country or friend, the first, perhaps, I would pick out, would be John Devoy. Change this line if you bring out a second edition. Of course you will remember me to all my friends. I wonder Donchadh has not answered my letter to him. Good-bye. May God bless and strengthen you. Tim grew wonderfully big, entirely out of proportion with that moustache of his. I suppose all your brothers and sisters have moved forward also. If you would not be jealous, I would desire particular remembrance to Isabella. I suppose your little son has grown big, too.

Yours, dear Mollis, ever fondly,
JER. O'DONOVAN ROSSA.

STRAND HOUSE, CLONAKILTY, COUNTY CORK, April 27th, 1870.

MY DEAR ROSSA: You are annoyed with me, naturally and justly, for my seeming negligence in writing to you. I do not know what excuse to form, for I am ignorant of any that ought to be sufficient to exonerate me from my guilt of procrastination. I have put off from day to day the letter I intended to write you, each night thinking "I will surely write to-morrow," and each morrow finding me either beginning a letter doomed to remain unfinished, or so engrossed with the usual occupations of my position as a servant of the public that no time remained to write. Now I am home for a week or two with a tiresome throat affection, I have neither business nor fatigue to prevent the fulfillment of this little duty, and so I begin.

What do you suppose I have been doing all day?—cleaning an old broken picture of yours ('twas broken in Cork the day you last sailed for America), and dispatching it with voluminous directions and an exact description of the color of your eyes, hair, beard and complextion to an eminent artist, that he may get me a decent oil painting from it, to console me, now that Mr. Gladstone refuses to give me the original. And if you only knew where that little Cork picture has been all the time! Do you remember any young lady who would feel so deep an interest in you that she would not scruple to bribe a servant to steal it from my unoccupied room at home for her; and after "illegal" possession of it for a couple of years, would find her conscience—quickened in view of a journey to the other side of the Atlantic—urging her to disgorge her unlawfully-gotten property, and face the ocean after restitution? Do you know where you might look for such a person? I won't tell you her name; but it is a fact that the little picture, after a mysterious disappearance of several years, has turned up very much the worse for wear, and we at home have gathered the information that one of the servants pilfered it, originally, for a romantic young lady of your acquaintance; that said young lady treasured it ever since; and that some time ago, as she was making up her spiritual accounts prior to her departure for America, the picture became a skeleton of dread to her conscience, and she had it conveyed back to the family mansion—whence it has gone on a fresh journey to-day. Now, isn't it quite refreshing to any masculine vanity the prison has not worn off you, that you can still hold your ground in the feminine heart despite of time and absence and newer suitors? I have heard men say, with an earnestness that adduced honesty, they envied you even in prison. But the world is very ill-advised and envious altogether, for I am positive there are many women who would gladly exchange positions with me. Very few types remain of that famous old "Miller of the Dee," who envied and was envied by nobody.

About two weeks ago I met Robert Eagar, at the Limerick Junction. I wouldn't have known him, but he came up and introduced himself. He was on his way to England, and wanted to know how he could get to see you. I gave him all the information in my power, and promised to write myself to Mr. Fagan to request that he may be admitted to see you. Now, don't get mad if I acknowledge I never wrote since till to-day; but then there is one extenuating circumstance: Mr. Eagar told me he would be a month in London, and any time before its expiration would do to get the pass, so I did not endanger any chance he has of seeing you. Papa told you in his letter about Mr. Gladstone's refusal to set you at liberty. I gave Mr. Moore no authority to return thanks to the Premier, for I considered I had nothing to thank him for—merely a civil and exceedingly diplomatic letter, after several weeks' waiting in suspense. My only consolation is, that neither in the tone nor wording of my letter of proposition was there anything I could regret or that you could wish removed. Let that satisfy you; your honor is safe in my hands as in your own heart. I do regret one step, and only one, I took since we were separated; that is the lawsuit against the Belmont-O'Mahoney Fund, into which your Cousin Tim hurried me. If *he* had not happened to stand in such relationship to you, I should have been less easily led. It is the only action in which I have suffered other people to entirely influence or direct my course or to cast a shade over my own judgment. You will laugh to yourself, and say I am growing very self-opinionated: I *have* doubts sometimes as to the advisability of getting so strong-minded—in view, you know, of some day being again called upon to "obey." I think you will lead a dreadfully unhappy life with me, for I have entirely lost that amiable dependency and timidity of provoking reproof which, I think, constituted my charm for you in old times.

Lest I forget it, I will mention here that I happened to be a fellow traveler of Mr. McCarthy Downing, on Saturday evening, from the Limerick Junction to Cork. 'Twas so late on reaching the city I went to the Victoria Hotel for the night, and had only just finished supper when Mr. Downing sent up to know if I would see him. I went down stairs and met my fellow traveler; found he, like myself, had had to break his journey to home in Cork, and that we would be as far as Bandon together on Sunday morning. He showed me that document you gave him some months since, but did not offer to give it to me, and I did not like to ask it, though I told him you regretted having written it. I was not at first agreeably impressed by Mr. Downing. I thought he looked and spoke like a man who had a big opinion of himself and a little one of everybody else; who would be prone to look at people and things through rather dark and narrow glasses; but my opinion improved on Sunday morning, when I heard him bring forth the most convincing arguments, and pour them overwhelmingly on a "loyal" Bandon physician who "couldn't see what in the world the people were continually complaining about." From that moment, when his pale grey eye dilated and lighted to his subject, while he mourned the exodus caused by the Coercion Bill, and inveighed against the short-sighted policy that led to it, I began to admire and like him, and was really sorry when the Bandon Terminus was reached and our roads separated. The doctor proposed to go look for a horse and car and bring me home, and he selected an exceedingly skittish, wild creature, that had to be held while I got on the car. Such a drive to Clonakilty! The day was a delightful one; the hedges are all in their earliest summer dress of snowy-blossomed blackthorn, tender-budding hawthorn, and long green grasses embosoming little purple violets and pale fragrant primroses; meadows thickly starred with daisies; fields in even brown furrows and corn-plats, with the young emerald blades shooting half a hand above the ground; then the singing of birds and the gleaming of the river, that, like a thread of silver in the sun, winds along a portion of the road homewards; the pure fresh air, the clear, mild sky—all made up a living picture not to be forgotten. I enjoyed my drive, even though it was a lonely one, and I very much enjoyed the wildness of the horse, whose frequent "vagaries" made it a clever feat for anybody to hold a seat on the car behind him. 'Twas Easter Sunday, and on arriving at the old house I found Papa and Tim were at the Island keeping the day. Mamma, who is, poor woman, but a shadow of her former self, was pleasantly surprised to see me. Will had gone off on his first voyage (he has taken a fancy to the sea and lately studied navigation). My sister Isa has grown to be a young woman; Alf is a hardy little man, and all the rest have grown so that you would not recognize them. James Maxwell has grown as tall and much stouter than Chroum was when you last saw him, and he is as like Denny, your eldest, as if he were a twin brother of his. This brings me to the subject I suppose second nearest to your heart—the fortunes of your boys. Denny, as I told you when at Chatham, is very like yourself in appearance and disposition, and I am inclined to hope much that is good from his ripening years. Jack I have heard nothing of lately, further than that he is still studying law with Mr. Lawless and begins to consider himself quite a young man. Jeremiah, who was always very quiet, good-natured and not over bright, is showing quite an unexpected aptitude to learn; in fact, is getting the name of "a genius." He is at St. Jarlath's College, Taum.

I was at Mullinahone the week before last and learnt the dumb alphabet, in order to talk to poor Charles Kickham. He is apparently in the enjoyment of pretty good health, though he complains of weakness and inability to pursue as arduously as he would wish his literary occupations. He is engaged at present on a serial story, entitled "Knocknagow; or the Homes of Tipperary," for the New York *Emerald*. I stayed at his place in Mullinahone. Some of the Rossa and Kickham Election Committee were also present with the ladies of their families, and we—sat up all night and went to bed at sunrise! Mr. Kickham monopolized me from the time I entered the house till I went to the Lecture Hall, and from my return to sunrise; you'd have been awfully jealous if you could only see the amount of attention he lavished on me, and how complaisantly I received and returned it. He came as far as Carrick with me when I started for Waterford, and—*kissed* me before all the people at the station, coming away! Now, don't you feel very much aggrieved? You need not, my dove—a million kisses from any other would not be sweet as one from you. (I had better qualify that assertion by saying "I think" at the commencement of it, for I have not put the belief to test, and if I ever do it may not stand trial!)

Saturday, coming from Waterford, I was for awhile alone in one of the first-class carriages; but at one station, a gentleman who had frequently passed where I sat, entered and took a seat. I was buried in a new book, and did not feel myself called upon to notice that anybody was making efforts to disengage my attention from it. At last I was interrupted by a polite interrogation as to whether I was not Mrs. O'D. Rossa; I bowed and resumed the page. Several questions followed, to each of which I answered yes or no, and then again turned to my book. At last—I forget his name, though he told it to me—my *vis-a-vis* said he had been "anxious to contribute to the fund for relief of the prisoners; he understood I was collecting for them, and"—here he produced a sovereign. I told him he had been misinformed; I was not traveling for that purpose, but simply as a Reader, but I would give him the address of the Treasurer for the Relief Committee. "Oh, no, he would prefer I should receive it and send it." I do not know will you understand what sort of pang it was that shot through my heart! wounded pride or dignity it may have been, for I knew in my soul that man under-estimated me, and that I was being put through the indignity of a trial which I should aggravate by appearing to see through, so I quietly and steadily met the bold gaze of the intruder (he had very handsome eyes, too, Carissa!); assured him I could not depart from my usual practice, and wrote for him the number of the Committee Rooms and the Treasurer's address. I thanked him, too, for the interest he expressed in your fate (though I didn't believe one word he had uttered), and then I took up my book as a bar to all further conversation. He left at the next station, with not quite so jaunty an air as he had worn on his entrance.

You were anxious I should write everything befalling me: that is one incident of my travels, and many more I might give you of something of the same character, but I doubt if they would be worth recording; unless, indeed, the absence of news would make any trifle acceptable to a prisoner, especially if it relate to one he loves.

It is close on one o'clock a. m. There *was* a fire in the grate some time since, but I have just discovered 'tis dead out; the room is consequently rather chilly, and I shall have to bid you "good night"—or "good morning"—soon, lest I retard, by acquiring from cold, the recovery of my throat. I am using iodine for it, and some horrid medicine that tastes like rank seaweed. The iodine is colorless, an improvement in "physic," which I have the honor of being the first to test. A very clever Tipperary physician, hearing me express a reluctance to use the usual iodine because of its dyeing properties and the saffron tint 'twould give my neck, set his wits to work to devise a remedy or a substitute: the result is, he has compounded an iodine wash equally effective and perfectly colorless and uncoloring. I have had to come home to use it and the medicine, and they are really doing me a great deal of good.

Well, it is so late, I must tear myself away from my talk with you. Good night, my love—ay, 'tis good morning, I may dream, but I hope I shall go to sleep without thinking of you. I am not so philosophic as not to be made unhappy by dwelling on what is beyond my reach. "If only land or sea," the old song says, "had parted him and me, I would not now in vain be wailing." Land and sea, and stronger than both in their dissevering properties—prison walls—arise between us. It must seem strange and exasperating to you, who always managed to have your own way in everything, that the force of your will and all its concentration of power, are powerless to level the walls of Chatham, or to bring you one step closer to any object you desire. It is—for the time—disheartening to me, that the object for which I strained all my powers is still at such an aggravating distance from me. Possibly we are blind to what is best for us. I am quite certain, though, that however beneficial they may prove to the country and the world at large, viewed in a personal light my trials are not conducive to my own proper salvation. I can't grow contented.

Oh! I'll have to wind up now; so good-bye, and a hundred kisses, from your affectionate wife,
MARY J. O'D. ROSSA.

THURSDAY, 21st April.

This morning the morning papers bring the intelligence of the sudden death of George Henry Moore. Great public regret is felt and expressed for his untimely end, and I am saddened very much to think that Ireland and the prisoners have lost so faithful a friend and so good an advocate in the British Parliament. Of the few who are generous enough to see the interest of the country before their own, or too independent to sell their sense of right, Mr. Moore was the most generous and the most fearless. It does seem as if we are doomed, and Heaven and the dark powers have formed a league against the welfare of this unfortunate land.

I do not know but I may be infringing on my privilege by writing anything that could be construed into political news; however, as you were before this allowed to hear the news of your election for Tipperary, you may be allowed now to hear the reason you were not re-nominated, as I was informed by the Election Committee. It was credibly stated that the Sheriff would not accept your name again, taking, it was supposed, his cue from the action of Parliament. To prevent Mr. Heron's return Kickham was at once nominated, and his name could not be refused. Unfortunately, Tipperary was so sanguine of success again it did not put out its full force in the second election, and Mr. Heron, it is said, has fraudulently secured a seat in the House.

When I read in Cashel a short time ago, about thirty young men, with the Tipperary Band, came all the way by car to be present and lend me their assistance. It caused quite a commotion in the "City of the Kings." The resident magistrate, who, it appears, is an excessively timorous man, had the constabulary out in full force. "Like an eagle in a dove-cot, he—fluttered the Volges in Corioli!" might be applied to the advent of your little wife, backed by the Tipperary Band, in Cashel. I enjoyed immensely the trepidation of the local authorities and the immense enthusiasm of the people. The priests are somewhat unfavorable to me—don't know why; but in Cashel they absolutely went round amongst their lady parishioners to prevent their attendance. I had not a paying audience in Cashel, for it seems the greater number of voters for you were found there, and all these told the door-keeper they had a right to free tickets. Some of the scenes on the lobby were most amusing. One mountaineer, with the remnant of a black eye, pointed to it as a corroborative proof of his assertion that he had *fought* for you; and another showed a dilapidated coat-skirt, made ragged in the same cause. Of course all these claimants got passports. During the interim, you should have heard the house singing songs in your praise! every verse ending with an assertion that they'll never be satisfied till their "Hero" is released to them. Several others also, in tribute to you, were sung by your "constituents" and chorused by the whole house, standing. 'Twas the strangest, the wildest, and yet most orderly meeting of a mass of enthusiasts that I have ever witnessed. On Sunday I went to last Mass, and found, when 'twas over, the congregation were waiting to give me an ovation on my return to the hotel. (By the way, that hotel is kept by a niece of Col. Doheny's.) The gallery stairs in the chapel were lined with people, and as I stood on the first landing and looked over the eager heads of a double line of people down the steps, spreading out into the sunny, tree-shadowed chapel yard, filling it densely, then swelling in still stronger numbers outside the gate and down and up the ancient street, my heart swelled to my throat with a feeling that was not vanity or mere personal gratification. While I paused, and felt my eyes fill with tears of national pride and gratitude, a tremendous cheer rang up within and without the sacred building; it was echoed and re-echoed down the street, and, as I passed with much emotion down the steps and out into the chapel-yard and street, every head was uncovered; the people fell back to give me a passage, and, while those near enough seized my hands and fervently kissed and pressed them, the whole mass of my country-people there murmured a blessing and a hope for the future of Ireland, of you and of me. I could not tell you how I was affected. The people cheered me to the hotel, and remained outside a short time in groups and knots, talking. Afterwards I went to see the Abbey and Cormac's Castle on the Rock, and another surprise awaited me there. The young men of the town had been watching for my visit, and as the guide unlocked the massive gateway of the castle, the voice of a multitude of people met me from within, crying, "Welcome to the Rock of Cashel!" and immediately an amateur band, composed of concertinas, cornopeans and accordeons, struck up "God save Ireland." 'Twas really a scene you might imagine taken from a fairy story. We stood in a grass-grown court-yard, very extensive, partially surrounded by the castle battlements and the ivied walls of King Cormac's Chapel. Through pointed archways and deep mullioned windows at one side, and over the ruined fosse and embankments at the other, the beautiful, grassy pasture land swelled and opened under the sun, and glimpses of silver rivers and rivulets met our admiring eyes; up the winding stairs of the castle to the very top we went, and up there the cheering from below again greeted my appearance. You have been at Cashel, I suppose, and looked from King Cormac's tower over the seven fair counties that lift their faces round. Then I need not describe them. On leaving the chapel of the rock, the guide indulging in a sudden fit of sympathetic romance and enthusiasm with the people, made me stand on an elevated slab at the end of the nave, and there impressively told me that I stood on the very spot on which King Cormac was solemnly crowned. I stepped off at once rather confused, but not before the delighted followers had made the chapel ring again and again with their approving shouts. I believe with all their pretended republicanism of feeling, they'd have crowned me there and then as really as they crowned me in their hearts, if they only had the power.

I am writing, I believe, in a more egotistical strain than I ever indulged in before; but I must do so in order to give you the faintest idea of the romantic devotion of the people. It is also gratifying to me, inasmuch as it is proof to me of the advanced spirit of the people. Liberty is the goddess they adore; you are her devoted martyr; me they take as a personification of the cause you suffer for. They invest me with all the virtues and brilliancies their affectionate hearts can devise; they put me clothed in these garments of their own weaving on a pedestal, and there they bow down voluntarily and pay tribute to their beloved goddess through me. It is an insecure height to have reached, and I often tremble lest the adulous breath of the people come sometime to my dizzy head in gusts and too strong for my safety, that like an unfastened statue on a facade, I shall be blown down some day by a strong wind or an adverse wind. "Hope and pray," say the chaplains. I don't pray a great deal. I think you have more opportunities for praying and you can do both our shares, while I will do all the hoping for you. Perhaps, though, that prayer would be a sort of ballast to the barque that hope would inordinately lighten. There is at least a little reason in the idea, and I ought to put it in practice.

Here have I written forty-four pages, and I really seem to have told you nothing, and to be only now in condition to begin. I am not usually so prosy, for I believe in business-like letters. I am afraid, too, the Directors will be alarmed at the length of this and procrastinate the reading of it as long as I have done the writing. I hope with all my heart they won't detain it from you, and I hope you will forgive the delay I made in despatching it. It does seem cruel to keep you in suspense, for of course you have no way of getting any outside information. But one is not apt to remember that always. The whole family send love to you, and with wishes for your health and resignation, I remain, my dear Rossa, ever your affectionate wife,

MARY J. O'DONOVAN ROSSA.

The Fenian factions in America had dragged my wife into their contentions. The "Belmont fund" was claimed by John O'Mahony, and she was urged by the opposing faction, and strongly advised by a lawyer cousin of mine, to put in a claim on my behalf for some of it.

It was painful to me to learn this, but I was quite powerless to prevent it. There was the usual amount of newspaper scandal in connection with the affair, and it is painful even now to read in the newspapers of the time such passages as the following regarding me:

"He (Rossa) lent £300, at 10 per cent. interest, for the purpose of sustaining the paper. THAT LOAN, HOWEVER, WAS DULY PAID TO HIM, WITH INTEREST, out of the proceeds of the Chicago Fair. This I have learned from Mr. James Stephens and others, who had personal knowledge of the fact."

The writer of this took the side of John O'Mahony, and undertook to prove I had no claim whatever on the fund, and there he was right; but when he says I was to get or got ten per cent. interest or any interest for any money I lent the *Irish People*, or that I was paid principal and interest out of the proceeds of the Chicago Fair, he says more than is known to me, or known to James Stephens, or known to any others "who had personal knowledge of the fact." As the man who wrote this is dead, I would not refer to it but that I prize my Irish reputation somewhat, and to find my name mentioned in connection with "10 per cent." on the advance of a trifle of money to forward the cause is as painful to me as it is foreign and false to my character. And yet the writer of the paragraph—James Cody, of Callan—was as truthful, as true, and as self-sacrificing a worker in Ireland as the movement produced. It only shows what unjust things are possible to be said when friends fall out.

The next letter in order is that of my lawyer friend, Timothy F. Donovan. His arguments to secure my co-operation or "silence" did not lack the necessary force, but I doubt that I wouldn't have spoiled his case had I the liberty of speech.

202 B'WAY, Sept. 3, 1869.

MY DEAR COUSIN: By my suggestion your wife a short time ago commenced legal proceedings to obtain out of a fund now in the custody of our Courts the amount due you for your outlay and services expended on the *Irish People* newspaper. The proceeds of the suit are to be applied to the education of your children, under the directory of a guardian, to be appointed by the Court. I may here state that your best friends in this city have warmly advised this proceeding, and under their direction the matter is being pushed. The suit would never have been brought, were it not that its successful termination is assured beyond a doubt. But a clique, headed by O'Mahony, are striving to obtain it for division among themselves. He has made his newspaper here the vehicle of a most villainous attack on your wife, with intent to break her down in her readings before the public—in fact, to steal away her bread, because she has foiled him, and stopped the money from going into his pocket. It is the fixed determination to apportion this fund to the children of the prisoners for their education and nourishment, and for that purpose your friends have put in a claim for your children to obtain your *quantum*. It is necessary, therefore, that you keep aloof in this matter. Do not give a negative or an affirmative expression either way, relative to the case—and this becomes the more important, as your wife's success in her readings may in a great measure depend upon her triumph in that case.

Therefore, keep up a steady silence about it; and please to return to me an authority to commence in your name all suits I may deem necessary to recover for your children your worldly goods—a mere expression to that effect will suffice. All the folks deploring your bad fate, and hoping to see you free once more, send their love to you. Yours, most truly,
T. F. DONOVAN.
To J. O'DONOVAN ROSSA.

MY LOVE: I send you back this ugly letter of my cousin's. There is the lawyer on the face of it. How you engaged in this Belmont-O'Mahony lawsuit, influenced by any one who could use such contemptible reasons to influence me, is what I cannot understand. If this is the only thing you regret since we parted, I suppose I may pass it over. But even though it may tend to make you self-opinionated, let it be a caution to you to beware of acting again on the advice of others against your own inclination. If you are much led by others, it is ten to one but you will be led astray.

As to your losing the lesson of obedience, in view of our re-union, I have not yet lost all confidence in my own powers of making you unlearn if you be stubborn. Yes—while you are left to your own resources for support, trust yourself alone.

You say that in America the party who befriended you most, of the factions, was the Roberts party. I must tell you Mr. Roberts did not make the most favorable impression upon me. I heard him say that he would have nothing to do with Fenianism if he knew there were so many difficulties to overcome. He tendered his resignation then and there. The Council pressed him, begged him to hold on, and it has often surprised me since to hear with what tenacity he *has* held on through such a sea of difficulties.

It is not often that tears start to my eyes, but I felt the woman in me at witnessing this scene. I said to myself, "This man will never do." Let it be acting, or what it be, he aroused a prejudice in my mind, and if I had heard any time since, that he withdrew from Irish politics I would have more confidence in him.

You could have sent me your correspondence with Gladstone. Your letter did not contain one word to show me that you received the one I wrote *en regle* (I sent this to her "surreptitiously") three days after your visit. You said you spent an evening at Mr. Moore's, in London. I don't know did he remember that it was your husband he met at Moore Hall, on one occasion. I liked him immensely well, and regret his death much. This spinal affection is troubling me. If I leave you entirely—then,

"A place in your memory, dearest."
Yours, ROSSA.

I am publishing the last letter under protest from my wife. She says there is no man in America who acted more friendly or more honorably towards her than William R. Roberts, and she grumbles at my expressing a weak thought about him at any time. But I am writing my prison life, and her likings or dislikings must not alter the record of anything I wrote or did. When Fenians and all my political connections seemed to care little whether my wife had a friend or a home in the City of New York, she found both with old-country neighbors of ours, Maurice and Kate Spillane.

Anxiety of mind and depression of spirits brought on an illness that rendered her unable to write, and her medical adviser said she should have rest and country air to save her life. Mrs. Spillane was making preparations to afford her these, when Mr. Roberts, learning the circumstances, sent his wife and his carriage for her and took her to his house on the Bloomingdale road, where she was treated for a few months with the greatest attention and kindness. This is an obligation that I have no way of requiting and for which I must ever feel indebted; but as most of my indebtedness comes from trying to serve Ireland, I cannot allow any of it to suppress a thought that was written when thinking of Ireland's interests. It is in the dark days of a nation's distress that the truest of her sons cling closest to her, and those who are ashamed to associate their names with her fallen fortunes, or who are scared away by dangers and difficulties from giving their assistance, are not the men fitted to raise her to a position of national independence.

In the Summer of 1870 the Governor of the prison informed us that a Parliamentary Commission was appointed to inquire into our treatment, and we could have the help of counsel to prepare our case. We immediately communicated with our friends, and when we learned the help of counsel was only a thing of nothing, that the Commission was to be a secret one, and no counsel allowed to appear, my companions pronounced the inquiry a sham and decided to take no part in it. I decided on taking a contrary course, and made up my mind to give evidence. My case was somewhat different from that of the others. I knew the truth or falsehood of matters that affected me were some of the principal questions in dispute, and I had such confidence in my ability to prove the truth of what the Secretary of State said was false that I was sure I could stick the lies down their throat if I got any fair play.

If I followed the example of the others and refused to give evidence, it would be a victory for the Government, for they would be only too glad to have it in their power to say that the reason I refused to go on with my case was because I was unable to substantiate my allegations.

I came to the conclusion to employ my wife as counsel. The authorities consented to allow her to consult with me; but they never gave her the permission to come till the day the Commission opened, though she came to London and remained there a fortnight appealing for the visiting order. When she returned to Clonakilty the visiting order followed her there, and then some advisers put it into her head that it was wrong for me to take a different course from the other prisoners, and she grumbled about coming.

The following letters passed between us before she came, and then during the visiting hours for six or seven days, between the several sittings of the Commission, we were put into a glass-room for consultation, with an officer looking on outside the glass door— for fear we should commit suicide:

STRAND HOUSE, CLONAKILTY, July 7th, 1870.

MY DEAR ROSSA: The printed letters, which I enclose you, will, if you are permitted to read them, explain why I am not present at Chatham. I can easily see how your disbelief in the honesty of the Inquiry, combined with your anxiety to talk unreservedly with me, have induced you to grasp at the offer of interviews held out to you so late, and to write wishing me to return. I have not done so; I will not do so, and—as Mr. Butt remarked—" wash my hands of the Commission" and all the false privileges the Commission can grant.

Even while I can understand another man putting aside all considerations but the satisfaction of meeting his wife, I cannot understand it in you, who have, since I first knew you, held public interest far in advance of mine or your own gratification. To take advantage of this permission "to assist you in preparing your statement for the Commission of Inquiry," when the inquiry was already about to be inaugurated at Chatham—to take advantage of it *merely* for the satisfaction of an ordinary interview, when we know that the fact would be brought against us to prove that the Government "gave fair means of preparation, which were availed of, and in their barrenness of corroborative result to the prisoner's complaints, made another proof of the innocence of the Government!"—this I would look upon as selling one's right, like Esau, for a mess of pottage—as putting one's character in pawn for an equivocal reward.

Do not fear for me. To endure has become second nature to me. I remember at school my class-mistress sometimes gravely rebuked me for the fact that if I were not *heading* her list, I would surely be found carelessly at the very bottom. This has followed me still. I want no compromises, no mediums. "*All* or nothing;" "Saint or sinner;" "Cæsar or nobody," have grown instinctively to be my watchwords. So I will have all my husband or none of him, and I will have all its promises from the crown or none of them; and as I cannot have the peaceful wedded life I hoped for once, why I can make up my mind to lead a strong single one. Don't, therefore, abate or alter, after so long endurance, any of your principles, beliefs or inspirations through compassion for me. I had asked Mr. Butt to take my order for interviews with you, if the orders were granted in reasonable time. They were not granted in reasonable time, and I would not insult him by offering it on Monday.

It is impossible for me, my dear husband, to enter into private or particular family matters, as you would wish, in my letters to you. I can but tell you what I would permit my greatest foes to know, lest at some time I find the Government making use of my information to you against you or myself. Besides, you cannot help me in anything. If I wish your presence you cannot come to me; if I wish your advice, before you could give it me the need for it would have passed away. We are *not* one, but two very distinct people, while English law stands between us, and we might as well recognize the fact, submit to it, and be content with our position until Providence will send *a full and perfect change*. Oceans could not so effectually divide us as your prison discipline, nor even could death so completely cut off communication, for in death the spirit is surely cognizant of the acts and prayers and wishes of those it loves. I have no doubt the Government will presently make important concessions, not only in favor of the prisoners but of the country for which they suffer. I can wait for these concessions, which *must come*, and that without my snatching at the small bait, in offering which the Government hopes to get the prisoners' friends to hold the whitewash pail while it (the Government) whitens its own dark acts.

My letter must needs be a short one to-day, as I wish to send it with as little delay as possible. I received yours from London yesterday. When I think of all the indignities I was put through in the capital of Great Britain, by British officials, I feel as if I could curse like a dragoon—only I'm trying to be a saint. "*Forgive* your enemies, *do good* to them that hate you, and *pray* for all that persecute and calumniate you!" Truly a hard rule to follow, yet none of us should cavil at it; for, *knowingly* or *unknowingly*, we have wronged, hated, persecuted and calumniated some other members of the human family, and we would gladly see those we have wronged, &c., ready to love, do good and pray for us, in return for our evil.

I enclose a likeness I had taken in London, in one of my stage dresses; one of Babe's also. I have been contributing every week to the *Irishman*, but can't put my hand on any of the verses this moment. I may find them before post hour. Meantime, with love from all at home to you, and kindest regards and good wishes to General Halpin, to McClure and all your fellow-prisoners,

I remain, my dear Rossa, your affectionate wife,
MARY J. O'DONOVAN ROSSA.

P. S.—I could not get a copy of Messrs. Knox and Pollock's Report. Mr. Pigott hasn't it, and I don't know who has, but Mr. Butt thinks the Commissioners had, or could get it.

I found some poems: "Ross Carberry;" "My Mother's Grave;" "A Protest;" "Prayer of Manasses," and "Shall We Tell Him So, My Boy?" I enclose them for you. Babe's likeness is miserable; he *wouldn't* be quiet, and was awfully frightened at being put in the middle of the gallery alone. Thought he was about to be shot at through the machine, I believe.

CHATHAM PRISON, SATURDAY, 5 P. M., July 9, 1870.

MY DEAR WIFE: I have just received your letter of the 7th. It is some ease of mind to me to hear from you, and it is a pleasure to me to hear that you are so strong. Well, I did surely anticipate the pleasure of having a history of your life from you, besides any information you could give me as to the course I would adopt at this inquiry. But I must tell you that, independent of any advice you or any one else could give me, I determined to pursue a certain course, and though your letter may lead me to think that you would disapprove of it, still I will not alter my mind. That course is to give evidence before the Commission, if they see there is anything relevant to their inquiry contained in a part statement which I laid before them on Monday, the 4th. I did not make this statement as a complaint. I only stated simply matters that I experienced by virtue of prison discipline, and left it to them to examine me or not as to the truth of what I stated.

I was led to adopt this course by thinking that the most of what I stated to them were matters that were, one way or another, canvassed and contradicted in the world, and whatever your opinion or my opinion of the Commission be, I concluded that I would not leave it in the gentlemen's power to say that my refusal to give evidence was proof that these statements could not be substantiated.

After a conversation with the gentlemen, and my expressing a willingness to be examined if they desired, the decision was: that they would take the paper I gave them as a part statement; that they would not go into my examination until they would come again on Tuesday, the 19th; that every day till then I could have my wife's assistance in preparing my case (that is if my wife came), and that then I could give them the rest of my statement if I wrote any more. Here is a paragraph of your letter: "Even while I could understand another man putting aside all considerations but the satisfaction of meeting his wife, I cannot understand it in you, who have, since I first knew you, held public interest far in advance of mine or your own gratification, to take advantage of this permission to assist you in preparing your statement for the Commission of Inquiry," when the inquiry was already about to be inaugurated at Chatham—to take advantage of it *merely* for the satisfaction of an ordinary interview, &c., &c. This I would look upon as selling one's right, like Esau, for a mess of pottage, or as putting one's character in pawn for an equivocal reward."

In your mind, as seen in these lines, you overvalue me and you undervalue me. Where you think too highly of me is where you think I have made much sacrifice of my happiness, convenience, or gratification for "public interest," and where you think too little of me is where you think that I would now put aside all considerations for the satisfaction of meeting my wife—where *you* think that *I* think so little of public interest as to sacrifice it merely for the satisfaction of an ordinary interview.

Well, I am not so much in alarm as you are in these matters. I will pursue the course I have indicated, if the authorities do what they have stated they will do, and I have no fears as to doing wrong or as to "injuring the public interests."

I cannot see, suppose nothing else but the "public interest" is concerned, how a history of my prison life to you would not counterbalance the advantage the Government would derive by saying that I had your assistance in preparing my case. However, ye outside know the world and ye must judge. Before I knew the offer would be made us of having an interview with our friends, I had applied for a private visit from you, and it was refused. I then applied for an ordinary visit, and it was granted, and now that I can have a private visit the public interest will not permit you to avail of it. This is rather hard.

It puts me in a very peculiar position, for if you know my mind, you know that I cannot at any future time, with any face, under these circumstances, go before a Director and ask him for a public or a private visit from you. He might say to me, "How do you know that your wife wants to see you?"

I am really pleased, Mollis, that you are so strong—that that sickness of expectation and "hope deferred" is left you, and that you have made up your mind for the worst, for it is only thus that you can act for the best.

I was in much suspense till I got your letter—but it is not a letter—it is only a note, and, therefore, by post return, write a long letter; and as it seems to me that you write under a misapprehension of the time for visiting me being past, and seem to be unaware that there is over a week yet, I would wish you to be final on this point, and it would be well that you would, by the car-driver, send a telegraph to Bandon for the Governor of the prison, saying whether you will come or no.

As I allude to this I will expect you to do it, and then I will make up *my* mind. I did not get the printed letters nor the poems, nor the photographs. I must, I suppose, wait till I can see Mr. Fagan.

When did you go home? Why did you not tell me? Did you go by Dublin? I have permission to write, while the Commission sits, on matters connected with it.

I wrote to Mr. Pigott and Mr. Downing, M. P., already, and you can tell them—your father and Mr. P. at least—they may keep on writing to me, if they have anything to say or send.

"Don't, therefore, abate or alter, after so long endurance, any of your principles, beliefs, or inspirations, &c." 'Tis funny to see you writing these words to me, if you are acting in this matter on your own advice. 'Tis so different from the threatening notice you sent me from America of not living with me if I neglected my family in future; but I am glad that you are at last strong.

Yours, dear Mollis, ever fondly,
JER. O'DONOVAN ROSSA.

SUNDAY MORNING—5 O'CLOCK—July 10, '70.

MY DEAR WIFE: After having slept on your letter, or rather after having spent the night awake on it, I write a more brief and more decisive note than the long "do-as-you-please" one which I wrote upon its receipt last evening.

If I have ever made sacrifices for public interests, I have liked to see my way, and I cannot, in this matter, see how your visiting me now is to injure public interests.

I do not intend to injure public interests. I have no fear that anything I will ask you to do will injure them, and I ask you to come.

I like to get my quill to accompany me in any direction. To serve public interests against my inclination is what I have not done, or cannot do. If I strive to accommodate one to the other, my friends and public interests should make some allowance for the weaknesses of poor human nature and the selfishness inseparable from man.

There is one condition, and one alone, on which I tell you stay; and that condition is, that *all the visiting friends of all the prisoners have agreed to avail not of the permission to visit until this Commission has done its duty, and that no prisoner is to have a visit from anyone.* If you have entered into such a compact as this, I will so far yield to the public opinion as to tell you hold to it. If you have not, I will not allow you to be swayed by any other advice than mine—not even by your own—and I ask you, with any authority you concede to me as a dead husband, to come.

Apart from public reasons, there are two other excuses for not coming, which I will hold equally valid. They are: the absense of any desire, on your part, to see me, or have a long private conversation with me, and the absence of money necessary to defray the expenses of coming.

I do not know, Mollis, but that there is some of the husband pride breaking out here, for I think I feel a little humiliation at being obliged to say to my companions, when I meet them by-and-by, at nine o'clock, "Oh, my wife wouldn't come."

I am to go through this inquiry whether you come or not, and your advice or assistance might not change the course I have struck out for myself, and that course I have determined with a view to public more than personal interests.

I only feel that I could go through it with a lighter heart if you could have cheerfully responded to my call. Equanimity, evenness, or peace of mind, is what alone has preserved my health in prison so far, and I must cultivate this, "for what is the world to me if my wife is a widow," and you must assist me if you are not otherwise disposed.

If you are coming, telegraph from Bandon to the Governor to tell me. If you are not, send the unwelcome message also by the first car-driver that passes for Bandon. Attend to this, for I had two or three days' work struck out for you.

I got from the authorities six of my suppressed letters to you, twenty sheets of "memorials" to the Secretary of State, and I had these for you to copy in large hand, for the Commission.

I will have to go at them myself if you do not come, and writing has become most unpleasant to me, as it painfully awakens this affection of the spine. The time is getting short, therefore telegraph. Remember to all. I got nothing but your letter.

Yours, dear Mollis, ever faithfully,
JER. O'DONOVAN ROSSA.

During our interviews at this Commission, to which I will devote the next chapter, you may be sure we talked very little about the inquiry or about the case I was to make out. I had all that settled before my wife came, and we spent the hours together getting and giving an account of our lives and all that concerned us in life. It was as curious a position as ever a married couple were seen in, to see us sitting in this glass house with Principal Warder King as sentry outside the glass door; and was it not a curious place for her to reproach me with ingratitude because I never wrote a line of poetry for her since we were married? When

I went to my cell that evening I wrote the following lines, and made her very agreeable next day by presenting them to her when we met in the morning:

> A single glance, and that glance the first,
> And her image was fixed in my mind and nursed;
> And now it is woven with all my schemes,
> And it rules the realm of all my dreams.
>
> One of Heaven's best gifts in an earthly mould,
> With a figure Appelles might paint of old—
> All a maiden's charms with a matron's grace,
> And the blossom and bloom of the peach in her face.
>
> And the genius that flashes her bright black eye
> Is the face of the sun in a clouded sky;
> She has noble thoughts—she has noble aims—
> And these thoughts on her tongue are sparkling gems.
>
> With a gifted mind and a spirit meek
> She would right the wronged and assist the weak;
> She would scorn dangers to cheer the brave,
> She would smite oppression and free the slave.
>
> Yet a blighted life is my loved one's part,
> And a death-cold shroud is around her heart,
> For winds from the "clouds of fate" have blown
> That force her to face the hard world alone.
>
> And a daughter she of a trampled land,
> With its children exiled, prisoned, banned;
> And she vowed her love to a lover whom
> The tyrant had marked for a felon's doom,
>
> And snatched from her side ere the honeymoon waned:
> In the dungeons of England he lies enchained;
> And the bonds that bind him "for life" a slave
> Are binding his love to his living grave.
>
> He would sever the links of such hopeless love,
> Were that sentence "for ever" decreed above:
> For the pleasures don't pay for the pains of life—
> To be *living* in *death* with a *widowed wife*.
>
> A single glance, and that glance the first,
> And her image was fixed in my mind and nursed,
> And now she's the woof of my worldly schemes,
> And she sits enthroned as the queen of my dreams

CHATHAM PRISON, July, 1870.

> "The longest days must have an end,
> And the dearest friends must part."

And so it was with us. Our six or seven days' communion with each other came swiftly to an end, and stone walls and prison bars again divided us. Without a word of preface I will close this chapter with the following two letters. What ingratitude! to write to me in such a strain after making such a sweet poem for her:

LONDON, 178 STAMFORD ST.,
WATERLOO BRIDGE, August 9th, 1870.

MY DEAR ROSSA: I know it is very ungrateful of me to have kept you in supense all this time. I have no excuse to offer for myself only one that makes my delinquency worse, *i. e.*, I hated to write.

I reasoned and argued with my disinclination, but I could get no answer from it but "Let me alone, I am miserable; bury Chatham—fly from it, forget it, for all my wretchedness lies there." So I groaned and turned my face farther away from that fortified town by the sea, and each day I said, "I will forget it yet to-day, and to-morrow I will force myself to write to him." It seems cruel to write in such a strain to you, especially as I know there are depths in me you have never sounded, and would not be able to understand—depths of capacity for suffering from reflections which would bring no suffering to you. Since I last saw you, I have sat for hours and hours with locked hands, closed lips and vacantly fixed eyes, actually *blank* with the load of invisible misery I seem to be carrying. It is grown to be a disease with me, this fearful weight of melancholy. It so overwhelms my soul that I cannot see in the future any *circumstance* that could reanimate me—anything that could bring me permanent joy.

"'Tis not on youth's smooth cheek alone
The blush which fades so fast,
But the tender bloom of heart is gone,
Ere youth itself be past."

No; I am so changed, so hardened, so disenchanted of my life, so utterly *dead* of heart and bare of hopes, that if the prisons poured forth their occupants tomorrow, I should be capable of no more than the general public rejoicement, for I am dead while I live. Life is not what I had hoped—it is bare, cold, wretched reality. It is not good for me to see you or to write to you. What is the use of concealing that the farther in soul and body I am away from Chatham the less unhappy I have ever been. Do not blame me. I cannot sit down to write to you without having my passive melancholy turned into active anguish. I am blameable if you will—I am weak, I am cruel, I am ungenerous, I am anything you choose to call me in anger. I do not defend myself. I have no reason for the fit of despondency which has increased from time to time on me—I *know* no cause unless it is madness—but I know it is exaggerated and intensified to a degree in which I cannot control my words when I collect my thoughts to write to you or to visit you.

It is a cruel thing to say it, but I would to God you had never seen me—that I had died at school, or gone into the grave with that fair young cousin of mine at whose wake and funeral I first saw you. Then I should have missed the pangs of earth, and been less unworthy of the bliss of Heaven. Now the spirit and the flesh both suffer. The light of Heaven seems no more to shine upon the darkness of my life. God Himself seems to have deserted me. As the pillar of light to the Israelites in their dark pilgrimage, between them and their enemies, so stood between me and the misery of my portion God's blessed love. It is gone from me—it has left me, I cannot see a star of promise, nor feel anything but solid darkness in my whole soul's horizon. I am barren of prayer as of earthly hope. "My soul is sorrowful unto Death!" but unhappily it is not "for its sins" it is so sorrowful. It is the sorrow of a soul so clouded and covered with *sorrowing flesh* that it cannot find a chink in its solid armor of discontent through which to look up to its native Heaven. Therefore, "air-tight" in the body, it is impregnated with the body's woes. Truly, a piteous plight; and I would thank forever whosoever would help speedily out of its contemptible and uncomfortable habitation my distressed spirit. If they would but give me a minute's grace to pray, I would consider myself fortunate to fall in with a band of desperadoes, covetous of my life—but pshaw! what's the use of allowing my pen to express so many words of nonsense. I will turn from the subject. When I left Chatham for London, I did so in a state of great disquietude, on my father's account, and on arriving in London I lost no time in driving to Paddington station. I reached it and actually had bought my ticket, and was importuning the porter to leave some other work and bring in *my* baggage, when the bell rang, the engine screamed, there was a final banging of carriage doors, and I had the mortification of hearing the train go "puff, puff, puffing" out of the station as the sulky porter got half way to it. I made a great complaint to the Inspector, but 'twas in vain—no other train was to be had in time to catch the Bristol boat. I telegraphed home to know if Papa was so ill that I should go by that horrible way of Dublin. I got no answer. I telegraphed again and put up at the Great Western Hotel. Friday, Saturday, Sunday—no answer to my messages. I got vexed and telegraphed to Papa himself, to sister Isa, to Tim, and to the party he boarded with in Cork, and on Monday evening I had an answer from them that would have made me exccessively angry, only it relieved my fears for Papa. Papa was ill, certainly, but it was not dangerous illness, and their anxiety to *see me at home* was their principal reason for alarming me about Papa. This I gathered from the dispatch, and next morning, in a letter from home, I was informed that from the extreme gloom and unnatural despondency of my letters to Tim and my father, they were afraid something awful would happen to me, and they thought nothing would bring me under their protection as quickly as a telegram of Papa's serious illness. Though I pretended to Tim I was outrageous at being unnecessarily alarmed, still I treasure up this fact as a proof of my family's great affection for me, so clearly as they read my mind from the mere tone of my letters! so promptly their love for me suggested the readiest way to bring me again under soothing home influences! Oh, may God bless my father. The poorer in heart, and soul, and purse, I grow, the richer he grows in love for me, and in devices to heal, to comfort and to lead me right. To his prayers that are always ascending to Heaven for me, I attribute my safety in many a past danger—to his advice where I have taken it, I owe all that is good and fruitful of good, and in every act that crossed my father's wishes, I have sown bitter, barren, thorny seed. If I can pray for nothing else, I can pray " God bless my father," and then I shall know one is blessed who will never forget to pray blessings on me. Tim told me there was no immediate necessity for me to leave London, and I therefore came back to my old boarding place, and wrote requesting Tim would come over to make arrangements for my readings in England. Unfortunately he has been really ill with congh and cold, and could not leave his room safely. Dr. Hadden told him, so I must wait for him even some days beyond to-day. Meantime, I have had a letter from the Rossa and Kickham Committee. It seems they are heavily in debt, and they naturally turn to me to get assistance in the shape of a few readings. I could not easily refuse, so I have at once consented. I would not grudge three times the labor I will have, to the men individually, but I feel some fears about associating my work with theirs in England. 'Twould be all right *in Ireland*, but I don't think it will serve me with Irishmen in England who have little sympathy with their petition failure. However, I am pledged to them now, and, " sink or swim," I will do my utmost for them.

I think my friends begin to feel it might be dangerous for them to show their faces here. I have only seen the visage of my old friends, the detectives (two occacasions excepted, on which " Counsellor O'C." called to inquire about you and Fitz, to ask about myself!) since I left Chatham, so I am utterly alone, friendless—left to my own sad thoughts. I went the evening before last with my landlady's niece to walk from Westminster to the end of the embankment. The boats had stopped running, the river was very quiet, and the moon was spreading a cloak of silver on the water. We leaned for a long time on the low granite parapet of the embankment. So softly the waves lapped up against their boundary! so gently, as the light of a woman's tender blue eye, the mild waters invited me to their breast, that I could not wonder many a poor wretch, deceived by a love of the world, should be tempted to throw herself into so soothing and placid a bosom as the Thames unveiled by moonlight. One could not help thinking that a dreamless rest might be got by trusting the weary limbs to such a soft and winning nurse. I wrote to McClure's family, and I wrote to Miss Crowley, but got no reply yet. I sent your poem as you " *commanded!*" to Mr. Pigott. I must say you are growing quite imperious of late, anticipating the royal honors you will receive if ever you live to be " King of Ireland," and the obedience you will demand. The Commission has not, to my knowledge, made any report of its labor yet, and I am therefore not working on any notes I took in Chatham. I am trying, by letting it drift rather indolently, to help my mind recover its balance, and with God's grace it may be lifted out of the " slough of despondency " into which it so deeply fell. " All is vanity but loving God and serving Him alone." Now, if I had a brave *Puritan* husband who would rather elevate my soul to the foot of Heaven by sympathetic faith, than weaken it as you do by going no farther than earth, I would be better able to bear my sufferings. But there is no sympathy between your *soul* and *mine*. I consider the first aim of existence is to serve God, and *unless done in His service*, I look on every noble act as wasted. But I am very weak. Oh! weak beyond belief; and though I have for whiles detached myself from earthly love, and fixed a faithful and unwandering eye on the goal of life toward which I have tried to train my uncertain footsteps, still outward influences coming from sources near enough to be strong, can shake to fragments my card-house of piety and leave me shivering and worthless in the blast of Fate. I have a cousin of your name, and if you were but like him in belief, in soul, I, reposing on you, should be strong though leagues, and laws, and death divided us. Withal my appetite for earthly things, there is in me a passionate yearning to rise to higher things, a desire to be either free to seek my way undeterred by earthly vassalage to the foot of God's throne, or (combination of earth and heaven) to seek it hand in hand, and more securely, with a stronger partner soul. For "what is it to gain the whole world and lose your own soul." What is fame? I could curse it. What is love but a rapid road to misery, if its links are not riveted by common and voluntary service to the spirit ot Love, which is God! Flung into the world, utterly alone and *belonging* to *nobody*, God will claim and hold me; but made half of another being, for good or ill, the *soul* of that other being must have an influence on my soul. If it will not help me to God, it will help me away from Him, and the least it will do is to distract and fling into indecision the spirit that had just strength, and no more, to keep itself "on its feet." I have no faith in human honor, in human virtue, or in human truth. If men who profess no religion do not rob their neighbors of their wives and goods, do not swear falsehoods and spill human blood, it is simply because they are not tempted to do any of these things, or they cannot without hurting some nearer interest to them, or they are afraid of human penalties imposed by human law. And in the matter of the wives—and maids too—men are honorable because of all the forementioned reasons, and added to them, that after overcoming all these reasons, the woman may not at all be inclined to be kind, and may leave him hopeless of success in his designs. I begin to grow tired of writing, sleepy too, for 'tis late. I think I shall leave anything else I have to say until to-morrow, yet I shall finish the subject I was on, *i. e.*, my disbelief in human virtue. You have said I am proud, and to my pride, and my love for yourself, you attribute the creditable figure I have made in my strange and most unhappy life. You are much mistaken. I am not prouder than was Cleopatra, nor, to come nearer home, than was Queen Elizabeth; and, if the stories be true that people tell of them, their pride was admirably accommodated *to their inclination.* And as for my love for yourself—why, the Devil has often whispered to me that you are the root of all my misfortunes, and that I have little reason to be thankful for the amount of affection you bestowed on me, as that did not tend to any worldly or spiritual advantage of mine, but only to the gratification of your own personal passion; and, again, I am convinced that had I married the least remarkable for mind, position, money or person of God's creatures at that time, I would have been a fond and faithful wife, as I am convinced every innocent, honorable, religiously reared Irish girl is to her husband. It is easy for people to say that love comes but once. I am sure I could love a hundred husbands (one at a time!) and except that I should naturally have a preference and give a sigh to one that perhaps had passed away, neither of them should find fault with me for undeserved coldness. I should scruple to say this to you, if I were your first wife, but you, who find no more difficulty in fitting yourself to a new marriage relation than to a new pair of gloves, must be prepared to expect an equal liberality in the mind of the woman philosophical enough or courageous enough to take you.

So I do confess that though I might have a preference for you, that preference would not at all interfere with somebody else's prospects. Therefore, I do not look upon "Love" as my shield from the sentimental ills of life. On the contrary, it is the enemy's mine under my feet, which I must tread over with the greatest caution, and hold in the holiest fear lest it at some time be my destruction. I told you once, and I tell you again, I had and I have no reliance but on God—no reliance but in Him—no happiness but where he allows it. My father is, and has been all his life, of a deeply religious turn. Tim, as he advances in years, is of my father's mind, and when I am at home and under their influence a blessed peace gradually takes possession of my stormy heart. In America I was often visiting with Frank Donovan's family, and one could not be unhappy or wicked in their vicinity. Frank's letters, like his conversation, breathed an apostolic spirit. They led me to peace as often as it left me; and *peace* is the only gift to be craved in this life—deep religious peace. Perhaps if I could get off to you a couple of letters like this you would come to understand me. You imagine you have always understood me, but I do not think so. I do not know how you could do so, seeing that while you were with me every natural impulse of mine was in obedience to my desire to be a "perfect wife," and when my feelings or my words would not have pleased you, I, so far from home, amongst perfect strangers, and dependent on your pleasure for my peace, took care to be silent. If I had married you, looking forward to spending my life with you, I *think* I should have acted less complaisantly on several occasions. I say I think, for I'm not sure but my natural softness would have bound me to your will anyway, but you knew, and I felt, that we had made a mad leap to reach a temporary island in a stream, which island would be washed from under our feet in one, two, three, or, at most, twelve months. Did you not tell me in those old letters that my father burnt, that, feeling that you had but a short span of life to run, you wanted all the pleasure possible in the time (you were not a law-abiding citizen!), and what could I do but help you to the best of my ability to make that poor "remnant of your life serene?" I argued to myself, as I dared the thing at all, it would be like "straining at a gnat after swallowing a camel" to object to anything else. There is one thing, Cariss, that you may be sure of—I will never take the same amount of trouble for you or for any other man again. Human love is selfish, except in the first enthusiasm of youth; after twenty (no one I believe passes that age without experiencing the divine sentiment) love is no longer conceived in such purity and nursed in such utter and sustained unselfishness. It becomes a selfish human passion, living only so long as the object gives pleasure, and ceasing when the object thwarts the will, offends the vanity, or fails to minister to the self-love, pride, passion, or power of the pretended lover. You often said you loved me, but I never put your love to proof, and I never believed but if I did put it to proof I should find it wanting. I remember I never showed the slightest inclination to interfere with your movements but a shadow, slight, yet perceptible to me, would come between us. I took warning from slight indications, and I forebore experimenting where I felt it likely I should, by testing, find myself unpleasantly convinced. How can you know anything of me, therefore, but that which I believed would be most pleasing to you? Love is easily tested. It is often found in woman, seldom in man; but its step-brother, Passion, takes its place and its name, and assumes to itself the honors, and the license, and the title of Love, while doing most unloving things. By their fruits love and passion are distinguishable. Love does not, as Passion does, take to itself its object for a slave and servant, but Love makes itself the slave of its object. Love does not gather its beloved from security and peace to garnish and render odorous his own uncertain and hazardous hours. Love does not that which, to bring comfort to himself, must bring detriment to the beloved. Love looks with unselfish eyes to the life-long happiness of the beloved. Love is pure and patient and all-trusting; love gathers to itself its beloved more dearly and fondly, for the poverty, the unjust revilements, the disappointments of life. But Passion, that covers himself with love's mantle! oh, he is cruel and selfish, and vain and ungenerous. He will snatch his object from a fortress, and plant her upon a precipice. He will enslave her. He will seek recklessly the gratification of the hour, if she should die of the effect in the next—and withal he is blind enough to imagine himself the legitimate representative of Love! Passion is unscrupulous, and making floods of protestations makes yet no effort to smooth the path of life for his object. He feeds himself with the notion that in gratifying himself he gratifies his object; and no fine care for her, no single thought for her separate ease or pleasure, gives the poor victim to understand that she is more to him than the dinner he eats, enjoys and praises, the coat he wears and finds comfortable, or the horse he rides and takes pride in. They are all ministers to his wants and wishes, and he has an unthought of, unconscious belief, I suppose, that the horse is happy to have such a master, and the coat done justice to by having such a wearer, but I doubt whether he would, on reflection, say the dinner was blest in having such an appreciative eater? Unless on the principle which seems to animate sham philanthropists, to whom all men are beloved and inexpensive brothers, and who cannot understand why those beloved brothers (albeit they are hungry and unclad) are not joyful in the Lord with them for love and blessings which they have all in a lump, but which the poor souls have none of. I could pursue the subject without half exhausting it till to-morrow night, but I am grown altogether too weary and sleepy now to write any more. I am trying to think, in a stupid, sleepy way, did you ever give me one proof of self-forgetting love? I can't remember, though I have often thought before on the subject. Perhaps I'd dream it, so good night.

Give my most affectionate regards to each and all your friends in prison. Don't forget to tell McClure I wrote to his family, and, in fact, have obeyed every direction with which I was entrusted by either. When I get news for them, from any quarter, it will not be my fault if they are not apprised of it. As the poor fellows do not have a great many letters, I think the Governor would not consider it incumbent on him to suppress a letter of mine to them.

If you wish me to take advantage of the Governor's permission to see you, tell him so, and I am sure he will be good enough to order his secretary drop me a line intimative of your wish. As it is, having nothing particular to say, I should not, for my own pleasure, take the trip to Chatham. Tim will be here in a few days, and when I have had a conversation with him I may be less barren of gossip for you; but, in any case, if you wish me to run down to Chatham, say so, and I shall go, even if you had no more desire than to find fault with this letter and myself.

Do not tear this letter in anger, for I shall be curious after awhile to know what I could have written in forty pages, and what you thought of a great deal I have for the first time expressed to you. The words are held together by so slight a thread as a hair from the head of your affectionate wife,

MARY J. O'DONOVAN ROSSA.

CHATHAM, August 13th, 1870.

MRS. O'DONOVAN ROSSA, 178 *Stamford St., London:*

By Jove! Mollis, I don't know what to say to you now, after the terrible revelations you made to me to-day. To think that you would marry another man if I were dead! Oh, 'tis awful! and I'll not die as long as I can live. But I suppose 'tis worse to think of it alive than dead. I should like to talk to you, as the Germans say—*unter vier augen*—"under four eyes," on those distinctions you draw between love and passion. The characteristics of the latter may hit off myself, you think, but I am not going to give myself to you at such a valuation. You are out in your estimation of me here, as much as you are out in thinking that in the presence of God I have little religion, because I might differ a little from you. What would you say if it would be in a religious spirit I would incur so much of your displeasure as to get you to threaten you would not live with me? This you could not see by my regard for the outward ceremonies, but if you could regard the eyes of the soul you may see them fixed on their Creator, in the hope that He would accept the sufferings that are to be encountered in this world by all who seek to elevate God's work—accept my share of them in the risks I run as some atonement for my sins. I told you that I had a particular mental prayer, " that if the Almighty interfered in the petty ways of this world, He would in His mercy send me my punishment here, and peace hereafter." This is a pretty hard prayer, when I make it in view of the possibility of living years of absence from you, and under the pains and penalties of this servitude.

Yet it calms my mind in view of the future world, for God knows my mind, and if the reason He has given me does not enable me to view Him with other men's reason, how can I help it? I cannot act the hypocrite to God, and trample under foot what He has given me for my light. You would not like this prayer if you thought it would be heard so as to keep me in this living grave for a number of years. No, and no wonder. Nor would I desire the long-suffering, either; but eternity is longer, and though you imagine I think but little of that, I do not imagine so myself. There is another thing in the prayer you will object to, and that is the "if;" but I will not, for I cannot, do away with it. I see too much injustice in the world, and I cannot bring myself to say that it is God's work. I cannot, with the historian D'Aubigne, assert that " the history of the government of this world is the annals of the government of the Sovereign King." I may be wrong; the ways of the Lord are wonderful and inscrutable, but where I see many works that do not bear the impress of Him, I cannot help keeping my " if." I would like to be all that you desire, love—if I may take the license yet to call you love—but my first duty here is not to you, and certainly you are not so narrow-minded as to think that all are utterly lost who do not think as you and your father and Frank Donovan think on religious matters. Look at this extract from a letter received to-day from a lady correspondent: " If Catholics and Protestants will only unite, and not think it necessary to fight over religious differences, Ireland would ere long be free and happy. Strange that the children of one Father should hate one another (because they do not all see alike), and anathematize one another. The one true religion consists in loving God and one another, and in doing to others what we would wish done to ourselves. This is the pattern that our Master set us." Yes, that is the one true religion; but to be " religious" and act differently, is what I despise. Perhaps you take to heart my saying to you that, seeing the way priests in Ireland had treated me, I was satisfied to leave myself in the hands of God. Perhaps you think there is no salvation for me without begging from those who repudiate me for my love of country. It is not deemed irreverent to give worldly illustrations in matters divine. The Government of England sends a Lord Lieutenant to Ireland; that Lord Lieutenant imprisons me, yet when you seek my release you apply not to him, but to those who sent him. The priests excommunicate me. Granted, that they are the messengers of God: certainly all God's power and mercy is not in their keeping, and though they, as the Lord's Lieutenant, will not release me, the King can. Enough on this.

Saturday Morning.—I fell asleep last night at half-past ten, and did not wake till half-past four this morning. 'Twas the best, the only sleep, I may say, I had since I saw you. Can it be that such a letter as you think would trouble me, only calms me? —selfish still you see; not looking to your troubles, but to my own rest, and your giving me your confidence contributes to this. 'Twas hard of you to leave me thinking so long, that perhaps another blow was given to you in your father's death. If you are dilatory any more, I will give you credit for attending to happier correspondents, and I will banish you—from my dreams. But here it seems I am powerless, too, for you took care to impress yourself too deeply in the mind. And I *have* strange dreams about you sometimes. Only think that since I saw you I dreamt twice that you were married and settled down in the North of Ireland: if I dream it a third time, I don't know what will happen to me. One thing in my dreams that I like is, that I find myself always faithful to you, and no seductions will woo me away from you. This must be the waking image appearing in sleep. I have my waking dreams about you, too, and they are laden with more anguish. Twice lately—and the last occasion was on Wednesday, when you were writing to me—I found myself exclaiming, "Oh, Mollis," and I vowed a vow that I would " banish you, banish you," not think of you at all this side of Christmas. But then you have imposed an obligation on me that makes me think of you night and morning, and when I do kneel down a thought comes into my head that brings you with it. I forgot once, but that was while you were here. I forgot last night, too, till it was ten o'clock. I can say the Lord's prayer with as much fervor as you can, every word of it. Wouldn't that save me with good works, if I could work them, and avoidance of injury or ill will to fellow mortals? "Thy will be done" seems to me holier than to ask for anything which might be against His will. I don't like that parable, where the widow is represented as being justified on account of the annoyance she gave the magistrate, and I will not think of God's mercy in a parallel light. If suffering comes to me from praying that "Thy will be done," I can take it; and you, with more religion, ought too. Neither of us like suffering. Christ, even, is represented as having prayed that *His* would pass away from Him. Can it be expected that we can have a stronger manhood? God, St. Austin says, " hath only one son without sin, none without a scourge. "Deus unicum habet filium sine peccato, nullum sine flagello." Socrates says if all humanity came together to throw their ills in a heap, and then take share and share alike, none would be satisfied; and Addison has a paper showing the discontent of each after a similar sharing—each anxious to throw away the new ill and pick up the one he was used to. I don't know that you or I would have much reason to fear discomfort in such a case. You say you could curse fame. Ah, that's all very fine. I could say it, too; but what we want is to be happy, and that is what no mortal ever got in this world. If you and I had the fruition of our desires to-day, new ills would be engendered. I would be no sooner outside the prison gate than other troubles would assail me, and the realization of yours, without feelings of the eternal longing of the soul for something—if nothing else, something imaginary—would be just as impossible. I wish I had ten sheets to reply to your ten; I can't "expand" here; the mind is imprisoned, too, and though it be shallow, no serene sun has shone in our days to show you to the bottom of it. How I should like to take you up in love and passion. What is love? rather where is it as you describe? Yes, you may realize it in a father's or mother's love, but the love that sets the world mad, where is it without passion? 'Tis where the bee is without his sting—in cold, icy death. And *you* told me once at Moore's you could love me with this love. Where is it now, or were you only simulating, or is it now that you find me worthy of opening your mind to me? That you married me to make "the remnant of my life serene" for two, three or twelve months, also folds up a mystery. What was in me? What had I done for you that you should sacrifice yourself for me? Well, I *did* love you—perhaps I had better add "passionately." I don't know do you give me credit for that even, and I suppose nothing but pity—"for pity is akin to love"—on your part, granted me your favors. Tho' you mightn't see it, I see much of unity in our souls' depths. Here was I hunting my barren brain to get an illustration for you to set your imaginary troubles at rest as to my thinking of dead loves, by asking you would your maternal love be divided by having another child, and all this time you understood what I was hunting for in what you say as to your being able to "marry one hundred husbands one at a time," and not wronging either by undeserved coldness. Perhaps, after all, the feeling represented by this expression is only a common one to human nature—that widows and widowers dying un-remarried is only in the order of old maids and bachelors dying unmarried for the want of being satisfactorily mated. You believe that I would marry again if I trod the world and found you dead or divorced? Well, now, don't be so sure of that. In the harvest of my years, with the reaper perhaps sharpening his sickle for me, I would have no chance of improving on you, and in the spirit of "Excelsior" I could not be happy in descending. Then there being for me no " higher"—not even a parallel rung on the ladder, the probability is, nay the certainty is, that I would live the rest of my days a virgin. Unless, indeed, that it was by divorce you had been separated from me, and that fortune offered me a chance by visiting you with the misfortune of making you a widow.

The lines below, beginning "My Love," were written a week ago. Then I got this sheet to send you a copy of that stray letter—the Governor thought he could get the original suppressed one for me, but up to yesterday it came not; and then I told him I would use the paper to answer yours. As to our visit, I told him if it was to be a private one I would have it, but if we could not talk without others being present we could not talk on what we desired, and I would not ask you to come: he said that any way he could not admit you without an order, that you should have to apply to the Directors. Do so and keep it—the order—by you, that you may be able at any time to take a run to see me, if the wish to see me should take possession of you at any time while giving your readings in England. I am to see Mr. Fagan, and will ask him as to our being allowed to talk privately, as at the Commission, giving my parole not to pass anything to you, and also as to writing that letter to Mr. Gladstone referred to below. But don't hope anything from it. I asked the Commissioners to publish in their report that "Mrs. Moore letter," and the reply is that they will use their own discretion. In that last letter, speaking of that railway occurrence—the Waterford one—I told you what you tell me now, that I placed no trust in the honor or virtue of men, that my trust was in yourself, and that if my belief in Dr. Cullen's politico-religious teaching was as strong as my belief in your ability and will to maintain and defend your own honor and mine, he would not be thinking of hotter hells for me. But the Ennis affair, Mollis, was worse. Why will you blame me for being solicitous about you, your safeguards are all in yourself combined with the elements of the danger. It is a principal one to see that danger, and to recognize it as ever present. "Virtue," Dr. Johnson says in his "Vanity of Human Wishes," grows distressed at scorn of danger, and scorn of her remonstrant calls," and

"Fired with contempt she quits the slippery rein,
And pride and prudence take her seat in vain,
In crowd at once where none the pass defend,
The *harmless freedom and the private friend*.
The guardians yield by force superior plied,
To interest prudence, and to flattery pride."

Get from some library Burton's "Anatomy of Melancholy," and Henry Taylor's "Notes on Life." Taylor says: "Great intellect, according to the ways of Providence, almost always brings with it great infirmities, and it is certainly exposed to unusual temptations; for, as power and pre-eminence lie before it, so ambition attends, which, whilst it determines the will and strengthens the activities, inevitably weakens the moral fabric." Even without the stimulant of self-love, some minds, owing to a natural redundancy of activity and excess of facility, cannot be sufficiently passive to be wise." If, however, a man of genius be fortunately free from ambition, yet there is another enemy that will commonly lie in wait for his wisdom—to wit, great capacity for enjoyment; this generally accompanies geniuses, and is perhaps the greatest of all trials to the moral and spiritual heart. It was a trial too severe even for Solomon, "whose heart, though large, beguiled by fair idolatresses, fell to idols foul." A great capacity of suffering belongs to genius also, and it has been observed that an alternation of joyfulness and dejection is quite as characteristic of the person of genius, as intensity in either kind." Sydney Smith says, "Wit is dangerous, eloquence is dangerous. Everything is dangerous that has efficacy and vigor for its characteristics. Nothing is safe but mediocrity." I do not wonder at your finding most relief when most distant from Chatham. The same thoughts culminate in me, when I, in half joke and half earnest, speak the word "Divorce," granting that Church, State, society, and yourself above all, would allow this. I do not think you would be happy with another husband while I lived. Your ills might be only imaginary, but they would be thorns, nevertheless. Suffering is what the world will have from man and woman. Yours is intense; and, if you would fly from it, the world would not be charitable. I speak of this word because it would bring more relief to me to see you so, honorably may I say, separated from me, than to hear of your being forgetful of yourself or of me in the whirl of dangers that surround you. As it is, I fear you do not escape the evil tongue. If they say you are the cause of my giving evidence before this Commission, it is not true. Have you not my letter "commanding" you to come? Your love for me is not what I rely on for your safety; nor your pride nor your religion either. I rely on all together, and other elements, besides, embodied in yourself. Any one alone would not assure me. Even in religion people fall. And even though forgiveness should follow in such a case, I could not feel easy with you if I had been unfaithful. I should confess to you before I could have full free happiness with you after. Esteem for you, honor, self-respect, domesticity and "passionate" love, with other things apart from religion, would go far with me to make me true to you, but I must close. Read Bacon's essay on man being lightly dealt with, and woman being denounced as infamous for love-slips, and his reasons why. I suppose in the matter of esteem with you I have lost it, by showing myself to you so clearly lately.

Yours fondly, ROSSA.

MY LOVE: The foregoing is an exact copy of that letter which went astray. The Governor gave me the original suppressed one to re-write it. This day week you paid me that running visit, and I am most anxious since, and most troubled fearing that some other ills awaited you thro' your father's illness. I am dwelling on the worst;

this is bad, but I cannot help it. You said you would write or telegraph, or be back in a week—the week is past, and there is no news from you. If I could learn patience regarding you, as I must and can learn it regarding much that concerns me, I would be all right, but I am a bad scholar here, and I fear I can never improve. Do you know what I did to-day? Well, I shut you up in a Nunnery; I had a picture of you fixed on my door, and I took it down and put it out of sight amongst my papers. I don't know that that will improve matters, for the image impressed on the mind is more life-like and cannot be so easily returned. Having my papers in hands I looked for that letter of yours about the Commission—"Cæsar aut nullus" when you spoke, too, of being strong at last. I like to read those things when I feel troubled about you, but I found the letter was gone, so that you must have taken it amongst your papers in mistake, as I meant to keep it. You will, however, send me something instead of it— I don't know will you remember all you said you would send me, and all you said you would write. I intended at our final interview to have given you my mind upon the matter of your asking me to write what I wanted on paper so that you would submit it to the Government after the Commission, but time did not permit. I have applied for permission to write to Mr. Gladstone. If I am allowed to do so, I will ask him for a copy of the report, and ask him for permission for you to visit me while you are reading in England, say once every two months; that you would take your English rests at your Chatham lodgings and have liberty to visit me for a few days each time *sans ceremonie*. A wife can visit a political prisoner in France upon showing her marriage certificate, and if, as you think, there may be a desire to make a distinction between us and other convicts, this may be granted; but if not granted, why, we must only make the most of it. I think very often of that fit of passion you got into about my offer of divorce, or my manner of offering it, and I am asking myself could I have possibly offered it in any way that would make it agreeable or acceptable to you? Tell me, Love. You made me think of refractory cells, &c. If you could see into my thoughts you would see very litle reason to think I meant to insult you, and if you showed your mettle to all who *would* insult you, as you showed to me on this occasion, you would be well able to protect yourself. If our future prison interviews are to be in presence and hearing of officers, I do not see the use of your incurring expense by frequent visits. There is little use in my "looking at you" or you "looking at me," when our mouths must be closed on the (non-political) personal matters that we desire to talk most about. You can keep writing and be more communicative than formerly as to what happens. Never think that anyone is to see your letters but me, or, if you must think differently, think that they are priests, who will not talk about our exchange of confidences. The immense sum of money you must have spent since you left America is saddening—spent to no purpose. You think of getting me out of prison some time, and wouldn't you try to hoard up a trifle just to enable us to start in the world, if fate would have it so. You say you will never live with me again as we did live; I do not blame you for that. Why I suggest this avaricious thought to you is, that, having something in view, even making money tends to engage the mind, and withold it from perhaps worse thoughts. You left in a very depressed state of mind. Ah, the "ambition," and "pride," and "individuality" of the first day was gone —gone entirely. Cannot you recover from me now that we are separated. I was about thinking when I heard you speak that you were a desperate case, and that even with a fair field I'd have something to do to win the old place in your affections. But I must close, and will do so by telling you to remember what you read to me one evening out of your favorite author, viz: "That many women were disposed to excuse improprieties, rudeness and impertinence, when the person puts his conduct to the credit of his inability to resist the attractions of the lady."

Yours, ever fondly and faithfully, ROSSA.

Lest you would be jealous of my having a lady correspondent, I must tell you that the lady I received the letter from is the Marchioness of Queensberry. It is a very pretty letter. Let you acknowledge my receipt of it, and tell her that I am one with her in the religious and political opinions expressed in it. I do not believe a word of your saying you would never take the same amount of trouble for me or for any other man again. Yours, Mollis, "CARISS."

P. S.—You might send me Shawn's letter and those other letters you promised me, and keep writing to me once every two months, and avail of the chance of writing a reply to this if it does not vex you terribly. I don't intend to vex you, tho' your words being held together by a hair of your head, would? I suppose, convey that they could be easily broken. I thought to ask you for that curl that hung in your forehead, but I forgot it. Send me that poem, if printed, that I may see it; and if you give readings, send scraps telling about them to the Governor. Do these things or get them done. If I do not get them, let not the reason be that you did not give the chance. Keep me "posted" as to yourself.

Yours, my poor woman, ever fondly and faithfully too,

I mustn't call you "Love" any more. ROSSA.

CHAPTER XXI.

THE COMMISSION OF INQUIRY—LORD DEVON CHAIRMAN—EXAMINATION OF DIRECTORS, GOVERNORS, WARDERS AND PRISONERS—OFFICIAL FALSEHOODS—MR. BRUCE, THE HON. SECRETARY OF STATE, A CONVICTED LIAR—THE COMMISSIONERS AGREE IN THEIR REPORT, BUT THE "DOCTORS DIFFER."

The Commissioners appointed to conduct the inquiry were Lord Devon, George C. Broderick, Stephen E. De Vere, Doctor Robert D. Lyons and Doctor E. Headlam Greenhow. They commenced their sittings on the 24th of May and ended on the 20th of September. They held sixty-three meetings; eight of which were in Chatham Prison. The fourth of July was their first day there, and during the three previous days Halpin, McClure, Mulleda, O'Connell and myself were kept from chapel, and kept in solitary confinement lest we might avail of our ordinary intercourse to combine in making up a case against the authorities.

I have their statements before me in a Blue Book, published by the Queen's printers, Eyre & Spotteswood, London, 1870, and I will leave a few words from each on record, to show that though they were prisoners in the hands of a cold-blooded enemy, they were still men, and fearless men at that, trying even in their bonds to uphold the standard of the cause for which they suffered. General Halpin writes:

"*To the Commissioners appointed to inquire into the treatment of Treason Felons in English Prisons*:
"CHATHAM PRISON, July 20, '72.

"GENTLEMEN: * * * From my knowledge of the capacity of some of the witnesses that should, and very likely will, be examined by the Commissioners to make false reports and lying statements in reference to the class of prisoners whose treatment is to be inquired into, I have no hesitation in saying that such witnesses will not tell the truth except under oath and through a strict cross-examination. * * * *

"I did not from the beginning believe that the Government would appoint a Commission to prove its own public statements untrue, or that it could afford such an investigation as would unveil the facts and lay the official sores open to public view, and I find the action of the State authorities, and the Commissioners since their appointment, justify this conclusion. First, the Commission is to be secret, and acting in the dark, refusing not only the representatives of the press admission, but even denying counsel to act on the part of the prisoner. Every artifice that cunning could suggest has been resorted to to keep us in the dark, and keep us from even knowing the cause of this inquiry. * * * * * * * * * * * * * *

"To comment on such acts would be a waste of time. The Commissioners give me permission to wirte to my friends on the subject of the Commission. Mr. Bruce takes that permission away. The Commissioners tell me I can have the assistance of a friend in making up my statement. Mr. Bruce says I cannot. What a mockery! what a sham is this whitewashing Commission, appointed by the Home Secretary to cover up his falsehoods and his frauds! The orders of the Commission, as well as those of the Home Secretary, are plainly meant for the public eye. They are intended to deceive; they pretend to confer rights in public which are taken away in private. Perfidy has long been the characteristic of England's rulers, and it appears they have no intention of shaking it off. I am, gentlemen, respectfully,

WM. G. HALPIN."

John McClure, born in America, concludes in this manner:

"GENTLEMEN: * * * I feel compelled, in justice to myself, to decline to take a part in the present proceedings, in consequence of experiencing a want of confidence in the impartiality and completeness of the present investigation. I may, I think, with propriety, add here, that a torturing and living death, with every circumstance specially adapted to render life miserable, has been an alternative which the public and my Government were led to believe was a singular act of clemency, when, in 1867, the Government of England awarded penal servitude for life in exchange for an unnatural but speedy death.

"I regret to be obliged to say that three years experience of this merciful alternative gives me every reason to view that apparent act of clemency in a totally different light, and strongly inclines me to look upon a power that could thus torture me as being

"Too 'merciful' in public gaze to take our lives away,
Too anxious here to plant in us the seed of life's decay."

"There has been a sad want of that magnanimity which is so much admired in, and expected from, a generous and humane victor, towards a fallen adversary. To treat me as if I had been guilty of some degrading or ignominious crime is hardly deserved.

"Such a proceeding but degrades the power that can inflict on honorable men the infamous punishments allotted to the thief and vile outcasts of society.

JOHN McCLURE."

John Devoy says:

"GENTLEMEN: * * * Five years bitter experience, to say nothing of the record of seven hundred more, have made me look with suspicion on everything emanating from the quarter in which your Commission had its origin. * * * In conclusion, I will say that I have never asked for an inquiry, because I believed that a complete and impartial one would not be granted, and that if friends of mine, or of the other prisoners, did ask, it was for a *public one*."

Henry Shaw (Mulleda) says:

"GENTLEMEN: * * * I—after calm, careful and deliberate consideration—came to the conclusion that I could not, consistently with the duty which I owe to myself, do otherwise than decline to make any statement. * * * I assure you that I am actuated solely by the conviction that I should be but aiding and abetting a delusion in acting otherwise, as I am convinced that nothing but a full, fair and public inquiry will ever succeed in eliciting the whole truth."

When I look over the proceedings of the Commissioners at Portland Prison, I find the action taken by the prisoners there was somewhat similar to ours. All refused to have anything to do with them. Governor Clifton is examined, and asked what each of the prisoners said when he offered them paper to make statements.

Question Number 2209.—LORD DEVON—What did George Brown say?—This prisoner declined to take the paper I offered him, saying, "I do not want to say anything; want nothing to do with it."

"2213.—Did Luby make any statement?—He asked if the Earl of Devon was the same nobleman who was on the Land Commission in Ireland. I said, 'I believe he is the same nobleman,' when the prisoner replied that Dan O'Connell said at the time it was like a jury of butchers trying a sheep.'"

"2216.—Did John O'Leary make any statement?—He declined to receive any paper, saying that they might have spared themselves all the trouble, as he did not intend to make any statement."

"2217.—Did Michael Sheehy make any statement?—The prisoner declined to receive any paper, and stated that while in British pens he would make no statement 'I have been treated badly, and I have plenty of complaints to make. Dr. Blaker knows the state of my health. If there are Irishmen coming over to sit on this Commission, they are in the pay of the British Government.'"

"2218.—Did Mortimer Shea *alias* Moriarty make any statement?—This prisoner declined to receive any paper, saying that he did not wish to have any connexion with the Commission."

"2219.—Did Edward St. Clair make any statement?—This prisoner declined to receive any paper, saying that he did not wish to have any connexion with the Commission."

"2220.—Did John McCafferty say anything?—McCafferty—this prisoner declined to receive any paper, or to make any statement until he goes outside, when he will do it upon oath. He further stated that he would not go before the Commission unless by force."

"2223.—Did Patrick Walsh make any statement?—This prisoner declined to take any paper, and when informed that he would not be sent out to work during the three days, said, 'I wish they were going to stay away. If they are my countrymen, they are humbugs.'"

"2227.—At the same time that you asked the prisoners those questions to which they gave the replies that you have now stated, were they singly brought before you? They were, my lord."

The Commissioners do not seem at all satisfied with this state of things, and sending for John O'Leary, the Chairman asks him:

"2542.—Do you wish to make a statement to the Commission?—Yes, I wish to say I asked for no Commission, I wished for no Commission, and, when I heard some time ago that some Commissioners were appointed I fully made up my mind to make no statement of grievances to any body of men that would be sent down; and as to anything that I have to say about my treatment in prison, whatever I do say, I intend to take my own time and place for saying. * * * * * * * It would seem that what you want to know is, whether we have been subject to any hardships except those incident to persons sentenced to penal servitude. I may complain that we have been treated no worse than murderers and thieves. It appears to me that it is at least an exceedingly consistent proceeding on the part of the author of the celebrated letters to Lord Aberdeen to be sent down here."

"2544.—Do you wish to make any statement on those points?—No, not to you; not that you should for a moment be under any delusion of my having more serious reason. You must, in fact, take us to be an extraordinary humble-minded class of men, to think we would make complaints."

"2551.—It appears to me, to ask a person of my political principles whether I got punished, would be like an Oliver Twist kind of business—asking for more porridge."

At the Invalid Convict Prison, in Woking, Denis Dowling Mulcahy has a long argument with the Commissioners. He requires all the conditions that are necessary to a fair and impartial inquiry, and, failing to get them, he refuses to go into his case.

"6489.—Did I understand your lordship to say that the report of Messrs. Pollock & Knox would not be allowed?

"6490.—It will not.—Well, my lord, I must say that I think that a very important document, for if I gave certain evidence to them which they have suppressed; I should think it very important and requisite to understand that."

"6491.—That is no part of our inquiry.—But I have learned from my friends that that report has been made use of repeatedly by the Home Secretary. I wish to show that I have stated many important matters to those Commissioners that were not stated in that report, and that report was used as evidence against us to prove that we were untruthful."

"6493.—We cannot go into that.—Very good, my lord."

"6494.—But you can go into anything that you think material in the absence of that report.—Yes, but if I had the report of Messrs. Pollock & Knox, I could show that I stated to them two or three very important facts with regard to the bread and water, and the hæmoptysis, and being sent to Dartmoor when it was known, as I can show from the very documents I have here now, which have come from the prison books, and which are the most meagre abstracts that they could make, that while I suffered from hæmoptysis I was sent to the quarries."

"8209.—CHAIRMAN—I think I must tell you, Mulcahy, that you have received all the papers which, under the sanction of superior authority, it is decided are to be given to you.—Very good, my lord; I consider that insufficient to prove the charges, and that the powers of the Commission are too limited to enable me to substantiate my case."

I myself had a long statement for the Commissioners. I will not reproduce the whole of it here, as it would be only repeating many things I have previously stated. In its preparation I took good care not to make any complaints regarding anything I suffered. One of the objects of the Commission was to inquire if we were treated "exceptionally," and I laid points and particulars of the treatment before them, leaving them to judge whether or not my examination thereon was pertinent to their business. If it was, I was their humble servant; if it was not, I had nothing to say.

This is how I met them:

"TO THE COMMISSIONERS OF INQUIRY :
"*Quod tibi fieri non vis alteri ne feceris.*"
CHATHAM PRISON, June 30, '70.

GENTLEMEN : If you were prisoners in France, under Napoleon the Third, as you might be if William the Conqueror and his successors had ruled England from France, instead of becoming English, and if you had been treated as I have been, and had been somewhat misrepresented and belied; and, after having had experience of one Commission of Inquiry being a sham, if you learned that another was coming on, you would be able to understand why I commence with the above quotation.

Taking it for granted that you may be determined to elicit the whole truth, I have reasons to fear you cannot succeed, and here is one of them : I was thirty-five consecutive days in this prison with my hands tied behind my back. I have reason to believe that this putting of me in irons was by order of the Board of Directors. Well, the story one way or another gets into the world ; and though it is in accordance with prison "discipline," the Government deem it proper to contradict it, and the Board of Directors who ordered the punishment, do actually, through one of their own body, hold an inquiry at this prison to prove that no such punishment took place. * * * Mr. Gladstone is at the head of the English Government at present. He is a writer as well as a statesman, and, if my memory serves me right, he has in some book written that in any nation or institution where publicity is guarded against and secrecy provided for, abuses must necessarily exist.

My letters are suppressed because I speak of my treatment, and the British Government defame my character by saying that it is because I have told lies in them. I have asked you to call for those letters to question me on them, and I hope you will do so.

"*Crimine ab uno disce omnes.*"

Mr. Gladstone, in speaking of the treatment of prisoners at Naples, writes these words; but where is the man coming to see an English prison can speak to an English prisoner and ask him for information as to the treatment ? That man is not to be found. The visitor will find everything in the nicest apple-pie order, and, as Mr. Gladstone saw in Naples, he will see excellent rules and regulations hung up in every corner; he will see a Bible in every cell, even in the one where the victim is chained and being starved; and if he comes on a Sunday he will see 1,500 men parading for chapel, each with a Bible and prayer-book exposed to view. What wonder if he says to himself, "Oh ! this is the paradise of saints ;" but he little knows the curses that are burning, the hell that is seething under this phylactery face which discipline makes her votaries assume, at the peril of losing their daily bread. If it be a digression to speak here of what does *not* tend to the reformation of these English children of misfortune, I will, for an excuse, again borrow the words of another, and say, "*Homo sum, humani nihil a me alienum puto.*"

I do not see any rule which authorizes discipline to deprive a man of the use of the Bible for six months, and yet this sentence was passed on me.

I do not see anything in the rules to warrant the authorities stripping me naked once a day for three or four months, and yet discipline does it.

I also fail to see any rule that obliges me to bathe in water in which other men had bathed and washed, and this I had to do often.

When I applied to the Director, Captain Gambier, for a sufficiency of coarse bread, and remarked that that was what England would not refuse as a right to the State prisoner of any other country, he refused it, with the observation that " England has no State prisoners now-a-days." England may not like to have the odium that attaches to any country having State prisoners, and she may try to get rid of it by labelling us as thieves and murderers. She would have her vengeance and her Christian character at the same time, and she hopes you will assist her. I can only hope you will be just.

As to exceptional treatment, might I not ask, how is it explained that I have been separated from the rest of the Irish prisoners and sent to Chatham, under the cir-

cumstances I state? How is it explained that in Portland I have been separated from the Irish prisoners and sent among a gang of English prisoners? How is it explained that, while in Portland, the rest of the treason-felony prisoners working in mid-winter in a shed, I was placed outside the shed, and prevented from having that little shelter from the poison-laden blast which the others had? How is it explained that, when under "report" the same day with some of my fellow-prisoners, on a charge of talking while at work, they got twenty-four hours on bread and water, and I got seventy-two hours on bread, with fourteen days' solitary confinement on penal class-diet? * * * * * * I remain, gentlemen, yours respectfully,
JER. O'DONOVAN ROSSA.

MR. WILLIAM PITT BUTTS, Governor of Chatham Prison, recalled:

6589.—CHAIRMAN—Have you a communication to make, Mr. Butts?—Yes, my lord. Rossa has just written that, and sends it to you.

6590.—The Chairman read the following letter:

" TO THE COMMISSIONERS OF INQUIRY':
" CHATHAM PRISON, July 19th, 1870.

"GENTLEMEN: The Secretary of State knows that since you were here I applied for a copy of Messrs. Knox and Pollock's report, and he leaves my application unattended to as yet. I have been shown by my wife an official statement emanating from that honorable gentleman, and I very reluctantly say there is something wrong in every paragraph of it. He says my letters to my wife were suppressed because they contained falsehoods. I present to you six of these letters; I undertake to show you they do not contain a single falsehood; and, with all due respect, I ask you to invite the Secretary of State to be present. I submit to you four or five printed letters—printed as from me. I write my name on each, to acknowledge the authorship, and I undertake to show you that they contain no falsehood.

" I remain, gentlemen, yours very obediently,
" JER. O'DONOVAN ROSSA.

" P. S.—I desire that all witnesses at the inquiry be examined on oath."

7067.—CHAIRMAN—You stated, just now, that three letters written by the prisoner, Halpin, to Mr. Motley, Mr. J. F. O'Donnell and Mr. Callan, were suppressed by order of Secretary of State?—They were, my lord.

7068.—Are you in possession of the Secretary of State's letter announcing that they were to be suppressed?—I am.

JEREMIAH O'DONOVAN ROSSA examined:

4901.—CHAIRMAN—We are a Commission, I should explain to you, appointed by Government, but entirely independent of the Government, for the purpose of inquiring into the treatment of yourself and the other prisoners under the treason-felony act, at present confined in prisons in England. I had better name for you the Commissioners first: This is Dr. Greenhow; this is Mr. De Vere; this is Dr. Lyons; this is Mr. Broderick, and I am the Chairman, Lord Devon. Our object is to receive, in the fullest and freest way, from any one of the prisoners into whose case we are going to inquire, any statement, orally or in writing, or both, which you may wish to submit. The statement will be made to us in a private room, and out of the hearing of any person connected with the prison, and, whatever the statement may be, it will in no way prejudice the future position of the prisoner as regards the prison in which he is. He will be none the worse for it in any way.

4907.—Do you wish to defer your examination until you have an opportunity of conferring with your wife, or other friends, to aid you in preparing your statement, written or oral, to be laid before this Commission?—Well, I have written something, and I am prepared to give it up to you; and I do not know whether it would be too much delay, but if you would look over it I then would be prepared to answer any questions you put to me, and be ready, when you come again, to be examined further.

4913.—But we think it would be better now not to enter on your examination. If you, after seeing your wife, wish to make a supplementary statement, it can be put in an envelope and handed to the Governor, who will hand it to us.—I have no objection, my lord, he should get a copy to send to the Director, or Secretary of State, or any others you wish.

4914.—Your examination being deferred to the 19th, is there any matter that you wish to state to us now before you withdraw?—Well, my lord, you said that any thing I would say would not prejudice me in future.

4915.—No.—Well, I have some experience of prison life, and I do not know how—though you may be very much inclined to protect me—how you could, if the authorities desired to keep punishing me; for they can get thousands of excuses to punish me and say that it is a breach of discipline; and I do not know how you would be able to learn it, or become aware of it.

4929.—Dr. Lyons—Is it your impression that you were punished with bread and water in consequence of having given evidence before Messrs. Knox and Pollock?—I could not say, Dr. Lyons.

4931.—Mr. Broderick—You were actually placed on bread and water in a dark cell?—Yes, in a darkened cell; not entirely dark. On those gentlemen coming to make inquiry, they said to me, "We have nothing whatever to do with prison discipline." And when I was laying before them the matters that concerned me, they said, "That comes under prison discipline, and we have nothing to do with it." Coming to make an inquiry under such circumstances does not appear honest.

Captain Stopford was one of the Prison Directors, and when the chaining of me for thirty-five days was questioned, he was sent down to Chatham to doctor up a report for the Secretary of State. He got the very men who tied me day after day to deny having done so.

He says: "The books are examined, and I find only one entry of the prisoner being handcuffed behind, and that was on the 17th of June, 1868."

Lord Devon, examining me, asks:

Question No. 7155.—Having read that, and observed what was stated there, do you still remain of opinion, and are you prepared to tell us that it was for thirty-five days?—Yes, my lord.

7156.—Mr. De Vere—And that those days were following one another?—Yes, Mr. De Vere.

7157.—Dr. Lyons—Why do you remember so distinctly that the number of days was thirty-five?—I fixed them in my memory at the time, and the suffering that I endured, and the cuts on my hands and everything made a very vivid impression on my memory; and, my lord, at the expiration of those thirty-five days, twenty-eight days bread and water commenced. The date of the commencement of the bread and water must be in the prison books, and from the time I committed the offence until I got the bread and water, until the Director's order was read for my punishment, I was in irons all the time.

7158.—After the thirty-five days you were put on bread and water?—Yes, Mr. Lyons.

7183.—Whom else do you refer to?—Another day I distinctly recollect Father O'Sullivan coming in, and from the blood that had trickled from the marks on my wrists, I had written on the door, "Might I not cry out ' blood for blood.' "

7197.—Did you suffer much from the cuts or scrapes?—No; they did not fester. I did not care much for cuts; only the *animus* that I thought was displayed in treating me so.

7220.—Mr. Broderick—I see that you say in the latter part of your statement that shortly before this offence was committed, the Governor came to you in your cell, and on your refusing to salute him, that he used the expression, "I treat you with contempt!"—That was not in the cell, sir. I was summoned; I was taken before him for refusing to salute him.

7222.—What passed upon that occasion when you were taken before him on this charge?—I said that I did not mean to be disrespectful towards him, or any officer of the prison, but that I could not conscientiously be paying salaams to authorities that were assassinating me.

7223.—Chairman—That you would not pay salaams to authorities that were assassinating you?—Yes, to authorities that were assassinating me. I used the word "assassinating." At the same time, I said it was not through disrespect to him, and he said, "I treat you with contempt!"

7224.—Mr. Broderick—You are quite sure that he used the expression, "I treat you with contempt?"—I am quite sure he did.

7226.—Mr. Broderick—What happened after that?—I thought he would treat me with contempt, as he said, but he came after that to my cell, and I just remained in the same position. Whatever position I was in when he came I remained in it, and for doing so I was again cited before him for highly insubordinate conduct and treating him with disrespect, and he gave me two days' bread and water for that, after saying he would treat me with contempt. That was not treating me with contempt. So when the officers came again and called on me to salute the Governor, I committed the offence that is stated.

7227.—Had the officers, before you committed that offence, used violence to bring your hands into the attitude of "attention?" Had they attempted to make you use the salaam?—Yes, they had; three of them, before the Governor in his office.

7230.—CHAIRMAN—What did the officers do?—One of the officers, Allison, came behind me and caught me; another officer came to this hand, and another to this hand, and kept them down. I went to the Governor and first stood this way (standing upright) before him, and that was "highly contumacious."

7247.—When Captain Du Cane came to the prison during that time, as you inform us that he did, did you not appeal to him against that sentence?—I did not, sir; oh, no, I did not; I knew I had committed the offence, and I took the punishment without making any appeal against it.

7248.—Do you remember on what account it was that you did come before him on that occasion?—I came before him. I was charged with this offence. He read out the offence for me, and he asked me what I had to say. I said I had nothing to say; that I committed it. "Well," says he, "It is getting worse, instead of better, you are. It is very brutal conduct." "It is just a reflex," said I, "of the treatment I received." I was sent back to my cell.

7250.—And you never expressed a wish to petition the Secretary of State on the subject?—No, sir.

7268.—Between the day when you threw the water in the Governor's face, and the day that you saw Captain Du Cane—which I see was the first of July—did you ever refuse to put on your jacket?—Yes.

7269.—Did you on several occasions refuse to do so?—Yes.

7270.—Did you tell the warder that he might do it himself?—Yes: "You can put it on, officer." I felt uneasy with the jacket on, and wanted to keep it off. I said, "You can put it on if you wish; I have more freedom without it."

7271.—That occurred four days. On the 24th of June you refused to put on your jacket, and you did the same on the 25th, 26th, 27th and 29th of June, according to this record?—That will corroborate that I had the irons on those days.

7282.—Are you quite sure that you were in irons during thirty-five days?—I am quite sure.

7283.—How do you know that it was thirty-five days?—I counted every day of them at the time, and they fixed themselves in my memory.

7284.—Are you quite sure that during the whole of that thirty-five days you were on light-labor diet?—Yes, sir, I am.

7285.—You think your memory does not deceive you about it?—Not in the least.

7286.—And during those twenty-eight days that you were on bread and water you were not in irons at all?—No, sir.

7295.—At the end of the thirty-five days during which you were handcuffed you say that you were again handcuffed for two days additional?—Yes, sir.

7296.—With heavy irons?—Yes.

7305.—When the handcuffs were put on you, were you perfectly quiet?—I was perfectly quiet.

7306.—You never resisted?—I never resisted.

7307.—You allowed them to be put on and you were perfectly quiet?—I was perfectly quiet, and I allowed them to handle me in any way they pleased.

7308.—But you did refuse to put on your jacket on several occasions?—Yes, that is so.

7311.—It was within your cell you usually refused to put on the jacket?—Within my cell.

7312.—On all occasions?—Yes; except I might meet the officer at the door, and I would perhaps just say I felt better without it, that the weather was warm, and he could put it on if he liked, and if he wished to put it on I would let him put it on.

7320.—When you were brought before Captain Du Cane did you tell him how long you had been handcuffed?—I did not, sir.

(Mr. Butts and Principal Warder King here brought in handcuffs.)

7330.—CHAIRMAN—Rossa, look at those handcuffs, and see which of those kind of handcuffs was put on you. Are those all the patterns of handcuffs used in the prison? MR. BUTTS—Yes, my lord. PRISONER—These are the kind that were on me thirty-five days.

(Principal Warder King puts the handcuffs indicated by the prisoner on Dr. Lyons, with the hands in front.)

7331.—CHAIRMAN—Now, Rossa, show how it was that your wrist was wounded?—PRISONER—If he pressed the spring this way it would catch, but if he pressed it this way it would not catch. If he made the pressure below it would not be fair.

7332.—DR. LYONS—If, in closing the spring, he held up the hand?—Yes, it would catch then.

7333.—Did I understand you to say that you were obliged to take off your jacket while you had the handcuffs on?—No, certainly not.
7334.—Dr. Lyons (with irons on his wrists, pours water into a glass and drinks it.) Prisoner—Yes, you could eat and drink with the handcuffs in front comfortably enough.

(The handcuffs were taken off and put on again with the hands behind.)

7336.—Dr. Lyons—For how many consecutive hours were you manacled with your hands behind your back?—From between six and seven hours in the morning—that is, from half-past five to twelve o'clock—and from about half-past twelve or a quarter-past one to about a quarter-past seven in the evening. That was something about thirteen hours.
7337.—Did you find it excessively fatiguing, or painful, or very distressing?—Oh, certainly, sir.
7344.—Chairman—Now, I ask you, O'Donovan Rossa, whether your punishment during the period of thirty-five days that you were under report was more severe or less severe than the punishment that you had to undergo after your sentence?—Well, it was as severe; it was more physically severe, but I did not feel the hunger that I felt in the twenty-eight days bread and water.

(The Commission deliberated for some time.)

7350.—Dr. Greenhow—Rossa, after being handcuffed and put upon punishment diet for twenty-eight days, you were placed for six months in penal class?—Yes, penal class diet commenced—a punishment of six months—but I was released from that punishment about the second of October, I think.
7352.—Dr. Lyons—Can you remember distinctly what your sensations were when you were put on the bread-and-water punishment?—On the first day that you were put on the bread-and-water diet what were your sensations as to hunger or otherwise?—Oh, I felt so hungry that I began to think of books that I read in my youth about men being pushed into places and eating rats and mice, and I recollect well the feeling I had in youth about men eating those things. I thought men could not do it. But I thought then that I could do it myself.
7353.—Was that the sensation you experienced the first day?—Oh, not the first day, but often while I was in prison.
7832 (Referring to the Mrs. Moore letter.)—Are you positive that the Governor used the word "intrigue," in speaking to you of this matter?—Yes, I am positive.
7841.—You did not show him the words "for Mrs. O'D.," on the first occasion?—No, he did not show me the letter on the first occasion—he did not show me the letter at all; but he used these words to me, "It was only yesterday that I saw for Mrs. O'D., in small writing. That I believe was only a subterfuge. I told the Secretary of State so, and I told the Board of Directors so. I said "you told them what was false."
7842.—Mr. De Vere.—Is it your wish now to state to this Commission, in as solemn a way as you can do it, without the sanction of an oath, that the letter now referred to was written for and intended for your wife, and for no other person whatever?—Yes, sir. I state that solemnly, and I will swear it if you desire.
7848.—What do you wish to have done in regard to this matter, when you state that you bring the matter before us with the view of our doing justice to you?—If what the Governor told me is on record in any official place; if he wrote to the Secretary of State or the Board of Directors that he believed the letter was for Moore's wife, I wish to have that destroyed, wherever that paper is, or any official record of it.
7849.—You wish to have it destroyed?—Yes.
7850.—Supposing that that cannot be done, what else do you wish?—I do not know what else can be done. A man does not know what happens after he is dead and gone; but we all know this, that State paper offices are ransacked and matters looked upon, and in twenty or fifty years' time this may come forward to defame my name, or be brought against my children.
7853.—If it was intended to go to your wife, why was it not addressed to her at once?—My wife was at the time, my lord, connected with the "Prisoner's" Fund Committee for relieving families of prisoners, and I calculated that the letter to my wife would be stopped in the Dublin post-office, her name being more remarkable; and Moore gave me the address of his mother. I asked him the address of his mother, because he told me previously that his mother used to go to my wife to get some of this money weekly from her.
7885.—Chairman—You state that with the distinct intimation that we shall go into this matter at Portland, so that any statement you make will be tested by examination?—I desired to be brought before Mr. Clifton in the presence of Messrs. Knox and

Pollock, but they told me that they could not do that, and they also told me that he and his officers contradicted all that I said.

7868.—Did not Mr. Clifton on a subsequent occasion use this expression to you, that he "could not be sending your love-letters to your wife?"—He did, sir.

7869.—Was that in reference to this former affair or not?—No, sir; it was in reference to a letter or words that I had written on a slate for him to copy. He told me that he would do this in consequence of a letter he received from my wife, asking permission for me to write to her, answering some questions. I wrote these words on a slate, and sent the slate to Mr. Clifton, and in about a month after, I asked him about the matter, and he said "I could not be writing your love-letters to your wife."

7871.—CHAIRMAN—Why did you write on a slate?—Paper was not allowed, my lord. I was not due for a letter.

7875.—DR. LYONS—Do you, after hearing what Cranston stated about your being manacled on the 16th of June, adhere to your statement that it was on the 17th it commenced?—I do, sir.

7877.—DR. GREENHOW—Each day when you went out to exercise, your hands were tied behind your back?—Yes, sir. I expected officer Goad would give fair evidence on the matter, being a religious man. One day he was tying my hands behind, and he must have noticed the cut, for he said, "I will not hurt you." "I do not mind," said I, "so long as a man does not intend it."

7983.—Have you suffered from any deficiency of clothing from that time till now?—I have in Portland; I felt so cold at one time that it induced me to leave off work and go into the cell one morning.

7984.—Were you then employed in the quarry work at Portland?—I was, sir, and my hands got sore—they got yellowish, the skin got whitish and then broke out.

7985.—Do you know what chilblains are?—Well, I never had anything like these before; never had chilblains, but in three or four places the flesh just melted out.

7986.—Did the doctor treat you for it?—I showed them to him in Portland. I asked him for inside work, and he said my hands were not bad enough yet.

7987.—DR. LYONS—He said what?—He said my hands were not bad enough yet to give me inside work.

7991.—DR. LYONS—What kind of gloves did you get?—They had no fingers. They fit on the hand like a bag. They call them "gloves." I was treated for the hands in Millbank, after leaving Portland. They kept sore for a few months up to May. I got ointment from the doctor in Millbank for them.

8030.—DR. LYONS.—Do I understand that you wish to send for Mr. McCarthy Downing?—My wife showed me a copy of some correspondence he had with the Secretary of State. If both attend, I would wish it.

8031—DR. GREENHOW—Both of whom?—Both Mr. Downing and the Secretary of State, on the treatment and the inaccuracy of the statement Mr. Bruce made in Parliament. Mr. Downing has written to him, saying he called to this prison and made a kind of examination among the prison officials.

The Commission deliberated.

8032.—CHAIRMAN—We are come here, O'Donovan Rossa, to receive any evidence which you or any person in your position may wish to render. If you wish to have Mr. McCarthy Downing examined, you can tell him so, and he can offer himself if he likes to do so, but the Commission do not see any reason for calling him?—Well, my lord, I will abide by the decision of the Commission. * * * * *

8741.—CHAIRMAN—Then your point is this, that Mr. Fagan granted you a visit from your wife on the 14th of June, and you wish to know why she did not come?—She told me why she did not come. I will ask another question, my lord. Did I understand from your lordship or any gentleman of the Commission, the first day of your coming here, that you told me or told any of the prisoners that any person they would have to assist them during the Commission would be allowed to them every day during the Commission?

8742.—No. We told you that assistance might be given by a friend before the Commission commenced the examination, but not afterwards.—I was speaking to other prisoners about my wife not being allowed to come, and Halpin told me that he distinctly recollected Mr. Lyons telling him so.

8743.—CHAIRMAN—No, we did not do that. We came to the conclusion, which we communicated to the prisoners, that as soon as the examination of a prisoner commenced, his intercourse with friends ceased.—Of course, my lord, I am in a very helpless position. It is very hard I cannot have a person to speak to.

8744.—We have decided that.—I will not press it, my lord. On Thursday evening I asked you about a witness named Douglas.

8747.—Do you know where the man Douglas is?—My wife knows where his wife is. I understand he is in Scotland.

8748.—He is no longer in the service?—No, my lord. I was just thinking that even though you have evidence enough to satisfy you that I was telling you the truth, still, he has one passage in his letter——

9748.—I may tell you at once that, as regards the length of time you were under handcuffs, we have entries in the prison books to show that you were handcuffed. They do not say whether you were handcuffed behind or before, but that you were handcuffed for thirty-four days, one after another, with intermissions, therefore you need bring no proof of that.—But the handcuffs behind, my lord?

8750.—If you wish to support that allegation you will bring witnesses.

8751.—Dr. LYONS—Are you still positive about that, that every day you were handcuffed with your hands behind your back?—Positive.

8752.—CHAIRMAN—You must bring evidence if you wish to support that allegation?—I do wish to support that allegation, my lord.

8780.—Dr. LYONS—I see entered here: "Monday, 1st of June, 1868, 9549, J. O'D. Rossa, three days' punishment diet"?—Yes, it commenced that day, Mr. Lyons.

8782.—Dr. GREENHOW—Why were you put on punishment that day?—I refused to work with the prisoners outside, after seeing the unpleasant life I led with them and the position in which I was.

8783.—Dr. LYONS—You got three days' bread and water because you refused to work outside?—Yes.

8786.—Dr. LYONS—On the expiration of those three days, were you again put on punishment diet?—Yes, Mr. Lyons.

8787.—When?—The 5th of June. After the three days expired then one day intervened, and I was on report for the next day. During the time that I was under bread and water I refused to salute the Governor. I desired to be left quietly in my cell to take my punishment. I was punished for highly insubordinate conduct; that is the insubordinate conduct, refusing to salute the Governor.

8788.—Is that what you call the salaam?—That is what I call the salaam.

8789.—Commencing when?—The 5th. I have the date here, Mr. Lyons.

8790.—Dr. GREENHOW—What words did you use that day, when you behaved in this offensive manner, as alleged?—I cannot recollect, sir, what words I used; but I recollect using the words before him in the adjudication room about assassination.

8791.—Dr. LYONS—On the 5th of June I find "J. O'D. Rossa placed in dark cell, by order of the Governor, at 7 p. m. on the 4th inst.?"—On the 4th.

8794.—On the 5th there is, I find, a further entry: "J. O'D. Rossa, three days' penal diet." Is that the case?—That is the case; yes.

8795.—That is the case?—Yes.

8796.—When again were you put under punishment diet?—June the 9th is the next.

8797.—That period, of course, would end on the 8th?—Yes; and then a day intervening to have me under report.

8798.—I find that you were twice reported on the 8th?—What is the second report, Mr. Lyons?

8799.—The first report states, "Reported by Warder Brown, for highly insubordinate and disrespectful conduct towards Captain Powell, on the morning of the 5th of June." Also reported again for "highly insubordinate conduct towards Captain Powell, at 7 p. m., in the penal cells, he being under punishment for a previous offence?"—Well, my lord, I would wish that whenever you examine the officers as to my violence, whenever they speak of it, that you would ask what are the particular acts of violence that were committed.

8800.—CHAIRMAN—That we will do.

8801.—Dr. LYONS—I find on Tuesday, the 9th of June, "J. O'D. Rossa removed to dark cell, by order of the Governor," apparently at twelve o'clock in the day?—Yes; I was for five or six days in the dark cell that time.

8802.—I find on the same day the entry, "J. O'D. Rossa, two days' penal diet." Is that correct?—That is correct, Mr. Lyons.

8803.—When next were you put on penal diet?—Have you the 12th, sir; the 12th of June?

8804.—I find that on the 11th you were "reported by Warder Brown for defacing the cell by writing on it, about 9.30 p. m. on the 9th; also insubordinate conduct to Captain Powell, the 10th, he being under punishment in the dark cell for a previous offence." Is that correct?—It is correct that I did not salute him under those circumstances. That is all I ever did.

8805.—I find also, on the 11th of June, "J. O'D. Rossa, 12.15, released from the dark cell this day, by order of the Governor." Is that correct?—I cannot, Mr. Lyons, recollect the particular dates.

8806.—Then I find on the 12th, "J. O'D. Rossa reported by Assistant Warder Cranston for refusing to leave his cell when under report, to go before the Governor, at 12 noon, the 9th inst.; also for highly disrespectful and insubordinate conduct towards the Governor, on the 9th inst.?"—Yes, I refused to go before the Governor. I said he could order his punishment, and let them go on with their assassin work without me, and that as he would not write down anything I would say there was no use going before him.

8807.—"12.40. J. O'D. Rossa, two days' punishment diet, and pay for damage to his cell door." How were you to pay for that?—Out of the gratuities. Prisoners get a gratuity.

8808—That was to be debited against your credits?—I have none at all, Mr. Lyons.

8812.—On Sunday, the 14th, I find entered," J. O'D. Rossa detained under further report," and on Monday, the 15th of June, "J. O'D. Rossa, two days' punishment, and pay for damage to gutta-percha pint?"—Two days on the 15th.

8813.—CHAIRMAN—Then this accounts for the period from the 1st of June to the 16th?—Yes, my lord.

8814.—Dr. LYONS—Sunday, the 14th, I find, "J. O'D. Rossa reported by Assistant Warder Hibbert for refusing to clean his boots and willfully damaging his cup, about twelve noon, this day." What did you do to the cup?—I do not recollect now, Mr. Lyons. Oh, yes, I now recollect. I found the cup that I got was a bit nipped. I caught it with my teeth and nipped a bit out of it, and kept it in my mouth with a feeling of hunger to be chewing it, and Mr. Alison saw it and had me reported, and then I took and broke the cup entirely.

8819.—Dr. GREENHOW—And you gave as your reason for refusing to work outside, that you would not be working with a gang of thieves?—Yes, sir.

8820.—Do you recollect a day on which you were found imperfectly dressed; that is, having no jacket on, on which you were ordered by Thompson to put your jacket on?—Yes, I think I do, sir.

8825.—Did you use those words: "Then you are not satisfied yet, you miserable, prejudiced wretch"?—Yes.

8830.—On the 9th of June, when you were brought before the Governor, did you refuse to stand to "attention," and did you lounge back with your hands in front of you?—Yes, I did, this way. (Exhibits the attitude.)

8831.—Then, on the 12th of June, you were ordered out of your cell for the purpose of going before the Governor, being under report, when you refused, saying, "You can go on with your assassin work without me." Do you think that is true?—Yes, sir; I acknowledge that.

8832.—On the 9th of June, did they find that you had written on your cell, and damaged your cell by writing?—Will you please read the charge?

8833.—The charge is, that "on inspecting the prisoner's cell on the 9th instant, I found he had willfully damaged it by writing on it."—Does it give what was written, sir?

8834.—It does not say what was written. (No reply.)

8835.—CHAIRMAN—Was that the occasion when you wrote those words in French, "Le sang rouge d'Irelande coule en Angleterre?—No, my lord; that was in Millbank.

8836.—Dr. GREENHOW—Have you written on the cell here?—Yes. I will tell you under what circumstances. When I could not get the Governor to take down my charge in writing, I would write on the cell those very things that I wanted him to take down, with a view that if I was reported for this the writing should be put on record.

8843.—MR. DE VERE—O'Donovan Rossa, with the exception of two or three days' intermission, you appear to have been on bread and water and in dark cells from the 1st of June until the 16th, when you committed this assault on the Governor?—Yes, sir.

8844.—The charges against you during that time appear to be for insubordination and disobedience. Was there any charge made against you during that time of assault or violence to any officer?—No, sir; there cannot be. I was never violent or attempted to assault any officer except on a few occasions that they laid hands on me. I was just as peaceful and obedient to them on those occasions too.

8845.—Dr. GREENHOW—Were those occasions when you were violent between the 1st and 16th of June?—I was not violent, but I refused to leave the cell, and then they would come and put hands on me, and I would go.

8846.—You went quietly and did not resist?—I did not resist, but went quietly.

8847.—MR. DE VERE—What effect on your health, spirits and character, do you conceive that long period of dark cells and bread and water to have had?—Well, I felt at the time, of course, that it would kill me; that was the feeling I had.

8849.—Will you state in what respect your health was affected?—Well, at the time, I did not feel it much affected; but I felt not well since; I got an affection of the back since, that I had not at that time.

8850.—Is it true that you have, on any occasion since that, expressed your regret for your conduct on the 16th?—No, I do not think it is, except so far as expressing it in such a manner as you have seen in that statement I gave you; that it was an act,—that it is an act I thought once I could never do. There is one report that I wish to refer to that I do not see here, that might elicit some evidence as to having my hands behind my back at one particular date, and that is officer Thompson's. He came to me one day after dinner and put me in irons.

8885.—CHAIRMAN—What day was that?—I cannot recollect the day, my lord, but I will say that if you can find the report it will be one of the days I was in irons with my hands behind my back. It is some date during the thirty-five days, Dr. Greenhow—perhaps at the middle of the thirty-five days, or about that time, he came in. You see the report about my tearing my clothes—that is when the irons were tied behind; I had no braces; I had some annoyance in trying to keep my trowsers up, and I just bit a hole in my waistcoat one day—two holes—and ripped the seam behind to keep the trowsers up, and Thompson, after tying the irons behind, set about unloosening the clothes and I could not tie them again. So I asked him was he ordered to do that. "Oh," said he, "that is none of your business." Said I, "Have you not done your duty, you mean wretch." So there was a report put on the books to that effect, and he will be before you for examination, if you have not examined him already.

8886.—DR. LYONS.—Did your trowsers fall down?—The trowsers used to fall down.

8887.—How did you keep them up after he unloosed them?—I had to leave it so.

8888.—Why had you no braces?—The prison rules do not allow any braces while you are in punishment cells, for fear a man would hang himself, I suppose.

8889.—Are you positive that the braces were taken away from you always in the dark cell?—Always from me.

8891.—Yes; here I find Assistant Warden Francis Thompson, who, being duly sworn, states, 19th June, that about 6 p. m. on the 19th instant I was on duty in the penal class separate cells, when I went to Jeremiah O'Donovan Rossa's cell for the purpose of changing his handcuffs from front to rear—they having been removed for him to get his supper, when I found him wearing his vest buttoned to his breeches, which he had ripped. I told him not to do that, and unbuttoned them, and he said in a snarly manner: "Have you not done your duty, yet, you wretch?"—I thought it might be some other date.

8893.—DR. LYONS.—I find that from the 1st to the 16th of June, you were every day confined under report and punishment?—Oh, yes, every day.

8894.—Then on the 17th of June, by your own statement, you were put in handcuffs and kept so during a period of thirty-five days?—Yes, on the morning of the 17th of June.

8895.—On the 23d of July, I find in this book an entry that you were then sentenced to twenty-eight days' punishment diet in close confinement, and six months' penal diet, from the 20th instant. That was so, was it?—Yes.

8896.—That twenty-eight days was carried out from the 20th?—Yes, from the thirty-five days after the 17th of June.

8897.—That would bring us to the 19th of August. Now, on the 20th of August I find you reported by Principal Warder Alison for gross insolence to Captain Harvey; and on the 21st. I find that you were remanded for the Director?—If you will ask Alison in his examination what this insolence was—

8801.—Do you not remember anything about it?—No; I only recollect that I was reported the morning after they trampled me in the cell. The day after, I was reported, and they sent the case to the Director, they reported me for assaulting three officers after they working their will on me.

8920.—DR. GREENHOW—Since Captain Du Cane said he would give you a chance of going on smoothly and let you go out to work, you have gone on well, and never been reported since?—Except once, that a letter was found on a prisoner, and I was charged with writing the letter, and I was put ten days in solitary confinement, awaiting report. The Director came after I was about five or six days in, and did not see me. I was taken out as if to be taken before him while he was sitting, and I was brought back to my cell again.

8923.—DR. GREENHOW—May I ask did you write the letter?—No, sir, I did not. I would tell you, sir, if I did, because I have tried to send out letters.

8934.—DR. LYONS—The offence was sending out a letter?—A letter was got in the prison with some prisoner. I was immediately put in solitary confinement as being the writer of this letter. I was not the writer of it.

9545—CHAIRMAN—We will go to the next paragraph. You say discipline required that in a blackhole cell you should be left during two nights without bed, blanket or even rug. When was that?—That was in this prison, my lord.

9550.—Were you, in point of fact, left without bed, blanket or rug?—Yes, two nights in this blackhole.

9564.—Dr. Greenhow—Did it ever happen to you to be deprived of your body clothes in the dark cell?—Yes, sir.
9567.—I am now asking if it ever happened to you to be in the dark cell and to have your body clothes taken away from you?—Yes.
9568.—What had you on that occasion?—Two blankets and a rug.
9569.—And a mattress?—No mattress.
9570.—Do you mean to say that you were in a dark cell without a mattress and without any body clothes?—Yes, sir.
9578.—Do you remember being in a dark cell from the 6th to the 9th of August, and on the 8th being removed from No. 3 to No. 2 dark cell, by order of the medical man?—Yes, Mr. De Vere; one day I was removed, for I reported to the doctor the stench of my cell or something, and he removed me, and I was a day or two in the second cell.
9584.—Mr. De Vere—On any of those occasions when you were confined in dark cells, were you ironed during your confinement in a dark cell?—Well, Mr. De Vere, I cannot say exactly. I recollect, any way, the state of my mind about these cells. When they deprived me of books in the light cells, and I could not get anything to pass away my time, I used to recite something, and try to pass the time as well as I could, and made a noise which passed me to the dark cell. When I was thirty-five days with my hands behind my back, I was allowed books, and tried to read by turning the leaves with my mouth, and I made no noise; but when the twenty-eight days on bread-and-water punishment commenced I made a noise. So I would not say I was in the dark cells during the thirty-five days I was in the irons, because I had books.
9585.—Were you on any occasion kept in irons at night?—Not in this prison; in Milbank I was.
9586.—During your thirty-five days in irons were you allowed books?—Yes, I was allowed a library book.
9587.—You described the manner in which you turned over the leaves?—Yes, I used to put the book on the block, and then turn upside down my cell-pot, and sit on it, and turn over the leaves with my lips.
9588.—Are you prepared to say whether that mode of turning over the leaves continued during the whole of the thirty-five days?—That was the way I recollect I used to do it.
9589.—During the whole of the time?—Yes. I recollect one of the books I hap that time, during a fortnight, was "D'Aubigne's History of the Reformation."
9590.—During the whole time of reading "D'Aubigne's History of the Reformation" do you recollect turning the leaves that way?—Oh, yes.
9591.—Dr. Lyons—You spoke of putting the book in a certain position—how did you do it?—I could use my hands so far as to put the book in the position. I sat down with my legs on each side of the block. You saw those blocks in the cells.
9592.—Will you take this printed copy of your statement in your hand, and look at the paragraph there commencing with the word "discipline." There are two distinct allegations made in that paragraph. Do you observe—just read it?—"Discipline required that in a blackhole cell I be left two nights without bed, blanket or even rug, and I should like to see the prison rule which authorizes it."
9593.—That is one of the allegations. The other follows that?—"To give me a rug and blanket, and deprive me of my body clothes in such a place, is also what I experienced often."
9594.—Did both these events occur?—Both these events occurred.
9595.—Did they occur together, or were they separated by an interval?—Separated by an interval.
9600.—Do you mean to say that on several occasions it happened to you that you were deprived of your clothes, and left in a dark cell with only two blankets and a rug, and no mattress?—Yes.
9603.—It occurred several times in Portland?—Yes.
9610.—Dr. Lyons—Was it because ——? I beg pardon, Mr. Lyons, it did occur in this prison, even more than once; because I now recollect that there was a question amongst the officers as to whether they would leave me my stockings, and another time whether they would leave me my drawers; so it did occur more than once.
9611.—Did it occur twice?—It did. I recollect one of the officers saying, "You can leave him his stockings." I do not know was it the same time about the drawers. This positively occurred, so that it must have occurred more than once.
9618.—Dr. Lyons—Was it not because you did not consider what was left to you of your clothes and those bed clothes sufficient to keep you warm, that you refused to take off your clothes?—Certainly, Mr. Lyons. Yes, I told them I would give my clothes, if they gave me a bed, but that I wanted to keep my body clothes if there was no bed.

9619.—You told them that?—I told them that, and Mr. Alison gave orders to strip me, and they rushed and threw me down. Might I ask if the doctor will be examined, and I be allowed to question him?

9620.—CHAIRMAN—Yes. Are there any other officers?—I have given the names, my lord. Have they stated my hands were not tied behind?

9621.—I cannot tell you what they have stated, or what our opinion is on it. In proper time we will make up our minds on that. If Cranston said —— (A pause.)

9629.—Yes, my lord. Regarding your decision about my being not allowed to ask those witnesses, whom you have examined, any questions, I will just observe that I do not object to any decision you may make. I leave myself entirely in your hands until the Commission is coming to a close, but if you then tell me you are not satisfied that I have told the truth, I hope you will give me some way for saying a few words.

9620.—You may rely that if we think it just to you to confront you with any witness we shall do so.—Yes, my lord, I recollect Dr. Greenhow's expression the first day, that your object was to know everything, and that you will give me every facility.

9631.—MR. BRODERICK—You recollect that we did confront you with some witnesses whose recollection was different from yours?—Yes

9658.—MR. BRODERICK—I think it is clear that on the first occasion you were two nights without bed, blanket, or rug; that there was a second occasion on which you were, at all events, without a mattress, namely, on the 19th of August, and that there was a third occasion, the date of which you cannot fix?—The 25th.

9666.—CHAIRMAN—I will go now to the next paragraph of your letter. You say, "To be confined for months in a darkened cell, specially furnished with a privy unfurnished with a lid, and one month of this without ever stirring out of it, except to the blackhole, and on 16 ounces of bread, and 40 ounces of water daily, may not be necessary for the preservation of health, but is deemed necessary for discipline"—when did that occur?—That occurred in '68, my lord.

9664.—"For months," you say. Were you in a darkened cell for months?—Yes, my lord.

9668.—How long was the period?—From the first of June to the first of October, my lord, in this prison.

9669.—Was the cell darkened all the time? Yes, my lord.

9670.—By a screen within?—By an iron screen, my lord.

9671.—Was there a privy in the corner of the cell?—Yes, my lord, there was.

9672.—Without a lid? Yes, my lord, it can be seen to the present day.

9673.—MR. DE VERE—How long were you there?—From the 1st of June to the 1st of October, I was in this darkened cell in punishment, and since I came to the prison in it without punishment.

9674.—You say, "One month without ever stirring out of it." You were taken out for exercise, were you not?—For the twenty-eight days I was not, my lord.

9676.—DR. GREENHOW—That was the period on bread and water?—Yes; I did not leave the cell these twenty-eight days.

9686.—MR. DE VERE—During the whole of that period that you were in the cell in which was a privy, was there a lid to it any part of the time?—No, sir; no lid at all?

9687.—CHAIRMAN—Was there any offensive smell from it?—Yes, my lord, there was.

9738.—Do you believe the doctor has neglected you?—I am not a medical man; I only state what passed between me and the doctor.

9739.—It does not appear to me that you distinctly state that he has neglected you?—I only state what has occurred and how I felt.

9756.—Is there anything that has occurred within the prison since you have been confined that you would refer to as the cause of that pain?—Unless that leap on my chest would cause it.

9757.—Were you very violently pressed on the chest on that occasion?—Yes; he stood up and leaped down on me, that way, with his knees (imitating the act).

9758.—Why did he stand up?—To turn me to take the trousers off. He leaped that way, down on me with his knees.

9759.—During that act, were you lying on the floor?—Lying on the floor.

9760.—On your back?—On my back.

9761.—Then, had they to turn you over?—To turn me over. He had his knee on my neck while they were taking off my clothes. If you ever saw a pig-trying for measles in Ireland, it was just the same as that.

9765.—You did not think you were hurt, on that occasion?—I did not; but I felt my chest; when he leaped on my chest a burst of air shot up my throat.

9766.—You did feel that?—Yes, sir.

9771.—You say in your statement, "I do not see any rule which authorizes discipline to deprive a man of the use of the Bible for six months, and yet this sentence was passed on me." Will you explain what you mean by that?—Yes. In Portland, my lord, a sentence was passed on me that I be deprived of books for six months, including the Bible.

9772.—Who passed that sentence?—It was, I think, sent by the directors, my lord. It was under the date—if you look on the records—of January 25th, 1867.

9773.—You were ordered by the directors, when at Portland, to be deprived of books for six months?—Yes, my lord.

9777.—Dr. GREENHOW—The sentence is, "Three days' confinement and punishment diet; 1,440 marks, 540 for remission; 25 days' penal class diet; to be degraded to penal class; to forfeit 540 marks remission; to be deprived of all books for six months; to be only allowed sufficient waste paper daily for the wants of nature, for having a book concealed in the work-shed containing improper writing, also letters." Was there any writing in the book itself?—Yes, I had written on the pages of the book. The book was concealed in the shed. I acknowledge to you that it was I who wrote in the book, but they had no evidence of it.

9788.—Dr. LYONS—What was the writing that was improper?—That is what I would wish to call his lordship's and the Commissioners' attention to, the way reports are drawn up. I tried to get the Governor to correct the report that the writing was not improper, but that I had it improperly in my possession.

9779.—CHAIRMAN—What was the writing?—A letter to my wife. The one in question about the book was, I think, a copy of a letter or memorial to the Secretary of State, which I have submitted to your lordship and the Commission.

9780.—You wish, then, to state to us that the book was not of an improper character, nor the writing of an improper description, but that what was meant was that the book and the writing were improperly in your possession?—Yes.

9781.—Dr. LYONS—What was the name of the book?—A prayer-book,—a "Think Well On It," or something of that kind; but not one of those supplied to me.

9782.—When you say that you were deprived of all books for six months, do you include religious books?—Yes; I recollect trying to get a Bible; I came to a punishment cell and there was a Bible in it; I suspected the officer would take the Bible and I hid it under the cell-pot, and he went looking for it, and found it out.

9783.—Dr. LYONS—Did he take it away?—He took it away.

9784.—Dr. GREENHOW—Was it a Protestant or a Catholic Bible?—It was Protestant; it is Protestant Bibles are in all these cells.

9787.—Dr. LYONS—I see that you have applied for extra books. Are you much given to study?—Yes; any time I have I like to read. I got great annoyance in the way of not getting books; I could never get books that I wanted.

9789.—When you say that for months you were "deprived of that waste brown paper which is supplied to every prisoner for purposes of nature," that was not the case at the time that all books were taken away from you on this occasion?—No, my lord.

9790.—Where was it?—That occurred in Millbank.

9791.—How long was it in operation?—I was four months in the penal class; in fact, I was about six months, I think.

9792.—Dr. GREENHOW—You told us that you wrote in that book at the shed; did you write in any other book?—No, I never wrote in any other book.

9793.—You never injured any library book?—I never injured any library book. Perhaps you will be told I wrote in my library books; but in my report I allude to that, where I say, you will do well not to believe it until you question me.

9794.—Dr. LYONS—What do you say about it?—" If you will inquire why, you will perhaps be told that I injured some of the books given to me; but you will do well not to believe it until you question me."

9795.—MR. DE VERE—You said that the Bibles placed in the penal cells are Protestant Bibles?—Yes, sir.

9796.—Are they supplied to Roman Catholics in the penal cells?—I cannot say, Mr. De Vere. I only speak for myself.

9798.—You are a Roman Catholic?—Well, I have never been at any other place of worship.

9799.—You are registered as a Roman Catholic?—Yes, registered as a Roman Catholic.

9800.—Have you ever complained to the visiting priest that you were supplied with a Protestant Bible?—Never, sir. I would not make such a complaint, because I do not want to get into religious subjects. Not with disrepect to you, Mr. De Vere, but I only express my opinion that I have no desire to get into religious matters of discipline.

9801.—In fact, you never made a complaint on the subject?—I did not.

9802.—DR. GREENHOW—Did you ask for "D'Aubigne's History of the Reformation" yourself?—Yes, I did.

9813.—I was just coming to that. It—the Bible—was given to you in Portland?—In Portland the Bible supplied was the Old and New Testament. In Milbank and this prison it was a Testament. But I applied for a Bible, and the reason I will tell you. In any studies I engaged in are languages; there are here German and Italian Bibles, the Protestant version, got up by the Bible Society, and I desired to have one of this kind, as I stated, having no other books of foreign languages to read. I got permission from the Catholic Chaplain to get one of these books from the Protestant Chaplain. I made application, and my request was attended to.

9814.—Dr. Greenhow—It was an English Bible then?—No, not in the English language. I applied for some Irish books: I could not get them, but the Protestant Chaplain was kind enough to lend me his own Protestant Bible, in the Irish language.

9815.—Chairman—In the Irish language?—Yes, my lord.

9819.—Dr. Greenhow—You state in page 4, that you were stripped naked once a day for three or four months?—Yes.

9820.—Where did that occur?—In Millbank.

9821.—At what period did it occur?—From February until May, certainly.

9822.—Do I understand you to say that you were stripped once a day?—Once a day, sir, assuredly. I had to go through positions to have them look at all parts of me naked.

9823.—In what place were you stripped?—I was stripped naked in my cell when the officers came, once a day.

9827.—Mr. De Vere—In page 4 you state that "On refusing one day to be the agent of your own shame, five officers seized you, and, giving you a terrible choking, left you naked on the floor!"—Yes, sir.

9832.—On that occasion were the five officers present?—Yes; there were five of them charged on me.

9834.—Was that stripping you naked, once a day for three or four months, part of the ordinary discipline to which you were subjected; or was it something extra in consequence of your being put into a punishment cell, or in any way punished?—No; but it was part of the ordinary discipline to which I was subjected without any charge being brought against me for having writing materials, or secreting anything in my cell. The order was given, for some reason I do not know, to search me once a day. I think, from what I have learned from prisoners who were out in the world at that time, that the order was given for precautionary purposes regarding my escape, because there was some noise at the time, they tell me, in Ireland, about Chester Castle. I think precautionary measures were taken, and, at this time, at night. I used to be kept in one cell during the day, and then taken from that cell and that ward and taken to another ward, and brought back in the morning again to the cell in which I was during the day.

9835.—Are you aware whether the other treason-felony prisoners were, during the same period, stripped naked and searched?—I did not hear that any of the others were searched.

9841.—Chairman—Are you tired—would you like to sit down?—Thank you, my lord. (Does not sit.)

9845.—Was there any particular reason why, on that day, you would not allow yourself to be searched?—Yes, I was disgusted. I had made up my mind that I would not do anything they wanted me to do, and that I would leave myself in their hands; but that I would not use my will and do any thing they wanted me to do. This all occurred after being punished for idleness when I worked. I made up my mind then that there was no use in my trying to get on with any satisfaction.

9849.—Chairman—In page 5 of your statement, you say, "the ordinary prisoner can pray, if so inclined, without an irreverent stare; but if the treason-felony prisoner prays, it is with three officers sitting on the bench in front of him, looking him in the face; and if the treason-felony prisoner goes to communion he has an officer parading him through the chapel, while the ordinary prisoner can approach the rails without such distinguished notice." First of all, is it the fact that when you are in the chapel three officers sit on the bench opposite you?—Yes, my lord.

9852.—They do not face you but they sit sideways?—Sideways.

9853.—But for a time they sat facing you?—Yes, my lord.

9854.—When you approach the altar rails, does an officer accompany you?—All the other prisoners, we see them on Sundays, go up leaving the officer, but when any of the treason-felony prisoners go to communion one of those three officers attends him up to the rails through the chapel and down again. Last Sunday week was the last time it was done.

9856.—What do you complain of in regard to the fact of prisoners being brought up to the rails and back?—*I do not put it as a complaint; I only state it as exceptional treatment. I do not make any complaint of it.*

9865.—CHAIRMAN—Look at the second paragraph on page 5. You say there, "I state that I was one morning in my cell; the gas was turned off pretty early, and left me unable to read a book I held in my hand. There was an iron blind on my window then, which has been since taken off." Explain what exceptional treatment you refer to there?—When I came to this prison, my lord, I was put in this darkened cell, and nine English prisoners were located in those cells, I believe, to prepare a place for me, and assimilate their treatment to mine. One morning the gas was turned off earlier than would allow me to read by the daylight, and I objected, that not being under punishment now, if I was in an ordinary cell I would have light to read the book. I thought I should be allowed gas-light under circumstances where others had the daylight.

9899.—DR. LYONS—I find that previously you applied for extra library books. Did you get them?—No, I did not, Mr. Lyons.

9900.—I find subsequently that you applied for permission to write to the Secretary of State to have more books allowed you. Was that permission allowed you?—No, it was not, sir.

9908.—MR. BRODERICK—The report is this, "Assistant Warder Thompson states that O'Donovan Rossa was very idle the whole afternoon. On my rebuking him for the idle manner in which he was working, he replied, in a most insolent tone, 'The wages I get are very poor.' His tone and manner were very insolent."—I spoke to him as blandly as I could speak. "Oh," said I, "Officer, the wages are rather light, too."

9913.—CHAIRMAN—You wish to have Alison asked if he had been told by Pratt that you had the newspaper, your allegation being that Pratt gave you the newspaper?—Yes, my lord.

9914.—Dr. LYONS—What do you expect to get out by that?—That there was some complicity between the officers and the prisoners to get me into trouble.

9919.—CHAIRMAN—You think they had Pratt as a sort of spy on you?—As a sort of spy on me? Yes, my lord.

9920.—Did you tell the officer that you were left-handed?—I did, my lord; and he told me put the hammer in the right hand, and he kept telling me the stroke was light; and after he repeated this to me two or three times I only said, "Oh, officer, the wages are rather light, too;" just quietly, and without any acerbity in my tone.

9929.—CHAIRMAN—We will go to the next point. You say that on one occasion in shaving that you cut your throat, that the blood flowed pretty freely, and that with the point of your slate pencil you wrote on the door of your cell, "Le sang rouge d'Irlande coule on Angleterre," thinking of an expression of a duke of Burgundy dying on a field of battle. What was the result of that?—I went to exercise immediately after that, my lord, and while I was at exercise an officer saw this inscription on the door, and I was put under report for it, and charged next day with the offence of having written on my cell door "The red blood of Ireland *will rise* in England." I tried to explain that that was not what was written on the door; that it was "*coule*," and that it should have been taken down properly if it was taken down at all. I do not know how the Governor managed the report, but I brought the matter before Captain Gambier again. I do not know how they managed it, but I had forty-eight hours' bread and water for it. It was the Deputy-Governor that adjudicated.

9930.—Mr. BRODERICK—The entry as it stands here, Rossa, in the copy furnished to us from the report book is, "Writing on his cell door with blood 'The red blood of Ireland flows in England?'"—It was corrected by Captain Gambier. Have you a copy from the original books the day I was before them, for it was originally written "will rise," and I made some efforts to get it corrected, you will find, if you see the book?

9931.—CHAIRMAN—I will take a note to examine the book at Millbank, and see if there is something in the original report erased, and something written instead?—The matter was corrected when I brought it before Captain Gambier or Mr. Fagan. I think that any way they said there was a gentleman in the prison yesterday, a colonel, that knew French, and said something about it.

9932.—CHAIRMAN—On another occasion you say, "I am on bread and water in a darkened cell, and to keep myself company I am repeating some lines. The officer addresses me and says, 'You must not be going on this way.' I reply, 'Oh, by Jove, I will;' and next day, in the offence charged against me it is 'By Jesus, I will,' which makes the affair look very wicked." When did that occur?—That occurred some time after the report of my being punished for idleness, when I was doing the work, because I never made any noise in a separate cell or other cell until after that; but I cannot fix the date.

9934.—DR. GREENHOW—You used the words "By Jove!"—"By Jove." I am not aware that I ever used the words "By Jesus." It is a curse I am not addicted to. It is an expression I never used, and I would not like to have it remain on the prison books that I used it.

9935.—DR. LYONS—You say that you never used the expression?—No; not as an oath or otherwise. I did not use the expression "By Jesus." Whatever badness I do, I have not used that curse.

9936.—CHAIRMAN—You say, "To have one officer set me doing one thing, and another another thing, and to have the first charge me with idleness for not doing his work, while doing the work of the second, is another way of getting up reports." When did that occur?—When I went to Millbank first, my lord.

9947.—CHAIRMAN—You go on to say, afterwards, that "while in Portland, the rest of the treason-felony prisoners working in mid-winter in a shed, I was placed outside of the shed, and prevented from having that little shelter from the poison-laden blast that the others had?"—Yes, my lord. I recollect one morning coming out from punishment, and at this time my hands were in that state that the flesh was rotting off my fingers. My block, where I used to work before in the shed, was inside, and all the prisoners worked inside; but this morning Officers Russell and Parsons made me bring my block into the open air, outside the shed, and set me to work outside.

9955.—"On the 20th, talking on the public works; the 22d, talking on the public works; the 29th, talking on the public works, and insolent when spoken to. On the 22d" you got "two days' punishment diet in penal class, and on the 29th you got three days' punishment diet and fourteen days' penal class diet." There was apparently an accumulation of offences in the prison books against you?—Yes; but these offences could be got against any of the other prisoners as well, for we all used to talk. But I was made a set on, and made to stand whatever was to be said. The Governor used to come to the works and tell the officer to report us for talking.

9956.—CHAIRMAN—Where was this?—In Portland. I recollect the Governor came to the works one day, and he said there was talking going on there. After he left, I had a conversation with the superior officer, and he said he should report some of the men; he told it to me himself. I said, "Report me. I do not want to get you into any trouble," said I; "I have been talking." He took down the names of six or seven to report, and he said he got orders next day not to report us. Just as the wind used to blow from Ireland, in these troublous times, they had a bark at us, or used to deprive us of a bit of our daily bread, or something.

9959.—Was the punishment that was awarded to you for that charge 72 hours on bread and water, and 14 days in solitary confinement on penal class diet?—Yes, that was awarded, Mr. De Vere, for that offence.

9962.—"Talking on the works, and insolence when spoken to, 720 marks; ordered 14 days' penal class diet, 84 marks reduced for remission?"—You must not consider that the loss of these marks might not be punishment, for it is punishment, and a severe punishment, because I have not spent one year in prison yet according to discipline, although I am five.

9965.—Then am I to understand that the punishment of the 29th of December, 72 hours' bread and water and 14 days' close confinement on penal class diet, had reference to what took place on the works on that day?—Yes, and certainly no insolence from me to any officer.

9970.—CHAIRMAN—On the occasion of your wife's applying to the Governor for leave for you to write to her on some matters connected with your pecuniary affairs, what did the Governor say to you?—He told me he had this communication from my wife, and to write on a slate what I had to say, and he would get it copied and sent to her. On something else in about a month I was before him, and I asked him if he sent this matter to my wife. He said, "No, I could not; I could not be sending your love letters to your wife, and, besides," said he, "it would lessen your punishment."

9971.—Are you quite sure he used those words?—Yes, my lord, I am quite sure he used those words.

9972.—DR. LYONS—Can you explain that?—I wrote on my slate what at his request I was to write, and he said he would send it to my wife; and in about a month after, or less, I asked him if he had sent the copy, and he said "No, I could not be sending your love letters to your wife; if I did it would lessen your punishment."

9974.—MR. BRODERICK—Did you understand him to mean that allowing you to communicate with your wife would be so so far a diminution of your punishment?—Yes, I did.

9976.—As to your treatment in English prisons, did you say anything?—Yes, my lord, I made some remark about being treated so in English prisons, and he said, "Your treatment is too good for you; twenty years ago you would have been hanged."

9977.—You say that at Millbank some writing was found on the person of another treason-felony prisoner?—Yes, my lord.

9978.—And that you were suspected to be the writer, though your name was not to it?—Yes, my lord.

9983.—This is the day which you speak of in your statement as being stripped three times?—Yes, in twenty-four hours, my lord.

9984.—Was there anything found on you?—Nothing was found, my lord. I was then put into a darkened cell, a refractory cell, not entirely dark, a cell with a hole in the middle of it, and I was left in this cell for three days, from Friday till Monday. Mr. Handy, one of the chief officers, then came and took me out of the cell, and said I was to go back to my own cell—that is, to the ordinary cell, and that it was decreed that I was not to be allowed to go to Chapel any more in the mornings. That was, I think, on Monday, my lord.

9986.—Mr. DE VERE—Was it with writing the paper that you were charged?—With writing this paper that was found on a prisoner named James O'Brien—James Xavier O'Brien. It is not necessary, I suppose, to tell the Commissioners, because it referred to me; whatever was written, was a note that spoke about the Director saying something to the prisoner Rossa, to me. The Director said to me, "So you think that of me." "Well," said I, "in anything I wrote about you, I wrote what I think." It was nothing disrespectful, but it presumed to state some interview between him and me, and he said he would, as punishment, stop a visit, the ticket of which had been sent to Mr. Pigott, of the "*Irishman*" office, Dublin; it was previously sent. It was on the day I asked to see the prisoner Duffy. Mr. Duffy was dying, and I said I would take seeing Duffy as a visit that was due to me, and he said I could not see Duffy.

9987.—Were you manacled in the dark cell?—Yes, manacled two days and two nights.

9989.—CHAIRMAN—The handcuffs were not unloosed during meals?—No, my lord.

9990.—Mr. BRODERICK.—Had you not destroyed the spoon?—Yes.

9991.—Dr. LYONS—Were the handcuffs that you had on, then, handcuffs with a small link connecting them?—No, they were the close handcuffs.

9992.—Quite close?—Quite close.

9993.—So that you could not possibly help yourself to your food, as you could have done if they were handcuffs such as we saw the other day with links?—Yes, and as I could not use the hands, I had to go on my elbows and knees, not having a spoon.

9994.—If you had a spoon could you have used it?—Well, I suppose I could; but in a dark cell——

9995.—CHAIRMAN—It was not an absolutely dark cell?—An absolutely dark cell, my lord, a story under ground, such as the cells you have seen that I have been in over here, with double, triple doors.

9996.—We have been in that cell in Millbank.—It is down under ground.

9997.—We have been shut up in it.—Well, my lord, I would not wish you would.

9998.—You had to go on the floor to eat your food?—I had to go on the floor on my elbows and knees.

9999.—Dr LYONS.—You lapped it out of the dish?—I lapped it out of the dish.

10000.—What size was the dish?—A dish of eight inches, perhaps, in diameter.

10003.—There was no stool, or table, or resting place on which you could put the wooden bowl?—No resting place. There is a bed-board, but that is only a few inches off the ground.

10004.—Was the cell absolutely dark at the time?—Absolutely dark, Mr. Lyons. You could not see anything.

(Principal-Warder Dalton is called in with handcuffs.)

10005.—Dr. LYONS—What are those technically called?—Figure of eight, sir. (He put them on Dr. Lyons.)

10006.—Are those similar to the handcuffs you had on? PRISONER—Yes, sir.

(Dalton removes the handcuffs and withdraws in order to bring a different kind.)

10007.—Were the handcuffs you had on closer or looser than these?—They were not so loose as these, for I sent to the doctor to represent to him that my hands were pained by one of them. This was in the dark cell, in the morning. I recollect the doctor came, and when the lamp was held up to my hand to see it, I saw that my wrist was bloody; that during the night it had wounded me some way. The gruel is thick, and will not run in the dish, and you cannot sip it.

10008.—CHAIRMAN—Was this for one or two days?—One day. I was two days in the irons, but I had not the opportunity of getting the food the second day in the dark cell.

10009.—Did you get food the second day?—I did; bread and water.

10011.—Were you able to eat it with the manacles?—Of course you can eat bread.

10010.—Or take a dish of water?—Yes.

10012.—But you could not have got at the gruel?—I tried to get at it, as I tell you, my lord.

10013.—Mr. BRODERICK.—Are you clear upon this point, that you were manacled during two days, day and night?—Not two consecutive days. There was some day between them; once, 24 hours, and another 24 hours.

10014.—But you are quite clear that the handcuffs were on two nights?—I did not get my bed the first night; the mattress was kept. I got only part of the bedding the first night; I got the whole of the bedding the second night.

(Dalton here returns with handcuffs, puts a small pair on Dr. Lyons, and, after taking them off, withdraws.)

10015.—Dr. Lyons—The cell that we examined was, I think, a very small one. Did you find that you had room to lie down on the bed-board of that cell?—No; I noticed that it was very small. I think it was rather short, too.

10016.—What is your height?—My height is about 5 feet 10, I think.

10017.—The length of the bed was 5 feet 4 inches?—I recollect—it made a fixed impression on my mind—the cold of the night, because when the clothes got off I could not put them on again.

10018.—Your height is recorded 5 feet 9¼ inches?—I am growing down, I suppose.

10019.—The length of that bed is 5 feet 4 inches; did you find that you had great difficulty in lying down in that space?—Yes; there is something in my mind that it was not long enough, or something uncomfortable.

10020.—Did it appear to you to have added to your suffering in that cell, that you could not lie down at length on the board?—Yes, Mr. Lyons; but what particularly impressed itself on me was the cold during the night, for the bed-clothes fell off, and I could not pull them on as I could not use the hands.

10030.—Then, on the 20th, it is stated you further broke the trap-door, wrote on the walls and the door, shouting "I am a Fenian," and singing Fenian songs?—That is an expression I never used. Of course, Mr. Broderick, I was what is called a "Fenian," but I never said it or sang Fenian songs.

10031.—Chairman—You distinctly deny that?—I distinctly deny that I ever made use of the expression "I am a Fenian," either in prison or out of prison.

10032.—Dr. Lyons—Did you sing Fenian songs?—I cannot sing. I do not know what are called Fenian songs, Mr. Lyons.

10033.—You cannot sing?—I cannot sing. Whenever any of my friends, who know me, would hear of my singing, they would burst out laughing at the idea of it.

10034.—Mr. Broderick—On the 23d, "Disfiguring a pint, writing on the cell wall, filling the key-hole with pieces of a broken bowl?"—My lord, I think I tell you in the report that, after being obliged to go on my face and hands to eat, I broke the bowl.

10035.—Chairman—How did you succeed in breaking it?—With my feet.

10036.—And did you put pieces of it in the key-hole?—I did, my lord.

10039.—In the paragraph at the bottom of page 8, you say, "One day I was yoked to a cart with those men, drawing stones, and I had a noose of the rope over my neck. The car heeled over, the shaft flew high in the air, and the rope slipped off my neck without doing me any injury: the danger was in its hitching on my neck. A second time that day the car heeled over before its time, and at this occurrence I was in no danger, for it had arrived at its destination, and the rope was off my neck or breast." Will you tell us what occurred at that time?—I was, my lord, the morning in question, yoked to this cart with a noose of rope around me.

10040.—With other men?—With other men, my lord. The cart was full of stones, and we were drawing it; two men were detailed to keep the cart from heeling, or "tipping," as they call it in prison, I believe; I do not know whether they intended it or not, but the cart tipped or heeled, the shafts flew up in the air, the rope round my neck was quickly taken off, and, had it hitched on my neck, I would have been hurt.

10046.—Mr. De Vere—You say that you were afraid to work with those men?—After that, Mr. De Vere, I applied to the Governor to be allowed to work in my cell, and not be put amongst those prisoners, and he would not give me permission.

10047.—That is, you wished not to be sent to work with those prisoners who put you in such danger?—Yes, I did not like to be with them.

10048.—Was your application granted to you?—No, it was not, Mr. De Vere.

10049.—How often did you ask it?—I asked about three times. I asked the Director. The Director only made matters worse, for he issued orders that these men were to be set a certain distance apart, and worked so that there should be no annoyance given to me; and these men being set apart in that way, and prevented from speaking, they got more unpleasant, and I felt the position more than before.

10050.—Did you get any punishment for refusing to labor with these men?—On two occasions I refused to labor before the 1st of June, and got punishment—three days at one time and two days at another.

10051.—Was your reason for refusing to work with them that you considered yourself in danger with them?—Yes, in danger, and in a most unpleasant position: these men, feeling that they were kept in a state of punishment, kept isolated from all the other prisoners, even in the chapel, and kept in punishment besides, and they were made to see that I was the cause of that isolation, because, any days that I was kept in on bread and water, they were taken outside the prison walls to work but never taken out when I was amongst them. I complained of that to the Governor and Director, that it was not fair to show them that I was the cause of their being submitted to such restriction.

10054.—CHAIRMAN—" Defacing his gratuity and library cards, writing on his cell door, and drawing on his cell floor."

10055.—Dr. LYONS—That is on May the 6th?—" Drawing on the cell floor" was making some geometrical figures while I was on bread and water; and "defacing his gratuity and library cards"—that was, my lord, in consequence of my inability to get the Governor to take down my words in writing—the answers to the charges. This morning, I happened to get a bit of lead; I found it in the yard, and I brought it in with me, and on those two cards that were in my cell, my lord, I wrote what I intended to be my reply to the charge against me, in order that I would get him to take it down in his book, the state I was in, and why I did certain things; and if he did not do that, that I would be reported for writing on the gratuity card. When I was taken before the Governor, and asked what I had to say, I took the cards out of my pocket and said, "I put it on these cards"; but he would not take down the reply. I pressed him as much as I could to take down the reply from the cards, but he would not do it. The report is here—" defacing his library and gratuity cards"; of course they were defaced, but I tell you under what circumstances.

10062.—CHAIRMAN—What happened on May the 25th?—The 24th was a Sunday, my lord; I was at the chapel, and at the chapel I put one leg across the other.

10063.—Dr. LYONS—Here is a report for disorderly conduct during divine service, and a further report for shouting, at 6 p. m.?—Perhaps, my lord, that will bear out what I was going to tell you.

10065.—CHAIRMAN—What had you done at chapel?—For putting my legs across—I believe he charged me with looking at another prisoner. When I came from the chapel I was reported for the offence, my lord. My cell was cleared out of all its contents. It seems I was under report under such circumstances. I did not commit a great offence at the chapel; but as I saw myself under report, I made some noise in my cell by reciting; I put no restraint on myself when I saw that the men were determined on persecuting me. This noise was added to the report next day, and now it appears the whole report was for shouting and singing, and highly improper language. I did not know what the highly improper language was. The officers of the ward, when I was before the Governor, reported that I was singing treason songs. I told the Governor distinctly, that what I was repeating that evening was this quotation from Cowper:

" We have no slaves at home ; then why abroad?
And they themselves, once ferried o'er the wave
That parts us, are emancipate and loosed.
Slaves cannot breathe in England ; if their lungs
Receive our air, that moment they are free :
They touch our country, and their shackles fall."

It is in Cowper's "Task."

10066.—CHAIRMAN—I know the passage:

" Slaves cannot breathe in England ; if their lungs
Receive our air, that moment they are free :
They touch our country, and their shackles fall.
That's noble, and bespeaks a nation proud
And jealous of the blessing."

10067.—Dr. LYONS—On the 24th, you were removed to the dark cell. On the 25th there was a report made in reference to the 24th : " J. O'D. Rossa, reported for defacing his cell by writing on the back of the door." And further : " J. O'D. Rossa, two days' punishment diet and removed from dark cell, by order of the Governor, 12:20, noon "?—On one occasion, my lord, I distinctly recollect that I was put into this dark cell without making any noise whatever; that Mr. Alison accused me of repeating in the cell when I was only speaking in a whisper; he said I should not be going on so; he went outside the cell and listened; I thought what I was saying in a whisper could not be heard outside; he listened outside, and he came in and sent me to a dark cell.

10068.—CHAIRMAN—When was that?—On one of these occasions when I was only speaking in a whisper, my lord.

10069.—Did Allison send you to the dark cell without speaking to the Governor at all?—Yes, my lord.

10070.—How was that?—He threatened that if I did not stop whispering to myself he would put me in the dark cell. He went outside and listened. I kept whispering to myself, not above a whisper, and he opened the cell door and put me in the dark cell for three days. On other occasions I used to make a noise.

10071.—How do you know that he did not communicate with the Governor about it?—Because he was listening at the door.

10072.—He put you at once into the dark cell?—Yes, my lord, he did.

10073.—He did not go away from the door?—No, my lord, he did not go away from the door.

10076.—Mr. Broderick—You have been often in the dark cells, I am afraid. Have you ever been brought before the Governor and asked what you had to say before being sent to the dark cell?—Never, sir.

10077.—Have you always been taken to the dark cell on the report of a warder'—Yes, sir.

10078.—And without giving you an opportunity of saying anything yourself about it?—Yes, I have, sir, always. I got three days' dark cells in Portland—it is recorded in the books—for refusing to salute the Governor, and using what is called insulting language in getting the affair of the *amour* corrected, my lord.

10079.—Dr. Greenhow—In one of your own letters published in the papers you say, "Let them flog us and starve us legally." As a matter of fact, were you flogged?—No, sir.

10080.—What do you mean by "Starve us legally?"—Well, I suppose I meant by that that I was starved without sufficient cause—for instance, being starved on a charge of idleness when I had my work done. Would you show me the passage?

10081.—It is a passage from your printed letter published in the Irish papers. I have taken down the exact words.

10083.—Have you any complaint with regard to the quality of your food?—No; I make no complaint as to the quality of my food: *I am here under the treatment of a convict, an English convict, and when the authorities consider that I am a fit subject for that treatment I am not going to speak or to complain of food or anything connected with it; but I always claim a right to speak of the treatment I receive. They may treat me any way they please; my duty is to bear what they impose on me and not to complain.*

10088.—Was that occasion when you found the hide in the soap the same as when O'Connell found the piece of hide?—Oh, I think not.

10092.—You say in the same letter that when you were handcuffed in Millbank, the officer seized you by the throat and used a club to strike you?—Yes, that is so. I cried "Coward, to strike a man chained." He raised his club to strike me, and the other officer said, "Don't hurt him."

10121.—You say, in page 3 of your statement, "My letters are suppressed because I speak of my treatment, and the British Government defame my character by saying that it is because I have told lies in them." What do you refer to there?—I refer to the statement that I gave you a few days ago, which, I understand, emanates from the Secretary of State, in which he states that my letters to my wife were suppressed because they contained falsehoods. That is in one of the paragraphs of a paper I gave you, and I have very good reason to believe, from the internal evidence in that paper, that it is an official paper, because it speaks of things that could not be spoken of by any one except a person connected with the Government. I gave you those letters to my wife, just to challenge any allegation as to their containing any falsehoods.

10123.—Dr. Lyons—You made a statement in a paper I hold in my hand, in which you applied for permission to write to your mother?—Yes.

10124.—Was that permission granted to you?—It was not, sir; I applied in Portland for permission; I applied in Millbank for permission, and it was not granted to me. I did that as a matter of duty, because she is an old woman, perhaps seventy years of age.

10125.—You did not get permission?—No, I did not get permission.

10145.—Was that suppressed letter not furnished to you amongst the others?—No, it is not.

10146.—It is not amongst those supplied to you?—It is not; and it is no wonder that I would feel a little annoyed. Of course, you cannot take into consideration or calculate those things; the fact of my wife thinking I am not writing to her, and of my thinking she is not writing to me. Here is a passage from her letter in America: "If what the Governor said was true about your breaking the rules so often, you certainly did not, or do not, care to write to me. I do not mean to write a long letter until I hear. Tell me, have you grown really so indifferent regarding what I think or feel that you make no efforts to gain the good will of your jailers and officers?"

10147.—Is that from your wife from America?—That is from my wife, sir. It is no wonder that I would feel annoyed at those things.

10158.—You have been in four convict prisons. In which of them do you consider you have been most kindly treated, and in which most harshly?—Well, it is much the same in all, Mr. Broderick.

10168.—DR. LYONS—Is there anything in that (handing the prisoner a document) that you wish to find out?—As you told me on the first day, my lord, that anything tending to corroborate another prisoner would be received—

10169.—CHAIRMAN—That another prisoner could be called to corroborate any statement you may make?—Yes, my lord. You may go to prisons abroad. Prisoner William Roantree may lay before you the treatment that he was subjected to. He was afflicted with hœmorrhoids and piles in Portland, and could not get relief. I saw him one day in Portland works, and he put his hand down his boot, down the side of his trowsers, and pulled up his hand all dripping with blood; not spotted with blood, but actually dripping with blood, and he said he was that way for months.

10183.—MR. DE VERE—You were twelve months in Millbank with the gas lighted in your cell at night?—Yes.

10189.—We have taken a note of anything that you have which may be a matter for inquiry. We have down many things that you said about Portland, to which we shall be obliged to refer. We will examine the Governor and the officers whose names you have mentioned to us?—There is one matter that occurred to me, my lord, in Portland. I point to it in one of those letters that I have given in, and I have not been asked about it, my lord.

10190.—What is it?—About removing a large stone one day on a barrow going up the quarry slope. I hurt my finger, and another prisoner seeing it came to take part of the barrow. The officer was looking on, and said to me, without any provocation whatever, "You are a man that would suck another man's blood."

10191.—DR. LYONS—Who said that to you?—Gunning was his name, Mr. Lyons. I went to the Governor the next day and ask him if that was language that could be used towards me. The Governor took the officer aside, and questioned him, and then said to me, "You were not sent here to be too sensitive, and nothing can make you more degraded than you are."

10192.—Are you quite sure that that occurred?—I am quite sure that Governor Clifton said this to me; also, "I suppose you expect the officers to tip their caps to you?" Mr. Clifton said these words to me.

10205.—DR. LYONS—Can you give any account with regard to Mulcahy's having spat blood while he was at the works at Portland?—I cannot, Mr. Lyons.

10207.—You did not see him on any occasion, in Portland, spitting blood?—No, I did not. In that memorial to the Secretary of State, Mr. Lyons, if you have gone over it, there might be some matters in it that would be relevant to the inquiry.

10217.—DR. GREENHOW—We are desirous of ascertaining the truth?—I made up my mind to lay myself in your hands, and to ask the request of you, if I have not satisfied you fully, of giving me an an opportunity of having those few things asked.

10218.—DR. LYONS—As it is easier to make out the points by means of a printed than a written paper, I leave my printed copy of your statement in your hands until to-morrow, for the purpose of facilitating you in your preparations for your further examination. (Hands prisoner printed statement.)—Thank you, Mr. Lyons.

10246.—Will you, from the facts that you have before you, put in a return of the number of days that you have been actually on bread and water during the whole period of your imprisonment, the number of days that you have been on penal diet, the number of days that you have been in dark cells, and the number of days, according to your own statement, that you have been in handcuffs?—Yes, I can do that, Mr. Lyons.

10261.—CHAIRMAN— Under what circumstances were you dashed against the wall?—When I was stripped of the clothes, when the officers took the clothes off and threw them out; I was stretched on the floor of the cell when all was off. The last man was at the door, and, as I was getting up, he turns back and dashes me against the wall.

10262.—Were you not trying to prevent the door being closed?—No, I was not.

10263.—CHAIRMAN—Were you lying on the floor?—I was lying on the floor, and got up.

10267.—DR. LYONS—Did he push you with force or violence?—With great violence, dashed me against the wall. My hand was cut the next day. In examining these men here, my lord, have you learned from them any expressions that I used towards them, anything regarding my being violent, or anything that way?

10268.—CHAIRMAN—Yes. By one man it has been stated that in the struggle you seized Alison by the private parts.—Oh no, my lord, such a thing was never attributable to me. I never did such a thing. I caught him by the coat tails, that way, and he told Giddings to strike me, and Giddings struck me on the hand with his staff, and I let go.

10271.—CHAIRMAN—It is fair to say that Alison did not say it himself.—I did not attempt any such thing.

10272.—Allison himself made no complaint of it to us.

10272.—MR. DE VERE—I do not think Rossa need trouble himself about that.

10284.—As to the gross insolence to Captain Hardy, that is one thing that I wished to know what it was, and perhaps it was not right for me to speak o him what I did, but he came in the usual way to pay the usual visit. I was in a very uncomfortable position, and I said, "Governor, I suppose there is no chance for a man getting eggs for breakfast here?" And they gave it down "Extra breakfast."

10285.—DR. LYONS—What you said was eggs for breakfast?—Eggs for breakfast. That was the ridiculousness of it—eggs in a dark cell.

10286.—Why did you say that?—With the position in which I was placed it was a poor place to joke, but I do not like to be reported in those books for gross insolence.

10287.—Was that all you said?—That was all I did say.

10288.—Are you quite sure?—Oh, quite sure. They themselves say I said no more than "extra breakfast."

10289.—CHAIRMAN—Is there any other point upon which you wish to speak?—Well, my lord, as to threatening to strike, I do not recollect that I made any such threat. Whatever I have done in prison I do not like to make myself ridiculous, to threaten to assault men who came in with certain orders.

10290.—MR. BRODERICK—It may be satisfactory to you to know that Alison stated you did not strike or attempt to strike any one, but merely gave them a good push.

10291.—DR. LYONS—He said that you heaved them off, one in one direction, and the other in another?—That is perhaps, the fairest account to give of it, but I did not draw my hand to strike a blow, nor did I strike them.

10292.—CHAIRMAN—We will take, as the version of what occurred, that which was given by Alison?—Well, about the "assassin dogs," my lord, and throwing the pot when the door was closed at the officer?

10293.—The Commission has considered what you are now saying, and instructed me to say, that we think we know exactly the entire of this occurrence. We have had Alison's evidence, which was given very fairly, and does not represent you as using the violence that one or two others speak of; and we are satisfied that there is nothing in that transaction which calls on us, in justice to you, to go further?—Thank you, my lord.

10294.—I may say, also, that in other points in which your evidence has been in any way contradicted, or any different statements given, we have asked all the questions which we think necessary to have put, in fairness to you, of the other witnesses, and of yourself also. We do not think, therefore, that fairness calls upon us to go any further in reference to these points. I mention that to you, so as to leave it to you to consider whether you think it necessary to put them further before us. We do not think it necessary to put further questions concering them?—No, my lord, I would not be doing justice to my feelings in going further after what you have said. As to the bathing in dirty water, my lord——

10295.—That is a point we have inquired into in this and other prisons?—It occurred to me in Millbank.

10296.—CHAIRMAN—We are going to Millbank and will inquire.

10307.—MR. DE VERE—That matter, I may say to you, has been fully seen into.—Thank you, Mr. De Vere. Have you, my lord, asked a question as to what I submitted in the statement as to the officers looking at me bathing?

10308.—CHAIRMAN—We have examined and shall ask further questions. There is great discrepancy as to how they stood?—While I was in the bath, my lord, the officer stood at the door, and kept his eyes on me, looking at me.

10311.—DR. LYONS—What do you object to in it?—I only just state it, that it was a matter which was painful to me.

10312.—It is the indelicacy of the act that you complain of?—The indelicacy of the act.

10322.—DR. GREENHOW—The only notice here is, "wetting his coir before picking it," and the only punishment is "admonished?"—Well, my lord, but the officers told me to wet the coir.

10323.—DR. LYONS—They told you to wet it?—Yes, to wet it; that it would allay the dust that was rising from it, and make it easier to be picked; and Brown admitted that he told me to wet it. Two others denied they did—Cooper and another. The very officer that told me to wet the coir, my lord, reported me for wetting it.

10359.—DR. LYONS—During the time that you were thirty-five days in handcuffs, were you taken to Mass on any of the Sundays?—No, sir.

10360.—During the subsequent time that you spent on bread and water diet, were you taken to Mass?—No, sir.

10361.—Were you taken to Mass during any part of the time that you were in penal class?—No, sir, I was not taken to the chapel.
10362.—Dr. Greenhow—Did you consider that a hardship?—Well, I did not, Dr. Greenhow. I do not give you that answer with the view of being disrespectful of religious matters or things I do not want to get into. Has the doctor been asked if he ever saw me violent, or insolent, or disrespectful?
10364.—We are going to examine him presently, and if you have any questions to put to him you can put them through me?—Well, I will reserve that matter, my lord. I recollect that on the report of Knell, I recollect asking what did he mean by making noise in the cell, and his answer was that I was walking up and down my cell.
10380.—Chairman—There are some questions which you wish to put to the doctor. I believe?—Yes, my lord.
10381.—Then you can remain here.
10836—Dr. Lyons—Now, O'Donovan Rossa, can you state to me the number of days that you were on bread and water in the several prisons in which you have been confined?—One hundred and twenty-three days, Mr. Lyons.
10837.—Will you specify the prisons and the number of days in each?—Portland Prison, twenty-nine days; Millbank Prison, thirty-two days; Chatham Prison, sixty-two days.
10839.—Dr. Lyons—Can you state how many days you were on penal class diet in dark cell, what variety of diet you were on, and in what prisons you were so confined?—In Portland Prison, penal class diet, thirty-three days; in Millbank Prison, one hundred and fifty-eight days; and in Chatham forty days.
10841.—Dr. Lyons—What total does that make on penal class diet?—Two hundred and thirty-one days.
10845.—Can you now state how many days you were confined with your hands tied behind your back?—Thirty-seven days, Mr. Lyons.
10848.—On what diet were you during those thirty-seven days?—On light labor diet during thirty-five of them, that was awaiting report, and on bread and water during two of them.
10849.—How many days and nights were you confined with your hands tied night and day?—Two days and two nights, Mr. Lyons.
10852.—With what sort of manacles?—Tight manacles. There was no link between the cuffs. No. 8, is what the warder called them, I think you said.
10853.—How many days were you in absolutely dark cells in the various prisons that you have been in?—I think twenty-eight days I allowed.
10855.—I cannot recollect the number here. I was put in dark cells so often, and taken out so often, that I took no account of them.
10856.—How many nights of this period were you without a bed?—I was two nights here without a bed, without rug or blanket or anything; and I was fourteen nights in the several prisons without a mattress and sheets.
10857.—Were you sent back to Millbank for a second period of probation of twelve months?—Yes; I was sent back from Portland.
10858.—Did you spend that twelve months in Millbank?—Yes, twelve months and a few days.

EXAMINATION OF CAPTAIN DU CANE.

1.—Chairman—Your are Chairman of the Directors of Convict Prisons, I believe?—I am.
56.—What was the total number of treason-felony convicts received into English prisons?—There are twenty-one in English prisons now; forty-five were sent to Western Australia; two have been discharged on license, and one is dead. One was transferred to Mountjoy Prison, and sixteen have received conditional pardons; that makes ninety-one as the total number who have passed through the English prisons.
93.—Is it possible that a very prolonged period of bread and water diet could have been enforced, as was alleged by some of the friends of the political prisoners?—They could not have been longer than twenty-eight days on punishment diet, certainly; but they might have been on penal class diet for six months.
115.—Dr. Lyons—It is alleged that the prisoners have been made to clean privies other than their own; has that been the case?—I think what that refers to is this: When these prisoners were at work out on the works at Portland, there is a certain privy which is set apart for the use of the prisoners on the works. I recollect some question about that, but precisely what it was I cannot say. I can inquire if you wish me to do so.
219.—By way of illustration, will you tell us, would O'Donovan Rossa have heard of his election for Tipperary?—I happened to be down at Chatham just after he was elected, and he asked me whether he was returned or not.
220.—Then he was aware that he was a candidate?—Yes, he was aware that he

was a candidate, because he had a visit from one of his friends. I told him I was not authorized to give him any information of a political nature at all. Then he asked me whether, if he was elected, he might be allowed to come to Millbank, in order that he might be convenient for taking his seat. I told him I presumed every consideration would be shown to him.

221.—As we have mentioned him, I do not know that there is any impropriety in my asking whether there has been any change in his prison character of late?—It has very much improved. He now conducts himself uncommonly well; as well as anybody. Up to the middle of the year 1868 he was a very difficult man to manage, and was always doing something against the rules; but I was fortunate myself in being able, in some way or other, to produce a little change in him.

222.—Can you attribute the change in O'Donovan Rossa's conduct to any greater indulgence in his treatment?—No; I think that he commenced his good conduct first, and then it was encouraged by any little things that one could do to preserve that state of things.

223.—Mr. DE VERE—*By little indulgences?—Little considerations. He was allowed to see his child, or his wife, when he would not ordinarily have been permitted to do so.*

249.—Will you furnish us with the cost per annum to the State of each political prisoner?—I cannot distinguish political prisoners from others.

10921.—Could a man be kept for a month in handcuffs?—No; the Governor sees him day by day, or the Deputy-Governor.

10922.—Could he, on that original order, be handcuffed for a month if he was in the separate cells?—No, he cannot be in the separate cells for a month under the Governor's order.

10923.—If there was a fresh order from the Governor for the continuance of the handcuffs should that order be entered as a fresh order?—Certainly it should.

10925.—Would you run your eye over the entries in that book before you, and see is there any entry that the re-imposition of the manacles was done " by order of the Governor?"—I do not see any.

10935.—Captain Du Cane, you tried O'Donovan Rossa on the 1st of July, 1868?—Yes.

10936.—Did you see him in person on that day?—Oh, certainly.

10937.—Was he in handcuffs when you saw him that day?—I cannot recollect at this distance of time.

10941.—Have you no recollection one way or the other about it?—No, I have not the slightest recollection whatever. I cannot say anything about it.

13272.—Has it been reported, or made known to you in any way, that their health had suffered in consequence of punishment?—Well, it is very difficult to say, unless I were to look through the reports of men who have undergone punishment. I do not at this moment recollect anything of the kind, but it must do so; if a man is perpetually put on low diet, and so on, he must, somehow or other, be affected.

13277.—They were located in those places because it was thought rather necessary to keep them secure. One treason-felony convict escaped in Ireland; I believe that was the reason, partly, that they were sent over to England. Therefore, we felt it incumbent on us to take particular care that these men should not escape, and they have not.

13279.—With whom would it rest to make the necessary regulations and arrangements for the transmission of prisoners from Mountjoy Prison to the English prisons?—It was concerted between our department and the Irish convict department.

13280.—Which department would officially have charge of them?—We sent over for them.

13281.—You sent for them?—Yes; we received them, I believe, at Kingstown; I am not quite sure. There have been two or three batches. Some I know were sent over in a gunboat to Portland. Those that came over to Pentonville first, I believe we sent as far as Kingstown for them; but it might have been to Holyhead only. There have been several batches brought over. The passage was all done in one day.

13330.—When a prisoner is put in handcuffs seventy-two hours, does it mean seventy-two consecutive hours?—I believe the Governor would be justified in keeping a man in, without breach of orders, for seventy-two consecutive hours.

13331.—If the continuity of the seventy-two hours is broken by removing the handcuffs at night, would it be right to keep a prisoner in handcuffs longer than three days without a fresh order?—I do not think it would; but I think that if the question was referred to me to investigate a case of that kind, and if I found that the Governor had kept them on more than three days, I should say he had not gone beyond the *letter* of his instructions; but I should say he had much better have reported at the end of three days as if the ironing had been consecutive, but there is a rule preventing him.

13333.—Then at the end of three days, whether the man was in handcuffs night and day, or only during the day-time, the Governor ought no longer keep a prisoner in handcuffs without communicating with the Board of Directors?—He would not break any rule so long as the man had not been seventy-two hours consecutively in irons.

13334.—Mr. Broderick—But after that he would?—He would.

13335.—Dr. Greenhow—Then a Governor may keep a prisoner in handcuffs every day for three months, provided they are taken off at night?—He might without breaking any written rule.

13336.—But would not that be breaking the spirit of the rules?—It would; I could not say he had broken a written rule, for the rule is usually regarded that it might be read the other way.

13348.—Then without breaking the letter of any existing rules, do you see any limit to the length of restraint in irons that the Governor may impose?—Well, I should say if a Governor did that kind of thing, it would come to the knowledge of the Director, and that would be a practical limit. That is what the Director is for—to see that those things are not exceeded.

13349.—I will only ask you do you think the possibility of its coming to the knowledge of the Director would be a sufficient safeguard?—I should say that if a man was restrained unduly in that kind of way, he would himself bring it to the notice of the Director.

13350.—If it were to appear that such a case as this might arise, of a man being kept in irons for a continuous period of thirty-four or thirty-five days, with the exception of the irons being taken off at night, and that it had not been noticed by the Director, would not that show that the safeguard that you allude to was not a sufficient one? —Well, it might, but the particular case that you allude was not under that circumstance; *it was known to the Director.*

13351.—Was it made the subject of any animadversion by the Director of the prison to the Governor?—No, certainly not. I quite approve of that man having been kept so; I take it entirely on my responsibility as Chairman; I take the responsibility on myself of approving of what Captain Powell did when he kept the man in restraint day by day.

13352.—Dr. Lyons—Did you, as a matter of fact, know in reference to this last question when you tried O'Donovan Rossa on the 1st of July, that he had been in handcuffs?—I was aware. I forget at this moment, but I think it is most likely that I knew he had been restrained in handcuffs very frequently, perhaps every day, since the time he had committed the assault.

13414.—Supposing a man was condemned to punishment in a refractory cell for a certain number of hours, and that a Sunday intervened, would it not be possible to allow him to attend religious service, and then put in a number of hours at the end of the sentence that would compensate for the time he had been absent from the cell? You might do that; but I think it would to a certain extent break the effect of the punishment. It is the continuousness of the punishment that tells on a man. If it is broken, he is to a certain extent deprived of its effect.

13420.—Are you aware of the size and position of the dark cells at Milbank?—Yes; I have seen them not very long ago.

13421.—Are you aware that they are under the level of the ground?—Yes; they are not all good places.

13422.—Are you aware that the beds are placed along the shorter walls, which are only five feet four inches in length?—No; I am not aware of that.

13425.—Do you consider confining a prisoner in a dark cell as distinct from a light cell, a necessary instrument of prison discipline?—Yes; I think it is. It is not one I like or should use often, as it is, I believe, used often; but it has an effect.

13437.—Supposing, Captain Du Cane, that the letter contained a statement as to his treatment in prison, and that such statement was not proved to the Governor to be untrue, but, on the contrary, seemed to have been well founded, would it be allowed to go out?—A letter to his friends?

13438.—Yes; a letter to his friends must refer to nothing about his treatment inside prison.

13442.—Mr. Broderick—I have here before me a statement in the case of one of the prisoners at Woking. The following note was made, I presume, in the books, from which he has been furnished with extracts according to his application. The note referring to his first application, respecting an answer to his letters is, "Was suppressed by the Director; the prisoner not to be informed?"—I do not know the specific case.

13445.—This relates to a letter which had been received for the prisoner?—Oh, I cannot undertake to say that when letters are received they are always told. No; I would not undertake to say that; because they are only allowed to receive a certain number of letters. I suppose if more than the proper number were written they would simply not be given to him. I will not say that they are always told it.

13446.—If news were contained in such a letter which it was important for the prisoner to know, such as the death of his wife, he would be told?—He would be told.

13452.—Dr. Greenhow—If an ordinary prisoner had committed the assault Rossa did, what would have been done?—He would have been flogged. If any other prisoners had done what Rossa did, he might have been flogged a dozen times.

13471.—Dr. Lyons.—Have you satisfied yourself as to the effects of certain punishments, such as dark cells and the use of bread and water, or do you merely act on what you have found in practice? Have you given any special attention to the consideration of the question of those two punishments?—I have by inquiry from those who have seen people under the effect of them.

13474.—Is it your opinion that, on the whole, they are successful in the objects intended?—Certainly they are, in most cases. Some prisoners are affected by different punishments, some by others.

13476.—Are you aware that both these measures of discipline and punishment are a good deal abandoned elsewhere?—I did not know that they were abandoned. I know that there are many persons that object to them.

13476.—Do you think, on profound consideration, and on theoretical grounds, that they are really useful as means of correcting a refractory spirit?—I think they are. I think they take the refractory spirit out of a man.

13477.—Have you not found very notable instances in which they failed, and in which another mode of action very wisely and very successfully put in operation—by yourself, for instance—in one case, had more effect than continuous dark cells, bread and water, and irons?—Certainly, they do fail: all modes of punishment fail, even hanging sometimes.

13481.—In some notable instances where they were long continued, have they not failed?—Yes. I may say that in educated prisoners, who do not care so much about food as others, the question of depriving of food is not always very efficacious.

13482.—Have you looked at the deprivation of food yourself, as to its efficacy; as to the results in producing what is expected of it—a power of coercion on the human will?—I know that a man who is put under that kind of punishment very often mends his ways.

13483.—Would you be surprised to hear that in abstinence from food, the sensation of hunger very often ceases at an early period?—Yes; I am told that it does.

13484.—And that it is succeeded by languor and weakness?—I dare say that it might do so. Yes, I should think most probably it would.

13487.—Do you think that with regard to the permission of letters inwards and outwards, without any serious ill result to the prison system of discipline, a relaxation of the rules now in force could be made?—I think the privilege of letters is one of those very few things which we are able to use as inducements to good behavior, and I think any relaxation of it will deprive us of that advantage.

13489.—We have in evidence that a prisoner was for a very lengthened period without knowing how his wife was?—Well, I suppose there was nothing the matter with the wife of that prisoner. If the prisoner was ill-conducted he was not entitled to a letter.

13519.—If a prisoner expeditiously completes the task-work prescribed to him, and then reads a book, is there any moral or prison guilt involved in it?—I should say that whilst working-hours existed he was bound to work. If the Governor had set him a task which did not take him enough, he ought to have asked for more.

13522.—In this particular case it was three pounds of oakum he was to pick?—During working hours I should expect a man to work, not to read. If he was tempted to read I should take the books out of his cell. I would not have him read when he ought to be working. He is not sent to prison to read.

13523.—But if he completes his work within the given time is there anything contrary to discipline in his reading for the remainder of the time?—I say that during working hours he ought to work. If he is so vigorous that he can do more work than ordinary people he must still work, according to my idea of propriety, during working hours.

13535.—Would it not be a great assistance to the Directors of prisons in carrying out the sentence on a prisoner, if, as you suggested, the Judge were to take into account the amount of moral degradation that was involved in the case, and that the Directors of prisons should therefore be able to modify the discipline of the prison as affecting the peculiar character of the man?—I think there might be disadvantages in that; but in the same prison I should be very sorry to see different systems. I should send him to a different prison.

That is as much as I need give of Captain Du Cane's evidence. The reader can readily understand that he is a man suited for his work. At Question 13351 he admits he knew I was thirty-five days in irons, and, as Chairman of the Board of Directors, he sends one of them down to Chatham Prison to get up a report that I was only one day in them. He admits that though there is a standing order not to keep a prisoner handcuffed more than three days, there is a way of evading that and keeping a prisoner handcuffed all the days of his life, if it be pleasing to the authorities. Mr. Du Cane played an important part this year at the International Prison Congress. How I wish I had him under examination there, in the presence of the representatives from the other nations, to whom he showed the excellence of his English system, with all the buchu plastering he could lay on.

Count Sollahule of Russia proposed the following question for this Congress, and I am sure my Director would not—at least for the Irish political prisoners—consider imprisonment alone sufficient punishment:

"No. 8.—Ought not the Congress to recognize from the start, as a binding principle, the fundamental proposition of 'Rossi's Treatise on the Penal Code : "*Imprisonment is punishment, par excellence, among all civilized people.*"

Mr. Du Cane would have a punishment that drove sixty-two men into the madness of self-mutilation in Chatham, during the year 1872, and that created 19,633 casualties for the doctor, that is an average of 53 each day.—(*See English Government Report of Convict Prisons,* 1872.)

MR. WILLIAM FAGAN EXAMINED.

3040.—CHAIRMAN—Mr. Fagan, you are one of the Directors of convict prisons?—Yes, my lord.

3045.—You would have power to inflict punishment which the Governor cannot?—I can inflict the punishment which a Board of Visiting Justices can. I can award corporal punishment to a prisoner; I can sentence him to close confinement on punishment diet for 28 days, vary only each fourth day by penal class diet. If he is a man who has committed an assault on a warder, I can place him in cross-irons, not exceeding six pounds in weight, and restrict him to a dress such that every officer will know he is a person who has committed an assault on one of themselves.

3096.—As a matter of fact, have you detained many letters which came for, or were sent by, treason-felony prisoners?—Formerly we have detained a great many.

3097.—Have you detained many letters sent for the prisoners?—Yes.

3098.—Have you detained many letters sent by them?—Yes; we suppressed them because they contained statements in abuse of myself, or of the Governor, or of the Government.

3116.—DR. GREENHOW—You ordered the treason-felony convicts to be kept separate from the other prisoners?—Yes.

3117.—Did you consider that an indulgence?—No; I thought it more a matter of security.

3118.—Not as an indulgence?—Oh, certainly not, but as a point of security. I considered the prison a weak one, and I was responsible for the safe custody of those men.

3122.—Did you gather that the impression on the minds of the treason-felony prisoners was, that their crime was of a different character, and that they ought not to be associated with ordinary prisoners?—Yes; they have always called themselves "State prisoners."

3124.—Now, is it a fact that they have had fewer visits than other prisoners?—Yes, I think, in point of fact, that they have had fewer visits.

3136.—In case of the death of a prisoner's mother, wife, sister, or brother, or any other relative, and that a letter was received announcing it, would the prisoner be allowed to receive that letter, although it was out of time?—He would not be allowed to see it until the time arrived that it was due, but the information in it about the death would be communicated to him at once.

3250.—MR. DE VERE—In the case of confinement in the dark cell, is there any system of periodical disturbance of the men at night?—Oh, yes; the same system exists here as in all prisons.

3251.—How often at night?—He would not be more than half an hour at night without being visited, but not necessarily disturbed.

3252.—And when disturbed, would he be awakened?—No, unless they cover themselves in and put their heads under the blanket. The officer when he visits must know whether the man is sick or dead, or there at all. If a man laid himself down with his blanket off his cheeks he would not be disturbed at all.

3253.—DR. LYONS—When a prisoner is in a punishment cell, and Sunday falls within the period of his punishment, is he allowed to go to religious worship?—No.

3257.—I wish to know is there any impossibility in the matter. Take the case of a Catholic, with whom it is the highest obligation to attend Mass on Sunday—would there be any impossibility of sending him to Mass on Sunday?—Except that it would be a violation of the punishment, and it would be treating him exceptionally with regard to his fellow prisoners."

This is Mr. Fagan, the Irishman and the Roman Catholic, who ordered that no Irishman or Roman Catholic be allowed to have any charge of us.

MR. GEORGE CLIFTON, GOVERNOR OF PORTLAND PRISON, EXAMINED.

2084.—CHAIRMAN—Mr. Clifton, you are the Governor of this prison, are you not?—I am, my lord.

2128.—During the time you have been here you have had under your charge certain prisoners convicted under the Treason Felony Act?—I have, my lord.

2135.—How long did they remain in the wash-house?—Only a day or two. I think it was five days; but that I could refer to and ascertain immediately, my lord.

2136.—Then it was in consequence of instructions given to you that they were placed in the ordinary public works?—I then received instructions to treat them as ordinary prisoners; that is to say, that they were to be sent on to other public works; but they were to be located by themselves, and they were to be worked in a party separate, by themselves, and they were so.

2138.—And has that continued to be the case to the present time?—It has continued with the exception of a day or two, my lord, when there was a great spirit of insubordination shown by them, and at the same time I was hourly expecting a mutiny amongst the prisoners here. At the very time that this exhibition of a turbulent spirit was taking place, information indirectly came to me that the treason-felony prisoners were going to assist in the mutiny; and I believe that it was on that occasion that for a day or two, on my request to the Visiting Director, two of the treason-felony prisoners were removed out of the party, as they, I thought, were leading the other men astray.

2139.—Who were they?—O'Donovan Rossa was one of them, and, I think, O'Connor the other.

2142.—They were separated from persons suffering under the same sentence as themselves?—Exactly, my lord; but I found, from the information I got in the party, they were doing more harm there than they were amongst themselves. I therefore put them back into their own party again.

2143.—I believe you then, or subsequently, moved them from the ordinary cells to the penal class cells?—I did, my lord.

2144.—Why was that done?—I looked on it as a more secure position.

2159.—Would the Visiting Director receive the evidence of another prisoner in charge, when it is borne out by collateral evidence?—I do not think he would ever directly take the evidence of one prisoner to support another.

2267.—Are the prisoners expected to salute the officers here?—No, they are supposed to salute the superior officers. For instance, when going around the cells of a day, if a man is lying down he stands up to "attention" and salutes, but only when he is visited by the Medical Officer, the Chaplain, the Priest, and the Governor, or Deputy Governor.

2318.—I think you stated that the rule of silence on the public works was formerly enforced against the treason-felony prisoners?—It was endeavored to be enforced. It was never strictly accomplished, but some of the treason-felony convicts were reported during the first month they were here for breaking that rule.

2319.—Do I understand you to say now that they were virtually permitted to talk freely?—Well, I must say they are, virtually so. They are virtually permitted to do so now, from the mere fact of the impossibility of preventing them; the alternative is, that they must either be confined under punishment, or be allowed to talk.

2471.—Dr. Lyons—The baths, I observe, are so arranged that, as I have been informed, three persons in succession use the same bath?—Yes.

2481.—What amount of clothing is given to a prisoner in Winter?—He has exactly the same as in Summer.

11951. Chairman How long, Mr Clifton, was the treason-felony prisoner O'Donovan Rossa under your charge?—Speaking from my memory, my lord, I think nearly twelve months.

11952.—Do you recollect during that twelve months the case of a letter which he was charged with endeavoring to send out surreptitiously?—I do, my lord.

12025.—Did O'Donovan Rossa afterwards state to you that if you had told the Board of Directors and the Secretary of State, that the letter was intended for another man's wife, you told them what was false?—I recollect of his telling me if I told the Board of Directors; I did not make use of the Secretary of State's name.

12026.—Was he punished for making that remark?—I do not know. It was highly insubordinate conduct, accusing the Governor in the presence of a subordinate officer, of having made it public in the prison that he had been carrying on an intrigue with another's man's wife. He upbraided me very severely, and I had intended to have him reported and punished, but I thought I might give him one more chance. I am under the impression that I mentioned it to the Director afterwards, but I am only speaking from memory.

12028.—To the best of your knowledge, is there any written account of the alleged fact that O'Donovan Rossa tried to pass out a letter to another man's wife appearing in the books of Portland Prison, or in any other book within your cognizance?—I think there is, sir. I think I might be able to put my hand on either the semi-official letter or the official letter that I sent up to Parliament street with the documents.

12033.—Dr. Greenhow—There are two lines here that I will read for you:

"The fatherland, the hope of years—
The friend, the child and wife."

Here is another:

"It freely flies to wife and child,
To friend and fatherland."

Now, after reading these lines, could you doubt that that letter was addressed to his wife?—(No answer.)

12038.—Mr. De Vere—Do you remember this matter having been investigated by a former Commission?—It was.

12041.—Do you remember the conclusion that the Commission came to?—I will read it to you: "We are far from saying that it was not so" (that is, that it was not satisfactory). "The letter may have been for Mrs. Moore the elder, not for Mrs. Moore the younger. 'Mrs. O'D.' might mean Mrs. O'Donovan Rossa, not Mrs. O'Donovan; but at least the matter requires explanation, and Rossa might have asked Moore's permission before writing either to his mother or his wife." That is their conclusion. Do you understand by that conclusion that the Commission leaves the matter in doubt as to whether O'Donovan Rossa was or was not writing a letter to another man's wife? —(No answer.)

12042.—Chairman—You must be cleverer than I am, Mr. Clifton, if you can put any other interpretation on it.

12068.—When you mentioned to Moore that O'Donovan Rossa had written to Moore's wife, did he evince any feeling of anger or resentment?—He was very indignant.

12074.—Did you think there was no danger to be apprehended from two men meeting one another under the impression that one of them had written to the wife of the other?—No; for the treason-felony prisoners send their love one to another and there is the greatest possible sympathy and friendly feeling between them, and they never forgot to mention each other.

12086.—Chairman—Rossa in his statement asks, "How is it explained that in Portland I have been separated from the Irish prisoners and sent amongst a gang of English prisoners?"—He was separated from the treason-felony prisoners on two occasions, my lord, when the treason-felony prisoners were showing a very insubordinate spirit and carrying it to such an extent that I recommended to the Director that the party should be broken up and distributed amongst the other prisoners, or at all events those who were the leaders. Looking on O'Donovan Rossa at that time as being their leader I removed him, and, I think, it was O'Connor, into another party of prisoners, where he was employed and was very much under my own observation and the observation of the officers. He created such a feeling of sympathy towards himself in the party that I saw that it would be dangerous for him to remain there. I thought it would be better, and for the safety of the prison at large, if he returned to the party and worked with them, and accordingly he was sent back. I was then in possession of written information that a meeting on a large scale was to take place at the prison; on marching back to the prison from the works the convicts were to rise *en masse*. They were to be officered or commanded by the Fenian prisoners and were to rush on the prison. It was just about this time.

12087.—He asks, "How is it explained that while at Portland, the rest of the treason-felony prisoners working in mid-winter in a shed I was placed outside of the shed and prevented from having that little shelter from the poison-laden blast which the others had?" Do you know anything about that?—He complained to me about that and I interrogated the officer at the time, but it was simply that he was misconducting himself and had been put outside the shed for a short time.

12089.—"How is it explained," he asks, "that when under report the same day with some of my fellow prisoners, on a charge of talking while at work they got twenty-four hours on bread and water and I got seventy-two hours on bread and water with fourteen days solitary confinement on penal class diet?" The date is 29th December, 1866?—The others were charged with simply talking on the works, while he was reported for talking accompanied with insolence; in fact, setting the officer at defiance at the time, and therefore he was awarded a heavier punishment than the other prisoners.

12092.—Was O'Donovan Rossa ever deprived of all books as a punishment at Portland?—I think he was on one occasion by order of the Director.

12094.—Are you able to state positively whether O'Donovan Rossa was for six months deprived of the use of the Bible?—I could not without reference to the Director's order in the case.

12095.—When a prisoner is confined in a dark cell at Portland would he have his body clothing at night, or would his body clothing be taken from him at night?—It is the ordinary custom that when a man is in a dark cell his clothes are taken from him.

MR. MORISH, GOVERNOR OF MILLBANK, EXAMINED.

12858.—MR. DEVERE—Do I understand that if a man by diligence and exertion had finished his work a little before the close of the working hours, he would not then be allowed to read?—No, not in working hours.

12893.—MR. LYONS—Would you show us the kind of bowl O'Donovan Rossa was furnished with to take his food out of?—Yes.

12894.—Had he any spoon on each of these occasions?—He would be supplied with a spoon, certainly, if he had not broken it.

12972.—Was O'Donovan Rossa searched very frequently?—He was searched very frequently because he was found to have forbidden things about him.

12973.—Do you happen to remember if he was searched daily for a considerable period?—Well, I could not state exactly whether he was, but I think it is very possible that he was.

12997.—Might they be naked searches?—Yes, if the man is a dangerous character.

13011.—How many baths have common water in them?—There are four separate ones in the reception ward.

13013.—How many of these baths have the same water?—I am going to speak now with regard to the time of the reception of O'Donovan Rossa. At that time two prisoners on an average used one and the same water.

13025.—I find recorded here on the 20th of December, 1867, this order: "He is to have no other spoon issued?"—Yes; but I think that does not refer to the cell he was in "for destroying his spoon, and scraping away the cement on the bottom of the cell window." On that occasion he had no other spoon issued.

13029.—How would he lift it, the hands being crossed?—Very well; I could do it without difficulty.

13030.—Your hands are not manacled now?—At all events, I am satisfied that persons have taken their meals with manacles on their hands.

13038.—I think your proposal to get the manacles on is a better way of testing it? Yes, but I do not know if we can get any gruel at present. (*Witness directs a warder to have some gruel brought in the bowl.*)

13051.—MR. MORISH—I consider that it can be brought up to his mouth this way (*witness lifts the bowl to his mouth.*) I think I could empty that bowl without much trouble.

JOHN D. BURNS, M. D., EXAMINED.

5664.—Have you noticed a bad smell as the result of bad drainage?—I have, sir. It is caused by not having sufficient fall.
5665.—The tide makes its appearance?—The tide makes its appearance.
5666.—Does the tide come into the prison?—The tide comes into the kitchen.
5667.—The tide has been known to come into the kitchen?—Outside the kitchen.
5668.—Have you made any report of the state of the sewers?—I have, and frequently.
5671.—Have you made medical reports to the Director, or the Home Office, or the Office of Works?—I have frequently.
5689.—DR. LYONS—Do you think that the boards upon which the treason-felony prisoners sleep furnish as comfortable a bed as the hammock of the other prisoners?—That is a matter of opinion, entirely. Some men would prefer to sleep in a hammock, and think it more comfortable. I think the others more comfortable, because in the hammocks they might fall out, and many do fall out, and the strapping gives way. I think it is more comfortable on the floor, where they are.
5747.—CHAIRMAN—Is it your opinion, Dr. Burns, that there is sufficient ventilation in the dark cells?—There is not, my lord; not quite so much as there ought to be.
6890.—MR. BRODERICK—Did you on any occasion, Dr. Burns, say to Underwood O'Connell that medicine was not what he wanted, but food, better food, and that you were not allowed to give him? Did you ever say that to him, or anything to that effect?—No; but he has suggested that idea to me. He has, for instance, put it to me whether better food and other food would be better for him. Certainly, I think it would.
6891.—And have you ever gone on to say that he required better food than you were allowed to give him?—Well, I think it very likely that I have done so."
6919.—It was stated to us that on his complaining to you, you said, "when the boot has worked a sore I will endeavor to mend it," that he then asked, "Is not prevention better than cure?" and that you answered, "I am not allowed to prevent anything of that sort in certain cases?"—Well, my lord, it is very likely—the statement of the prisoner about prevention.
6932.—Are not the treason-felony convicts in penal cells?—They are in the penal cells, but not in the dark cells. Rossa, I believe, is the only man who ever occupied one of them.
9044.—You stated, I think, in answer to Lord Devon, that it is most unusual for a man to have handcuffs on him in the dark cell?—It is.
9045.—And I think you also said that Rossa was handcuffed in the dark cell?—I think he was. To the best of my recollection he was handcuffed in the dark cell.
9058.—Did you at any time find that his health was suffering at any period between June and the end of August, 1868, in consequence of the discipline he was undergoing?—His weight and appearance were reduced, in consequence of the low diet that he was placed on; but beyond that I do not think his health suffered. He appeared reduced in face, and reduced in appearance, from the bread and water that he was placed on.
9059.—Do you think it possible that a man could be on bread-and-water-diet for twelve days out of fifteen, and in dark cells at the same period for eight days out of fifteen, without suffering in health?—I think that he would be reduced in bulk, but I do not know that his health would suffer. It would not be improved, certainly. His reduced diet might certainly injure his health to a limited extent, possibly, although not appreciably. I cannot say it would improve his health.
9072.—CHAIRMAN—On visiting O'Donovan Rossa during that time, did you consider it injurious to his health?—I did not, my lord.
9019.—For a great many days between the first of June and the end of August, he did undergo bread and water?—He did, a great many times.
9120.—Did you observe any deterioration of his health during that period?—I did not.
9121.—It seemed to agree with him?—No, I cannot say that it agreed with him. The man used to emaciate on it.
9134.—He made no complaint?—He made no complaint at the time.
9162.—Do you consider him constitutionally a strong man?—I think him a very strong man indeed, very.
10382.—CHAIRMAN—What questions do you wish to put to Dr. Burns? PRISONER—I do not desire, my lord, to go into the question about the irons, if you have examined about it.
10383.—I do not think it necessary that you should.—Very well, my lord. Well, my lord, a question: Would you ask Dr. Burns if he ever saw me violently or insolently disposed towards him or any other person?

10384.—Have you ever, Dr. Burns, had occasion to complain of the conduct of O'Donovan Rossa towards you, as being insolent, or in any way unbecoming? DR. BURNS—No, my lord, never.
10441.—You state that you observed, on the third day, that he was manacled with his hands behind his back? DR. BURNS—I think he was; to the best of my knowledge, I think.
10445.—Then, it is possible that you may not recollect what position the hands were in on the fourth, fifth, sixth and subsequent days? DR. BURNS—It is quite possible.
10446.—O'Donovan Rossa, in what position were your hands manacled on the fourth day? PRISONER—This way. (Puts his hands together behind his back.)
10447.—Repeat it in words, so that the short-hand writer may take it down? PRISONER—Behind my back; but if the doctor came at dinner time my hands would be in front.
10448.—On the fifth day, in what position were you manacled? PRISONER—My hands behind my back.
10449.—Do you positively assert that? PRISONER—Positively; every day for 35 days.
10618.—CHAIRMAN—Dr. Burns, are you in professional attendance on the Rev. Mr. O'Sullivan, Roman Catholic priest of this prison?—I am, my lord.
10629.—Is he in a state in which he would be able to give evidence?—He is in a very weakly state indeed. He has hardly been able to crawl about. He is lying on a water-bed or air-bed this morning.
10620.—Is his ailment mental or bodily?—Bodily; and he has had hæmoptysis—vomiting of blood and spitting of blood. He can hardly bear any excitement.
10621.—Then you would not consider it advisable to examine him?—I would not consider it advisable to examine him. There is a note to tell me his state to-day.
10660.—I fancy that Rossa, when he first came here, was at harder labor than the other Fenians.--I remember something of that kind. It is no doubt on record.
10873.—CHAIRMAN—What is O'Donovan Rossa's present weight, Dr. Burns?—154 pounds—the lowest he has ever been.
10874.—You weighed him just now?—I did my lord.

This is the Dr. Burns who tortured Daniel Reddin by piercing his feet with needles and plunging him into cold water. The unfortunate prisoner is now paralyzed in Kingstown, Dublin. When he left prison he went to law with Dr. Burns, but the English judges threw his case out of court. Like the men who tied my hands behind my back for thirty-five days and afterwards forgot they ever did it, Doctor Burns and his agents were able to satisfy the courts that Daniel Reddin's story was false, as they were able to satisfy the Secretary of State and the Secretary of State able to satisfy Parliament that all I said was moonshine. Any one who reads this chapter I am writing can form a pretty fair idea of the little reliance that ought to be placed on the evidence of English officials when they are examined by Parliamentary or other Commissions on any question affecting the management of English institutions. Such quibbling and contradictions and "forgetfulness" *I* have never read of, as I witnessed myself. I wanted to have the Rev. Mr. O'Sullivan produced to give evidence about his seeing my hands cut by the irons, and his seeing the writing on the door in blood, but the priest was pronounced "too ill to appear."

JAMES CRANSTON EXAMINED.

7499.—CHAIRMAN—Are you an assistant warden in the prison?—Yes, sir.
7536.—DR. GREENHOW—Are you quite sure that the handcuffs were put on O'Donovan Rossa on the 16th?—I am, sir. I was present, sir.
7543.—MR. DE VERE—On what day was it you heard him complaining of being hurt, and say "Don't pinch me?"—I think it was next morning, either after exercise,

or when he was dressing himself for exercise. The officer was putting them on, and he said "Don't pinch me." I do not think he said anything more about it.

7684.—CHAIRMAN—As your statement, O'Donovan Rossa, differs from Cranston's, we think it right to call you together. Cranston has stated to the Commission that he was frequently on duty in the penal wards at the time between the 17th of June and the middle of August, and in answer to the question put to him by us he has expressed his belief that you were not for more than three or four days with your hands handcuffed behind you. Now, that being his statement, differing from yours, we think it right that you should have an opportunity of putting to him, through me, any question that you might wish to ask him which you think might tend to show that your version is correct and that he is under a mistake. It is stated that you were not more than three or four days with your hands manacled behind you. That is a correct statement of what you told us, is it not? CRANSTON—Behind, sir.

7685.—Do you believe that he was not for more than three or four days with his hands handcuffed behind? CRANSTON—Yes.

7686.—Do you wish to put any question upon that statement through me? O'DONOVAN ROSSA—Ask him, my lord, if you please, how often did he take off or put on the handcuffs?

7687.—How often did you take off or put on the handcuffs during the period referred to? CRANSTON—Frequently during this time, to take his food and exercise. ROSSA—Please, my lord, to ask him could he make a guess at the number of times?

7688—When you say "frequently," can you define the number of times; eighteen, twenty, or thirty, or how often? CRANSTON—Not exactly the number of times, sir.

7690—But you cannot tell the number of times the handcuffs were so changed? CRANSTON—No, not exactly, sir. ROSSA—Ask him, my lord, did he change them six times during the whole time?

7691.—Did you change them six times? CRANSTON—Yes, more than that. ROSSA—Ask him, did he change them ten times, my lord.

7692.—Did you change them ten times? CRANSTON—Well, I might say I have.

7696.—Do you think that you changed them twelve times? CRANSTON—I cannot say exactly. ROSSA—Is he sure of ten times, my lord.

7697.—Are you sure of 10 times? CRANSTON—Yes, I say 10 times.

7698.—You have no doubt of 10? CRANSTON—No, my lord. ROSSA—I ask these questions for the purpose of having the same questions asked of them all, for the whole number of times could be taken and then the sum divided by the number of times a day.

7703.—ROSSA—In the 10 times that he changed the handcuffs, my lord, how many times did he change them at the dinner hour?

7704.—How many of those 10, when you changed the handcuffs from rear to front took place at the dinner hour? CRANSTON I think I done it twice or three times after dinner."

This man saw me with my hands bound behind, nearly every day during the five weeks.

W. T. ALISON EXAMINED.

8414. Do you recollect, in June, receiving instructions from the then Deputy-Governor to put the prisoner, O'Donovan Rossa, in irons?—Yes, my lord, I believe—yes, yes.

8419. What did you do in consequence? Was there any mode specified in which you were to put on the irons or handcuffs?—To the best of my belief, my lord, it was to "put him in handcuffs behind."

8437. Except that one day, is it your impression that you have seen O'Donovan Rossa in handcuffs behind some other days?—I believe he was more than one day in handcuffs behind, but I do not think, to the best of my knowledge, my lord, that he was more than three days in handcuffs behind.

8464. CHAIRMAN—What do you say?—I never saw such punishment carried on, sir.

8467. CHAIRMAN—The reason you do not think it might have been continued for thirty days is that you never saw such punishment imposed?—I did not, my lord.

8573. I now finally conclude that you have no means of saying, although the order was given to you, on what day, or what period of the day, O'Donovan Rossa was first put in irons?—I am unable to say,

8600. Was he put in irons in consequence of that offence of allowing the water to run waste?—No, I think not, sir; I think not. I am not aware. Yes, sir, here it is. The Governor gave orders for the prisoner (Rossa) to be removed to another cell, and to be placed in handcuffs during the time some alterations were being made to the tap of the closet.

8614. Did it ever happen in your experience of prison life that a prisoner was handcuffed in any way, either in front or behind, for such a period as 35 days?— Never, sir.

8615. Never?—Never.

8617. I ask you what is the longest period in which, in your experience, you have known a prisoner to be handcuffed in any way?—72 hours.

8627. If he states positively that he was handcuffed with his hands behind his back for 35 days consecutively, do you, having seen those entries there of his being daily handcuffed for so many days consecutively, think it likely that he was handcuffed with his hands behind his back, in accordance with the first entry?—I should not think he was, sir.

8628. Why?—I do not think that ever there was such an order given. I do not think there was ever a man that underwent that punishment for 35 days.

8650. Did he resist the application of the handcuffs on those occasions?—No, sir.

8651. He was perfectly quiet?—I believe so.

8652. He did not make any resistance which would cause you to hurt him in putting on the handcuffs?—No, sir.

8654. Did he show you any marks on his hands?—Well, it was just very slight, sir.

8657. Was there only one mark, or was there more than one?—That I am also unable to say. There might have been two. He complained, and I made the remark that the most carefullest man might nip a person in putting the handcuffs on.

8684. Do you recollect any occasion of a second offence being committed, say at the time in which he was on penal class diet?—After he had been released from the handcuffs, according to his own statement, they were put on again. Who put them on again after letting the water run?—I labor under the impression that it was me, my lord; I think so, but I am not sure.

8685. Were the irons then put on in front or behind?—Behind, I believe, my lord.

8691. Mr. Broderick—Do you recollect having to assist O'Donovan Rossa in buttoning or unbuttoning his clothes during this period that he was in irons?—No, sir, I do not; I might have done it, but I do not recollect.

8692. Do you recollect his having made holes in his clothes in order to keep up his trousers?—He had no braces on, my lord. He might have done so. I cannot recollect.

8693. Do you recollect on any occasion telling him that there was a place near the prison called "Jilligum," and that any prisoner who did not obey the rules very soon found his way to it?—I do not recollect that sir, but I might have done so. I have often given that caution to prisoners that would persist in coming from the cells. I have told them that very same thing, and advised them to keep out of it.

8694. What is "Jilligum?"—Gillingham Cemetery.

8714. Mr. Broderick—Referring once more, Mr. Alison, to the occasion in August, 1868, when O'Donovan Rossa was confined in the dark cell, do you remember refusing to give him any clothing?—Yes, sir.

8722. Did you or either of the others, to the best of your knowledge, lift yourself up and leap with the knee foremost on his chest?—I cannot say, sir. If there was anything occurred it was a regular up and down thing.

8724. Dr. Lyons—Is he so strong that he could resist three of you?—I had a great many men to remove to the dark cell, but I never got a wetter shirt from any man than I did from O'Donovan Rossa. I never had a more difficult task in my life.

What a convenient memory this Mr. Alison has! He can't remember anything he did, but he can invent lies, for I never gave him any trouble going to a dark cell. I always went, in obedience to the order, "come on."

ALFRED BROWN EXAMINED.

12178. Do you recollect an occasion on which O'Donovan Rossa committed an assault by throwing water on the Governor?—Yes, sir.

12198. How many times, I am asking you, did you put the handcuffs on? Did you put them on five times, or ten times, or twenty times?—Yes, sir, I dare say I put them on five times.

12199. Did you put them on more than five times? (No answer.)

12200. Can you not recollect whether you put them on more than five times?—It is so long ago now, sir, that I cannot remember the time.

12232. Supposing the first entry is "handcuffed behind his back," and then it goes on for twenty days, say, with the word "handcuffed" without the words "behind his back," would that imply punishment in the same way during the whole of those twenty days?—No, sir.
12233. Would it imply that it did not go on more than the first time?—That he was handcuffed?
12234. What would it imply, supposing, on the second day, the entry simply is handcuffed? (No answer.)
12235. You say that he was handcuffed with the hands behind the second days and yet the entry does not show it. How do you account for that? The entry on the second day is just the same as the entry on the tenth day. You say he was not handcuffed behind on the tenth day, but was on the second day. Why was not the entry put on the second day? Can you answer that question? (No answer.)
12257. Surely, you were about him every day, and you can remember about how many days he was handcuffed after that assault?—No, sir; I cannot.
12258. Do you think it was a week?—Handcuffed all together sir?
12259. Yes? Either behind or before?
12260. Yes; either behind or before?—No; I couldn't say, sir.
12261. You cannot say whether it was a week or a month?—No, sir; not at that one time.
12262. And yet it was your duty to attend to those cells?—He may have had a month on and off.
12263. Are you quite sure that, during that month when he had them on and off, he was not handcuffed with the hands behind every day?—I am positive of it, sir.
12286. You have already told Lord Devon that the handcuffs were put on behind for three days, and that they were taken off and put in front whilst he ate his meals. You now tell me that they were taken off altogether. Now, consider, were they taken off for him to eat his meals or not? (No answer.)
12287. CHAIRMAN It is a simple fact. Can you tell us whether, or not?—It is so long ago, sir, that I cannot remember these things.
12288. DR. GREENHOW—In fact, you remember nothing about it, is that the case?—Not any dates, or anything of that sort, I cannot.
12290. And is it a common thing for men to be handcuffed for about a month? —No, sir.
12291. And would not such a circumstance attract your attention?—Not, in the way O'Donovan Rossa conducted himself, it would not, sir.
12292. Would not the very way he conducted himself lead you to pay attention to the handcuffing; it seems to me that the man's having conducted himself badly would lead you to pay greater attention to the circumstances of his case? (No answer.)
12308. Supposing a man is ordered to be handcuffed behind, would it usually last three days?—I don't remember he having them on any way, sir.
12360. You repeat over and over again a period of three days; but I want to know have you any reason for stating that he was only handcuffed behind three days?— Well, I don't know that I can state any particular reason.
12363. Now, will you look at this book; whose handwriting is that (an entry in the separate cells book)?—Mine, sir.
12364. Is that your entry (another entry)?—Yes, sir.
12365. "J. O'Donovan Rossa placed in handcuffs behind, by order of the Governor;" is that your handwriting?—Yes, sir.
12366. Is that your handwriting (another entry)?—Yes, sir.
12367. "J. O'Donovan Rossa, handcuffs removed from behind by order of the Governor;" is that your handwriting?—Yes, sir.
12368. On the 18th there is another entry, "J. O'Donovan Rossa replaced in handcuffs by order of the Governor;" is that your handwriting?—Yes, sir.
12414. Is that?—Yes, sir. (Witness identifies several other entries as his handwriting.)
12416. From the 17th of June down to the 21st of July, the majority of the entries here which have reference to the handcuffing of O'Donovan Rossa are in your handwriting?—Yes, sir.
12423. DR. GREENHOW—Do you recollect distinctly that you put them on yourself? —Yes, sir.
12424. DR. LYONS—You see that is not consistent with what you said a little while ago? (No reply.)
13425. You feel, no doubt, that after the prisoner throwing the water on the Governor, you shut the door of the cell yourself?—Yes, sir.
12475. DR. GREENHOW—You have just been cautioned on the subject. We have seen the evidence you gave on the trial of the case before Captain Du Cane. I want

to know how you reconcile your statements. You have told me that you shut the door yourself; on that occasion you swore that O'Donovan Rossa shut the door violently. This is your evidence and is signed Alfred Brown: " Being duly sworn states, on Tuesday the 16th of June, 1869, at about 12.10 p. m. I accompanied the Governor on an inspection of the cells in the penal class. When in the usual way I opened 449, prisoner Jeremiah O'Donovan Rossa's, door and called him to " attention," he being at the time sitting on stool close to the door, when he rose up off the stool and made a movement I thought, of picking up a jacket to put on as he was sewing it, instead of which he picked up his cell-pot and threw the contents over the Governor, which covered him from head to foot and myself. He then slammed the door to, in the Governor's face, in the most violent manner."

12487. How do you reconcile what you have three times told me distinctly, that you shut the door, and here I show you that you swore Rossa slammed it out himself; how do you reconcile that?—I am wrong there, sir.

You are, and in several other places also. But *you* are only one of the small fry. Let us take a look now at your superior officer, Captain Wickham Talbot Harvey, "an officer and a gentleman," and see the figure he cuts in truth-telling.

CAPTAIN WICKHAM TALBOT HARVEY EXAMINED.

12505. CHAIRMAN—You are, I believe, at present Governor of the convict prison at Portsmouth?—Yes, my lord.
12598. How long, according to your recollection, was O'Donovan Rossa handcuffed at all, whether in front or behind?—Well, I should not think more than five days at the outside, as far as I can recollect.
12604. Have you ever known a prisoner handcuffed for as many as 34 days?—No, never.
12620. Then if it should appear that these three books (the senior officer's book, Alison's book, and the Governor's book, which was probably kept by Harvey himself), kept by different officers, all men of the highest character, concur in showing that O'Donovan Rossa was handcuffed continuously day after day for a period of 34 or 35 days, would it make you inclined to doubt the accuracy of your memory? I should prefer the entry of those three to my own memory, certainly.
12642. Was O'Donovan Rossa very violent on the occasion of that assault? He was. He threw Principal Warder Alison, who was a troop sergeant-major of the 16th Lancers, clean over his shoulders as if he was merely a child.
12643. When was that? I cannot remember.

I am willing to give him credit for telling the truth here when he says he "cannot remember," for such a thing never happened between Alison and me; but he soon again relapses into lying by saying I was violent during the handcuffing.

12713. You say Rossa was violent during the period of the handcuffing?—Yes.
12714. Are you quite sure of that from personal observation?—Yes. The fact is that when I went round I used to speak to him in as friendly a manner as I could, and I used to advise him to keep quiet and so on. I told him he was only making matters worse for himself. Sometimes he used to laugh and sometimes break out, and my impression is that a great deal of this outbreak on his part was that he was under the impression that, sooner or later, it would bring his case before the public. It was my impression all along that he would somehow or other manage to establish a case of ill-treatment, because on more than one occasion when he tried the temper of Principal Warder Alison he looked as much as to say, " Well, it is curious you have done nothing to me."
12745. DR. GREENHOW—You spoke some time since of the language that O'Donovan Rossa had used towards the warders. Can you give any instance of it?—Well, I cannot exactly recollect the language.
12746. DR. LYONS.—Was there anything in Rossa's language that you describe as violent, more than what you mentioned to Dr. Greenhow, that he characterized them as being minions of the British Government? I mean, did he use foul language?—No; I cannot say that he used foul language. Oh, no, he did not, but it was of an irrita-

tive character. "Servants of a tyrannical government," and "eating the bread of," I don't know what; I can't recollect now.

12752. MR. DE VERE—You said that seeing those entries makes you feel somewhat distrustful of the accuracy of your memory?—They do; there is no doubt about it.

12753. Would it make you somewhat more distrustful if you were aware that the chief medical officer, and the Governor, Captain Powell, have both given evidence that O'Donovan Rossa was under restraint in one way or other from 30 to 35 consecutive days at that time?—Of course, anything further that can be adduced of an opposite character would shake my confidence in my memory.

Hibbert was the man that leaped upon me, and Giddings was the man that struck me softly with the club, and it is strange that they were the only two that could speak anything like truth to the Commissioners. They ought to be promoted. I recommend them to the consideration of my friends, Captain Du Cane and Captain Gambier.

WILLIAM HIBBERT, EXAMINED.

9195. CHAIRMAN—Had you charge of treason-felony convict O'Donovan Rossa?—I had, sir.

9210. CHAIRMAN—Did you see him with the hands manacled behind on more than one occasion?—Yes, sir.

9213. How many times did you see him manacled behind?—A few, sir. Five times? Yes, more.

9215. Ten times? It may be more. In my opinion—a month altogether to the best of my opinion.

9238. MR. LYONS—Are you positive that when you saw him at night for the purpose of having the handcuffs removed, and having him released for the night, he was in most instances handcuffed behind?—Yes, sir.

JOB GIDDINGS, EXAMINED.

9269. CHAIRMAN—What part of the prison were you in, in the months of June, July and August, '68?—In the separate cells, sir, at different periods of the day; not all day, sir.

9270. Did you during that time see the prisoner O'Donovan Rossa?—Yes, sir.

9282. Did you ever see him with his hands handcuffed before him?—Yes, sir, during the time he was at his meals.

2983. Excepting that time, do you think that the hands were always handcuffed behind him?—Yes, sir.

9284. Always?—Yes, sir.

9285. For a month?—For, I cannot say how long; several days I should say.

9286. Several days?—Yes, sir.

9287. Was he in handcuffs, to your knowledge, for more than a month? Well, I could not say, sir.

9300. Are you clear in your recollection that you saw him 10, or 15, or 20 days, during the period he was in handcuffs altogether, and that of that time such a portion as you name you saw him with the hands behind?—My duty was to take his supper things away from him and place his handcuffs behind him.

9301. How often did you do that?—Every night, or nearly every night, sir.

9302. For a week or two?—Yes, sir.

9303. Three weeks?—Well, it might be that, sir.

9304. MR. BRODERICK—When you took away his supper things, did you find his hands before or behind?—Before him, sir.

9305. Did you ever leave him after supper with the hands before him?—No, sir.

9306. You never failed to replace the hands behind?—No, sir.

9313. Do you say that you distinctly remember unloosing the manacles which bound the hands in front, and replacing them behind the back?—Yes, sir.

9314. Do you remember doing that distinctly, on several occasions?—Yes, sir.

9315. Night after night, after you took away his supper things?—Yes, sir. There was another officer with me at the time.

9316. Who was that officer?—Mr. Hibbert.

9317. You actually took off the manacles from before and put them behind?—Yes, sir; we used to do it; took off one cuff.

9318. Describe how you did it?—We took off one of the cuffs from the wrist and turned it round.
9319. You turned his hand round?—Rossa would put his hand this way (witness put his hands together behind his back) and I would put the handcuffs on.
9320. Do you remember distinctly, unloosing one cuff, placing the hands behind, and then putting on the handcuffs?—Yes, sir.
9321. You cannot be deceived in your recollection of it?—No, sir.
9322. Mr. Broderick—Did he ever resist on any of those occasions?—No, sir; never.
9323. Dr. Lyons—He always yielded quietly to have the manacles changed from front to rear after meals?—Yes, sir.

I now proceed to convict the English Secretary of State of *deliberate, intentional lying*. I lay before my readers the following documentary evidence, and if they do not bring in a verdict of " guilty," I will be very much disappointed.

[*From the Irishman of June the 12th,* 1869.]
THE TREATMENT OF O'DONOVAN ROSSA.
REPLY OF THE GOVERNMENT AND PRISON OFFICIALS TO SIR JOHN GRAY'S QUESTION.

"On last Friday week Sir John Gray asked the Secretary of State the following question, notice of which he had given *two* days previously:
Sir J. Gray asked the Secretary of State for the Home Department if his attention had been directed to the statement published in one of the Irish newspapers, apparently on authority to the effect that the prison authorities so secured the hands of one of the political prisoners by manacles behind his back, that he could neither dress nor undress, or raise food to his mouth, and continued this cruelty for 35 days; and, if the statement was true, was the circumstance reported to the Home office, and was there any objection to place the report before the House, with a statement as to whether the officer guilty of this cruelty was reprimanded or otherwise dealt with, and how?
Mr. Bruce replied—I am obliged to my Hon. friend for making this inquiry, for it is clear that the statement he has just made, if true, ought to be explained; if not true, it ought to be contradicted. Now, the facts with regard to this unfortunate man—O'Donovan Rossa—are these: He was committed to Pentonville on the 23d of December, 1865. Under ordinary circumstances prisoners would be detained there nine months before being sent to the convict prison. But it was thought more humane, and more conducive to their health, to send these prisoners at once to Portland, which, if I may use the expression, is the most cheerful, and certainly most healthful of all our convict prisons. His conduct there was so violent and outrageous, and produced so bad an effect upon the other Fenian prisoners, that it was found absolutely necessary to send him to Millbank, to which place he was removed in February, 1867. What his conduct was while at Portland is described in the reports of Messrs. Knox and Pollock. The House will, perhaps, allow me to read an extract from this report, more especially as it is stated in the report from which my Hon. friend quotes that O'Donovan Rossa was of a gentle and tractable disposition. The report says:
"The convict Rossa is a dangerous man, and must remain the object of unceasing anxiety and vigilance to the authorities. The senior warder at Millbank, a man of no mean experience in convict life, said that in the whole course of his career he had never met with the equal of this most unfortunate man, Jeremiah O'Donovan Rossa. He had no ill-usage to complain of—no severity but of his own seeking. He must amend his ways, or abide his fate."
Again it was said:
"As long as the treason-felony convict Jeremiah O'Donavan Rossa was at Portland, so long were these prisoners in a state of chronic discontent, which found its expression in daily acts of insubordination and words of insolent defiance. He has most properly been removed to Millbank, and an entirely different state of facts prevails. Since Rossa's removal the prison authorities express themselves as far more satisfied with the conduct of the treason-felony convicts ; the convicts declare themselves far more content with the treatment they receive from the outhorities. 'At present I find the state of things here almost relatively perfect happiness,' said treason-felony convict O'Leary to us. 'The conduct of the convicts has been far better, they are far more industrious, and far less insolent,' was in effect the language of the warders, many of whom in terms attributed the change to the removal of Rossa.

After spending a year at Millbank, he was removed to Chatham on the 24th of February, 1868, and during the greater part of the time he continued at Chatham the conduct which he had exhibited while at Portland. I will not weary the House by reading a list of the offences for which he has received punishment, but will refer only to those which occurred in June last. On the 5th of June he was reported for highly insubordinate conduct, using abusive language, refusing to get out of bed, and disturbing the quiet of the penal class, and he was sentenced to three days' close confinement on punishment diet. On the 9th of June he was reported for insubordination and disrespectful conduct to the Governor, wilfully damaging two vests, highly insubordinate and disrespectful conduct towards the Governor, and defacing his cell door, and he was sentenced to two days' close confinement. On the 15th of June he was reported for refusing to leave his cell and disrespectful conduct to the Governor, for refusing to clean his basin and damaging his vest and a gutta-percha pint, and sentenced to two days' confinement. On the 17th of June he was reported for throwing the contents of his cell pot in the Governor's face, when under punishment in the separate cells. The prisoner having committed these acts of violence, and being a very powerful man—so powerful that it required three or four warders to master him—was for a while manacled with his hands behind his back. But, so far from being kept in this condition thirty-five days, he was only so for a part of a day."

The "last Friday week" mentioned at the beginning of this quotation, was the 4th of June; and, looking to page 59 of the Report of Lord Devon and his brother Commissioners, I find under the head of that date the following reply from the Governor of the Prison to a telegram from the Board of Directors, London:

"CHATHAM PRISON, June 4th, 1869.
"SIR: With reference to your telegram requesting to know how many days Reg. No. 9,549, Jeremiah O'Donovan Rossa was placed in handcuffs after his assault upon me, I have the honor to inform you that he was placed in them on the morning of the 17th of June and kept in them each successive day, as a measure of precaution to prevent his repeating a similar act when visited by either myself or an officer of the prison, till the 20th July; the handcuffs being invariably removed each day at 7.45 P. M., and not replaced till the following morning,
"WM. FAGAN, Esq. "T. F. POWELL, Governor."

There is no doubt but that this information was required for the Secretary of State, and that he had it in his possession the same evening when he made his statement in the House of Commons. But should any of my jury hesitate, I will not press for Mr. Bruce's conviction yet awhile. I will give the Secretary three weeks additional time to get the information from the Board of Directors, and I will direct the attention of the jury to another debate in the House of Commons on the evening of June the 29th.

George Henry Moore has reason to doubt the truth of the reply given to Sir John Gray, and he introduces the subject a second time. I quote from the *Irishman* of July 3d:

"The following supplement gives that portion of Mr. Moore's speech in full where he introduces the Warder's evidence:
'Now, the incessant infliction of such frivolous severities is one of the principal subjects of complaint which runs through the whole of the statements of these prisoners. But that is not all. Weighing these various statements one with the other, and with regard to corroborative evidence of impartial witnesses, it is impossible to doubt that the penal labors to which these men were sentenced was, with deliberate purpose, made unnecessarily galling by the connecting it with insulting concomitants and ignominious associations; that the fact that they were felons, and to be treated as other felons, was thrust constantly upon their notice; and that their resentment of these indignities was visited by punishment which was intended for obdurate ruffians

and not for the sensitive impatience of high-spirited men. We have heard of the dreadful outrage committed by O'Donovan Rossa on one of the authorities of the prison; but who can know of the long tale of cruel provocations which goaded that rebellious nature into the mad attempt to repel indignity with indignity? One part of his story was published to the world, and was subsequently contradicted in the most peremptory and circumstantial manner by the Secretary of State. But I have been furnished with a formal deposition, professing to corroborate the original statements in all their essential particulars. It has been sent to me by Messrs. Merriman, solicitors, in this city, who state in their letter to me that they have taken it down from the deponent's lips, and here it is:

"JUNE 25, 1869.

"Joseph Kay, of 16 Cross-street, Palace-road, Hackney, late assistant warder of Chatham Prison, was assistant warder from April 5, 1865, till November 5, 1868, states that the prisoner Rossa, in the months of June and July, 1868, was handcuffed for about six weeks during those months with his hands behind him, from ten minutes past 5 a. m. till 7:30 p. m., his hands being removed in front of him, though still handcuffed, while he took his meals. The first meal, the breakfast, occupied from 5:30 till 6 a. m.; dinner from 12:15 till 1:15 p. m.; supper 6:15 till 6:45 p. m., and at 7:30 the handcuffs were removed on his going to bed. During the whole of these six weeks he was confined in a separate cell, the handcuffs on him behind his back, excepting when partaking of his meals at the above stated intervals."

"This statement is quite inconsistent with the terms of the contradiction forwarded by the prison authorities to the Home Secretary, and stated by him to the House. I trust that the Right Hon. gentleman will cause such an inquiry to be made into the matter as will elicit the truth. There is only one more observation which I wish to make before I sit down. I have not justified, nor do I seek to justify, a single act of the Fenian conspiracy, nor of the insurrection to which it gave rise; but I am convinced that there is not one man who lost his life or his liberty in that enterprise who would have saved his life or would now purchase his liberty by the admission that there was guilt or shame in the cause for which they suffered imprisonment or death. Nor can I, on their part, or on my own, make any such admission. They entered into a conspiracy, the object of which was to make Ireland an independent nation, and the effect of which has been that the First Minister of the Crown has hastened the hand of the Parliamentary clock to accomplish an act of which, in his pre-Fenian mind, he had regarded as indefinitely remote. I have already quoted the prophetic words of Mr. Charles Kickham on leaving the dock for penal servitude. They are already fulfilled. Some have died, and many more have suffered in the same cause as he. But in the gilded chamber over the way to-night "their souls are marching on." One act of justice is all but accomplished; another is treading upon its footsteps, and a third may yet be seen " no bigger than a man's hand " in the horizon, and which will yet all but accomplish what these humble martys died and suffered to advance—vague and shadowy, as may have been the views and the purposes— the means, they were yet the shadows of real things—real misgovernment, real misery, real reasonable, resolute, disaffection. Above all, they are the shadows of all that is left of national life in Ireland—an abiding purpose and an immortal hope, which have never been conquered, and which never will die."

Bravo! George Henry Moore! Long will your memory live in our souls.

"Mr. Bruce said the House would recollect the very remarkable statement made a short time ago in that House relative to the treatment of O'Donovan Rossa—namely, that he was handcuffed for 35 days with his hands behind his back, that his only food was gruel. Two or three days ago the Hon. member gave him notice that he intended to controvert the statements he had made on this subject. He applied to the Hon. gentleman for the name of his informant, but he declined to give it. [Mr. Moore: "I had no permission to give the name."] He gathered from the statement of the Hon. gentleman that his informant was a warder who had been dismissed, but if he supplied his name he could have made inquiries as to the reasons for his dismissal, and whether his testimony could safely be received. At all events, he had left the establishment. [Mr. Moore: "I know nothing about it."] He presumed he must have left the establishment in November, as the circumstances to which he spoke occurred between June and November, 1868. It certainly would have been more satisfactory if the Hon. gentleman had given him an opportunity of inquiring into the character of his witness (hear). He, on the contrary, believed in preference, the testimony of the Governor and Deputy-Governor, who stated that after the horrible assault, which he had on a former occasion described, the hands of O'Donovan Rossa were manacled behind his back for half a day."

It was only reasonable that Mr. Bruce should believe the testimony of his officials in preference to any other. You have read the evidence of the Governor admitting I was 35 days manacled, and you can read the evidence of Captain Du Cane, the Chairman of the Board of Directors, admitting he knew I was all the time in irons. It was through these Directors the Secretary of State received all his information, and now it will be worth your while to go back a few pages and read the evidence of Captain Wickham Talbot Harvey, the Deputy-Governor, on whom Mr. Bruce relies. He cuts the sorriest figure of all the witnesses I ever saw on a witness table. The Commissioners do not believe a word he says, and I will end my case by giving some extracts from their report, on the strength of which I demand a verdict not alone against the Secretary of State, but against Mr. Gladstone and the whole English Government for their disgraceful treatment of the Irish political prisoners:

"Report of the Commissioners appointed to inquire into the treatment of treason-felony convicts in English prisons. London: printed by George Edward Eyre & William Spottiswoode, printers to the Queen's most excellent Majesty for her Majesty's stationary office. 1870:"

26. It appears that medical officers of convict prisons are not required to possess qualifications both in medicine and surgery, and that in some instances, and at certain seasons, the sole medical charge of a large infirmary, and of 1,200 or 1,500 convicts out of hospital, devolves upon a single officer having only one professional qualification.

29. In the public works' prison and in parts of the invalid prison at Woking, the cells, being designed mainly for sleeping, are much smaller, and, as we think, too small for health, unless further provision be made for ventilation. All the dark cells, but especially those at Millbank, appeared to us imperfectly ventilated, a defect which the entire exclusion of light renders the more injurious to health. The dark cells (Pentagon V, Millbank), from their restricted dimensions, their bad position, and their exclusively defective ventilation, demand immediate attention.

33. The restrictions now imposed on the writing and receipt of letters, may, in our judgment, be somewhat mitigated without prejudice to discipline. We think, moreover, that when even a letter is surpressed, whether addressed to a prisoner or written by him, the fact and the reasons should be forthwith communicated to him.

26. The somewhat arbitrary use of handcuffs as a measure of restraint calls for notice in this place, though we refer to a later part of our report, the observations which arise out of one particular case to which they were employed.

38. We have to report that there does not appear to us to be that uniformity in practice, or that unanimity in the interpretation of the powers entrusted to Governors, which we should deem to be desirable on so important a subject.

39. We find a very great concurrence of opinion that manacles may be imposed for a period of 72 hours and longer. Finally, the Chairman, while admitting that the period of 72 hours cannot be exceeded without reference to a director, stated that in his opinion, under a literal construction of this rule, provided the full period of the order is not exhausted by the continuous imposition of manacles for 72 consecutive hours, day and night, at any one time, a prisoner may, if the Governor deem fit, be kept in manacles an indefinite time.

41. We are moreover of opinion that, except for the immediate control of personal violence, and for a short period to be defined by the Directors, manacles should not be imposed without the written order of a Governor or Deputy Governor, after a hearing of the case; that the order should in all cases specify the manner in which the manacles are to be applied, whether in front or behind, and the period for which they are to be so continued.

42. At Pentonville and Dartmoor, the Governors informed us that refractory prisoners are not kept in dark cells for more than four hours, whereas at Chatham we have found that a prisoner has been frequently so confined for a period varying from

one to three days. We are of opinion that confinement in a dark cell is not to be justified as a simple measure of restraint, since the admission of light is consistent with the adoption of every necessary precaution against violence. It is, in fact, a very severe punishment. We think also that a prisoner in a dark cell should be allowed to retain his bed, blanket and rug while confined therein.

43. Punishment for prison offences by diminution of food or alteration in the kind given, is common to all prisons we have visited. Bread and water diet, under which one pound of bread is allowed daily, is frequently employed for a period of from one to three days by a Governor's sentence. It may also be extended to twenty-eight days, by the sentence of a Director, with penal class diet every fourth day. Penal class diet may likewise be imposed by a Director for six months, and may immediately succeed twenty-eight days' bread and water. We cannot but call attention to the very serious consequences which may result from continuing such punishment too long or repeating them too frequently. In our opinion twenty-eight days confinement in a penal cell, on bread and water, varied with penal class diet every fourth day, or penal class diet for six months, can hardly fail to be in some degree injurious to ordinary constitutions.

47. With regard to those in the Infirmary, we think that arrangements should be made to facilitate the attendance of all who are able to leave the sick ward; and as regards those under punishment, we entertain grave doubts whether the reason given for prohibition, viz., that the attendance at Chapel would be a temporary mitigation of the punishment enforced, should be allowed to outweigh the spiritual advantages which may accrue to every person from attendance on religious service.

48. Proceeding to the second branch of our inquiry, viz.: "Whether the treason-felony prisoners have been subjected to any exceptional treatment in any way, or have suffered any hardships beyond those incidental to the condition of a prisoner sentenced to penal servitude." We think it more convenient to state, first, the general allegation applicable to some or all of the treason-felony prisoners, with such remarks upon each as may appear to us necessary.

49. We should premise, however, that certain allegations were made by two of the prisoners in reference to circumstances attending their transmission from Ireland, into which we were not in a position to inquire fully, but which we think of such a character that the attention of the proper authorities should be directed to them. It is alleged that due consideration was not shown by those in charge of the prisoners for the inconveniences incidental to a sea voyage and a long journey. Should it be found that such circumstances occurred as were detailed to us, we think it important that due provision should be made against their recurrence.

50. *Searches, &c.*—Of the general complaints made by the treason-felony convicts, the first had reference to the practice and mode of searching, as well on their first reception in prison as at certain periods during their confinement. The rules which prescribe and enforce searching are, with slight variations as to the frequency of the periodical searching, common to all convict prisons, and it did not appear to us that the treason-felony prisoners were subjected, in this respect, to any exceptional treatment, except at Pentonville, where some of them had to undergo weekly searches, as a measure of precaution, for a short period after their first arrival.

51. It was stated strongly to us, by all the prison officers whom we questioned on the subject, that the maintenance of the practice of searching is necessary for the exclusion of prohibited articles, and for the personal safety of those who are charged with the custody of the prisoners. * * * We therefore do not feel justified in suggesting any change other than that the naked search of a prisoner should not take place in the presence of other prisoners, and should be conducted by selected officers.

52. In the case of some of the treason-felony prisoners, complaint was made that, when at Pentonville, they were obliged at bed-time to put out their day clothes and cell furniture. It was explained to us by the Governor that this measure, though somewhat exceptional, was enforced, not as an indignity, but as a precaution against escape, as a course uniformly adopted in similar cases.

53. *Deprivation of Flannels.*—We find that on arrival at Pentonville the flannels supplied to the treason-felony convicts at Mountjoy Prison were taken from them. We are of opinion that, as they arrived in mid-winter, and as some of them appear to have been men of delicate constitutions, and one was of deformed and weakly frame, flannels should have been given to them without waiting for the intervention of the medical officer, in lieu of those which they had worn up to that time, and which it was necessary to send back to Mountjoy Prison.

54. *Association.*—Another general complaint of the treason-felony convicts was that, whereas the offence of which they had been convicted was of a special character, implying, in their view, no moral degradation, they had been associated with other prisoners undergoing the sentence of penal servitude for gross and heinous

55. Waiving, for the present, the question of principle involved in this complaint (to which, however, we shall hereafter advert), we proceed to state the facts.

57. At Dartmoor, none of the prisoners have been confined except Mulcahy and Lennon. Mulcahy was transferred to Dartmoor on the 8th of February, 1867, and thence to Woking on the 8th of May, in the same year. During that period, he was associated with the ordinary prisoners. Lennon was transferred to Dartmoor on the 30th of December, 1868, and is still there. He, also, is associated with other prisoners.

61. At Chatham, except in the infirmary, the treason-felony prisoners have, as a rule, not been associated with other convicts, or employed on the public works. It appears, however, that some of these prisoners themselves applied to be allowed to labor on the public works for a short time. J. O'Donovan Rossa was, for some time, the only treason-felony convict in this prison, and he was then worked in association. On a subsequent occasion—1st June, 1868—as a measure of punishment, he was compelled to labor with ordinary prisoners on the public works. After some days, he refused to continue at work, in consequence, as he alleges, of "the unpleasant life he led with them." For this he was reported and awarded three days' bread-and-water punishment.

63. *Occupation.*—Several complaints were made by these prisoners of their having been obliged to perform certain tasks of work of a degrading character—*e.g.*, to wash the clothes of other prisoners, to clean out cells, and even privies.

64. It is perfectly true that those who were received at Portland were, on their first arrival, and for a few days pending the receipt of instructions from the central authority, placed in the wash-house, but they were subsequently, as stated above, placed on the public works as a separate party.

65. * * * It is true, indeed, that in the Winter of 1866, during a storm of unusual severity, the rain was driven in through the walls of Hall D., Portland Prison, and the cells occupied by certain of the treason-felony convicts were partially flooded, and their beds and clothes became a good deal wetted.

67. In one instance only, the Commission detected portions of meat unfit for human use in the supply sent in for the infirmary. This occurred at Chatham on July 4th, 1870, when three pieces of mutton of greenish color, in parts, and of very bad smell, were pointed out by the Commission.

69. We have, therefore, to report that while it is possible that, as alleged by some of them, the treason-felony convicts have on some occasions been served with rations more or less tainted, this did not occur—nor, indeed, is it alleged by themselves to have occurred—except at few and distant intervals. With reference to the allegations that such foreign substances as a mouse, entrails of a fowl, or other refuse, have found their way into the prisoners' diet, we have to observe that if such articles got accidentally into the soup cauldrons, even a few hours before the soup was served, they would be boiled down into a condition in which they could not be recognized. * * * It must be admitted as barely possible that, in transition from the kitchen to the prisoners' cell, by accident or design, a foreign object of small size might find its way into a convict's ration.

70. It is, no doubt, true that some of the treason-felony prisoners have been in the habit, from time to time, of returning various articles of diet, and, in some instances, their entire rations.

72. * * * At Portland, the prevailing whiteness of the stone and the glare of the sun, in hot weather, appear to us to require the addition of a good peak to the prisoners' cap, with a shade for those who have weak or tender eyes. In trenching and excavating operations in the open air, greater facilities for shelter against severe weather might perhaps be provided.

74. Various charges have been made which come under the head of medical treatment. They have chiefly had reference to alleged want of proper attention to the prisoners' complaints or calls for medical aid on the part of the medical officers.

75. We have already expressed our opinion on the general system of medical attendance and for infirmary management in convict prisons, and we shall have occasion to discuss the more important of the specific complaints at a future stage of our report.

JEREMIAH O'DONOVAN ROSSA.

77. This prisoner, described as the publisher of the *Irish People* newspaper, was convicted of treason-felony, at Dublin, December 13th, 1865, and sentenced to penal servitude for life. He was received into Mountjoy Prison on the same day, and thence transferred to Pentonville, 23d December, 1865. He was removed to Portland on the 14th of May, 1866; placed on second probation, at Millbank, on the 20th of February, 1867, and removed to Chatham on the 24th of February, 1868. He handed in a written statement, and was, on several occasions, examined by us upon it.

78. Two special allegations were brought under our notice by this prisoner. The first and more important of them was that he was on one occasion, at Chatham,

kept in handcuffs for thirty-five days, and that, with the exception of his meals, when his hands were brought to the front, and, during the night, when the handcuffs were taken off altogether, he was manacled for that whole period.

79. We examined many witnesses in reference to this allegation. It appeared that, on June 16th, 1868, after numerous and repeated breaches of prison rules, for which he had been almost continuously under punishment since the 1st of May, O'Donovan Rossa committed an assault on the Governor, Captain Powell, by throwing at him, on the occasion of his visiting the punishment-cells, in discharge of his daily duty, the contents of his chamber vessel.

80. For this he was ordered on the next morning to be "handcuffed behind" and placed under report, to await the consideration of his offence by the visiting director. The director did not visit the prison until the 1st of July. He then heard the case and awarded, provisionally, a sentence which he submitted for the consideration of the Chairman. Premising that, in the ordinary course, Rossa would be punished for his offence by flogging, he recommended that, in case that punishment should not be inflicted, the prisoner should undergo twenty-eight days' punishment diet, in close confinement, and be placed in the penal class for six months. He also recommended that all movable articles should be removed from his cell, and that he should be kept in handcuffs in the day-time. This sentence was confirmed on the 7th of July, but without mention of handcuffs. The period of twenty-eight days' punishment diet did not take effect until the 20th of July.

82. The allegation is that O'Donovan Rossa remained, with the exception of nights and meal times, with his hands manacled behind him from June 17th to July 20th.

83. We carefully examined, with reference to this allegation, the entries made at the time in the Governor's journal, the chief warder's report book, and the seperate cell book. These entries substantially tally, and are perfectly conclusive on one point. They place beyond all possible doubt the fact that O'Donovan Rossa had handcuffs on, either before or behind, with the intervals already reffered to, for 34 days.

84. Dr. Burns, the medical officer, Principal Warder Alison, Warders Brown, Hibbert, Giddings, and others testify to the fact that for the first three days the prisoner was handcuffed with his hands behind his back, except at meal times, when they were placed in front, and at night, when they were altogether removed. The sworn evidence of assistant warder W. Thompson, given on the 1st July 1868, and recorded in the prison books, leaves no doubt that the prisoner was handcuffed on the 19th June, with his hands behind his back.

85. As to whether the handcuffs were during the remaining portion of the 34 days before or behind, the evidence is very conflicting. The first entry in the separate cell book under date of the 17th of June is as follows: "J. O'Donovan Rossa to be placed in handcuffs behind, by order of the Governor;" but all subsequent entries simply record the removal at night, and re-imposition in the morning of handcuffs, without showing in any way whether they were placed behind or before.

86. Captain Harvey, then one of the deputy governors, speaking from memory only, stated that he visited Rossa's cell frequently during the period refered to, and that Rossa had then no handcuffs on. When shown the entries in the prison books, Captain Harvey declared himself unable to reconcile them with his own recollection, on which he was unwilling to rely in the face of such evidence.

87. Dr. Burns, though he cannot fix the exact time during which handcuffs were worn, states, though not very confidently, that the prisoner was not handcuffed in either way for so long a time as is alleged. Alison, too, as well as several other warders then employed in various offices about the seperate cells, deny, more or less positively, that the handcuffs were continued behind after the first three or four days.

88. On the other hand, the inference to be drawn from the evidence of two of the warders, Hibbert and Giddings, is that the manacles were put on behind for a period of about three or four weeks. These officers were among those whose special duty it was to take off and put on the handcuffs.

89. Other evidence of a less direct nature has been laid before us, both orally and otherwise; and we have not failed to give due weight to whatever might in any degree throw light upon a transaction which, in the course of the last two years, has been the subject of so many contradictory statements.

90. There are two considerations which greatly weaken, in our judgment, the force of the evidence against the allegation, repeatedly and consistently made by O'Donovan Rossa, that he was manacled with his hands behind for at least 34 days. In the first place the majority of those who denied that allegation appeared to lay greater stress on the strong improbability of such a measure having been enforced, than upon a clear recollection that it was not enforced. Secondly, we cannot but notice that most or them denied with equal confidence that O'Donovan Rossa could have been manacled at all for so long a period as 34 days, whereas that fact, as we have a1——— stated, has been established by proof which we regard as irrefragable.

91. It is to be borne in mind, too, that there is no entry or other proof of any alteration or modification of the original order, and that, in the absence of any such counter order, the duty of the warders would be to act upon the original one.

92. On the whole, we are of opinion that the preponderance of testimony is in favor of the supposition that, except at meal times when the handcuffs were placed in front, and at night when they were taken off altogether, O'Donovan Rossa was manacled behind for the peroid which intervened between June 17th and July 20th.

93. Whether this continuous use of handcuffs is to be regarded as a measure of restraint or one of punishment has not been clearly shown to us. We are of opinion that handcuffs should never be employed in any case as a measure of punishment, and upon a review of all the circumstances we fail to discover any sufficient justification for their employment for so long a period as a measure of restraint.

94. The second matter of complaint brought before us by O'Donovan Rossa was as follows:

95. In November, 1866, a letter was found in the Roman Catholic Chapel at Portland Prison, inserted between the leaves of a book of devotion, signed by him, and addressed as follows: "Mrs Mary Moore." In the corner of the cover, at the back of the letter itself, and also at the foot of the last page in the inside, were written the words: "For Mrs. O'D."

96. O'Donovan Rossa was reported for an attempt to send out a letter surreptitiously, and brought before Mr. Clifton, the Governor, on the morning after that on which the letter was found. That charge he admitted, as well at that time before the Governor as in his evidence taken by us.

97. The result of our consideration of the subject has been to satisfy us that the Governor acted and spoke under misapprehension in reference to this letter; that the letter was bona fide intended for O'Donovan Rossa's wife; and that O'Donovan Rossa is clear from the imputation of any endeavor to carry on a love intrigue.

102. It is fair to add that Mr. Clifton had not, previously to his examination by us, compared the two letters; but we cannot but express our regret that he did not take that course, since such a comparison, coupled with the strong internal evidence supplied by O'Donovan Rossa's letter, could not have failed to prevent him from harboring the suspicion, or communicating it to others.

103. We examined O'Donovan Rossa on several other topics of complaint included in his written statement, and we think it right to express our sense of the candid and straightforward manner in which his testimony was given. These topics related almost exclusively to a series of punishments incurred by him during the first three years of his imprisonment. We investigated such points arising out of them as appeared to merit explanation, and the evidence respecting these will be found appended. We consider it, however, less necessary to deal with them here in detail, inasmuch as many of them have been anticipated in our more general remarks; while O'Donovan Rossa himself did not disavow most of the specific offences against prison discipline for which he was punished. What he virtually alleged was that, finding himself a marked man from the first, and branded as a bad character when he was unconscious of deserving it, he was led to assume an independent, not to say defiant, attitude, and thus became involved in a protracted struggle with the prison authorities.

CHARLES U. O'CONNELL.

105. He has been for a considerable time in the habit of returning portions of his food unused. His diet has been occasionally chainged, but with only temporary improvement of his appetite and general condition.

106. It is necessary to state that Dr. Burns is of opinion that this convict's loss of weight is due to his wilful refusal of food, and that he has sometimes been malingering or shamming since the occasion of a visit paid to him in the early part of last year. After having gone fully into the evidence given by the medical officer in support of this view, we are compelled to state that he (Dr. Burns) himself admits that he did not take any special means of testing whether the prisoner was or was not malingering; nor did he lay before us ground sufficient, in our judgment, to warrant this assumption.

107. In the preliminary evidence given before us by this prisoner, he states that he has been frequently placed on bread and water punishment, sometimes for periods of 70 hours. We find, on reference to the prison books, that he has in fact been setenced on two occasions to close confinement on bread and water for three days, and on four occasions to a like punishment for one day. Assuming that he was then suffering fron aortic disease, he would, in our judgment, have been unfit to undergo such discipline.

108. He further alleges that his father and other members of his family were prevented from communicating with him or receiving news of him for a period of four years, and that four out of five letters written by him to his family have been suppressed. His father is in America. He has placed before us certain of his suppressed letters which he read in full to the Commission.

110. While we in no way desire to recommend any interference with the proper censorship of prisoners' letters, we are of opinion that it would have been better to forward the letters addressed by the prisoner to his nearest relatives, erasing or removing such parts as the prison authorities on due consideration deemed improper to be communicated.

112. In conclusion we have to state in regard to this prisoner that his health and condition are such as to make his ultimate location and treatment a question which demands the special attention of the authorities.

PATRICK LENNON.

114. His main complaint is that his lungs were injured by prison fare at Millbank, and that his disease was neglected by the assistant medical officers at Millbank and Dartmoor.

116. During the early part of 1869, he more than once applied to the Governor and expressed himself discontented with his medical treatment. In September his appearance attracted the notice of the medical officer, and he was shortly afterwards admitted to the infirmary for a boil. On the 16th of that month he was ordered to be weighed, and found to have lost 19 lbs. since reception. * * * We cannot but express our opinion that a closer examination of his chest would have been desirable when he fell off so remarkably in weight, and that it may be matter for consideration whether he should not be removed from Dartmoor before the coming winter.

PATRICK RYAN.

119. He was examined before the Commissioners at Woking, July 1st, 1870, and was then in a very weakly condition. It was necessary to provide him with a seat, and to give him refreshments several times during his examination. He was suffering from diarrhœa, to which he seems to have been for a considerable time constitutionally liable.

120. His complaints for the most part referred to the hardships of prison discipline, diet, and clothing.

122. Ryan complains of the naked searches to which he was subjected at Millbank and Woking. His statements are not contradicted. We refer to the general observations which we have elsewhere made on this mode of search.

125. Ryan states that on one occasion only he objected to work. It was on a Sunday, when he was about to receive the Holy Communion. He alleges that he mentioned this to the officer, and requested that he should not be required to work at the pump, but that the officer refused, telling him that to work at the pump "would do him more service." Ryan could not state the name of the officer, and it was not, therefore, in our power to investigate the complaint. We do not doubt, however, judging from the respect for the religious opinions of the prisoners uniformly manifested by the higher prison authorities, that, if such language had been proved to have been used, the officer who used it would have been severely punished.

JOHN MURPHY.

133. This prisoner, now 61 years of age, was convicted at Mullingar, on the 17th of July, 1865, and was sentenced to seven years' penal servitude. He had spent five months in Mountjoy prison before his removal to Pentonville, on December 23d, 1865. * * * He made few complaints before us, and disclaimed any wish to complain.

134. His chief anxiety seemed to be that his term of seven years' penal servitude might be considered as dating from his first trial (when no verdict was returned), in March, 1865, instead of from his conviction, on the 17th of July, 1865.

135. Like other treason-felony convicts, he spoke of the frequent stripping for searches at Pentonville, and of having to put his clothes outside his cell at night, as harsh and unusual precautions; and he stated that he had suffered from the deprivation of flannels. The observations which we have already made on this subject apply with special force to a man of his age with a rheumatic tendency. The prison records show that he was supplied with flannels on January 12th, 1866, so that he was left without them nearly three weeks. He also found some fault with the prison food at Woking—especially with the shin-of-beef soup, the cheese, and the suet pudding.

136. The only other annoyances which he mentioned were the rough languauge of one warder and the vexatious conduct of another (no longer in the prison), who used to wake him up at night, and whom he reported four times to the Governor. This annoyance, he stated, was at last stopped on his threatening to report it to the Director. On the other hand, there are but two reports against him on the prison books, neither very serious. We learn from his case-sheet that his health, in prison, has been indifferent, and that he has been frequently under medical treatment for rheumatic affections.

WILLIAM FRANCIS ROANTREE.

137. This prisoner, aged 39, was convicted, at Dublin, on the 24th of January, 1866, and was sentenced to ten years' penal servitude. He is described as a butcher or mercantile clerk, but he informed us that he never followed the former occupation. He was received at Pentonville, from Mountjoy, on the 10th of February, 1866; was transferred to Portland on the 4th of May, 1866; was invalided to Woking on the 8th of February, 1867, and still remains there.

139. His own representation is, that, "since his arrest, he got piles"; that he was almost rid of them when he was removed from Mountjoy prison to Pentonville; that, at Pentonville, they were aggravated by purgatives administered under the doctor's orders; that, nevertheless, he was an able-bodied man when removed from Pentonville to Portland; that he was there kept working at the quarries while bleeding profusely from the effects of the disease, and that Dr. Blaker, the medical officer, grievously mismanaged him; that he is now, and has been, since his removal to Woking—three years and a half ago—a confirmed invalid, "with a permanently injured constitution;" and that a studied disregard of the conditions necessary for health has been shown, in his case, by the prison authorities.

140. * * * It is not disputed—indeed, the medical records prove—that Roantree has suffered piles at frequent intervals throughout his imprisonment. * * * At Portland, he was three times under treatment for this affection—once for a period of 168 days. * * * He was invalided to Woking, in consequence of piles, and has since been repeatedly subject to bleeding, sometimes complicated with prolapsus. Dr. Campbell does not take the same serious view of the case as the prisoner himself. * * * We have no means of judging whether, on his arrival at Portland, he was in a fit state for working in the quarries, or ought to have been admitted earlier into the infirmary, though it is right to say that there is some evidence to show that bleeding occurred on more than one occasion while he was at work. * * * During twenty-four months of his imprisonment at Woking, he has been an inmate of the infirmary, performing no work at all, but Dr. Campbell positively states that he is perfectly capable of hard labor, and would be put to it if he were an ordinary prisoner.

141. It would be obviously impossible for us to review his medical treatment in detail—still less can we undertake to pronounce an opinion upon the demeanor or manner of the medical officers and others, whom he accuses of unfeeling conduct.

142. There are several minor grievances alleged by Roantree which fall within the scope of our remarks on the general treatment of the treason-felony convicts. Such are deprivation of flannels during the first four days at Pentonville, the constant searching, and the nightly removal of body clothing at the same prison, and the rule of silence, which he represents to have been introduced for the special annoyance of the treason-felony convicts on the Portland works. * * * The penalty in respect of diet, to which he was sentenced on one occasion, appears, it is true, somewhat disproportioned to the offence. * * *

DENIS DOWNING MULCAHY.

158. This prisoner was convicted at Dublin on the 20th of January, 1866, and was sentenced to 10 years penal servitude. Having been received into Mountjoy Prison on the 19th of January, 1866, he was transferred to Pentonville on the 10th of February, 1866. He was removed to Portland on the 14th of May, 1866. On the 15th of November, 1866, he was re-transferred to Mountjoy Prison, whence he was sent to Millbank, the 1st of December, 1866. He was again sent to Mountjoy Prison on the 16th of January, 1867, brought back to Millbank on the 26th of January, 1867, transferred to Dartmoor on the 8th of February, 1867, and finally invalided to Woking on the 11th of May, 1867.

159. He is 30 years of age, 6ft. 1¼ in. in height, and is stated on his prison record to have been a student of medicine. He weighed, on his reception at Pentonville, 170 lbs., and at Woking, on May the 16th, 1870, 155. He has thus lost weight to the extent of 15¼ lbs.

161. When removed to Portland he was returned as fit for "hard labor," and was placed to work at stone-dressing. While so engaged he was attacked by blood-spitting, and we find it officially recorded that on two occasions, the 21st and the 23rd of July, 1866, he was laboring under hæmoptysis. He further complained of cough, and was seen and prescribed for at intervals up to September the 7th by Dr. Basan, then assistant surgeon to the prison. He was kept at work during this period, and having regard to the nature of the work upon which he was so employed, and the occurrence of blood-spitting on two occasions, we cannot consider that he was fit to be continued at hard labor, or that due care and caution were exercised in his regard.

162. It is further alleged that in Portland prison this Prisoner was served with tainted soup, and that on one occasion he found the entrails of a fowl, and on another a mouse, and "other vermin," in the diet served to him. We have fully considered this charge in connection with others of a similar character.

163. On his arrival at Dartmoor, he was reported by the medical officer as fit for, and was put on, full labor. He was placed at work on the moor, his occupation being that of trenching and clearing land. It is alleged that he was compelled to carry slabs of stone on his back; and although this is stated by the Governor to be contrary to the rule and practice of the prison, we find the allegation fully corroborated by the evidence of principal warder Hodge.

165. After about three weeks at full labor, this prisoner's health gave way. The medical notes of his case taken at this period by Mr. Ascham, then medical officer of the prison, have been accidentally mislaid. It is alleged that the prisoner suffered from hæmorrhage from the lungs. He appears to have spent about half his time in this prison in hospital in consequence of the blood-spitting, and on the representation of the medical officer, the then Governor, Captain Stopford, wrote a report to the Directors, and requested " that he should be removed, for the climate might not agree with him." Captain Stopford further adds that Mulcahy, while at Dartmoor, was never reported for misconduct, nor ever punished. He was invalided to Woking in May, 1867, the ground of invaliding being hæmoptysis.

166. It is alleged that during a period of 10 weeks he was unable to consume more than 20 ozs. of solid food daily, and that during this time no sufficient inquiry was instituted by the medical officer as to the cause of his rejecting or not using his food. As the prisoner did not furnish the dates in reference to this charge, and as he finally declined to submit any detailed statement to the Commission, we had no opportunity of going into the particulars of this allegation.

167. The same may be said in reference to the general allegations that he frequently suffered from dyspepsia, diarrhœa, rheumatism, and neuralgia; that he was subject to punishment in consequence of his evidence given before Messrs. Pollock and Knox, and that in the month of February of the current year he suffered much from keen blasts and insufficient clothing.]

BRIAN DILLON.

168. Brian Dillon, described as a law clerk, is a very weak and deformed man, of middle age, and delicate appearance.

169. He was tried at Cork before a Special Commission on the 14th of December, 1865, and sentenced to 10 years' penal servitude.

173. *Discipline.* Dillon, in common with other treason-felony prisoners, complains of the naked searches to which he was subjected at Pentonville, which he describes as having been of a very minute and offensive character. He also states as a grievance, that when at Pentonville, he was obliged to put out his clothes and cell furniture at night. On both these subjects we have already expressed our opinion in our general remarks.

174. Dillon in many parts of his statement complains of the nature and amount of his work. He says that at Pentonville, "the long working hours, from 6 in the morning till a quarter to 8 at night, during which he sat at a table sewing," contributed to shatter his health. We must point out that in this statement no account is taken of intermissions for meals and exercise.

175. He states that in the Winter of 1867, when at Woking, he was placed to clean a heap of frozen bricks partly covered with snow, and that he suffered much from the cold.

176. He states that when discharged from hospital, and still very weak, he was employed to cut bricks in a narrow wooden shed, that the weather was very cold, and that it was necessary to keep the bricks soaking in water. In the Summer of 1868, he had to work, he states, when suffering from dysentery, under intense heat, hoisting up bricks by a rope and wheel, and exposed to continual danger by the falling of bricks from the scaffolds.

177. We feel bound to say that some of the work on which Dillon appears to have been from time to time employed, was of a nature hardly suitable to his delicate and deformed frame. His weight is 7 stone 4½ lbs., his height is 4 feet 10 inches, and the delicacy of his constitution is clearly shown by his personal appearance, and by his frequent admissions to hospital, especially during the last two years. Dillon's condition, at the time of our visits, in consequence of an accidental fall, appeared to be such as to render him incapable of any manual labor. He is hardly able to walk without assistance.

178. Dillon complains that on his passage from Ireland much suffering was unnecessarily inflicted upon him by being handcuffed with another prisoner affected with sea sickness and diarrhœa, from whom he was not allowed to be even temporarily separated. We have referred to this subject in our general observations.

181. He further states that at Pentonville he was forced to bathe in water rendered foul by having been used by other prisoners. Having inquired into the

facts, we found this to be substantially true. We have already commented on this practice.

187. We are bound to remark that a man who, at the commencement of his prison life was pronounced by the assistant medical officer to be capable of doing a little light work, seems to have been long employed at work of a laborious description, and under much exposure to heat and cold, and this at a period when he was a frequent applicant for medical relief. This occurred in the Summer of 1868. On the 6th of August in that year, he was, after several applications, admitted to hospital.

190. *Clothing*.—Dillon states, that on his arrival at Pentonville in January, 1866, from Mountjoy, he was stripped of his Mountjoy clothing and supplied with a Pentonville suit, in which flannels, such as he had habitually worn, were not included. A reference to the matter of complaint is to be found in our general observations.

193. One of the most frequent complaints put forward by Dillon, as well as by other treason-felony prisoners, is that he was associated with ordinary convicts. We make this most important subject a matter of observation in our general remarks.

195. *Letters*.—Dillon complains that the Governor has erased portions of his letters to his friends at Woking, without letting him know that he had done so. We believe this is not unfrequently done. A letter written to Dillon, on the 3d of April, 1869, was suppressed, and bears the following indorsement, " suppressed by Director, the prisoner not to be informed." In our general remarks we have commented upon the practice of suppressing letters, or parts of letters, without informing the writers of the fact and of the reason.

200. A considerable part of Dillon's complaint refers to the treatment of other prisoners. He especially dwells on the cases of treason-felony convict Lynch.

201. When Lynch died an inquest was held, at which his prison treatment was considered. Dillon stated before the coroner that Lynch attributed his illness to being deprived of flannels at Pentonville. * * * The coroner's jury returned a verdict of "death from natural causes," and it would be manifestly improper for this Commission, even if legally competent, to re-open the investigation of this case, after a long lapse of time and in the absence of the contemporaneous evidence adduced at the inquest.

208. There are certain incidents of treatment which we have commented upon with disapprobation in our remarks upon the cases of individual prisoners, but we have no reason to believe that in any of these instances the conduct of the prison authorities was influenced by the fact that the prisoners were treason-felony convicts.

209. A further question was forced on our attention in the course of our inquiries, though it does not strictly fall within the letter of our instructions. It is the question whether prisoners convicted of a crime so exceptionable in its nature that it has been thought right to modify prison discipline in their case to a certain extent, might not with advantage be more completely separated from the general body of convicts. We cannot be insensible to the difficulty, not always unattended with danger, of allowing any exceptional indulgences to a few individuals in the midst of a large prison population. Bearing this in mind, we are led to the conclusion that the difficulties attendant upon the location and treatment of political offenders, may perhaps be most readily and effectually overcome by setting apart, from time to time, a detached portion of some convict prison for prisoners of this class, and we recommend this subject to the consideration of Her Majesty's Government.

We remain, Sir,
Your obedient humble servants,
DEVON,
GEORGE C. BRODRICK,
STEPHEN E. DE VERE,
ROBERT D. LYONS,
E. HEADLAM GREENHOW.

3 PARLIAMENT STREET, September 20, 1870.

REPORT ON THE CASE OF J. O'D. ROSSA, BY DR. LYONS.

LONDON, Sept. 10, 1870.

While I fully concur in, and have appended my signature to, the general Report of the Commission, which includes the case of this prisoner, I think it necessary to call attention in a more especial manner to certain parts of it, and to some considerations of very grave importance which appear to me to arise thereon.

It is necessary to premise, that whereas the assault on the Governor of Chatham

Prison by O'Donovan Rossa took place about noon, on the 16th of June, 1868, he was not manacled until 8:50 a.m. on the 17th, a lapse of nearly 19 hours. If handcuffs are a means of "restraint" and not of punishment, I fail to recognize the propriety of their use after such an interval, unless called for by a renewed act of violence, which has not been established in this case.

In view of rule 15, hereafter cited, which limits the power of a Governor in the imposition of manacles to a period of 72 hours without the written order of a Director, I am of opinion that it was beyond the competence of the Governor or Deputy-Governor of Chatham Prison to keep the prisoner in handcuffs day after day, from 17th June to 1st July, 1868. No renewed acts of violence demanding the continuous employment of manacles as a measure of restraint, for which purpose only does their use appear to be onjoined and justified by the prison rules, are recorded against the prisoner in that interval. No written or other instruction from a Director to authorize the continuous handcuffing of this prisoner within the days above named has been produced to the Commission, and it was not until 1st July that the prisoner was tried by a visiting Director. The prisoner asserts, and in this he is not contradicted, that the handcuffs were removed when he was brought before the Director on that day. It is not on record that he had attempted to commit any act of violence since the 16th of June. It is even admitted by the warders that he submitted quietly to the daily imposition of the manacles. He was, notwithstanding, ordered by the Director "to be kept in handcuffs" apparently for an indefinite period, as no time is specified. Having regard to the fact that the offence for which he was tried had been committed fifteen days previously, and that no new act of violence is recorded against him in the interval, as also to the consideration that handcuffs are enjoined to be used as a measure of restraint only, I am of opinion that the Director on this occasion acted *ultra vires* in ordering the prisoner " to be kept in handcuffs," and that this was an arbitrary and unjustifiable exercise of authority, and that the order itself was defective inasmuch as it did not "specify the cause thereof, and the time during which the prisoner is to be kept in irons." In the confirmation of the sentence by the Chairman of Directors on 7th July no allusion is made to the handcuffs.

The sentence at the trial on the 1st July, ordering amongst other things that he "be kept in handcuffs," was not confirmed by the Chairman of Directors until 7th July, and it was not communicated to the prisoner until the 20th July, on which last-mentioned day only that part of the same sentence of the 1st July which ordered 28 days' punishment diet and six months' penal-class diet commenced to take effect.

I have, therefore, to report that in my opinion both the Governor and the visiting Director exceeded the power and authority entrusted to them, by keeping this prisoner in handcuffs, under the circumstances above referred to, from 17th June to 20th July, and I further desire to add that it is much to be regretted that more prompt action was not taken by the Directors to secure a speedy trial in a case of such gravity, as pending his trial and the carrying into effect of his sentence the prisoner was kept under the most rigorous restraint, which in itself constitutes a very severe form of punishment, although, as I am fully aware, it is not technically so regarded in prison discipline.

15. "*Governor's Powers.*—In a case of absolute necessity he" (the Governor) "may put a prisoner in irons, not as a punishment but only as a restraint, such irons, however, not to be continued on an offender for a longer period than 72 hours without the written order of a director, specifying the cause thereof, and the time during which the prisoner is to be kept in irons, which order shall be preserved by the Governor as his warrant." (See rule No. 15, p. 10, of the Rules and Regulations for the Government of the Convict Prisons. Approved by the Secretary of State for the Home Department. 1858.)

11. "*Director's Powers.*—In cases of necessity a director may, by order in writing, direct any prisoner to be kept in irons, such order to specify the cause thereof, and the time during which the prisoner is to be kept in irons. The irons on ordinary occasions to be common handcuffs." (See rule 11, p. 5. of the Rules and Regulations for the Government of the Convict Prisons. Approved by the Secretary of State for the Home Department. 1858.)

I may be here allowed to observe, that having carefully considered the Acts of Parliament, as well as the Standing Orders and the Rules and Regulations for the Government of Convict Prisons, supplied for the information of the Commission, by the Directors, I have not been able to find, and the Prison Department has not succeeded in producing to me Statutory authority for the powers exercised by the Directors, of ordering manacles to be imposed, for, apparently, indefinite periods, and leg-irons, 4½ to 6 lbs. weight, for a period of six months.

I desire further to remark, that the powers deputed by the Directors to Governors, by Standing Order No. 325, of imposing manacles for a period of 72 hours, are largely in excess of those granted by Act of Parliament to " Gaolers " of county and other prisons. The Act 2 & 3 Vict. c. 56, in part repealed, limited the Gaoler's power, as to irons, to 24 hours. "The Prison Act, 1865," expressly limits the powers of "the Gaoler" in the imposition of irons to 24 hours without an order in writing from a visiting Justice, see 28 & 29 Vict. c. 126, sch. 1. No. 59).

As a constitutional principle of great importance is here involved, I beg leave to recommend that the whole question be referred to the Law Officers of the Crown, with a view that if it should be found necessary, the powers to be entrusted to the Directors of Convict Prisons may be more clearly defined by Act of Parliament.

I have very fully considered all the charges which this prisoner has brought forward. He candidly admits himself that he has committed numerous prison offences. Some of these have been of considerable gravity, and necessarily entailed, in accordance with prison rules, severe punishments, and the emylyment of measures of restraint; others of the charges against him have been of a less important character, and I am not satisfied that in certain instances, as, for example, that in connection with coir picking at Millbank, in July, 1867, it was proper to punish him at all.

On various grounds, and in different prisons, O'Donovan Rossa was awarded a very unusual amount of prison punishment during the first three years of his imprisonment. He asserts, and is substantially borne out by the prison records, that he has undergone 123 days of bread-and-water punishment diet, 231 days of penal class diet in a darkened cell, 28 days in the absolutely dark cell, and that he has been, in all, 39 days in handcuffs. He admits that he acquired a bad prison character, but he attributes the attitude of resistance to prison discipline, which he assumed, to the manner and conduct of the authorities towards him. It is, I think, but just to him to add that during a long period when he was almost constantly undergoing report and punishment, his applications to the Governor and the Secretary of State show him to have been frequently asking for books of instruction. It is also worthy of remark that the almost continuous employment of bread-and-water punishment diet in the case of O'Donovan Rossa, in the months of May and June, 1868, did not prevent him from committing the assault, already referred to, on the Governor, on the 16th June; that the handcuffing which followed from 17th June to 20th July in punishment cells did not prevent him, when liberated, from committing a further offence, for which he was, after an interval of two hours and a quarter, again put in handcuffs for two days, and that the infliction of 28 days bread-and-water punishment diet, carried out from 20th July, did not prevent him from committing additional offences, for which he was further reported, and tried by the visiting Director in October, 1868. The marked and immediate effect of the few well chosen words of Captain Du Cane, accompanied by a total remission of the punishments undoubtedly incurred by the prisoner's conduct, show in well defined contrast the influence of moral agency, as against the failure of long-continued measures of coercion, accompanied with a total of more than 40 days' bread-and-water diet, spread over the period from May 1st to October, 1868.

I am of opinion that a more discriminating treatment of this prisoner by some of those under whose authority he has been placed would have been in all probability attended with more satisfactory results as to his prison history. * * * The signal failure of all repressive measures in this case, furnishes a most forcible illustration of the necessity of separating prisoners of this class from ordinary criminals. Such a conspicuous and successful defiance of discipline is in itself a scandal of prison life, and a most dangerous example to the other convicts. As the consciousness of guilt breaks the spirit of the ordinary convict committed for a crime which involves moral turpitude, and all the more readily if he have been, as sometimes happens, a man of education or position, he recognizes at once and submits to the dictates of prison discipline. But the political prisoner, purely such, is, on the contrary, led to a higher and even exaggerated sense of his position by confinement in association with ordinary criminals. He considers that his sufferings ennoble his acts, and he rebels against prison rule.

The history of the case of J. O'Donovan Rossa in itself furnishes a cogent argument in proof of the necessity of dealing otherwise than as at present with the class of prisoners to whom he belongs. This is a subject to which the Commission has already specially alluded.

ROBERT D. LYONS.

MEMORANDUM. BY E. HEADLAM GREENHOW.

I have signed the Report on the treatment of treason-felony convicts in English prisons, because I agree entirely in the main conclusions set forth in it.

The *sixth* allegation states that O'Donovan Rossa, at Chatham prison, had his hands tied behind his back for 35 days.

After the fullest possible investigation of Jeremiah O'Donovan Rossa's case, we came to the conclusion, as set forth in the Report, that the preponderance of testimony was in favor of this statement being a correct one; excepting that the manacles were always taken off at night and removed from back to front during meal times. It seems, however, to me, only fair to the prison authorities to add, that what was undoubtedly an exceptional and irregular proceeding did not appear, in my opinion, from the evidence, to have been intentional on their part, but to have been a lapse consequent on the misunderstanding of verbal instructions. The Governor of the prison, Captain Powell, on his return from a three days' absence, immediately following the gross assault upon himself which caused O'Donovan Rossa to be put in handcuffs, abstained from visiting and taking control of the prisoner whilst he was awaiting his sentence of punishment from the Directors for that offence. Captain Harvey, the Deputy-Governor, who gave over charge of the prisoners on the return of his superior officer, did not consider that he was any longer responsible for the treatment of O'Donovan Rossa; consequently the warders, receiving no countermand of the original order, continued to apply the handcuffs behind in accordance with it during the time stated. In truth, O'Donovan Rossa's language and conduct throughout his prison course, previous to his assault upon Governor Powell had been so exceptionally violent and insubordinate, and had made him appear so intractable and mischievous a prisoner, that the warders may perhaps, not unnaturally, have taken for granted as intentional any measure which would keep him quiet without doing him harm. He had on numerous occasions resisted the officers, and once, after breaking his cell-pot, had put the pieces in a towel, so as to make it into a weapon of defence, with which he threatened the first person who entered his cell. He had at different times broken his utensils or furniture, and even the walls or door of his cell, and for several weeks before the day on which he committed the assault upon Governor Powell, by throwing over him the contents of his chamber-vessel, he had been almost constantly under report or punishment for breaches of prison rules, or willful damage of prison property. On the other hand, it is but justice to O'Donovan Rossa to state that, subsequent to the period in question, up to the time of the investigation of his case by the Commission, his conduct had been good; and, that his honesty in admitting to us most of his prison offences, and his anxiety not to overstate what he considered his prison grievances, made a very favorable impression.

John M'Clure, according to the statement of the medical officer at Chatham has had only a single fainting fit, from which he recovered almost immediately; it occurred on May 3d, 1869, in very hot weather. He has been occasionally in the infirmary, but has required very little medical treatment, though he has frequently refused thefood. He has never been put to hard labor at Chatham. Mr. Gover, of Millbank Prison, states that he took him off penal diet on the same grounds as Devoy. He is obviously a man of weakly constitution, and has gradually lost weight during his three years' imprisonment to the extent of 17 pounds.

In the matter of clothing it was alleged that the treason-felony convicts, on their arrival at Pentonville, were deprived of the flannels they had brought with them from Mountjoy Prison; and that, although their arrival was in mid-winter, they were not supplied with others, to the great detriment of their health.

The facts of the matter are these. For obvious reasons prison rules require that the clothing belonging to one prison should not be retained by prisoners transferred to another; and, therefore, on the arrival of the treason-felony prisoners at Pentonville Prison, their Mountjoy clothing, which included flannels, was necessarily exchanged for Pentonville clothing. But at Pentonville Prison, which is constantly warmed during the Winter, and the temperature kept up to a fixed minimum, flannels formed no part of the ordinary prison dress, and were only supplied on the recommendation of the medical officer.

In conclusion, I feel compelled to state that I am unable to concur with my colleagues on the Commission in the suggestion made in the final paragraph of the Report, for the setting apart, from time to time, of a detached portion of some convict prison for the reception of prisoners of the treason-felony class. As is stated in the paragraph itself, no such question was comprised in the subjects referred to us for inquiry and I cannot but regard it as beyond the province of the Commission to recommend to the consideration of Her Majesty's Government a measure involving, as it appears to me, the virtual establishment of a special prison for prisoners of the class of the treason-felony convicts. E. HEADLAM GREENHOW.

CHAPTER XXII.

ONE OF THE COMMISSIONERS IN IRONS—LETTERS—MR. GLADSTONE AND MR. BRUCE—MR. M'CARTHY DOWNING—"AMNESTY"—BANISHMENT BY "VICTORIA, BY THE GRACE OF GOD"—A PRIVATE LETTER AND MY REPLY—LEAVING CHATHAM AND LEAVING HALPIN BEHIND—THE CUBA—FORBIDDEN TO TOUCH IRISH SOIL IN THE COVE OF CORK—ARRIVAL IN NEW YORK—A GENERAL JUBILEE OF WELCOME—I MUST BE A TAMMANY MAN OR CEASE TO BE AN IRISHMAN—I REBEL AGAINST THIS, AND SACRIFICE MY POPULARITY TO MY INDEPENDENCE—IRISH-AMERICAN POLITICIANS AND AMERICAN POLITICS—COLLECTOR MURPHY—EMIGRATION—TAMMANY WAR CRIES: "GRANT AND MURPHY," "MURPHY AND GRANT"—I COMMIT POLITICAL SUICIDE WITH THE IRISH PEOPLE BY RUNNING AGAINST TWEED, AND KILL MYSELF ENTIRELY BY BECOMING A COMMUNE AND JOINING TENNIE CLAFLIN.

If you have read this book through and perused the last chapter carefully, you will see I have been corroborated in everything I stated regarding my prison life. It was somewhat vexatious to find myself flatly contradicted by Doctor Burns, and Warders Goad and Cranston, and all the others I met, in presence of the Commission, but I had been a long time learning patience, and my schooling stood to me on the occasion. The Commissioners themselves behaved like gentlemen; but Doctor Greenhow did not at all seem to like the developments I was making, and looked as if he wished me to break down in my case. See how he differs with Doctor Lyons on the question of treating political prisoners as thieves, and tries to explain away how it was by a mistake I was kept so long in irons. Mr. Broderick was very deferential all through the inquiry, and I conceived a particular liking for him. My four or five days' acquaintance with Mr. De Vere was rendering him quite familiar to me, and I had much sympathy once for Doctor Lyons, when I saw his hands chained behind his back, and saw the agonized look he gave when he asked me if *my* hands were actually tied in that manner for thirty-five days. He was after taking lunch; his flask lay on the table, and when his hands were loosed he poured out some whiskey in a tumbler and offered it to me. My habitual modesty made me decline at first, but he pressed me, and, as it was such a novelty to touch anything so Irish in this quarter, I made the introduction of this friendly enemy of ours. Lord Devon offered me a chair, but I felt too independent to sit in such company, and continued giving my evidence standing.

The labors of the Commission having come to a close, I returned to my companions and to my old trade of stocking-mending. We speculated on the further developments that should necessarily arise when the Report was published, for I knew I had floored the officials, and the Secretary of State and Mr. Gladstone should stand convicted as false witnesses. True enough: it was on the very day this Commission Report was published that the announcement was made of our banishment from prison. They took from July to December to prepare the book, during which time I kept preparing to carry on the war of reporting progress to the public, in case of foul play.

All this year there were large amnesty meetings holding in Ireland and England, and what are called petitions were gotten up to the Queen, or to the Queen's manager, Mr. Gladstone. The one that came when events made it judicious for him to release some of us was presented by Mr. M'Carthy Downing, the member for Cork. The first to sign that petition was the Lord Mayor of Dublin, and through him Mr. Gladstone conveyed the news that we were to be released on condition of leaving the country.

DOWNING STREET, 16th December, 1870.

"GENTLEMEN: I have to inform you that her Majesty's Government have carefully considered the case of the convicts now undergoing their sentences for treason and treason-felony, and that they have recommended to the Crown the exercise towards them of the Royal clemency, so far as it is compatible with the assured maintenance of tranquility and order in the country.

"They will, therefore, be discharged upon the condition of not remaining in, nor returning to, the United Kingdom. W. E. GLADSTONE."

A few days after this announcement the Governor of the prison informed me I had received a conditional pardon. My sentence was changed from perpetual imprisonment to banishment for twenty years, and unless I accepted the conditions the pardon could not be granted. I would leave the country, but would give no promise not to return. If I *did* come back before the twenty years, let the Government take whatever course it deemed proper, but it should not be said I had made a promise and broken it. I got paper to give a reply, and here it is:

DECEMBER 22d, 1870.

To the Governor of Chatham Prison:

SIR: I don't think I can give a fairer reply to the official document you read for me to-day than to give you this paper which I withdrew from Mr. McCarthy Downing, and to tell you that I will abide by its words. Here they are:

"MR. DOWNING: Your having asked me if I would leave this country or Ireland on conditions of my being let out of prison, I reply that I would, and with the understanding that if I am found in England or Ireland again, without the permission of the British Government, I render myself liable to be re-committed to prison.

"Very respectfully, JER. O'DONOVAN ROSSA.
"March 22, 1869."

When I handed this paper to Mr. Downing, he said it was most satisfactory. I thought Mr. Downing had some intimation from the Government to ask me the question, and when I learned, in a few months after, that he had not, I deemed it becoming to withdraw the paper from him. But now that the Government offer me a conditional release, I repeat my words to them.

My children are in Ireland, and I would wish to see them. If the authorities impose upon me the obligation of going straight from the prison to the ship, I will do so; but if they can afford me a few weeks' citizenship in Ireland, by my giving an assurance of carrying myself as privately and silently as possible, I will give them that assurance.   Yours respectfully,   JER. O'DONOVAN ROSSA.

Director Fagan visited the prison next day, and said my answer was quite satisfactory, but that some others of the prisoners were giving a little trouble. In saying something about the Portland prisoners John O'Leary's name came up. I thought I might write to him, and he offered me paper to do so; but on consultation with Hal. we decided it was more prudent not to write, lest it should be considered I would do so to influence the Portlanders any way.

My wife had come to Chatham on the first announcement of our release. She wanted to get me clothes, but she would not be allowed to do anything for me till I was outside the gates. Though it was Christmas week, she could not get me out before the holidays. She telegraphed, but, getting no satisfactory reply, she went home to Ireland.

She was after having written a letter thanking Mr. Gladstone for the "amnesty," which brought her this answer:

CHESTER, December 24.

MADAM: I thank you for your letter, and I take your writing it as an act of much kindness. It would, I am sure, have been most agreeable to my colleagues, as well as to myself, had it been possible to make all the needful arrangements and to effect the actual release before the Christmas festival. It is much more agreeable to me to address you now than it was on a former occasion, and you will not misunderstand me when I ask you to accept my wishes for yourself and for your husband.

I remain, madam, your faithful servant,
W. E. GLADSTONE.

Every prisoner was asked where he would go to, and I at first said Australia. My wife was willing to face any part of the world with me, and I was anxious to evade the factions of Fenianism in the United States. I knew enough of things there, and knew enough of my own nature to know I could do very little in the way of following up my past life there; but I was no longer my own master. I was now public property, and public opinion was to master me. While my wife was in Chatham she went to London every evening and came to Chatham every morning. She met some of the men who were prominently interested in the Irish national movement, and they, one and all, declaimed against my going to the Antipodes. I would be going under the British flag; I would be looked upon as deserting the cause. No; I should go to America, where we would be able to unite the factions and do everything we liked for the men at home.

I trampled my first impulses under foot. I changed my mind— no, that isn't correct, I only changed my course—and I made ready for the sacrifice, and made known my intention of going to New York. It is well known to my companions that we left prison having decided to take no action in Irish politics in America unless we were able to unite all into one party; and how we were dragged and cajoled into a course that we decided against is a story in itself.

Mr. Fagan came to Chatham on the 5th of January, 1871, and brought with him all the necessary papers. A saloon passage was engaged for us, and we were each to be supplied with a suit of clothes and five sovereigns for pocket money. I was the first he sent for, and he presented the patent of pardon, asking me to sign an acceptance of it. I wrote:

"I accept this 'patent of pardon.'
"JER. O'DONOVAN ROSSA."

"Here, I suppose that will do, Mr. Fagan."

"Well, I don't know, I think there is something else wanted; say without mental reservation or something that way."

"Would you please write out what you think proper, and if I don't see anything hard in it, I will make a copy and sign it."

The Director wrote as the prisoner directed, and I copied and signed the document, putting quotation marks around "Ptaent of pardon."

I, Jer. O'Donovan Rossa, having seen and heard read the conditions of my release from prison as contained in the "Patent of Pardon," accept them unconditionally and without reserve.
JER. O'DONOVAN ROSSA.

He then gave me possession of the parchment with a round plaster of wax about two pounds weight tied to it, which is called the seal. It is a curiosity in its way.

After presenting me with this I asked Mr. Fagan if he would give me all my suppressed letters. He could not do so, but there were some which were made up to be given me; the rest I could not have. He proposed to have them burned, and, as I could not get possession of them, I consented.

CHATHAM PRISON, January 5, '71.

"Victoria, by the grace of God of the United Kingdom of Great Britain and Ireland, Queen Defender of the Faith and soforth, to all whom these presents shall come greeting, Whereas at a Special Commission of Oyer and Terminer and General Jail Delivery, holden at Dublin in and for the county of the city of Dublin, on the eighteenth day of December, in the year of our Lord, One Thousand Eight Hundred and Sixty-five, Jeremiah O'Donovan Rossa, late of Skibbereen, in the county of Cork, was in a lawful manner indicted, tried and found guilty of certain felonies, and was duly sentenced to be kept in penal servitude for the term of his natural life: And whereas, in consideration of some circumstances humbly represented unto us on behalf of the said Jeremiah O'Donovan Rossa, we have thought fit on the conditions hereinafter contained, and expressed, to extend our royal mercy unto the said Jeremiah O'Donovan Rossa. Know ye, therefore, that on the conditions hereinafter contained and expressed, we of our special grace, certain knowledge, and mere motion by and with the advice and consent of our right trusty and well-beloved cousin and councillor. John Poyntz, Earl Spencer, K.G., our Lieutenant-General and General-Governor of that part of our said United Kingdom called Ireland, and according to the tenor and effect of our letter under our royal signature, bearing date at our court, at St. James's, the thirty-first day of December, in the thirty-fourth year of our reign, and now enrolled in the Record and Writ Office of our High Court of Chancery in Ireland aforesaid, have pardoned, remitted, and released; and by these presents we do pardon, remit, and release the said Jeremiah O'Donovan Rossa, or by whatever other names or additions of name, office, art, mystery, or place, the said Jeremiah O'Donovan Rossa is known, called or named, or was lately known, called, or named, the felonies of which he stands convicted as aforesaid and all and singular convictions and attainders thereupon, and save as hereinafter mentioned all pains, penalties, and forfeitures thereby by him incurred as aforesaid, or incident or consequent upon the said felonies or any of them, or the commission thereof, or the judgment had thereupon as aforesaid; and our firm peace to him, the said Jeremiah O'Donovan Rossa, for the same. We, on the conditions hereinafter contained and expressed, do give and grant by these presents, forbidding that the said Jeremiah O'Donovan Rossa, by the justices, sheriffs, excheators, baliffs, coroners, or other the officers or minister of us, our heirs and successors on the occasion aforesaid, may be molested, disturbed, or in any manner aggrieved for the same, so that on the conditions hereinafter contained and expressed, he, the said Jeremiah O'Donovan Rossa may stand right in open court, if any person against him should be willing to speak on the occasion aforesaid. And our further will is, and by these presents for us, our heirs and successors, we do grant that these, our letters patent, or the enrolment thereof, shall be in all things firm, good, valid, sufficient, and effectual in the law, and shall be as well to the said justices and sheriffs, escheators, bailiffs, and coroners, as to all others the officers and successors, a sufficient warrant and discharge in that behalf. Provided always, and it is hereby declared, that these our letters patent, and the pardon, remission, and release hereby granted, are expressly subject to the several conditions following—that is to say, that these, our letters patent, be enrolled in the Record and Writ office of our High Court of Chancery in Ireland aforesaid, within the space of six calendar months next ensuing the date of these presents. And, further, that the said Jeremiah O'Donovan Rossa *shall forthwith depart out of the United Kingdom of Great Britain and Ireland, and shall remain out of the said United Kingdom for the space of twenty years from the date of these presents.* And, further, that the said Jeremiah O'Donovan Rossa shall not during the said space of twenty years, exercise, or attempt, or claim to exercise within the said United Kingdom any capacity, right, access, or privilege of which he was, or has been, deprived, or which was or has been lost, forfeited, extinguished, or suspended by the felonies aforesaid, or any of them, or by reason of his having committed the same felonies, or any of them, or been convicted of, or adjudged guilty of, or sentenced or attained for such felonies, or any of them.

"In witness whereof we have caused these our letters to be made patent. Witness, John Poyntz, Earl Spencer, our Lieutenant-General and General Governor of Ireland, at Dublin, the third day of January, in the thirty-fourth year of our reign.

"Enrolled in the Record and Writ Office of her Majesty's High Court of Chancery in Ireland, on the third day of January, one thousand eight hundred and seventy-one. "M. J. BRADY, A. C. R. & W.

"RALPH CUSACK, Clerk of the Crown and Hanaper."

"Now," said he, "I have a sealed letter for you which I have never read, nor do I know what it contains. I am instructed to give it to you after you receive your pardon, and here it is."

LONDON, Dec. 20th, 1870.

MR. O'DONOVAN ROSSA: I have for some time past looked forward to congratulating you on your release, and expressing my sincere good wishes for your future career. I do not feel that I have the right, nor would it become me to offer you any advice, and especially of a political nature. Though you and I are nearly of the same age, our experiences of life and views of life are very different; nor would it be reasonable to expect that you should regard Fenianism in the same light that I do. At the same time I would venture to implore you, before connecting yourself with it again, either in the United States or elsewhere, to take counsel with the wisest and most disinterested friends that you possess, with your good wife, and, let me add—with your own best feelings and highest aspirations.

I will say no more, except that I shall always hear of you with friendly interest.

Indeed I should not have said what I have said had I not formed a conviction which I have freely avowed, that you are worthy of a happier destiny than has yet been yours.

I rely upon your honor to regard this letter as confidential, and remain, though little known to you, Your friend, ———.

CHATHAM PRISON, January 5, 1871.

SIR: It is a poor thing to thank you in words, and I have no other way to thank you for your kind letter, and your very kind wishes for my welfare. Our experiences in life are, as you say, different, yet if we could speak our minds to each other our views regarding "Fenianism" may not be so far apart as you think. I would expect your enlightened mind to regard me as it would the inhabitant of any other conquered country, and I would allow you the right of the conqueror to maintain his conquest. But we cannot talk, and my time or opportunity does not permit me to write, even if my acquaintance could warrant my speaking freely and candidly to you. I should wish to see Irishmen and Englishmen friends as well as neighbors. Now-a-days, when mighty armies and weapons of destruction are before our eyes, and the possibility of their being used in the interest of tyranny so patent, I would much rather see, between the people of these Islands, a strong bond of Union and Brotherhood, such as would repel any thought of aggression, than to see the ever-recurring efforts of the one to bind down the other. Would English statesmen turn their talents to our union, and not to our division, it would lighten my exile.

I do not know how winds will drift me, but this you may be sure of, that no course of life will ever find me fostering ill-will between Englishmen and Irishmen, and if you, as a writer, make a similar endeavor to dissipate those prejudices which exist and seem to be by some influence cultivated between the two people, I will ever remember you with kindness.

You possibly have one time or another in your life experienced that pain of thought resulting from being led by your opinions—by your consciousness of rectitude to express yourself and to act in a manner that would not be entirely agreeable to some one you respected. It is such a feeling I experience now, in the desire to respect you, and to be consistent with myself.

You do me overmuch honor in your opinion of me. Some fortune (perhaps a misfortune) has followed me through life in making people see more in me than I feel or see myself. You are the agent at present, and if I could speak imperatively to you, I would say, you must correct yourself on this head.

I will, as you desire, consider your letter a private one.

There is one matter of concern to me, which I will communicate to you; it is this: I am leaving prison, and—what I do not like—I am leaving behind me, among the soldiers and Manchester men, some whom I have influenced into the course which led to their imprisonment, and this cannot tend towards my rest. If I had time in the country, I intended to ask the Secretary of State if there were any conditions of release for these men? I thought the Government might altogether close this open sore of political prisoners in England. Could you do anything in the matter? If you could, I would ask you and request you to send me a line to meet the Cunard steamer in Queenstown on Sunday next.

I remain, sir, yours very respectfully,
To——   (Signed)   JER. O'DONOVAN ROSSA.

P. S.—A message has reached me from one of those Manchester prisoners, and here are the exact words: "They have me nearly dead. I am now doing twenty days' bread and water, and have no bed at night. My name is Dan Reddin; I am one of the Manchester men."

This is enough. The man has been repeatedly under punishment. I am expected to make his case known when I get out of prison—and I tell you honestly, I have no desire to rush into print. I intend to speak to Mr. Fagan to-day, with a view to his relaxing the discipline in this man's case. Perhaps the most becoming way for me to do it is to lay this letter before him.   J. O'D.

The Daniel Reddin referred to here is the young man who became helplessly paralyzed in prison, and who tried to get an indictment against Dr. Burns and other officials on account of the ill-treatment he received from them.

The snow was thick on the ground at the time of my release, in January, 1871, and he was then starving on bread and water, without a bed at night.

My correspondent did not write to me to the Cove of Cork, but when I arrived in America I received a letter from him saying he was out of London when mine came. In this he spoke very kindly and promisingly; I would let you read it but that it might betray who he was, and he "relied upon my honor to hold it as confidential."

When I came to New York I was *forced* into public politics, as I will afterwards explain; and as this was taking the course my correspondent would dissuade me from, I felt delicate about replying. I could not feel it manly or gentlemanly to follow up the favors I expected from him in the release of the soldier prisoners, and as this was the principal subject of my last letter, I did not reply to it. Could I have foreseen the little good I could do here for the cause of Irish independence I would have taken a contrary course. I would rather look back now to the release of Johnny O'Brien or Sergeant M'Carthy three years ago, than to anything I have done, or seen done, by Irishmen in America to forward the cause of Irish revolution. This may give consolation to the enemies of Ireland, but if it shame her so-called friends into more honest and energetic action for her freedom, I don't begrudge the others their little pleasure.

Halpin refused to sign any conditions. He intended prosecuting the perjurers who swore against him as soon as ever he got out of prison, and signing this paper would be signing away his right to do so.

Everything having been made ready for our departure from Chatham, we took a last fond look at our cells and descended to the courtyard. We stood and made a request that Halpin be brought down to us to bid him adieu. It was granted, and it was as painful a parting as you could imagine to see us in our broadcloth bidding adieu in his convict grey to him of whom we were all so fond.

We took our seats in two coaches, two warders seating themselves with us, the Deputy-Governor entered a gig, some one shouted out "All right," the heavy prison-gates swung on their hinges, and in a moment we were outside them; but though outside and on our way to freedom, yet were we prisoners still. In that land that affords a refuge to all the political prisoners of the world there was no resting-place for us—no freedom until we were placed beyond its boundaries.

"The foot of slave thy heather never stained."

We had the accursed brand of English slavery upon us, and our tread should not pollute the soil.

We were driven to the railway station in Chatham, and, having been conducted into a carriage, the Deputy-Governor entered the next compartment to us and the train started. Arriving in London, we were placed in coaches, and driven to the station from whence the train starts for Liverpool. The Deputy-Governor told us there was time to have refreshments, and if we liked we could have some. We consented and were conducted into a private room in the building; here there was a table already prepared for us. We had sandwiches, wine and ale, and could have anything we liked. We ate and drank, and thanked the Deputy, who, now that he wasn't a jailer, was a very amiable gentleman. He made himself as agreeable as possible, and telegraphed to have everything ready before him as he went along. Detectives were here and there and everywhere that we made a stop or changed cars or coaches. It was deemed necessary to observe the greatest possible secrecy regarding our removal, lest any troublesome demonstrations should spring up on the way, and our escort did his best to hide us.

Having taken such a lunch as we did not enjoy for the past five years and four months, we, with detectives behind and detectives before, were stealthily conducted to the train, and after a ride of four or five hours found ourselves in Liverpool.

There was a crowd at the station there, and Mulleda, who was well known by the Irishmen of Liverpool, had lots of friends around him. Coaches were drawn up to receive us, and as I stepped out on the platform one friend kindly gave me his arm, and his kindness was imitated by another who saw I had another arm to spare. I thought they were some of our friends, and we had a great laugh afterwards when we learned they were detectives who thus acted so politely towards every one of us. Another hour's driving through Liverpool brought us to the river-side, where there was a tugboat in waiting to convey us on board the steamship Cuba. She lay in the middle of the river, ready to sail next morning. It was about ten o'clock when we got on board, and the Deputy ordered a supper. We had a grand time of it. Jailers and convicts and ship's officers fraternized over the champagne. We tried to make ourselves as genial as possible. We toasted the Deputy's health and he toasted ours; the doctor of the ship made a speech; some of the prisoners, being called upon, became humorous and gave excuses for short orations by saying they were a good while out of practice under the silent system. Altogether we had a good night of it, though we were still prisoners. The doctor went so far as to boast of being an Irishman, though he wasn't a Fenian or a Catholic, and when he heard our opinions as to how little we thought the name "Fenian" or "Catholic" or "Protestant" should influence a man in the discharge of a duty towards his native land, and other opinions of ours also, he appeared pleased that there seemed so little difference between us. It was a regular straight-out liberty, equality and fraternity party. There were the head jailer and his deputy warders and their prisoners sitting at the same table with the ship's officers, all toasting each other's health, in utter disregard of those distinctions of caste so necessary to "discipline," and discipline herself outraged in treating us as gentlemen while holding us as felons.

We retired to our berths about two o'clock in the morning, and the two warders did prison duty over us by remaining up and keeping guard outside our doors.

About nine o'clock, just before the ship sailed, the Deputy asked us into his room, and laying before each of us five sovereigns, said he had instructions to give us so much for pocket money. As we had decided to receive everything given us, under the circumstances that our friends were not allowed to give us anything, we took the English gold, and shaking hands with the officer as a form of bidding him good-bye, he went on board the tug-boat, and the Cuba steamed down the Mersey. But though the Deputy left us, *his* two deputies did not. We were prisoners still, and they had charge of us until we started from the Cove of Cork, where the ship was to take up the mails.

An hour after starting from Liverpool, I made the discovery that we had a stow-away on board. Strange as it may seem, he knowing that I was on the ship, sought me out and gave me his confidence. He represented himself as a correspondent of the New York *World*, he had been "interviewing" me all the morning but could not draw me out, and recognizing the vast importance of having my opinion on the questions of the day for the American world, he had hid himself on board, as he could not otherwise secure a passage from Liverpool to Cork. I thanked him for the compliment paid me, but begged to be excused from giving my opinions, as I had been shut in from the world and in utter darkness regarding all the affairs passing in it. Yet he would not be put off, he should have something from me for his pains, and he went to the trouble of telling me of the Irish Tenant Right bill and the Irish Church Disestablishment bill, which Mr. Gladstone had lately passed, asking my opinion on them. I told him I had not faith enough in Mr. Gladstone to pass any bill that would give the Irish tenant any right against the right of the landlord to eject him and rackrent him whenever he thought proper, and in this I was not far astray, for it is now seen that Gladstone's Tenant Right bill is only a second edition of Deasy's bill, or any of the other sham bills that have been passed to gull the people.

As to the Church Disestablishment bill, I reasoned thus when my interviewer asked me if I thought it should not quell agitation and make the Irish contented. A robber seizes your house and property, expels you, and in addition to this he imposes upon you the duty of maintaining one of his bastard children. His neighbors are witnesses of this injustice, and to look well in their eyes he tells you he will not tax you with the support of his child any more; that that much of the injustice is taken off your shoulders. Are you then to forgive him all the other injustice done you and to look upon him as a benefactor? It was in such wise that I spoke to this gentleman. I was a little on my guard, as I did not know but he may be an English spy sent to sound us, but probably I was mistaken here, as I afterwards saw in the New York *World* something purporting to be an account of what passed between us. I got sea-sick and went to my berth, but this did not prevent him from trying to prosecute his mission. He came into my room, but I got such a violent attack of retching whenever he asked me a question as induced him to have compassion on me and go away. On Sunday morning as we were approaching the Cove of Cork, he made for me again and I made the best of my way to evade him.

Ireland once more. There she lay before us, with her hopes and the high hopes of our youth blasted. As we drew near to land the jailers drew nearer to us, and we were reminded we were not allowed to go on shore.

Twelve years before I lay in the County Jail of Cork, and this same harbor received the Neapolitan exiles who had broken loose from their jailers while at sea. Mr. Gladstone championed them: he and all the English people were jubilant over their escape and heartily welcomed their arrival in Ireland. Now Mr. Gladstone is Prime Minister of England, and not alone has he countenanced in his prisons the very treatment which he vehemently condemned in the Neapolitan ones, but when we approach our native land on our way to banishment he prohibits us from setting foot upon its soil.

As soon as we cast anchor, the necessary relay of police and detectives came on board to keep us to our quarters during the five or six hours we stayed in the harbor. The Cove pilot informed me that my wife had arrived in town the evening before, and I enjoyed the prospect of having her a fellow-passenger to America. Small boats came from shore and in them I recognized two of my Portland companions, Pat. Barry and Jerry O'Donovan, with several others of my old-country friends. None of them would be allowed on board, but as the mountain would not come to Mahomet, Mahomet went to the mountain, and seeing Davey Riordan and a few others begging for leave, and refused, to be allowed shake hands with me, I jumped over the side of the ship into their little boat. You'd think this was the signal for an outbreak, there arose such a commotion. The detectives ran here, the jailers ran there, every one ran somewhere, but after having a few words and a shake hands with my friends around I climbed up the side of the ship and delivered myself quietly into the hands of my keepers.

During the day, four or five steamers from "Cork's own town" crowded with "God's own people" came down the river and kept hovering around our ship. The cheering was immense, and the enthusiasm showed us the old cause was still uppermost in the hearts of the masses of our people.

A committee presented us with clothes and money: they had an address for us also, but one of the conditions of allowing them on board was that this should not be presented.

My wife and youngest child met me here, and accompanied me to America.

Approaching New York a pilot was taken, and the newspapers he brought showed us we would be placed in a very delicate situation arriving in the New World. The Irish people were heartily joyous at our release, and the politicians of the city were, as a matter of course, at the head of the people. As our ship neared land, torches blazed and cannon boomed. "Ship ahoy." "Government cutter." The ladder was let down: a portly brown-haired gentleman stepped on board, and I was introduced to the Collector of the Port of New York. On the part of the Government of the United States he tendered me and my companions the welcome and the hospitality of free America. The Government steamer was alongside to receive us, and apartments for our accommodation had been engaged at the Astor House.

I thanked him; but as I was only one of five, I desired the Collector to see the others with me. During our interview some of the City Fathers had come on board from another steamer, and having met some of the other prisoners, were tendering us a welcome and hospitality on behalf of the great City of New York. The city steamer was alongside, and apartments had been engaged for us at the Metropolitan. I saw immediately that the question of our reception had grown into a party fight. It was impossible for me to get a word with one of my companions without half a dozen surrounding us, half of whom would be at one side and half at the other side, bawling out, "Rossa, go this way." "Rossa, go that way."

The Collector asking if he could have a few private words with me, I went with him to the Captain's room, and he spoke to me somewhat in this manner:

"Mr. O'Donovan, I am an Irishman myself; I am not without some sympathy for your cause, and I wish to see our people respected in their new home. I am pained at what you have witnessed here to-night. You have been years in prison, you are banished from your native land, you turn your face here, the National Government come to receive you, and a faction that has been for years degrading the character of our race steps in to create disturbance. The Irish people are glad of your release; they are honest, but they have got into the hands of a party of thieves and swindlers, who on every important occasion strive to use them against the interests of the country, and, as you see here to-night, to our common disgrace. Tammany Hall is not greater than the National Government, and, if you take a broad, statesmanlike view of the case, you and your friends will come on board the cutter with me."

I had not time to reply when the door was burst in, and I was seized bodily and borne to the centre of the saloon. Room was made for the five prisoners to come together to receive an invitation of welcome from the Municipal Government. We were introduced to John Mitchel and Richard O'Gorman, one of whom read the address, and then a scene arose that baffles description.

A college professor from the West, who sat at our table during the voyage, whispered me aside and said, "Rossa, if you would excuse me for offering an advice it would be this—Receive the invitation from the Nation first. Let the Government cutter receive you from the English ship. Let the national flag carry you to American soil, and when you are landed in the city, you can, with propriety, accept the other invitation, if you wish."

This was sound advice, but the increasing din of voices, the up roar, the shouting and shoving, forbade a quiet thought to be given to anything. We saw acquaintances now at both sides of the house warmly contending one against the other. All of them were our friends, but the fight had waxed so warm that we saw we could not get out of making half of them our enemies if we accepted either of the invitations.

In the midst of the melee, Dr. Carnochan, the Health Officer of the port, came and ordered the ship to be quarantined, as there was a case of small-pox on board, and no passengers should be allowed on shore till further orders. The Health Officer was on the Tammany side of the house, and this was a clever display of the tactics of the party. If we accepted the national invitation the Health Officer could not allow us to infect the city with small-pox; if we accepted the city invitation, there mightn't be much danger of the contagion.

We craved a short time for consultation, and were allowed it. We retired, and decided we would go to a private hotel, and after twenty minutes we returned to the saloon and read the following reply to the invitations:

ON BOARD THE "CUBA," Jan. 19, 1871.

To the Gentlemen of the several Deputations for Receiving the Irish Exiles.

GENTLEMEN: We thank you for all your invitations, and we will try to accept all, but we are only a few of many. Our fellow-prisoners are on the way hither, and we will take no public step until they arrive. You may look upon us as representing the cause of Ireland, for the interest of which cause we desire that all Irishmen should be united. It is painful to us to-night to see so much disunion amongst ourselves. For what your reception concerns us as individuals we care little compared to what we feel about it in connection with the interest of Irish independence, and as you have not united cordially to receive us, we will not decide on anything until the arrival of our brothers. We will remain on board the ship to-night, and go to a hotel to-morrow.

We remain, gentlemen, yours, very respectfully,
JER. O'DONOVAN ROSSA,
CHARLES U. O'CONNELL,
JOHN DEVOY,
JOHN McCLURE,
HENRY S. MULLEDA.

If this did not please any one, it calmed the elements a little, and the storm began to subside. By and by I found myself sitting in the parlor listening to a very spicy debate between the Collector and Mr. O'Gorman. They hit at each other pretty hard in a gentlemanly way but some less gentlemanly person present joined in the debate, making use of the rude and vulgar observation that he knew the Collector many years ago when they boarded in the same house, and that he was not then as big a man as he was now. This turned my sympathy to the side of Mr. Murphy—which I found to be the Collector's name. I don't know that he is as Irish as his name indicates, but he is the most prominent and influential Irishman in the city to-day. He was born in 1823 in Ballinacht, Garryowen County, and his father, John Murphy, who was land agent to old William Wise, of Cork, brought the whole family to America in or about 1832—man-servants, maid-servants, et cetera—in all seventeen souls.

The morning after our arrival we left the steamer and went to Sweeny's Hotel, telling the proprietor we were ourselves to pay for our board, and requesting him to receive money from no one on that account. A sum of money had been subscribed previous to our arrival, which lay in the hands of Mr. O'Gorman. He presented us with fifteen thousand dollars of it for "the exiles," and when we came to inquire about our hotel bill we found it was also paid.

Deputations, invitations, addresses and congratulations continued to pour in, and morning, noon and night the hotel was besieged with visitors. Our hands got swollen and sore from hand-shaking. It was a hearty, generous welcome of the people, but we were heartily wishing it would come to an end.

We made up our minds that we would have nothing to do with either of the political parties, and, as we did not land in the Government steamer, we determined to have nothing to do with Tammany Hall. But here a difficulty arose. It was thought we could not well refuse a public reception, offered by the City, without laying ourselves open to the charge of treating the authorities with contempt, and this position we did not wish to be placed in. Knowing that the eyes of England were upon us also, we accepted the invitation, and the programme laid down by the City Fathers was to have us taken to Tammany Hall and to have the procession start from there. Once we placed ourselves in the hands of the authorities we, in all decency, felt bound to acquiesce in their management of the proceedings. I felt bitter to think that, after all the efforts we made to steer clear of party—to act straight between all and give neither side a victory or defeat—we were now being taken to a place that would give our existence a political complexion.

While laboring under the vexation of seeing the cause of Ireland brought into this question of American party politics, I was called upon to speak, and I spoke something that seemed not pleasing to the leaders.

I said if I went to Ireland, and that the Orangemen there offered me a welcome, I would joyfully accept it as a tribute to the cause we represented, and coupling the name of Tammany in some infelicitous manner with this observation, "I put my foot in it." It was in the original programme to take us into the City Hall when passing it. As we approached the place there was a halt of about an hour, but what I said threw cold water on everything that was prepared there, we were not invited in, and the official part of the ceremony ended ungraciously.

The Common Council of Brooklyn voted us a public reception also, and we had to appear in state there another day. The Mayor and Aldermen of Jersey City followed suit, but we decided on having no more public honors. Alderman Harrington, a Dunmanway Irishman, was in New York every day pressing us to accept the Jersey offering, but we reasoned him out of his anxiety to fete us.

The representatives of the nation, in Senate assembled in Washington, welcomed us in a resolution introduced by the Hon. Benjamin Butler, and the State representatives in Albany sent us their greeting through the Governor:

{STATE OF NEW YORK, EXECUTIVE CHAMBER,}
ALBANY, Feb. 18, 1871.

SIR: I take pleasure in transmitting to you herewith a copy of a "resolution of welcome" to this country, which had been unanimously adopted by the Senate and Assembly of the State.

Very respectfully, JOHN T. HOFFMAN.
To JER'H O'DONOVAN ROSSA.

STATE OF NEW YORK, ASSEMBLY CHAMBER,
ALBANY, Feb. 16, 1871.

Resolved, if the Senate concur, That the Legislature, in the name and on behalf of the people of the State of New York, extend to Thomas Clark Luby, Jeremiah O'Donovan Rossa, Charles Underwood O'Connell, John O'Leary, Thomas F. Bourke, and their associates, the Irish exiles and patriots recently landed upon our shores, a most hearty welcome to our country, and that a copy of this resolution be transmitted to them by the Governor of this State.

By order, C. W. ARMSTRONG, Clerk.

IN SENATE, Feb. 15, 1871.—Concurred in without amendment,
By order, HIRAM CALKINS, Clerk.

The whole affair is now past and gone; the excitement is all over; there seems to be no Ireland—no Irish revolutionary cause alive in New York; the "exiles" have sunk to their natural level of humble private individuals; but whatever can be said of them—whatever be their faults and failings—it can never be said they availed of their position then to forward their own interests—to feather their own nests. No; Ireland's Cause was uppermost with them; they sank their own individuality to raise that; and if it is now

"Down in the dust, and a shame to be seen,"

they had no hand in dragging it down.

Place and position were within easy reach of them; the ruling powers keeping pace with the exuberant outburst of welcome were generously disposed. I myself might have been a lord to-day—or a Sing Sing convict—had I grasped the treasures laid before me. The man who gave Mr. Green control of the City of New York paid me a visit at Sweeny's Hotel one of these days. Mr. Sweeny told me he was coming, and asked me not to be out. I remained in, and when Mr. Richard B. Connolly was announced I admitted him. Mr. Sweeny ordered up a bottle of champagne, and as we were drinking it the Comptroller lamented the death of his deputy, Mr. Watson, who was killed a few days before. He wanted a man to fill his place, and he did not know where to get one. He looked inquiringly at me. I felt confused, and only said he ought not to have much difficulty there, with the number of smart men New York contained. I shoved this away from me as I would any other honors that could be offered me at the time by either Collector Murphy or Comptroller Connolly. I would not be so scary of accepting them now. "There is a tide in the affairs of men," but I went against the current of mine when it was high water, and I am no way sorry for it.

The newspapers differing in political opinion agreed in admitting that we had behaved ourselves becomingly; the Black Republicans and the red-hot Democrats gave us their meed of praise. Here is a specimen from each:

THE RESOLVE OF THE EXPATRIATED REBELS.

(From the New York Irish Democrat.)

"On all sides we hear unqualified commendation of the reticence and retirement of the Irish exiles since their arrival amongst us—of the good taste and considerate feeling that declined an ovation until their fellow martyrs could participate in the honor, and of the sound judgment that preserved them from being made the mere shuttlecocks of political parties. The temptations were great, and the resistance was proportionately creditable. But from the antecedents of the men we could have expected no other result; they were not patriots for mere pageantry—no kid-glove nationalists, to expend their zeal on platforms—they strove nobly and nobly suffered; and there was no nobler characteristic marking their career than their conduct now."

HEAD LEVEL.

(From the New York Standard.)

"The highest compliment that can be made to a man on the Pacific slope is to credit him with carrying his head level, and we can think of no more appropriate or forcible expression by which to designate the public esteem for Mr. O'Donovan Rossa since his arrival in this country. As the principal among the first arrivals of Fenian exiles, he has been regarded as the expounder of their will, and he has certainly added much to the reputation of Irishmen by the delicacy and determination of his method of management.

While the Metropolitan Hotel and Astor House were secured for the reception of himself and brethren, where they could live in state on a par with the Japanese princes, he preferred the retirement of a modest hotel, kept on economical principles. He cut the gordian knot which released Tammany and the Irish Republicans from tearing his coat, by politely but firmly resisting the overtures of either, and what promised a row will end in an ovation. Never had man a fairer opportunity of living on the fat of the land, for the next six months, at least; to be feasted at Washington, paraded at Philadelphia, or whiskeyed at Louisville, to his heart's content.

He is obliged, for the consistency of things, to accept the ovation of his thousands of admirers on Thursday next."

We had two difficulties to encounter in our desire to steer clear of politics. There were two phases of the mania raging—the Irish one and the American one—and of the two the former was the worst. The different sections of what is called the Fenian element, surrounded us, all calling aloud for "Union," "Union," "Union," and when we turned our attention to their call, we found the union that each party wanted was an adhesion to itself. Let us join them and all the other factions should come in or die out. We were called upon by all to start something that would embrace all. If we did not do so we were most culpable and guilty of letting the opportunity slip of doing good. We, on leaving prison, had resolved, as I said before, not to mix ourselves up with the Fenian question here, but if we did not respond to this call made upon us it would be said to-day and evermore, that we had shirked our duty. We started the Irish Confederation, with a platform broad enough to give standing room to every kind of Irish society existing in the country, but the very men that called most loudly for action on our part, were the first to set their faces against the success of our work. When they saw they could not swallow us up, they raised the cry that the exiles were tyrannical, "they wanted to control everything," and this cry has—in the interests of division and disorder—been kept up to the present day.

When I saw I could do no more in America than help to build up another faction or party where so many existed, I gave up the Confederation.

I was disgusted with the Irish politics of the country, disgusted with hearing and seeing societies organizing to aid Irishmen in Ireland to fight England, and not sending one red cent to buy arms, or anything else. No, but worse than that; the very men that were most energetic in calling for money to help "the men at home," were cutting the throats of "the men at home," by industriously circulating the lie that they were not fit to be entrusted with the use of money.

God blast your falsehoods—you do-nothing drivellers. Only for the men at home, only for their action and conduct there, the name of Irish liberty in America would stink, on account of your work in the sacred name of it here.

If you had the opportunity; or, having the opportunity, if you ever had the courage to work *with* "the men at home," you would not work against them now in this manner.

One of these men at home is worth a thousand of *you* here, is worth a thousand of *us* here, is worth a thousand of *themselves* here, for Irish revolutionary purposes. One John Kenealy in Ireland is worth a thousand John Kenealys in San Francisco. We degenerate when we leave the old land. We have no enemy to rouse the blood into a healthy circulation.

Seeing that the great hurra of our reception in New York and the great popularity it brought me, brought me no power to do any good for these men who expected something from us, and seeing they were under the impression I could do anything I liked if I exerted myself, I found myself getting out of humor. I did not much mind how soon I was relieved of such popularity. I sometimes got into company, and sometimes talked American politics, and I was very often given to understand that I could be nothing—should be nothing unless a Tammany man. If I wasn't Tammany I wasn't Irish, and the very people who leaped for joy at my release from prison would repudiate my being an Irishman.

This set me thinking. I had stood up as a freeman in an enslaved land. For this I had suffered six years' imprisonment, and in prison I tried to keep my soul unshackled. I was now in a free country, and my mind revolted at being told I should hold myself as a kind of slave. I found myself becoming a "rebel" again, and nursing a determination to sacrifice my popularity to my independence whenever an opportunity offered.

In company, one day, the conversation turned on the "exiles'" reception, and, while admitting the demonstration was genuine on the part of the people, I asserted there was more of the American politician in it in the end than of anything else. I also asserted that we Irish of New York are American politicians before we are Irish, or anything else. I am not saying this is wrong. The Irishman has done as much as any other man to make America; there is as much of his sweat and blood in the soil as of any other man's; and, having no country of his own, his existence is wound up more closely than any other foreigner's with its institutions, and it is only natural he should take a primary interest in all that concerns the public where his lot is laid. But what I don't like to see, and what I think I do see here, is Irishmen kicking up their heels as if the whole country belonged to them, as if they had no taint of slavery connected with them. The man in Ireland that would ride with boots and spurs, and cut up a shine at fair or market, while his mother was in the poor-house, would soon be made to lower his head by some cutting remark from a passer-by, and I never can listen to an Irishman here "bouncing" about his being a free man, without thinking of his mother in the poor-house. When a man gets married to a young woman, his obligations to his mother do not cease; he is considered bad if he throws her out of doors.

In this company I speak of, Captain Tom Costello disputed what I said about our people being more American than Irish, and I promised him I would try it in a small way at the next election. I thought it well, also, to make a lesson for my countrymen in Ireland, who thought that the people who threw up their hats on my landing would throw me into the presidency if they could.

An opportunity soon offered, and everything was propitious. Mr. Wm. M. Tweed represented the most Irish district of the city; his term of office had expired and he was up for re-election. I went to Collector Murphy and told him I would run against Mr. Tweed if he gave me any support. He got me the nomination and one thousand dollars, and I got seven thousand votes counted for me against Mr. Tweed's thirteen thousand. He was then charged with the robberies for which he is now undergoing a sentence of ten years' penal servitude. It was the Irish people "elected" him. I say it to show how much they were in the hands of those trickster politicians that use them to the shame and disgrace of our national reputation.

A cry was immediately raised against me. I had gone against Tammany Hall; I had gone against the Irish, I was a renegade. I had done what no public Irishman did here before. A club of the Irish Confederation in Memphis or some Southern city wrote saying they could not have confidence in contributing any more money for Ireland while I was on the Directory, and I received several evidences that I committed political suicide.

An Irishman writing in the *Globe* of Nov. 6th, 1871, said:

> "O'Donovan Rossa did more within a few years to bring about the disreputable state of Irish national sentiment, than all the *fiasco* mishaps and blunders of ten years' mismanagement of Fenian organizations." "Is it not most lamentable and most pitiable that all future efforts for Ireland's redemption by true men is marred and sullied by this man's stupidity? Oh, Ireland's patriots and martyrs, how you and your great cause is blurred by the mercenary conduct of Rossa." "Oh, shame, where is thy blush." Mr. Rossa's course of conduct in this matter has done more damage to Irish nationality, and more to destroy a future confidence in so-called Irish patriots, than the treachery of all the perjured informers for hundreds of years! "How absurd and stupid, because of an inconsistent and coarse stubbornness on his part whilst in prison, gained for him a notoriety, that when a free man to act and perform, had not brains enough to guide his political conduct into a consistent and legitimate channel." Rossa's political floundering in the interest of Tom Murphy, Grant's Ku-Klux whipper-in, absolutely proves him to be purely a man of chance, who was pitchforked into Irish national notoriety! "Would not Mr. Rossa command much respect from Irishmen and Americans, etc., if he became attached to the only legitimate Irish party in the country, and not be a tool of Grant?" Alas, poor Yorick! O'Donovan Rossa's work for Ireland is over and done, his political career is passed; his grave is made and will be forever closed on Tuesday next. "What a name! what vast renown! what imperishable honors he and his country would gain if England's bloody government never pardoned him."

God help you, you poor pitiful slave! you have Rossa's prayers for your restoration to light and freedom.

I opposed Tammany! Tammany—the only party that ever gave any representation to an Irishman! I was lost. My career was ended. But I was satisfied, and the Irish people may be satisfied that while I live I will oppose Tammany while Tammany disgraces the Irish character by the men she takes to represent us. John Mitchell is a consistent advocate at that side of the house for the last twenty years. Hostility to England's government of Ireland is the grand characteristic of the Irish character, and he is the the grandest representative of that in America. Has Tammany taken him to represent the Irish people? No, he doesn't want it; he doesn't go the right slavish way to seek favors; they are not offered to him, but are given to men who are only fit to be the representatives of slaves, who, having Irish names and rowdy manners, degrade and lower our character by presenting in their representative persons to the beholders, a spurious standard of our manhood and intelligence.

Even though I may oppose Tammany, I have enough of Irish pride and feeling left to make me wish that when they *do* select Irishmen for the purpose of securing the Irish vote these should be respectable independent men, and not disreputable slavish ones.

Apart from anything else I have been saying, if I could become an American politician and go into American politics with the same soul that I could go into Irish politics, I would differ with this Tammany party on pure principle alone. Its strength is made up of foreign-born men—of hard-toiling men, too, who leave their native land and come here to earn higher wages. The blacksmith that gets three or four shillings a day making *graffawns* in Ireland comes here and gets three or four dollars a day. He joins a trade society to protect him in retaining this wages and to help him in getting an increase of it; but at the very same time he commits the inconsistency of joining Tammany, that is working to keep his wages down—Tammany, that is laboring with all its might to get *graffawns* that are manufactured in England brought to America free of duty, where they can be sold cheaper than the mechanic can make them, and the mechanic must necessarily lose his business or lower his wages if Tammany principles prevail.

I am touching now on the question of Tariff or Free Trade. If principles were respected, and if I had to take sides actively in American politics, I would unquestionably be on the side of those who advocate the imposition of a duty on foreign manufactures. Even at the present day, seeing the number of men that are in want of employment in New York and other places, I don't know that it would not be for the interest of the country—it would at least be for the interest of the unemployed—to impose a tariff on the importation of further emigrants until those we have are provided with labor.

The Common Council of New York, this week, passed a resolution that no outsider coming to New York should be employed there while there was a six months' resident of the city out of employment. Let this be taken to heart by my friends in Ireland who intend emigrating, and let them not be coming out here and going back again disappointed, as many have done this very present year.

I have had something to do with emigration since I came here, but I am not so wound up in making a fortune at it as to let it prevent me from giving a word of advice to the men at home.

I know many of them are forced to leave the old land, but I know many more of them are cheated into coming here. For instance: Conn Callaghan comes to America, induced by letters written home by Morty Downing, who stated he was making a fortune. It is Conn's turn to write home, and as he was as good and industrious a man in the old land as Morty, he must stand still as good, and he writes that he is making a fortune, too. Then their brother-in-law Johnny Shea must try his luck, and he breaks up house and brings a large family to New York, knowing he has friends there well off, who will help him. He takes his family, bag and baggage, to Conn's or to Morty's, and he finds them in a fourth story floor in Cherry street, with hardly spare room enough to give a cat a night's lodging. Johnny must write home and be as good as the others, and so the deception goes on. I have witnessed several cases of this kind within the past year, and I have seen the bitter tears of disappointment shed when the friends met.

As my feelings have dragged me into these observations, I cannot close without a few words more to emigrants. There is plenty of room in this country for all the oppressed peoples of the world if they go *into* the country and are able to settle down on land, but if they are not able there is no living being here to assist them. My countrymen may hear and read as much as they please about Irish benevolent societies and Irish emigrant aid societies, but these are all money-making concerns, and the new-comer arriving in New York poverty-stricken or stricken by sickness finds himself miserable and pitiable, and finds no Irish benevolent or aid societies to lend him a dollar or a helping hand.

This is not as it should be. The Germans do better for their people. They have organizations to help them out West. The Irish have only Tammany, and Tammany has governed these emigration departments for past years to the enrichment of office-holders and the neglect of the emigrants' interests, and the interests of the nation.

I am not saying that things are any better now that there is a change of rulers, nor do I say things are going to be better. With many of the influential men of all parties here, dollars seem to be more prized than principles, and the rush for emolumentary position will allow nothing to stand in its way.

I know many good and honest Tammany men who think as I do, whose principles incline them the other way, but who *are* this way because principles of themselves are not respected, and there is little show or consideration for Irishmen at the other side. They say when an Irishman is put on the "Republican" ticket there is such a prejudice against him, particularly if he be affected with the taint of Catholicity, that he "runs far behind his ticket." The party he has been working with will vote for a "Democrat" before voting for him. If this is so—and I believe it is to some extent—the "Republicans" may blame themselves for having Tammany Hall so strong with the Irish, and Republican Hall so weak. If they only treated the Irish fairly, my countrymen would act fairly by them. When bigots are allowed a standing-place in countries where there is less freedom than in this, I suppose it is only fair they should be allowed a standing-ground here, but it is as unfair or them to claim the sole right to possess the country as it is to claim the sole right to heaven.

The most saintly of them cannot claim a longer priority of right than two hundred years, and while we respect that right and all the other rights established by the Constitution, there should be no place for hatred of race, creed or color in the breast of any man treading that soil which the great founders of the Republic contemplated to be a home for the oppressed, tyrant-stricken people of the Old World.

And as to this religious prejudice against the Irish, is it not old-womanish and contemptible in this age? Ought not those saintly bigots know that the way to Heaven is through long suffering, sore trial and sorrow, and that consequently there is not a people on the face of the earth have a fairer prospect of entering the Kingdom than the Irish people. Yes, holy, sanctimonious bigots! you may mar the happy progress of the people's union in civil and religious liberty; you may grudge us the privileges which the charter accords to all; but, have nothing to say to us about Heaven, we are before you there—do not refuse us the graces you hold by being before *us* here, and we will be only too happy to reciprocate.

You ought to know that the Irish are more likely to be found loyal to the flag of the Republic in a time of danger, than any other adopted citizens. Suppose we had a war with Prussia, it would pain the German, and one of his arms would undoubtedly be paralized. A war with France would unquestionably make another arm of a Frenchman powerless, but give us a war with the ruling powers of Ireland, and *both* the Irishman's hands would be raised to strike down the English flag, and *every* Irishman would rush to arms.

It is said the bigots are again striving to revive that ugly spirit of "Know-Nothingism" that marred the happy progress of the nation's peace and prosperity, and left such bitter memories behind; and that its *animus* now is more directed against the Catholic Irish than against any others. I hope they will desist from such an undertaking, and consider well before they commence such a crusade against a people that are surrounded by all the favorable circustances that qualify them to "become more American than the Americans themselves."

Some of the "Republican" newspapers do much also to scare Irishmen away from the ranks of that party. When my countrymen take a prominent part in electing a Tammany ticket, these newspapers assail the whole Irish race in America with low, vulgar abuse, as if there was not a decent man amongst them. It is jokingly said that you must bore a hole in a Scotchman's head to get a joke into it; but if you want to get the decent, manly principle that is in an Irishman, out of him, you will never succeed if you attempt it by cracking his skull.

Collector Murphy has some controlling influence in the "Republican" party; he is certainly free from those prejudices I speak of. Has he no power to dispel them from the minds of others? If he had, he would remove the greatest barrier that stands in the way of the manly portion of the Irish people, taking that side to which their opinions incline them.

If my memory serves me right, Mr. Murphy often lamented to me that the Irish citizens did not treat politics as the Americans did, and range themselves on different sides, according to their judgment, instead of running *en masse* to one side and making it appear to our native born citizens that they acted from impulse and not from judgment. He trusted I would "instruct" them whenever I got an opportunity, and this being the only opportunity I get to say a calm word on either side, I tell him if he does his best to allay those prejudices I speak of, he will be doing more than a hundred like me could do to strengthen his party.

The Collector told me he also regretted that our people, who had struggled seven hundred years for liberty and won the respect of Americans on account of that struggle, before they came here, should be found, as soon as they arrived, rushing in a body into the ranks of a party that supported slavery, that advocated free labor, and that would hold the Irish in the same bonds as the nigger was held if it so happened that the white Irishman had been born their property. That in place of joining a party whose officials all understood that the doctrine of that party was "Thou shalt not steal," they joined a party who believed in the principle "Thou shalt not steal," with word "not" left out—a party who did not think "the laborer worthy of his hire." While he seemed to wish the Irish citizen should vie with the American citizen in the performance of every duty belonging to a good man, he repudiated the idea that he should not retain that affection for his native land that a child should for its parent. There was nothing to clash in the nature of a man's affection for his wife and for his mother, or in the nature of an Irishman's discharge of duty to America and to Ireland. If Irishmen would take *his* advice in this direction, they would be doing all that would be expected from any citizen, and adding to the future greatness of a country that will eventually be their children's home—the greatest country and the best government on the face of the earth.

But to be just to both sides, I must admit that all the bigotry and hatred of Irish Catholics is not entirely on the side of the "Republicans." The "Democrats" have their share of it, and Mr. Murphy gave me numerous instances of where Irish Catholics on the "Democratic" ticket were black-balled by the "Democratic" Americans, who voted for the opposing parties in preference to them.

And yet the Irish amongst the "democrats" never resented such conduct. They always voted blind "democrat" for whatever candidate was put before them by the party, no matter though that candidate were a bitter Know-Nothing and hater of their name and race. He instanced the case of Fernando Wood and James Brooks and President Pierce, the latter of whom voted against the repeal of a law in New Hampshire which forbade to any Catholic the right to hold office.

These men, he said, knowing the impulsiveness of the Irish and their love of country, could lead them any way that answered their interests, with the cry of "*Fag-a-Bealagh*" or "*Erin-go-Bragh*." Oakey Hall in a suit of green on a Patrick's Day, and standing on the steps of the City Hall as the processionists passed, could elicit cheers from them that would be a sure pledge of their forgetfulness of his past Know-Nothingism, and of a continuance of their support at some election in the future.

This brings to my mind a story about a Patrick's Day in Dublin, which I will tell to illustrate my subject.

On the 17th of March, 1864, I was sitting in the editor's room of the *Irish People* office in 12 Parliament street, when Pagan O'Leary rushed in, and, throwing up the windows, seized the little pots of shamrocks that Jerry O'Farrell was nursing there, and dashed them one by one into the yard. He then laid hold of my hat, and snatching the shamrock out of it, trampled it under his feet. I ran to save my hat lest that would be trampled too. The Pagan's rage was aroused by seeing a dog wear a wreath of shamrocks. The Castle yard was near our office, and the Pagan walked in to see the Patrick's Day pageant. The Lord Lieutenant was on the balcony with the ladies of the Castle around him, and one of the lap-dogs, with the political instincts of an Oakey Hall, clothed himself in a garland of shamrocks, and in the arms of his mistress exhibited himself to the multitude with the National emblem around his neck. To see it worn by a dog set the Pagan raging, and to talk shamrocks to him since would be as much as your life was worth.

There are many Irishmen in New York politics wearing "shamrocks" who care very little for the cause of the green sod—who are ashamed to have their name associated with it when their shamrocks have blossomed into diamonds. There are enough of manly Irishmen in America, no matter to what party they belong, to punish any man of any party whom they would find making a dog-collar of Ireland. But they are not organized; if they were, the examples of Irish politicians deserting the Irish cause when they had attained their political object would be less rare. In consequence of the conduct of these dog-collar men, the name of an Irish-American politician stinks in the nostrils of good Irishmen; and they do not interfere much in the elections, in consequence of which the dog-collar dodgers have full play in getting into positions. It is by *their* standard the character of our people is measured. This is not as it should be, and I trust the good men will correct it.

In writing the words "republican" and "democrat" I have put them in quotation marks because I do not know what they really mean, more than that they are party cries. My small share of education tells me that republican comes from two Latin words meaning public-affairs, and democrat from two Greek words meaning people-government. Now there is no "democrat" in America who is not interested in public affairs, and consequently must be a republican; and President Grant, being a governor chosen by the majority of the people in people-government form, must necessarily be a democratic President.

But you would realize how beautifully all those things are muddled if you were listening to some fuddled Tammany democrat making an election speech. I heard a few of them at the late election, and instead of Grant being elected by the people you'd think the whole thing was done by some Connemara man, playing the devil with something in a Custom House. It was "Grant and

Murphy," "Murphy and Grant," at the beginning and ending of every sentence, with the "Custom House" coming in somewhere in the middle. With the unfortunate Boss Tweed booked for ten years' imprisonment, and the fortunate Andy Green having charge of the money books of the city, and all the old Tammany hacks still "running the machine" and grabbing at office, and at everything else within their reach, I was not at all possessed with the belief that that public virtue which is the vitality of republics had at last found its way into that machine which turned out such dirty work lately.

A people with any national self-respect would avoid the vulgar practice of flinging low personal abuse at their nation's Chief Magistrate—whether he be "Democrat" or "Republican." But this seems to be the stock-in-trade of every defeated party during a presidential term. That of George Washington itself was not an exception.

One observation more will finish me on politics. Tweed and Oakey Hall were sterling "Democrats." They led the Irish in that name, and used them to their shame and disgrace. But they enriched themselves, and those about them. When Tweed the great "Democrat" was resigning he gave his place to Van Nort a "Republican." When Oakey Hall the great "Democrat" was losing his power he gave Richard O'Gorman's place to Delafield Smith, a "Republican." Let my red-hot "Democrat" countrymen ponder on this, and let them not be disposed to break my head because I refuse to be a slave to the prejudices that blind them to see such chameleons as these in their proper light.

I have said that in running against Tweed I committed political suicide with the Irish people, but I now come to finish my career with an act that "killed me entirely." I became a "Commune," and as the story of all sudden deaths are somewhat tragic I will tell mine.

While I was in prison in England I was treated pretty harshly, and publicity of my treatment was the only protection I had for my life. There was a French exile in London named Gustave Flourens. He became interested in my case—more interested than many Irishmen, and more interested than that very good Catholic Bishop who sent this telegram from Rome when the Irish people were crying out to have us amnestied:

"FROM MONSIGNORE M'CABE, ROME, TO REV. J. REYNOLDS, LONGFORD, IRELAND.

"Your letter received. Let all unite and prepare for contest. Let no one be intimidated. I am more convinced than ever of the necessity of opposing Fenian candidates. *No priests to sign the new amnesty petition.*"

Gustave Flourens did not do anything like this, but he translated an account of my treatment into French and German and had it published in the continental papers. This vexed England a little and she conceded a Commission of Inquiry to the voice of public opinion, which Commission established the truth of our ill treatment and led to our release.

When the French war broke out, Gustave Flourens went to France. After the "war of the Commune" he was charged with having engaged in it and he was shot. Rossell and others were shot twelve months or more after the cessation of hostilities.

Without entering into the discussion of any bad acts that might have been committed in war times, when the blood was hot and there was killing all around, I hold it was cruel to be knocking men on the head so long after the war was over, and when I hold an opinion I never withhold any act or expression that is necessary to back it when required.

A funeral for these men was held in New York, and, like many others, I went to look at it. As I was standing on the corner of Fifth street and Bowery, General Ryan, who was lately murdered in Cuba, seeing me, came out of his carriage, and invited me in. A few weeks before this he had written me a letter offering his sword and himself to Ireland whenever there was any fighting to be done against England, and believing he *would* fight, and fight bravely— as bravely as he died—in our cause, I had some respect for him. I declined his invitation to a seat in the carriage. "What!" said he, "don't you disapprove of the shooting of these men in cold blood now that the war is over?"

"I do, certainly," said I.

"Then is it afraid to attend their funeral you are on account of the cry of 'mad dog' that has been raised against them—you know that cry was raised against yourself?"

This nettled me a little. I bade good-day to O'Feely Byron, who was with me. It was a cowardly thing to be afraid, when my conscience told me I was right, and with a "Come on, then, General, I'm not afraid," I went to my grave.

As I am writing my own obituary, there is one point on which, for my domestic peace, I do not wish my character to stand defamed. The Irish religious—the ultra-Catholic press that often hit at me for my connection with Irish revolution—hit at me now for being a Communist and being a free lover, and for my connection with Tennie Claflin. She happened to be in the funeral, but let me solemnly assure 'my readers I never laid an eye on her that day, or any other day before or since, and I never spoke to the woman in my life. This, I hope, will satisfy my friends of the Boston *Pilot*, and all other friends.

I desire to take my leave in words of peace. My course in the Old Land has brought me the esteem of the people there. It is more than a reward to me for anything I have tried to do to uphold the Irish name. Anything I have done since I came to this country has been done in the effort to make my present and future life consistent with the past. My personal interests alone in view, I have made mistakes and will possibly make more. I have retained my opinions and my independence when it was expected I would run in ruts laid down by political tricksters of every kind, for Irishmen to travel in.

I will not be a slave if I can live otherwise. With all due respect for others who hold opinions contrary to mine in the politics of America, I will take my own course there. But as regards the politics that lead to the Independence of Ireland, to the helping of the revolutionists there, I am not so independent as not to be prepared to bend in any way their real friends deem necessary to bring them practical aid.

I desire to retain the good opinion of the "men at home," and indeed, of all men. If I am anything, it is Irishmen have made me it, and without their aid I can do nothing or become nothing further.

It is to do my part towards enabling my countrymen to judge justly of my conduct that I introduce this matter of the "Commune." Those who know me need no explanation. Those who do not, may read the following extract from some of Gustave Flourens' letters on my behalf:

THE FRENCH PRESS ON IRELAND.
GUSTAVE FLOURENS ON O'DONOVAN ROSSA IN THE "MARSEILLIASE."

"While the Olliver Ministry holds the prisoner in St. Pelagie, the deputy of the first circumscription of Paris—Henry Rochefort; in England the Gladstone Cabinet, a Cabinet of *honest men*, also gets tortured by its *shirri*, the Irish representative, O'Donovan Rossa. The *Marseillaise* has already published a moving letter from this unfortunate victim of the English "Liberals." The IRISHMAN has just published a second. This letter has been reproduced by the English press, the *Standard*, too, which has accused us of inventing the first letter of the citizen Rossa.

I send you the literal translation of the letter given by the IRISHMAN. All commentary is superfluous. At some steps from the splendid mansion from which the House of Lords governs England are to be witnessed : cities which had no parallel even in the Neapolitan prisons of the Bourbons—those same prisons which so horrified Mr. Gladstone.
* * * * * * * * * * * * *
I do not know Rossa, but I love him for his simplicity, the calmness and the firmness with which he relates his frightful torture.

GUSTAVE FLOURENS."

The man who would "run me down" for going to that man's funeral must be very hard to please indeed.

www.ingramcontent.com/pod-product-compliance
Lightning Source LLC
Chambersburg PA
CBHW032004300426
44117CB00008B/898